M. Kemal Atatürk

1881 — 1938

Birinci Baskı: 1982
İkinci Baskı: 1991

ATATÜRK KÜLTÜR, DİL VE TARİH YÜKSEK KURUMU
TÜRK TARİH KURUMU YAYINLARI
XVI. Dizi - Sa. 39²

ATATÜRK

by
JORGE BLANCO VILLALTA

Translated from Spanish
by
WILLIAM CAMPBELL

3. baskı

TÜRK TARİH KURUMU
ANKARA, 2014

Blanco Villalta, Jorge Gastón, 1909 - 2003
    Atatürk / Jorge Blanco Villalta ; translated from Spanish by
William Campbell. — 3. baskı. — Ankara : Türk Tarih Kurumu, 2014.

    xvii, 505 s. : portre ; 24 cm. — (AKDTYK Türk Tarih Kurumu
yayınları ; XVI. Dizi – Sayı 392)

    Bibliyografya ve indeks var.
    ISBN 978 - 975 - 16 - 0372 - 2

    1. Atatürk, Mustafa Kemal, 1881- 1938. 2. Türkiye _ Tarih _ 20. yy.
I. E.a. II. Campbell, William, çev. III. Dizi.

923.156
956.1024092

Atatürk Kültür, Dil ve Tarih Yüksek Kurumu Yönetim Kurulu'nun 24.04.2014
tarih ve 687/14 sayılı kararı gereği 2000 adet basılmıştır.

ISBN 978 - 975 - 16 - 0372 - 2

Baskı:
Salmat Basım Yayıncılık Ambalaj San. ve Tic. Ltd. Şti.
Sebze Bahçeleri Cad. (Büyük Sanayi 1. Cad.)
Arpacıoğlu İş Hanı No. 95/1 İskitler-Ankara
Tel: 0312 341 10 24 · Faks: 0312 341 30 50

CONTENTS

PART FOUR
TOTAL EFFORT

PART FIVE
THE REPUBLIC AND THE SOCIAL REFORMS

Dedication

This first English edition of my book
"Atatürk" is dedicated to

Fahri Korutürk

Atatürk's illustrious successor as President of the

Republic, and in whom the ideals of his Great Fel-

low - Citizen remain alive and active, and to

The Armed Forces

of the

Turkish Republic,

Faithful guardians of the historical

legacy of their immortal creator.

THE TRANSLATOR

William Campbell is a permanent officer of the British Council. He has worked in Spain, Indonesia and Iran, besides spending two tours of duty in Turkey. In 1961 - 1963, he taught English at Çapa Eğitim Enstitüsü, and since 1973 he has been Director of the Ankara Centre of the British Council, with responsibility for the Teaching of English.

PROLOGUE TO THE FIRST ENGLISH EDITION

I wrote the last paragraphs of this biography of the great and wellloved figure of Atatürk during the sad days of his passage into immortality, in November 1938, and it was published in Spanish in early 1939, by the publishing house "Claridad," of Buenos Aires. It attracted considerable attention in Latin America. It has therefore been my fortune to have been the first author in the world to write a biography of that great reformer, after his death.

I have poured into this book the experience derived from five intense years spent in Turkey, from 1930 to 1935. I was able to share the experience of the events of those historic years, as passionately as any Turk. The merit of this biography rests only upon its documentary value.

Thanks to my father's position as Consul-General of Argentina in Istanbul, and my own position as Vice-Consul, at a time when my country had no Embassy as yet, I had the privilege to attend receptions of an official nature attended by Atatürk. I had the honour to shake his hand many times. Since there had not yet been built in Ankara headquarters for most of the diplomatic representations, part of diplomatic life went on in Istanbul.

I also found Kemal at the Park Hotel, where he was in the habit of going, and where he used to dine with his friends and enjoy dancing, in the hall on the lower floor. He was interested in the way I danced the Argentine tango, the steps of which I sometimes used to show off as I went past his table. On one occasion he spoke to me, showing his great kindness and his smile, which was short, but extremely friendly.

I have retained a vivid and close memory, and a deep feeling of devotion, from his incomparable and charismatic presence.

Within the frame of world history, the great figure of Kemal Atatürk has imprinted his indestructible profile upon the broad history of political thought.

As a military leader, his genius in strategy places him among the most outstanding of those captains whom history has raised high, and it is enough to remember him as the victor in those legendary scenes at the Hellespont and on the high Anatolian plateau, in battles which remain as lessons in the military art, and in amazing strength of will. Again Kemal the statesman succeeds the general, and in a matter of a few years causes his people to advance centuries along the road to progress, through a revolution both in law, social affairs, politics and economics; along the true road to spiritual and material progress.

Now that thirty-eight years have gone by since he passed into those regions where time loses its sway, we can more accurately assess Atatürk's presence in the environment of history, and appreciate his true dimensions there. Kemal outstrips the limits of his own country, as a man who could change the course of history.

At the close of the First World War, when the Turkish people had been beaten in one war after another, driven from Europe, oppressed in their own home in Asia, and betrayed by their feeble Sultan and his courtiers, Kemal led them to defy their fate. Raised to red heat by their military hero's preaching, the Turks revolted against the arbitrary decisions of the victors of the First Great War, collected into the Articles of the Treaty of Sèvres, Turkey's sentence of death.

The whole world, with its statesmen and international political forecasters, was left stupefied by the apparently impossible: the victory, all- subduing, of a people in arms, with poor weapons and bottled up in Anatolia, over the truly formidable armies with which the Allies attempted to impose their unjust law.

Decades have passed since then, and we can now see that the victory was not merely a local triumph, as was then thought. No; it was the sign of the deliverance of all the oppressed peoples of the East and Africa, the beginning of the end of colonialism, and the advent of so many countries' struggle for freedom and their entry to the international community. Atatürk is the banner of all those who believe that all peoples and all men should have equal rights and opportunities.

However, he did not only make a change in the direction of political history at world level: also transcendent are the principles on which he founded the organisation of the new Turkish State which he created; principles which were realistic and advanced, sufficient for the urgent needs of the moment, yet which have been shown sound in retrospect through time. Kemal was against any theocratic form of government, yet he allowed religious belief to labour in the broad field of the individual's free conscience.

Kemal Atatürk held a powerful interest for me after my arrival in Turkey in 1930: there I found his will, moving every activity, inspiring every hope: as he himself would have put it, there was a particle of his spirit within the spirit of every Turk.

I remember Kemal walking past me, with a quick step, and the grey glint of his penetrating eyes, whose expression of intense will gave greater concentration to his thick eyebrows. This man was without doubt one of the great founders, of the stature of those whose names are picked out by history, and revered by nations.

In spite of his belief in democracy, Atatürk had to act on some occasions in a dictatorial way. He was forced to do this through circumstance: otherwise it would have been impossible to achieve the transformation of the country: reaction would have hurled down the reforms and driven progress back. It was impossible to move, without any transition, from the Ottoman autocracy to the most advanced form of democracy. A period of education and acclimatisation was required. Kemal was a Teacher of Democracy, and never ceased training his people in the understanding of its ideals. History has fully justified him.

Atatürk has passed beneath the bronze arches of history not so much as one of the greatest commanders of all time, nor as a man who liberated a nation and built a new, modern and prosperous state, but rather and principally, as one of the greatest philosophers of political theory. He contributed a political plan which has wide possibilities for the future of man: a system which at the moment it was proclaimed was completely revolutionary: a political system of an economic and social character, in which the direction of the economy is the fundamental responsibility of the State, which intervenes as far as is necessary and useful, and no further; and a people which is absolutely free to elect its rulers, free to adopt its own ideas, free in conscience, and possessing the right of choice.

At the end of the War of Independence, Atatürk made it an accomplished fact that his country stood equidistant from East and West. He created a Turkey which was free of any bond of any kind, which might tie her to either of these poles of power, and able to make her own decisions. In this aspect, the Hero of the Sakarya can be seen as the precursor of the Third World.

Atatürk belongs not only to Turkey but to Humanity.

After forty years, fate has brought me back to this country that I love. I cannot express in words the emotion with which I bent before the tomb of the immortal Creator of the Turkish Republic. Privileged by the honour of guarding the ashes of that great man who loved his people so much, Atatürk's Ankara is now the Holy City of the new Turkey.

BLANCO VILLALTA

Ankara, 1976

PRONUNCIATION OF TURKISH NAMES

The Latin Turkish alphabet, introduced by Atatürk in 1928, is an extremely clear and consistent one. Most of the letters have sounds very similar to their English equivalents, with the following exceptions:

1. *Vowels*

    i. Turkish vowels are normally short. They are long in some words derived from Arabic or Persian, and are then written with a circumflex accent:

    > Nâzım, Nâmık

    However, the circumflex has another function when it follows l, g or k (see below). The circumflex, and long vowels generally, are falling out of use because of the elimination of foreign words under the Language Reform. Soft g also lengthens (2. iv).

    ii. The vowel İ, ı, (always written *with* a dot on the capital as well as on the small letter), corresponds to the English vowel in 'fect,' but is shorter. İsmet.

    iii. The vowel I, ı, (always written *without* a dot, both in capitals and small letters), stands for a vowel made by shaping the lips as for an English 'ee' as in 'feet,' but trying to say an English 'oo,' as in 'food.' The result is something like the English vowel heard in unstressed positions, such as 'baker,' 'around.' However, the Turkish vowel can carry a full stress: Atıf (stress on the second syllable).

    iv. The vowels ö, ü, are similar to French 'eu,' 'u' (he*u*re, pl*u*me), or German ö, ü.

2. *Consonants*

    i. c stands for the English 'j,' as in '*J*ohn.'

    ii. ç stands for the English 'ch,' as in '*ch*urch.'

    iii. g usually stands for English 'g' as in '*go*,' but 'gy,' before i, e, ö, ü, û and â.

    iv. Ğ, ğ *either* simply lengthens a preceding vowel: 'ağ' (equivalent to English 'ah'), *or* when placed between two vowels, shows a movement from one to the other. Depending on the vowels, it sounds more like an English 'w': 'soğuk,' 'kuğu,' 'boğa,' 'dağın,' or more like an English 'y': 'değer,' 'öğe,' 'derneğin,' 'kütüğü.'

v. h is always pronounced, including at the end of syllables: Falih.

vi. j stands for the English sound in 'pleasure,' 'confusion.'

vii. K stands for English 'k' in '*k*ing,' except 'ky' before i, e, o, ü, â and û.

viii. l stands for English 'light l,' as in '*l*ick,' '*l*eft,' and for 'dark l,' as in '*l*ook,' 'wa*ll*.' There is no difficulty for English speakers, as Turkish uses the two kinds of 'l' in the same places as English, except when a circumflex vowel follows. Thus 'lâle' has a 'light l' at the beginning, where we would expect a dark l.

ix. ş stands for English 'sh' as in '*sh*op.'

x. v is pronounced like English 'w,' when next to a, ı, o or u, elsewhere as English 'v.'

3. *Stress*

The stress on a Turkish word usually comes on the last syllable, and this is always the case with the names of people : K*emal*, İs*met*. However, place names regularly have the stress on the first syllable: *Ankara, Sivas*. Some exceptions to this are: *Istanbul, Antalya, Amasya, Antakya*.

OTHER WORKS BY JORGE BLANCO VILLALTA
(IN SPANISH)

The Turkish People. El Ateneo, Buenos Aires, 1936.

Scenes from Contemporary Istanbul. El Ateneo, Buenos Aires, 1937.

Turkish Literature. University of La Plata, La Plata, 1940.

Comtemporary Turkish Literature. Claridad, Buenos Aires, 1941.

Conquest of the Rio de la Plata. Atlántida, Buenos Aires, 1945.

Ritual Cannibalism in America. Emecé, Buenos Aires, 1946.

Montoya, Missionary to the Guaranis. Kraft. Colección Cúpula, Buenos Aires, 1955.

Organisation of the American States. Buenos Aires, 1958.

Nobrega, the First Chronicler of the Conquest of Brazil, Argentine Academy of Letters, Buenos Aires, 1965.

The Diplomats (with the help of Manuela de Blanco Villalta). Acleón, Buenos Aires, 1968.

Cannibal Rites in America. Casalardo S A, Buenos Aires, 1970.

Turkish Art and Literature. National Museum of Oriental Art, Buenos Aires, 1975.

JORGE BLANCO VILLALTA

PART ONE

THE BACKGROUND AGAINST WHICH
KEMAL'S PERSONALITY EMERGED

FIRST STIRRINGS

Macedonia — chains of mountains collide with each other forming great masses which, breaking in terrible convulsions, are dismembered into separate sheer-sided peaks. The rainwaters can find no peace there, but are immediately changed, breaking from rock to rock, into small impetuous torrents, and are driven where the tortured terrain wills them, giving birth to rivers which must suffer interminable cascades along their paths. After passing through narrow valleys in which a few willows dare to approach their crumbling edges, they leap down slopes proudly bearing forests of planes and poplars, which then extend in broad fertile plains, pasturing numerous herds of cattle.

These are the courses of the Struma and the Vardar, great rivers which water Macedonia, a region whose inhabitants have throughout all time followed the example of their convulsed mountains, by continually fighting each other.

The Orestians, Elimians, Paeonians, Macedonians, Eordaeans and Lyncestians, who were the first known tribes to inhabit the area between the Pindus chain and the Rhodopian mountains, maintained bloody struggles amongst themselves, from which emerged the victors those who gave their name to the land which was to become the home of Alexander.

Macedonia became the mistress of an enormous empire. She thought her internal peace secured, but this was not to be. In the second century before Christ, her last King, Perseus, fell defeated by Aemilius Paullus, and she was invaded by the Romans; later, Macedonia became a Province of the Eastern Empire, suffering devastation by the hordes of Alaric I. Later Macedonia became the Kingdom of the Marquis of Montferrat, but was then reconquered and Theodore of Epirus was proclaimed her Emperor. Then she was governed by the Byzantines, then by the Serbs in the 14th century and by the Ottomans in the 15th.

Different races and religions have met there, and have always met in battle. Hatreds have remained endemic and produced sharp crises. There are few regions where the differences of faith, language and race are as pronounced as in Macedonia or where they are intertwined in such a complicated way. Many times these inevitable clashes have sparked off cruel wars.

We can take the year 1822 as the date which marks the beginning of the state of rebellion in Macedonia against the feeble Ottoman Government.

The destiny of peoples who live on the plains is to suffer, if they are defeated, the yoke imposed on them by the invader; that is not so in the case of mountain peoples; they retain something of the liberty which belongs to the eagle, their brother. So the minarets erected by the Moslems on the plains showed that the Turks were masters; but when one climbed the first slopes, near some limpid stream, a church, or a Christian Monastery, Greek, Bulgarian or Serbian, marked the beginning of the rough places, where men were guarding their faith, and where an orthodox priest would be speaking in exalted language of religion, race and liberty. The mountain Christian was reminded of his beliefs by icons painted in ecstatic styles, and crosses of rustic wood showed him his way.

Eagles carefully watch a noble bull in its last death throes, eager to seize upon its flesh, still beating in the last spasms of death; from the mediaeval monasteries, monks who had followed each other in succession for more than four centuries, dreaming of that great day when Macedonia would become a Christian land again, were following step by step the rapid decay of the Ottoman Empire.

That moment was approaching in which the ideal of the Greeks would begin to become a reality; now all the orthodox peoples found themselves united under the cross, ready for the crusade against the infidel lord. This, it was believed, would lead to the Resurrection of the Eastern Empire, which would have three capitals; Athens would be the intellectual centre; Jerusalem redeemed, the Holy City, would be the religious capital, and Constantinople, set between two seas and two continents, was destined to be the political one. The Greek Emperor would attend a solemn mass following the orthodox rite in the cathedral church of Santa Sophia. Beautiful dreams for a Greek.

But when the decay of the Ottomans became so obvious that no one in the Balkans would have any doubt that sooner or later the Turks would have to abandon Macedonia, the orthodox lost their unity, and nationalism arose. The Bulgarians, Serbs, Greeks and Romanians fell out with each other; the time for sharing the spoils was approaching, and it was this share out which was to cause some years later the Second Balkan War.

At the beginning of this century, Macedonia was populated by very different elements, distinguished by race, religion and language. The Bulgarians inhabited the southern slopes of the Rhodopian mountains, the area around Üsküp was occupied by Serbs, and the upper valleys of the Vardar by the Albanians. Most of the Greeks were to be found in lower Macedonia, while in the central plateau there lived Wallachians and Turks. In the cities, especially Salonika, one could find fair-sized colonies of Turks, mainly composed of Government employees and army personnel; however, the population was predominately composed of Greeks and Sephardic Jews, descendants of those Jews who were expelled from Spain in the 15th century.

It was at that same city of Salonika, situated on the shore of the gulf of the same name, which connects to the Aegean Sea, that there was born in 1881 in the old Turkish quarter, with its winding alleyways, and little houses with faded paint and dried-up timber, their windows covered by the traditional grille which veiled the patriarchal life of those Turkish homes, Mustafa, the son of Ali Riza and Zübeyde.

The comfortable house in the street called İslahane, which was one of the widest and passed through one of the better neighbourhoods, had nothing to distinguish it from those on either side of it; nor did the parents of the new born child show any unusual circumstance. The young mother Zübeyde was a pious Moslem, of traditional opinions, unlike the master of the house, who was a man of liberal ideas and a declared partisan of the westernization of the Empire. His wife did not share his views, but as custom demanded, she refrained from arguing about them.

A Moslem woman was condemned to seclusion. She could only go out into the street covered from head to foot by the traditional "Çarşaf" and by the "Peçe" a thick cloth which covered her face. It was not even permitted for her to walk through the streets at her husband's side. She was supposed to follow him a few paces behind, and after sunset no woman was allowed to be found in the public streets. Her happiness depended exclusively on the lord of the house, whom the Koran always regarded as being in the right and allowed to punish her or expel her from the house whenever he wished. A woman might think herself lucky if she was her husband's only wife, as was the case in most humble families, as polygamy was an expensive business.

One can easily imagine that the education received by a Turkish woman, who would have had to leave school at a very young age, was rudimentary. Those ladies whom Pierre Loti calls "désenchantées" belonged to powerful families who could afford the luxury of foreign governesses for their daughters. To Westerners, the life of Turkish women would certainly have seemed painful and filled with humiliation and betrayal; in general, it was not so bad as one might have believed. The religion, which was the foundation of the Islamic law, was also that of the family and of the Empire; its precepts were obeyed without question by believers, and in particular by the women, being further removed than the men from the experience of life and civilisation. "God is great! God knows what is good for you and you do not know it," says the sacred book.

The Turkish woman resigned herself to her destiny, and her days went past monotonously, but serenely, in her home which was for her the whole world; her children and her husband treated her with gentleness and respect. She was considered to be a pure being, separated from the miseries of the world and even from the dust of the streets. There are other factors which make the commandments of Mohammed bearable; kindness, which he considered the first of all virtues, is a quality natural among the Turks. Their kindness extends to everything which surrounds them, to other people and even to animals. They even wish their kindness to continue after their death; one frequently sees on Moslem tombs cavities made in the shape of a heart, which collect rainwater so that the birds can drink from them. A particularly endearing characteristic of this people is the respect which young people show towards their parents, teachers and the aged. One sees the harmony of their family life, and the gentleness of their thoughts reflected in the expression of happiness to be seen on the faces of children, whom one hardly ever hears crying, and in the serenity of the old people.

So it was then, that from his earliest years, Mustafa found himself between two different conceptions of life; the past represented in his mother, and the future in his father. He came into the world at the moment in which one epoch of the old theocratic Empire was dying and a new epoch was beginning to appear. It was to be the destiny of that child to be the soul of a nation's transformation.

Many years later, Mustafa recorded certain events of his childhood, which had a decisive importance in determining the direction of his life. "From my earliest childhood only one event has remained engraved on my memory, but with an inerasable clarity. This was my entry into school, a question about which my parents thought in different ways. My mother remained faithful to the old traditions and customs; a quiet and gentle Religiosity, but one which was unshakeable, formed the essence of her character. For that reason she wished to place me in one of the schools directed by "hocas," holy men, in which the teaching followed the severe traditions of Islam. I believe that she insisted upon this, more than anything because by custom the entry of a child to one of these schools was accompanied by a religious ceremony. That day had to be distinguished from others by a special holy act, so that the child would thus understand that from that moment onwards he belonged, above the bonds of family relationship, to the great community of believers, and that he must fulfil the duties which that community demanded from its members.

"My father, on the other hand, was a man of liberal views, rather hostile to religion, and a partisan of Western ideas. He would have preferred to see me go to a lay school, which did not found its teaching on the Koran but on modern science.

"In this battle of consciences, my father managed to gain the victory after a small manoeuvre; he pretended to give in to my mother's wishes, and arranged that I should enter the school of Fatma Molla Kadin, with the traditional ceremony. On the morning of my entry to the school, my mother dressed me in a white suit and decorated me with a band of golden linen, with which she wrapped my head like a turban; in my hand she placed a golden branch. Then the schoolmaster, a hoca, followed by all his pupils, presented himself in front of our door, which was decorated with green branches; a prayer was said, and then after touching my breast and forehead with the tips of my fingers, I bowed to my parents and to the school master and kissed each one of them on the hand.

"Finally, amidst the cheerful shouts of my new companions, we progressed through the streets of the city to the school, which was situated near the mosque. As soon as we had arrived there and recited another prayer in unison, the schoolmaster took me by the hand and conducted me to a room, empty and domed, in which the mysteries of the Koran would be revealed to me.

"Six months later more or less, my father quietly withdrew me from the school of Fatma Molla Kadın and took me to that of old Şemsi Efendi, who directed a free preparatory school according to European methods. My mother made no objection, since her desires had been complied with and her convictions respected. It was the ceremony above all else which had satisfied her."

Mustafa, who was then seven years old, felt a tender veneration towards his mother. For her part Zübeyde poured out the whole tenderness of her heart upon her son; she did not feel that her little daughter Makbule merited such love or attention; a boy was something superior; as the Prophet has said; "men are superior to women, because God has given them predominance over them." Throughout all the stages of his career, Mustafa retained his original feelings towards that good lady.

Ali Rıza Bey, a gentleman and a government employee, dreamed of giving up the monotony of his work and his meagre salary, which he usually received considerably in arrears, for a life of commerce and free activity, where each man's intelligence and perseverence could win him a better future. He had before him the example the Jews and Greeks, who held the commerce of Macedonia in their hands, while Turks aspired no higher than obtaining a job or entering the army.

Ali Rıza realised his ambition, and established himself as a trader in timber. The rich forests of Macedonia were being cut down mercilessly, to such an extent that the climate was clearly changed. The tree trunks, either whole or sawn up were exported at prices defeating all competition. Perhaps in his new profession Ali Rıza would have managed to accumulate a sizeable capital, but bis life failed to reach even a pessimistic expectation. His wife and children were left without resources.

His neighbours and friends brought his rough coffin of white wood, covered with a green cloth embroidered with verses of the Koran, upon their shoulders from the house where he had died. They bore it towards the nearest mosque, hurrying, because prayers for the dead are recited at noon.

Passers-by who professed the religion of Mohammed joined the funeral procession, and as is a custom and a fine one, helped to carry the dead man in his final journey, at least seven paces. From the mosque to the Moslem cemetery situated on the edge of the town, it is a long way to go on foot.

The grave was prepared and Zübeyde and some of her friends waited beside it. Now began the saddest part of the ceremony, the moment when the muezzin sings his lament, and the grave-digger saws through the coffin as it hangs inside the trench suspended on pulleys, when the women weep and the men move aside so as not to see the shrouded coiose fall into the bottom of the pit. The heavily turbaned imam raises bis voice in prayer, and extending his hands at the level of his white beard monotonously ends with the words, "Radi Allahu anh!" May God have mercy upon him.

Zübeyde prepared her luggage that same night. She could not remain in the same rooms which brought her so many memories which she could not beat at that time; frequently she interrupted her work to weep; little Mustafa watched her curiously, but with a profound seriousness. He could not understand what had happened. He knew that his father had gone forever, but was it forever? What a strange thing! He loved his father very much. His father was very good, and he could understand clearly everything which he said, which was not the case with their friend the hoca, who sometimes said things whose significance he could never understand. His father had died. Death! What a strange thing! In his heart he felt pain and grief, and his throat was hurting him, but he did not weep like his mother. Why should he weep?

Then they went to live in the country, in an uncle's house, near the village of Langadhas two hours distance from Salonika. Mustafa preferred this free country life a thousand times over that of the city; he was interested by the farm animals, whose habits he observed, and sometimes he went out riding on horseback. His white skin became a copper colour, tanned by the strong sun and fresh air which blows down from the mountains. He had fair hair and his eyes were grey-blue, sometimes the grey predominating in them and sometimes the blue, just as the sea varies in colour through the influence of the sky; his mouth was small, almost without lips. His whole features combined to suggest a strong will and observant personality. His uncle instructed him in the rudiments of agriculture. He thought that he would make a countryman out of this strong lad; the prospect did not appear to displease the boy, and he worked enthusiastically at the small country jobs which were given him to do.

Zübeyde had a close desire to set her son off on a career, as she knew he was intelligent and hard working; it would have been her dream to see him wearing the green turban of the Doctors of the Law. Faithful to her intentions, she made every possible economy and succeeded after two years in persuading a relative in Salonika to take him in as a paying guest, until such time as she could herself manage to instal herself in the city, which occurred a few months later.

Mustafa began his studies again; he was then eleven. In the first weeks the walls of the school seemed like prison to him, accustomed as he had become to the wide open spaces of the countryside, and he had rather lost the ability to take jokes from his fellow students. Being of a sensitive nature, he quarrelled with them several times and fought with them; he was admonished, and one day when he was fighting ferociously with a stronger comrade who thought that he could beat the obstinate Mustafa, the teacher of Arabic came to separate the belligerents, and since he believed that Mustafa had been the originator of the disturbance, he beat him in front of all the students. Mustafa said nothing, but as soon as he could he went home and told Zübeyde that he would never set foot in that school again. Disconcerted though his mother was, she had to accept the inevitable. But to what school could she now take him? There was no abundance of schools in the town; Mustafa had made his decision long before; he envied the fine uniform of his neighbour Ahmet, who was a student at the military academy. He was also attracted by the elegant officers whom he frequently saw. Thus it was that there awakened in him an irresistable desire to become a soldier, to show himself off in gold braid like them and carry a sword. On his own initiative, he asked an officer who had been a friend of his father to help him in his plans to follow a military career. The old soldier was amused by the formal request made to him by the little twelve-year-old, and since he knew the director of the military preparatory school in Salonika, he arranged that his protégé should be admitted to the entry examination.

His mother accepted Mustafa's declared vocation, although it would not have been the career that she would have chosen for him. The military schools, which were supported by the government, gave a young man who wanted to study a future, without his having to undertake any expense, and this helped Zübeyde's difficult financial situation considerably.

Mustafa succeeded completely in his examinations, and quickly put on the uniform of his dreams. He enjoyed himself in the cadet school; he distinguished himself from his classmates by his quick learning and his seriousness. He showed signs of an exceptional gift in mathematics; that exact science fitted his positive spirit perfectly. Captain Mustafa Bey, the mathematics teacher, was very proud of his student, treated him as his friend, and gave him the privileged post of monitor. In his second year of studies, during which the progress made by the young cadet had brought him to the top of the class, Captain Mustafa, wishing to reward his perseverance, called him in front of all the class and gave him the sur-name of Kemal, an Arabic word which means "perfect;" this would, the teacher added, serve to distinguish the names of master and student. From that moment onwards he used it alongside his own name, although at that time surnames were not used by Turks.

The brilliant student felt the delights and griefs of love for the first time, when he was barely fourteen. The daughter of a neighbour was the cause of the awakening of these sentiments, and as happens in first love, their intensity was great. She would show herself to him with her face uncovered, at one of the windows of her house, and her admirer took every opportunity to pass that way. During the nights he spent long periods waiting, before the wooden grille, from behind which Beauty was surely likewise attempting to discover him hidden in the shadows. Love did not make him break the rhythm of his studies nor lose him his first place in the class, for his heart was never able to dominate his brain.

As soon as the four years of preparatory school were finished, and he had successfully passed the final examinations, he was sent to the cadet school at Monastir.

This city, second in importance in Macedonia after Salonika, and built on the banks of the Dragor at the foot of high mountains, is of unusually great strategic importance, as it is the junction of the roads which join Durres, an Albanian port on the Adriatic, with Üsküp, Adrianople and Salonika. The imperial government therefore gave special importance to this key point in their Balkan territories and amongst other military installations there was situated the cadet school.

In this school Mustafa Kemal formed his character, and there was where his personality was born. The whole influence which he had unconsciously absorbed from the ambience and cosmopolitan character of his native city, was here revealed to him through his higher studies in history. His customary manner, which showed a mingling of keen observation and strong will, acquired from then on the characteristics of a man of thought, who looked inwards upon his personality, and who reasoned with himself.

The strict military life was very different from that which he had known so far, living with his mother; he had come to expect words of solace for his worries from the kindly Zübeyde. Mother and son were alike, not only physically, with the same mouths and eyes, but also with kindred characters, dominant and fixed in their beliefs. Mustafa had also inherited something from his father, his definite realism and his minute observation of things which he had seen. In this he contrasted with Zübeyde, less educated than Ali Rıza, who based her wisdom on the holy book of the Koran, and on the words of the Prophet. The only arguments which even for a short time disturbed the complete understanding between mother and son concerned the Word of the Prophet, and mysticism.

Mustafa was passionately interested in study, and in particular the study of the life of nations and men.

What profound teaching could be found among those pages of those history books, books full of lessons from the past! There was room in them for unsuspectedly wide horizons, and amazing figures rose out of the past, with their glorious trains of escort. Napoleon, Selim, Mehmet, Oğuzhan, Hannibal, Alexander-Alexander! Like himself a son of this country, who knew and loved these mountains, who emerged from that place, conquered the mysterious East and created an enormous empire. History also taught him, on the other side of the coin, that all the great empires existed only for a limited time; and then invariably decay attacked them all.

He now realised that the hour had come for the Ottoman Empire, as it bad for all the others, whose domination had been imposed with the edge of the sword.

Let us see what the course of that Empire had been.

In Anatolia, which from remote times had been a theatre for events of great historical importance, and the cradle of important civilisations, there flourished in the thirteenth century a Turkish Empire, that of the Seljuks; thousands of years before, other branches of the great Turkish family from Central Asia had arrived in great migrations to these same lands.

A part of the Turkish tribes, who had remained behind, were converted to Islam in the eighth century, and placed beneath their rule nearly the whole Moslem world before setting off, three centuries later, towards Asia Minor, under the protection of the Seljuk Turks of Iran. In the middle of the eleventh century the Anatolian Seljuks controlled the other Turkish states which had arisen in different parts of that peninsula. Two centuries later, they began to decline with the invasions of Turco-Mongol hordes, belonging to the armies of Cengiz Han. However, the Mongol dominance was of short duration; after its disappearance, anarchy reigned, which allowed the development of small Turkish principalities. Amongst them, in the region near the frontier with the Byzantine Empire, was situated the principality of the sons of Osman, who were to make their fame known to the entire world. The eponymous hero of the tribe, Osman, considered himself to be an independent sovereign, amidst the confusion which then existed amid the ruins of the Seljuk Empire. At the same time, it was a propitious moment for him to extend his frontiers at the expense of the decayed Byzantine Empire, a task to which he dedicated himself without delay.

The period of glory began, and conquests followed each other. Osman's son Orhan took Bursa in 1326, and made it into the first capital of the Ottoman Empire. Orhan was as good an administrator as he was a warrior, and he laid the. first foundations of the government and justice which were necessary to a state, and also founded the Corps of Janissaries. These troops, who took part brilliantly in the Turkish conquests, were formed of men who had been seized from their families in the conquered territories. Later on, to provide them with recruits, there was instituted the levy of children by the "Devşirme," which ensured that their ranks were never depleted. The children who were recruited were brought up in the Moslem Religion and instructed in the arts of war; they then entered the Corps of Janissaries, from which they could aspire to all the honours and high positions of the Empire. Since at the time of their first conquests there were not many Turks who gave allegiance to the house of Osman, the Empire would never have achieved such rapid glory without the help of these converted Christians, who usually did not know where their parents had lived, and who besides were soldiers gained from the conquered territories.

The Eastern Empire, in its decadence, offered a wide field of action for the conquerers from Asia. The Emperors were obliged to appease the anger and ambitions of the Sultans by paying them large tributes.

Orhan mapped out the route of conquest; the coasts of the Marmara Sea, then Thrace, to encircle Constantinople. One after the other, he took Nicaea and Nicomedia, and his cavalry, whose appearance and tactics were similar to those of the hordes of Central Asia, sacked Thrace on several occasions. The third Emperor of the Dynasty, Murat, conquered nearly the whole Balkan peninsula and established the capital of the Empire at Adrianople.

The advance of the Ottomans suffered an interruption, with the destruction of their army and the imprisonment of the Sultan Beyazit in 1402, after the battle of Ankara fought between him and the Turkish conqueror Tamerlane. After Tamerlane had taken possession of nearly the whole of Anatolia in his usual blood-thirsty fashion, he was surprised by death in Otrar, while he was preparing to conquer China. On the death of Bayezit, who was nicknamed "Yıldırım," the Thunderbolt, an interregnum followed, during which his four sons fought each other for the possession of the inheritance. European historians have counted Süleyman, who at one moment was nearer to making himself accepted as sultan than his brothers, as the fifth Ottoman sultan and the first of his name, but Turkish historians do not agree with this; this prince never became sultan and the successor of Beyazit was Mehmet I, Süleyman's brother.

The obvious weakness of the Ottoman Empire provoked a new attempt on the part of the Christians to expel the invaders from Europe. The army of the coalition which was formed, commanded by King Wladyslaw VI of Poland and John Hunyadi the Voivode of Transylvania, arrived at Varna on the Black Sea in 1444, and was there defeated by Murat II, the King of Poland being killed. Sultan Murat, a nightmare for the Christian armies, died in Adrianople after a reign of military glory; he was succeeded on the throne by his son Mehmet. Since the victories achieved by his father ensured that he need not fear attacks either in Asia or in Europe, Mehmet was able to dedicate himself completely to putting into effect his plans to capture Constantinople, this city having so far resisted all attacks, protected by its formidable walls.

The desire to conquer that great city prevented Mehmet from enjoying the pleasures of life; he was tortured by insomnia, and his plans for attack and its possible consequences occupied him ceaselessly. The thousand-year- old Byzantine Empire, from which the Ottomans were tearing vital parts on all sides, was now reduced in this tragic time for the West merely to the city of Constantinople itself, a strip of land of some hundred miles to the North and West of the city, and half of the Peloponnesos. The Emperor John VIII had gone in person to beg help from the West; he had had an interview with the Pope Eugenius IV, and the Council of Florence in 1439 the schism between the Roman and Greek churches was brought to an end. The Emperor believed that by this he had assured the help of the Western Powers, but it never arrived. Neither the Byzantine clergy nor the people accepted a return to Catholicism, and although mass was said in

Santa Sophia according to the Roman rite, there were voices outside which said "Rather live beneath the turban than beneath the tiara."

On the 29th May 1453, after a memorable siege, "the City well-guarded by God" fell into the hands of Mehmet II. This date has been chosen to mark the end of the Middle Ages and the beginning of the Renaissance.

The Emperor Constantine XIII fought with extraordinary heroism; death caught him sword in hand in the middle of the fight. This was the last glorious page in the history of the late Empire.

Now master of the city, Mehmet Fatih, the conqueror, advanced towards Santa Sophia followed by his brilliant train; he had promised Allah to transform the great temple into a mosque. In the forum of Augustus, covered with dead bodies, and onto which opened the gates of that temple whose capture he had dreamt of, the conqueror stopped his procession, and with eyes shining with happiness contemplated the greatness of his conquest. Nearby, still showing its last defiant expression, was exposed the head of Constantine, last Emperor of Byzantium. After giving the Patriarch Gennadius the charge of governing his new Christian subjects, Fatih continued with his conquests. His military career had met with almost complete success. Now he showed himself a great administrator also; he revised and codified Ottoman legislation in a book of laws called the "Kanun Nameh." Osman had established the basis of the new Asian Empire. Mehmet organized one which was to be powerful on the continent of Europe.

In the next century, the sixteenth, there stand out two great Sultans, Selim and Süleyman. Selim the Grim, one of the most glorious conquerors of his dynasty, deserved that title. He is accused of having poisoned his father, and it is certainly true that he caused the death of his two brothers and five nephews. His most favoured vezirs were decapitated for the slightest reason. He was a fanatical Sunnite, and fought against Moslem of the other persuasion, the Shi'ites, slaughtering them in thousands. In this same persecution, he made war against the Shah of Iran, Ismail, also a Shi'ite, and captured his capital, Tabriz. He conquered Syria, Palestine and Egypt where he ordered a horrible massacre of the Mamelukes. He forced the last Abbasid Caliph to relinquish to him the dignity of Calif of the Moslems, which from then onwards was a title of the House of Osman. With Süleyman the Law-Giver or "The Magnificent," as he is more usually known in the West, the Empire reached its highest point, and greatest extension. His reign from 1520 to 1566, is notable for the capture of Belgrade, and the castle of the knights of St. John in Rhodes, a stronghold which had constantly threatened the communications between the Ottoman possessions in Africa, Asia and Europe; also for the final conquest of Hungary and the siege of Vienna, which however he was obliged to raise. Süleyman I placed special importance on the formation of a strong fleet, which at the orders of the fearless Barbarossa, terrorised the Mediterranean and extended Ottoman rule beyond Oran. Later on the Sultan brought the frontiers of the Empire up to the Persian Gulf.

Süleyman consented in 1535 to sign with Francois I, some commercial treaties, which were called "capitulations." Apart from their commercial clauses, the treaties stipulated, in favour of the King's subjects who were resident in the Ottoman Empire, the right of being judged by their own courts. The treaties which were agreed between the successors of Süleyman and other powers contained greater privileges in favour of these same people, which finally became abused, and allowed the establishment of foreign governments within the Turkish state.

On the death of this Sultan and the accession of Selim II, the Empire entered a period of stagnation, which lasted until the second siege of Vienna in 1683, which date marks the beginning of its decay. During this period the Empire was governed by foolish men, such as Murat III, an epileptic with few of the requisites of a man of state, the bloodthirsty Mehmet III, who was obliged to abdicate, being considered to be mentally defective; then Murat IV, a strong character, managed to revive for a fugitive moment the glories of the past; however he was succeded by Ibrahim, a prodigal libertine, who tried to vie in his luxury with Persian satraps and even the Pharaohs, whose example he followed by having his beard adorned with costly pearls. He had grown up amidst the luxury of the court of one of the most powerful Empires in the world. He abused the pleasures of the harem, until his nervous system collapsed.

At the end of the reign of Mehmet IV, in which took place the second siege of Vienna, resulting in a defeat for the Turkish army, there was heard in Europe with renewed vigour talk of the Eastern Question, by which was meant the expulsion of the Turks from European soil. The period of the conquests had been followed by one in which the Empire had contented itself with holding on to the territories it had seized; now the Empire lacked strength and the European nations would be able to force the invader to retreat to where he had come from, in Asia. The Ottomans had not assimilated the conquered populations, but had permitted them to continue in their beliefs and customs; all they had exacted was the payment of taxes. In fact they had accomplished merely a military occupation.

After the second siege of Vienna, the Turkish Armies suffered defeat after defeat. Fortune showed the Sultans who followed that she had abandoned them, in their battles against Eugene of Savoy and Peter the Great.

With the treaties of Karlowitz in 1699, which recognised the loss of Hungary and Transylvania, and Passarowitz in 1718, which lost Northern Serbia, Montenegro and Dalmatia, the decay of the Empire accelerated.

Catherine II, who reigned during the second half of the eighteenth century, was Turkey's great enemy. She encouraged the rebellion of the orthodox subjects of the Ottomans, and even proposed to the German Emperor the partition of Turkey, as a result of which Russia would take possession of Constantinople and the straits. However this plan could not be realised because of Austria's opposition. It can be said that from this moment onwards the Russian and Ottoman Empires were continually, though from different motives, in a continual state of war.

We thus come to Selim III, 1789 - 1807, the kindly and cultured Commander of the Faithful, for whom Western civilisation held no secters. He thought to reform the Empire whose progress he could see to be flagging; he was the beginner of the reform. The ulemas, or Moslem clergy, and the janissaries declared themselves enemies of the Sultan and his progressive ideas. In particular the janissaries, protesting against the creation of new types of military units, attacked the imperial palace, obliging Selim to give the throne over to the rebel's own candidate. The second reforming Sultan was Mahmut II; he showed that he possessed great statesmanlike qualities and had the willpower and bravery to impose Western ideas of progress, in spite of the opposition and violent criticism, which were met with at every new step in this direction. It was his fortune to have to reign during a period of extraordinary difficulty, for rebellions and wars succeeded each other during his long period on the throne, almost without interruption. The ulemas and the janissaries were his declared enemies; but the Sultan decided to break the power of the latter, since they had become a constant menace towards the internal peace of the country, and concerned themselves more with politics than with the defence of the Empire. He ordered a general massacre of the janissaries, and it is calculated that twenty thousand of them died. Russia hurried towards the realisation of her old dream; her troops reached as far as Adrianople and without the intervention of France and Great Britain, Constantinople would have fallen into her hands. Greece declared herself an independent country through the treaty of London in 1830. Another of the misfortunes which overshadowed the life of Mahmut was the rebellion of Egypt. The armies of Mehmet Ali, Viceroy of Egypt, defeated the Ottomans in all battles, occupying Konya. Mahmut called upon the powers to aid him but only Russia agreed to help, since peace existed between them at that moment. In 1833, the Russian fleet presented itself in the Bosporus; but the other powers, seeing Russian armies in Constantinople, hastened to serve as intermediaries between Egypt and Turkey, with the object of seeing them go away again. Nevertheless, Mahmut organized a strong army which marched against Egypt, but was defeated. Mahmut died a few days later, his efforts to delay the dismemberment of the Empire having proved unavailing.

The great powers, who since the capture of Constantinople by Mehmet Fatih, had employed their forces with the intention of undermining the Ottoman power, now considered its ruin to be a dangerous prospect. Some state might benefit by it, and thus transform itself into one which would be more dangerous than the dying Ottoman state, "the sick man," as it became known. Diplomatic and military pressure was put upon Egypt. Mehmet Ali and his descendants were recognised as the lawful government of Egypt, although they continued under the nominal sovereignty of the Sultan, and thus the war came to an end.

Reform required a new champion in the Sultan Abdülmecit. In 1839 he announced the Edict of Gülhane, the foundation of the new imperial constitution.

Russia had not given up her designs to open a way through to the Mediterranean. The Tsar Nicholas I renewed this drive, yet again was held up by the Western powers, France and Great Britain, who signed an alliance with Turkey and declared war on the Tsar, a war which ended favourably to the allied forces in 1856, and which has become known as the Crimean War, after its principal field of action.

In the treaty of Paris, which ended that conflict, the Ottoman Empire was treated, in appearances, as being at the same level as its allies the Great Powers, and in fact it did assure the integrity of its territory and its political independence.

Abdülaziz, who was the only Ottoman Sultan to leave the frontiers of his Empire, when he visited the universal exhibition in Paris in 1867, was dethroned by a conspiracy led by Mithat Paşa; two days later the former Emperor was found dead, the veins of his forearms open. The new Sultan Murat V was not able to enjoy power for long, as his brother Abdülhamit, an intriguer and astute politician, succeeded in replacing him in 1876. The Russian Tsar Alexander declared war on Turkey. The heroic resistance of the Turks could not prevent the Russian troops from reaching as far as San Stefano in the outskirts of Constantinople, where was signed the peace treaty which divided up European Turkey; however, the Great Powers, led by Great Britain, succeeded in forcing a revision of this treaty, which was done in Berlin in 1878, giving results more favourable for Turkey.

Mustafa Kemal walked out to breathe the evening air, a book under his arm as was his custom; naturally it was a history book. He walked down a road lined on both sides with tall poplars whose leaves seen from underneath were white. He heard the sound of the bells from a far-off monastery, far out of sight. This sound, the voice of Christianity, was tolling the knell of the Ottoman Empire in Macedonia; in all these monasteries and churches the word "expulsion" resounded. Armed bands of Bulgarians in a state of open rebellion roved the mountains at their pleasure. In Greece, Serbia and Albania men only waited for the right moment to begin the war of liberation; but the Colossus was still able to defend himself, as he had just demonstrated in a war against Greece which had recently finished. He had to be undermined little by little, so that his huge weight would bring him down with greater tumult. The malcontents counted on the support of Europe.

Kemal thought how far away were now those glorious days of the Empire, when in the middle of the seventeenth century it controlled the whole coast of the Black sea, part of Poland, Hungary, and the whole of the Balkan Peninsula; in Asia, it ruled as far as the Persian Gulf, Arabia, and in Africa it reached further than Oran. Now there was a threat even to expel it from the Balkans; he thought that perhaps one day he would see his birthplace in the hands of others.

He stopped at a bend in the road; behind him the Char Planina twisted, and at his feet the Dragor went searching for the Vardar, with whose waters it must mix its own, and flow with them into the far-off gulf. He contemplated that countryside, now invaded by shadows which veiled it like the future; he realised that Macedonia was a land of protests, of rebellions; a land of warriors, and had always been so. It was in these plains that King Philip, the father of Alexander, created the famous phalanx. There was not a single place in the valleys or the plains which had not been covered by the body of a fallen hero. Even the Turks themselves were beginning to feel this spirit of rebellion; they complained about the administration of the Empire, which was extremely bad; they complained about its politics, which were deplorable, being based on concessions and prevarications. The decay of the Empire could be seen by all. Day by day the great powers squeezed it with renewed force between their oppressive talons; they offered loans in exchange for its pride. The shadow of the capitulations grew larger. Europe was the enemy of the Turks, a protector of their declared enemies; so it was that in the last war against the Greeks, the effect of the Turkish victories had been extinguished by European interventions, and while the Turkish soldiers returned victorious from the fields of battle, they returned defeated by the hatred of the champions of the Eastern Question.

The young cadet soon got over these black thoughts; he felt himself able to achieve glorious campaigns, and there must have been many other subjects of the Padişah who would have certainly rivalled those warriors who had reached the very gates of Vienna, who were victorious in every battle, and who carried the crescent standard in the conquest of a huge Empire. Kemal was then seized by an extraordinary enthusiasm for war. A thousand battles passed through his mind in disordered haste; he gazed upon the mountains fearlessly, his eyes full of terrible defiance; if it were left to him, not one of the enemies of his fatherland should remain alive in any of their own.

One holiday evening, Mustafa's classmates found him sitting on a garden bench, a book open upon his knees; his gaze was lost amongst the violet peaks of the distant mountains. They asked him why he had not taken the opportunity of that day to amuse himself, and what was the point of sacrificing himself so much to his studies, "I would like to become somebody" answered that strange cadet. "We hope that you are not imagining that you are going to become Sultan," they answered jokingly. "No," he replied, turning his gaze once more towards horizon. "I would like to become myself."

But this demeanour, in which we can identify a crisis in the formation of his personality, did not last for long. In general, his pleasant conversation, generosity and correct behaviour made him a companion. He did not suffer from egotism, a defect very common in all countries. One of his contemporaries at Monastir, speaking of Kemal in those years in the college, has described him thus: "He generally kept himself separate from us; he retired into himself and did not form deep friendships with anybody. Nevertheless he was not disagreeable or gloomy; on the contrary, his character was cheerful and his manner amiable. The strange thing is that although he never attempted to impose his will upon us, we allowed ourselves to be commanded by him without even noticing it. He read a good deal and thought even more, meditating about the contents of a book three times more than the time which was necessary merely to read it."

He would spend his annual holidays in Salonika; however, he did not live in the house of his mother, because she had remarried, this time to a merchant from the island of Rhodes, who had a comfortable living. Mustafa was very annoyed by this decision of his mother, though he forgave later on; however he always refused to meet his step-father and never mentioned his name.

He employed his free weeks in attending the school run by the Christian fathers in Salonika. He followed their courses of French, a language for which at the beginning he had no facility, as his teacher in the military school had to remind him. This was enough to make Mustafa decide to learn it, and he succeeded so well that he was able to command it as well as his own tongue. His deep knowledge of French brought him the advantage of being able to move through the wide field of French literature, and to read books which brought him knowledge of the social progress and politics of the West. All the French classics passed through his hands, the books which took more of his time being the works of the encyclopaedists, which left deep doubts within his heart.

In the Empire there was complete freedom of instruction. Under the protection of the capitulations, the European powers maintained schools in which their subjects received an education similar to that established in their own capitals and in their own language, without troubling at all about the offical language of Turkey or her history. Since the teaching received in these schools, especially in the French ones, which were all directed by members of religious orders, was superior to that which could be provided by the native institutions of Turkey, those Turks who could begin sending their children to them. Thus it was that the French language became popular and a movement of sympathy was established towards France.

Kemal returned to school eveiy year with pleasure; he was thinking of the future and in his own future. What did fortune have in store for him? However, anything could be achieved with determination and the will to overcome. For the moment he wanted to do better than his comrades, and obtain better marks. He himself later related that his comrades had the same intention : "They were all trying to be the best and felt within themselves the spirit of emulation that belongs to pushful youth, for which the fountains of science had remained for a long time shut off, and the ardour of a people that desired strongly to fill as quickly as possible the gap which separated them from the European nations."

The three years which were required for him to graduate as a sub-lieutenant were over. Throughout this time Mustafa had been an exemplary student; they had been years of great intensity for his spirit, and when the new sub-lieutenant arrived at Salonika, it was a concientious man who came. He laughed little, almost never; what pleased him was to talk about political affairs or military subjects, and his thoughts often absorbed him and made him forget his surroundings.

Mustafa Kemal did not go to the Mosque; essentially he was a realist, and did not believe in religions. He knew that a God should exist, a creator of all things, but that God was so far away from his preoccupations, that he really could not trouble about him. He considered religions as being more political entities than as having any real mysticism. In Salonika he was in contact with various of them; there the Jews had built about thirty synagogues; the domes of the orthodox churches and the Moslem minarets profusely adorned the city in its beautiful amphitheatre, and there in front, on the opposite shore of the Gulf that Mount Olympus, which had been sacred, recalled still the fabulous history of its Gods.

Religion in Macedonia, having been placed at the service of nationalist interests, was fomenting hatreds. Enmities amongst the orthodox themselves had reached the point of separating them into independent churches, mortal enemies of each other, first the Romanians, then the Serbs and finally the Bulgarians. Nevertheless Kemal viewed them with tolerance, since they were, he felt, continuing a work of merit in keeping alive in the people their nationalistic aspirations, quite the opposite of the Moslem religion, which there did nothing but debate puerile theological problems, when it could have done so much for Turkey.

The Sub-Lieutenant Mustafa Kemal Bey left his native city for Constantinople, "the Queen, the Eternal Enchantress of the East", as it had been called by the poet Tevfik Fikret. He was there to enter Harbiye, the famous military academy. He intended there to follow the highest studies which were provided for the soldiers of the Empire; after five years he would receive his diploma as Staff Captain. On occasions this seemed an enormous length of time for him, but he was a man of willpower and he was going to achieve his plans because he understood that he must achieve them. He would be Staff Captain at twenty-five, with a brilliant future before him. He did not have ambitions, but expectations.

His mother remained in Salonika. There Kemal left behind all that he wished to remember; the white marble column on which the name of his father was carved, lost amongst innumerable others, beneath the cypress foliage which guards the rest of the dead, of those who sleep the sleep that has no dreams, no dawn, no worries, no awakening, as says Omar Khayyam; he left the garden of his far-off childish games; and he left the poplars of Monastir and those horizons in which there often appeared, as if sculptured on those same rough rocks, those great heroes of Plutarch.

Yet he bore, carved on his character, the influence of that land, the powerful mountains, the impetuous rivers, and the spirit of rebellion, which like the winter winds roar across the narrow gorges of the mountains.

The continual contact with men of different races had led him to know what man is; the arguments between the clerics of different religions, and their schisms, had given him a true and deep insight into them. The cosmopolitan spirit and Western ideas which circulated in Salonika with complete freedom had transformed it in a spiritual sense into a European city.

Ever since the times when King Cassander founded the city which he called Thessalonica in honour of his queen, the sister of Alexander the Great, it had been a centre of Western culture. Salonika was part of Europe; this explains the reaction of the future liberator, when confronted with Asiatic Turkey, which had lagged so obviously behind.

As Alexander had done many centuries before, Mustafa Kemal left Macedonia for the East. Kemal did not go as a conquerer, nor did there follow him powerful armies or brilliant followers; he went alone, perhaps sometimes apprehensive before the unknown future, and awed by the name of Constantinople The Marvellous, the great capital of the Empire, just as Alexander would have been before the mysterious Gods of the East.

CHAPTER 2

POLITICAL ORIENTATION

Mustafa Kemal wandered about Constantinople, the ancient Byzantium, which had been the splendid capital of the Roman Empire in the 4th and 5th centuries, and of the Eastern Empire until the 15th. Its grandiose monuments, outraged by the ravages of time and the intrusions of other buildings, displayed its aristocractic tradition; there still processed through the city the ghosts of the Emperors, some of them glorious, like Constantine the Great, himself the banner of Christianity, who converted Byzantium into the capital of his Empire, Justinian I, builder of the great church of Santa Sophia; Constantine XIII, heroic defender of Constantinople as she died; or others of more sombre memory, such as the vice-ridden examples of Michael the Drunkard and Michael Calaphates. Other strange ghosts wandered through the imperial mosques, whose tall sharp minarets rise like lances thrust into the Christian land by the power of Islam; first were those of the mosque of Fatih Mehmet, conqueror of the city, and following his example, each new Sultan altered the profile of the city with new domes and new minarets. Every imperial mosque, a colossal monument representing the strength of the whole Empire, bore the name of one of the first Sultans who reigned in the Pearl of the Bosporus; it is their spirits which are evoked by their names, their spirits which can be felt present sometimes in the porphyry and bronze balconies erected by the Moslem Califs, next to the holy Mihrab, the altar which shows the direction of Mecca, and sometimes in the silent and venerable imperial mausolea, surrounded by tranquil gardens, set around the mosque itself.

Mustafa Kemal sought out the places which had been the scenes of historical events. There he reconstructed in his mind what the books had told him. He climbed one of the ninety-six towers twenty metres high, bulwarks of the principal wall of the fortifications of Constantinople, and which represent in their proportions the most colossal work that has ever been constructed for the defence of a city; at his feet there extended the far- spreading city of the dead, with its thousands of grave stones, showing where there reposed the remains of the valiant Turkish soldiers who fell before the walls of the city they dreamed of capturing. One could still see the breaches opened by the powerful Turkish cannon shells, when they were beating against the walls of Theodosius; there was the place through which the first Janissaries penetrated.

He crossed the square called the Atmeydanı, which occupies the site of the famous hippodrome, which had room for one hundred thousand people; there are still standing some of the monuments which formed the "Spina," which served as the backbone of this huge stadium. This was the heart of the city, where the people found amusement, and which was also a theatre for its passions and tragedies.

He visited Santa Sophia, a magnificent temple opened 14 centuries before by Justinian and Theodora, and which Mehmet had transformed into a mosque. He spent much time in the Topkapı Palace, which is more a small city than a palace. It was there that the Sultans lived through their hours of glory in the Empire's greatest days; there, in those cold rooms with thick walls, were celebrated the victories of Yavuz Selim, who tried to emulate Tamerlane, and those of Süleyman the Magnificent. Later these same walls would have been witnesses of the grief of the Sultans and their court, when after the second seige of Vienna in 1683 there began the decay of the Crescent. Lepanto, Ofen, the Morea and Mohacs were names whose echo would never have been given back by the domes of the throne room, so quietly would they have been pronounced.

The record of history provided by that gloomy succession of buildings bathes them in blood; in them were plotted evil intrigues, and bloody vengeances were achieved, some by the Sultan's wives, concubines and slave girls, in order to obtain the favours of the lord and supremacy over their rivals, others by aspirants to the throne itself. How many Vezirs and how many women of the imperial harem must have paid tribute with their lives to calumny and envy? In that room there died by strangling the cruel voluptuary Ibrahim; it was to be the fate of the kindly Selim III to die murdered by Mustafa IV, favoured by the Janissaries; he in his turn was to be hanged by the order of his brother Mahmut II. Murders followed each other, marking off periods in the long silences of doubt and indecision of the descendants of Osman.

Kemal thought for a long time about the historical evolution of the Empire, and for even longer about the autocratic regime of the Sultans, who governed the country at their whim; even at that time of general social progress, they still wielded the noose and the knife, as was the case with Abdülhamit II, who had been Sultan since 1876. He had reached the throne through intrigue and murder. His first victim had been Abdülaziz. During the last years of Abdülaziz, who had visited the West, the financial chaos in which the country had been struggling, and the increase in taxation, had provoked a growing discontent among the population, which showed itself in rebellions. The "Şeyhülislam," chief religious authority after the Calif, and other dignitaries including Mithat Paşa, forced the

Sultan to abdicate. Two days later the Sultan was found dead, it was said by suicide.

There then ascended the throne a nephew of Abdülaziz, named Murat V, but he was very quickly replaced by his brother under the pretext that he was mentally defective, and incarcerated in the Çırağan Palace. The mystery of the death of Abdülaziz was covered up by several murders. The mystery was in any case merely relative. Mithat Paşa himself was murdered by the order of the Sultan. That general, one of the leaders of liberalism in Turkey, had travelled a great deal in Europe and had held the post of governor in several regions of the Empire, in every case providing a benevolent government and attempting always to unite the Turkish and non-Turkish populations, and make the life of both more bearable. Mithat Paşa, like any young man who might have graduated from a European University, where religious fanaticism did not exist, wanted to from an Ottoman state in which the citizens would all be under one law, and where the religions and the races would not, as they then did, make it into an ungovernable mosaic. Guided by these ideas, he took an active part in the dethronement of Abdülaziz. It was then hoped to find a Sultan who would accept a constitutional regime; Abdülhamit gave the appearance of being a convinced liberal, and was accepted, replacing Murat, and once enthroned he named Mithat Paşa as Grand Vezir as had been stipulated. After a year he exiled Mithat Paşa, since he could not bear that anyone should impose their will upon his own. He was not satisfied with that, because he feared that liberal patriot, and offered him the post of Governor of Damascus. Mithat, the "King Maker", believed that the Sultan had repented of his ill will returned to the Empire, only for the Sultan's emissaries to murder him in the fortress of Taif.

In the same year in which Abdülhamit girded on the sword of Osman, the equivalent in Turkey of the coronation of Western Kings, salvoes of artillery proclaimed the establishment of the Ottoman constitution; there was created a parliament with two chambers, a Senate, and a Chamber of Deputies. It was consultative in character, and laws were presented to it by the Padişah. This parliament, in 1877, had to take the responsibility of declaring war on Imperial Russia. This war ended with the Russian troops at the gates of Constantinople, at San Stefano, where was signed the peace treaty which dismembered European Turkey.

Parliament met for the second time in 1878, but was immediately closed "sine die," Abdülhamit had already began to show his true sentiments. The Red Sultan, as he became known because of the blood which he caused to flow, was a continual enemy of progress, and in contrast to his immediate predecessors, who had followed a policy of Westernisation, bad turned his eyes upon the East, and was dreaming of a possible panislamic state, of which he would be the head, by virtue of his title of Calif of Islam. Against civilisation and modern methods of government he opposed the old tactics of the seraglio, imperious autocracy and caprice.

In 1894, a little before the arrival of Kemal in Istanbul ("the Turkish name for Constantinople"), the world was disturbed by the massacre of Armenians, secretly encouraged by the Red Sultan. Those who did not know him could not understand his attitude, since years before he had chosen Armenian Vezirs and counsellors, and appreciated their work. The Armenians were a people of ancient tradition, but Balkanized between Russia, Iran and Turkey. The Armenians within the Empire lived amid a majority of Turks, in the area around Lake Van and Mount Ararat. The tragedy which befell them had its origins in the policy of Russia, which was to excite the nationalism and religious fervour of the Christian peoples who were subjects of the Ottoman Empire, in order to hasten the Empire's ruin. Russia therefore tried to attract the Armenians, and preached to them, as to the Bulgarians, the crusade against Islam. In the treaty of San Stefano, Russia demanded certain improvements in the treatment of the Armenians, a clause which Great Britain viewed with mistrust; sympathy for the Armenians would dangerously extend the influence of the Tsar over Ottoman territory.

From that moment the Sultan became the enemy of the Armenians, who it seemed had become allied to his enemies; he removed them their high positions, and gradually, by using against them the Kurds, who were traditionally the enemies of their Armenian neighbours, managed to provoke bloody disturbances, which turned into massacres. These reawakened two years later, at the same time as other disturbances in Crete. The Great Powers, unable to agree on a policy because of their mutual rivalries, did nothing but .protest. The third persecution took place in the capital itself, where many thousands of Armenians had taken refuge. The crucial factors were some terrorist acts perpetrated by some Armenians from the building of the Ottoman bank and the fears of the Sultan, who terrified of the possible repetition of this, decided to make an example. In 1897 the problem of Crete began a war with Greece. It was ended through the pressure and mediation of the Powers, and the Turks had to content themselves with an indemnity, although they had won a series of victories, and had to accept against their will a Greek Prince as ruler of that Island. This was the first step in the loss of Crete.

Abdülhamit lived constantly tormented by fear of attempts against his life; however, this did not prevent him from ordering his secret police, a terrible organisation which he licenced to kill, to poison or get rid by any possible means of perfectly honest people, simply because one of his spies had wanted to display his zeal, in the hopes of the usual prize.

The Red Sultan had taken refuge in the luxurious palace of Yıldız, protected by high walls and overlooking the Bosporus. Fear of assasination and death made him consider dangerous all the other palaces, including that of Dolmabahçe, the official residence of his predecessors.

Every Friday morning, a remarkable parade of troops wearing multicoloured uniforms would assemble in compact lines between the main gate of the palace of Yıldız and a small white mosque situated not far from it. Between this double wall of humanity and protected by the bodies of ministers and other high dignitaries, the imperial carriage passed at the greatest speed that was permitted by the legs of the aged Vezirs which accompanied it. During the brief minutes occupied by this fearful transit to the place of prayer, Abdülhamit would be peering through eyes darkened by mystery and suspicion, seeking any possible way for the assassins of whose existence his spies and he himself were certain, to give him the cowardly stroke which they were preparing for him. He might well give more severe orders to his secret polite. His worst enemies were those young Turks who were studying in Europe, a perverted group living in infidel territory; it was they who were pretending to dethrone him in the name of "progress." But thanks to Allah, these centres of anarchy and conspiracy were efficiently watched.

The Turkish military academy in Harbiye, which had been founded in 1834 by Mahmut II and from which had come since that time the officers of the Ottoman General Staff, was situated close to Pera, the foreign quarter, which was inhabited also by Turkish subjects who were not moslems. In that area were to be found the buildings of the Embassies and Consulates, and the headquarters of the foreign capitalist companies, which monopolised almost all the commercial activities of the country.

Pera had little resemblance to a Turkish quarter, and Turkish was little heard in its streets, while the reverse was true of French, Greek, Spanish and Armenian. The beliefs of the population were shown by the number of Catholic, Orthodox, and Gregorian churches, and Synagogues. The sight of Catholic processions, Christian Priests, and a population dressed completely in European style, would make any casual visitor think himself in any Western city. In the reign of Süleyman I, one would not have found amidst the vines and fig trees which covered the hills where Pera, now called in Turkish Beyoğlu, later stood, anything more than some summer villas, mostly owned by Greeks. The Ambassador of the King of France liked that place, and begged permission from the Sublime Porte to build there a residence for himself and for the Franks under his protection. It was thus that it became more populated. This was the origin of the foreign quarter, that of the "Frenks," that is to say Foreigners belonging to any nationality or religion, born or domiciled within the realms of the Padişah. Because of the enermous advantages which they gave to foreigners, the capitulations attracted a great number of them, who found indeed greater advantages than in their own countries. Thus was created the cosmopolitan city.

The quarter called Pera, which could really have been called a city, was a true product of the capitulations. These treaties, which had their origin in a gesture of friendship from Süleyman to the King of France, acted as an instrument of oppression in the hands of the Western Powers during the decay of the Ottoman Empire. The capitulation treaties gave to foreigners a series of privileges; amongst these, was the exemption from any taxation or customs duties except those approved by their governments; all foreigners enjoyed extra-territoriality, and had the right of being judged by consular tribunals.

The economic, legal, and even political independence of the Empire suffered definite restrictions, and the Empire quickly became a kind of colony. It was in complete financial ruin, and had to apply to the capitalist countries of the West in search of loans. However they, doubting the solvency of the "Sick Man of Europe," demanded that in order to ensure the servicing of their debts, the control of the country's sources of wealth should be transferred to an administration created in 1881 under the title of the Council for the Ottoman Public Debt, which was of course composed of the representatives of the Great Powers.

The long-established foreign and levantine communities, whose wives were as elegant and well-educated as European ladies, and travelled frequently to the great Western capitals, to follow in Istanbul the same customs and fashions as they found on their travels, had made of Pera a small city which was completely Western, with the luxuries and pleasures of the West. Kernel having lived all his life in the provinces, was not accustomed to the life of the great world, nor to associate with such beautiful women as these, dressed in extraordinary luxury, who regarded his timidity with amusement. He quickly habituated himself to this kind of life; he frequented dances and fashionable bars, and took even more care that the cut of his uniform fitted better to his body, which was slim and of good proportions. He was not tall, but his narrow waist and broad shoulders gave a certain harmony to his figure. The fair-haired Sub-Lieutenant had some amorous adventures and thought himself in love with a lady of international society. He tasted the pleasures offered unsparingly by the beautiful Istanbul, truly a bridge between Europe and Asia, where the refinements of both continents were intermingled. In this critical age in the life of a man, he was not swept away by a whirlwind of pleasures, as his strong will ensured that he would be able to follow the path that he had traced for himself, succeed in his studies, be accepted, and become somebody, "become himself."

Mustafa Kemal looked at the panorama shown by the ruin of the Empire. There was Pera, a city of traders, and a busy centre of foreigners, who were masters of the customs, the ports, and the railways, and were creditors to the extent of more than five thousand million francs; compared to it, Istanbul, the contemplative city of the peaceful and fatalistic Ottomans, appeared to be fast asleep. Continuing at this rate, with this mentality, and while the sultan continued to be aveise from all progress and Westernization, Turkey would quickly pass from semi-colonial to definitively colonial status.

All this was being talked over by a group of young soldiers in the school at Harbiye, and Kemal was part of that group. It was he who expounded very clearly the government's defects, its bad policies and worse administration, and he rebelled against the tyranny of the Sultan. The number of malcontents grew day by day.

The non-Moslem populations, annoyed by the Sultan's pro-Islamic policies, were gaining their independence one after the other, thanks to outside help. A great idea arose from the hearts of young progressive Turks. They wished to give the word "Fatherland" such a wide significance that it could contain within itself all the religions and races which formed the Empire; they would reduce the importance of the religions, including that of Islam, to a matter of personal conscience, each man believing in what most appealed to him, but all considering themselves citizens of one state, Turkey. Unfortunately, these fine desires were practically impossible to realise; the Islamic religious leaders, and the faithful who followed their admonitions, had offered the most determined opposition to those reforming Sultans who had tried to do something of the kind before. Could it be possible to make infidels and the faithful equal in status?

Kemal and his friends formed a secret society, which they called "Vatan" the Turkish word for "Fatherland." They published a newspaper written by hand under great precautions, which circulated amongst the members, together with revolutionary books brought from Europe. The passionate poems of the great poet Namık Kemal, a man of advanced conceptions and fervent patriotism who died in exile, made the idealists of Harbiye feel their hearts beat wildly within them, and lift their breasts higher in search of a better air to breathe, the air of liberty. The oppression in which they lived was insupportable to them. They felt the need for a revolution, for the destruction of the theocratic regime and the building in its place of a Turkey which could be taken for one of the other states of civilised Europe.

Kemal was the member of the executive committee who gave it most impetus. He wrote many articles, in which were mingled juvenile enthusiasm and mature logic. The revolutionaries held their meetings in secret and secluded places, always changing them as soon as any suspicion made them feel unsafe. At the meetings, after listening in silence to the discussions, and the putting forward of various points of view, by his companions, Kemal would speak; he would give a brief resume of the ideas expressed by his comrades, then after describing the political situation of the country, he would propose the next step, the next effort they must make towards the realisation of their ideals.

The Sultan's Police received information that even in the school of Harbiye there were to be heard criticisms of the Commander of the Faithful. It was something serious when there malcontents in the army, in which his power trusted. Possibly some of the students who were not of the same opinion as the liberal group were those that gave the alarm. When information reached the inspector of higher military schools, İsmail Hakkı Paşa, he demanded explanations from the director of the school, Rıza Paşa. The director denied that his students were partisans of a subversive movement; at any rate nothing had occurred to arouse suspicion in him. The inspector agreed with this; and he reported as much, adding that this proved that Rıza Paşa lacked the necessary capacity to direct a school.

Rıza made public the investigation which had been made by the inspector, and those whom it concerned, who apparently were not unknown to the director, ceased their dangerous meetings. It was certain that the Sultan's efficient police would go to any lengths of zeal to discover who the conspirators were. Their military careers and their very lives were in danger.

The young student was generally of a sombre manner; during recreation periods he would retire to the most secluded places; seeking solitude, and feeling tired and sad. However his mind was in constant activity. He could not concentrate the manifold thoughts which followed each other through his brain; there was one which because of its insistence dominated the others; rebellion, that is rebellion against everything which surrounded him, against the whole ambience and against the course of history which his country was following.

One day one of his comrades pointed out to him for some time he had noticed that Kemal was not awakening in the mornings at reveille, and that the duty officer had to go and make him get up. His friend asked Kemal why he was living in this way. Kemal's reply was evasive. Many of his friends asked him the same question. They were curious and interested to know why their comrade, ordinarily of an active temperament, had changed his way of life. Mainly because he understood the hints of criticism, Kemal saw that he would have to explain. He told them. "My friends, when I go to bed I cannot sleep as you do; I stay awake until dawn and only then can I go to sleep. Thus when the reveille sounds I do not hear it. A man with a stick in his hands moves my bed and shakes me out of my slumbers. That is why I get into a bad temper because my body and spirit are tired. The friends I meet in the classroom are happier than I am." Later he would talk for a long time to his intimate companions who shared his ideals, about the ideas which tortured him in his nights of sleeplessness.

Kemal attracted the attention of his teachers in the staff academy. In the subjects of tactics and strategy in particular, he showed himself an exceptional student, and succeeded in obtaining his diploma as Staff Captain within the allotted five years. He was then twenty-five years old.

The discontent of the students at Harbiye had naturally increased during the years, while the Sultan's vices had made themselves more pronounced. In Pera it was easy to find French books full of liberal ideas. These were the favourite reading of everybody who, unlike the Sultan, understood that spiritual and material progress were necessary, and had to be looked for in the West. Since there were usually several weeks to wait between leaving the school and formal entry into the army, the new officers took advantage of this time to begin their secret meetings again. The members of the Vatan society attacked with renewed vigour the existing state of affairs, and in particular the unbridled autocracy of Abdülhamit. They counted the names of the people who had been murdered by his secret police, whose members, charged with the duty of systematically preventing the penetration of the corrupt progress of the West into the dominions of the Padişah, committed unspeakable atrocities against those suspected of sympathy with the liberals. The Red Sultan did everything he could to make barriers between Europe and the Empire, barriers which would isolate it intellectually from the western world and thus prevent the contamination of the new Turkish generation.

The spies of the Red Sultan were legion. Every activity of every social class was invigilated by them, and the master of terror, himself terrified, had to spend sometimes the best part of his day listening, and trying to evaluate the possible truth of the innumerable informations and new traps which his spies pretended to have discovered. The prodigality of this Sultan towards his most efficient spies was such, that they all aspired to rival Fouche. The imperial treasury suffered from chronic anaemia, caused by the continual bleedings which were made in favour of the "eyes and ears of the Padişah."

The malcontents of Harbiye, now better organised to resist the fear of Abdülhamit's secret service, held their secret meetings in private houses, and in the back rooms of certain cafes. They also had the use of a small apartment, in which the revolutionary newspaper was composed, and the most important meetings were held. There was no shortage of people who wanted to enter Vatan. Only those who had been previously examined, and who inspired absolute confidence were initiated.

On one occasion they made a sad mistake. Fethi Bey, formerly a comrade, made himself appear a man of vanguard, ready to unite his strength with those of Vatan. The new recruit made himself useful at once, and since he claimed to be short of money, he asked to be allowed to live in one of the unoccupied rooms of the association's headquarters, and this request was granted. He thus attended all the meetings and knew the identity of those who wrote articles in the revolutionary newspaper. A short time later he proudly announced that he had converted a friend of his, who now desired to be admitted to membership of the association.

Careful as was their custom, the "contaminated" decided to examine the candidate in one of the cafes which they frequented near the Galata Bridge, near the port. At the day and time which had been arranged, the main nucleus of the members had gathered to wait for Fethi and the candidate for admission. Indeed they both arrived, but the latter gentleman informed them that the place was completely surrounded by police and that they were under arrest.

This trick was the work of İsmail Paşa, the inspector, who desired to show his zeal in the Sultan's service in an area which the latter would most appreciate, the discovery or frustration of a plot. The detainees were imprisoned in separate dungeons before anyone could speak to them. Their situation was desperate. They knew the methods which were used at Yıldız, and that it could well happen that some night they would be executed without anyone hearing more about them. During this time a military commission was studying the proofs which had been obtained, and considering the greater or lesser culpability of each person; all of them could be accused of disloyalty to His Majesty. The situation of Kemal was particularly delicate, because of the tone of the articles he had written, and because he had been one of the main leaders of the organisation.

İsmail Paşa had several interviews with the Sultan on the subject, and he advised the wisdom of taking extreme measures, and punishing the culprits in a way which would serve as an example to the army. The director of Harbiye, whose fortunes were also in question, was also called to the palace to give his opinion to the Sultan. In order to improve his position with the latter he spoke in favour of his pupils; they were so young and they were at such a romantic age, and their absurd ideas did not go further than that; as they got older they would understand that the place of a patriotic soldier and a good Moslem was at the side of the wise descendant of Osman. He added that an exemplary punishment, such as hanging an officer of such intelligence, as the inspector advised, would make people think that the army was no longer obeying the Padifah wholeheartedly, and that this would be an unwise step.

The astute Abdülhamit, whom one must accept to have been a diplomat of the first order, preferred not to give too much importance to the question. He decided to send the discontented officers to serve in the garrisons which were furthest away from the capital, in the evil climate of the South, where they would have plenty of time to meditate and correct their faults; failing that, they could always be eliminated. Mustafa Kemal had to appear before a military tribunal which met in Yıldız Palace. It seems that on certain occasions the Red Sultan would watch, from a hiding place, the changing directions of the judicial arguments, and that the judges would hear from him that word which would tip the balance of the scales of fate.

Captain Kemal Bey was not convicted, but he was sent, one could say as a prisoner, to the far-off garrison at Damascus. It was pointed out that His Majesty had been merciful to him, by allowing him the opportunity of rehabilitation, and that it was hoped that the reports that his future commanders would make about him, would demonstrate that he had given up his foolish ideas, and was dedicating himself to the fulfilment of military duties.

The next day Kemal left by sea for Syria. His place of exile had been well chosen. There, amid the rocks of the Hawran, there was in progress a bloody struggle against the rebellious Druzes.

CHAPTER 3

IDEALS

Kemal had hardly arrived at Damascus, that city whose beautiful gardens are irrigated by the Barada, in the fertile valley of the Gutah, when he had to depart for the ill-defined and far-extending line of battle.

The Druzes had recently revolted, and protected by their natural allies, the huge grey rocks of the Antilebanon Chain, were defying the Sultan's forces. The Druzes are a strange people of unknown origin, who speak Arabic, a language which Islam and their contacts with the Arab peoples have imposed upon them. Although their religion has a basis of Islam, it is in the greater part of its precepts contrary to that religion. These who practise this religion are not advised to observe either the Ramazan Fasts, regular prayer, the pilgrimage to Mecca, or circumcision.

The creator of this religion was Hamza Bin Ali, a Persian with prophetic pretentions, who visited Egypt where there was reigning at that time, the eleventh century, the Fatimid Calif Hakim, a person of doubtful sanity; amongst his other deeds, it is recorded that like an African Nero, he ordered Cairo to be set on fire. He became possessed by theology and mysticism; this was the moment which the prophet Hamza Bin Ali took advantage of to declare that he recognised in Hakim the spirit of God upon the earth. These two men founded the religion that is practised by the Druzes. According to the Fatimid dynasty, it was Hamza who caused parts of the Koran to be excluded, and other parts added. Both the founders died martyrs' deaths, murdered by the people, but their powerful religion reached as far as Syria.

The Druzes, believing that Hakim was the true God, and who still expect his return to this earth, had to find refuge, as had the Maronite Christians, in the mountains of Lebanon, where they were able to live and defend themselves from the Moslems, who persecuted them because of their beliefs.

This indomitable people, masters at guerrilla warfare, owed obedience to the Ottoman Empire from the beginning of the sixteenth century, but all the efforts made by the Sublime Porte to subject them effectively had proved in vain. It is almost impossible to extend firm rule over regions like those difficult of access because of their terrain, inhospitable because of lack of water, high temperature and absence of vegetation. The Lebanon Chain, with its forests of oaks, firs, olive trees and a few of the famous cedars, stands in contrast to the parallel range of the Antilebanon, an area of lofty peaks, arid, a chaos of stone which indicates the proximity of the desert. The Antilebanon is the Druze's preferred refuge, and their massive fortress.

The Druzes obtained first sympathy and material help, and later spiritual inspiration, from Lady Hester Stanhope, who was proclaimed by the Arabs, her first friends in the Orient, "Queen of Palmyra," standing in the middle of the desert before the venerable ruins of that city. She was a new Zenobia, Queen of those ruins which Aurelian had left of what had been a grand city. Lady Stanhope was the neice of William Pitt, and admired by King George III. In her turn she admired Brummel, because she despised the prejudices and meannesses of the society of that time. She left England and arrived in Syria after an eventful voyage. Her interests lay in adventure and mystery. There was plenty of interest offered by Syria in those days of anarchy. The "Queen of Palmyra" achieved remarkable fame, and her influence became important; it was to her that the rebellion of the Druzes much later owed its origin to a great extent. She died in the greatest poverty. Her tomb is in Chihun, on one of the steepest peaks of the Southern Lebanon.

In 1840, İbrahim Paşa, son of the Viceroy of Egypt, conquered Syria. However the European Powers obliged him to return it to the Empire. Twenty years later, because of the enmity existing between the Christian and the Druzes, fomented by the Sublime Porte, for the principle of "Divide et Impera" was well known there, bloody battles took between these antagonists, which degenerated into a war which took the tragic toll of more than eight thousand dead Christians. As the Empire became yet weaker, the Druzes made ever greater demands, paid their taxes more reluctantly, and even dreamed of possible autonomy. To these ends there occurred frequent disorders and insurrections, such as that in which Mustafa Kemal first saw the realities of war.

It was an exhausting campaign for the young officer, who was not accustomed to the hot climate, nor to the deprivations and exigences of war. However, the game attracted him; sometimes the mountains were quiet and he was sent on inspection missions like a policeman, through the Syrian Desert, rock and fire. The little skirmishes without warning against the Bedouins had a particular interest for Kemal Bey, who found in them a training ground for greater battles. The endless excursions and fights beneath the desert sun accustomed his eyes to encompassing immense distances, and his body to tolerate exhaustion. In mountain guerilla warfare, if one wishes to dominate the enemy, one must climb to the highest peaks by scrambling up the rocks, no matter how.

However nothing distracted him from his intention; to fight without rest until he succeeded in making the voice and interests of his people heard; until the constitution should be respected, until the powers of the Tyrant should be restricted, and a government should be elected which would have the power to make the Empire progress, following Western lines. The financial situation, the interference of the Great Powers, the Empire's policy towards its subjects and towards the ambitions of the other great states, required men with sufficient qualities and willpower to be at the helm of government, not backward-looking like the Sultan, surrounded by his favourites, who listened to the intrigues of the Harem and of his court full of spies.

Kemal tried to win to his cause several of his companions in arms; the situation was propitious for this because several of the officers had like him been exiled from Istanbul because they had aroused suspicion. In October 1906 he had founded in Damascus the Association for the Fatherland and Liberty. He had lately been posted to Jaffa, and there he began his activities again. Then, helped by good friends and influential people, he left that city, which had been conquered by Bonaparte and in which many of the latter's soldiers had died of pestilence. The help of Ahmet Bey, the local commander, was of great value to Kemal. He not only procured for him what he needed for the journey to Salonika, where Kemal was proceeding in order to give information to the great centres of revolutionary thought about the situation obtaining in Syria, but also promised to keep complete secrecy about his escapade and to warn him immediately if, despite all their precautions, it should be discovered.

He went to Salonika by crossing Egypt and Greece. Our captain found the situation in Macedonia worsened. Under the pretext that Abdülhamit had not kept his promise of reforms, the Great Powers had obliged the Imperial Government to allow into Macedonia a body of foreign officers, who were supposed to reorganise and command the Ottoman Gendarmerie, and to protect the Christians, who were complaining about the exactions of Abdülhamit's regime. The programme for the pacification of Macedonia, which had been enforced by Russia and Austria, became known as the programme of Mürzsteg, after the name of the castle near Vienna where Franz Joseph and Tsar Nicholas had met in 1903, and had established the basis for intervention in that turbulent Ottoman province; naturally the advantages which both these great persons expected for their respective states were taken into consideration. Two years later, the demands of the Powers reached the point of proposing that there should be a foreign financial intervention, which was imposed after an impressive show of naval force.

The secret society "Union and Progress" began in those years a wide revolutionary movement, providing a central point for the activities of all the bands of malcontents. Thanks to its establishment in Salonika, the most Western city of the Empire, far from the palace spies, and which enjoyed easy communications with true Europe, this society was in the best possible situation to keep in touch with the Turks living in the West, and also to prepare in this region hostile to the Sultan a possible armed force. There was in Paris a group of expatriate politicians, writers and students, who formed one of the most important groups in Union and Progress. These men plotted in complete liberty; they printed a newspaper and pamphlets, which were sent to the centres of revolution in the Empire through the foreign Post Offices in Turkey, which enjoyed inviolability. The pamphlets, threatening or ridiculing, often turned up stuck on the very walls of Yıldız. There were also revolutionaries of the Union in Berlin, who were planning to establish modem ideas in their country, under the leadership of Prince Sabahattin, nephew of Abdülhamit.

There also worked in alliance with Union and Progress the masonic lodges scattered through the Empire, though they were relatively few because of the persecutions of Abdülhamit's police. Their main gatherings followed the Grand Oriental rite. Apart from progressive Turks, the active part of these centres was composed of Jews from Macedonia, Istanbul and Izmir, who were attracted by their completely liberal tendencies. The central nucleus and driving force of the association consisted of carear officers.

Mustafa Kemal did not think it wise to appear in public, and he took refuge in his mother's house; from there he got in touch with those friendly officers who had urged him to come to his native city. Kemal knew of the existence of the Committee, although not in any great detail, and that it had ramifications in foreign countries, in the army and even in Yıldız itself; the reason why he had come was to become a member of this powerful association, which sought to direct the country's new policies. For many days his friends refused to give him any concrete information about the mysterious Committee, or about the possibilities of his joining it. They submitted him to long interrogations, in order to give more information to the leaders of the Committee. Finally he was admitted to the Committee of Union and Progress, but he decided not to join the Masonic Lodge.

Kemal was certainly one of those young enthusiastic officers who directly affected the policy adopted by the Committee of Union and Progress, which was also known as "The Young Turks." The power which could be acquired by a well-organised secret society had already been shown by the "Internal Revolutionary Organisation" created by the Bulgarians, with the motto of "Macedonia for the Macedonians," and against which the Ottoman army and the Gendarmerie had been powerless.

Kemal's presence was discovered; an order for his arrest arrived from Istanbul. The Committee's spies, who were to be found in every army unit, contrived his escape in time. He returned to Jaffa, and from there with the help of Ahmet Bey, he proceeded towards the Gulf of Aqaba at the northeast comer of the Red Sea.

The frontiers with Egypt were carefully watched, since the British, with their long-held hopes of hegemony over the Arabs, were becoming dangerous neighbours. The second in command at Salonika, Cemil Bey, and the commanders and officers at Jaffa all agreed to asseverate that on the date when Kemal was accused of having been absent without leave, he had been on the Egyptian frontier. This produced confusion in Istanbul and the investigations were brought to an end, perhaps because there were more important things to think about.

The ever-increasing influence of the Committee of Union and Progress within the army obtained Kemal's posting to Macedonia a year later. It was intended to bring together the best officers for the struggle which could be seen approaching. It was there, in Macedonia, that the destiny of the country was being forged, and from there would arise the movement of renewal. Mustafa Kemal, full of hope, wanted to give all his energies to the plans which he had so often studied.

Chapter 4

DISAPPOINTMENTS

Kemal was back in Salonika, whose citadel kept watch over the Gulf. Though he could not see them, the young Captain's imagination brought before his eyes the triumphal arches, built in that city in Roman times, and beneath which had paraded victorious warriors. The triumphal arches in his mind's eye were huge. Beneath them he saw passing the patriots who bore the new ideals, who defended the constitution and justice.

Nevertheless, there were waiting for him sad disappointments, even there, where he had so confidently placed all his enthusiasm. Kemal was still young, and it requires a long apprenticeship before one can have true knowledge of men, of their mean ambitions, and the envy which is to be found within their hearts.

He immediately got in touch with the Committee and its leaders. The Committee was now a formidable institution, with a great many members in all spheres. It was assumed that when the right time came it would become the master of the Empire. Now the men who had brought about this remarkable organisation were looking at each other with suspicion. The revolution would triumph, who could doubt it? But what would happen then? For whom would there be honour, fame, and high positions?

A political battle was going on in the heart of the Committee; those who hoped to become the great men surrounded themselves with their friends, and tried to gain more supporters by campaigns and promises. Kemal found it repugnant to enter such competition, and realised that at the bottom of the conversations he had had with the possible great men of the movement, there lay the fact that the liberal doctrines which they preached were for them merely a means of getting to power; having done so they would show the same vices as were traditional in Ottoman leaders, and the new promised government would be far removed from the liberalism and fraternal spirit which motivated the sincere idealists. Although Mustafa Kemal was respected for his soldierly qualities, his powerful intelligence and the services he had made to the cause in Syria, whither he had been sent by Abdülhamit's police, itself a reason for congratulation at that time, he could not compete with the influence and strong personalities of those who were directing the Committee in Salonika. He did not wish to give his support to this or that leader, and retired from the internal political debate of the Committee of Union and Progress, with distaste and disappointment. Nevertheless he did not lose faith in its ideals, and went on working for its cause, although more or less anonymously.

The commanders of the Third Army, to which he had been posted, decided at one point to send him to Monastir, but they soon had cause to appreciate his value and kept him in the staff headquarters at Salonika. He was entrusted with the inspection of communications; strategic routes, railways. This job obliged him to make frequent journeys, and to follow very varied itineraries. He took advantage of the possibilities which his official duties gave him, in order to visit any place he wished without incurring the suspicion of the high command, so that he could take upon himself the task of uniting the interior of the province with the central Committee. Sometimes he had to transmit urgent orders of extreme importance.

In his memoirs Kemal describes the life enjoyed at that time by the revolutionaries in Salonika. Groups of soldiers, mostly young, and civilians of many social classes would gather in the back rooms of the main cafes and restaurants of the cities. There they engaged in vehement discussion about politics and on plans to overthrow the government. Once Kemal had become aware of these meetings, he went one night to the cafe Nonyo, and went through into a very small room, which communicated with the main salon through a small hidden staircase. The room was full of people, all revolutionaries. Kemal went towards a table occupied by some fellow soldiers and sat down. The conversation was turning upon the need for great men, to be able to direct the revolution, men whose qualities and intelligence would mean security and hope. One could tell that the people gathered there were hoping that they themselves could show some similarity to these ideal people. Someone expressed an opinion to the effect the Cemal Bey deserved to be one of the leaders, and this was approved by enthusiastic acclamation from everybody else.

Kemal knew Cemal Bey intimately. Cemal was later to become one of the masters of the Empire. At that time he was commander of the general staff of the army in which Kemal was serving. This model for a "great man" was chubby, with a lively darting gaze, always smiling, willing to please, and dedicated ardently to politics. He had great influence in the Committee, and despite his modest military rank, he had an authority much greater than one would have expected from that.

The others at Kemal's table turned towards him, wondering why he remained silent. Kemal looked at them calmly and steadily; he wanted them to understand with this gaze many things which he could not say. Was it absolutely necessary for a people which longed for liberty and progress to find a man who was the incarnation of its ideals? Was not that people's own consciousness sufficient? Kemal had already taken the measure of Cemal, as of other influential persons. This man, who had been made in the old pattern, was incapable of adapting himself to the new conceptions of life in the civilized countries of Europe. He was a selfish man, and was looking for political success. He was relying on liberalism, in order to win; for him the triumph of the revolution meant everything : honours, riches; his thoughts hardly touched upon the question of national culture, and the benefits which the nation expected. Kemal realised that his enigmatic expression had annoyed his friends, with whom, being a new arrival at that garrison, he did not feel yet much confidence. It occurred to him that they might think of him as follows : "This gentleman, who has no experience, probably thinks himself a great man, which proves that his judgement must be so perverted that he has been unable to recognise true greatness: this man cannot be one of ours."

"That night and at that table," says Kemal, "I formed two distinct opinions, one positive, the other negative. One was, that it was important to be a great man and then save one's country; the other, that it was not possible to become a great man by a word. Before all else the country must be saved, and even after that there was no reason to talk about greatness." These were the ideas which passed across Kemal's mind as he sat in the back room of the cafe Nonyo, amongst his first contacts with the Unionist patriots.

On one occasion Cemal Bey published an article, unsigned, in a Salonika newspaper. On the tramcar which was taking them to the city centre, after their duty at the general staff, Cemal, who had taken a particular liking to Kemal, offered him a copy of the newspaper and asked him if he had read the article. Kemal said that he had not, and at his commander's request, did so carefully. Cemal asked his subordinate's opinion. "It's a pretty trivial article, written by a rather ordinary journalist" was the reply, "Marvellous!" exclaimed Cemal. "It was me that wrote it!" Mustafa Kemal then said to him : "Please excuse me. I did not know that, and I would have wished that you had not been the author. Cemal Bey, you should not allow yourself to be flattered by the applause of people who have only the brains of birds. It is merely vanity. Greatness consists in neither flattering nor deceiving anyone, in not seeing and not going beyond the true ideal of one's country. You will have the whole world against you, all trying to divert you from your path. Yet you will continue upon it. Endless obstacles will build up in your way; you will overcome them, not considering yourself a great man, but as little, weak, helpless, as though you were nothing and without the hope of anyone's help. And if after that they call you great, you will laugh in the face of those who call you so."

We can see in these sentences the spiritual maturity of that young officer, and his better understanding of humanity. His imprisonment, his exile in Syria, and above all his disappointments at discovering that the ideals of the Committee were in the hands of men who forgot them for their own personal ambitions, had a powerful influence upon him.

In June 1908, Tsar Nicholas II and King Edward VII met at Reval, a Russian port on the gulf of Finland. For the diplomats of Europe this action gave a glimpse of a series of possible interesting combinations for the future, concerned with the Eastern Question; as for the Sublime Porte, the Ottoman Government, these discussions were to bring a tragic echo.

The political problem of the Eastern Question consisted, in the years of the ascendancy of the Crescent, in the efforts\of the Christian powers to expel the Turks. When the Empire was in decay, caused largely by its inability to assimilate the conquered populations, the Eastern Question turned into that of who would finish up with the richest spoils, the much desired straits and Istanbul. For its comparative health, the Empire was indebted to the rivalry of the Great Powers, which as soon as they saw one of their adversaries on the road of conquest to Istanbul, rushed out to meet him with reasoning, and failing that with force. The Crimean War was a good example of this. The Eastern Question invariably brought the danger of a general conflagration. France and Great Britain protected Turkey against Russia, and Russia in her turn prevented them from laying their hands upon "the Sick Man," as they called her. But seeing that Austria, another interested power, had for certain reasons turned against Russian policy, the Tsar had a meeting with his enemy in the East, Edward VII. With France and Italy already in agreement in external affairs, and their rivals also co-operating with each other, there appeared no alternative for Turkey except to give in to the demands of both groups up to the very end, from which would come the Empire's complete dismemberment.

The meeting of the two Kings showed quick results; there would be an intervention in Macedonia, in order to establish there an administration under the auspices of those powers of which the two Kings approved. Intervention would be both juridical, financial and military, so that that province would certainly become separated from the Empire sooner or later. The Young Turks faced the problem, and considered that the time had come to shake the mouldering Empire from its vaccilating policies. It was urgently necessary to solve these difficult problems with energy and dignity. The people must be consulted, and the idea of nationalism must arise from the constitutional regime.

At the beginning of June 1908, the Central Committee gave the signal for revolt. A few days later General Şemsi was assassinated in Monastir, and the troops who supported the rebellion retired to the mountains, where their natural defences made up for their numerical inferiority. The forces sent against them immediately by the high command crossed over to the side of the rebels.

The Padişah was terrified by the increasing danger. He could no longer count on the troops in Macedonia; he therefore concentrated thirty regiments in Izmir, imagining that the men of Asia Minor would not be contaminated with the ideas of those traitors. The order went forth to embark the troops from Izmir and land them at various points on the Macedonian coast. But the Red Sultan was wrong; the officers in Anatolia agreed in the majority with the Young Turks and favoured their programme. Some regiments refused to leave, others arrived on European soil and joined the revolutionaries.

The Young Turks, now masters of the situation, sent an ultimatum to Abdülhamit, announcing that unless he accepted the proposals they made to him, the Third Army would immediately march upon Istanbul. They did not have to wait long for the reply of the clever Sultan. He had already consulted the commanders of the troops in which he had blind trust; their answer, interrupted by declarations of loyalty, was that they also wanted the Constitution. Having lost all hope, the Sultan ordered that a favourable reply be sent, and we are assured that he let slip the following phrase : "One can do anything with bayonets, except sit upon them."

The imperial telegram was in the following terms : "In view of the desire expressed by the people, the Constitution promulgated in 1876 and suspended for certain reasons, is again in effect from this moment."

The joy which the quick triumph of the revolution produced throughout the Empire reached extraordinary proportions. For the first time in nearly thirty years, the people, used to keeping silent, were able to show their enthusiasm freely. In Macedonia, the Greeks, even the Bulgarian comitajis, and even the Turks who were considered to be supporters of the Padişah, the hojas with their great turbans, and the Greek priests fraternized amid popular rejoicing. An era of happiness appeared to be about to start. Before the magic word "Constitution" there disappeared the ancient rancours between the heterogeneous peoples who, united by force, formed the Ottoman Colossus.

Surrounded by the main revolutionary commanders, among them Kemal, Enver Bey, the idol of the moment, spoke to the people in the square which was later named Liberty Square, as follows "We are all brothers. Bulgarians, Serbs, Greeks or Romanians, Moslems or Jews, we are all Ottomans. It matters little that some of us go to the Synagogue, others to the Church or the Mosque. Beneath the fair sky of our country, let us be proud to bear the name of Ottomans."

The Sultan immediately called new elections, in which the Young Turks had a large majority. The first months of the revolution were promising; the political programme of the Committee of Union and Progress offered equality to all the subjects of the Empire, the universal vote, liberty of instruction, of assembly, of the press, and from obligatory military service. Abdülhamit pretended to accept the new state of affairs with relish: he blamed his favourites, and proclaimed himself as the protector of the Young Turks. He thus assured himself the possibility of continuing to reign, although it was only in appearance, for he believed that he would eventually do so effectively once again.

The Great Imperialist Powers, following sophistic reasoning, considered it natural that they should ride, and when the opportunity arose, divide amongst themselves the small countries, amongst which they classified "the Sick Man." They were amazed at the unusual spectacle; the aged Ottoman Empire, its energies exhausted, was fighting back; progressive ideals had achieved the humiliation of the all-powerful Calif. Europe unleashed her clever diplomacy, and studied carefully the consequences which the revival of the Sick Man, by an injection of young blood, might engender.

Their doubts were soon allayed; the revolution was unable to take advantage of its great moral strength, and its popular ascendancy, in order to give true new basis to national consciousness, but was held up in the search for forms and methods. The existence of the Constitution could not prevent Austria-Hungary declaring that it had annexed the provinces of Bosnia and Herzegovina a few months later, or Bulgaria from proclaiming herself an independent Kingdom.

Difficulties were piling up before the leaders of the political party of the Young Turks, who were also at the same time the leaders of the whole country. They had had no preparation for governing, and they were ignorant of the fine touches of politics. Their enemies, the traditionalists, attacked them with the same weapons that liberalism had placed in their hands, the freedom of the press and of assembly. The "leitmotiv" of the campaign was, that the Young Turks with their imported ideals, were forgetting Allah, and more than that, were denying him. The faithful would see themselves made equal to the infidels. The clerics joined the movement. In Turkey it was a serious matter to go against religion, the Koranic Law, the "Şeriat," the basis of the state's very structure.

The Young Turks were afraid of making themselves unpopular amongst the Moslems, and in order to stay the growing murmurings which accused them of atheism, gradually abandoned their original policy of universal equality, and at the same time came nearer to an intransigent nationalism. Those who were not Moslems, seeing their hopes for autonomy frustrated, on the one hand resisted confusion with the Moslem peoples, and yet on the other hand did not wish to give up their own prerogatives. This caused them to feel the repression of older days. They decided to commend themselves to their traditional protectors, the Great Powers. According to the Powers, democracy and progress, which clashed with traditional Islam, would not be acceptable to the great mass of Moslems. The Turks were, they went on, incapable of governing themselves according to the methods of civilized countries. The Powers intervened again, by diplomatic means, in favour of the Christian populations. The supreme experiment had been unsuccessful.

The Parliament which had been so longed for was composed of two-hundred and seventy-five members, of whom one hundred and thirty- three were not Moslems; these held opinions and voted against the wishes of the Committee of Union and Progress in matters concerning the Turkification of the Empire. They were afraid and wished to hinder the return of the nationalism of Abdülhamit. The first sympathisers of the movement were thus brought into alliance with those who defended the disgraced regime. A tacit agreement was made between them against the Young Turks. It was clear that the dreamed-of unification was merely a utopia.

There were other disappointments to surprise the inept and shadowy leaders of the country. The Prime Minister whom they chose, Kamil Paşa; from whose friendship with Great Britain they hoped would result a change in her policy of alliance with Russia, realised that the forces opposed to the Committee were more numerous than its supporters in Parliament, and tried to escape from the pressure which the Union was exercising upon him. He expelled from his cabinet two ministers who were fervent Unionists. It was a rather hasty action, for the Committee was not yet sufficiently weakened in prestige. A representative group of officers threatened Parliament, and it voted for Kamil's dismissal. Under the new Prime Minister, Hüseyin Hilmi Paşa, the enemies of the Young Turks did not rest either; on the contrary, they redoubled their campaign against those masons and Jews, enemies of Allah, who were, it was alleged, bringing with their base ideas the moral and material ruin of the Empire. The Sultan was certainly feeding this mystic flame. The signal for the counter-revolution in the name of Islam was given by an event which was never explained.

An obscure journalist of conservative opinions was found murdered on Galata Bridge. The Committee were considered responsible for the murder. This first victim of the freedom of the press was borne off to an imperial mausoleum, accompanied by a multitude rarely seen there for a funeral. The coffin was carried high, balanced above turbans of various shapes belonging to the ulemas, hojas and dervishes. Whole congregations of these formed green islands amid the red sea of fezzes which advanced like a vengeful wave, to the rhythm of the prayers intoned by choirs of müezzins.

On the following morning, that of the 13th April 1909, the soldiers of the garrison of Constantinople rendered their officers powerless, eliminating those who resisted, and supported by Abdülhamit's formidable guard, placed the city under occupation. They forced the resignation of the cabinet and of the parliamentary speaker, the choice of a new government faithful to religious principles, and the punishment of those officers who had been involved in the Young Turks' revolution.

The Red Sultan came forth triumphant from the shadows. In an "irade" or imperial decree, he vouchsafed a complete pardon for the excesses which had been committed. The post of Grand Vezir was given to a veteran politician of the old regime, Tevfik Paşa. This happy day's work was celebrated magnificently in the mosques, as was the effective re-establishment of the country's fidelity to the ancient Şeriat, while the fanatical troops, wild with joy, shouted in honour of the Padişah. He smiled with satisfaction at his own cleverness; the Empire was going to be his once more, and the word "Constitution," which some months before had given him some worry, no longer meant anything at all. In these days the non-Moslems lived in fear of riots by the populace and the troops, who seemed to have revived the spirit of the bloodthirsty Janissaries. It was possible that there would be a persecution of the kind which Abdülhamit was fond of. However nothing happened, apart from some murders in pursuit of revenge.

The Sultan wanted to show himself as a guarantor of good order to the Great Powers, from whom he was hoping for help, particularly from the United Kingdom, which he thought would look approvingly upon the return of the old theocratic regime in the Empire of the Calif, whose sluggish stupor was more conducive to the tranquility of her oriental colonies, than those echoes of revolutions in the cause of democracy and above all the hated word "Freedom." Great Britain aided the Lord of Yildiz, and considered the Young Turks' movement as merely a frustrated coup d'état. The unionists were to remember this, when at the beginning of the World War they had to decide in favour of Germany or Great Britain.

The Third Army in Macedonia, stronghold of the Young Turks, declared itself ready to march on Istanbul. A number of Greeks and Bulgarians joined the movement; this was a new fraternisation, this time sincere, among Turkish subjects of different religions. The Second Army, at Edirne, proclaimed itself in favour of those who wished to restore the rights which had been won in the previous year. At the head of the liberating forces was placed the General Mahmut Şevket, an Arab by birth, and a man who had great influence over the leading officers in the Committee.

Kemal, who had recently arrived from Tripolitania, was appointed the Chief of the General Staff of the "Army of Repression." This was an appointment of historic importance, and the moment was of extreme seriousness, not only for the Young Turks but for the whole Empire, since civil war could have resulted from an attempt to take the capital. The Red Sultan, surrounded by his guards and by the whole of the garrison army, without counting the human reserves which might be sent to him through the open door of Anatolia, would make that expedition a risky one.

The revolutionary army established its camp within sight of the walls of Istanbul, without being attacked. From the city there came favourable news. The troops, whose officers had been dispersed, imprisoned or killed, had repented after the first moments of excitement, and had become inactive in the fear of severe punishment. The opposition press was silent, and the religious men, after deep thought, had decided to abstain from any propaganda; the bourgeoisie and the non-Moslems desired, for their peace of mind, the re-establishment of the liberal regime.

The forces of Mahmut Şevket entered the age-old city by night and through various entrances. By the morning the city was in the hands of the so-called Army of Liberation, after some sporadic resistance. Two weeks had not passed since Abdülhamit had once again become master of the Empire. He had been less fortunate than the Great Corsican. His second reign was to last a mere fourteen days.

That same night a delegation appeared at the Palace of Yıldız where Abdülhamit awaited them in fear. He must certainly have remembered all those whom he had put to death, and saw again the faces of those who had been his friends only to lose their lives at his hand; now his turn too had come. What kind of death had they chosen for him? But it would be impossible for them to kill him, the Representative of God upon the earth, the Shadow of Allah! Yet in those moments of terror, such bombastic phrases sounded hollow to his ears, since he was no longer convinced of their truth. No, he thought, nobody would come to save him. He gave himself up to despair. The visitors who he thought were to be his executioners informed him that he must leave the palace that same night, and that they had chosen the city of Salonika as his place of detention. Abdülhamit listened to them; the gloomy expression on his wizened features, crowned with a red fez, acquired a yellow pallor; his impenetrable eyes stared with an angry intensity. He now suspected that death was now awaiting him through poison or strangulation, so that nobody would be held responsible for the murder. He who had once been all-powerful besought them thus: "I have always worked for the good of my people," he said. "I submit myself to the will of the nation. May I at least feel secure that my life will be spared?"

Some hours later he crossed the fair gardens of his park in a modest carriage; it was a pity, he thought, that it was too dark for him to see the exotic plants on which he had lavished such care, and which were just beginning to flower in these spring days.

It came as a surprise to Mehmet Reşat to see the approach of the delegation which announced to him his accession to the throne of Osman, and his ascension to the dignity of Calif of the Moslems. Being a timid person, he did not know whether to accept or decline these lofty offers, but as the delegates insisted, he said; "I will do what I can for the good of the country." He was therefore conducted to the Ministry of War, where were waiting the new leaders of the country, whom he would have to obey. The Şeyhülislam raised his voice in prayer, and after the imperial personage had sworn allegiance to the Constitution, the accession of the new Padişah, Mehmet V, was announced to the people by salvoes of artillery.

This aged Prince was then sixty-seven years old, having spent the last thirty years of his life in almost complete isolation, since his brother Abdülhamit saw in him a possible usurper. Mehmet Reşat was a kindly, inoffensive man, a docile instrument in the hands of the Committee, who now began to rule the country in earnest.

The new government's first acts consisted of reprisals against the reactionaries. Gallows of classical pattern and economical construction were erected beside the most populous places; left swinging there were high functionaries who had been the allies of the disgraced Sultan, and all those upon whom suspicion fell. We need not speculate on the fate of the once- feared spies.

The job of forming a cabinet was given to an old politician, since the leaders of the Committee, with truly Ottoman wisdom, preferred to remain in semi-obscurity, from which they could rule the country at their pleasure and without any official responsibility.

The power of the Young Turks depended on the army, and to please that element, the most important political positions were given to several officers belonging to the Union. This admixture of the army in political affairs had become one of the reasons for arguments between Kemal and the leaders of the Committee. He knew the weak points of the army, and understood that it would be dangerous for it to intervene directly in the government. On several occasions he expressed an opinion that the Empire ought to follow a path of democratic renewal in accord with the popular movement, and that the army should return to its proper area of activity, which was to look after the defence of the country, which was after all in danger. He discovered that his theories about the "great men" were indeed correct. These men were ignorant of the true principles of the constitutional regime which they preached, and were not the men of the new mentality which Turkey needed; they showed the same defects as those whom they criticised; their spirits were those of satraps. Kemal took his own decision to break with the politicians of the Union. He did not expect to obtain preferment after the march on Istanbul; he preferred to dedicate himself with all his enegry to work which concerned his career. His studies, together with his intelligence, and the practical experience of war which he had received in the years of fighting within the frontiers of the Empire, had made him into a brilliant officer. His natural ability to command foreshadowed the leader that he would soon show himself to be.

The Committee, although they felt his cold and systematic opposition to them, attempted to win him over by attractive propositions. He was offered therefore the chance of going to France, in order to observe the progress of that country's military manoeuvres, which were being executed in Picardy. Kemal was pleased to accept this prospect of travel, so that he could go away and perhaps forget this first great disappointment of his life, which had left a sad expression chiselled upon his features.

PART TWO

THE DEFENCE OF THE FATHERLAND

Chapter 5

TRIPOLITANIA

The train ran across France, which Kemal was now leaving on his re* turn to the Empire. His mission had lasted only ,a few months; however, he had taken away a clear vision of the French army and its efficiency. He compared it with its Ottoman counterpart, and its organisation, which continued to be defective, in spite of the fact that since the beginning of the previous century, under the reforming Sultans, foreign experts had laid the foundations of reform for the primitive army.

The fair country of France, which respected the most diverse ideologies, and generously received all men whom their own countries' politics had expelled from their native lands, the mother of the rights of man, had conquered the heart of that Turkish officer, who had already been predisposed to this by the long tradition of mutual friendship existing between the two countries. Süleyman the Law Giver and François I had created this current of friendship, which had not ceased to flow, despite the occasional clashes of material interests.

Paris had with her stone memorials stirred noble feelings in his soldierly spirit and his heart full of idealism, patriotism and love of his fellow men. Les Invalides! That silence, those immobile standards which had known the brutal shock of nations in arms, the epic charges of the cuirassiers of the First Empire, which began with the clarion call and ended with the yells of victory; great names for which there was scarcely room beneath the dome : Austerlitz, Jena, Wagram, and down there a tomb, sunk down under the weight of the remains that it holds. It is that of Napoleon, the warrior, whom Kemal, as a soldier, admired and whose genius overpowered him. A man whose spirit contained great qualities, but who at the end of his career, led by eagle standards and followed by glory, found death as a prisoner on an arid and solitary rock, while France slowly arose from her ruins amid grief for her dead. Such was the end to which his ambitions of glory led. For Kemal the Marseillaise brought a closer emotion. They too, who fought against the Red Sultan, with the fervent enthusiasm and self-denial of those who suffered with grief for their country, were marching, soldiers and civilians alike, from the Marseilles of Macedonia to the Bastille of the Empire, to the rhythm of that hymn of liberty. For the first time the violin of Rouget de L'Isle would find its echo in the hearts of men of the East.

Just as in the revolution of 1789, the new knowledge had broken the absolutism of the autocrats, had restored or rather given a constitution, and now the "Unionist Convention" was trying to defend the frontiers of the country. The French people had seen their hopes disappointed after the 18th Brumaire, with the rise of personal ambitions which deluded with mirages of glory. There too, in Turkey, there were some amongst her hidden leaders, those "great men," whose dreams of power and unbridled power worried Kemal, who had learned to understand them. France left Kemal with some hope; he had realised that neither Voltaire nor Montesquieu had spent their lives in vain, and that their philosophy, so humane when it speaks of individual conscience and liberty, and of the respect which those principles deserve for the great happiness of nations, had truly triumphed there.

In Istanbul he joined the general staff. He now studied the situation of his country, or rather compared it, and from these continual comparisons which he made between it and the West, using an eye which had the ability to see simply the true size and value of things, he concluded that the old Empire was backward in every field, and confirmed the opinions he had already formed. He made plans for directing the country towards the West. He felt that he loved his country with great intensity in spite of all, as one might love a dying father; he was ready to give his life for it, and more than that, he would passionately dedicate all his time and all his efforts to saving it and seeing it prosper. If he only had a situation in the government, what benefits he could achieve! He felt that he could even bring himself to make up his differences with the Committee; however, this rapprochement would be useless. They and he were going by different roads.

Sometime after his arrival from the West he was given a military posting to Salonika; he was made commander of a regiment, and achieved some constructive work, putting into practice the lessons he had learnt in France. The Minister of War, Mahmut Şevket, received accusations against Mustafa Kemal for subversive activity which he was alleged to be making in the army. The one thing that was certain was that his popularity in Salonika was increasing, and that, with his usual frankness, he was continuing to uphold among his friends the ideas which had divided him from the Young Turks. The Minister ordered Kemal to return to the general staff, far away from the Balkans, a dangerously ebullient area.

The Grand Vezir Hüseyin Hilmi had resigned at the beginning of the year 1910. He refused to be a puppet, or to allow himself to become a mere man of straw in the hands of the leaders of the Union. These leaders had set themselves up as the champions of the defence of the rights of the Empire, but saw that the mere fact of obtaining power was not sufficient for them to prevent the Empire's progressive dismemberment. On the contary, the Great Powers were alarmed at the danger of a possible resurrection of the "Sick Man" and were trying to hasten his collapse. The Unionists, in disappointment, allowed their anger to carry them away. They took the path of extreme nationalism, fighting against any interference by the Powers in the internal affairs of the Empire, and took the dangerous expedient of trying, too late, to Turkicize the regions of the Empire which were not Moslem. If the Ottomans at the peak of their power had not been able to assimilate the peoples whom they ruled, how could they attempt to do so now, when their decadence was so clear?

Kemal was convinced that this policy would only result in providing motives for foreign intervention and in the more rapid dismemberment of Turkey. Perhaps he was already thinking at that time of a Turkey which would be homogeneous, inhabited exclusively by Turks, although her frontiers would be far less extensive. At least such frontiers would be realistic, and not imaginary as in those days. The new government had before it a problem without an apparent solution; how could they reconcile truly Turkish interests, with the freedom which had been promised to the Christian subjects of the Ottomans? It was clear to Kemal that the Moslem clerical establishment, which the Unionists found themselves obliged to treat with respect, was an obstacle which hindered the Union of the Ottoman populations and the modernisation of the Empire. A break with Islam would have meant ai complete loss of prestige for the Young Turks in the eyes of the generations which had been educated under Islamic law.

The sky of Turkey began to cloud over in the year 1911, and the storm which fell upon her lasted twelve years. For that reason the sun of peace which shone forth after the sufferings of the Turkish people were over appeared the more brilliant.

In September 1911, the Italian Chargé d'Affaires suddenly presented to the Sublime Porte an ultimatum from his government, in which Italy demanded that the Ottoman provinces of Tripolitania and Cyrenaica should be raised to a level of culture necessary for the Italian interests which existed there. It announced Italy's intention of taking upon herself this civilising mission by means of a military occupation. This news surprised the Unionist Government, since their diplomats had given them not the slightest intimation of the intentions and material preparations which Italy was making. This lamentable lack of foresight brought about the immediate fall of the cabinet.

Italy had set in movement her plans for these provinces in 1900, when she signed a secret treaty with France, according to which France would, in return for Italy's recognition of her dominance in Morocco, assure to Italy the right of preference in the Ottoman part of Africa. It was clear that the Powers were only waiting to lay hands on the only part of the African coast of the Mediterranean which had so far eluded their control. That moment seemed to have come, aided by the isolationist policy of the Young Turks; in addition it was expected that victory would be easy because of the mouldering state of the imperial forces, the incontestable superiority of the Italian fleet, and the long distance separating those provinces from the Ottoman capital.

Nevertheless, although they expected that the result of the war would be unfavourable to the Crescent, the government took what measures it could to offer resistance, at least an honourable one. It was not so much a question of holding onto territory, as of showing the Moslem peoples that the Calif was not abandoning them.

The Italian fleet immediately attacked the port of Tripoli, which surrendered after a heroic resistance of six days. The same happened at Benghazi and Derna. The Italians had information that the Turkish forces were very small, and lacked officers; it seemed to them that the conquest of Libya would bring them plenty of cheap glory. They saw their hopes disappointed by the shadow of the Representative of Allah, who called upon the faithful to war, and repeated to them the words of the Prophet: "Fight against your enemies in the war declared in the defence of religion." He added that those believers who did not abandon their country and fought for the faith could expect divine mercy.

Kemal, accompanied by several officers who were his friends, obtained permission to go to the African front. The Italian fleet prevented them from going by sea; they therefore had to travel across Anatolia, Syria and Egypt, a hard journey. Great Britain hoped that the war would end in Italy's favour, and did whatever she could to prevent the entry of Turkish officers into Cyrenaica. Kemal had difficulty in crossing the frontier with that province, but he did succeed in getting in touch with the leaders of the Turkish forces.

Like Kemal, other patriots had come to the defence of the Empire, amongst them the Lieutenant-Colonels Ali Fethi and Enver, one of the heroes of the Unionist revolution. Enver hoped that his military victories would surpass all those he had already gained as a politician, and thought Tripolitania a suitable field for the collection of laurels. Although he was only a Lieutenant-Colonel, he was given the supreme command of the forces defending the Region of Benghazi. He organised resistance, disciplining the Arab tribes and Berbers. He flattered their great chiefs, receiving them in his tent, which was comparable in luxury to those used by Harun al-Rashid. He talked to them in the flowery language which they liked, and acquired a great ascendancy over them. He was after all soon to become a "Damad," the title given to the sons-in-law of Sultans, for he was beloved by the Sultana Naciye, daughter of the Calif of the Moslem world.

The Sultana Naciye admired the young hero, who was reputed to be arrogant and extremely dashing; however when she saw him from behind the grille of one of the windows of the imperial harem, his soft, almost, effeminate aspect, and his apparently timid expression caused her to fall in love with him. They were brought into communication by discreet friends, and the princess, who had been destined for one of the sons of Abdülhamit, obtained her royal father's permission to engage herself officially to Enver Bey. The all-powerful Unionist Leader was a son-in-law not to be despised, even by the Sultan himself. For the young officer, who like nearly all the leaders of the Committee of Union and Progress was of humble origin, relationship with the house of Osman was the summit of his immense vanity.

The first important place which Kemal reached was Tobruk. He began to reconnoiter the positions of the troops, and succeeded in convincing the General Staff that he should attack without delay, which resulted in a victory.

With the help of their fleet, the Italians succeeded in conquering nearly the whole coast in two months, but they suffered reverses in the interior of the country, such as their defeat at Shorashot, Sidi Mesri and Henni, which made them understand that in order to achieve victory they would have to fight seriously, and bring in a greater number of troops than they had expected.

The defenders fought with an indomitable courage, and fought guerilla warfare in an unfriendly temperature. They lost no opportunity of attacking the invaders. Enver, the lord of the desert, was looking for any opportunity of the triumph he dreamed of, which would allow him to return to Istanbul for the third time as a victor. He was determined to reconquer Derna, and he sent his best troops to that sector, without achieving his aim. Kemal was frequently in contact with his commander on military subjects; their characters were opposed, and this generally put them in disagreement. However they did resemble each other in one thing, the power of their personalities, which were wilful, and this increased the tension of their relations. Kemal lived in a modest tent, and took no part in the entertainments which Enver gave to the Moslem dignitaries, tribal chiefs, and to his tribe of flatterers, who called him the "little Napoleon." Kemal preferred to make long journeys on horseback, to inspect the troops, and to occupy himself in a practical way with the progress of the war.

Kemal criticized the faults which he found in the tactics followed by Enver, and in many other aspects of the campaign. For his part Enver told his friends in a disdainful way, that Mustafa Kemal suffered from jealousy.

In November, the Italian army was increased to over a hundred thousand men; yet even with that and after seven, months of fighting the invaders were unable to advance more than ten kilometres inland, and consequently, and to avoid greater sacrifices, they decided to use their fleet. The fleet attempted to force the Dardanelles with the intention of threatening Istanbul, but the fortifications of the straits forced them to give this up. They therefore occupied the Dodecanese Islands in the Aegean Sea.

The serious events which were occurring in the Balkans obliged the Empire to give up the defence of its last African provinces. In October 1912, a conference was held at Ouchy near Lausanne, between the two belligerent states, as a result of which the Turkish troops were to leave Libya, and the Sultan said to its inhabitants : "I concede to you a full and complete autonomy."

Kemal, who had received the rank of Major for his services in the war, arrived at Istanbul, at the moment when the Balkan war had begun and the first Turkish defeats had become known.

CHAPTER 6

BALKAN WARS

From the beginning of 1911, there occurred disturbances in Albania caused by the Union's policy of Turkification. These were repressed violently. The antipathy of the non-Moslems towards the new government was increasing. The Bulgarians redoubled their activities against Turkey, and suffered reprisals. However when Italy declared war against the Empire, the Balkan states understood that the moment of liberation had arrived.

The Eastern Question was reaching its solution. The mighty pincers which were to smash the Crescent were closing their grip : Italy would expel it from Africa and they, the Balkan countries, would do the same in Europe.

The Young Turks were in disgrace. They were being held responsible for the loss of the African provinces, for the Italian occupation of the Dodecanese Islands, and for the menacing situation in European Turkey. A conglomerate political party formed from the various groups hostile to the Young Turks, was established under the name of "Liberal Union."

The Unionists, seeing that danger was near, called elections before the appointed time. They obtained once more a crushing majority. Rough methods were thought to have been used, but the pretence of an election did not produce the desired result, since those officers who had been corrupted by politics, and were tired of the dictatorship of the Committee, declared themselves rebels under the name of "Saviours of the Country." The Committee had to go into retreat, and in July 1912 the old Marshal Ahmet Muhtar formed a cabinet containing the greatest enemies of Unionism, including General Nâzim, a young and ambitious man, who received the Ministry of War. The other Ministries were given to a group of old Vezirs, some of them former servants of the Red Sultan. Thus the first reign of the Young Turks came to an end.

Russia, that eternal enemy of Turkey, who had been spying out the possibilities of the latter's sickness, was quick to arrange an agreement among the Balkan states which were already ready and armed, that they should attack the land of the Crescent. Thus on 13th May 1912, while the Turkish forces were gathering in Africa, a treaty of alliance both offensive and defensive was signed by Serbia,

Greece, Montenegro and Bulgaria. In this treaty there was laid the basis for the coming division of European Turkey, while to Russia was reserved the right to arbitrate over any difficulties which might arise from that division.

In September everything was ready for the action long dreamt of by the orthodox communities; it was the Bosporus and the Dardanelles which were to be the targets for the crusade.

The Grand Vezir Ahmet Muhtar tried by all means to reach an agreement with the Balkan countries and the Great Powers. To the former he gave renewed assurances that the promised reforms would be put into practice. But it was too late, for the ideas of the nations of the Balkan peninsula of freeing their brothers from Islamic domination had sent down deep roots. More than that, Greece was hoping to rebuild her territory along the lines of her history, for which the first stage would be the reconquest of Salonika and the Aegean Islands; Bulgaria considered that she had the greater right, from a racial point of view, to become the mistress of the greater part of Macedonia and Thrace, and she needed also to have ports on the Aegean and thus avoid having to pass through the straits; Montenegro felt suffocated in her tiny territory, and Serbia, in despair at the annexation by Austria of Bosnia and Herzegovina, was taking the opportunity of annex territories which would bring her nearer to the Ionian Sea.

The formation of the Balkan league was soon made known, and its partners made public their demands, which were inadmissable to the Ottoman government. The disagreement became so acute, that the Great Powers warned of the danger of war contained in this situation. Apart from Russia, none of the Powers was interested in the outbreak of a general conflagration in which they had nothing to gain. Furthermore the "Sick Man" was in such a state of gravity that, paradoxically, it did not worry anyone. The French Minister Poincare, with the agreement of the British government, gave a warning to the Balkan countries. They were not to undertake anything which could disturb the peace or affect the "status quo," which existed in the Balkans. Otherwise, the Great Powers would combine their forces to restrict the area of conflict and bring it to an end.

These fair wishes remained a dead letter, since the events which were bringing war closer precipitated it to such an extent that by the end of September the four allied states had mobilized, and in the first days of the following month Montenegro declared war against the Empire. The Ottoman government also mobilized, but continued with discussions, trying to gain time while she achieved the conclusion of peace with Italy. As soon as that was done, the war was declared and hostilities began with extreme violence, the initiative being taken by the allied states.

The Ottoman army had somewhat improved, in comparison with what it had been under Abdülhamit, when it had clearly been left behind by the armies of the day. The Ottoman ranks lacked enthusiasm; the Calif would call upon his faithful subjects to war and no-one failed to appear, through sheer habit. Among the soldiers of the allied armies, on the other hand, patriotic enthusiasm reached exalted degrees, and could be compared only to the religious fanaticism which also possessed them. The most terrible adversaries were the Bulgarians, who threw themselves into a formidable attack towards the Bosporus, with the war cry of "Tsaregrad! Tsaregrad!," their name for Istanbul. They were commanded by Tsar Ferdinand, who had been encouraged by the Russians to have great thoughts of the tall gates of Santa Sophia. He would pass through them as through arches of triumph, as he entered that great temple as bearer of the Cross. The Tsar's army did not waste time over capturing the stronghold of Edirne, which they besieged, but marched on Kırklareli which they captured brilliantly on the 24th October. One week later they defeated the imperial army on the banks of the river Ergene and marched towards Istanbul.

The armies of the other allies were no less victorious : Greece captured Salonika, along with an enormous number of prisoners, and her fleet occupied the Turkish Islands of the Aegean; the Montenegrins besieged Shkodër in Albania; the Serbs entered Üsküp and defeated the Turks in Kumanovo, then came down the river Vardar and reached as far as Durres on the Adriatic. This in fact meant the loss of Turkey's European territories.

The world still remembered the stories of the terrible Turkish conquerors who had on many occasions come from the depths of Asia to sow terror in the European lands with their savage attacks. All were now amazed to see them retreat, suffering defeat after defeat, towards the point from which they had departed centuries before.

The victorious Bulgarian army had to receive the fiercest part of the Ottoman resistance, for necessary reinforcements were arriving across the still unassaulted straits from Anatolia, an inextinguishable granary of men. The lightning advance of the Tsar's army was stopped for the first time, as the Turks fortified themselves in Çatalca, a little over thirty kilometres from Istanbul. General Savof brought in reinforcements and artillery, and prepared an offensive which would break down all resistance. The Bulgarian victories must continue. So near were they that they could see the minarets reflected in the Bosporus!

An attack of colossal size this time was launched against the lines of Çatalca. The clash of battle could be heard as far as Pera itself. Foreigners sought help from their respective countries. What would happen if as seemed probable the

Turkish army was defeated? They were certain that the army would retreat in confusion towards Istanbul and cause through its passage massacres amongst the non-Moslems. Also the Bulgarian invasion would bring other dangers. The Great Powers hurriedly sent warships and troops, who took charge of the defence of their compatriots. The Powers intended not only to be present when the shareout was made, but also to face the possible future master of the straits.

The Empire resisted in Çatalca. It seemed as if the walls of Istanbul had advanced over those intervening kilometres to hold up the invader. The Bulgarians redoubled their attacks, and rivers of blood flowed. The fortifications were dynamited, but the Turks formed new walls with their own breasts. The Bulgarians charged again and again, but in vain, for the defenders now knew that they were now fighting for their wives and children and for their homes. "They shall not pass!" Something was still left in the soul of that warlike race, some great thing which had not died with the last victories of the great Sultans. There was a calm bravery, and a spirit of sacrifice which could not be moved. The decay of the Empire was a sickness caused by its excessive extent and by its governing classes, the Sultans, weakened by pleasures; but the Turkish race was a young one, which had no knowledge of those vices, thanks to the very backwardness in which it had lived. Kemal knew this, and later on, when the country knew dangers infinitely greater than those of the Balkan War, he had faith in his people and love for his people. From such factors as these great things can be made.

The Bulgarian attack and the dreams of their Tsar fall defeated. The armies remained face to face, exhaushed. Now either of them might leap upon the neck of his adversary; the situation had altered.

Cholera broke out on both sides, followed by dysentery. Mortality was high. Istanbul trembled. One danger had passed only for a more terrible one to threaten it. Long lines of refugees from Thrace arrived every day, with buffaloes yoked to their rough carts; they carried with them the little that they had managed to save; a few domestic animals, a few sticks of furniture. The terror of invasion, of hunger, and of suffering was reflected still on their faces. Any refuge was too small for so many refugees. They filled the courtyards of the mosques, the squares, and the barracks, until they could be taken across to Anatolia. It was really extraordinary that cholera did not appear in Istanbul, where there was constant contact with the soldiers camped at the city gates.

It was in this sad circumstance that Kemal had been appointed director of operations with the army corps commissioned to defend the northern shore of the Dardanelles. The influence of Kemal on the commander of the army corps and of its chief of staff was considerable. He showed clearly his competence, and even more his well-tempered soldier's spirit. He seized on every chance and took advantage of it, both in victories and defeats, thus succeeding in forming a mobile front which in the last resort held, and achieved its objectives in those days of consecutive disasters.

Once the allies had achieved their objectives, and the Bulgarian army had come to a halt, the Great Powers thought that the time had come for them to intervene. They had not agreed with this war, which had defied their influence, and from which they saw a new power emerging; this was Bulgaria, which was aspiring to control Istanbul and the straits.

Hostilities ceased, and on December 3rd 1912, after the signature of an armistice, the belligerents decided to take their negotiations to London under their inevitable aegis of the Great Powers. On the banks of the Thames the allied demands proved to be of a character unacceptable to the Sublime Porte. They were demanding the cession of Adrianople, Shkodër in Albania and Yannina, cities which they had not even captured. The Empire would have come round to giving up the last two, but it refused absolutely to cede Adrianople, the ancient capital of the Empire, which was the pivot of the defence of the straits. The negotiations were suspended at the beginning of the following year.

In Turkey the year 1913 began with very serious political events. The government, from which the Young Turks had been excluded, wanted peace. A "Divan," or National Assembly was called, to decide whether to accept peace or to continue the war which had so far proved disastrous. It inclined towards peace. When the result of the Divan became known, the Young Turks, whose warlike ideas and fanatical patriotism were well known, protested furiously and moved from words to deeds. Thus, on the following day, the 23rd January, a group of them led by Enver Bey, penetrated into the Sublime Porte, seat of various ministries, and of the Prime Minister. Hearing voices raised in an unusual tone, Nâzım Paşa, the Minister of War, went out into one of the corridors, only to meet Enver, who blamed him for the Turkish defeats. An officer named Yakub Cemil who stood behind Enver immediately shot the Minister dead. After this bold stroke Enver obtained an interview with Mehmet V and obtained from him the appointment of Marshal Mahmut Şevket as Prime Minister. The Young Turks put the blame for all the Turkish defeats upon the regime they had deposed, and, instigated by Enver, sought to try the fortunes of war once more. They made rapid preparations for hostilities.

The fighting began again, but with much less vigour than before. The Bulgarian army made some attacks at Çatalca and in the direction of the Dardanelles against the troops of Hürşit Paşa, amongst whom Kemal was serving. In the first week of February, Enver convinced the military authorities that it was an opportune moment to attack the Bulgarians. Enver was a man of great ideas and fantastic projects; he thought up triumphs in his ardent spirit, instead of planning them in cool reality. His mentality was diametrically opposed to that of Kemal, and their different characters caused constant disagreement between them. Enver's plan aimed no less at obliging the Bulgarians to raise the seige of Adrianople by disembarking strong contingents in Şarkoy on the shores of the sea of Marmara. At the same time the forces in Gallipoli were to attack the Bulgarians on their right flank. Kemal noted that the enemy were occupying all the high places of Şarkoy, which would make disembarcation almost impossible, especially as the wretched Turkish fleet would be unable to give sufficient support; in addition the Bulgarians' internal lines were perfectly well fortified. However Enver was in command and his plan was accepted.

This attractive plan of attack by land and sea brought a sad disappointment to the Unionists, to which was added the fall of Yannina to the Greeks and that of the holy city of Adrianople. There was no other solution but resignation. On 30th May the representatives of the Empire signed over the total loss of their European territories. After five centuries of rule all that remained to them were the straits and a strip of land to the north of them. Austria and Italy were pleased at the creation of a new country, Albania, which prevented Serbia from having access to the Adriatic. The Great Powers were to keep the Turkish Islands close to the coast of Anatolia under their lofty protection, while their fate was decided; naturally, Crete would pass immediately into the power of Greece.

This first phase of negotiations brought no difficulties; the next stage however, which was the division of the conquered territories among the allies, brought heated discussions, whose intransigent character did not augur well. Serbia, Bulgaria and Greece had conquered Macedonia jointly; however Bulgaria, which had a racial preponderance there, and which during the war had borne the hardest part of the battle and obtained the most brilliant victories, expected to remain with the lion's share. Serbia and Greece did not wish to accept this reasoning, and put forward claims of their own; Russia reminded them of the pact they had signed and invited them to submit to the arbitration there stipulated, but since it was considered that Russia would favour Bulgaria, this was not done.

On the night of 29th June, the army of Tsar Ferdinand took everyone by surprise by launching a general attack against the Greek end Serbian forces, with the obvious aim of separating the armies of her former allies and occupying Macedonia. However, the Bulgarians' star had ceased to shine, and they were defeated all along the line. The Greek and Serbian armies entered Bulgaria, and the Tsar's ambitions received the coup de grace from Romania, whose army crossed the frontier and camped a few kilometres away from Sofia. It came on the pretext of imposing peace, and moderating the predominance of Bulgaria in the Balkans; on the way however, the Romanians took the opportunity of fulfilling their ancient desire to increase their territories by the annexation of the rich region of the Dobruja.

It was obvious that Turkey would not miss this chance of regaining Adrianople. Political struggles began again, following the bloody impulse given them by Enver with the murder of Nâzim Paşa. The enemies of the Committee of Union and Progress wanted to revenge themselves on him and weaken him. They chose the Prime Minister Mahmut Şevket as their victim. On 13th June 1913 he was murdered in the beautiful square of Beyazit, which is overlooked by the mosque of the same Sultan. This event was more useful to the Young Turks than to their enemies, for the leaders of the latter party were accused of complicity of the murder. In that same Beyazit Square, where the doves wait for the grains of maize thrown to them by pious passers- by, gallows were erected to establish more firmly the power of the triumvirate which from then on was famous, that of Enver, Talât, and Cemal, who thenceforth were the masters of the Empire.

They entrusted the functions of Grand Vezir to the Prince Sait Halim. These functions were now merely honorary, since power was entirely in the hands of the triumvirate. Unlike that triumvirate formed by Pompey, Caesar and Crassus, or the French Consulate, its members had a perfect understanding between themselves, and were complementary to each other; Enver was as brilliant as a star, Talât, on the other hand, was a realist, a clever politician completely occupied with reflection and reasoning, who left the honours to Enver, living in a plain apartment, while the other lived a luxurious existence in a palace on the shores of the Bosporus. The reins of government were however in Talât's hands: Cemal was the least important of the three. In spite of his modest origins —it was said that his grandfather had been an executioner in the time of Sultan Mahmut —, he made conquests in European society and in the Embassies of Istanbul with his amiable and pleasant character. Much of this sociability was a pretence; he was at heart an Asiatic, and knew how to control his impulses.

Sheer chance which one could call good fortune favoured them well. The Bulgarians' disaster gave the Turks the opportunity to become again masters of their ancient capital, and they took it. They reconquered Lüleburgaz and Kırklareli, scene of funeral memory, and entered Adrianople without a fight. The Turkish troops were received with indescribable demonstrations of joy. The ma-

jority of the population of that part of Thrace is Moslem; The Bulgarian occupation had been extreemly hard to bear.

Kemal, as Chief of Staff of the army at Bolayır, had the pleasure of being
one of the first to reach the ancient city. Adrianople, in Turkish Edirne, stands at
the junction of three rivers which cover it with vegetation, and it is a wonderful
city, both from point of view of its beautiful situation, and from the magnificence
of its buildings. This typically Turkish city is the most important city of Thrace,
and the Sultans had enriched it with proud mosques and solidly built yet artistic
bridges. Russia wished to make a demonstration of force, in order to force the
Empire to respect the treaty of London and evacuate Edirne, but the other Powers dissuaded her from this idea, thinking it more prudent to make diplomatic
approaches, which were pursued in Istanbul with great politeness.

Bucharest was the scene for a disaster to Bulgaria, who was despoiled of
nearly all her conquests in favour of her former allies and, in addition, of part
of her own territory to Romania, which won the Dobruja without the slightest
effort. Through the treaty of Istanbul in 1913, Bulgaria recognised the Empire's
possession of Edirne.

CHAPTER 7

WORLD WAR

The reconquest of Edirne made people forget somewhat the loss of European Turkey and the sufferings of the war. This revival of spirits made a hero of Enver, who in his high position as Minister of War began to direct not only the army but also external affairs. This was a delicate charge at the beginning of a year in which a world war was to break out.

The wishes of the triumvirs became facts so quickly that it is reported by eye-witnesses that when the Sultan was reading a newspaper one morning he dropped it with an exclamation of amazement, saying to his aide-de-camp: "I read that Enver is the new Minister of War. That really cannot be possible; he is still too young."

The last wars fought by the Empire had been disastrous for it. The Great Powers, especially France and Great Britain, were pressing financially upon her; the capitulations were suffocating her. Russia was a constant danger through her eternal wish to control the straits and have the Mediterranean in her reach; the Empire had lost its African possessions; the influence of Great Britain in Egypt and Arabia, that of France in Byria, and that of Russia in Persia foreshadowed further dismemberment. Where could Turkey find a counterweight to these menaces and help to escape from such oppression?

Already some years before there had been approaches and offers from Germany. Kaiser Wilhelm, whose main policy was that of pan-Germanism and the "Drang nach Osten" or impulse towards the East, was looking for new markets for the Reich's abundant industrial production, and larger colonies in which to settle her subjects and from which to obtain raw materials. Great Britain and France were successfully keeping her out of the few territories left available. The Kaiser was most worried about the first of these Powers, which was mistress of the sea. He dreamt again a dream of Napoleon, who like him had been oppressed by that fleet which reigned over the waves : he would go to the East along Alexander's path, and there, with the power which those regions give to those that possess them, he would deal Great Britain a wound in her arteries and later vanquish her.

The frontiers of pan-Germanism ended in Serbia, the centre of Pan-Slavism, whose frontiers stretched far to the East. Serbia was the barrier which blocked the route towards the dominions of the Shadow of Allah, the spiritual head of the Moslem peoples. It was true that these were in decline, yet they did inhabit extensive and rich areas, from the sea of Marmara to the sea of Oman and from Turkestan to the Mediterranean.

The Kaiser Wilhelm II set himself up as protector of the Moslem peoples. With his Empress he visited Palestine and Syria in the autumn of 1898. Following Napoleon's example, he showed respect to the external appearances of the Moslem religion; he entered the holy Mosques with his hat on, and put the famous slippers over his boots, then went to Istanbul, where his friend the Sultan Abdülhamit was to receive him as guest of honour. The Sultan's clouded imagination was faced by a situation which caused him serious doubts; he would be obliged to visit his illustrious guest, and in one of these dangerous journeys the murderers who were in the pay of his enemies would not fail to make an attempt against his sacred life. Suddenly a brilliant idea made him smile with satisfaction. Ah, how he would trick those traitors! He ordered a luxurious palace to be built immediately, next door to his royal mansion, just there, protected by the wall of Yıldız and his faithful Albanians.

Wilhelm and Abdülhamit embraced each other, while the Empress smiled amiably; the Sultanas did not appear before the Emperor's friend, for religion did not permit this. The Kaiser praised the Sultan and his pan-Islamic policy. He spoke to him of the respect which there existed throughout the confines of his dominions and in the heart of all Moslems towards the Commander of the Faithful, recognising that he represented a great moral force. Then he went on to talk about the ambition of the enemy powers, who were in fact the adversaries of both of them, and offered the Sultan his support, in a Germano-Islamic union, which the Sultan accepted. The Kaiser showed on a map the enormous area of the world which they ruled between them. The Calif ought to be in greater contact with the faithful; railways should be built, which would increase his power considerably. In this way the competing powers who had penetrated Syria and Egypt would lose the race. Abdülhamit agreed, and gave the most important railway concession to a German firm. This was the Baghdad railway, a direct threat to the British colonial power, and which would open with its rails an era of brilliant hopes for Germany. German influence was also evidenced by a request for military instructors.

The two autocrats understood each other and spent whole hours together. The Shadow of Allah showed off in his greenhouse the exotic plants which were his pride; he also reared animals, rarities in Istanbul which had been sent from far-off provinces. The traditional dwarfs, eunuchs and clowns of the luxurious palace, the grilled windows of the mysterious harem, which was populated by the fairest examples of oriental beauty, the minarets cutting the horizon, and the serenity of the Bosporus all made Wilhelm feel orientalised. Napoleon also experienced this sensation and once wrote : "I saw myself on the road to Asia, riding on an elephant, a turban on my head and a new Koran in my hands." This memorable visit left a fruitful seed for the friendship between Turkey and Germany. Wilhelm II wanted the fact to be recorded in stone: he presented to the capital of Islam a kiosk which pretended to be in the oriental style, but was noticeably reinforced with Teutonic solidity.

Amongst his great projects Enver had one which dominated his heart. This was to rebuild the Ottoman Empire, and bring it back again to its peak of the seventeenth century; to revive past glories. He was a Germanophile, having studied in Germany, to return later as Military Attaché. Enver and the Kaiser were on good terms; the interest of both sides allowed Enver to forget that Wilhelm had been a friend of the dethroned Abdülhamit. Although like the majority of the Young Turk rulers he was an atheist, he already thought of using the green cloak of the Prophet to attract the Moslem peoples.

The new Minister of War decided that the army should be reformed completely on new basis; its defects made this necessary. He expunged from the army list a large number of Generals and Colonels whom he considered useless, and amongst whom were all his adversaries. Through his influence a request was sent to the Kaiser for a well organised military mission consisting of good staff officers. This did not delay, but arrived in Istanbul before the end of 1913. There were forty-two chosen officers, led by General Liman von Sanders. The military mission had a difficult task, since the Ottoman army had deteriorated noticeably in the last war. Enver Paşa, for he had just obtained that title, wanted to command a powerful army, since this was the only way of realising his fantastic projects.

Mustafa Kemal, who had been promoted to Lieutenant-Colonel on the occasion of the capture of Edirne, was then in Istanbul with his mother and sister. Since he was separated from politics and from the Unionist leaders, his situation was not remarkable if compared with that of many of his contemporaries who formed Enver's court. Enver, who graduated from the Military Academy two years before Kemal, had achieved an amazing career, aided by his diplomatic character, pliant politics, and ability to advertise himself and make himself appear more than he was. His ambitions grew disproportionately with his success; he had even managed to relate himself to the House of Osman, by marrying the Princess Naciye. Kemal thought that Enver was a man of the past, full of unrealizable dreams, such as that of wanting to rebuild the Empire within its old frontiers, without realising that times had changed, and that the true strength and welfare of the country lay in social and spiritual progress, in achieving economic independence and thus creating an educated and free nation. The Empire's frontiers and its oppression of its population hindered this perfection.

Kemal protested against the arrival of the German military mission, which was equivalent to putting the Ottoman army under the command of 'the German general staff. He realised that Enver intended to give himself over to the Kaiser. Kemal asked for an interview with the Minister of War, but the latter refused. Being a man of soldierly rectitude of character who possessed a deep feeling of personal honour and self respect, he felt this offence painfully. He told Enver of his feelings by letter, and did not fail to explain to him why he had vainly attempted to see him.

Enver thought it would be a good idea to move this troublesome person to a distance. Should he give him a command? No, for he had already had to be removed from one in Salonika for having incited the army against the government. But what should be done with him? The best known way of solving cases of that kind was to give the undesirable person an official mission abroad. An occasion arose for this. Ali Fethi, a friend of Kemal's, was leaving for Sofia as Minister Plenipotentiary, and it was decided that Mustafa Kemal should accompany him as Military Attaché.

On 19th July, on the level ground of Bebek near the capital, there was held a military review in imitation of those which were held in other countries in those months leading up to the Great War. Enver had organised it to show the excellence of German methods and his own power. The stands were filled with people, the German officers were placed in seats of honour and great personages arrived in carriages. At the sound of a fanfare, the crowd stood up, the troops presented arms, and a squadron of imperial lancers, wearing beautiful red uniforms and capped with traditional kalpaks adorned with beautifully coloured feathers, came in leading the Sultan's carriage. At the Sultan's right hand, Enver cavorted on his pure Arab steed. "Long live the Padişah!" cried the soldiers. The audience applauded, but their applause was for Enver, the idol of the army.

The foreign military attaches were impressed by the parade, which was magnificent from every point of view. Near the throne of Mehmet V two proud palfreys reared up at the sound of the strident marches; their two Negro grooms, wearing gold-faced tunics, could barely control them. These were the Sultan's horses; however he no longer led his troops to war, as had his far-off ancestors, nor did one any longer hear the phrase "approach the imperial stirrup." The descendant of the Prophet was a grotesque shadow of a Sultan. Enver turned his eyes towards his father-in-law; those troops, full of strength, full of life and vitality deserved a better commander. He himself felt that he had more than enough qualities to become a glorious Sultan. Up to that time, for six centuries, the blood of Osman had flowed through the veins of every Sultan, but the dreams of Enver had no limits.

A new life for Kemal began in the capital of Bulgaria. This was the life of the salon, led in diplomatic circles and high society. His studies, his intrigues in Istanbul and Salonika with spies following him, his different military posts, and the wars he had fought, could not have helped much to make him into a drawing-room man, a man of refinement and good-natured frivolity. Nevertheless, he moved through embassies and palaces with complete naturalness from the first moment, without pretending to have other manners than his own, though these were naturally correct. He preferred listening and observing to setting forth his ideas, and above all he tried to associate with military men, and to discuss with them subjects which were within his knowledge or which concerned politics; the conclusions which he drew after a few moments thought were brief, but the depth of their meaning contained the solution or explanation of a problem.

Kemal fulfilled his mission with the same energy and vitality which he displayed in everything he undertook. He attended military manoeuvres, about which he wrote reports which attracted attention for their concise understanding. He became friendly with General Savof, his old adversary, with the most distinguished officers of the general staff, and with his diplomatic colleagues. He always found conversation with these interesting, and he knew how to turn the conversations to the subjects that he wished.

We are now in the tragic year of 1914, and unease reigned in Sofia, as in all the other capitals of Europe. Discussions went on incessantly about the great problems, between the diplomats and politicians who were most involved with them.

The scene for the drama had been set long before. The nation which had been mistress of the world saw, at the end of her nineteenth century, her Victorian era, the rise of a competitor who was acquiring the proportions of a giant, and whose efficient industries were threatening her markets and challenging her dominion over the seas, which were her seas; finally, after everything had been shared out already, this rival was aspiring to create a colonial Empire, and had set her sights on the East. However, the great fleet was powerful, and when the French fleet was allied to it they would form an impassable barrier protecting their colonial dominions. Prince Bismarck had the foresight to prepare a road

to the East by land. He began to build it over Austrian territory, but was unable
to finish it because an obstacle had arisen. This was Russia, in the Slav Balkan
countries. The Tsars were also looking in that direction, and had done so before
he had; much Russian blood had been spilt to reach the Bosporus, and at the
decisive moment the Western Powers had deprived Russia of her royal booty,
Istanbul and the straits.

Now the great problem was posed for Germany. She must pass the Slav
barrier, and reach the East, in order to conquer a colonial Empire and control
the seas and their approaches. On one side Russia would try to hinder her in the
Balkans, and on the other side were France and Great Britain. Amid his dreams
of rebuilding the Empire, Enver was seeking, reasonably, for German support in
the war which was so probable; he bad absolute faith in the German army and
a German victory. Von Sanders' mission had given the good results that he had
hoped from it. While preparations for war continued at a rapid rate, compulsory
military service was in force even for non-moslems.

Kemal became passionately interested in the games of international politics;
he held to his first idea and told his Turkish friends, that Enver, with his secret
alliance with Germany, was carrying them towards disaster. The Kaiser did not
have victory assured and if he won it would be worse for Turkey, since she would
then have to depend on Berlin. What obligation had they to take part in the war?
Was it not better to wait upon events in an intelligent neutrality, which also had
its value? His friends thought that Mustafa Kemal, though an original thinker,
was this time completely mistaken and many of them, even some of the friends
he most valued, began to doubt his intelligence. How could he have any doubts
of the omnipotence of the army of Germany and Austria-Hungary, so perfectly
trained? And how could he doubt the excellence of the Prussian General Staff?

It was the irridentism of Serbia which produced the long-awaited spark in
the powder keg of Europe, by contact with intransigent Germanism. With the
support of Russia, the Serbs began a campaign of protests against the annexation
of Bosnia and Herzegovina which had been achieved by Austria. The spark took
flame from the guns of two young Bosnians, when at the end of June they murdered the Archduke Franz Ferdinand of Austria and his wife the Duchess of
Hohenberg in Sarajevo. They were visiting Bosnia to observe some manoeuvres.
This murder produced deep feeling throughout the world. Vienna and Berlin formerly accused Serbia of responsibility; Vienna sent her an ultimatum some days
afterwards. The activity of the governments of the countries concerned reached
fever pitch. On the advice of her protector, Serbia accepted the terms of the ultimatum. That however was not the desired result. The war was fated to happen,

and must one day or other break out; it was better to do it then, when the occasion seemed propitious.

For her own part, Russia did not accept the frustration of her advance towards the East or the loss of all hopes to dominate the Straits. It is possible to understand the enthusiasm which both Russia and Serbia had for the idea of war from the discussions that have been passed on to us by the French Ambassador Maurice Paléologue in his masterly book about imperial Russia. On the 22nd July, a few days before the Russian mobilisation, the Grand Duke Nicholas and his wife the Grand Duchess Anastasia, who was the daughter of King Nicholas of Montenegro, told the Ambassador, without trying to hide her own enthusiasm, that they were living through historic and holy days. She added that she had just received a telegram in cipher from her father, telling her that they would be at war before the end of that same month of July. As a result Austria would be destroyed, and the Russian and French armies would penetrate as far as Berlin. Germany would be annihilated. Great Britain was preparing to enter the conflict, and as one of her final preparations had gathered her fleet in Portsmouth. After Sarajevo, and in view of the attitudes of Austria and Russia, there was no longer any question of vague fears and suppositions. War was inevitable. Ultimatums, heralds of death, followed each other and crossed the gloomy atmosphere of Europe in all directions. Europe suffered under a horrible tension, as her peoples threw themselves simultaneously into the assault.

Turkey had not been dragged in by the first whirlwind, and confined herself at the beginning of the drama to closing the straits, ordering partial mobilisation, and completing her preparations. The influence exercised by the Germanophiles Enver and Talât, supported by the majority of the Committee of Union and Progress, made it clear even to those furthest removed from secrets and political combinations, which side the Turkish bayonets would turn to.

An incident which is remembered as one of the interesting episodes of the World War occurred to re-inforce that opinion. Two German warships, the Goeben and the Breslau, managed to elude the vigilance of the French and British fleets and penetrate the Dardanelles, after a dramatic and skillful journey across the Mediterranean. They took service under the Turkish flag to reinforce thus the defence of the straits. These two ships made up in a certain way for the two ships which had been ordered by the Empire and which had been almost completed, but which Great Britain had confiscated as soon as the straits were closed. The moral effect produced in Istanbul by the arrival of these ships can be considered to have been a great weight set in the hovering balance of Turkish public opinion. Although the majority of the Unionist leaders were convinced pro-Germans, the generally greater popularity of France kept bourgeois opinion until that moment opposed to the Central Powers.

The German Admiral Souchon was appointed Commander-in-Chief of the Imperial fleet. Neither the fleet nor the strong points of the Straits were in the state of military preparation required by the time and the circumstances. German aid in the shape of experts and sufficient materials proved precious. After this first step, there only lacked the main one; this was, to provoke hostile acts that would make it inevitable that the Empire should enter the war. Souchon proposed to bombard Russian ports or her fleet. The proposal entailed a heavy responsibility, and Enver, who had decided upon the abrogation of the capitulations amidst a chorus of protests, was unwilling to take this new measure. However the Admiral managed to convince him, and set the so-called Turkish fleet on course for the Black Sea in the greatest secrecy. On the 19th October this fleet bombarded the port of Odessa. Russian public opinion reacted violently to this prelude to war with the Ottoman Empire. The lot was cast, and Turkey had to follow the Central Powers in victory or defeat, a fact which recognised by the Allies, who withdrew their Ambassadors.

Tsar Nicholas delivered a manifesto to his subjects which ended with the following words : "The ill-considered intervention of Turkey will do nothing more than accelerate events, fatal for that country, which will open to Russia the way towards the solution of that problem which our ancestors have bequeathed to us on the shores of the Black Sea." He was clearly referring to the Byzantine dream of the reconquest of Istanbul. Russia declared war on her old enemy on 3rd November. On the same day the Anglo-French fleet bombarded the forward fortifications of the Dardanelles. This warning decided the Turkish-German General Staff to reinforce the defence of the Straits, since they now expected a full attack of great intensity.

On the 5th France and Great Britain declared war on Turkey and on the 12th Turkey did so on the Allied Powers. Soon afterwards, the Sultan and Commander of the Faithful, standing before the green flag of the Prophet, proclaimed a Cihad, or Holy War. He called upon all Moslems to join in saving the prestige of Islam. However, this manoeuvre did not bring the success the Unionists hoped for; the heroic days of the first Califs were forgotten, and the Ottoman Empire suffered the pain of seeing that the very Arab peoples themselves, from the desert of Syria as far as the holy city of Mecca, had joined with the Christians, to attack and cruelly maltreat the soldiers of the Calif.

The first Turkish army to engage the enemy was the Third Army, which was defending Ottoman territory from the Russian invasion in the Southeast Caucasus. The Turkish troops did well and the Russians were held back. From this first success there germinated in the fantastic regions of the mind of Enver, now Vice-Generalissimo of all the armies of the Empire, warlike adventures which were worthy of Alexander or Hannibal. He immediately embarked for Trabzon. He had already prepared some interesting plans : he would conquer the Russians, for this appeared an easy matter; then he would cross Afghanistan and enter India. This would be a rude shock for Great Britain, which would suffer a simultaneous attack along the Suez Canal. Of the three corps which composed The Third Army, Enver used one to hold the enemy along the road from Erzurum to Kars, while the other two were to make an encircling march leftwards across the gigantic mountain walls of Armenia, to surprise the army of the Grand Duke Nicholas on the flank and from the rear. The Vice-Generalissimo had much imagination but little practical sense; he paid little attention to assuring himself of the condition of the tracks which his soldiers would have to use along with their baggage. Winter was beginning and cold and snowstorms were a great danger for a large army having to march across those lofty mountains.

The Vice-Generalissimo was impatient to show the world what a military genius he was, and ordered his plan to be carried out immediately. The cold was terrible, the tracks were covered with snow, and the regiments lost order. His strategy paid off, as the Russians were indeed surprised on the flank; but the Turks, who had been decimated by the inclement weather, and weakened by the loss of part of the army which had lagged behind or got lost altogether, suffered a crushing defeat in Sarıkamış on 4th January 1975. The Russians pursued their enemies mercilessly as they retired in disorder, and the scenes of horror which accompanied the withdrawal of Napoleon's army across the Russian steppes were repeated with an equally dramatic intensity.

Of the ninety-thousand men who made up The Third Army, only twelve thousand escaped their victors and the cold. Enver's fantastic scheme and his inexperience had written in the book of history a bloody disaster for the imperial armies.

Following her declaration of war, Great Britain disembarked an expeditionary force in the Persian Gulf, with the intention of seizing Baghdad, which was the terminal of the famous railway which ran from Hamburg via Istanbul. This railway whose rails were to carry German influence to the Orient was still under construction. In addition Great Britain declared that Ottoman Sovereignty in Egypt had ceased, and made her annexation of the island of Cyprus definitive. All this was answered by the supreme Turkish command with the surprise attack they had prepared against the Suez Canal, lifeline of the British Empire, and around which her policies necessarily revolved. It was defended by a concentration of troops, war-ships, and the most efficient precautions. The triumvir Cemal took charge of the Fourth Army, in Syria, and with the help of German officers prepared to march sixteen thousand men over the sands of the desert of El Tih.

The army arrived, secretly, at a point near Ismailia. There it was impossible to remain concealed. British patrols appeared, and seeing their surprise attack discovered, the expeditionary force retired under cover of darkness. Those who hoped to compete with British imperialism had suffered a second reverse and a new disappointment.

Now that hostilities had begun, the British thought it was time to exert a decisive pressure against the Turks. The naval commanders examined a plan already devised to force the Dardanelles and occupy Istanbul. This was considered to be too dangerous to achieve, without the occupation by a disembarking force of the peninsula of Gallipoli and the Asian coast. In a war council held in London in the middle of January, the first Sea Lord of the Admiralty proposed an attack, naval only, by the combined French and British forces. Land troops would not be required until the Straits were under the navy's control. Lord Kitchener supported this plan, which did not require him to send his men ashore except onto land already secured, for the British army commander was reluctant to commit his reserves. This was the plan decided for the ill-fated operation.

In mid-February the Anglo-French fleet was stationed opposite the Dardanelles, with bases in the islands of Lemnos, Imbros and Tenedos. It received orders to destroy the fortifications which defended the entry of the Strait, and to sweep away the mines from that area. Having done this, the fleet was to destroy the fortifications further in, cross the Sea of Marmara and make a demonstration of force outside Istanbul. The first part of the programme had been completed by 25th February. The outer fortifications were reduced to silence, and some detachments of troops which had been disembarked reached them without being molested. The fleet went on with its work of clearing away the mines from the mouth of the straits for about a month, under the fire of the mobile Turkish batteries.

Mustafa Kemal, seated at his work table, covered with books and maps of the region shaken by the war, was analysing the situation. Pencil in hand, he reproduced on paper the movements which had occurred on the battle front. He traced rapid plans, changing the disposition of the armies, and moving them into different formations; then seized by visible nervousness, he paced up and down in the room. Kemal had fervently wished that his country should have remained neutral; however, being a soldier before all else, he had set his own point of view aside and wished only for a place in the battle. During the last weeks of November, he waited anxiously for the order to give his services to the army. Since this order was delayed for an unreasonable time, the Military Attache telegraphed his old comrade Enver Paşa, pointing out that his place could no longer be in the diplomatic salons of Sofia, while other officers were sacrificing themselves and dying in the battle. But the Lieutenant of the Supreme Commander had not forgotten his ill will; apart from the generals and colonels whom he expelled from the army, over a thousand other officers received the same treatment, while others disappeared and it was also known that many were prisoners; these were the men from whom Enver feared a reaction. The so-called Red Prison of Abdülhamit returned to service, this time more energetically.

Enver had classified Kemal as a dangerous man. He preferred to keep him away from the army which he might contaminate with his opinions, which were against the alliance of Germans and Unionists. He therefore replied to him with great courtesy that he had always had for him a post ready in the army; however, since it was felt that his remaining in Sofia would be particularly advantageous, he was leaving him there. Kemal could not control his feelings on receiving this reply. He did not hide them in a letter which he wrote to Enver, in which he tried to make him understand the usefulness of the services which he could give, services such as the country greatly needed in those difficult times. The Vice-Generalissimo left this letter unanswered.

Kemal then sought help from the minister Ali Fethi; together they made all kinds of approaches which brought no result, and Kemal, thus condemned to remain inactive, felt a double grief, on hearing of the disaster of the Eastern front and the failure of the attack on Suez. He considered that Enver was to blame for the disaster which had befallen the Third Army, which had been sacrificed to that man's pride and needless caprice. How was it possible that a commander could throw away men confided to him by his country into a mere adventure, or fail to realise because of his own egotism, that an attack of such a scale was impossible to realise? Kemal had found out the details of the Caucasian episode, through the loud boasting of Russian diplomats in Sofia and of the other representatives of the Allied Powers, since Turkish communiques had not allowed any importance to the affair. A rigorous censorship had been established; to speak about the Caucasus was enough to bring down the wrath of Enver and his satellites.

Bulgaria had remained neutral, but was pleased at the outbreak of war, and was anxiously observing the way the operations went, before declaring herself for or against either side. The Embassies in Sofia, divided into two groups, vied with each other in their ardour to conquer the hearts of the Bulgarians; they wished to show at all costs that the war was favouring their side and every battle won was exploited by one of the groups of diplomats, whilst their opponents denied it and tried to take away the importance of such victories. The Entente offered Bulgaria part of Macedonia and Thrace. The Allied Powers were more generous; they offered a port on the Aegean and sizeable slices of territory from the neighbouring enemy states. They would thus have an ample vengeance.

The military circles of Sofia viewed the chances of the Russian Bear with pessimism; they expected that the Germans would soon inflict a decisive defeat upon it. It was obvious that as soon as the German army was free of her enormous though feeble adversary, she would attack Serbia, which she would naturally destroy. The victor's friends would then be lords of the Balkans.

Holy Russia for her part, being traditionally of mystic temperament, gave an exaggerated importance to her first victories. In February, on the day of the reopening of Parliament, the Prime Minister Goremykin said, amidst applause: "Turkey has allied herself to our enemies, but her armies have been militarily defeated in the Caucasus, and every day there shines more clearly before us the radiant future of Russia, there, on the shores of the sea which bathes the walls of Istanbul!" The Russian government informed France and Britain that they should give more explicit undertakings on the future of Istanbul. It requested them that their respective countries should proclaim clearly that on the day peace was declared, they would accept Russia's right to annex that city. Those two countries answered favourably, and announced at the same time the compensations which they intended to reserve for themselves : France was to receive Cilicia, Syria and Palestine; the United Kingdom was to be assured that the central region of Iran would remain under her influence. Russia was happy to accept.

Turkey's fortunes would have been sad, had it not been for the revolution already incipient in the great Russian masses, and which took root in the armies which were fleeing, defeated and hungry. The Eastern Question had reached the time of its solution, in a way which would have filled her most cruel enemy with satisfaction.

There came a time when it was impossible for Kemal to continue any longer as a spectator of the war, on which there depended the very existence of his country. He made his final appeals, and allowed himself a certain time, after which he would definitely leave for Istanbul, without considering the consequences this disobedience of orders might bring him; at worst he intended to enlist as a private soldier. Having arranged his journey, Kemal moved his belongings to the Embassy and began to wait for this time to expire. Before it did so there arrived the order for him to return, signed by the Quarter-Master General of the Ministry of War.

We can imagine how happy Kemal was when he held the telegram in his hands, and knew that he had been appointed commander of the Nineteenth Division. He had scarcely time to make his official farewells, before taking the first train to Istanbul. His tense nerves found repose only in the monotonous symphony of the moving carriages.

On arrival in Istanbul, he went to the Ministry of War, and found there some comrades of earlier campaigns; however nobody could tell him anything about the division which he was to command. Osman Şevket, Director of Personnel, assured him that his appointment had been made by order of Enver Paşa. Kemal was gratified that Enver had conducted himself as a Minister should, by forgetting old scores and giving command of troops to an officer whom he knew could serve well. The Lieutenant of the Supreme Commander was now in Istanbul, and attended the Ministry. Hearing that Mustafa Kemal was in the building, he called him to his office. Perhaps his grief at defeat had made him more human. Kemal found him thinner and subdued. After an exchange of correct military salutes, there remained silence; the Lieutenant-Colonel was the first to speak. The conversation confined itself to short sentences about the progress of the war and Enver's health. Kemal then thanked him for having been pleased to give him command of a division, and asked him where it was. The minister did not know, and advised him to enquire at the General Staff, where they would give him all the necessary information. There was nothing left for them to say to each other.

Kemal had to visit several offices in the General Staff without being able to trace his division; nobody had heard of it. He was determined to find it, and decided to visit every office. He opened the door of each one and said loudly, "Lieutenant-Colonel Mustafa Kemal, commander of the Nineteenth Division." This search produced no results. Later on Kemal confessed that at times he had the impression that people thought he was an imposter.

Eventually someone told him that it would be better to see the chief of the General Staff of General Liman von Sanders. This commander could give him no news of his division either; however he thought it likely that it had been proposed to create the Nineteenth Division within the army corps which was stationed in the Gallipoli peninsula, being part of the First Army, commanded by von Sanders. He added that if the Lieutenant-Colonel could take the trouble to go there, he would certainly find all the information he needed. It seemed extraordinary to Kemal that he should have to go as far as the Dardanelles to find out if his division existed or not; however since he had to find it he had to go there.

The chief of the General Staff wanted to present the new commander to the German general; Kemal was received with every courtesy by Liman von Sanders, the man entrusted with the defence of the Straits, a well-known military person-ality and perfect gentleman. He was interested by Kemal's career so far, and hear-ing that he had just arrived from Sofia he took a noticeable interest in his conver-sation with him. Kemal answered the questions made to him, and explained the situation in Bulgaria, pointing out that the Bulgarians wanted to be certain of the superiority of one of the armies over the other before deciding in favour of the Allies or against them. The Prussian general was annoyed by this reply. What? Did the Bulgarians still doubt the power of the army of the Reich? And how could this be repeated by a Turkish officer, an ally? Yon Sanders asked why the Bulgarians did not believe that the German armies would win. Kemal answered that the government in Sofia were waiting to see first some great victories. The general became more and more angry against this mere youth, who was allowing himself, with excessive calm, to consider as anything but all-powerful the perfect machine which was the German army. He calmed down a little and fixing his gaze in the clear and calm eyes of the young officer asked him a question which placed him in a difficult situation. "And what do you think?" Kemal reflected for a few moments, and after a rapid examination of his own conscience decided to speak frankly to the man who had the defence of the straits in his hands. "I think the Bulgarians are right," he said.

Von Sanders got up as if propelled by a spring and gave a cold dismissal to his new subordinate, whom he was soon to begin to know better and to appreciate, and who was to become his most remarkable collaborator during the course of the war.

The great naval attack which was expected to be made against the Dar-danelles was becoming imminent. Military opinion appreciated that if it were successful it would influence the final result of the European war. It had been feared in Turkey for some time already that the allied fleet might reach as far as Istanbul, so that measures had been taken to defend the city and to remove the government to a city in Anatolia. The formidable baggage train of Mehmet Re;at and his harem had made themselves ready by February to cross the Bosporus, and return to those regions in which the Ottoman Turks had prepared their conquest of Europe.

The capture of the imperial capital by the Anglo-French fleet could be achieved if a strong army were disembarked in Gallipoli. The Unionist govern-ment gave the German officers the task of frustrating the various possible enemy plans : Admiral von Usedom was made commander of the defences of the Straits : Admiral Merten was sent to Çanakkale on the Asian shore of the Dardanelles, with the title of inspector responsible to the general staff: Admiral Souchon was commander of the fleet, and the First Army, divided into six corps which were placed in the straits and on the coasts of the Sea of Marmara, was given to von Sanders.

The 18th of March 1915 was chosen for the date of the full attack, on which so many hopes rested and which Russia was awaiting with a truly religious anxiety; ships laden with arms would then arrive quickly and the Bosporus would become a Russian canal. On the result of the attack Bulgaria would make up her mind, and if the fleet were successful, the Central Powers would find themselves besieged. The idea which found most favour in the combined Turkish and German General Staff was that of reinforcing as far as possible the fixed and mobile artillery in the Dardanelles. It was hoped to strangle the attack there, as the defence of Istanbul was thought problematical.

At the last moment, Admiral Carden, commander of the allied fleet, declined to take responsibility before history for the direction of the battle, which was to be the most formidable of its kind ever seen. We cannot be sure if it was his nerves that gave way, or if his experience and the conclusions which he drew from it allowed him to foresee the defeat in which the planned attack was to result. His successor, Vice-Admiral de Robeck, received an unequivocal order from the Admiralty to advance at any cost.

The plan having been finalized, de Robeck began by having the powerful dreadnoughts bombard the Turkish fortifications, from long range, while the other units advanced with the intention of silencing the forts and innumerable mobile batteries carefully hidden, which could fire on the ships which entered the Straits practically at point blank range. Those who took part in that titanic struggle were always to remember the thundering of the artillery, the burning of the town of Çanakkale, the thick smoke of burnt gun powder which was wafted in all directions, warships sinking into a sea which boiled from the impact of projectiles, and the mines which exploded against the flanks of those colossi of the sea.

The forts resisted, and so did the mobile batteries; however it was the floating mines, carried along by a favourable current, which gave the signal for the defeat of the great fleet and its allies. The fleet withdrew, with a sad casualty list from that memorable day. Three warships were sunk : the British "Irresistable" and "Ocean," and the French "Bouvet," along with several torpedo boats. A large number of other ships were seriously damaged; for example the "Inflexible," which had been hit by a mine, was saved thanks to the spartan character of her captain, who ordered the closure of her protective deck and all the exits from it, thus isolating the part which had been destroyed from the rest of the ship. Captain Phillimore knew that that order condemned to death many of his brave sailors who had just fought with great valor; however he did not hesitate more than a few seconds before sacrificing them in order to save His Majesty's ship.

CHAPTER 8

GALLIPOLI

After the failure of the fleet, even those who had supported the idea of an entirely naval attack had to realise the necessity of combining the seaborne forces with a strong expeditionary force by land, whose disembarkation they could protect efficiently with the ships' guns. They therefore decided on a joint action of the fleet and the army; they had to efface the bad impression caused throughout the world by the fleet of the Queen of the Seas.

In the month of April, the Turkish general staff received from their information services worrying news of concentrations of strong contingents of British and French troops in Egypt, and on the islands of Limnos and Imbros. Quays had been constructed on the islands, and enormous quantities of food, munitions and war materials of all kinds were being disembarked there every day. The figures given were exaggerated and so were those given of the number of soldiers. In brief, the general staff received the impression that a mixed attack of great size was about to be made. They were on the eve of a desperate struggle for the possession of the Dardanelles.

A special army, the Fifth, was created. Its mission was that of resisting the allied assault against the shores of the Straits. Von Sanders was given command of this army of extreme importance.

It was not possible to foresee at what moment the disembarkation would be made, since its best hope of success lay in surprise. The defenders would have to remain ready, guard the extensive coast and combine to dislodge the enemy from those points as yet unknown where he would attack. Von Sanders dedicated himself to the practical study of the terrain; the narrow peninsula of Gallipoli, "Gelibolu" in Turkish, which forms the northern shore of the Dardanelles, is extremely mountainous and almost entirely lacking in vegetation. Three points on the peninsula were considered suitable for a disembarkation. These were : first, the extreme southern point of this peninsula attached to Thrace, since this was completely at the mercy of the fleet's guns; second, a low-lying area, which crossed from the Straits to the Aegean Sea; if the invader managed to penetrate that valley, he could attack the fortifications of the Dardanelles from the rear; third, and most dangerous, the point at which the peninsula joins the continent, an isthmus only seven kilometres across. The Turkish troops on the peninsula would find themselves in a critical situation, isolated from Thrace by land; in addition, the attackers could instal artillery there, which would in its turn prevent Turkish ships from having access to the Straits. On the Asiatic coast, it was thought that a disembarkation could be made on any part of the coast opposite the island of Tenedos, which was controlled by the Allies.

The surprising thing about the war in the Dardanelles, which became one of the most discussed actions of the First World War, was the insistence of the allied General Staff on repeatedly attacking in those places which were most difficult to capture, without using such places as the Asiatic shore and the isthmus, where their efforts would have given appreciable results in the course of the operations.

The Turkish forces consisted of a little over sixty thousand men, divided into six divisions; two of these were in Asia and the other four on the peninsula. The Nineteenth was one of the latter. Von Sanders, with characteristic military genius, ordered each division to concentrate its forces and conceal them as much as possible, as the terrain allowed; the coast was to be watched by patrols, so that when a disembarkation was made one or two divisions would fall upon the place and make their weight felt.

There passed days and long nights of waiting, and whole weeks, without the attack beginning.

Kemal was satisfied with his appointment. He knew the peninsula perfectly, since he had maintained bloody conflicts with the Bulgarians during the Balkan Wars when they were trying to conquer the Straits. With his rare energy and activity he dedicated himself to the organisation and training of the troops which had been entrusted to him, and which formed the Nineteenth Division. Within a short time they had reached perfect battle readiness, having been subjugated by the strong personality of their commander.

Kemal fully realised the importance and gravity of the days which were coming. Both the Allies and the Central Powers found themselves in a difficult situation. The German plans had been shaken by the spirit of resistance they had met in Belgium and France. The Germans had had to withdraw along the Marne, and in that spring of 1915 the Kaiser had again thrown his formidable army against the front at Ypres without success. It began to be thought that the war in the trenches would not allow the victory of either side, unless one gained a notable superiority in numbers. The war in Russia had taken from the Western front a large part of the armies of the Reich and Austria-Hungary; however, Russia would seem to be on the edge of defeat. This would give the war a different aspect, since the Central Powers would then be able to dispose of all their divisions on the front which they chose. This prospect however was compensated for to some extent by the falling of an important card into the hands of the Allies. This was Italy, who had left the triple alliance and was now on the other side.

An allied victory in the Dardanelles would allow the Tsar's innumerable subjects to be equipped for modern warfare, and would oblige the Central Powers to keep their armies separated. Apart from cancelling out Turkey, such a victory would have incalculable effects on morale; the undecided countries would move to the side of the victors of the day, very probably those of the future. For the Ottoman Empire and her allies, a victorious defence would mean the promise of solid triumphs in the future.

Kemal watched the movements of the ships of the Grand Fleet through his binoculars. Why were they taking so long to make up their minds? He wanted a face to face meeting with the British, the oppressors of the East; he wanted to make them feel that they, the Turks, were not a decadent race, like those whom the British had easily subdued. Almost every morning at dawn, he would put one or other of his regiments through manoeuvres. He visited different parts of the coast, pretended a disembarkation, and showed his men how to combat it, while at the same time gaining better knowledge of that rugged land which months later was to become an enormous cemetery.

Protected by the last hours of darkness on 25th April, five large groups of warships and transports approached as many places on the coast of Gallipoli and on the Asian shore. At dawn, the fleet's innumerable guns opened an extremely violent fire against the Turkish positions, while landing craft laden with soldiers left the sides of the transports and made rapidly for the land.

The French succeeded in disembarking near the fortress of Kumkale in Asia, and began a terrible battle there. British troops managed to establish themselves on the extreme south of the peninsula, after a hellish bombardment with heavy artillery from three sides at once. In the depression which runs from the Aegean to Maydos, a third disembarkation was made, with equally lavish munitions and fire cover. As for the two other places, which had also been bombarded, and which were the areas of the isthmus of Bolayır, in the Gulf of Saros, and in Asia opposite the island of Tenedos, the transports moved around without attempting any disembarkation. Their movement was in fact a mere feint; however they succeeded in deceiving von Sanders, who took a day to realise his mistake; he had remained immobile with the Seventh Division in the area of the isthmus. It was soon clear that the French attack on the Asian shore was not dangerous; on the other hand, the battle on the central and southern fronts of the peninsula was becoming fiercer. The enemy was disembarking more troops constantly, protected by the deadly fire of the fleet; the Turkish generals found themselves forced to use the last man they had in reserve.

At five-thirty in the morning of the day when the long and bloody Dardanelles campaign began, Mustafa Kemal was beginning some manoeuvres with his troops which were to guard the inner slope of the hill of Conkbayrı, which together with the hills of Kocaçimen and Anafarta form a line of natural defence which composes one of the main keys to the peninsula. The general staff of the Fifth Turkish Army had anticipated the allied plans : they would disembark in Kabatepe on the Aegean Sea, advance right through the valley to Maydos on the shores of the Straits, and from the neighbouring heights would reduce that fortress to rubble by their artillery. From Maydos, the British would be able to surprise the Turks from the rear in their positions on Conkbayrı and the neighbouring hills. In addition, they would make a frontal assult from Cape Arıburnu, a little further to the north of Kabatepe.

The first part of this plan suffered an alteration; through an error of the ships' officers, the boats towing the landing craft touched land a mile further north than the point indicated, so that the frontal attack was directed against Conkbayrı.

Kemal went forward at the head of his men. In his nervousness he almost ran; he must arrive in time before the British, for if he did not it would be impossible to expel them from their positions with the weak forces he had. He had not considered whether to ask for permission to commit his forces; every minute might mean years of slavery for his country, and he wanted to save every minute. He was the first man on the crest overlooking the sea. The huge ships, monstrous as whales, and in a wide semi-circular formation, were inflicting a terrible bombardment on those places which were thought to be held by the Turks. About four hundred metres below Mustafa Kemal, the Australian column was climbing the steep flank of the hill.

He had arrived in time. Dividing his men into columns, and cheering them on by word and gesture and by the flashing light of his steely pupils, he gave them the cry of attack, Hurled downwards by the gradient, the attack of the fifty-seventh regiment became an avalanche. The Australians could not advance a single metre, but fought bravely. The two remaining regiments of the Nineteenth Division arrived in sections, tired and breathless. Kemal seemed to have grown in size in the fight, and to be in many places at once. He led them to the attack in person, and passed on to them his bravery and energy. He straightened their lines, helped them to position their artillery, and controlled the direction of fire.

Nor did he forget to call for hot food or to relieve those companies who had suffered worst punishment.

There came a moment when the battle became so fierce that not a single man remained in the rear guard, in spite of all instructions to keep something in reserve. Everything was thrown into the fray, no effort was spared, nor was even the slightest detail omitted which might help to move the faith- fill to fight for their country. The Turks fought incessantly throughout the day; some of their attacks reached such extremes of violence that they could be held back only by the artillery of the fleet.

Night came, yet brought no rest to those heroic defenders. Kemal attacked in all sectors at once, yet the Australians did not yield. Losses were very high on both sides; the Australians were the better armed, but the Turks, under the personal control of their commander, had the better position. The Turks had been decimated and were physically exhausted; they had dug trenches and were protecting themselves behind enormous rocks. The attackers, who were pinned to the slope were at a disadvantage and were also fatigued; their effort had been roughly halted by those Turks whom they had considered unworthy of comparison with themselves. Had they not lost the last wars, destroyed by the Russians in the Caucasus? It is an error, often a fatal one, to depreciate the qualities of an adversary and not to investigate carefully the causes for any earlier defeats he may have suffered.

Kemal enjoyed the satisfaction of having held that strategic point, thanks to his military genius, his quickness in taking decisions and his tenacity in putting them into practice; if he had failed to do this, and had waited a few more minutes in doubt or in seeking for orders, in order to escape from responsibility, the interminable columns of British soldiers would have entered the heart of the peninsula through that point, and taken the defence lines in the rear. These would then have collapsed.

After five days of savage fighting in which the "Anzacs," a word formed by the initials of "Australian and New Zealand Army Corps," tried in vain to break through, with the fleet's support, Kemal decided to attempt to throw the invaders back into the sea. This operation was a complete success against the land forces, which in some sectors began to reembark; however Kemal was not only fighting a land army, but also against a fleet which distinguished itself by its good aim. The Nineteenth Division was forced to take refuge in its fortifications after a hail of missiles. The Anzacs were almost immediately reinforced, and reoccupied their positions.

It was not so easy for Kemal to obtain reinforcements; it was more difficult every day to obtain supplies, which were brought by caravans of camels or in carts pulled by water buffalo. Sea communications were made difficult by the presence of enemy submarines in the Sea of Marmara; there was a shortage of water, especially in those days of confusion, and the troops fought the campaign in wretched clothing. Because of two wars full of disasters, and an administration of similar character, Turkey did not have the means to sustain in better array the huge armies which this new conflagration demanded. She was fighting in the Dardanelles, in Eastern Anatolia, in Mesopotamia and in Arabia, regions which were separated by colossal distances.

Fighting ceased on the Asiatic side of the Strait, for the French had reembarked. The south Gallipoli front was rich in terrible events. There the Turks were more sure of the places in which the enemy would attempt to disembark, waited for them with every precaution against the event, and inflicted a memorable slaughter upon them with machine-gun fire. The British succeeded eventually by sheer force, in making a front and occupying some important points, but only after actions similar to that which involved the coal ship "River Clyde" at the beach of Sedd-ül-Bahr. The "River Clyde" anchored off the coast as planned. A plankway was immediately begun on top of a line of boats, to allow the two thousand men to reach the shore, protected by the fire of the machine-gun unit-installed in her bows. The "River Clyde" had to contend with formidable obstacles : the Turkish machine gunners had her in easy range from the neighbouring fort and from the steep slopes of the cove, and the laying of the planks was made difficult by the current. After incredible efforts it was ready. The first company risked the short passage from the "River Clyde" to the shore, but it was only a few men who arrived; the companies that followed them were torn to pieces by invisible marksmen. Then the planking gave way and the men who were still upon it fell into the water and were drowned under the weight of their equipment. The planks were put in place once again, and the company of men continued their race to destruction. General Napier, other senior officers, and the great majority of all the officers and troops lost their lives.

The small area of ground which the Allies had gained with such terrible sacrifices had to be maintained by even greater ones. It was not only that the Turks continually attacked them, but the terrain was inhospitable and the sun of that summer, which was excessively hot, heated up the stones in the trenches and thickened the stench exhaled by the unburied corpses. On the southern front, the allied lines were able to move northwards after the arrival of strong reinforcements, but at the same time they realised that it would be impossible to conquer the peninsula in this way; they did win a few metres of ground but they lost a great dream. So passed the months, made up of enormous numbers of painful minutes. It was no less uncomfortable for the Turks than for their enemies, for the climate was the same for all of them, and their positions and the whole peninsula suffered continual bombardment from the grey ships. Their enemies had come to recognise that the sober and silent Turkish soldier possessed, in addition to his terrifying bravery, a complete indifference to life in defence of an ideal, and those greatest qualities for a warrior, simple nobility, generosity to the defeated, and absence of personal hatred. When collecting their dead and wounded, the Turks often went as far as the allied lines in order to hand over a wounded allied soldier. The opponents exchanged glances; there was no hatred in the calm expression of the Turkish soldier; on the contrary, his manner showed some pity for the dying man. General Gouraud, commander of the French expeditionary force, who lost an arm in the campaign, wrote thus in his orders of the day : "The Turks are not our enemies, but our adversaries. Treat them as adversaries, not as enemies." General Hamilton has recorded his respect for the nobility of the Turkish army.

According to mythology, Vulcan, the god of fire and metal, resided in the island of Limnos; the Argonauts had visited that island on their visit to the East in order to capture the Golden Fleece. Now following the example of such heroes of antiquity as Castor, Pollux, Jason, Hercules and Orpheus, thousands upon thousands of warriors were disembarking on that island from which they were to reembark for the East, to continue the ever- renewed struggle of Occident against Orient.

From its island massifs, formed from extinct volcanoes, one could see the hills of the Thracian Chersonese and the Asian coast. In that same historic area, a titanic struggle was giving ample material for a new Iliad, with Greek mythology and epic poetry as a backdrop.

The Hellespont is accustomed to the sight of bloody wars and great invasions. Xerxes, continuing the campaign begun by his father to conquer Greece, passed his immense army across it on a bridge of rafts. Along the straits at Aegospotami, a river of the Gallipoli peninsula, which in antiquity was called the Chersonese, the Spartans defeated the Athenians in 403 B. C., in a decisive battle which brought the rivalry between Sparta and Athens to an end; across the same straits passed the armies of Philip and Alexander, and those of Rome and of Islam.

There were so many men and so much activity in the island of Limnos, that the soldiers who remained there a few days while awaiting transport to the trenches of the peninsula compared it to an enormous anthill. The cannon fire which could be heard from far away made them think of the horror of the days that were awaiting them, as they suffered the total inclemency of the climate and of the war itself. Would this Troy fall, or was the fate of Patroclus reserved for them? To the north they could make out the island of Samothrace as a violet-coloured shape. These modern Argonauts, who were journeying eastwards in search of the Golden Fleece which they hoped to find in Istanbul, thought insistently of the figure of Victory; but that victory, which had seemed so sure at the beginning of the campaign, had already broken wings.

Vice-Generalissimo Enver Paşa went to Gallipoli to inspect the fronts and to congratulate the defenders. After his disastrous campaign in the Caucasus he was not pleased to observe Kemal's success. The latter had been promoted to Colonel on 19th May. Enver was unable to control his feelings and was heard to say on many occasions that Kemal's performance did not deserve special praise, since other Turkish and German officers had comported themselves more brilliantly. This offended Kemal, not only because it concerned him personally, but because it reflected upon his junior officers and the whole division, so that he told von Sanders that he had decided to resign his command. However, the German general managed to dissuade him from this. Kemal felt great respect for his commander. He said of him : "Liman von Sanders was a rarity among chiefs. We did not always agree with each other and sometimes our discussions degenerated into quarrels, but in the last resort, he always allowed me freedom to do what seemed to me best."

Kemal rarely left the line of fire, and remained in continual contact with his men; he did not only take care to get for them all the material benefits which the general situation allowed, but also paid attention to keeping their morale high. One evening he happened to be sitting near a trench, when a British battery opened fire in that direction. A bomb fell near Kemal, a second one exploded nearer yet, and it was clear that if the direction of fire continued, one of the next bombs would destroy him. Some officers who were inside the trench begged him to hurry and conceal himself beside them. At that moment the third bomb fell. The earth which was thrown up by the explosion covered the Colonel, so that the officers repeated their pleas with insistence, but Kemal told them calmly : "No. It's too late; it would give a bad example to my men," and lit a cigarette. The battery directed its fire in another direction, leaving Kemal in the eyes of his soldiers with the double aura of bravery and divine protection.

The British divisions were wearing themselves out on fruitless attacks, and General Hamilton, commander of the Expeditionary Force, saw that it was necessary to employ intelligence, and carry out some strategic plan which would change the military position in the peninsula; he accepted a plan presented by

General Birdwood, which technically would give the allied armies a crushing victory. In general terms the plan was as follows : they would reinforce the central front in Gallipoli, gain control of the heights of Conkbayrı and other hills, which formed the massif of Sarıbayır, from whose crest one could see the Straits and the forts which guarded them. These forts would then lie within range of the artillery which the British would bring up onto the top of the massif. Simultaneously with this first phase of operations, a large number of regiments would be disembarked as quickly as possible to the north of Arıburnu in the bay of Suvla. These forces would be able to encircle the natural fortress of Sarıbayır without meeting much resistance, and surprise the Turks from the rear. If this new plan was realised in the manner envisaged by Birdwood, the patient defenders would suffer a terrible disaster.

General Hamilton sent these plans to London, presenting them in the most favourable light; in order to bring them to a happy conclusion, he asked for enormous numbers of men; he argued that the Turks would have to give way, before a mass attack. Lord Kitchener and the British Government approved the plan. They had no alternative, since if they gave up the enterprise which had cost so many sacrifices already, and which was being closely watched by the Eastern nations, by the vacillating Bulgarians, the agonized Russians and all the world on the sidelines, it would be counted as a defeat with the gravest consequences.

Hamilton dedicated himself body and soul to the preparation of this bold plan, which was the last chance to establish the good fortune of the allied armies in the Dardanelles. From the experience gained already, the expeditionary force was this time properly equipped to achieve the various phases of the plan. Unfortunately for the Allies, it was not possible to conceal their intentions and menacing preparations. The alarm was given, and the defenders brought to Gallipoli all the artillery that they could find and all the men that were available.

General von Sanders had no information of the plans of the enemy general staff. The Turkish army kept vigil by day and even more by night : the enemy might emerge from the darkness like phantoms, at any moment and at any place. Von Sanders had still not given up his idea that the enemy would try to disembark on the Isthmus of Bolayır and he established defences in that place, which in fact was never attacked. Another place which aroused his worries was the empty space between Arıburnu and the southern front. He placed a whole division there, but no one came to attack it.

At the start the Birdwood plan went according to its creator's optimistic forecasts. In three consecutive nights, and without arousing the enemy's suspicion, the reinforcements reached their hiding places on the Arıburnu front, so

that in this small space with a total front of 1 1/2 kilometres there were concentrated thirty-six thousand soldiers and seventy-two guns.

A general attack was launched in the evening of 6th August 1915 both on
that front and on the southern one; it achieved its purpose in forcing the Turkish
divisions to remain in their trenches, while General Birdwood was realising his
double mission of trying to gain control of the heights of the complex Sarıbayır,
and also of distracting the Turks' attention while the disembarkation was going
on in the bay of Suvla, further to the north. The manoeuvre had only partial
success, for although they succeeded in taking up positions on Conbayrı, they
presented an easy target to the Turks because of the number of their soldiers and
the shortness of the front, and suffered very severe casualties.

As resilient as ever, the Turks counter-attacked fiercely and the battle continued with unabated intensity until midnight, by which time the British had
still not succeeded in occupying the heights of Conkbayrı. An idea of the bloody
nature of this conflict can be gained from the fact that the Duke of Wellington's
Regiment, originally consisting of seven hundred men, was reduced to fifty-three.

The attacking forces, exhausted, began to lose heart, for the army corps
which was to have surprised the Turks in the rear showed no signs of arrival.

General Cox's column, which was making forced marches by night to- wars
the hill of Kocaçimen, managed to reach its summit and to see at dawn the
famous Straits, half hidden by the mist. The Ninth Turkish Division, which
had passed under Kemal's command as its own commander had been seriously
wounded, threw back the British from the crest of the hill. They retreated down
the north face, and remained there quietly, while Kemal fortified the rocks which
he had conquered. It was of great importance for the defenders to keep control of
this summit, for its situation and height would allow the enemy to fire in enfilade
on Kemal's trenches which were defending Conkbayrı, and this would mark the
beginning of the Turkish defeat.

Despite their resistance, the Turks' situation was critical. They knew now
that whole divisions were disembarking in the bay of Suvla, and had a free approach to them. Von Sanders, who was completely surprised by the Biritish plan,
sent out repeated orders, which could not be obeyed as quickly as he wished.

Fortunately for Turkey, the British divisions which disembarked in the Bay
of Suvla did not take advantage of the situation, and appeared to have forgotten
why they had disembarked at all. The generals did not want to advance before the
arrival of the artillery, food, reserve munitions and above all water. The officers
became flustered by the difficulties of controlling so many thousands of men,

many of whom were on their first campaign. Pushed forward by the increasing number of troops which were arriving, the Eleventh Division advanced through the valley of Anafarta and occupied the crest of Mestantepe. Throughout the following day and the day after that the British remained quiet, whilst the soldiers on the Arıburnu front, who were hoping to see their companions arrive at any moment, were falling in thousands.

In a desperate assault, the Arıburnu army seized Conkbayrı. Kemal was unable to dislodge them despite counter-attacks. The enemy also succeeded in capturing Kocaçimen, and also occupied the ridge which separated that hill from Conkbayrı. Kemal's men were now at a disadvantage as their positions were on the southern slope of the hills and were enfiladed by the enemy fire; Kemal's officers advised him to withdraw his lines to a more secure front. Kemal thought it out impassively under enemy fire; he would resist, regain the lost positions and win. His orders were brief, his language spartan, but his orders were indisputably right, for they brought back hope and certainty to revive both officers and soldiers. Amid the horrors of the battle and when fortune was against him, Kemal appeared like a hero of Ferdowsi, indifferent to danger, his energy and infectious enthusiasm making him seem larger in the eyes of his men.

The figure of the Turkish commander renewed the vigour of his men; their lines proved unbreakable, and they forced the enemy to retreat. This time fortune was on Kemal's side, though he never trusted to fortune, but in his own efforts. The fleet, which as one need hardly say had been bombarding the Turkish positions intensely, brought under its deadly fire those British soldiers who had succeeded in reaching the crest of Kocaçimen at the cost of bravery and lives. They had to abandon their positions after suffering serious casualties.

Liman von Sanders called Kemal to his General Headquarters. He had now recognised in him an extraordinary commander and a military genius. He needed him at his side. Von Sanders had exhausted himself with the tension of these days. On the night of the sixth he ordered the Seventh and Twelfth Divisions to advance as rapidly as possible to the plain of Anafarta and attack the British; by the eighth they had still not arrived there. In the meantime von Sanders had ordered them to attack at nightfall, but this order was also not carried out. When the commander of these troops was asked the reason he replied that his men were too tired for them to reach their objective. The commander was removed from his post and von Sanders decided to place all the forces between Conkbayrı and the plain of Anafarta at the orders of Kemal. When informed of this, Kemal received the news calmly. He accepted without asking any questions since he knew what was expected of him. He must attack the British on the plain of Anafarta, where for some mysterious reason they were failing to occupy the important positions which were within their grasp, positions which the Turks made a show of defending but where their troops did not consist of more than a few battalions placed in the strategic points, and which could have been overrun; at the same time he must continue the fight to reestablish his old positions on Sarıbayır. In a few words, he had to break the Birdwood Plan. Kemal at once went to meet the laggard divisions, which had finally managed to arrive at the place appointed for their assembly; the soldiers were exhausted by a march of more than thirty kilometres. Kemal gave them a few hours to rest themselves, and called a meeting of the general staff and commanders to study the situation. He decided to attack at dawn.

On the enemy side, the British were planning their long-delayed advance. It had proved necessary for General Hamilton to come to Suvla to find out the reason for the mysterious hold up in the plan which had been agreed. He obtained the vacillating generals' promise that they would attack on the following morning. The British and Turks clashed furiously at dawn on the 9th August; however, the men led by Kemal fought with extraordinary courage, in spite of their fatigue, on both sides of the Azmakdere, and the British were driven back to the coast at some points; however, the hill of Mestantepe remained in their possession. During the following night the Fifty- third Division disembarked and threw itself into the attack, without success. The encircling movement could not now be realised, for the British had passed from being the attackers to putting themselves on the defensive behind a line which they had to fortify. The plain of Anafarta had been closed to them.

During Kemal's absence from the front at Arıburnu, the Anzac troops had amplified their positions on Conkbayrı, from which they were firing on the trenches of the Nineteenth Division from the flank; counter-attacks failed to dislodge them and tension spread throughout the Turkish lines, while the soldiers demanded Kemal's return. Why had he abandoned them? A telephone call was made from the general staff of the Nineteenth Division to Kemal, who was at that moment directing the victorious battle of Anafarta. He calmly asked them to hold out for another twenty-four hours, after which he would come quickly to join them.

In fact he reached Conbayrı at night; he made a careful reconnoiter of the new enemy positions, and worked out a plan of action which he gave to the commanders in a few words. In the early hours of the tenth, all the troop movements ordered by Kemal were achieved under his control; for the last time he went through the compact ranks of his men speaking to them in the simple language which they liked, and advising them above all not to be in a hurry to join battle;

he would choose the opportune moment, leaving the trenches, and raise his hand to show the moment when they should follow him.

The Turkish soldiers, heirs of so glorious a tradition, waited impatiently for the figure of their commander to come forward through the pale clarity of the dawn. He was a hero, he had thrown back the great British attack on that same front during the night of the 6th, throughout the 7th and the following day; he had been made to repeat his prowess in Anafarta, then return from there, without showing any sign of fatigue, spend the night preparing the attack, and now it would be he himself who would be the first to defy the enemy's machine-guns. Men of this calibre must have been those commanders who had led the Turks to the conquest of their colossal Empire.

The Turkish artillery concentrated its fire on the British positions at dawn on the 10th August. In the trenches Kemal looked at the time by his watch, which he kept in the upper pocket of his jacket : it was time. He leapt out of the trench and went forward several paces; the British bullets whistled close to his body, the marksmen corrected their aim, and Kemal's watch stopped a bullet. The Turkish batteries finished their work; the commander turned towards his men, who could already see in his eyes an expression of indomitable energy, which was to illuminate the legend that would become known to future generations; he gave the agreed signal and advanced resolutely, his men following him in a magnificent and reckless charge. No breakwater could have held back that flood; the'[1] British of the Wiltshire Regiment died in their lines, while the other regiments turned in retreat, the North Lancashires fled, and the whole British front was broken up. The pursuit began, but His Majesty's ships came to protect his army, and found easy targets in the Turkish battalions which were coming down the slopes. They suffered heavily, and were compelled to take refuge in their original trenches; nevertheless, the whole of Sarıbayır was free of the enemy. Kemal had smashed that castle of dreams which the allies had built upon the Bird- wood Plan.

Hamilton insisted on continuing with the campaign, on which prestige depended. He disembarked two more divisions, and attacked with these reinforcements on the 15th, on the most easterly part of the new Anafarta front, intending to surround the enemy positions. Kemal received troops from Asia, to whom he allowed no rest before sending them to the front. His battalions climbed painfully up the slope and advanced with great difficulty over its crest, which was swept from the flank by the cannons of the fleet, whilst the British infantry were machine-gunning them from the front. In spite of all these obstacles and their severe losses, Kemal's battalions succeeded in occupying the dominant points, this time for good.

After this new reverse, Hamilton tried to join the fronts of Anafarta and Arıburnu, which he succeeded in doing with great loss of life. This united front was all the practical result gained by the Birdwood plan. As on the front at Sedd-ul-Bahr, trench warfare continued on that front until the month of December, when the expeditionary forces were completely evacuated on the advice of Lord Kitchener. The Dardanelles campaign had proved to be a serious reverse for the Allies both at sea and on land; as a result of this, Bulgaria had joined her fortunes to those of the Central Powers in September, while Russia remained condemned to her sad fortunes, and a wide highway was being opened between the Ottoman Empire and Germany.

Great Britain and France abandoned Gallipoli; six brilliant generals had perished there, and an enormous number of officers and soldiers remained there also. The saddest part of the story was the tragic fate of British regiments composed of young men sacrificed by the inexperience and inertia of the commanders responsible for them. The theatre in which the struggle took place makes it appropriate to quote here, in posthumous homage to each of those lives which were cut short, Homer's phrase : "The veils of death enwrapped him, his soul left his body and flew to Hades bewailing its fate, its youth, its strength."

The Allies admitted to three hundred and thirty thousand losses in the Dardanelles. The Turks calculated theirs at two-hundred and eighteen thousand.

The bloody battles of August, which became known by the name of Anafarta, will always evoke the name of Mustafa Kemal. It was those gigantic battles which mark the culminating point of the campaign, and after which there remained no hope for the attacking forces. At Arıburnu, on Conkbayrı, and in the depth of that mystery which inclines fortune to one or the other side, we can see Kemal, now leading a picket which boldly surprises and holds up an enemy of infinitely superior numbers, now reviving the spirits of exhausted battalions and divisions, from which he knows how to exact a supreme sacrifice by his own example. In the Hellespont, his great figure joins those of the other glorious captains who have fought there in the course of the millennia.

CHAPTER 9

CAUCASUS

Mustafa Kemal, who was already known as the hero of Anafarta, reached Istanbul at the beginning of 1916. His military renown had reached all parts; he was considered to have saved the capital and he received fulsome praise from the newspapers.

Since the beginning of the war, power had been in the hands of the triumvirate; the other members of the cabinet, including the Prime Minister, had only a very limited influence. A new period of terror in Turkey was begun by an efficient police force and an even more efficient force of spies, organised by Cemal Paşa. Fear of reprisals taken by Cemal, who had become an Ottoman Duke of Otranto, and the cruelty with which he crushed any subversive movements, or persecuted those who thought differently from the Unionists, caused liberal opinions to disappear from the political scene during the years of the war. In spite of this harsh regime, military conspiracies multiplied, though on a small scale it is true. Some of these were discovered in the first months of 1916, but their origins and their punishments remained half-concealed. These attempts at revolution expressed the opinion of the army, which was becoming every day more opposed to the way in which the Germans, under the protection of the triumvirate, were exerting pressure on the Turkish army. The long months of the Great War had dissipated the enthusiasm which had been raised in its first days, and had brought the shortages so frequent in war-time. The Germans had been making themselves unpopular, and there had been many disputes and quarrels between Turkish and German officers. Enver was criticized for his devotion to the Kaiser, and public opinion had begun to ask what had happened to those promises of brilliant victories and of the easy triumph of the armies of Wilhelm II.

After the assassination of Nâzım Paşa, which restored power to the Young Turks, the ailing Empire lived amid convulsions; the non-Moslem populations felt the oppression of the "reactionary liberals." At the end of the year 1913, the Unionist Government had to support the indignity of accepting foreign interference in the person of two inspectors, who were charged with assuring the security of the Armenians; the idea of provincial autonomy gained support in Arabia, and the movement assumed such proportions that the Unionists thought it wise to make the Arabs extravagant promises of improved conditions, which they failed to fulfil except in insignificant respects. Even the Kurds, whom Abdülhamit had employed to persecute their Armenian neighbours, rose in revolt in their turn, with aspirations of autonomy.

When the Unionist leaders declared their programme of government after the victory of the revolution, they declared that their mission was the transformation of the ancient and theocratic Turkish autocracy into a government based on the Constitution, which would respect the principles of human rights. It was believed that they were speaking sincerely and even firmly desired to bring about what they had preached; both the country and the Great Powers believed them. Kemal also believed that they were sincere; however he predicted, which earned him the enmity of the Unionists, that in practice they would change their attitude, and that they were not men who were able to realise the miraculous transformation of the Empire; he believed that power would bring them personal satisfactions out of all proportion to their feeble spirits, and that they would give themselves up to the soft cushions of the divan of power, so that, lacking the necessary qualities, those same men who claimed that they would shake the old Turkey out of her evil customs would themselves fall into them.

The year 1915 which had just finished, and which had seen the Turkish armies crowned with glory in the defence of the Dardanelles, also saw the disastrous campaign of Enver Paşa in the Caucasus, where by July nearly the whole of the ancient Armenia had fallen into the hands of the Russians. In Mesopotamia, the British had been held in their advance towards Baghdad; however it was clear that they would persist in their efforts with greater forces. In Egypt, it was now realised how difficult it would be to effect an attack against the Suez Canal strong enough to have a noticeable effect on British communications, while the clandestine political activity of the Powers of the Entente in Syria was attempting to undermine Ottoman resistance there.

Her alliance with Bulgaria, recently her enemy, brought to the Empire an important advantage. First, the heroic armies of the old King Peter I of Serbia, who were bearing up against the attacks of Austria with extraordinary courage, and had managed to recover Belgrade, were destroyed by the Bulgarians and forced to retire across the mountains of Albania. The road of which Bismarck had dreamed was now open; through it Turkey would receive the arms she needed, whilst her government would supply provisions to the Central Powers in their besieged position.

On the West European front, the war continued without giving a marked advantage to either side, and both had been forced to give up mobile hostilities in favour of trench warfare; in the East, the armies of the Tsar had suffered serious defeats at the hands of the Germans, which had saved Anatolia from a Russian invansion, for the Third Turkish army, in its shattered state, would have been unable to hold back the Grand Duke Nicholas.

The conduct of Holy Russia towards the Armenian subjects of the Ottoman Empire brought forth fatal fruit in 1915. Russia continually maintained a policy of encouraging Armenian nationalism and the religious feelings of that nation; her intention was to create difficulties for the Ottoman Empire and to prepare herself for the annexation of that region, on the day when it was expected that the colossus would be shared out. However, Imperial Russia would not have allowed the creation of a free Ottoman Armenia, since this would have provided a very bad example for Russian Armenia, which she had no intention of losing.

The Armenians are a race which lived for thousands of years in the region included between the sources of the Euphrates and the Tigris, the Black Sea and the Caucasus, and had lost their independence centuries before. They hearkened to the words of encouragement from beyond the Caucasus, and nationalist societies were formed with revolutionary intent.

The events which had occurred in the time of Abdühamit and the sufferings of the Armenians under his rule had caused them to view the Young Turk movement with pleasure. When the movement triumphed, the Armenians believed that they were on the road to independence, and had the unfortunate idea of holding demonstrations and religious processions in the eastern provinces and in Cilicia, a region in the south of Anatolia, where the Armenians had formed a state in the time of the Crusades. Apparently the Armenians took the opportunity of revenging themselves. This has caused serious disturbances and a strong reaction amongst the Moslems, leading to a resumption of killings in April 1909. The Young Turks then deprived the Armenians of that equality before the law which they had preached, and the Armenians were again treated as undesirable aliens.

Once war had been declared on the Entente, and confident with the German army behind them, the triumvirs thought that a good moment had arrived to solve once and for all the continual problems which arose because of the minorities, and which gave pretexts for the European nations to intervene in Turkey. Since Mehmet Fatih had conquered Istanbul, the orthodox Christians, Jews, Armenians and others had been governing themselves; they had no obligation to fight in wars, and they were only subjected to a payment of tax. This liberal treatment was disastrous for Turkey, since the peoples, or "Nations" as they were called, retained not only their religions but their nationalist spirit, and continually tried to seek foreign support in obtaining their independence. The result would have been quite different if the Turks had been in truth the barbarians and fanatical religious proselytisers which the Christian world accused them of being. In the days when the Ottomans were all-powerful it would have been easy for them to Turkicize the conquered people by violence or persuasion. A crusade for the Faith, which other creeds had found an excellent reason, would have served to cover up any repression.

The new rulers understood that the only solution to the problem, in the twentieth century, was to expel the Armenians from the regions where they lived and which they considered their country, and deport them to Mesopotamia and Syria. Whole populations of Moslems would be removed to the regions vacated, and in this way the Armenians and to a lesser extent the Ottoman Greeks, Nestorians and others would lose their dreams of independence through being dispersed.

The Armenians depended on the victory of Russia, France and Great Britain, who had been their protectors, though also the cause of their sufferings. On the day of that victory they would see the aspirations of their race achieved - an independent Armenian state. They therefore treated the Tsar's army as liberators of their race, and innumerable Armenian volunteers crossed over to the enemies of Turkey. Since they knew the secrets of the high mountains, they contributed much to the Turkish defeat, and when the beaten Turkish armies were retiring in disorder they were harassed by bands of Armenians.

Enver Paşa was ashamed of his defeat and he accused the Armenians of treason, also using them as scapegoats to excuse his own wretched strategy and his megalomania, which drove him to headstrong decisions. Enver received support from Talât and other leaders, and initiated the programme which was to lead to a mass deportation of the Armenians. But the Armenians had arms which they were receiving from Russia, and fought tenaciously with them. They were able to resist the government forces for many months, since the troops sent against them were few because of the needs of the battle fronts. The deportation programme degenerated into battles followed by atrocities.

The wrath of Enver fed more fiercely the blaze which extended itself over all the area inhabited by Armenians. The favourable or unfavourable developments in the war did not diminish the intensity of the incidents, whose protagonists, Enver and Talât, took care to rekindle them continually. When the Allies received definite news of these events they published a declaration in which they declared the Ottoman Ministers responsible for the killings.

In the first weeks after his arrival in the capital Kemal spent his time visiting friends and people connected with government and political circles.

He realised that although the power of the triumvirate was great because of the methods used to maintain it, general public opinion was not in favour of it. Kemal found sympathy for his ideas amid the silent opposition and those who regretted the entry of Turkey into the war; in the end, whoever won, the country was going to be faced with problems the solution of which would be to the detriment of its independence.

He had an interview with Talât Paşa, to whom he thought he would be able to explain his ideas and conclusions on matters of vital importance to the country. The minister received Kemal amiably, which encouraged him to speak freely. Talât was unfavourably surprised that the soldier who visited him should seek to get mixed up in political affairs, since they, the Unionist leaders, thought they had perfect ability in diplomacy and politics. Talât continued to appear communicative so that he could thus discover Kemal's opinions, with which he had never been able to agree. Some days later the minister boasted to a mutual friend that he had made fun of Kemal on the political questions that they had discussed, which proved that Kemal had very little idea of these matters. Kemal found this out, and was thereby convinced of the ill-will of the triumvirate.

He then obtained an interview with the Minister of External Affairs, Halil, who had studied in the School of Political Science in Paris, and who had argued against Turkey's giving up her neutrality in the Council of Ministers. Kemal believed that he had found a man able to understand him. When the hour of the interview arrived, Kemal had his presence announced; however, the minister received before him many people who had arrived later than he. Kemal passed the long period of waiting talking to a friend; when the usher came to him to tell him that His Excellency would deign finally to receive him, he replied drily "Let him wait!" He continued his conversation for some further minutes.

During the interview the minister described the general situation of the country in extravagantly optimistic terms, to which Kemal replied by producing facts which refuted what he had been told; the minister began to lose ground in the discussion, and his visitor took advantage of this to speak his criticisms freely. Halil was annoyed by the way in which his importunate visitor was taking it upon himself to blame the government, and told him that it was better for him to distinguish himself in a useful way in the General Staff, since he was evidently ill-informed. Kemal observed that it was useless for him to go to the General Staff, since it was in fact non-existent apart from the German military mission. The conversation ended coldly. The minister told his cabinet colleagues of the tone of the interview, and asked that Kemal should be reprimanded. Kemal heard of this, and when he came to record this years later he added the thoughts which he had had in those days :

"I found out some days later that His Excellency the Minister had complained to his colleagues and asked that I should be punished. This amused me. It was believed generally at that time that this Mustafa Kemal, whoever he was, could be punished without difficulty by a government which thought it was strong, because it rested upon the nominal head of a dynasty which was degenerate both morally and physically. But I was certain that all those men, who had come from none knew where, and each of whom believed himself the one a professor, another a genius,, another a dictator, another one a doctor, could do nothing against that humble Mustafa Kemal. It was true that they could resort to the force of their bayonets to have me hanged, but I wished more than anyone that in such a way as this my rebellion should become known to all. They were not brave enough to do it. Why? I think it was because they were not certain that they could do it with impunity."

The leaders of the government contented themselves with removing this dangerous individual from the capital and centre of politics. They knew that before everything he was a soldier, and that he would immediately accept his place in battle. He was offered the command of the Sixteenth Army Corps which belonged to the Third Army, which had been destroyed by the Russians. In Diyarbakır he received his official appointment as brigadier.

The disaster of Sarıkamış in 1915 had reduced the Third Army to a mere twelve thousand men, without organisation, and afflicted with eruptive typhus. The Commander-in-Chief Halis Hakkı himself had died of this terrible sickness. These meagre forces were supplemented by about twenty thousand recruits, many of whom succumbed in their turn to typhus, malnutrition and the lack of hygiene and medical supplies. The main reason for these misfortunes was the enormous distances which separated the Caucasian front from the last station of the railway, which varied between five hundred and six hundred kilometres of rough terrain. Travel by sea was considered impossible since the Russian fleet would be able to stop it.

Amid all the horrors of the defeat and its terrible consequences, the Turkish General Staff had the satisfaction of seeing that the Russians, distracted by their operations on the European front, had been unable to take full advantage of the victories that they had achieved. Some months later in 1915, the Tsar's forces made a general advance from the Black Sea towards Lake Van. The cities of Malazgirt, Van and Bitlis fell into their hands; the Armenians joined the invaders, and the feeble Third Army had no alternative but to withdraw all along the line.

In the autumn of the same year the Grand Duke Nicholas took personal command of the troops in the Caucasus, which pointed to the prospect of new Russian attacks. Indeed, a strong attack was made against the Turkish front one year after the battle of Sarıkamış. The fortress of Erzurum fell, and a Turkish division to the west of that city was destroyed. The Turkish army withdrew further, in the direction of Erzincan, suffering heavy losses.

It was necessary to send reinforcements to this front, the defence of which was of vital importance; however, through lack of foresight, three of the five Turkish armies were concentrated in Thrace, where there were no enemies, while the two remaining armies had to sustain all the attacks which Turkey was suffering. The feeble reserves that were sent reached the Eastern front exhausted, after a march which recalled that of the Ten Thousand, through the same area. The reserves were unable to prevent the fall of the important port of Trabzon. When the General Staff finally took alarm, a plan was worked out which consisted of throwing a whole army against the left wing of the Russians, so as to make a way through the enemy lines and attack the centre of their army from the rear. We can seem to see in this brilliant idea the style of Enver Paşa and we can be equally sure of its results.

The Second Turkish Army was the one called upon to fulfil the most difficult part of the plan, for which it began to collect itself in April 1916. However, the High Command in Istanbul believed that because of the course of the war the Russians would have been forced to take away a large part of their forces stationed in the Caucasus in order to move them to Europe; they therefore ordered that the Turkish army should move onto the offensive at a time when only a part of the reinforcements had arrived at the front. The Russians had foreseen their enemies' intentions, and in July made an attack with superior numbers against the exhausted Third Army before it had been able to join up with the Second. The Third Army suffered another crushing defeat. The withdrawal of the Turkish centre turned into a flight, as the enemy cavalry penetrated their lines in two places, starting a panic.

It was in these disastrous circumstances that Kemal Paşa took command of the Sixteenth Army Corps, which was defending the Turkish right wing. In the village of Silvan, to the east of Diyarbakir, he met his most senior officers, General Kâzım Karabekir and Colonel Ismet, who was the head of the General Staff of the Army Corps. As soon as Kemal understood the true situation of the divisions placed under his command, he toured the advanced posts, the reserve echelons, and the hospitals; he spoke to the soldiers in order to find out the level of their morale after the defeats and privations which they had suffered. His conclusions were extremely sad.

There were shortages of food, ammunition, personnel and medical supplies. The new brigadier realised that he had a large number of soldiers dressed in summer uniforms and others who, in spite of the prevailing intense cold, had their feet wrapped up in rags; they were being fed only a third of a normal man's diet, so that they were in an extremely weakened state. In the advanced positions, it was common to find whole sections of men dead from cold and hunger. Since it was impossible to give the sick men the necessary treatment, an average of nine hundred men died every month. They were in a shocking state of wretchedness and filth.

The operations of the supply department left room for doubt about its honesty; even when the soldiers were in such a wretched state of suffering, having gone there to give their lives as a sacred offering for the salvation of their country, the speculators still hoped to obtain material benefits, which were the greater as the army became weaker. Kemal punished these men severely and attempted with his usual energy to set some order amid that agglomeration of unfortunates, who were more reminiscent of that scene in Dante's poem, when he describes the punishment by ice in hell, than of an army which would have to resist the attacks of a powerful enemy.

Kemal advised the Ministry of War of a series of important measures which must be taken urgently; he received only an evasive reply. He sent a telegram to Enver, who had been the cause for all these misfortunes. Kemal thought that the Russians would begin to attack again before the end of winter, since General Brusilof had achieved an offensive on the European front which had resulted favourably; in August, Romania had entered the war as an ally of the enemies of the Ottoman Empire; on the Western front, it seemed that Verdun could not be captured, and all the efforts which the German Crown Prince could make were doing no more than weaken the German Army; Verdun was the Allies' Gallipoli. The battle of the Somme and the Italian offensive would allow Grand Duke Nicholas to find sufficient troops to continue his advance in Anatolia.

If he did not receive the immediate help he had requested, how could Kemal turn those tatters of an army into a force able to resist the shock? He answered the question by his own will-power. As in the memorable days of Anafarta, Napoleon's words "Activity! Activity! Speed!" which he had written down in his note book, were to be his guide.

On the 7th and 8th of August he made a clever manoeuvre to recapture the cities of Muş and Bitlis. A new weight had just been placed upon his shoulders : he was entrusted with the command of the whole Second Army "ad interim." He had to face the problem all over again, on a larger scale.

Like some earlier ones, a plot against Enver and his colleagues had been discovered, but could not like the earlier ones remain unknown. Although he had not had the slightest involvement in it, Kemal found himself implicated in this dubious affair. The plot had been made by a discontented commander, Yakup Cemil, who lost his own life and seriously endangered that of Kemal, whom Enver would have liked to have had the opportunity of hanging. One day when Kemal was already on the Caucasus front, at a meeting of a large number of conspirators, Yakup Cemil made bitter criticisms of Enver Paşa, the Committee of Union and the Cabinet. Enver, he said, should be removed, along with several of his accomplices. Someone then asked who would have the right personality to take charge of the government. Yakup Cemil, who had a great admiration for Kemal, and knew of the respect in which the army held him, suggested his name. The means of overthrowing the government should, he said, be a bold coup similar to that which had brought Enver to power.

Two of those who had attended the secret meeting reported the conversation, and Enver conceived a stratagem in order to discover the size of the conspiracy. It was a serious matter, for if as everything seemed to suggest, Kemal was the instigator of the plot, abundant proofs of his guilt would have to be found before they could arrest the new rival of the Minister of War in the army's admiration.

Enver had known Yakup Cemil for some time. He had been a member of the Committee of Union and Progress, and was one of the group of "volunteers" whom the Committee employed to carry out dangerous missions. On one occasion he had promised him the command of a division, but had later pretended to know nothing of his promise, which angered the "volunteer" to an exaggerated degree. Enver's plan to find out exactly who the conspirators were consisted in making Yakup Cemil believe that he was making him commander of a division, which was to be formed from the deserters who were then scattered all over the country, and for whom an amnesty was to be given. Yakup immediately stopped speaking ill of the Vice-Generalissimo, installed himself in the quarters assigned to him in the Ministry of War and immediately began his task; he collected his closest friends and appointed them commanders of the various sections of the imaginary division. In this way Enver had a Targe number of possible conspirators within his grasp.

A long interrogation began, but threw no light whatever on Kemal's guilt. However, Yakup Cemil was hanged. When Kemal Paşa heard of this he declared that he had not approved of Yakup Cemil's attitude since he did not agree with the achievement of power by such methods.

In the Caucasus, Kemal was engaged in a titanic struggle against adversity. Plague arrived to add itself to the evils which afflicted the Second Army. Their medical defences were so weak that in one month alone forty- two Turkish doctors died of that disease. The areas occupied by his army were half depopulated because of the persecution made against the Armenians, and since the fields had not been cultivated in the usual way it was difficult to find stocks of grain and other food. The total losses of the Second Army were reckoned at sixty thousand, of whom only a minority died at the front; the rest succumbed to hunger, cold and sicknesses.

In these circumstances, he was ordered to go to Damascus, familiarise himself with the plans of the command of the Fourth Army, and then take charge of the operations in the Hejaz. Kemal obeyed the instructions he had received. In Damascus he studied the possibilities of success that might be found in the operations which he had been ordered to direct. His impressions were entirely pessimistic. He discussed his point of view with Enver and Cemal, Commanders of the Fourth Army. Kemal believed that the far-extended front would require to maintain it much larger numbers of troops than those available; it was preferable, and more than that an urgent necessity, to evacuate the Hejaz and reinforce the Syrian front. His way of thinking seemed logical from every point of view, and was thought worthy of acceptance; if it had been put into practice, the Ottoman Empire would have avoided several disasters. However in the event, other opinions were adopted.

Kemal gave notice that since the job that he had been ordered to do would cease to have any reason to exist if his view was adopted, he requested an immediate return to his army in the Caucasus. He took substantive command of the Second Army at the beginning of 1917.

Kemal's career could be considered brilliant; he was thirty-seven and already commander of an army. Enver, still younger, had reached the highest rank through politics; Kemal on the other hand had obtained his success entirely by his merits in war, since he was not a person whom the government favoured.

The Russian revolution, which broke out in the spring of 1917, saved Turkey from the serious problem of defending the eastern front. Soviet propaganda sowed the seed of desertion amongst the Russian armies, and the Tsar's troops scattered like sheep, as if by magic. It is true that at the beginning, some armies managed to keep themselves together, thanks to the ascendency of their commanders, but warlike spirits were paralysed, and no offensive could hope for success now that their worst enemies were behind their own backs. Kerensky wanted to continue the war and ordered Generals Brusilof and Kornilov to attack; however the power of the extremists was clearly rising, and the generals found that their armies and that of the Caucasus had disappeared.

The struggle between the heirs of Imperial Russia and the allies of the dying Ottoman Empire was to be ended by a separate peace.

CHAPTER 10

JOURNEY TO THE REICH

Some painful news, which augured sadly for the fate of the whole Empire, brought grief to every Turkish heart : Baghdad, the ancient capital of the Abbasid Califs, had fallen into enemy hands. The loss was doubly painful because the Turkish armies on the Mesopotamian front had achieved remarkable successes, and it was not expected that the city would cease to remain Turkish. Sultan Murat IV, who in the 17th century had reconquered the city of Harun ar-Rashid, the centre of Islamic power, must have been turning in his sumptuous grave from rage and impotence. Only the Tigris remained to recall the apogee of the "City of Salvation," and its golden centuries, the 10th and 11th, when it housed about two million inhabitants. Its bazaars, where the merchants of a hundred different nations traded, were famous throughout the whole world. That great city died, one can say, under the Mongols, who seized it in the 13th century; in the next century it was ruled by Tamerlane, and then fought over by the Persians and Turks until annexed to the Ottoman Empire in the 17th century.

However the fair city was in decay, and was no longer even a remote shadow of what it had been. Any vitality it still possessed was due to its important commercial position, in rich Mesopotamia, terminus of innumerable caravan routes. Baghdad was a place of utmost importance in the game of the Great Powers who had an interest in the control of the East. It was for this that Germany had paid court to Abdülhamit, so as to gain the concession for the railway which was to reach as far as that golden-domed city; in this way the road to India would lie open and Berlin would take a step nearer the East

The United Kingdom was defending her colonial Empire at Suez and on the route of the Baghdad Bahn, and attempted to seize Baghdad in November 1915. General Townshend thought that it was a good moment to fall upon the city by surprise, after a forced march across ancient Assyria. His plans were ruined by the Turkish resistance, and he was defeated at Ctesiphon. He was able to take refuge in Kut-el-Amara, where he remained in a besieged and critical situation. He surrendered on the 29th April 1916, along with thousands of soldiers and a rich booty of armaments.

If advantage had been taken of this victory, and enough forces thrown against the invaders to drive them out of Iraq, Baghdad and all she meant to the Turks' morale would have been saved; but this was not done.

Enver went to Baghdad in May. After studying the situation, he agreed with the German plans. Under the slogan of the "Liberation of Iran by Germany and Turkey, to the exclusion of all selfish policies," Germany was trying to bring Iran to her side. Iran had so far remained neutral in spite of the preponderant influence of Russia. At the German request, Enver sent the Thirteenth Army Corps towards Iran. In this way, and as always acting against common sense in matters concerning the war, he weakened the army which was defending Baghdad, in order to form an expeditionary force whose usefulness was doubtful.

Great Britain returned to the attack to recover the military prestige she had lost in the Dardanelles and in Kut-el-Amara, so near to her colonial Empire, and because of the real importance which the capture of Baghdad would have in the progress in the war. Finding themselves unmolested, the British built a strategic railway, and collected an army which it would be difficult to halt. In the event, a determined British offensive in January 1917 surprised the weakened Sixth Army. The Turks fought bravely along the Tigris, between Kut-el-Amara and Baghdad, but they were unable to prevent the Anglo-Indian army from entering the city of Harun ar-Rashid in March.

This disaster, for which Enver was responsible, had grievous repercussions in Turkey at all levels. The triumvir saw the shaky ramparts of his prestige cracking; his pride shattered, he went to his German allies, and gave himself up to them like a beaten man. The German general staff agreed to help him, but on new conditions. He must recognise Teutonic superiority, bow to it and obey it. Berlin decided that an army group should be created for the purpose of recapturing Baghdad. Since the beginning of the war, Germany had helped Turkey by providing instructors, officers and parties of specialists; now however there was to be a great army, whose commander would have to be a German. Its general staff would be almost entirely formed of officers of the same nationality, and in addition German soldiers, special groups and officers in large numbers would serve in it; in short they intended to create a German expeditionary army with Turkish soldiery, in the same way as that in which the British and French were using coloured soldiers from their colonies.

The army group was given the name of "Yıldırım," the Thunderbolt, surname of the Sultan Beyazıt, a man of remarkable energy who contributed to the expansion of the Empire, but who was defeated by the conqueror Tamerlane. Its command fell upon General von Falkenhayn, formerly commander of the German army which had recently achieved fame by destroying Romania at the end of 1916. His General Staff was composed of seventy-five officers, of whom only nine were Turks. Kemal was appointed commander of the Seventh Army, part of the Yıldırım group.

After the desperate winter in the Caucasus, which increased the sufferings of the Turkish soldiers, the enemy began to withdraw, until the end of April. Kemal's forces followed the Russian withdrawal closely, but he avoided useless fighting, not only because of the poor state of his troops, but because after every battle he always felt an uncontrollable sadness when he thought of his comrades who had fallen, whether they were officers or soldiers. At all times, he took care of the lives of the men entrusted to him, and tried to limit the number of dead by his military skill; if as happened at Gallipoli, he ever sent even the last of his soldiers into the assault, it was because he knew that this effort would influence the result of the war.

Kemal believed that his task had finished on that front. It was unlikely that after the final efforts of Kerensky's provisional government, Russia, torn by convulsions, would return to the attack; all the indications were that her troops would withdraw back to her former frontiers with the Empire. One problem remained, that of the Ottoman Armenians who inhabited the areas occupied by the invader, whose entry they had assisted. Many of these had withdrawn along with the Russian troops, and the remainder were not molested by Kemal. He was a soldier and considered that political questions did not concern him when they did not concern his mission; he disapproved of the Armenians' attitude, but since he knew the causes which had started the Armenian problem, he was thinking of new ways of solving it. One day he was to achieve this, by methods very different from those used by Abdülhamit and Enver.

On receiving notice of his new posting, Kemal handed over command of the Second Army to General Kâzım Karabekir; this man was a good officer with a high capacity for work. He had an eye for detail but was not capable of conceiving great strategic plans; however he had those qualities which make a soldier love his commander.

Kemal set off for Istanbul, with the intention of discussing with the General Staff those operations which were being made necessary by the British activity and successes in Mesopotamia and Syria.

In January of that year of 1917, Talât Paşa had taken the position of Prime Minister; the triumvirate wanted to increase its strength to prevent so far silent criticisms from being made public; Parliament was docile, and German help made itself felt in the defence of Germany's friends. The triumvirate thought it had a long life to come.

On the general scene of the war, the huge advantage brought by the complete defeat of Romania, the defeats suffered by the Italians, the success of the submarine war and the disappearance of the Russian army was counterbalanced by the entry into the war of the United States, which was both a military and financial power. The main part of the struggle moved therefore to the Western front, where the recently created Hindenburg line had given satisfactory results.

After giving up for lost all hope of forcing the Straits, the allied High Command decided to execute their plan to send an expeditionary force to Macedonia, with a base in Salonika. This army would help the Serbs, who were in a desperate situation; it would also be a threat to Istanbul, and Greece would be forced to turn to the side of Venizelos, who favoured the Allies. This in fact happened, and a new enemy appeared in the Balkans; Greece, Turkey's historic enemy.

Enver wanted to impress his friends, and quickly agreed to send Turkish divisions to the European fronts. From 1916 onwards he sent up to seven divisions one after the other. Any of their cadres who were weak or imperfectly instructed in the arts of war were replaced by men who were strong and experienced fighters, taken from those fields of battle which were defending the life of Turkey.

With the creation of the German Yıldırım army and the arrival of von Falkenhayn, German influence degenerated into oppression; it was not enough of merely military affairs to have to follow her directions, but the same must be true of internal political matters. The Prussian character, with its terse way of giving orders and its imperious will to be obeyed, did not agree in the least with that of the Turks, and when such a way of thought left its own element, the army, and began to concern itself with questions of national honour, the Turks rebelled. On the other side German military prestige was on the wane, and had reached the level which Mustafa Kemal had assigned to it before the war, contrary to the expectations raised by Enver and his partisans, in order to move public opinion in favour of the Central Powers.

Kemal was already disappointed by the Germans' political mistakes, when he learned of the plans of von Falkenhayn, a former Prussian Minister, at the Yıldırım headquarters. Von Falkenhayn wanted to recapture Baghdad, but Kemal thought this was inopportune, since he was; certain that the Allies would attack the Palestine front in order to relieve the front in Iraq. As a result of such an attack, the Turkish army would find itself in serious danger, since its forces were not strong enough to resist an attack in Iraq and at the same time another in Palestine. The argument with the commander of Yıldırım was renewed at every meeting. Enver, who was also in Aleppo, naturally supported the German's views. Kemal brought data to prove the truth of what was later to become reality.

Kemal was infuriated as a patriot by von Falkenhayn's activities, which he pursued in close collaboration with the German Embassy, involving himself unashamedly in political questions, and by his way of treating the Turks as inferior beings.

One action of von Falkenhayn demonstrates how far he was mistaken in his assessment of the commander of the Seventh Army, and his opinion of the Turks. One day Kemal was visited by two officers, one Turk and one German, sent by von Falkenhayn, who brought him a small box containing a large number of gold pieces. The officers were not able to give a clear account of what this money was for. Kemal made a list of the contents, and obliged the emissaries to take a formal receipt for it. The German general had thought that this present would win over General Mustafa Kemal, a man whom money had never had the slightest interest, and for whom on the contrary, his honour was an integral part of his personality. Von Falkenhayn showed himself to be a very bad psychologist.

Soon after this, Kemal resigned his command, against military regulations. It was an act of rebellion, and by doing so, he hoped to make public his disapproval of German interference. Enver did not wish to punish the rebel, as von Falkenhayn wanted him to, for this would have raised opinion in the army against him; Kemal was respected and loved for his brilliant military prowess and his honesty. Enver preferred to let the incident pass over in silence, but asked him to reconsider his decision; he succeeded in getting the German general to write a letter to Kemal, containing phrases which would have allowed another man to take back his words. But Kemal's attitude was not governed by common feelings of vanity; after all, how could he take pride in the fact that his predictions of the unfavourable issue of the war were being proved correct?

He handed over that same box which he had taken against receipt to the man who replaced him. The latter sent it .to von Falkenhayn with his aides, with the order not to return without the original receipt, and to tell the German; "Here is your money; but the signature of Mustafa Kemal, which is worth more than this money, may not remain in your possession." To save appearances, which was what Enver was most concerned with, he appointed Kemal once more to command the Second Army. However, Kemal was not angry with one of the armies but with the direction of the army in general, so that he made up an excuse, and decided to leave for Istanbul. Enver did not give way, but arranged that the General Staff should give Kemal leave of absence for health reasons. There was nothing to add.

When on the point of departure he had so little money left that it was impossible to begin the journey. He decided to give up his horses, to which he was very attached, being a fine rider. He had twelve magnificent thoroughbreds, the majority of which were gifts from his friends who knew his taste. With a heart full of pain, he ordered one of his aides to sell them as quickly as possible at the market in Aleppo. He received not a single offer, for the officers who might have been interested could not afford such a luxury, while private citizens did not dare to buy them, since they might be requisitioned at any moment in time of war. The triumvir Cemal heard of the difficulties besetting the man who had been his subaltern in Salonika, and advanced him two thousand Turkish pounds in gold (a Turkish pound was worth a little less than a gold Pound Sterling) against the horses, and undertook to find a buyer for them and send the rest of the money later. This he did, and soon afterwards Kemal received in Istanbul three thousand pounds more, which had according to the triumvir been realised from the sale of his chargers.

Kemal's mother and sister had been obliged to leave Salonika and were living in Istanbul. Kemal did not go to live with them on his return from Aleppo, since his independent spirit preferred to be in complete freedom. From his infancy onwards he preferred always to live alone; he could not even enjoy living under the same roof with his own family or his friends, and this was a custom which he never gave up. He also confessed : "I have another peculiarity. This is that I cannot stand my mother, sister or near relations when they give me advice about this or that according to their mentality and point of view. Those who live in a family know that it is impossible to escape from the observations, no doubt disinterested in character and sincere, which come to him from right and left. He is then in a dilemma; he can obey, or he can take no notice of all these warnings and advice. In my opinion both these solutions are bad ones. What if I obey? If I accept the advice of my mother, who is twenty or twenty-five years older than me, is this not going back to the past? But if I disobey, it would mean wounding the heart of a mother who in my eyes personifies virtue, sincerity and all the qualities of a great lady. It would not be right either."

Kemal established himself in the luxurious Pera Palace hotel, as befitted his high military rank. The windows of that hotel look out over a wide and gloomy quarter of wooden houses, an undulating mottled surface splashed with minarets. The Moslem cemetery of Kasım Paşa reaches out towards it with its unmoving armies of cypresses and tomb stones; further on, on one of the bare hills over which the city is scattered, one finds the Jewish cemetery, sown with great stones which seem to have been thrown at random, with no tree or anything on which the eye could take refuge, in its flight from the horror of the thought of death, brought forth by the desolation of this Dantesque place. At the foot of that gloomy hill there flows the mud-filled

Golden Horn, forming a magnificent natural harbour. From the Pera Palace, one can also clearly see the white sanctuary of Eyüp, lifting its two tall minarets like skeleton arms imploring heaven.

It was a melancholy vista which faced Kemal from his window and fitted well with the feelings woven into his spirit. He searched for some sign of hope that his country could be saved, but he saw obsessively the contrary sign as that to which all the roads were leading. He realised with infinite pain that his predictions were proving correct. How could he turn back the current of mistakes made by those who thought themselves able to guide the nation? He was familiar with a group of politicians and high officials, as discontented as himself; it seems that they made several suggestions to attempt a coup d'état. Kemal did not listen to these proposals; this was not the moment for internal strife. The expression of his face reflected in the portraits of him which are known from the period up to that date and in some years which followed, invites us to study it closely. His features are not moved by any expression; however his calm eyes shine forth with a remarkable melancholy, and in his mouth and in the closure of his lips, one can detect a twist of pain. Until that time, all the years of his life had found him in continual opposition to what was happening to that which most interested him, the destiny of Turkey. The unsuccessful wars, and his vision of the future, had put his heart into mourning.

In that month of February, Sultan Abdülhamit was dying in the Palace of Beylerbeyi on the Asian shore of the Bosporus. He had spent his years of idleness in cabinet-making; he constructed pretty commodes in a complicated damasque pattern, filled with little drawers with false bottoms and little hiding places, as he lived out the consequences of his old mania.

Kemal did not appear to be plotting but Enver thought it unwise to leave him without occupation. An opportunity arose with the journey which the Crown Prince was to make to the Reich, representing the Sultan at the Kaiser's invitation. The Kaiser visited Turkey in October 1917, and toured the battle fileds of the Dardanelles. With his dynamic personality, optimistic forecasts and promises, he tried to win back the sympathies of the Turks, but we would be wrong to think that he succeeded.

The Vice-Generalissimo offered Kemal the chance of joining the official party. Kemal accepted, because it was the only way of escaping from his inactivity. Enver also thought that if Kemal visited the German fronts, his opinion of

German power would be altered by the impression of strength which he would receive.

Two days before the day fixed for their departure, Kemal and his old teacher from the school of Harbiye, Naci Paşa, who was also part of Prince Vahdettin's train, were received by the Prince in audience. When they arrived at the palace, they were taken to a hall, where the only furniture consisted of a sofa and two chairs. A large number of gentlemen wearing the famous 'Istanbulines' which were obligatory in the palace were also waiting. Another personage, also dressed in a long coat, entered the hall; Kemal failed to recognise the Crown Prince, but realised that it was Vahdettin Efendi through the demonstrations of respect which the new arrival received.

The Prince was tall and thin, and his weak shoulders carried his head in a forward position; his movements seemed to be restricted by extreme lassitude. He approached the sofa and sat down at one end of it. The two generals were told to do the same on the two solitary chairs, which faced the sofa. For a long moment His Highness remained with his eyes closed, as if absorbed in profound thoughts. Opening them, he looked at his visitors and, as if making a real effort, said slowly to Kemal, "It is a real pleasure to me to have met you," after which he closed his eyes and remained silent. Kemal has related the circumstances of this interview with these words: "I reflected on what would be a convenient reply to such a flattering remark, but what could I reply? I looked at Naci Paşa, who seemed to be lost in his own thoughts. I decided to remain silent also and wait until the Prince again spoke. In fact, he did manage to reopen his eyes and say: "We are going to be fellow-travellers, aren't we?" "Yes," I replied rather shortly, "we're going on a journey."

Kemal thought that he was talking to a madman. The interview came to an end; the generals got up, reminding the Prince that their departure was fixed for two days later, and retired. Kemal and Naci gave each other their impressions; Naci felt pity for this man who one day or other would be Padişah. Kemal made bitter reflections on the fate of his country which would have a creature like that as sovereign.

On the day of departure, a large crowd had gathered at the station to see the future Sultan off. He arrived dressed in civilian clothes, and reviewed the guard of honour, saluting them and also the multitude in the oriental fashion, with both hands and in an affected style. Kemal was surprised that the Prince was not wearing uniform, since the object of the journey was for him to tour the battle front. He remarked on this to the Prince's proud master of ceremonies, who did not deign to answer him; Kemal however, not being intimidated by proud palace lackeys, repeated his remark more brusquely. The courtier was used to bowing down before masters, and immediately changed his tone, explaining courteously that His Highness preferred to wear civilian clothes because of some arguments which had occurred between him and the army commanders about his military rank.

Kemal went off to look for the compartment that should have been reserved for him, amidst the to-ing and fro-ing of the Prince's companions and servants. It turned out to be in one of the places most remote from the Prince's carriage, and had been made into a short of depository for trunks and baskets. He complained about this to the director of Vahdettin's civil list, and asked for his accommodation to be changed so that he would be nearer to the Prince, whom he wanted to know better, since he had been ordered to accompany him in Germany while on official visits; this new courtier treated him as if he was a young officer, and replied that His Highness preferred to surround himself with his servants. Kemal reflected that the man talking to him was indeed remarkably well fitted for a servant's office

When the higher hills of the capital had disappeared over the horizon, and the train was running freely over the Thracian plains, an officer informed Kemal that His Highness was waiting for him. Kemal was sorry that he had accepted the mission, and followed the officer unwillingly, through the throng of courtiers. He was alarmed that he would soon have to accompany a man with a sick brain, who would be the laughingstock of the German leaders. Alas for Turkey in her death-throes! What 'would be thought of her when her own sovereign looked like a corpse in an overcoat, moved along by feeble springs?

He was to have an enormous surprise; instead of the soporific Prince, he found himself in front of a man with a firm gaze, whose manner was even authoritarian, and whose expression and quick comprehension contrasted completely with the spectre whom Kemal had seen before. The Prince began by apologising for not having known the name of the general who was to accompany him on his journey before the interview in the palace. He then said that he was pleased and honoured at the same time that it should be Mustafa Kemal, the hero of the Dardanelles, who had been chosen. Vahdettin knew all the details of Kemal's actions there, and talked about them at length. Kemal was still astonished: he became convinced that if this man were well advised, he could be useful to his country.

Vahdettin Efendi, brother of Murat V, Abdülhamit and Mehmet Reşat, had managed to make himself such a consummate actor, that there were very few people who realised he was tricking them. He had had long practice. He had been educated from infancy by the Red Sultan, whom he had frequently seen, and had gained his sympathy and confidence. The Sultan had lavished on his younger brother all the money which he needed to maintain his well-stocked harem, to which he was very much attached. Unlike his other brothers who lived as prisoners, Vahdettin was liked by the Red Sultan. Being very clever, and advised by the examples of Murat and Reşat, who had fallen victims to the ambitions and suspicions of his benefactor, he adopted from an early age the manner of a man who was worn out by the pleasures of the harem, lacking both will-power and ambition, and above all inoffensive.

Vahdettin's education was lacking in some respects, but given the example of his protector, he could not fail to be a master of palace politics, espionage and intrigue, and a convinced autocrat. The West, which he visited when over fifty, was unknown to him; its progress only made him suspicious.

He should not have been the heir of the throne, since according to the custom of the Ottoman Empire, the throne did not necessarily descend from father to son, but to the most senior member of the family. When Mehmet V was raised to the throne, his cousin Yusuf Izzettin Efendi was declared Heir Apparent. It is known that the Committee of Union and Progress considered putting this Prince on the throne, as being younger and more wide awake than Mehmet Reşat, who had become torpid by his long seclusion. Enver destroyed the claims of this Prince. The peaceable Mehmet was much more suited to the achievement of his dictatorial ambitions than was his rival, in whom Enver had discovered, under an insignificant exterior, a will that was difficult to bend. In Yusuf's breast there slept the autocratic and self-willed inheritance of the sons of Osman.

A dark hatred against the plebeian Enver took root in the Prince's heart. The heavy curtains of the palace let through the loudest threats and arguments between the two men in the days preceeding Turkey's entry to the war. Yusuf favoured neutrality. Enver managed to make the Heir Apparent seem to the leaders of the Committee of Union and Progress, a threat to the Committee's future

The Prince was informed that he was not in favour. Yusuf Izzettin retired to his palace, on the Asian shore of the Bosporus. It stood on a fair hill, beautified by a multitude of fruit trees and flowers, near to that other hill which is covered by the holy cypress grove of the cemetery of Karaca Ahmet, the largest of the cemeteries which populate the hills adjoining the Bosporus with their white stelae, constantly reminding us of the fragility of life. Opposite, on the European side, there apeared cut out against the limpid sky that other forest, the forest formed by the minarets of Istanbul, while the palace of Dolmabahçe raised its walls of hand-worked marble beside the waves of that magnificent channel. The presumed Emperor-to-be saw that place as if removed from him by enormous distances, which he would never succeed in crossing. The triumvirate, and especially Enver, was capable of anything including murder; that lowborn man had not hesitated in hanging the husband of an Imperial Princess, as if to warn those who thought themselves protected by the blood of Osman.

After the Prince Yusuf Izzettin had committed suicide, Vahdettin Efendi then advanced to the rank of Heir Apparent. He was a few years younger than his predecessor, and wished to become Sultan at all costs, to which end he continued playing the role of a man mentally exhausted. He did not want the masters of Turkey to see him as anything but a clown. The death of Yusuf Izzettin served as an eloquent example to him.

Seeing his hour approaching through the Sultan's delicate health, he cleverly continued to play his part meticulously, to present the appearance he wished to the triumvirate's spies, and above all to be as little noticed as possible. He knew perfectly well of the ill feeling between Kemal and the Unionist leaders; he was overjoyed at the chance which had put him in touch with the famous general; it was possible that later when he was on the throne, this man could serve him as an instrument in the struggle which he might have to undertake against the Young Turks in defence of his own rights.

Now far removed from the spies, he enjoyed long conversations with Kemal, trying to understand him, and decide what kind of services he could obtain from him. For his own part, the general, who had found in that overcoated skeleton a lively intelligence concealed beneath, loyally expounded to him his ideas about the events taking place in the Empire. The Prince was particularly pleased to hear Kemal's criticism of the triumvirate. A relative intimacy was bora between the two men during the train journey.

Kaiser "Wilhelm received the Turkish Heir Apparent with the greatest deference; Hindenburg, Ludendorff and the whole General Staff had congregated to greet the delegation. The Emperor and future Sultan embraced each other and exchanged courteous words; Naci Paşa was the interpreter. Vahdettin began to present his companions to His Majesty. When he pronounced the name of Mustafa Kemal, the Kaiser extended his right hand to the man presented to him and said in a loud voice; "Sixteenth Army Corps! Anafarta!" On hearing these words, the whole crowd turned to look at that man, whose military fame had reached the highest rulers of Germany.

The Prince and his party were comfortably lodged in the Emporor's own headquarters. Vahdettin began to make his courtesy calls, accompanied by Naci and Kemal. They visited the office of Marshal Paul Beneckendorf von Hindenburg, Commander-in-Chief of the German army since 1916, a noble figure who gave Kemal a very favourable impression. As soon as the visitors were seated, and contrary to the custom on visits of courtesy, which do not usually touch on matters of importance, the marshal gave an optimistic account of the situation, which reassured the Prince. Lieutenant- General Heinrich von Ludendorff was no less friendly and attentive. He talked with insistence about the great offensive with brilliant results which he was going to lead against the allied front on the 21st March 1918. That gigantic battle would end with the definite victory of Germany and her allies. German air power was demoralising the enemy cities, and their new long-range cannons had Paris at their mercy.

In his interesting "Memoirs," Kemal recounts the short conversation which he had with Ludendorff during that interview : "We knew about this offensive : but for my part, I was impatient to hear from Ludendorff's own mouth what results could be expected from it. I realised that this was not the point of his conversation with me, and that when he talked about the offensive in which the army was engaged, he was only looking for opportunities to lift the morale of his country and his army, and also that of all his allies. It was certainly to clear up this suspicion that I asked the general a short question.

'To what line, approximately, will the offensive be continued?' Asked this sudden question by an officer in the Grown Prince's party, Ludendorff interrupted his remarks, thought for a moment and said to me, looking me in the eye, 'for our part, we will effect the offensive. After that we will see what will happen.'

I replied :

'I don't think it is necessary to wait for events in order to appreciate the results of this offensive, because as I see it we are concerned with only a partial offensive.'

Ludendorff looked at me again. He had understood perfectly what I meant. However he said nothing."

Kemal later read General Ludendorff's own memoirs; he was not surprised that there was no mention of the brief question which had been made to the general by the companion of the Crown Prince, nor of the silence which was the only answer it received; however when he came to speak of that interview, Kemal did not want to let his readers forget an exchange which showed that he had not been mistaken when he assured the future Sultan that Germany was a long way off winning the war, despite what her military chiefs were telling him.

Enver had arranged that the journey of His Highness should coincide with the great offensive; he felt sure that that would make the Prince an admirer of German power, and if as his doctors feared, the Sultan were to die, the new sovereign would probably continue with a pro-German policy, and the triumvirate would prolong its reign.

On one of the first days after their arrival, Vahdettin and the generals Naci and Kemal were having an animated discussion in Naci's room, about the optimistic forecasts given by the supreme commanders of the German army. Kemal later reported the subject discussed. "I tried to explain to the Heir Apparent that it was useless to try and propagate in Turkey the ideas which were held by the commanders. I was driven to maintain this by the attitude taken by Ludendorff following my small question. It seemed to me that he was prepared to entrust himself to the divine fortune of arms. The Prince showed signs of agreeing with my exposition. At that moment a cry was heard through the hotel, approaching so that we could hear it : 'The Kaiser! The Kaiser!' There was a knock at the door, and the Emperor and King announced his arrival. We hurriedly went to meet him, the Kaiser entered the room, and we all sat down.

"The Emperor, who expressed himself in a very gentlemanly way, spoke of the faithful Ottoman state, which was a precious ally for Germany; he added that Enver Paşa was showing by the way he was performing his duties that he was fully conscious of the lofty meaning of that alliance. Through Naci Paşa as interpreter, Vahdettin replied more or less as follows :

'The words which Your Majesty has pronounced, concerning the fidelity of Turkey towards Germany, and on the possibility that the allies of the Empire can soon see their desire realised, have produced a feeling of happiness in me. Nevertheless, if I may abstract us from the reflections which may be inspired by an examination of the general situation, I feel that I must make clear one particular point. The attacks which are being made against the very heart of Turkey are not diminishing; every day they are stronger, and if they continue, Turkey will be destroyed. I hsve not had the fortune to discover in your declarations any assurance which will allow me to hope that these attacks will be neutralised. Your Majesty would be very kind if he could give me some information on this point which would make me feel a little more comfortable.'

'Honourable Crown Prince, I think I understand that there are some people who are trying to sow confusion in your heart. Is it possible that after I, the Emperor of Germany, have told you of the future and of the succes that is approaching, there could still remain doubt in your heart?'

"The Heir Apparent replied that his worries, in spite of everything, had not been dissipated. The Emperor got up, and we understood that he was about to leave. As he left, he shook the hands of Vahdettin and Naci, who were near him; I was standing a little further off, and he looked at me and went on his way. He had not given me his hand and he had no reason to do so. Was it necessary for him to salute any general, even if he was a companion of the Crown Prince? It was for that general to ask for the honour of shaking the Imperial Hand. I confess my fault; for some reason which I do not know I was standing in the attitude of a tired and distracted person. After taking two or three steps the Emperor half turned and came towards me. 'Pardon' me' he said, 'I did not shake your hand.' I gave him my hand, and I felt honoured with this delicate and noble gesture."

The Emperor gave a dinner in honour of his guest, the brother of his old friend the Red Sultan. Around the table there was also seated a German Prince, Hindenburg, the Turkish Ambassador, Ludendorff, the Prime Minister and the aide-de-camp of Vahdettin. Their host told Ludendorff in German to talk to Kemal, who was seated on the latter's right. Whatever subjects were touched upon by the Chief of the General Staff were not of sufficient importance to have remained graven on Kemal's memory. After the dinner, the guests moved to an adjoining room, where the Turkish general tried to begin a conversation with the victor of Tannenberg, whom he described as follows : "I saw before me a tall and imposing personage, whose noble gaze appeared to have been made especially to detect realities, but who knew how to keep a prudent silence." The conversation turned upon the affairs of Syria, which Mustafa Kemal knew so well. He there-fore informed Hindenburg of the true situation, concluding thus : "I fear that my words will not agree with the information which you have received, but you can be sure that they reflect the truth. You must believe me that the situation in Syria has not improved. In addition, marshal, you are in these days making an important offensive, but I do not think that you should have much confidence in it. Can you tell me between ourselves what objective it is that you feel confident of achieving?"

"Would this great soldier," Kemal writes, "such a circumspect individual, be able to reply to my question? I had no right to expect him to do so. It contained a certain indiscretion on my part, but perhaps this was due to the effect of the excellent champagne which we had been given. The marshal appeared to give close attention to what I was saying, and his reply was simple and original. In the centre of the room there was a small table with cigars and cigarettes.

'Excellency,' he said to me, 'can I offer you a cigarette?' Hindenburg con-tented himself with this answer for all my questions. We went to the table and he gave me a cigarette in his hand. Apparently the Emperor, without ceasing his conversation with Vahdettin, was observing our conversation with interest and asked the marshal in German: 'What does he say?'

"Hindenburg replied : 'A few things.'

"After lighting my cigarette I moved away from Hindenburg and came nearer to Vahdettin. I asked him : 'Well? You have been speaking to the Emperor of Germany in person. Has he said even a single word which can alleviate our worries?' 'No.' replied the Prince. 'You should continue talking to him about serious questions,' I added. 'Do not hesitate to tell him of your scruples. I do not think it will please him very much, but he will know that there are people in Turkey that are able to see the truth.'"

Some days later, the Prince and his companions began the tour which had been prepared by the German General Staff, which would allow them to visit different parts of the Western front and contemplate a gigantic spectacle : a struggle between several millions of men, armed with the latest advances in the science of killing and destruction. They arrived at a headquarters of minor importance, where the Prince was told, with due deference, how the battle in that sector was proceeding, in every way favourable to the German army.

The technical language of the commanders, and the way in which they used ground plans to back up what they said, confused Vahdettin, who whispered in Kemal's ear, "What is he talking about?" The general replied : "You should express a desire to see on the ground the position which they are showing us on the map." The Prince followed his advice, and the whole group went towards the line of fire. As they approached it, the German officers brought out a map which showed a route through which they ought to pass in order to reach the place which they had chosen. Kemal proposed to leave that path and go to some other place which he had chosen himself; naturally, this proposal was not accepted and the company followed the itinerary worked out by headquarters.

Still in his "Memoirs," Kemal says : "There awakened in me the obstinacy of a soldier, and I did not follow them. Following a map which I had managed to obtain, I went off towards another point in the line of fire, and stopped under a tree, behind the line. I was surrounded by several officers; in the tree there was a young officer as lookout, who came down and told us what he had discovered. I asked permission to climb up the tree, and was able to confirm that his observations were exactly correct. However, what was important to me now was to find out what dispositions they were thinking of making in order to meet the situation. I therefore asked : 'Can you tell me what means, forces and reserves you are going to use to oppose the enemy formation?' Being proper front-line officers, they did not hesitate to tell the truth to an officer of an allied army; the infantry was reduced almost to the point of insufficiency. They told me that cavalrymen had been dismounted in order to replace the infantry. The reserves did not contain either the quantity or even the quality of men that was necessary. I was very surprised by what they said, and replied :

'If that is true, you are in danger.' 'Oh, no!' they replied." From his visit to the front, Kemal obtained a clear enough impression of what was meant by the great spring offensive, and of the state of exhaustion in which the German Empire was fighting, while losses on the opposing side were compensated for by new men arriving from America. In Alsace, after they had finished touring the front, the Governor gave a reception to the Turkish party. He was tactless enough to blame the Turks for the misfortunes of the Armenians, in the presence of Vahdettin. The Prince defended himself by explaining the truth of what had occurred, and to support his statement called up Kemal, saying at the same time to the undiplomatic Governor;

"I have with me a general who has returned from that front. Would you care to listen to him too?"

"I heard from the Prince," says Kemal, "that the subject was that of the Armenians. The Governor believed that they had been inspired by the best of intentions, and was accusing the Turks of using undeserved rigour against them. I was astonished to see an official of a friendly nation and ally, and of which we were the guests, seriously discussing such a subject with the future Emperor of Turkey. I began to reply as follows :

'It surprises me that in such an important province a German Governor, who is without doubt a man of worth, should have chosen such a subject of conversation to bring before the Heir Apparent of Turkey, your ally, who has sacrificed to that alliance her whole moral and material existence, and to speak in favour of the Armenians, who are attempting to deceive the world in order to reestablish a national existence which has been lost in the darkness of history.'

"I could not avoid adopting a sarcastic tone in speaking to this Governor, who seemed very badly informed about Turkish affairs and who, despite our sacrifices, believed that the Armenians' pretentions were legitimate. I ended the conversation as follows:

'Mr. Governor, we are a mission charged with visiting the front lines. We have come here not to talk about the Armenian question, but to inform ourselves of the situation of the German army, which is our comfort and support. We have gained the information we wanted and are returning to our country sufficiently instructed."'

After the visit to the front, the party moved to Berlin, where the Kaiser continued his hospitality to them. Luxurious rooms had been reserved for them in the Hotel Adlon. Apart from visits by officials, the Heir Apparent was visited by several journalists, and was pleased to give them interviews. Vahdettin was certainly enjoying himself in a foreign country, after such a long voluntary seclusion in his palace, with the constant fear that he might share the fortune of an infinite number of members of the dynasty who had been murdered by members of their own family, or of appearing suspicious in the eyes of the politicians who ruled in Turkey.

One evening, Vahdettin and Kemal were left alone after the end of an audience given by the Prince to some journalists. The subject of discussion with the newspapermen had been, as usual, the impressions gained at the front, and they had also discussed the various ways in which Turkey was involved with the war. The spirits of the Heir Apparent were evidently clouded with the worries which he had to conceal. He looked at Kemal and asked for his advice, as if asking for support: "What should I do?"

Before answering, Kemal waited a few seconds. He was a man of instantaneous decision, as we have seen in the fields of battle from which heroes emerge, yet the words he was about to speak would need the deepest consideration; for the first and only time, they would provide a channel for the free- flowing torrent of his feelings. He did not know that if his proposal had been accepted, it would have changed the course of Turkish history. He spoke as follows:

"We know Ottoman history; it has brought dangers which give you reasonable grounds for fear and disquiet. I am going to make a proposal to you, and I promise you that if you accept, I will place my life at your disposal."

"Tell me," said Vahdettin to the man whom one day he was to condemn to death.

"You are not Padişah yet. You have seen that in Germany the Emperor, the Crown Prince, and the Princes have each their position. Why must you remain separated from affairs of state?"

"What can I do?"

"When you return to Istanbul, ask for the command of an army, the Fifth Army. I will be your Chief of Staff."

That was the army which had successfully defended the Dardanelles, and represented the largest force in the neighborhood of Istanbul at the time when the important conversation which we are examining took place. It could therefore have a decisive influence towards the solution of possible political struggles, which would naturally take place in the capital. Vahdettin replied, resignedly:

"They will not give it to me."

"Ask for it all the same," insisted Kemal.

"We will think about this when we return to Istanbul."

The return journey began. Kemal was returning with the impression that Germany and her allies had already lost; the future Sultan agreed with this view, but beneath the similarity of their opinions, two diametrically opposed reactions were produced. The cautious Ottoman was overrun by fear, though without noticing it; his only wish was that the German defeat should not prevent him from achieving the throne. For Kemal the patriot, it went without saying that he was prepared to sacrifice himself on the high altar for the good of his country; he also was looking for a way to defend Turkey from the greater evil, to break once and for all with the policies of the Committee, and to find an honourable solution somewhere else, such as through a separate peace. The "Sick Man" was about to die; his enemies' greed would make them leap ravenously on the remains of the dismembered colossus.

Kemal had hardly arrived in Istanbul when he began to feel internal pains. According to the diagnosis, he was suffering from an infection of the left kidney. In spite of the attention of his friends the military doctors, he was forced to stay in bed for a whole month, racked with pain, without experiencing more than an insignificant improvement. The seriousness of his illness decided his doctors to advise him to take a trip to Vienna, to consult a specialist. He saw that he had no other course. The specialist whom they chose thought it necessary to put him into a sanatorium called the Cottage Sanatorium near Vienna. He spent another long month there, and remained in bed, suffering a drastic treatment; after that he was told to take a cure at the mineral waters of Karlsbad.

Kemal had spent the last few years of his life on the battlefield, suffering the privations and worries which belonged to that; above all, his active temperament had made him seem divided into many men. His junior officers and even his front line troops would find him with them on marches, at meal times, and in the midst of battle; his superior officers would find him working at a desk in the General Staff. It is recorded that during the battle of the Dardanelles he disguised himself as a noncommissioned officer, and helped to collect the dead during periods of truce, in order thus to see the enemy positions at close hand; all this physical effort had finally caused the crisis in his kidney, which was already delicate.

Mehmet Reşat, Sultan of Turkey, died in the first days of July 1918. His reign had passed ingloriously; he was the first of his dynasty who had not governed. In the name of the word "Constitution" and its fellow-traveller "Parliament" the Young Turks had relegated the Sultan to a level of minor importance. As we have seen, those words held for them only a very relative value; the autocracy of the triumvirate had replaced that of the Ottomans. The new Sultan ascended the throne with the title of Mehmet VI. Kemal found himself unable to give himself an exact account of the reasons for the emotion which came over him on hearing this news. There was no reason to lament for the death of Mehmet V, a totally undistinguished figure, nor for the accession of Vahdettin. His excitement was more due to his hope that perhaps with this change of sovereign there might appear for Turkey new and less obscure horizons. What would the new Sultan do about Kemal? Would he remember their intimate conversations? It was a great misfortune that his sickness, from which he had not yet recovered, should have kept him away from Istanbul in those days; the triumvirate and the leaders of the Committee would be working incessantly to gain control over the new Sultan Mehmet. If they succeeded, all was lost.

The news which began to come out showed that the Sultan was having his own way; it seemed significant to Kemal that the Emperor had appointed Izzet Paşa to the office of General Aide-de-Camp, since he was known to be pro-Ally, and had always shown deference and friendship to Kemal. Kemal sent the Sultan and Calif a telegram of congratulation, which was promptly answered; he decided to continue his cure in Karlsbad. Two enigmatic telegrams from the officer who acted as his personal secretary asked him to return to the capital, and made it understood that this was desired by a high personage. Kemal thought it was wise to undertake the journey.

The state of his health continued to delay him. He was laid low by Spanish influenza in Vienna, and had again to take to his bed. When he finally managed to reach the city which had once been called "the City well- guarded by God," he found out that the personage who had such an interest in his return was Izzet Paşa, who knew all about the good relations between Vahdettin and Kemal which had begun during the journey to Germany; he thought that it would be useful for Kemal to renew these relations.

Kemal quickly succeeded in obtaining the audience he desired, through the influence of Naci Paşa, who had recently been made Aide-de-Camp to the Sultan. The Sultan received him with great friendliness and with demonstrations of respect, even more than he had been accustomed to receive from him when he had been Heir Apparent; Vahdettin even offered him a cigarette from his own hand, and lit it for him. After such a reception his visitor thought he could begin talking about the subjects which they had discussed on other occasions. He begun by congratulating the Sultan and showing his happiness at seeing him on the throne, although he had reached it at a critical moment; he then asked permission to speak with the same freedom as before, and Mehmet VI agreed.

Kemal explained his point of view clearly and finished with this summary:

"You should personally take the supreme command and nominate me, not as your lieutenant, but as Chief of the General Staff. It is essential before all else to have control over the army, because only then will the measures which you take be carried out."

As in the first interview, Vahdettin closed his eyes. After a prolonged silence he asked:

"Are there other military commanders who think like you?"

"There are," replied Kemal.

"Let us reflect upon it" was the answer.

There was nothing which he could reply to this, and the visitor asked permission to leave. He did so feeling little satisfaction. What was happening to the Sultan?

Another interview followed, this time at the initiative of Mehmet Vahdettin, who expressed his wish that Izzet Paşa should also attend it. This time the discussion was about general subjects, since the Sultan gave them no opportunity to discuss anything serious. It ended without any result.

Kemal insisted in seeing His Majesty alone, and the audience was granted to him. This time, and without preamble, he began to expound the ideas which he thought were right, and which Vahdettin had agreed with. The Sultan, to end this conversation, said:

"Paşa, I find myself with the most urgent obligation to feed the population of Istanbul, which is hungry. Until we can remedy that, any measures we take will be in vain." Having reasoned in this way, he closed his eyes, as if to change the subject or avoid replies. Kemal has confessed his sadness when he discovered that he was faced by an intriguer, lacking in courage to speak clearly. In spite of the Sultan's hints, he could not refrain from awakening him with a short but frank speech, as follows:

"The observation which Your Majesty had just made is very just; but the measures which must be taken to feed the population of Istanbul cannot make it unnecessary to resort to the decisive and urgent measures which are needed to save the country. Perhaps Your Majesty does not agree with my point of view; however I am obliged to affirm to him that the first act of a new Padişah is to make sure of his power. So long as power, which is the safeguard of the state and the nation, is in the hands of others, you will be Sultan only in name."

"Evidently," says Kemal, "I had not been very clever. In his reply, the Padişah let fall the following phrase: 'I have discussed what should be done with Their Excellencies Talât and Enver.'" Kemal realised the whole significance of that phrase. He asked permission to withdraw; the Sultan held his hand out to him, with his eyes closed and without saying a word.

Vahdettin was giving himself over to the Committee. Talât and Enver had manoeuvred him cleverly, or perhaps they appeared to the eyes of the new monarch a force that would be difficult to defeat, because of the strength which years of power had given them, and their supporters consolidated by presents. Could he struggle openly against Germany's protégés? Would a separate peace be opportune, or was it not already too late? Should he risk his throne, which he had so long desired and waited for with the sacrifice of his pride and self-respect, in order to bring Mustafa Kemal to power? And what support would that general be to him? None. He had no party to back him; it was true that the army loved him, but one must not forget that Enver systematically placed his personal friends in the highest military positions. It could not be denied that Kemal had great qualities as a soldier and administrator; however, Vahdettin had no confidence in him as a diplomat or a politician, and he was also afraid of Kemal's authoritarian character. If the force of which Kemal had spoken were created, the Sultan could not see where it might lead. The Sultan's energies were exhausted; in addition to the disposition he had inherited, and the existence of which had been proved by his three brothers and himself, his character had been weakened by the pleasures of the harem, where he took refuge to forget the dangers which surrounded him.

Sometimes the Sultan would catch himself shutting his eyes, and find that he had fallen in real life into the character which he had previously assumed in pretence. He was afraid of Kemal. Throughout history there were so many cases of fortunate soldiers who had become the founders of dynasties; he preferred to ally himself with the triumvirate, who had already lost the support of public opinion and did not represent a serious danger for the throne, but rather were seeking support themselves. He decided to remove Kemal from his side. Mehmet Vahdettin was wrong in this, and one day he would pay for this mistake by the loss of his throne and the disappearance of the ancient and once glorious dynasty of Osman.

It was then that Kemal conceived the idea of a revolution. Something had to be done. Turkey was exhausted both militarily and economically, and it was necessary to stop her rapid descent on the slope by which she was sliding into the abyss. But where could he find the support he needed? It would be difficult to seek it amongst the people, or the Committee's Police would discover the agitation from the start; it was a better idea to take soundings in the army, which was the only effective force; that was the way. Kemal did not want to alarm anyone, or attract suspicion to himself; as required by his rank of general, he attended the Friday Selamlık in the mosque of the palace at Yıldız, the same mosque which the Red Sultan had attended, ever beset with fear, before his dethronement. The Selamlık was a religious ceremony, followed by a reception in which the Padişah was greeted by the high dignitaries of state and of the foreign Embassies.

Kemal tried to give the impression of a general looking for a better situation or the command of an army. On one of these Fridays, after the muezzin had called the Faithful, and the Padişah, Princes, Enver and other important persons had made their prayers, Naci Paşa came up to the hero of Anafarta and told him that His Majesty wanted to see him in his private room, where he was waiting with some German generals. Kemal preferred to see the Sultan alone, and told this to the aide-de-camp who had summoned him. It turned out that the aide-de-camp had already tried to achieve this, but it seemed that the Padişah had some reason for wanting the German soldiers to be present.

The Commander of the Faithful wanted to erase the memory of the coolness with which he had last parted from his former travelling companion, and also to prepare him to receive the news he had to give him. He received him standing, with his eyes wide open and smiling; after shaking his hand, he presented Kemal to the commanders who were there, with these words: "This is a general of whom I think highly and in whom I have complete confidence." They then sat down, and the Sultan told him that he had decided to give him command of the Seventh Army on the Syrian front. He spoke to him of the difficult situation pertaining there, adding: "I beg of you not to let those areas fall into the hands of the enemies. I have no doubt that you will brilliantly accomplish the mission which I have entrusted to you." The Sultan turned to the German generals and said to them: "This commander is perfectly capable of doing what I have commanded him." Kemal had no alternative but to thank the Sultan for the honour which he had bestowed on him, since the Sultan's verbal order could not be argued with. He had to accept the idea of returning to the command of the Seventh Army, which he had left some months before, and which had later suffered disasters, as had all the armies belonging to the Yıldırım group. He was being sent to defend an already lost cause. It was Enver who was speaking through the mouth of the Sultan, whom he had won to his side against Kemal's expectations, in order to give Kemal an order which was the equivalent of a humiliation for him; he must now take back his refusal of that command made in Aleppo.

As he was crossing the anti-chamber filled with men in uniform, after the end of his interview with the Sultan, Kemal was approached by Enver, who was smiling; Enver was satisfied and wanted his enemy to know it. Kemal said to him: "Well done! My congratulations. You have won." But he was angered by that smile; his voice became serious, and he told Enver that there was on the Syrian front no army, no strength, no positions to defend except in name. He went on, looking hard at Enver:

"You have achieved a pleasant revenge by sending me there." This time Enver laughed, but it was a nervous laugh; it was now Kemal who was smiling. Enver, proud in the extreme and favoured both by fortune and his gifts as a pliant politician, possessed a military record full of serious disasters; Kemal, on the other hand, who was in rebellion against the government, his commanders, and everything else, had written pages of glory, to scintillate amid the death throes of the Empire. The revenge he spoke of was the one which the Vice-Generalissimo was awaiting: to see Kemal leading an army in defeat.

At that moment a group of generals, with their chests covered with medals and insignia, courtier-soldiers, were having an animated conversation at one end of the room. Kemal's attention was drawn by the subject of their conversations, which made him forget his own affairs. One of them was saying :

"Gentlemen, one can do nothing with Turkish soldiers. They are cattle, with an intellect only able to conceive the idea of running away. I would not wish anyone the burden of commanding a pack like that, lacking in any noble sentiment."

Did the victor of Anafarta hear correctly? Could there be anyone who despised the manliness and valor of the Turkish soldier? And was it a Turkish officer who was proclaiming this, and also Turks who were listening to it without protest, when throughout history their own enemies had allowed the Turks the best qualities that could be desired in a soldier? He went straight up to the man who was talking and interrupted him with these words :

"General, I am a soldier too, and I have also commanded in this army. The Turkish soldier does not run away, and does not understand such an idea. If you have ever had the chance to see his back turned, the reason is certainly that on that occasion the commander-in-chief had run away. It is not fair to blame the disgrace of the commander's flight upon the Turkish soldier." The general who had received this rebuke did not know who was talking to him in this way, and before replying, asked his neighbours who it was. When they told him, he said nothing, and Kemal went on his way.

CHAPTER 11

SYRIA

The new Commander of the Seventh Army began the long journey by train. It took him across Anatolia as far as the mountain chain of the Taurus. There the tunnels were still being built, so that the mountains had to be crossed by other methods of transport which were very much slower. Then he resumed his journey by train, leaving behind the cities of Aleppo, Hama, Homs, then Baalbek and Damascus, and finally crossing the Jordan, he approached his destination, the city of Nablus.

What ideas were crossing Kemal's mind? Turkey had fallen into bad hands. Germany was in no state to help her; far from that, she had *seen* her famous spring offensive bogged down in the Marne. Her supreme effort had reached that point; but there were no reserves to maintain that position. Foch rose to meet her, and threw in an enormous counterattack with a sufficient number of fresh men and modern materials. The battle was now going on to the north of that French river, and indicated that decisive hours were approaching for Europe.

Turkey had already lost Egypt, Palestine, Arabia and Iraq; now she was struggling to hold on to areas whose defence was difficult for the exhausted Turkish forces. Enver continued with his mad dreams of great conquests. Kemal did not know this, but Enver was going to take away troops and all kinds of munitions so necessary in Syria, so as to throw himself into an assault on Georgia and Azerbaijan. This was to be the reason for the great defeat in Syria.

What had happened? How had it been possible to lose such an enormous area, from the sea of Oman as far as the Dead Sea? What had been the determining causes of the Arab revolt and the enmity of the Christian populations? For the Arabs, the main reason was the desire for independence, fomented by British gold and protection; the Christians had been attracted by the deeply rooted influence of France, Britain and Italy, and promises of independence. The Allies took clever advantage of the factors favourable to them in order to give independence to these peoples, by which was meant independence from Turkey, so that they could fall under the Allies' own control. One must admit that the Ottoman administration left much to be desired; it was certainly very liberal, but it had amounted to keeping the countries it had ruled in a state of great backwardness.

What could the Sultan's government do in the far-off areas, when people were living in the very heart of Turkey, Anatolia, in a way so contrary to contemporary progress? The Young Turk Revolution had brought a spark of hope as far as the Empire's frontiers. Syria, Palestine and Arabia had all waited for the benefits which the Constitution, equality and fraternity were expected to bring quickly. When their patience brought them nothing but disappointment, the southern peoples looked to their own resources or towards the West, to those countries whose influence reached them continually, and which presented themselves as tutelary divinities, and promised them better days.

From the first centuries of the Christian era, groups of pilgrims had been travelling to the Holy Land, to visit the places which had known the gentle figure of the man born in Bethlehem, who died at Golgotha. Another religion was born in the seventh century, the one preached by Mohammed, a fiery religion, pursued by war and politics, which under the scimitars of the first Califs built one of the most brilliant empires of all those which have arisen in the course of the centuries.

The followers of Mohammed, the Moslems, soon conquered the country known as the Holy Land. From that time on, the Christian pilgrims found that country more difficult to reach, and insecure. Charlemagne, Emperor of the West, made an agreement with Harun ar-Rashid, the powerful Abbasid Calif of Baghdad, and obtained from him at the beginning of the ninth century full assurances for the safety of the pilgrims and of the Christians who lived along the routes they followed. The flow of pilgrims began again, stronger than before, and the King of France, who had been recognised as protector of the Holy Places and the Eastern Christians, received the keys of the Holy Sepulchre.

The crusades greatly increased Frankish influence in the East and deepened the divisions which existed between those who practised the different religions. The "Franks" (the name given by Arab historians to the crusaders) who came on the First Crusade, managed to seize Jerusalem, after suffering innumerable vicissitudes and privations, and after overcoming the desperate resistance of the city's inhabitants. These had to suffer a horrible massacre, which bathed in blood the Mosque of Omar, where the Moslems took final refuge, and also the streets and markets. Godfrey of Bouillon founded a Latin Kingdom which reached its highest point of power under his successors in the twelfth century. In the next century however, the rapid decline of that Kingdom and Moslem attacks gave the alarm in the West. A new crusade was preached by St. Bernard, and it set off to help the Kingdom of Jerusalem under the orders of Conrad III, Emperor of Germany, and Louis VII, King of France.

Conrad's army fell to the Turkish swords amidst the defiles of the Taurus and the French army was reduced to a few warriors after several defeats. The Second Crusade was unable to bring the help needed at Jerusalem, and the city had to surrender to the Sultan Saladin, lord of Egypt and Syria.

Europe stirred herself. An enormous crusade left by different routes. The most powerful Kings marched towards the city described by St. John the Evangelist in his Revelation, thus: "She was surrounded by a great light: high were her walls, and she had twelve gates; on each was written the name of one of the twelve tribes of Israel. She had no need of illumination by the sun or by the moon, for the Glory of God was her light. None that is blemished can enter her; they only shall enter whose names are written in the Book of Life."

One of the three legendary figures who led that Third Crusade, Frederick Barbarossa of Germany, marched to Asia through Istanbul, and was drowned in the river Cydnus in Cilicia. The other leaders were Philippe-Auguste, King of France and Richard the Lionheart of England. These two fell out with each other and returned to their countries without having achieved anything except the capture of St. John of Acre. The Holy City remained forbidden to the Christians; the Kingdom of Jerusalem would not arise again. In the last crusade the efforts of St. Louis, King of France were also in vain. The end of the crusades was marked by the capture by the Moslems of St. John of Acre, in ancient times Ptolemais, in 1291.

After the destruction of the Latin Empire of Jerusalem, the Mameluke Sultans held Syria until the sixteenth century, when it fell into the hands of Selim the Grim. During the Mameluke period, Frankish influence prospered, thanks to the acceptance by the Sultans of consular representatives of Western countries. Also the Sultans permitted, from the thirteenth century onwards, the creation of consular courts which tried cases between Franks and Saracens. For their part, the Popes lost no chance of taking an interest on behalf of the Christians, and letting the protection of Rome be seen to the eyes of the Syrians. French protection was exercised more freely following the reign of Süleyman the Lawgiver and the capitulations which he conceded. Richelieu increased the advantages which they had obtained, and amongst the Popes Gregory XII and Urban VIII did more towards the development of public education, which was a good means of penetration. The French King Louis XIV took a special interest in the fate of the Ottoman Empire's Christian subjects; the Convention and the Republic which followed him continued this policy, which was crowned with eventual success, since after the 1914 war Syria was recognised as a French protectorate.

The Turkification programme introduced by the Young Turks angered not only the Arabs, who were forbidden to use their language for any administrative purpose, but also the Syrians, who were disappointed in the hopes which Unionist propaganda had raised in them. These two great elements of the population of Syria united against their common enemy. The Powers happily took advantage of this new opportunity in order to continue their campaign to win the definite sympathies of the different races which populate the Middle Eastern mosaic.

When Turkey entered the war, the command of the Fourth Army in Syria was given to Cemal Paşa, then Minister for the Navy, and he also received extraordinary administrative powers over the country. He arrived in Syria with the airs of a proconsul, and set in motion the strategic plans for the expedition against the Suez Canal; he then decided to cut off at the root the pro-Ally movement in Syria, which had been encouraged by the enemy powers.

Cemal organised Selamlıks at Damascus in his own honour, in imitation of those of the Sultan in Istanbul. He considered himself as a real Viceroy, but his situation was extremely difficult; the two great attacks against the Canal were unsuccessful and after August 1916 the roles were reversed; it was the British who moved from the Canal into the attack across the Sinai peninsula, following a well thought-out plan.

Not only was there a tense internal situation in Syria and Palestine, because of the Allies' plots and the energetic reprisals which were made against any anti-Turkish demonstration, but Arabia had also begun to boil over. The proconsul saw that there was a danger that the allied fleet would protect the landing of a strong army on the long coast of Syria, where it would be welcomed by the natives. A widely ramified movement for the liberation of the Arab peoples from Turkish rule had been discovered. Heavy punishments were imposed. Another harsh measure was taken when the army cut communications between the peoples of the interior and coast. This, together with the general shortage of food in time of war and invasion of locusts, caused terrible famine to appear in several places, claiming thousands of lives. All these measures of the Governor Cemal caused the Syrians to turn finally against him and against Turkey; from that time onwards the Turks were in enemy territory in that country. The Sherif Hussein, a descendant of Mohammed, had worried the Red Sultan by some war-like activities some years before. The Sultan invited him to live in Istanbul, under his shrewd custody. He was afraid of those shifty Sherifs, who thought that they were entitled to aspire to the Califate, After the Unionist revolution, the Sherif was allowed to return to Mecca, and he was given the title of Guardian of the Holy Places of Islam, and of Emir of Mecca. He was there when the World War broke out, a man disenchanted with the Young Turks, who were trying to Turkicize the Arabs a people who were proud of their national traditions.

Hussein stood out amongst the other Arab Princes, and Great Britain intensified her campaign to obtain his support. In August 1915, he was told that Britain desired to help the Arab peoples to recover their independence and the dignity of the Califate, which should fall upon a descendant of the Prophet. An agreement was reached: the Arabs were to rebel and attack the Turks in every way possible; the United Kingdom would send arms and cooperate in the struggle against the Ottoman Empire with a powerful army. Emir Hussein then raised the standard of revolt, and sent emissaries to all the Bedouin tribes of the desert and to the coastal peoples, inciting their leaders to rise in arms against the Turkish yoke, and the godless government of the Young Turks; the chivalry of St. George had finally convinced them.

The revolutionary movement began in Jidda, on the shores of the Red Sea, in June 1916. The city was bombarded by British ships and captured by the rebels. The Sherif directed the capture of Mecca in person, and it fell after two weeks of fighting. The Sherif's picturesque forces had less good fortune in Taif, where the Turks resisted for three months, and in Medina, where the Prophet Mohammed is buried, which remained in Turkish hands until the end of the war. Fahrettin Paşa was the hero of its defence.

The revolt brought no more result than that. The Bedouins proved unable to fight even minor battles in an orderly fashion. Months passed without bringing any change in the situation. The British tried to give greater impetus to the movement, urging Hussein to push on with the fighting, now that the British troops were advancing with the support of a strategic railway and under the protection of their fleet.

At this decisive moment there appeared on the scene a small and mysterious person, familiar with the customs and languages of the inhabitants of the Garden of Allah, as the Arabs called the desert. We are speaking of the man later famous under the name of Colonel T.E. Lawrence, the uncrowned King of Arabia. From the moment he met Emir Hussein and his son Feisal, this man became the spirit of the revolution. Dressed as a Bedouin he travelled great distances on camel-back to convince the lords of the desert with sufficient talk and gold. He yielded neither to thirst nor fatigue, and his drive gave the rebellion a vitality it had not known before.

In November the Emir Hussein proclaimed himself King of the Hejaz; now that he felt confident of his strength, he began to have dreams, which Lawrence

did not dispel, of a new Arab Empire, which would stretch from the sea of Oman
to Cilicia and from the Mediterranean to the Persian Gulf. France and the United Kingdom thought otherwise; after the capture of the city of the Califs, these
Powers defined in the Sykes-Picot treaty the zones which were to remain under
their respective influences, and which were then part of the Ottoman Empire.
This treaty did not allow for the possibility of the creation of an independent
Arab state.

After the failure of the last attempt to reach the Canal, the Turks were moving gradually back towards Palestine, under the close vigilance of the British. El
Arish was evacuated and with it the whole Sinai peninsula. A defensive front was
made from Gaza, near the Mediterranean, as far as Beersheba, situated half way
between the Mediterranean and the Dead Sea. The Turks threw back two strong
attacks along this front in March and April 1917.

The Yıldırım Army Group took responsibility for the defence of Palestine.
This front acquired vital importance, because the British High Command sent
heavy reinforcements to the Syrian front to prevent Yıldırım from trying to recapture Baghdad. A well-known general, Viscount Allenby, was sent as Commander-in-Chief, with the order to proceed as soon as possible to a large-scale
attack.

In the meantime in Mesopotamia, the British continued their advance towards Mosul, the next objective after Baghdad.

General Allenby made large-scale preparations; he collected seventy- six
thousand very well-armed soldiers, supported by five hundred guns, and several
squadrons of aeroplanes; the fleet was ready to protect the army. The attack was
made on 31st October, against Turkish expectations, and their front was broken.
General von Falkenhayn formed a new line of defence a long distance further
north, from the port of Jaffa to Jerusalem. When the first of these cities was attacked, the demoralised Turkish and German troops abandoned it.

The situation in Jerusalem could not be maintained; her defenders withdrew
on the 9th December. Thus, after holding it for four centuries, Turkey had lost
the city chosen by David the Warrior-King as capital for his kingdom, where
his successor King Solomon built the great temple on the place of Abraham's
sacrifice, and which had seen one of the best-known episodes in the history of
mankind, the passion and death of Jesus Christ. The Ottoman Turks had never
hindered the Christians from visiting the Holy Sepulchre, or the Jews from bewailing the past glories of their race before the wall of the ruined temple.

The Ottoman Army reacted vigorously, and managed to hold the conquerors slightly to the north of Jaffa, along a new front which crossed the Jordan higher than Jericho, and reached the railway station at Amman on the line to Medina.

Cemal Paşa had acquired the deadly enmity of his temporary subjects; given the history of those peoples and the policies of the Allies, it is easy to understand that no matter how good a Turkish governor had been, the inhabitants of the lands south of the Orontes would still have been hostile to him. One can therefore imagine the atmosphere which surrounded a governor whose cruelty was well-known, and who had shown no hesitation in hanging Turks of importance. His companions in power begged him to return to the Ministry of the Navy; perhaps that would prevent the situation in Syria from becoming worse. The triumvir gave in, and the Fourth Army was put under the control of Yıldırım.

The Kaiser sent a brilliant officer to watch Vice-Generalissimo Enver, whose military qualities no longer convinced him; General von Seckt took over the position of Head of the Turkish General Staff. This completed the Germans' control over the army. All the same, senior German officials had found ways of always blaming the Turks for the defeats which the Empire suffered during the Syrian campaign; yet in fact Enver's mad dreams of grandeur had found a favourable echo in the heart of Wilhelm II, who through his ignorance of Turkey gave his support to adventures which were excellent for those wishing to emulate the Argonauts, but were inappropriate for a war in which one could say that the whole world was against the Central Powers.

Von Falkenhayn had been deprived of his command by the Kaiser because of the bad results of the plan against France, and was now also removed from his command in Palestine; he was replaced by Liman von Sanders. This general, for whom Kemal felt great respect and recognised as an excellent soldier, directed all his efforts to the reinforcement, as far as possible, of the long front. It was defended by troops in such inferior numbers that the enemy could break it at any point they chose. Nothing had happened apart from a few skirmishes and two battles of minor importance on the Jordan, which had proved favourable to the Turks. In August, Mustafa Kemal took command of the Seventh Army.

He set out from Nablus, seat of the Headquarters of that army, to review the front line. It was held by three armies; the Eighth and the Seventh covered a line of seventy-five kilometres as the crow flies, beginning on the Mediterranean north of Jaffa, crossing a stretch of completely open country for about fourteen kilometres, and then through steep, bare and rugged mountains as far as the river Jordan. On the east of the river, arid regions and enormous plains stretched as far as the Great Syrian desert. The Fourth Army occupied the eastern bank of the

Jordan and of the Dead Sea, and also the route of the railway, suffering guerrilla attacks by the Arabs, who were well-armed and led by British officers.

Kemal was shocked by the dreadful state in which he found not only his own troops but those along the whole front. When he had assumed command of the Sixteenth Army Corps in the Caucasus, misery and cold had been decimating his troops. Here there was even greater misery, made more acute, by the torrid heat, since the great depression through which the Jordan *flows* is hundreds of me-tres lower than sea level, and is absolutely airless. Dysentery and malaria carved through the thin Turkish ranks and the field hospitals found themselves unable to accommodate, let alone treat the enormous number of sick. There were few provisions, and the men suffered from hunger and thirst, so that most desertions were due to their inability to support such a life full of punishments and depriva-tions. Their skin was hurt by their ragged uniforms, since the underclothing of most of them had become unwearable months before, as had their boots, which the more fortunate had managed to replace with the famous Turkish "pabuches," made of sheepskin and fitting the foot very approximately. The General Staff ac-cepted suggestions made by Enver Paşa and the German High Command. Their plans for campaigns in Transcaucasia and Azerbaijan, which in the last resort had no effect at all on the result of the war, needed for their success the despatch of an enormous army. In August 1918, six Turkish divisions had been gathered in those areas, each of then* containing nine thousand soldiers.

The Vice-Generalissimo was persisting with his idea of becoming an eastern Hannibal and threatening Great Britain through Northern India. He thought that the Indian Moslems would rise against their oppressors on the arrival of the German-Islamic army, and that the Damad Enver, so-called because he had married an Imperial Princess, would make a triumphal crossing of the Indus. It seems incredible that Enver did not realise that religion had no strength in the face of personal interest, although he had before his eyes the spectacle of the very Emir of Mecca, who had allied himself with the infidels and was tirelessly attacking the armies of the Calif of the Moslems. Who of the faithful had rallied to the call made by the Calif beneath the Prophet's standard? After such examples as these they must have been blind who thought of deriving military advantage from religion.

It surprised many people that the Turks should march in conquest of foreign countries, while their Empire was losing at an alarming rate Moslem countries which it had controlled for centuries. Kemal saw completely the damage which these crazy plans were doing to the front which he had just reviewed. Those who fell on the field of battle, succumbed to illnesses or whose nerves failed and led them to desert, were replaced by bad troops collected from behind the lines, mainly Arabs, who would go over to the enemy at the first opportunity. They were poorly armed, and since the railway was functioning irregularly because of a shortage of coal, the artillery had to think hard before deciding to open fire; the Air Force could do not more than make observations, so long as the strong British squadrons allowed; the Turks had nothing to answer them with except two anti-aircraft guns.

But there was still something worse which shocked the realistic and practical Kemal. This was Enver's obstinacy, for political and religious motives of doubtful value, in holding on to the holy city of Medina, hundreds and hundreds of kilometres away, surrounded by a land in revolt and joined to Turkey by the railway, which had to be defended by very large detachments. It was better to withdraw the army from Medina, destroy the railway and establish a short front, where, according to his dispassionate calculations, it would be possible to resist successfully.

Allenby was only awaiting his orders before what he considered would be the final phase of the operations in Syria. The allied High Command was to order him to advance at the same time as the army in Salonika. The storm was approaching; the propaganda for a Turkish defeat began a period of unprecedented activity. With the help of the Arabs, the exhausted Turkish soldiers were presented with news which showed Turkey as being near to the greatest calamities: when the allied planes were not machine-gunning the trenches at leisure they occupied themselves with throwing down subversive leaflets and picture books, showing the material comforts enjoyed by the Turkish prisoners through British generosity.

Kemal firmly believed that everything was lost without remedy. However his subordinate commanders, General Ali Fuat and Colonel Ismet, the same Ismet who had been with him in the Caucasus, only saw him as a great enlivener of spirits.

The Commander of Yıldırım, Liman von Sanders, who had been given the title of Marshal in the Turkish army, received Kemal happily, as he knew from his own experience what a magnificent soldier he was; he was a man born for victory. The Marshal thought the future of their front was very doubtful.

As a result of the extreme fatigue induced by his wish to put that army into a state where it could be used, Kemal suffered a reoccurrence of his kidney complaint. His physical discomfort was increased by the heat, and his spirits suffered from being forced to remain in bed. Some weeks passed slowly in this way. One day, the 17th of September, he received news from *an* Indian deserter which made him think deeply. This sergeant told him that the British were ready to move onto the attack two days later, and that the assault would mainly be made in the coastal sector. Kemal had been drawing a number of plans showing the enemy's possible strategic movements, and having studied the weak points of the Turkish army, he came to the conclusion that the Indian's news was true.

Dressing himself with difficulty, he called his staff and the commanders of the corps which formed his army. He took the necessary measures, and sent information of them to General von Sanders. The latter, who had established his headquarters in Nazareth, did not believe his subordinate's conclusions, and answered him, with a touch of irony, that there was nothing wrong in taking precautions. Von Sanders thought that the information given by the captured sergeant was merely a bluff by the enemy command, which was trying to distract the body of the Turkish forces towards the coastal region, whereas in fact the important objective was the railway, where the main operational bases were located. Kemal had fallen into a trap, but he would not.

Soon afterwards he received news that the railway to Damascus had been attacked by strong Arab forces. Von Sanders believed that these attacks were a prelude to larger assaults on the same sector. He ordered the troops who were in reserve in Haifa, on the coastal sector, to move by train to Dera'a, on the other sector.

Kemal, sick with a fever, was still on his feet; officers and orderlies entered and left his room constantly. His army, weak and sick like himself, was also on foot, ready for anything.

The sector occupied by the Seventh Army was violently attacked during the night of the 18th; had they not been on the alert they would have been torn to pieces. At three o'clock in the morning, the enemy artillery began a strong bombardment against the poorly protected positions of the coast, and as soon as the sun rose, the British air squadrons took wing and began to bomb all the strategic places.

From seven o'clock in the morning onwards there was no news from the Headquartes of the Eighth Army, whose right flank was defending the coastal sector, but it became known that its front had been broken and that a very strong cavalry force was advancing northwards. This was the beginning of the disastrous retreat of the Eighth Army, as the routes by which it could retire were threatened. A mob of soldiers who had lost their formations, carts, and artillery trains, were filling the road which led to the railway crossing the Jordan south of Lake Tiberias. These enormous human snakes were furiously attacked by the British planes. The road was blocked by dead men and carts whose draught animals had been hit from the air by machine- gun fire. The soldiers' nerves were exhausted, and they no longer looked at the eagles of death, but continued their desperate march; if they had to die, that was their fate; perhaps it was to be preferred.

The Seventh Army, controlled by its commander's powerful character, was also in retreat, but an orderly one, and facing the enemy, who were unable to overrun it or break its line, despite furious attacks. Kemal was not withdrawing because of the British pressure, but because the Eighth Army which had been protecting the right wing of the Seventh no longer existed, it was essential to avoid being encircled. The Fourth Army, on Kemal's left, was also withdrawing northwards.

Von Sanders had to recognise, though late in the day as we have seen, that Kemal's warning had been the product of long thought in a well-endowed brain. In the early morning of the day following that which Kemal had indicated as a possible date of the attack, the town Nazareth, the Headquarters of Yıldırım, was surprised by a British cavalry brigade. The general escaped because the patrol which had been ordered to capture him mistook his hotel, and instead of going to the Casanova where he was staying, attacked the Germania, where they took many prisoners. The attackers were finally thrown back, but the Headquarters of Yıldırım was moved to Damascus.

The withdrawal to Damascus lasted for ten days, which were marked by innumerable difficulties. At the beginning, while the troops were able to move forward, over a wide front, they held the enemy at bay, but later when they entered the narrow valleys between Bet Hassan and Besan, planes flew almost incessantly over them at low altitude, to waste neither a bullet nor a bomb. They needed the command of a general such as they possessed, to prevent them from trying to seek refuge amongst the mountains.

The Commander-in-Chief ordered the formation of a temporary front, further to the north, at the level of Rayak, where the Beirut branch leaves the main railway. He left orders for Kemal at Damascus to hand over his army to the commander of the Fourth Army and leave immediately for Rayak to organise that front.

Kemal reached Damascus, the garden of the desert, on 29th September. The city was in fact lost; but it was necessary to resist until it was possible to make an orderly retreat. Painfully marching columns of wounded men were flocking into the city; convoys of soldiers and of ordinary families in their carts produced a traffic blockage whose intense misery did not lessen for many days. The population showed its hostility to the Turks; bands of armed Arabs were coming as far as the outskirts, while others, supported by British armoured cars, harassed the groups who were on the march.

In this way the Ottoman Empire lost Arabia and Palestine. Far away there lay the Holy City of Mecca, cradle of the Prophet, the venerable sanctuary of the Kaaba, and the land from which the first four Califs set out to conquer the world: Abubakr, Omar, Othman and Ali, hoisting high the standard of the new faith with their naked scimitars. Jerusalem, conquered by Selim, and which the Calif Omar once entered riding on his red-skinned camel, had passed into other hands, along with all the lands of Canaan.

The fighting in the last few months had been going on in biblical surroundings; every watercourse, every hill, every plain and every city for which they fought evoked the memory of the history recounted in the Old and New Testaments. The city of Jericho, the first to fall to the Israelites when they entered the promised land after forty years wandering in the wilderness; the fields in which they fought their eternal enemies, the Philistines, at whose hands fell the three sons of the first King of Israel on the heights of Gilboa; the river Jordan, in whose waters St. John baptized and on whose shores he announced the arrival of the Messiah; Nazareth, sweet-smelling city where Christ's spirit flowered; the paths of his journeys, the places of his sufferings for the salvation of men.

Emir Feisal made his entry into Damascus on the 1st of October, almost on the heels of the Ottoman rear guard. On the same day the British fleet entered the port of Beirut, and this decided the commander of Yıldırım to order a new retreat towards Homs.

Kemal talked with the Commander-in-Chief at Rayak; together, they inspected the forces on which they could rely; they found very little, except an agglomeration of soldiers who had no idea of what formation they belonged to, demoralised and exhausted. If they found food it was by chance. Kemal ordered officers in whom he had confidence to gather these men together and form new companies with them. Kemal and his officers went with Von Sanders to the Headquarters of the "Asienkorps," the name given to the group of exclusively German battalions. There, the colonel who commanded the group explained the movements which his troops had made and their present situation, which he represented as being brilliant, amidst the disasters which had befallen the Turkish army. When he had finished, Kemal asked the general if that colonel was under his (Kemal's) command; on receiving an affirmative answer, Kemal asked the Commander of the Asienkorps to be kind enough to tell him where his troops were and what was their strength and conditions at present. The German officer, apparently taken by surprise, stammered "I can't give you a clear answer. The troop movements make the situation rather complicated."

Kemal replied: "Colonel, my country is at stake. Those who have the task of defending her cannot be satisfied with approximations. Can you tell me what you have that I can count on?" "The colonel," Kemal tells us, "was an intelligent man. After thinking for a moment, he told me the truth without hesitation:

'Sir,' he said, 'I have to admit that I have no forces which can be counted on.'

'That is equivalent to saying that I see before me a colonel and his general staff, and nothing more?'

'That is right,' he answered."

While Kemal was going on with his work of reorganisation in Rayak, he was informed that the general who had been commanding an army corps which had surrendered had just arrived. Kemal ordered him to be brought before him. "You know," he said, "that an army corps is the most important complete military unit, from the point of view of strength and possibilities of action. Whatever the reason and circumstances for it may have been, the fact that you have handed over to the enemy a unit of this kind, without saving a single man, in order to save yourself, is to some degree reprehensible. I would like to forgive you, but on one condition; is your morale sufficiently good to be in command?"

After thinking for a moment the general replied: "Yes, my morale is good."

"In that case you must go to meet your comrade Fuat Paşa, who is at Baalbek; tomorrow I will again give you command of a unit."

The deserting general thanked him for this noble gesture, but instead of stopping at Baalbek he continued to Istanbul.

Kemal, as always controlling every impulse, thought about the situation in which he found himself; Damascus and Beirut were lost, the other cities of the coast were on the point of being lost, the Turkish army only existed in name, and on the other front, Bulgaria had been defeated by the Salonika army and had just capitulated, so that Turkey was now isolated from the Central Powers. At this rate the war could not last much longer. What was the use of trying to salvage crumbs of ground which all in all were foreign territory? It was better to take the remains of the army to the border of Turkish Anatolia, at the foot of the bulwarks of the Taurus. There the Turks, exhausted or not, would become lions defending their own territory.

The order given was that all forces should move northwards towards Aleppo.

The columns of fugitives had gone; nor was there any sign of the enemy. Kemal ordered that the railway station at Rayak should be burned, and that any military equipment that could not be evacuated should be destroyed. After doing this under fire from the furious population, Kemal left for Baalbek. He went on by train as far as Homs, where as soon as he arrived he went to the Commander-in-Chief to justify the movements he had ordered. Kemal spoke to him frankly and Liman von Sanders agreed. "But after all" he said "I am only a foreigner, and I can not take a decision of that kind. Only the sons of your country could do that."

"In that case," answered Kemal, "the order will be carried out."

In Aleppo, and in spite of his poor state of health, Kemal began the task of forming fugitives into divisions which would be capable of defending Turkish soil. By the 11th of October two resplendent divisions had been formed.

The Turkish military authorities were worried by the nationalist excitement in Syria; they had intelligence of a possible allied disembarkation in the Gulf of Alexandretta, which would take the defending army in the rear. The British resumed their advance with large forces and Emir Feisal also advanced, leading twenty thousand men. Kemal ordered the evacuation of Homs and Hama, followed by the careful destruction of the bridges over the Orontes and the railway installations.

In those days Kemal realised that Turkey was in danger of losing her own existence as a nation. The war was lost without remedy, but there was still time to take measures which could save the country from the abyss, even at the cost of separating her from her allies. No useful decision was to be expected from the cabinet of Talât Paşa and his accomplices, who were responsible for Turkey's misfortunes. It was essential to form a cabinet which could adapt itself to the new situation. In a telegram sent to the Sultan, Kemal put forth his views briefly, suggesting that Izzet Paşa should be given the task of leading the new government. He also appended a list of the people who he thought would be worthy assistants.

Soon after this, the second reign of the triumvirate ended, with the flight of Enver, Talât and Cemal.

Izzet Paşa was given the task of forming a cabinet, in which many of the men suggested by Kemal took their places; Kemal himself had shown the desire to serve as Minister for War, but he received a telegram from the new Grand Vezir, which amounted to telling him that he would have to wait until time of peace for providence to call for his help. Kemal was grieved by this news and answered: "If I asked to be Minister of War, it was because we shall pass through difficult times before peace comes, and in that time it will be possible for me to give notable services to the country. I am well aware that in peacetime there will be found men much better qualified than me, who will fulfil these functions calmly. For that reason, it does not seem to me that it is either indispensible or useful for us to work together in peacetime."

In Aleppo the Bedouin emissaries of Emir Feisal incited the people to recognise the Arab government and to harass the Turks; the last contingents made their retreat through every kind of hindrance; British planes bombarded the Turkish troop concentrations and the railway stations. Kemal ordered that ail unnecessary war materials and all the wounded and sick should be evacuated to Adana.

An important battle took place to the south of Aleppo on the 25th of October. Kemal's troops faced the enemy with the spirit of earlier days; the attackers, were thrown back all along the line, to their considerable surprise, as they had expected these exhausted men to withdraw at the first shots. The Arabs were likewise surprised, but a band of fifteen hundred of them managed to enter the city, seize the fortress and the government headquarters and attack the Hotel Baron, where the Seventh Army's headquarters were situated.

Kemal was tortured by the implacable grip of his sickness, and was only able to stand for short periods thanks to his indomitable willpower. He was caught in the Hotel Baron by the Bedouins, who had been joined by a large part of the town population. Already, on the previous day, the car in which he had been driving towards the east of the city had been surrounded and stopped by a menacing crowd. Kemal had forced them to move back and let him through, by his air of command and strokes of his whip.

With the help of some officers, he succeeded in expelling the attackers from his headquarters, and then organising the defence of the city. Fierce street fighting went on for hours until the attackers had to flee in defeat. On the same night Kemal moved his headquarters northwards out of the city, which he evacuated.

The Turkish divisions were ordered to move northwards. Kemal had chosen a definite front at the foot of the outlying hills of the Taurus, about forty kilometres north of Aleppo. The line he had chosen would cover the main roads entering Turkey, which in the past had been used by two great warriors: first Tamerlane, the fierce wanderer who razed Syria and burnt Aleppo, where he had wide and lofty towers made from human heads; the second was Ibrahim, son of

Mehmet Ali, Viceroy of Egypt, who penetrated as far as Konya, where he gained a further victory over the Sultan's forces.

At his headquarters in Qatma, Kemal issued his first orders and formed the first nucleus of what was later to become a famous organisation for the defence of the country. He foresaw that the Turks would one day have to fight for their own land. He gave out his excess armaments to the inhabitants of those areas, with the intention of forming irregular forces which would be very useful in those mountains.

Ali Cenani, a helper and friend of Kemal, has recorded an interview which he had with him in Qatma, where he had arrived from Istanbul. Kemal asked him where he was going. Cenani answered that he was going to the city of Antep, where his family were living, as he wished to take them to a safer place, since when the Turkish army withdrew the enemy would sack and capture Antep. Kemal said to him: "Are there no men left in the country? You should be thinking how to defend yourselves." Ali Cenani appeared surprised and asked how they could do this. Kemal said: "Organise yourselves, establish a national force and defend yourselves, I will give you the arms you need."

On the night of 30th October, the day when the Empire signed the armistice at Mudros, von Sanders received a telegram from the Grand Vezir in which he was asked to hand over the command of Yıldırım to Mustafa Kemal and return to the capital as soon as possible. The German troops in that area were to do likewise. As soon as Kemal received news of his appointment, he left for Adana, where von Sanders' headquarters was located.

During the journey his persistent kidney pain became more intense; this was the result of his exhaustion in the last few days. In spite of that, he was experiencing something which could be called happiness. It was not exactly because of the high honour which had been conferred upon him, since that had come too late, but more probably because in his new position he would be able to speak directly to the government, to make his thoughts known to them and suggest ideas to them, his ideas, at one time rejected, but whose soundness time was going to show.

Liman von Sanders received his successor with the greatest deference, but advised him first of all to rest from the fatigue which his ashen features showed. A few hours later these two noble commanders faced each other in the official room of the Commander-in-Chief: Liman von Sanders, the prototype of the Prussian officer, tall, stiff and correct; Mustafa Kemal, a figure no less correct and more harmonious in appearance, but emaciated, so that his eyes seemed wider open than usual, as if absorbed in visions of the future.

In handing over his command, the German general did so sadly, and with phrases which showed his emotion: "Your Excellency," he said, "I made your acquaintance at close hand when you were commanding on the front of Arıburnu and Anafarta. At a time when I see myself obliged to leave Turkey, I entrust the armies placed under my orders to an officer for whom I have had high regard since my arrival in this country. Amidst this general defeat it is impossible not to feel the whole weight of such a great misfortune. I have only one consolation: the knowledge that it is you who are taking over command."

The two brave soldiers sat facing each other, lit cigarettes and as they slowly drank the traditional Turkish coffee, Kemal recalled in silence the years which had passed amidst the whirlwind of the war. Nearly four years had passed since he had met von Sanders in Istanbul, when he had been searching for his Nineteenth Division, which no one knew about. Then there had been the intense struggle in the Dardanelles, long months they had spent together, and now the disappointing days of defeat. Only now he realised how quickly those years had passed, like a desert wind overthrowing the cracked walls of the Empire. There opposite him von Sanders also smoked in silence, also consumed by gloomy reflections. Kemal would have liked to express how much he esteemed the general, but his austere soldierly character and perhaps the emotion he felt hindered him from finding the words to do so: the glittering in his eyes spoke for him.

Von Sanders and the German officers left Adana the same day for Istanbul; Kemal went to see them off, accompanied by all the officers in the city, while the guard of honour presented arms.

The orders of the day in which von Sanders announced his departure began as follows: "At the moment at which I have to hand over the command of the Army Group to His Excellency General Mustafa Kemal, who has passed the test of many glorious battles, I express my most cordial thanks to all the officers, administrators and soldiers for the services which they have rendered to the Ottoman Empire under my command. The glorious days of Gallipoli, through which I have lived in close comradeship with many officers and soldiers of this Army Corps, will never be forgotten in the history of the world."

CHAPTER 12

MUDROS

The Tsar had abdicated in March 1917. Kerensky's government was also unable to hold back the Bolshevik movement, which seized power in November, and Vladimir Ilyich Ulyanov, known as Lenin, took control of the government of that new state which rose from the ruins of Holy Russia. His social and political ideas were completely new; he brought Communism into practice, whereas it had so far remained only on the level of theory; it was a dangerous experiment. Bolshevik propaganda reached its peak in those months; more and more mass desertions occurred on all fronts. In December the last Russian troops left the Caucasus. On the 7th December an armistice was signed between Soviet Russia and the Ottoman Empire; the Empire prepared herself to reconquer the territories she had lost, but her activities on other fronts, and the bad time of year, prevented her from achieving this.

The Tsarist administration had disappeared in Transcaucasia, as it had in many other regions distant from Moscow and inhabited by non-Russian populations, who saw in Russia's weakness possibilities of independence for themselves. The Central government authorised them to organise their own administrations. National congresses were held in Armenia, Azerbaijan and Georgia in December. By common agreement they formed the Comissariat of Transcaucasia, covering the whole of that region which is bounded on the north side by the chain of the Caucasus, on the south by the Armenian massif, to the west by the Black Sea and by the Caspian on the east; it had a population a little under eight million, of whom some 60 % were Moslems. Its natural resources, which were in agriculture, cattle, mining and above all in deposits of oil, attracted the attentions of Germany and Great Britain, so that after the Russian Revolution these powers made efforts to seize Baku, the centre of oil production.

The Transcaucasian peoples remained faithful to Russia; however, the ambitions of the actors on the scene of the Great War made their situation difficult; the Allies were seeking possession of those areas, and to create a fighting force which would distract the largest possible number of Turkish and German soldiers; the Reich needed raw materials and food, and her only recourse was to seek these in the East; the Ottoman Empire, apart from her ambitions of recapturing the territories lost in 1878, hoped to extend her influence eastwards, along the route marked out by the Turkish tribes during their successive invasions. The Ottomans enjoyed the greatest popularity amongst the Turco-Tatars of Transcaucasia, and could count on their support to reach as far as the other Turks in Asia, who had founded five autonomous republics in that same year, those of the Tatars, the Crimea, the Kırgız, Khorezm, and the Northern Caucasian Union, which were legalised by Bolshevik policy, since it recognised the right of all peoples to control their own lives and government.

The Turkish plan was of colossal dimensions, and found an enthusiastic supporter in Enver. The war had shown that pan-Islamism was an impossible dream and the Turkification of the non-Turkish populations of the Empire led to rebellions and violent reactions, but it was to be Pan-Turanism which would be the great salvation of Turkey. The Turkish language or one of its dialects could be heard from the Adriatic as far as the river Lena in Siberia; all these areas were populated by the Turkish race, and now that Europe was driving out the most important Turkish group, the Ottomans, into Asia, they would return to the pure fountains of the race, journeying eastwards to receive new inspiration.

The Turcologist Jean Deny calculated at the beginning of the World War that there were more than thirty-four million people of Turkish race living in Anatolia and Central Asia. This was a force worthy to be taken into account, and when the Russian Revolution occurred, Enver thought that the time for the union of the Turks had perhaps arrived; the great Empire of which he dreamed would extend over land exclusively Turkish.

Pan-Turanism is an expression derived from an old word "Turan," the name given to the Turkish people living north of Iran, which is used as a symbol for the whole ethnic group. This idea had already had supporters and propagandists, including the poet Ziya Gökalp, one of the first theorists of Turanism, who had a strong influence on his contemporaries and who recorded in poems the memory of the great Turkish conquerors: "My heroes! Attila! Cengiz! Glorious figures of my race! Oguz Han has filled my heart. The land of the Turks is not Turkey nor yet is it Turkistan. It is a vast, eternal region: Turan!"

After the winter, the Turkish forces on the Caucasian front began their march towards the Ottoman frontiers of 1914, which they recovered in March 1918. A little before that, in the Treaty of Brest-Litovsk, signed by the Bolshevik government and her enemies, Russia agreed to evacuate immediately the areas of Kars, Ardahan and Batum. A conference between representatives of the Commissariat of Transcaucasia and the Turks was unsuccessful, so that the Ottoman government sent an ultimatum to the Comissariat, and the Turkish forces advanced beyond the frontiers of 1914. The Georgian army was put to flight, while the Armenians evacuated Sarıkamış after setting fire to it, and retired towards Alexandropol. The old frontiers of 1877 were reached in April. Armenia refused to agree to some of the conditions imposed by the victors: for example, she refused to accept the loss of the districts of Kars and Ardahan, or to declare herself on the side of the Central Powers. The Turkish army attacked the Armenian army, which was destroyed, and Armenia accepted all the conditions on the 26th May. The defeat of Armenia brought the Transcaucasian Union to an end. Armenia was reduced to powerlessness, while Azerbaijan, mainly populated by Turks, was sympathetic to Turkey. Georgia placed herself under Germany's protection in order to escape Turkish ambitions to control Batum.

The Soviet government had no means of opposing a Turkish invasion in the area of the Caspian Sea, and even less a general rebellion of the Turks hitherto Russian subjects. The Germans occupied the Ukraine, while the Czechoslovaks armed by the Entente had found their way to the Urals; Alexeiev's voluntary forces were on the banks of the Kuban; Soviet Russia was in complete chaos. The strong Turkish army began to march forward under the orders of Halil Paşa. This general, who had been Commander of the Iraq front and was convinced of the soundness of Pan-Turanian theories, said one day: "What importance have these Arabs for us? Let us leave this cursed desert full of sand to the British; we will go there, to Turkistan: I will found an Empire for my little Cengiz" — his son.

In Georgia, the Turkish advance clashed with the Germans, who had guaranteed that country's independence; the conflict assumed a serious character, as several German detachments who opposed the Turks were made prisoners of war. Negotiations between Germany and Turkey resulted in the Ottomans' leaving Georgia to one side and continuing towards Baku.

This city, the capital of Azerbaijan, was then occupied by the British. The British Empire, after its victory in Mesopotamia, had formed further plans for the construction of a wide zone of safety to protect India, and of seizing the oil-bearing regions of Mosul and Baku. The force commanded by General Dunsterville occupied Baku, but was expelled from it by the Turkish left wing. The first forces who entered the city were composed of Azerbaijani Turks, who knifed to death about fifteen thousand Armenians as a reprisal for the slaughter of Moslems which had happened some months before.

The Turks did not delay in Baku; they continued northwards, towards the Turkish republics of the Volga and the Urals; they entered Daghestan and reached Petrush. Meanwhile, the right wing of the Turkish army was occupying the city of Tabriz and continuing its advance towards central Iran, when the defeats in

Syria and the victories of the Allies in Macedonia obliged the High Command to bring back several divisions of the Caucasian army, in order to defend the capital against attack.

In their despair, the triumvirate fell to quarrelling; Talât and Cemal contented themselves with putting the blame on the wild dreams of Enver, who had not given up any of his determination; he still hoped to be able to hold back the allied army, which under the orders of Franchet d'Esperey had already broken the lines of the Turks and their allies at Dobropoli. But there came a time when Enver bad to realise the reality of the defeat of the Ottoman Empire, now impoverished and without strength. Of the two million eight hundred thousand men who had been called for military service since the beginning of the war, only five hundred and sixty thousand were left. The dictatorship of the Young Turks was now hated even by many of their old supporters; there was only one solution, the resignation of the triumvirs.

Izzet tried to sound out the Allies about peace, on the basis of the fourteen points proclaimed by President Wilson in January 1918. Wilson, a professor of International Law, based his theories on the principle of nationalities, believing that every nation had the right of governing itself. The Allied Powers accepted this basis for peace, with the proviso that the theories were not to be applied in their own territories. Mr. Wilson's gospel of peace specified that complete sovereignty would be given to the Turkish regions of the Ottoman Empire, but that autonomy would be given to those inhabited by non-Turks; the Straits were to remain permanently open.

In trying to begin peace negotiations, the Grand Vezir met with some difficulties; he was informed that no one would listen to him unless an armistice was signed. He saw that he had to deal with Great Britain. That Power considered that she was the true victor over Turkey, since she had contributed the largest sacrifices in the tragic Dardanelles campaign, and also won the victories in Egypt, Palestine, Arabia and Syria. Since the Russian Empire, which had been promised Istanbul and the Straits, no longer existed, who could stand against Great Britain to deprive her of the fruits of her victory? She felt that none of her allies had such great interests in the East as she had; she should be entrusted with the final solution of the Eastern Question, and Lloyd George was to be the man who would resolve this ancient problem.

The British General Townshend, who had surrendered at Kut-el-Amara in 1916, enjoyed full freedom as a Turkish prisoner of war, lived in the capital, and frequented its society. He was invited to go to Mudros, the allied Naval Base on the island of Limnos, and obtain the cessation of hostilities as a matter of great urgency. The Turkish government was allowed to send its plenipotentiaries to Mudros in order to begin conversations on an official footing. The Turkish mission, led by Rauf Bey, Minister for the Navy, heard the conditions which Great Britain wished to impose with sad surprise; General Townshend had exaggerated British generosity. The first article of the agreement demanded that the Dardanelles and the Bosporus should remain open, and that the Allies should occupy them with troops. Although it was not mentioned by name, Istanbul was included in the area to be occupied. Voices of protest were raised in the Sublime Porte; but the Sultan suggested that it was preferable to accept. The remaining conditions were not as harsh as might have been expected; Great Britain, who had not told her allies anything about these negotiations, was in a hurry to conclude the armistice and assure herself of being the first to arrive at the city so much desired.

The text of the armistice, known as the Armistice of Mudros, was ready on the 30th October and was signed on that date by Admiral Gough Calthorpe in the name of all the Allies, and by the Turkish mission. The text consisted of twenty-five articles, of which eleven assured the British fleet of the complete control of the Straits; the Turkish army was to be demobilized, the garrisons of the Hejaz, Yemen, Syria and Mesopotamia were to surrender, while Article Seven placed Turkey at the mercy of her conquerors; for it said: "In the event of a situation arising which threatens the security of the Allies, the Allies will have the right to occupy any strategic points."

Thus the document ending hostilities between the Entente and the Ottoman Empire had been signed on board His Majesty's Warship 'Agamemnon.' The Turkish government foresaw that Turkey would be reduced to Anatolia and part of Thrace; however, they were confident that the Allies, who preached the right of nationalities to live in freedom, would assure the freedom of the Turkish peoples within their national frontiers.

Rauf Bey stood up to address the British admiral; he declared that he believed that the documents that they had signed would finally end the long bloodshed, and that he was also certain that the great British nation and her Allies would honour their signatures. Calthorpe replied that in signing the Armistice he was promising in the name of his government and in the name of all the Allies, to respect all its articles rigorously, and turning to the officers present, he asked them: "Is it not true, gentlemen, that Great Britain always keeps her word?" All replied: "Yes."

Thus amid the pain of her defeat, the Empire had hopes of the "justice" of the victorious Great Powers.

PART THREE

BIRTH OF THE NEW STATE

CHAPTER 13

DEATH THROES OF THE EMPIRE

From the moment at which Mustafa Kemal received command of the scattered remains of the Yıldırım group, on the day following the conclusion of the Armistice of Mudros, he devoted himself to the task of reorganising and making ready for battle the forces which had been called together to make Turkish soil respected along its southern frontiers. He had confidence in his men, who numbered about twenty thousand, and were almost entirely tough fighters from Anatolia. The officers understood that it was their duty to remain with their commander and help him to create this new army, since an equally new spirit had arisen to delay the hour in which those soldiers would be able to kiss the faces of their dear ones, which they had dreamt of for years like a sweetly renewed hope.

Kemal was fortifying with all speed the front which in his retreat from Aleppo he had ordered his troops to defend at any price. Later on, when the exaggerated ambitions of the victorious Great Powers reduced Turkish territory to a part of Anatolia on the Black Sea, her people gathered in assembly swore to rebuild Turkey, the true nucleus of Turkey, in her logical frontiers. To define the southern frontiers they chose the line which had been marked out by Turkish bayonets, the front established by Kemal. When he recorded the discussions which were aroused within the assembly at that time, Kemal said: "Poor Wilson! He did not understand that no principle can protect a frontier which is not defended by bayonets, strength, or feelings of honour."

At the same time the commander of Yıldırım had to set about putting into effect the articles of the armistice. In the first place, the tunnels of the Taurus, which were the keys to Anatolia, were to be occupied by the Allies, but it had not been specified how they were to reach them; then it was necessary to fix the frontier between Syria and Anatolia, since the British military authorities were using in their notes the historical name of Cilicia instead of the province of Adana, claiming that the northern frontier of Syria reached as far as Maraş, much further to the north than that established by the Empire. Consulting their atlases, the British demanded the surrender of the Seventh Army, as it was, they said, in Syria. Thereupon, they sought to disembark in Alexandretta and asked the Imperial Government for permission to use the road between that port and Aleppo, giving as a reason the necessity of supplying that city.

Kemal immediately understood what they were aiming at\ the Gulf of Alexandretta was the most vulnerable point of Anatolia; if they disembarked there, and at the same time occupied the tunnels through the Taurus, it would mean the end of any chance that the Empire could,try to recover Syria. Also, and this was what Kemal decided to prevent, the occupation of the road between Alexandretta and Aleppo by the British forces would cut off the retreat for the Seventh Army which, like the Sixth Army in Iraq, would then be obliged to surrender with its arms and equipment.

The Commander of Yıldırım ordered that the endangered army should withdraw to the north of the road, and until this operation had been completed, the British should be prevented from disembarking in Alexandretta, by force if necessary. This provoked diplomatic discussions which culminated in an ultimatum: the city of Alexandretta must be handed over; otherwise General Allenby would be authorised to use force. Kemal had already achieved what he wanted, the safety of his army. He saw no reason to countermand any of his orders since he had taken into account the possibility of using force while he was executing the withdrawal operation, which had now ended. Izzet Pa;a maintained with Kemal a violent discussion by cable, though it was covered by a veneer of friendly diplomatic language. The Grand Vezir was clearly terrified by his general's manner of behaviour; he tried to make him understand that it was impossible for the Empire to continue the struggle and that it was completely defeated, that the British representatives had given him assurances and that they were behaving like gentlemen. Kemal answered that he felt that he was lacking in that kind of generosity which would be necessary to prevent him seeing that the deceptive acts of the British contained more than mere chivalry, and that, in any case, since it went against his character to carry out orders which were intended to justify those who originated them better than they could themselves have done, he asked that a commander should be appointed to replace him as soon as possible.

The Grand Vezir repeated that he had confidence in him; but in view of the British ultimatum he telegraphed the following message to him, accompanied with exhortations to prudence: "If the British inflict such a terrible response upon us today, it is most probably due to the discourteous reception which the Commander at Alexandretta has given to the first steps made there by the Powers of the Entente." Kemal was surprised by this interpretation of the situation, which would make one think that it was due to the discourtesy of the Commander of Alexandretta that the British wanted to occupy that city, together with the strategic road, surround the Seventh Army and force it to surrender. He told the Grand Vezir of his opinion, and added with his usual frankness: "The reasons for the recent British reply, which you find so terrible, have to be found elsewhere. We can be certain that replies of this sort will only go on multiplying themselves until the whole country is invaded."

Kemal's forecast was to prove true. Already one of the first steps taken by the United Kingdom, in her race for absolute control over the old Empire, had been the arbitrary occupation of Mosul and its rich oilfields, two days after the signature of the Mudros armistice.

The allied fleet anchored beside the walls of Istanbul on the 13th November 1918. It had not arrived earlier because of the mines, which it had had to sweep away on its journey. The Admiral's pennant floated from the mast of one of His Britannic Majesty's ships; his armies would also soon arrive at that city, the possession of which, according to Napoleon, was worth an Empire. The Bolsheviks who had overthrown the Empire of the Tsars involuntarily helped the interests of Great Britain; no one would now dispute that country's right to the overlordship of the Straits and Istanbul, and it was she who would realise the lost dreams of the Russian Emperors. It did not matter that General Franchet d'Esperey entered through the gates in the walls of Theodosius, as Commander of the Army of the Entente; France would naturally have her share of the royal booty, but her influence in Turkey was going to pass into British hands.

The only idea of Sultan Mehmet VI was to win the good will of the conquerors in order to keep his throne, in those days which were fateful for many dynasties: the Emperor Nicholas II had been shot; the Habsburg Emperor Karl had taken refuge in Switzerland at the beginning of November, while Wilhelm II looked for asylum in Holland. However, Vahdettin was confident of British protection. He made much of the importance of his title of Calif of all the Moslems, and now that the British Empire ruled the immense majority of those who professed the religion of Mohammed throughout the world, the Calif felt that he could make a useful association with the British, by placing his moral authority at the service of the oppressors of the Moslem world, on the condition that Great Britain protected the Sultan's throne.

The heart of this Ottoman was untroubled about the Turkish people, their happiness, respect for their glorious traditions, or their disgrace. His new ally obtained from him all she wanted. Lloyd George could rub his hands together in satisfaction; the Eastern Question was to be solved in a magnificently advantageous way for his country. He could well smile to think what Lord Beaconsfield would have said of his success. He would certainly have been jealous. Beaconsfield's success in preventing Russia from obtaining her objectives in the Bosporus in 1877, in obtaining a revision of the treaty of San Stefano, and obtaining the island of Cyprus for the Crown, were when all was said and done very small things, compared to what had just been achieved and what could be still achieved with a little cleverness. It was therefore necessary to hold back the conclusion of peace as long as possible, and to try to extract the greatest advantage from the East.

Izzet Paşa was going on with his task of obeying the articles of the armistice and putting Turkey on a peacetime footing, while the Powers were penetrating cautiously into Ottoman territory. Kemal received a telephone call from the Grand Vezir. The Grand Vezir told him that he was giving up the direction of the government and that he thought it would be wise for Kemal to come to Istanbul. Since the army group under Kemal's orders had been disbanded, he decided to follow Izzet Paşa's advice.

Kemal saw from the railway station at Haydar Paşa in Asia, at the end of the Anatolian line, the incomparable silhouette of Istanbul, cut out against her marvellous sky. The city had the same appearance as in her happier days, but as the ship bringing him from the station to Galata Bridge came closer, he saw with greater and greater clarity, the vision of the Empire in its death- throes. The Powers had lost no time in forwarding their ambitions for complete domination in Turkey. When he went ashore, he saw patrols of forcign soldiers, making a sad clatter on the pavement as they marched by.

In Pera and Galata, the quarter inhabited by foreigners, mostly Greeks, he saw great activity. These people were happy at the Turkish defeat; the capitulations were going to bring them back to their privileged situations. The foreign city had put out its flags, and the allied troops had received a triumphal welcome when they entered it; the Greek national colours of blue and white could be seen on all sides; and the pictures of Venizelos, at which the orthodox Greeks looked with smiles of hope, were always decked with flowers.

The destruction of the fortifications of both the Straits was going ahead at a rapid pace, and the great fleet was rocking majestically upon the waters of the Bosporus. The Turks found the atmosphere heavy to breathe, and Izzet Paşa was attacked for having accepted such a disadvantageous armistice. The political parties could see nowhere to go. Dejection ruled.

With a clouded countenance, Kemal visited Izzet Paşa. The latter explained why he had resigned; the Sultan was angry with him because he had been in favour of the flight of the triumvirs; the Sultan would have preferred not to annoy the Powers and to have handed over the former dictators to them. The Prime

Minister had defended his view, saying that national honour was at stake, but when Vahdettin's remarks wounded his self-respect he gave in his resignation. His successor, quickly appointed, was a well-known Anglophile, Tevfik Paşa. It was clear that at the bottom of this affair lay the fact that Izzet was not a person completely trusted by the British, and the Sultan therefore wished to remove him from power.

Kemal managed to convince the former Grand Vezir that they must prevent the aged Tevfik and the Sultan from accepting the ignominious conditions which, as it was already possible to see, the Allies were going to dictate to the Empire. Izzet agreed to form a political front, to cause the fall of Tevfik's cabinet and replace it by a strong one, which would be able to defend the national interests with dignity.

Kemal spoke to his friends and acquaintances who were Members of Parliament. The Committee of Union and Progress still held a majority there; the general tried to get into communication with them and with all political parties, to whom he expounded his thesis: there should be a strong government, nonpartisan, to establish order. The politicians listened to him with respect; the hero of Anafarta had become, after Enver's escape, a figure of the first magnitude. His behaviour had invariably been correct and his patriotism was beyond dispute, so that he well deserved these demonstrations of respect.

Accompanied by his friends, Kemal made his first visit to the Parliament building at Fındıklı on the shore of the Bosporus. It was the very day on which the vote of confidence asked for by the Grand Vezir was to be debated. If the opinion of Parliament went against him, he would be forced to give in his resignation; this would be the moment to make the Sultan understand, with the weight of Parliament behind it, that Izzet should return to power. After Kemal had discussed and set forth his ideas to small groups in the parliamentary corridors, he was called over by a large group of members who wanted to listen to him before entering the chamber.

Kemal, who as a general was unfamiliar with politics, gave them an explanation of how he saw the situation, leading to the conclusion that Tevfik should not be given a vote of confidence. The Members of Parliament seemed to be decided to follow his advice, and to have a majority in numbers. When they were called to the session, Kemal went up into the gallery to await the result of the vote. He noticed that there seemed to be a certain optimism. The President announced the result. Tevfik had easily won the confidence of Parliament.

The soldier who had always lived apart from parliamentary life was amazed by the result he had just heard. The members who had seemed to respond so sincerely to his call had been many; however it was clear that those same men had voted for Tevfik. Kemal hurriedly left the Houses of Parliament, filled with a confusion of impressions and ideas.

Parliament felt the danger of being dissolved through the influence of the Powers over the Sultan, and selfishly decided to temporise with the Allies and humble itself before their ordinances. One could see from the windows of the Houses of Parliament the steel monsters of His Britannic Majesty and his allies, floating nearby on the blue Straits; it was their power which had frightened the feeble politicians.

The Selamlık was coming to an end; Kemal had attended it, and thereby had according to protocol performed an act of devotion towards the Commander of the Faithful. After the prayers were over he was called by the Sultan. The Sultan received him amiably; however he was more enigmatic than ever now, and more absorbed in his internal world. His sentences were separated by long pauses. Kemal began to unfold the theme which had been his reason for coming to the Mosque, but Vahdettin cut off his speech with a tiny gesture and said to him slowly: "I am persuaded that the commanders and officers of the army have a high regard for you. Can you promise me that they will not make any attempt against me?" Kemal could not understand what was meant by such a question, so unexpected and completely irrelevant to the course of the conversation which he had begun, and in order not to compromise himself he answered with a question of his own: "Has Your Majesty been informed in any more or less explicit way, of any movement directed against Your Person by the army?"

This trick could not be played against that clever Sultan, who closed his eyes and repeated his question. Kemal had to reply, but did so in an evasive way: "To tell you the truth I have only been in Istanbul a few days, so that I do not know the situation well; however, I do not think that there can be any reason for the commanders and officers to rebel against Your Majesty. I can therefore assure you that you have nothing to fear."

"I am not speaking only of today" said the Sultan, this time looking Kemal straight in the eye, "but also of tomorrow." Kemal gave a reassuring reply, and as he spoke he thought over the words which he had just heard. "Was if that the Padişah was considering the possibility of doing things which might anger the army? What plans were being thought out behind the eyelids which always shadowed those lifeless pupils? It would be nothing honourable, and if the Sultan was thinking that he could obtain Kemal's help in his machinations, he was wrong.

The Padişah opened his eyes after a final meditation and brought the long interview to an end with these words: "You are an intelligent officer, and I am sure
that you will know how to use your influence to calm your fellows."

As he left the audience chamber he met a large number of people, worn out
by the long wait of more than an hour, who were looking at him in a meaning
way. He did not understand the reason for these looks until the following day.
That was the 21st December, and Mehmet VI decreed the dissolution of Parliament, without fixing a date for new elections. This arbitrary measure was taken
by the Sultan with the agreement of the foreigners, who were advising him to
make himself absolute ruler. In order to calm public opinion, the Sultan had cleverly arranged to talk to Kemal, in a way which could not pass unnoticed, after the
Selamlık. The conversation had been deliberately prolonged by the Sultan, and
was interpreted by the public as an interview in which the Sultan and Kemal had
jointly decided upon the dissolution.

The Unionist press violently attacked the Sultan's decision; there found their
way into print some of the secret letters which the then Prince Vahdettin had sent
to the Red Sultan, and which had turned up at Yıldız. These documents showed
Vahdettin as a cynic, a common spy and informer and an expert smeller-out of
possible enemies for Abdülhamit. The opposition to him grew day by day, and
the power of the Union was still great; there was talk of revolutionary movements.

The Allied High Commissioners in Istanbul were alarmed by these rumors
and demanded a harsh repression. Vahdettin then achieved his old desire; this
was to nominate as Grand Vezir his brother-in-law Damat Ferit Paşa, a man who
in addition enjoyed the full confidence of Great Britain. In effect, the fossil-like
Tevfik had been merely a bridge for this ambition.

The Unionist leaders and rebellious persons were imprisoned, and the Sultan and his brother-in-law made themselves absolute masters of Turkey with
British support. Turkish and foreign spies watched over the city; the occupying
forces imposed silence, and every suspicious person was arrested. Beneath the
government of the two brothers-in-law, the clerical party and the court, it was the
British who held the power. It was the policy of those first three elements that the
country had to win the goodwill of the Allies through obedience, and since Great
Britain was the chief victor, by asking for her beneficent aid.

The artifice of the Selamlık and the dissolution of Parliament had removed
from Kemal's heart any hope of succeeding in getting the Sultan to do anything
to the advantage of Turkey. One can understand the rage of the hero of Anafarta
at seeing himself as a helpless spectator as his country was dying wretchedly, and

what was worse, to see it dying without honour, something which could never have been dreamed of by the Turks of the times of Süleyman the Great. He could see no path to follow, no far-off glimmer of light which might show a way out of that tangled forest of choking misfortune.

Kemal rented a house in a wide avenue in the modern quarter of Şişli, where there lived many Turks who had emigrated from Salonika. He often visited his mother and sister though, as always, he did not live with them. He spent long hours alone, unless one can call a cigarette company. He smoked extravagantly; he needed to smoke to calm his nerves and worries. He also felt the need to go out and find some kind of amusement. He attended aristocratic clubs and large hotels; he listened to the conversations and assessed the varied opinions of the various Turkish and foreign circles. The British police, seeing the general who had been so feared dissipating himself in this way, decided that he was not dangerous. His reputation of being a friend of the Sultan contributed to this mistaken belief, though it was extremely beneficial to the Sultan himself.

In those days of depression, the majority of Turks believed that the country as a whole could not be saved except with the support of a Great Power. Some were in favour of asking for an American mandate, others a British one, others French. The most important of the associations which were formed with this intent was the one called "Friends of Britain." The Sultan became its first member, followed by Damat Ferit and many other personalities and some British people, including the Pastor Mr. Frew who was the true leader of the association. The "Friends of Britain" openly aimed at a British protectorate through the Lloyd George cabinet.

Kemal in his house at Şişli did not favour these unworthy solutions, which were against logic: had they any idea whether Great Britain intended to keep the Empire together as a unit? The treaties and arrangements which she had made with the other powers and the Arabs made such a possibility out of the question. But above all else, Turkey, the Turkish people, had the right through their ancient traditions of culture and glory to live freely within their own frontiers. "No!" thought Kemal. "Turkey must save herself or perish!"

The Ottoman Empire had collapsed. Her enormous territory was now occupied by her conquerors, who were not going to give it back; there remained Anatolia, Turkish land, cradle and tomb of innumerable generations of Turks. The life of Turkey was there, and there lay her hope, in the hearts of that people silent then, worn out by long wars, bled dry, fearful of the invasion which was expected on all their frontiers, yet full of life and love for their mountains, their fertile plains and rivers, indomitable defenders of their hearths.

Kemal believed in his people; he had been able to see their fine self- denial and stoicism on the fields of battle. Such a people deserved to know a better future. He was sitting beside a wide window which allowed the cold sun of the last winter days to enter through the net curtains; through his half-shut eyes he felt coming from every corner of Anatolia the life of his people, and he felt their pain, equal to his own. In the wide avenue outside, a British patrol broke through his patriotic thoughts with their rhythmic step; there was born in his heart the idea of armed opposition to foreign intervention.

Kemal had found the way to salvation: it was not the way of a beggar, imploring the protection of foreigners or making oneself a tame slave, in the fashion of other weaker eastern peoples; nor was it to trust in the Sultan and Calif or in his divine inspiration: in the Turkish people, where there lay intact the virtues of his race, there lay hope! The Ottoman Empire was dead, but a new Turkish state must be born, which would be founded on the sovereignty of the people.

Kemal kept his plans secret; he continued his worldly life, and did not let the impassive mask which he had adopted reflect the anger which he felt at the offences daily received by the Turks from the occupying forces and the foreigners in Pera.

On the signature of the armistice, the victorious powers began military occupation of those zones of the Ottoman Empire which they had awarded each other previously through treaties. The British, who were established in Arabia, Palestine, Syria and Iraq, penetrated the frontiers of Anatolia, into the ancient Cilicia which they handed over to France in the middle of 1919. Italy disembarked troops in the south-west of Anatolia, in the ancient areas of Pamphylia, Caria and Lycia, which areas she kept under her charge.

In 1915 Italy had received offers of territory if she entered the war on the allied side. A year later, when France, Great Britain and Russia clarified further the possible division of the Ottoman colossus, Italy also demanded to know more exactly which part would be given to her. At the conference of Saint Jean de Maurienne in 1917, she was given rights over important regions of western Anatolia.

Apart from controlling the Straits, the three Powers sent strong contingents to the cities which lay along the great Anatolian railway. In December 1918 the allied forces of occupation on Turkish soil were forty-one thousand British, forty-nine thousand French and seventeen thousand Italians.

The Christian elements took part in this systematic invasion, hoping to see Turkey disappear not merely from the map of Europe but even from that of Asia. The Greek Orthodox Patriarchate of Istanbul was openly collaborating with the

Greek patriotic society "Mavrimira," which was engaged in powerful anti-Turkish propaganda. The Greek government was in continuous contact with the Patriarchate, and both were working towards the creation of a Greek state on the shores of the Black Sea, with its capital at the port of Samsun. Numerous secret societies, including the one known as "Pontus," scattered through the areas which had been captured from the Empire, were in feverish activity. Large numbers of armed men were disembarked at those places and maintained at Greece's expense. The Armenians were equally active, since they had no doubt that a free Armenia would be created by the Supreme Peace Council; the Kurds too believed that they had a right to independence. A remarkable network of spies and an excellent propaganda machine, supported by ample funds, had the task of destroying the effective forces of Turkey, creating a cancer within the country, and it was the Christian minorities among whom this political culture was grown.

In order to provide some opposition to this gangrene, groups of patriots appeared in many places who, joining in associations, trifed to find a way of defending Turkish soil and preventing the creation of Christian states. The most important to appear was the Association for the "Defence of the National Rights of the Eastern Provinces." The association was born from the fear that those provinces would be ceded to Armenia, and its objective was to use every means to defend the historical and national rights of the Moslem population of those provinces.

The excitement which was growing day by day in Anatolia worried the Allied Powers' representatives in Istanbul; in addition, one of the three armies to which the Turkish forces had been reduced was taking longer than the others in dismissing its troops and handing over its arms to the officers representing the allied intervention. This was the army which was then in the Eastern provinces, and which had conquered Tran caucasia only to retreat after the end of the war. The Allies intended to croate an Armenian state; the town region of Kars had been occupied by the Armenians, who had committed cruel acts against the Turks. The Turks reacted angrily, and the High Commissioners, foreseeing serious clashes, asked the Sultan to send there a trustworthy and energetic man who would be able to impose order and would have the wishes of Istanbul carried out to the letter.

Kemal had some friends in the government. Ali Fethi, the former ambassador in Sofia, was Minister of the Interior; Cevat Paşa was Chief of the General Staff; Ismet, his subordinate in the Caucasus and Syria, held the post of Under-Secretary of War; Rauf was Minister for the Navy. All these men had the highest opinion of Kemal, and also knew something of his secret plans to begin a movement to show the Supreme Council in Paris and the civilized world that Turkey still existed, that she expected justice, from the nations who at that time were trying to reform the world, and that she would demand her right to live, in accordance with the principle of the rights of nationalities.

The projects shaped by Kemal's powerful mind went much further than that; he was, however, afraid of letting them be known, and making himself appear to some people a suspicious person and to others a mere utopian. He, preferred to go on leading his life automatically through the social circles of the capital, and to pass his long hours absorbed in thought in the silence of his house. Sometimes the inference of his thoughts led him to see in the future a new Turkey, as yet unknown to all, which would be free from chains, oppressions and prejudices, and with something which no one had dreamed of, a new mentality.

His physique had suffered from his spiritual pains. It seemed as if ten or fifteen years had passed through the lines of his face, and marked the signs of premature age in grey tones. If they had seen that man sitting motionless in a chair, as if paralysed, his soldiers who had accompanied him in so many battles would scarcely have recognised in him the commander with nerves of steel and inexhaustable energy; yet if they had been able to see the vistas which were contained in the depths of his deep pupils, they would have discerned an intense vitality. It was in that white house in Şişli that Kemal conceived the soul of the new Turkey.

The general awaited his orders, knowing full well the historical problems of his country arising from the Eastern Question, and foresaw what would happen to it through the fateful repetitions of history; since the invasion of Europe by the Ottoman Turks in the fourteenth century, the European countries had been afraid of the threatening Turkish power, which they had opposed with little success whilst the Empire was strong, but with greater effect when it was in decay. This decay had now reached such an extreme, that the European conquerors found only a void before them. Now they were afraid of the Empire's weakness; a formidable unknown factor had appeared, which ambitions and jealousies would not allow to be solved. Who was going to be the main heir of the colossus? Who would make the Pearl of the Bosporus her own? No one felt that their strength was equal to their ambitions, with the exception of the Russian Empire, which, since the reign of Ivan the Terrible had constantly yearned to reach the open sea through the Turkish Straits. She found her aspirations always frustrated, even after the impulse given by Catherine II and her successful wars; the truth was that the Ottoman Empire was already in decay, and the Western Powers did not wish to see Russia as the mistress of Istanbul.

After the Empire of the Tsars was shown this truth in the Crimea, the un-known factor again appeared, — who was to be the heir? Diplomats advised their respective governments to bide their time; for the time being it was necessary to prolong the weakness of Turkey, to give strength to the "Sick Man," to stop him from dying. It was to defend this principle that the era of foreign intervention began; the doctors tried each for his own advantage, to win the confidence of the Sick Man, in the hope of winning the larger fee. Naturally rivalries arose, as the doctors spied on each other and intrigued in every way. One of them came out on top: the Berlin doctor. He had worked methodically and tenaciously; he had won the friendship of the nurse Union and Progress and together they had led the patient into a new war. The other doctors, especially the Paris doctor, were extremely offended. So many years lost in prolonging the death-throes of the patient, only for him to die at the hands of someone else!

In fact, as that man in Şişli realised, the Ottoman Empire was dead, but its Russian heir had predeceased it; that heir was out of the reckoning, so that the British, French, Italian and Greek heirs, with greater or less expectations, were looking at each other with distrust: who was going to carry off the biggest slice? It was easy to see what disagreements would soon be boiling up between the conquering allies. For the present, the High Commissioners had full powers to hasten the complete dispersal of the Turkish forces, and to carefully watch the activities of their colleagues.

A hope was born in Kemal's heart. He now began to see that it might be possible to achieve his plans. The other heirs would form a block against the greediest and strongest one, so that their forces would be divided. The people of Europe were demanding the return of the combatants to their homes, because they wanted to forget the years lost in the mud of the trenches, and the multitude of privations which they had suffered; humanity yearned to enjoy life: Kemal thought that it would be very difficult to convince such people that they should throw themselves into a new imperialist war; the dismemberment of Turkish soil would be achieved by diplomatic rather than military means. If he could organise the defence of Anatolia, and create a powerful army, Turkey would be treated in a different fashion.

In obedience to the request from the High Commissioners, the Turkish gov-ernment decided to send a trustworthy man to the Eastern provinces to hold down the resistance movement. Some members of the old power circles, who were not altogether happy about Kemal's silence, thought that it was not impru-dent to remove him from the capital. They therefore proposed to the Sultan that he should be sent to Anatolia, and the Sultan, who thought the same way as they did, agreed.

The British authorities spent some days considering whether it was wise to confide such a delicate mission to a man who had shown so much opposition to them in Alexandretta. Finally, after having informed themselves sufficiently about his activities in the capital, they gave their agreement. They thought that Kemal would carry out the mission entrusted to him as meticulously as was always his custom; in addition, his orders would be obeyed by the Turks, and since he was an enemy of the Committee of Union and Progress, he was the right person with which to fight it.

Kemal was called to the Sublime Porte, where he was informed of the government's decisions. He accepted in principle, but he pointed out that he needed special powers and authorities, to carry out the mission better. Kemal's friends in the General Staff proposed that he should be charged with the inspection of the Ninth Army, which was to be renamed as the Third Army soon. Kemal insisted on obtaining civil authority apart from his military functions, and the Grand Vezir made no objections to this.

In this way Kemal, who had had the resolve of going to the heart of Turkey in order to put himself in communion with his people and begin resistance, found himself unexpectedly the representative of Sultan Mehmet Vahdettin, and still more incredibly, a man trusted by the Powers who were the executioners of his country.

Life flowed back into Kemal's limbs. In hours he completed work which others would have taken days over; he put all his affairs in order, and arranged a secret code with the Chief of the General Staff and with Ismet so that they could communicate behind the backs of the allied watchers. He had somewhat more open conversations with his friends in the government, and these exchanges of views gave him the impression that the majority of Turks would prefer to fight than to watch the final dismemberment of Turkey with folded arms.

The Grand Vezir invited the man appointed Inspector of the Army to dine in his residence at Nişantaşı, a suburb of Istanbul; the Chief of Staff Cevat Paşa was also to be present. Damat Ferit wanted to know exactly the way in which the new inspector was going to carry out his mission.

Kemal was the first to arrive. After exchanging the necessary courteous phrases, they remained in silence. Ferit kept looking at his watch. Why was Cevat taking such a long time? Finally Cevat arrived, and the three men went into the dining room; at the table, words were also scarce. The host let his eyes stray

over the artistic objects placed on the furniture, or on the designs of the hang-
ings on the walls, thinking perhaps how heavy was the responsibility which the
Padişah had placed on his shoulders. The guests respected his silence, and devoted themselves to their own thoughts. When they had finished dinner, they went
to a small room, where the Grand Vezir suggested: "Why don't we bring a map,
so that the Inspector can explain to us?" As they looked at the map ofAnatolia,
Ferit asked, "What do you think of doing in the region of Samsun?" What the
government wanted was that he should combat the guerrilla warfare which the
Turks were maintaining, albeit on a small scale, against the Christian groups
which had been inspired by the Patriarchate and the foreigners, announcing the
creation of a Greek state in that area. It was difficult for Kemal to reply to this;
however, he answered with calming phrases: "It will be possible to decide what
are the best measures to take after study of the situation on the ground. You can
feel assured." The Grand Vezir was not assured, and went on with his questions
and soundings. Cevat Paşa helped Kemal throughout to try to satisfy Ferit. Since
the Chief of the General Staff appeared to give little importance to the question,
and Kemal's replies were logical, they managed to clear away the clouds of worry
from the Grand Vezir's brow.

A few minutes later, two men were walking quickly through the streets of
Nişantaşı. One of them said to the other, in a friendly tone: "Are you thinking of
starting something there, Kemal?"

"Yes, general, I am thinking of doing so."

"May God help you and bring you victory."

The hero of Anafarta went to say goodbye to his mother. Zübeyde was old
and ailing; she had spent many painful days waiting for news of her beloved son,
who had for the last eight years been exposing his life constantly on the fields of
battle and had often been ill. She could see a fatal issue hanging over the Empire;
all the sacrifices had been in vain, and she herself had had to fly from Salonika;
now in the capital itself, residence of the Representative of Allah, it was the foreigners who were the masters, and what would happen tomorrow?

She listened to her son, whom she could scarcely see; she heard him quickly
telling her of the latest events, his marching orders, then of his journey, and then
there was silence, those desperate moments which precede that farewell, which
may be the last. Kemal came close to his mother, kissed her hand and lifted it
to his forehead, as if the custom of the Turks, so respectful to elderly people.
Zübeyde took her son's blond head in her hands, and kissed him on the forehead
for a long moment. Perhaps she foresaw that this man was going to Anatolia with

the firm intention of starting serious disturbances there; naturally she could not give any form to what she felt; but she understood that hours of bloodshed were waiting for the Turks, and that she would continue anxious for her endangered son. In a way which she had never shown before in the sadness of parting from him, she placed on that farewell kiss a mighty hope, and a resolve to sacrifice all that she loved.

On the same day, the 16th May, a day of high spring on the Bosporus, the spring which is the most beautiful and full of life of any that there can be, Kemal stood on the upper bridge of the "Bandırma," as there disappeared from view the city of Mehmet the Conqueror, which he had made Turkish at the death of the Byzantine Empire, and which now in the decay of the Ottoman power might pass into other hands. The lamentable policies of the Sublime Porte, which was expert at composing diplomatic notes, begging favours from the Powers and attempting to excite their pity, was not what was required in order to obtain any satisfactory result; nor could that be achieved by the Sultan, whose sole ambition was in keeping his throne through the protection of Great Britain. From Istanbul nothing could be hoped for: her own inhabitants, foreigners and Turks who were not Moslems, worse than declared enemies, were happy at Turkey's shame. Istanbul was a corrupted city. Mustafa Kemal turned his back upon it and looked towards the shore of Anatolia with shining eyes, breathing with pleasure the reviving breezes of the south.

Chapter 14

THE GREEK INVASION

Eleutherios Venizelos, born on the island of Crete in 1859 under the rule of the Crescent, lived his life in continual struggle against Ottoman rule. He was one of the best known of the Orthodox leaders who wanted the island to be annexed to Greece. Having achieved that ambition, he dedicated himself to politics in Athens, and in 1910 became Prime Minister of that kingdom. Possessed by policies of expansion and of the conversion of his little country into a great power, and imbued with grand Hellenic ideals, he dedicated himself with all his soul to the creation of the Balkan league, and to strengthening it. The Balkan wars against the Ottoman Empire brought Greece large and rich territories.

At the beginning of the World War, Venizelos, who was a convinced supporter of the Allies, advocated the entry of Greece into the war on the side of the Entente, from whom he had received enticing promises of territory in Anatolia. He had to struggle against King Constantine, who was related by marriage to Wilhelm II, who wanted to keep Greece neutral at all costs. At first Constantine had the upper hand, and the Cretan politician retired to Salonika at the end of 1916, while the city was occupied by the allied army. There he formed a provisional government, opposed to the government of King Constantine.

The victories of the so-called Salonika army persuaded the provisional government to declare war on the side of the Allies in November 1916. Constantine abdicated in June of the following year in favour of his son Alexander. Venizelos had won. His first action was to bring the Greek army into the war, and thereby give the Greeks the right to part of the booty in the event of victory. There was a logical connection between Venizelos's expansionist ideas, and his furious determination to bring his country onto the side opposed to the Ottoman Empire: Greece had increased her territories through the dismemberment of the Empire, and Great Greece was to flourish over its ruins. As soon as the Armistice of Mudros had been signed, Venizelos began negotiations in Paris. He was a fine diplomat, and knew that promises made at moments of necessity are later forgotten. Another man, like him born an Ottoman subject, was to serve the interests of Greece, his adoptive country: this was Basil Zaharof, the mystery man of Europe; a man of modest origins, he performed every kind of function in Istanbul. He loved travel and adventure, journeying by any means. He got to know London and obtained the agency of an armaments factory, making this his career: he would visit countries where international or civil war was threatening before his competitors could get there, and by his activity or intelligence place the largest amount of arms sales, preferably on both sides, obtaining security for payment.

During the years when the world was suffering tragedies, but which were for him the years of the fat cattle and heavy ears of com, his fortune reached fabulous proportions. He helped Venizelos through his influence, the press which he controlled and with his money, in order to ensure Greece's adhesion to the allied cause, and he did not leave his side when the time came to present the Great Powers with the bill for the services they had been rendered. The bill was inflated, but there would be time for bargaining. Venizelos, like any good Greek, was a good businessman.

At the conferences of Paris, Venizelos talked of the greatness of President Wilson's principles. With the triumph of right and justice, he said, the moment had come when the Greeks of Western Anatolia, who had suffered the heavy Turkish yoke for centuries, would once again live freely under the blue and white flag and the Christian cross. He brought a superfluity of documents, statistics and precedents from history to prove the truth of what he said, and displayed them earnestly before the great judges, Wilson, Lloyd George and Clemenceau, who were, it was supposed, engaged in reforming the world and creating a peaceful future.

Italy was another country which had come in late, but for that very reason received larger promises, and had according to the treaty of Saint Jean de Maurienne a right to the provinces of Smyrna and Aydın. This was a vital question for Venizelos: the claims maintained by Greece over Smyrna must win the day. Fortune favoured him. The soldier poet D'Annunzio seized Fiume for Italy in a hazardous campaign, although the reformers of the world had already awarded it to the bright new Kingdom of Yugoslavia. This caused a formidable disturbance in the Supreme Council. Orlando, who personally represented the Kingdom of Italy, withdrew immediately from the conference. Venizelos did not lose the opportunity of claiming that Italy was pretending to make herself into a great Mediterranean power, and make the Adriatic an Italian lake; if she were given Smyrna as well as South-east Anatolia, her position in the Mediterranean would allow her to scheme with impunity. France and Great Britain listened to this and brought their attention to bear on this new problem.

The discussions which arose from the Fiume incident allowed these two powers to do what they thought best; in any case, the agreement of Maurienne had not been ratified by Russia, one of the four signatories, so that in the event it could be considered void. The Greeks had to be rewarded for their services; if they were given Smyrna and the adjacent areas they would be satisfied and forget their extravagant pretentions to Istanbul, since that city and the Straits would probably become an international zone. In this way they would prevent Italy from extending her coastline along the Mediterranean.

After this decision had been taken, it was only necessary to prepare the scene. Venizelos piled up in front of the delegates telegrams, reports and eyewitness accounts to prove the lack of security which existed in Asia Minor and especially in the province of Smyrna; they bore witness to the danger which the Greeks and other Christians were suffering, threatened by Moslem fanaticism; bands of Turks were said to be pillaging and murdering the non-Moslem population. In order to secure order it was essential to occupy Smyrna with allied troops, which was allowed by the Seventh Article of the Mudros Armistice. The Supreme Council authorised Greece to occupy the city of Smyrna in the name of the Allies.

Venizelos was almost deified by the Greeks. The clever Prime Minister succeeded in preventing any commission from being sent to Smyrna to check on the truth of the tragic situation which, according to the Greek representatives and the Zaharof press, was facing the Christian population of Western Anatolia. Later on an international commission was sent to investigate the area, and was able to show how false these declarations had been.

The day dawned without any apparent sign of the tragedy which it was going to 'witness. The radiant spring sun was happily bathing the beautiful harbour of Smyrna. That 15th of May was for the Turks an unforgettable day: it was an indescribable ordeal, in which European nations such as France, Great Britain and Italy, who had gone to great lengths to try to show how much more civilised they were than Turkey, showed that their pretentions were baseless, by consenting to the outrage which befell Turkey under their very eyes. Their prestige collapsed and from then on the Turks were able to look upon these Powers without any false haloes, and see them as thay really were.

At seven in the morning, the Greek warships "Averof" and "Limnos" followed by several transport ships anchored off Smyrna. They immediately began to land several infantry regiments. The troops lined up on the quaysides; the Greek population was at first silent, but then began to acclaim Venizelos, Greece, and the soldiers who were disembarking. Enthusiasm mounted; the priests, who had been worked up into a high state of emotion, harangued the populace. Then, a huge Greek flag was hoisted at the head of an Evzone regiment, and the troops began to march forward. A thick crowd of foreigners, Greeks and other non-Moslems repeated the cry of the Evzones: "Zito Venizelos!" — Long live Venizelos!

The Turks stayed in their houses and their troops stayed in the barracks. It was to the barracks that the delirious crowd went. It was occupied, apart from its garrison, by officers of other regiments and services. They had collected there under urgent orders; the soldiers laid down their arms and waited for their unknown fate. The invaders arrived. Some shots were heard from the barracks; it has never been discovered who was to blame, but it is logical to suppose that some Greek agent was given the job of provoking them in order to provide a pretext. It seems that this had been expected, since machine-guns were immediately heard in action, and rounds of rifle fire followed rapidly. The barracks guard fell without firing a single shot. There was great confusion inside. The men ran from one side to another looking for a refuge, and many were killed or wounded. The garrison was seized with panic. At last an officer came out to parley at the main gate, holding a white cloth, but this was not respected and he fell dead. The Greeks entered the building, collected all its occupants and formed them into a long line to which was joined another formed by the Governor and all the employees who had been found in his palace.

As the line of Turks moved silently and with lowered heads towards the harbour, they were insulted by the populace, who reached a paroxysm of excitement. The rough soldiers threatened the Turkish officers with their bayonets and struck them with their rifle butts; those who were wounded by this were helped along by their comrades, since to leave them on the way would have been to condemn them to a horrible death. Their enemies also amused themselves by making the prisoners shout "Zito Venizelos!" laughing at them, and if anyone was unfortunate enough to resist, pulling off his fez, which was the worst insult which could be done to a Moslem; many refused, and their blood immediately ran upon the pavement. Colonel Süleyman Fethi, head of the recruitment board of the Seventeenth Army Corps, who despised the threats and held his fez on with both hands, fell with his skull smashed by a rifle butt.

Suddenly, when they were already on the quayside, the long line of prisoners was attacked by machine-gun fire. Sixty men fell to the ground, and those who survived were roughly put on board the Greek transports. In the city there began looting of Turkish houses and institutions, and there were more insults in the streets. When Moslem women came, wild with grief, in search of news of their sons and husbands, the veils were torn from their faces and they received insults with words and deeds.

The fifteenth of May ended with a sad reckoning: three hundred Turks had been murdered and six hundred wounded. The events of that day's work shook the great mass of the Turkish people out of the torpor in which the war, the Armistice and the allied occupation had sunk them. Censorship was established, and the details of the first days of the Greek occupation did not reach the European public. Only in Istanbul itself were certain rumors to be heard. On the 17th, the echo of the atrocities which had occurred brought a powerful feeling, since the refugees from Smyrna had told of the horrors they had seen; indignation boiled amongst the Turks. It was clear, they thought, the Powers had decided that Turkey must die; the proof of it was that they had acted as a shield for the massacre in Smyrna.

Massacres followed each other in the ruins of Anatolia, lit up by the ruddy light of fires, and to the accompaniment of the cries of pain of the victims as they fell before the thundering of the artillery on the battle fronts, and the clamour of protests against the West. The 15th May 1919 was the beginning of the interminable years of suffering which fate still held for Turkey.

had invaded the whole of the province of Smyrna and that of Aydın, towards the south, bordering on the Italian zone. The horrors of Smyrna were repeated throughout the area. The untruth of the statistics which Venizelos had produced was made clear, since the Moslems were far greater in number than he pretended to show, and since they were determined to defend their homes, they suffered further massacres. It was not simply the exaltation produced by victory which had led the Greeks to commit those first atrocities, but racial and religious hatred.

Kemal took immediate steps to get in touch not only with the two corps which composed the Third Army, which he had been sent to inspect but at the same time with the others which belonged to the First and Second Armies which were in Anatolia. It was first essential to sound out the opinion of the army and obtain its support. Of those forces which were reviewed on the plains of Bebek by Enver and the military attachés of the Powers, and which had raised such hopes in Berlin, there was little left. It would be true to say that of-the nine army corps into which the Turkish army was divided when Kemal reached Samsun, and which nominally contained fifty thousand men, only the Fifteenth Corps in Erzurum, commanded by Kâzım Karabekir, was more or less in a state where it could be used, whereas the others were mere skeletons.

A few days after his arrival in Samsun, Kemal moved to the town of Havza, which was outside British control; this was a first step towards the heart of Turkey. It was from there on the 28th May that he wrote a letter to the military commanders and provincial governors, inviting them to begin the struggle to save national rights.

The mission to which Kemal the patriot had consecrated his life seemed then to be enormously great. Innumerable difficulties and obstacles rose before his eyes, and he foresaw even greater ones in the future. The Powers were occupying important strategic points, such as the Straits and the railway to Syria. Greece was invading Western Anatolia, Italy the Southwest, Great Britain Cilicia and Iraq, and the Armenians the area around Kars. There were also hanging over the country, like so many swords of Damocles, the separatist movements of the non-Moslems and Kurds, each favoured by the interests of one or other of the allied powers. Thus, Armenia, Kurdistan and a Pontic State were being drawn upon the Turkish map. Yet there were even greater enemies than this; there was Vahdettin, Emperor of Turkey, whose only ambition was to maintain his peace of mind and his throne, which he would do through despicable means; the British, the principle heirs of Ottoman power, held in him an obedient tool.

Kemal's plan was to create a new state which would be essentially Turkish, and essentially free. This would certainly be fought by the Sultan, who would, with his inherited ability to discover anything which might threaten his throne, realise that there would be no place for him or for his dynasty in this new state. After that, or rather before it, Kemal would have the hardest task of all, the conquest of the people. He was familiar with mass psychology, knew his history well, and could anticipate all the displeasures which he would suffer in such a basic task. Until the invasion of Smyrna, the people had endured all the measures which the Allies had taken with their traditional stoicism, which sometimes appeared mere insensibility; they still kept their faith in the justice of the civilized nations, and in the good faith of Wilson, a man born in a continent they knew hardly anything about. The Turks had turned their eyes back to their homes, and their strips of land, which they had begun to work again after a long absence, to their children whom they returned to find grown up and whose childish games they had been unable to witness. But now they were angry to realise how they had been tricked. Peace was not possible, for it seemed that the Greeks, ferocious conquerors, desired their extermination.

Kemal knew the noble and patriotic spirit of his people, and was easily understood by them; he was able to make them see that their hopes could be realised, and make them vibrate with enthusiasm and faith, that faith which is the indispensable factor in great victories. The people would follow him, because in following him they would follow their own ideals.

Avid to breathe Turkish air and to feel the beating of his people's heart closer at hand, Kemal moved on to Amasya, the old city of the Danishmendid Turks, whose mosques still stood to show the importance of that civilization through the beauty of their architectural lines. The Yeşilırmak, or Green River, which hurries past the city, carries Anatolia's nostalgia in its waters to the Black Sea.

The Turks of the province of Smyrna, under the direct threat of violent Greek agression, hurried to fight back. One can picture the state of excitement which reigned, reaching a kind of collective madness, as peaceful men gathered in their villages to decide what to do. They sought for arms, but found few. No preparation had been made, and the burning of towns went on faster and faster. They were forced to suffer every atrocity of which a fanatical soldiery can be capable. While in Amasya, Kemal heard that in Ayvalık, a small port on the Aegean, a group of patriots had resisted in hand-to-hand combat, until they had forced back a Greek regiment. In this way the Turkish people began to defend their country, on the 28th May.

At this first reverse, the Greeks reached a paroxysm of fury. The troops *from* this sector fell back upon Menemen, fearing further surprises. Whether to revenge themselves for what had happened, or as a warning, they spent three days in that town committing reprisals and pillage, murdering the Turkish officials.

The National Front quickly formed a continuous line, surrounding the fan-shaped zone which the Greeks had invaded. This front was broken through by the Greek army, and the defenders had to continue guerrilla warfare in small groups. They harassed the enemy tirelessly, but what could they do against troops which were well organised and equipped with the best munitions?

Fortunately for Turkey, there existed a man who through his abilities as an organiser and statesman, and through the prestige he had won as a successful fighter and dedicated patriot, would be able to unite the whole nation under the banner of his ideals. He made an appeal to the various patriotic associations, of the same tone as that which he had sent to the civil and military authorities in Anatolia and Thrace. His initiative was received with general approbation. He began by intensifying nationalist propaganda and invigorating popular enthusiasm. Territorial integrity must be maintained at all costs; the cabinet of Ferit Paşa, through weakness or treason, was to blame for the dismemberment of Turkish soil, of the land of her people.

Before a month had passed since Kemal had landed in Samsun, patriotic meetings were held in public places in every corner of Anatolia and Thrace and even in Istanbul; exalted speeches were made to deeply emotional audiences, and tears flowed freely. The people began to look towards the centre of Anatolia. They did not know yet what would arise from that quarter; but in those bitter times they wanted to have faith and to believe that this man, whose past many of them knew nothing about, could be their saviour; his words and deeds were passed on to them, myths, truth, exaggeration, all came mixed together. At times he seemed to be deified, at others it seemed he could not be a real person. Could he be the saviour sent by Allah?

First in the times of migrations and later under the dynasty of Osman, the Turkish people had never known any other form of government but autocracy. Parliamentary government, which had been established during the Empire's decadence and without proper foundations, had been a sad experience, as the Unionist dictators had taken the place of the Red Tyrant. Now indeed it was one man who, amids this great tragedy, was letting the people hear words whose deep meaning they understood; in him they found the incarnation of their desires. He was supported by the main military commanders, and he could have followed the easy road of the coup d'etat, which often lifts a man to power without the people's consent; but Kemal was beyond such little things and selfish ideas; he wanted to achieve a great work, and succeed in making the people their own master, expressing their will through their lawful representatives. Now that the Sultan and his government were Great Britain's prisoners, power ought to pass to the people.

As a first step, he channelled all his activity and that of those that had come to help him, towards the creation of a national assembly, which was to meet in a city of Anatolia. This assembly would represent the nation's will, and from it power would emanate. The city of Sivas was chosen as the place for this meeting, because of its distance from the zones which had been invaded.

On the night of the 21st June a secret meeting was held in Amasya. Kemal had invited General Ali Fuat, commander of the Twentieth Army Corps at An-kara, who arrived accompanied by Rauf Bey, who had resigned from his post as Minister for the Navy since the fall of the Izzet Paşa's Cabinet in November 8th, 1918, and wished to join the nationalist cause; also there was Colonel Refet, re-cently appointed Commander of the Third Army Corps in Sivas, who had sailed to Samsun with Kemal on board the 'Bandırma.' The four soldiers decided to op-pose the dismemberment of the country and Kemal insisted that it was necessary to convoke a national assembly in Sivas. He dictated to his aide-de-camp a note in which these decisions were recorded; Rauf and Ali Fuat were happy to sign the draft, but Colonel Refet refused. He said that he had not understood well the objective and the usefulness of calling such a congress; he saw in it the beginning of a state within the state. He mistrusted Kemal, as he was worried by Kemal's powerful spirit, and found it difficult to believe that he was disinterested. Kemal was upset by the mistrust shown by his comrade's attitude, and his lack of faith. He told this to Ali Fuat, who spoke seriously to Refet. The latter set forth his objections, then took the draft and signed it in an unintelligible fashion.

Generals Kâzım Karabekir and Mersinli Cemal, who was the Inspector of the Second Army in Konya, informed him of their agreement by telegram.

All the military and civil commanders of the country received invitations to the Congress of Sivas. It contained a well-defined plan; the nation was invited to send her representatives, through whom she would take her decisions. There was no place for parties in this assembly; it should represent the whole people. For the first time the basic principles of democracy were applied: the way was opened for the sovereignty of the people.

Kemal wrote many letters to several important people in Istanbul of patriotic opinions, giving a summary of his projects for saving the country through the efforts of its people.

A great step forward had been made. Kemal found, as he had expected, that the noble and brave soul of the Turks was ready for the greatest sacrifices for their country. Together they would perform deeds which would amaze the East and the whole world. It was true that Turkey's powerful enemies remained, with growing appetites, but who could stand against a nation which was demanding by every means its right to liberty and life?

Before the Congress of Sivas, a partial congress was to be held in the city of Erzurum.

From the Green River, it was a long and difficult succession of roads which Kemal had to follow before he could reach Erzurum, the Turkish city which was threatened with capture by the Armenians. Kemal had to make the journey, for his presence was needed at the preparations for the coming congress. The date of his journey was determined through special circumstances.

The national awakening and Kemal himself were to meet implacable enemies. The first of these was Ali Kemal, Minister of the Interior, an abject partisan of the Sultan. Through his position, he came to know of the relations which the Inspector-General was creating with the people and authorities, and he received complaints from the British High Commission on this score. The Minister began a tenacious struggle against Kemal. He was not powerful enough in Anatolia to have him arrested; he thought that it would be wiser for him to return to the capital on some pretext or other, and the Sultan agreed with his opinion. Ali Kemal's position as Minister of the Interior was becoming uncomfortable in the face of the growth of nationalism; his power was slipping from his hands. On the 23rd June he sent a circular telegram to the authorities throughout the country, in which he announced the dismissal of Kemal from all his powers.

Ali Kemal's telegram had some of the effect he intended; in some circles which were friendly to the government campaigns were begun against the Inspector-General. It was in Sivas, the city chosen by the nationalists as the site of the Congress which they had announced, that greater activity broke out. Posters appeared on walls of houses in the city, accusing Kemal of treachery and rebellion. The instigator of this movement was Colonel Ali Galip, recently appointed governor of Elazığ, and who happened to be passing through Sivas, accompanied by a small number of people whom he was appointing to posts in his administration. These companions tried to raise public opinion against Kemal, and the bright new governor himself incited his colleague in Sivas to use force against the pernicious person who was soon to arrive there, saying that he should arrest him and send him to Istanbul as a prisoner.

Kemal knew all about this, and decided to make a surprise arrival at Sivas, supported by mounted troops of the Fifth Division; in this way he would frustrate the plans of Galip and his followers and put an end to his hostile propaganda.

Sivas stands on a round plateau, surrounded by mountains which grow higher towards the East. In those mountains is born the Kızılırmak or Red River, which describes a wide curve before pouring its waters into the Black Sea. The poplar trees of Sivas surround the city with greenery, defending it like a wall against the dry plain; the houses are of kneaded clay, painted white. Many minarets rise towards the sky, most of them belong to the "medreses," or religious schools, for which that city was famous in Central Anatolia. The Blue Medrese, or Gök Medrese, which has been well preserved since the thirteenth century, is a building of mystic beauty; its monumental doorway, decorated with verses from the Koran and flanked by its two rose-coloured minarets, is a symbol of Moslem philosophy, elevated towards God. Sivas, a reserved and silent city, lived guarded by her mountains and her poplar trees, under the protection of her minarets in eternel prayer.

In such a place the news of the massacres in Smyrna seemed inconceivable, and raised the excitement of the inhabitants to fury. It was heard that the general who was giving his life for the defence of Turkey had arrived; no one failed to run to meet him and to declare their loyalty to him. Sivas was one day to become a historic name in the life of the new Turkey; a name disproportionately large for such a small town, huddled around the Kızılırmak.

At a farmstead which still exists in the neighborhood of Sivas, Kemal met one of his aides coming from the city, who told him of the situation. He also told him that the Governor, Reşit Paşa, had given him instructions to keep the Inspector-General at that place, in order to give time to organise his reception. Kemal very shrewdly suspected that probably they vere seeking time to prepare not a reception but an ambush for him, and decided to go on to Sivas immediately. Just as he was getting into his carriage, the Governor arrived in his. After the necessary greetings, the Governor asked Kemal whether he would not prefer to rest for a few moments; Kemal told him that he was not tired and immediately invited him to take a seat in his car at his side. The Vali (Governor) showed excessive modesty and could not make up his mind to accept such an honour; however, he could not convince the general, who saw that the person of the Governor would be the best shield he could have wished for. Together they entered the mystic city; the crowds received the patriot with delight.

Kemal immediately went to the Headquarters of the Third Army Corps and ordered Ali Galip and his men to be brought into his presence. He told them in plain language his opinion of them and their masters. Then accompanied by Rauf and other persons, he held a conference with the Vali, who promised complete loyalty to his cause and his full support at the approaching Congress which was to be held in the city.

They took to the road again, and the kilometres were counted in hundreds; the springs of the Red River were left far behind, but another current could be heard murmuring, that of the upper Euphrates, the Karasu, which Kemal's small party were crossing.

Whenever they stopped, Kemal spoke to the people who had gathered to hear him. How well he knew the heart of his humble compatriots, in those distant, almost unknown places! His words revived their faith and exalted their patriotism.

The countryside grew ever more fantastically-shaped, and awe-inspiring. The mountains curled like frightful waves in a sea of granite, and in the midst lay Erzurum, the fortress city, surrounded by mountains nearly three thousand metres high. Erzurum is a tragic city; the Romans named it Theodosiopolis, fortified it and made it into a bulwark against the invasion of the Eastern hordes; it was seized by the Seljuk Turks, and from then on was called Erzurum. Its later masters were Tamerlane who sacked it in 1387, then Mehmet in the fifteenth century; it was captured by the Persians and recaptured by the Ottomans. During the time of the Russian drive towards the Aegean, Russia seized the city on three occasions and thrice again had to give it up under the terms of treaties. The last of these was that of Brest-Litovsk in the collapse of the Empire of the Tsars.

When the Turkish forces retired within the 1914 frontiers under the Armistice of Mudros, three republics remained in Transcaucasia, - Armenia, Georgia and Azerbaijan. At the Paris peace conferences, Armenia claimed by virtue of her ancient and medieval history, and her preponderance of population, the annexation of the Eastern Turkish provinces and of Cilicia, which in the Middle Ages was called Little Armenia. Her arguments were not consistent, since in modern times there had never existed an Armenian majority in any of the regions which she claimed. The Turks in those provinces lived in continual anxiety; great or small, an Armenian state would be established there by the power of the Entente. There was also insistent talk of the creation of Kurdistan, under the protection of Great Britain, as was the Greek state of Pontus.

Kemal thought that since this area was in imminent danger of being separated from Turkey, it was urgent for him to go there and take some serious decisions; he had for some time been in contact with the leaders of the "Association for the Defence of the Rights of the Eastern Provinces."

Kemal entered the tragic city, whose solid walls and fortress still give no sense of security in comparison with the granite masses which surround it. The great majority of the population, which was less than forty thousand, came to meet Mustafa Kemal Paşa, who had made such a long journey to come to the defence of the endangered Turks; this man was speaking in a language until then never heard from the mouth of a ruler; he talked of the people, their ideas, their rights and their destiny, sought their approval, caused them to meet and give him their views.

News of the agitation in Anatolia reached Istanbul through hundreds of telegrams and reports, sent to the Sultan and the representatives of the Entente. The officers of the Control Commission announced that the situation was about to become dangerous; the various patriotic associations were joining together and everything pointed to the likelihood of their moving from words to deeds. One name was constantly repeated, Mustafa Kemal. The representative of the Sultan and Calif, a man in whom Great Britain trusted, was turning himself into the worst enemy of both, the head of the resistance movement.

Kemal was then invited to return to Istanbul. In Erzurum he received more categorical orders; he must put an end to his official functions. On the night of the 8th of July, after an excited telegraphic correspondence with the palace, Kemal's official mission was declared at an end. At the same time Kemal sent in his own resignation, not only from his task but from the army. Istanbul ordered the civil and military authorities to cut off all relations with Kemal, who had been expunged from the army lists.

The situation of the ex-general was critical: now that he had lost his official powers, and was in the situation of a rebel, would he not lose the support of the army and people? He would be persecuted by the Central Government, and so would all those who followed him; to pronounce in his favour was to follow his uncertain fortunes. Kemal was assured that the people would not desert him so long as he did not lose his love of his country and of freedom. What did the decrepit Damat Ferit, a man sold to the British, mean to him? He received support from the people and the authorities in Erzurum, and the echo of popular loyalty reached him from all over the country. The Sublime Porte too heard the voice of the people raised against it, and so did the allied authorities. From that moment the Turkish resistance movement could feel secure, but the Allies had confidence in their strength. When the Peace Commission gave its verdict and Turkey was dismembered as they expected, the armies which were charged with the realisation of that operation would smash through all opposition as through an insignificant thing, and force those fools to bite the dust. The national opinion worried the Sultan and his Grand Vezir much more. Fortunately, they thought, they could count on British support and it was ridiculous to be worried.

Kemal was occupied with the organisation of the Congress which was to be held at Erzurum, and at the same time took care to unite and bring the armed forces into harmony with the civilian movement, as this was of essential importance. Damat Ferit began to withdraw commands of troops from those soldiers whom he suspected of helping the revolutionary cause; reasons were found to call them to Istanbul, whence it was naturally difficult for them to escape. This happened to Mersinli Cemal, Inspector of the Second Army. Kemal sent his directives to all the military commanders; he established the principle that the national will was sovereign in the conduct of the destinies of the state and the nation, and that the army should be its docile servant.

The national forces, which had been formed with the object of defending the nation's independence, were there to defend it against any defects or interference.

On the 23rd July the Congress of the Eastern Provinces finally met in a modest school hall. This was the first step on the road to the new state of which Kemal had dreamed, of which he still did not speak, for the tradition of the Sultanate, glorious in its origins, and the Califate's halo of divinity were instititions venerated by the simple Turkish people. It was not wise to attack them; on the contrary, when occasion arose he spoke of them respectfully. The Sultan was another matter. He was not popular, and the sword of Osman had changed hands violently many a time.

Kemal was voted president of this memorable Congress in Erzurum. The delegates made a truly oriental picture, as many of them were dressed in ancestral fashion, wearing different costumes according to the regions which they represented. Kemal spoke to them in a language which was intelligible to all those turbanned and fez-capped personages, men little used to subtle speech. He set as objectives for the labours of the Congress the creation of an assembly which should rest upon the national will, and the constitution of a government deriving its power from that will. The turbans and fezzes nodded their approval at the words of this lean man with the pale and wasted features, but whose voice was firm and gaze penetrating. During the Congress sessions, the Minister of War ordered Kâzım Karabekir to dissolve this anticonstitutional meeting and arrest Kemal and the other organisers. The Commander of the Fifteenth Corps, loyal to his promise to Kemal, refused naturally to make even the slightest move against the nationalists. In every one of the orders which were disobeyed, Ferit's government lost part of the little prestige which it retained.

Two events, which were beyond the control of that Congress, happened to strengthen the will of its delegates and to make the decisions proposed by Kemal appear less audacious. The Imperial government was invited to send a delegation to Paris for the Peace Conference. The Grand Vezir felt proud of himself; the wise policies of the Sultan and himself were now giving fruit. They had succeeded in making the Powers deign to listen to them; little by little they would gain ground. On the other side, those madmen who were fomenting disturbances in Anatolia were only succeeding in discrediting the Empire in the eyes of the Supreme Council, just at the moment when it was beginning to show benevolence to Turkey after so many sacrifices.

Damat Ferit made a ceremonious journey to Paris and spoke before the Allies. He claimed that the blame for Turkey's entry into the war and the Armenian massacres belonged entirely to the leaders of the Committee of Union and Progress; he made an appeal to justice and to the noble Wilson principles; he asked that the Empire should receive back its old frontiers with the addition of some adjacent regions which were inhabited by Turks; he promised autonomy to the Arab provinces, and assured the delegates in high-sounding phrases that his country would in the future show itself worthy of European culture.

In his speech, the Grand Vezir employed all that small amount of tact which he was reckoned to possess, and showed that he was somewhat out of touch with the diplomatic questions which were determining the decisions of the conference like invisible puppet strings. Clemenceau was charged with answering him, and did so with alacrity. The Tiger sharpened his claws and made the first slash at the over-confident Turkish delegation. With biting irony he pointed out that there existed victors and vanquished; he then described the Turks as barbarians and destroyers, and congratulated the Grand Vezir for the desires he had expressed that his country might find a way of civilizing itself. The Empire had had its hearing, and the Turkish delegation again took the road to the Bosporus, disheartened.

Among the nationalists of Anatolia, Clemenceau's words sounded like the midday prayer, the prayer which is said for the dead, as if it had been pronounced over the corpse of the Ottoman Empire. There could be no doubt now that Kemal's words had been prophetic: "Only by its own will and energy can the independence of this nation be saved."

The second event was the Treaty of Versailles which was imposed on Germany. If such a powerful western nation could be treated in such a way, what fate could the other members of that alliance expect? On the 28th June 1919 the treaty was signed in the Gallery of Mirrors, depriving the Reich of all her colonies, reducing her European territory in size, forcing her to hand over astronomical sums of money as reparations, and forcing her to accept many other details, which in comparison with the other clauses were small. These precedents, which passed like birds of ill-omen across the skies of Turkey, encouraged the members of the Erzurum and Sivas Congresses to take practical decisions, which formed the foundations of the "National Pact." All the parts of the country which were included within the national frontiers formed an invisible whole. The national frontiers, in Europe, were those drawn after the Balkan wars; in the South, they included the areas occupied by the Turkish forces at the moment the armistice had been signed, while the eastern frontiers were those which existed before the war of 1877. The nation would defend itself against any foreign attack or intervention. In the event of the Central Government being incapable of assuring the country's independence a provisional government would be formed, whose members would be appointed by the National Assembly; if the assembly had not been convoked, the appointment would be made by the "Representative Committee." It was necessary that the national forces should begin action, and that the national will should exercise its sovereignty. The possibility of accepting a mandate or a protectorate was ruled out and finally, it was resolved to call a National Assembly immediately, which would assume the role of controller of the government's actions.

The decisions of the Congress of Erzurum, in which only the Eastern provinces were represented, were to be presented to the Congress of Sivas, which would be a National Congress, meeting some weeks later. The Erzurum declaration, in which could be seen the influence which Kemal exercised over the delegates, was made public not only throughout the country but also to foreign representatives.

Sultan Vahdettin, upon whom no attack had been made, but who had more than one reason to feel himself threatened, decided to change the direction of his policies. The Sultan's struggle against the nationalists began to become more virulent. The clever Vahdettin would leave no weapon unused; he decided to call parliamentary elections, for a parliament which would meet in Istanbul, beneath his control, so that the danger of a second government in Anatolia would disappear. He also, like his brother-in-law, wanted to suffocate the nationalist movement by the use of force, but he had no confidence in the loyalty of the army. He therefore secretly fomented the creation of armed groups who provoked disturbances in the neighborhood of the railway, and violence against the Christians, hoping through all this to discredit the nationalists in the eyes of the Allies and perhaps to obtain military help from the latter. Under Kemal's direction, the activity of 'these groups was neutralised as far as possible.

Vahdettin wished at all costs to prevent the Congress which had been announced from being held at Sivas; he found a valuable helper in Ali Galip, a strong supporter of his whom he had nominated governor of Elazığ. With the help of this man, and helped by some of the feudal lords of the area, descendants of the "Beys," he planned once and for all the extinction of this obsessive nationalism and the capture of its leaders, whom he would soon have swinging on the gibbet. Vahdettin dreamed of repeating the words pronounced by Vitellius, a few days after he had vanquished his predecessor, the Emperor Marcus Salvius Otho. Vitellius was touring the battle field in the company of his officers when some of them gave signs of being unable to stand the fetid smell exhaled by the still unburied corpses; the Emperor commented to them: "An enemy's corpse always smells sweet, especially if it is that of a compatriot."

Ali Galip promised the Kurdish tribes of the region even autonomy, in the name of the Sultan, on condition that they should assist him by falling upon Sivas in sufficient numbers and making prisoners of the Congress delegates. The Kurds agreed to serve the Commander of the Faithful on these conditions. The groups gathered around the city of Malatya, to the south of Sivas. Ali Galip was being advised by the British Major Noel, who had officially been sent to that area of Anatolia in order to find out the prevailing percentages of Turks, Armenians and Kurds. The representatives of France and Great Britain had made their own plans for some measures to intimidate the nationalists and prevent the meeting of the Congress, although they did not dare to put them into effect.

The election of delegates was slowed down somewhat by the actions of Istanbul. At the end of August it was learnt in Erzurum that the representatives of all parts of the country were already on their way, and that several of them had arrived at Sivas. Since it was necessary for the Eastern provinces to be adequately represented, in order to maintain the national character of the Congress, efforts were made to find representatives for them, but this presented difficulties. Since most of the delegates to the Erzurum Congress had returned to their far-off regions, it was decided that the "Representative Committee" which had arisen from the Erzurum Congress and of which Mustafa Kemal was president, should take this charge upon itself. Of the eight members of the Committee, only five were able to attend the approaching discussions in Sivas; these were, apart from Kemal and Rauf, Sheikh Fevzi, the religious leader Raif Efendi, and Bekir Sami, former governor of Beirut.

On the 29th of August, these delegates set out for Sivas by car together with a small escort. Before they arrived at the defiles of Erzincan, the party was informed by a picket of gendarmes commanded by a few officers, that the defiles had been occupied by the Kurds. To drive them out, reinforcements were necessary, and they had sent for these. All this went against Kemal's plans; he was expected in Sivas on the 2nd September, and if some inconvenient factor of this sort held him up for a few days, his reputation would be obscured and both the delegates themselves and all the supporters of his cause would fall into anxiety. Kemal did not believe that the road was held effectively, and even if it was, he decided to attempt to pass through it. He ordered one car to lead the way through, armed with machine-guns directed by men who were ready for anything; if the road was cut by the Kurds, they would have to leave their vehicles and fight a way through. Fortunately nothing happened; the Kurdish ambush turned out to be a mere threat, with which the circles friendly to the government had thought that they could detain the man whom they called the ringleader of the subversive movement.

Now that all the delegates had gathered in Sivas, the historic Congress opened on the 4th September. The meetings were held in the town lycee, a plain building surrounded by gardens. The hall where they deliberated was large, with six wide windows. At one end, under the arms of the Empire, stood the presidential tribune. Notable people of the town had sent rich carpets, which were decorating the walls of the hall.

The principal aim of Kemal, who had again been elected president, was to extend over the whole country the effect of the resolutions taken in Erzurum, and in this he succeeded. Greater strength was given to the "National Pact." It was given a new form, expressing open hostility to the Allies. The last part of the name of the "Association for the Defence of the Rights of the Eastern Provinces" was changed to that for "the Rights of Anatolia and Thrace." There were violent discussions on the advisability of asking for a North American mandate. Many delegates saw in that the only solution for their present difficulties, and against the terrible threats which were approaching; this idea had supporters even amongst Kemal's most important collaborators.

Kemal spared nothing of his abilities as an orator, his persuasive eloquence and his dexterity, to prevent the nationalist movement which had been begun with such sacrifices from being brought to nothing by the cowardly acceptance of a protectorate. At a heated point in the midst of the discussions, one of the speakers on the other side declared; "Let us accept the mandate in principle; we can discuss the conditions afterwards." There was heard again the opinion of the former Grand Vezir Izzet Paşa; according to him, the nation did not have the necessary strength to stand a new war; she should take refuge in the protection of the Powers, no matter what it cost. At last Kemal succeeded in having a proposal accepted, which would invite the government in Washington to send a delegation to Turkey, formed of Members of Congress, in order to study the country at close hand. In this way the imminent danger of a mandate was exorcised.

Discussions and political meetings were being held amongst the Congress delegates, some of them involving Kemal's closest friends; there was also present the monster envy, that evil counsellor which knows how to play upon the pride of men and undermine their noble feelings. It was to be the fate of Kemal, as of all those who attempt to achieve some great work and to bring about a higher mission, to entangle his feet in the morass of human wretchedness, calumny, jealousy, and ingratitude. What should he do? Should he linger among them or break through them? This is the moment when weak men are beaten; Kemal was strong and the nation demanded that he went forward. This he did, but with the shadow of sadness in his soul.

At Erzurum, some of the Congress delegates had privately expressed an opinion that it was above all important to show the nation and even more so to show the foreigners, that the revolutionary movement was essentially a national one; however, if Kemal appeared always at the head of the movement, being a man who was in a state of rebellion against the government, the movement might begin to seem a personal affair. An attempt was made to remove Kemal from the Representative Committee, the argument being that the delegates should have been chosen in the. provinces which they represented, and that he had not so been in any province. At Sivas, Rauf, Bekir Sami and other persons decided to oppose the reelection of the former general to the presidency. Kemal knew of this, but he was not prepared to let it influence him or divert him from his course. Everything pointed to him as the man who could unite the forces of all, and if he was going to have to wait at every step to submit himself to other people's opinions, many of which were dictated by some feeling quite apart from the welfare of the country, his strength would be lost amid Byzantine discussions and useless theorisations. In his book of "Speeches," Kemal has defined his concept of the leader; "History shows us irrefutably that for great tasks, the presence of a leader of great ability and inflexible energy is a sine qua non condition of success."

The majority always gave him his vote of confidence, and the people gave their support. After all, what other man was there to be seen in Turkey, who could have been able to achieve Kemal's historic work through all its stages? No rival can stand cool comparison with him.

As the Congress sessions proceeded, information arrived that groups of Kurds and gendarmerie forces which were loyal to the government were gathering themselves to surprise the assembly and capture the delegates. Thanks to his prestige as leader, Kemal was able to calm their justifiable nervousness. He took charge of directing the operations against these groups, but without appearing to give great importance to the question.

None the less, the President of the Congress felt some anxiety; he was not only worried about the activities of Ali Galip, Major Noel, and the Kurdish bands, but by the fact that the military commanders of the area were not making up their minds, and were holding back from crushing the Malatya conspiracy, fearing to commit themselves. The commander of the regiment at Malatya said he had insufficient forces; the regiments which were stationed in nearby areas did not get from their commanders the order to march upon Malatya, although Kemal insistently asked for this to be given. Finally on the 9th of September, some cavalry detachments began to move towards the city. At their approach, the commander of Malatya decided to arrest the individuals in question. They heard of his intention and fled.

Ali Galip was fortunate enough to be able to reach territory occupied by the Allies, but he was unable to destroy his private records, which were sent to Kemal. Kemal was thus able to prove that directly behind this incident were the Sultan, the Grand Vezir and the foreign Commissioners.

Kemal directed the general indignation against the cabinet of Damat Ferit, which was the cause of these intrigues, which could well be called criminal, against the victory of the nationalist movement. The Grand Vezir was playing his own game without keeping the Sultan informed of the true situation. By avoiding attacks on the Padişah, Kemal was trying to avoid giving nationalism an antimonarchical character. There were elements in the country who would be offended by such a tendency, and prudence is an important factor, which Kemal did not despise.

The Sivas Congress adopted some well-defined decisions; it had seven days of labour, discussion, fears, all of which were dominated by the willpower and faith of its President. On the day that the Congress closed, Kemal sent to the Ministry of the Interior a telegram containing amongst others the following harsh words: "It is time for you to react. Do not forget that the nation will take account of the responsibilities which you are incurring, when it pronounces judgement on the infamy you are committing by selling your consciences to foreigners, who are the enemies of our country."

Kemal decided to base his campaign against the cabinet on speaking directly and exclusively to the Padişah, so that the latter would withdraw his confidence from Damat Ferit. In the name of the Sivas Congress he demanded the dismissal of the Grand Vezir. Damat Ferit defended himself, by ordering that the telegrams addressed to the Sultan should previously pass through his own office. This could not prevent a revival of the telegraph warfare being conducted from Sivas.

On the day after the closure of the Congress, the Representative Committee sent an ultimatum to the Sublime Porte: if communications with the palace were not reestablished, all communications between the provinces and the capital would be broken off. When the period of grace expired without them receiving any reply, the Representative Committee gave instructions to the civil and military authorities that they should neither receive nor transmit correspondence or news from Istanbul. The telegraph offices in Anatolia were put under military occupation, the lines which were not controlled by the nationalists were cut, and those functionaries who resisted the orders of Sivas were dismissed from their jobs. In a short time Istanbul became completely isolated.

Since the country could not be left without a government, the Representative Committee took provisional executive power, as had been anticipated, with the authority of the Sivas Congress, Kemal published the resolutions they had taken on the night of the 13th September, and submitted them to the judgement of the military and civil authorities; their substance was, after expressing loyalty to the Sultan, that the affairs of state would continue to be administered in conformity with the prevailing laws, and in the name of His Imperial Majesty, until such time as the wishes of the nation could reach their sovereign, and it was possible to form a government worthy of the national trust.

This proposal brought Kemal violent criticism, which he received directly by telegram. It was not that his critics disagreed with the breaking of communications with Istanbul, or with the formation of a provisional government; it was Kemal that they were attacking. Nevertheless, the decisions which he had been offered for consultation were sent out again as ordinances. As President of the Committee, Kemal became de facto head of the nation. Political jealousy could be seen now amongst Kemal's own supporters; it was murmured that this dynamic general was an ambitious and authoritarian man who aspired to power, to be the master. Would he not be a new Enver? Kemal was a good psychologist, and soon understood these worries and envies; he hurriedly calmed them down, making them see that the present objective was to force the Sultan to get rid of Damat Ferit and entrust the task of forming a government and calling elections to an honourable person.

In Istanbul, the Padişah, Grand Vezir, cabinet, court and foreign circles were in a chaotic confusion. It was clear that the nation was responding to the call of nationalism. Vahdettin, abandoned by his people and his army, turned to the representative of Great Britain, who were expecting him to sign the treaty by which he would accept the British mandate and place his spiritual influence as Commander of the Faithful at the service of that Power, the leading oppressor of Moslems; in compensation for this, his throne would be guaranteed to him. That was all the Sultan wanted, and at his brother-in-law's advice, he signed the secret treaty on the 12th of September. Lloyd George believed that he had fished prosperously in the turbulent river of the moribund Empire.

After his double treachery to his country and his religion, Vahdettin felt happier. The British representatives told him that they were ready to use force for the compliance with the new treaty, but they advised prudence and cleverness as better cards to play. Why not agree to appoint a new Grand Vezir? Why not call elections? If he opposed the Committee of Sivas, he would only strengthen it. It was better to give way, legitimise the revolutionary movement, convert it into a political party, and make it parliamentary and constitutional. No one was attacking the glorious Calif; the hatred was all directed at Damat Ferit.

Vahdettin listened to all this with his eyes shut as always and with his marked expression of fatigue. As he saw it, Great Britain did not want to interfere directly in the Empire's internal politics; it would therefore be a good idea to follow her advice. He decided to dispense with the services of his brother-in-law, but before that he made some tentative approaches of reconciliation with Sivas, not so much in order to save Ferit but to preserve the principle of his authority. An emissary of his was able to talk to Kemal. The man chosen was Abdülkerim Paşa, one of Kemal's old comrades. He was known to be a member of a religious sect, and that he attended certain "tekkes," dervish convents, giving himself the titles of "Great Excellence" and "Sublime Excellence," taken from Moslem mysticism. He also gave pompous names to his friends, according to the merits which he discovered in them. He called Kemal" The Pole of Poles."

Kemal agreed to exchange ideas with this man and they maintained a telegraphic conversation more than eight hours long. In his bombastic and picturesque style, His Great Excellence did all he could to reach an agreement, but the points which had been the reason for the rupture remained unsolved.

There was no other remedy but to ask Damat Ferit to resign, leaving him disillusioned about Great Britain and the Sultan, who had both abandoned him in this way because he was no longer any use to them.

From the day on which the country began to be ruled by the Representative Committee, of which Mustafa Kemal was the spirit, he had to endure acts of disobedience and attacks from the nationalists themselves, frustrate the plans and counter propaganda of the Central Government, direct the struggle against foreigners and administer the country.

It was an incomprehensible error of General Kâzım Karabekir to allow the publication of the Sultan's manifesto, some days after the relations with the government had been broken off. The manifesto showed the situation of Turkey vis-à-vis the Powers of the Entente in an optimistic light, while condemning as extremely harmful to the country rumors which were current abroad of discord between the people and the government. One can imagine that it was easy for this string of baseless fantasies to disturb the naive mentality of some of the population.

The best retort against the Imperial manifesto was to be the peace treaty which was going to be imposed on the Empire. Kemal's intelligence, with its marvellously wide understanding, always succeeded in penetrating the future. Some have seen him as a visionary, but he was quite the opposite. His ideas were born from his knowledge of history and mankind, and he deepened them by hard examinations; there never escaped him even the smallest factor which could cause the unexpected, which had caused the miscarriage of great enterprises, defeats where no one expected anything but success, and the fall of empires. Whenever Kemal wanted to take a decision or to consider the possible development of some event which was preoccupying him, he would first inform himself, and when he felt that he had a clear idea, he would not adopt it until he had met with people who in his judgement had the capacity to understand the case. He set out his point of view, discussed it, learned the ideas of all the others, and if it seemed logical to him corrected his first notion and reiterated it. He placed great value on constructive criticism and long conversations with men of ability. His genius was founded upon logic, analysis and understanding. These conversations were useful to him, because they polished his own ideas. He preferred this method to solitary meditation. It was one of the methods he used to bring himself closer to the people, and to remain in contact with the nation.

The large numbers of detachments of foreign troops stationed at strategic points, on the Straits and on the railway to Syria for the most part, and the growing hatred of the Turks towards the Allies, which was increased by the Greek invasion, remained a delicate problem for the Sivas Congress, since a clash, whether provoked or not, could arouse complications. That was exactly what Ferit wanted, and he sent armed groups to Anatolia with the intention of starting some conflagration, but the vigilance of the national forces prevented any disagreeable consequences.

One incident did occur in the time between the break with the government and Ferit's dismissal, but it was provoked by the British. General Solly Flood, Commander of the British forces in Eskişehir had Atıf Bey, the Commander of the nationalist forces in the same region, arrested. Sivas protested, and there was great public indignation; were the British now involving themselves with Turkish politics, despite their declarations? Kemal took energetic measures against the protectors of Ferit, natural enemies of his country; he had to make well-understood the difference between the Turkish people, which was ready to make the greatest sacrifices to retain its dignity, and the other Moslem peoples, who were the slaves of Great Britain.

The Turkish forces advanced towards Eskişehir and occupied positions in the outskirts of the city. The British general tried to excuse himself and assured the Turkish commander that the British had no intention of involving themselves with the internal affairs of Turkey. This was disproved some months afterwards.

The nationalist movement now held the attention of the civilized world; Journalists and important people from the West had made the journey to Sivas, in order to write down their conclusions about this revolution which was different from all the others which had boiled up during the evil days of countries beaten in the last war. It had no point of contact with Communism, which had been the inspiration for the revolutions in Russia, Germany and Hungary. It was a revolution that was perfectly described by the word "Nationalist."

There arrived at Sivas in that month of September an important American mission, led by General Harbord, which was making studies in Anatolia. The American general and the Paşa had a long and interesting interview. "The Paşa" was the name by which Kemal was now universally known. There were an enormous number of Paşas in Turkey, for the word was applied to generals, and was also given as an honorific title to civilians. But when "The Paşa" was spoken of, it was understood to refer to Kemal. Kemal explained to General Harbord the essential causes which had brought about the creation of the nationalist movement. Harbord asked him a question which went deep: "Suppose that after all your efforts and after every imaginable sacrifice, you are defeated-what will you do then?" The Paşa replied: "A people which expends all its efforts and every imaginable sacrifice in order to ensure its freedom and independence cannot see its wishes frustrated. That would mean admitting that that people was already dead. For that reason, one cannot speak of defeat whilst a people is alive and ready for every sacrifice." General Harbord left that interview convinced that with a commander like that, the Turkish people would achieve great things.

CHAPTER 16

THE DEFENCE

On the 2nd of October General Ali Rıza formed a new cabinet, which would take over the reins of government if the nationalists approved of it. Ali Rıza was a man of advanced age, a stranger to politics and apparently of danger to no one; he was charged with the task of reconciling Sivas with Istanbul. In his cabinet there appeared some of those who had worked with Damat Ferit; the Ministry of the Interior was entrusted to another relative of the Sultan, Damat Şerif, while the Ministry of War was given to Mersinli Cemal Paşa, who was considered to favour nationalism. When Kemal learnt the name of the new Grand Vezir, he announced it to the nation, at the same time laying down three fundamental points which were necessary before he could recognise him: these were that the government should respect the organisation of the Congresses of Erzurum and Sivas and the objectives established by them; that no binding decision should be taken until Parliament had met; and that the delegates who were to be sent to the Peace Conference should be men who were aware of what the nation desired. All this he also communicated to the Grand Vezir by telegram.

Kemal had a long correspondence with the new cabinet, and found himself opposed by its ill will. The old tricks of the discredited Sublime Porte had once more been put into practice. Some days later the delegates in Sivas discovered that a double game was being played; this was not exactly the policy which was required by the grave situation in which the Empire was, since it was already near the condemned cell, for the masters of the peace were quietly preparing to pass sentence upon it.

The Grand Vezir first showed his indecision in the reply he sent to Kemal's telegram; His Highness was busy, and had to attend the palace in order to take the customary oath, so that he would answer on the following day. In place of the reply which had been promised, Kemal received a surprising telegram: "The Council of Ministers does not know the nature of the organisation of the Congresses of Erzurum and Sivas, or the objectives they have agreed upon." This was absurd, since the aspirations of the nationalists, which had after all caused the fall of the previous cabinet, must have been perfectly well-known.

Kemal saw in this reply a stratagem by the palace to avoid committing itself; however, reacting as if the affair was completely logical, he sent that same day a copy of the manifesto of the Sivas Congress to the Grand Vezir. The expected reply was received quickly, but it came without indication of the addressee or any signature; it only stated at the end: "Grand Vezir's Office." It then became clear that the cabinet was not agreeable to entering into official relations with the Representative Committee. In his telegram the Grand Vezir declared that he found the aspirations of the nationalists perfectly natural and gave to understand, with a trace of irony, that they were no different from those of the Imperial Government. When he heard of the way in which Ali Rıza's cabinet was facing the situation, Kemal lost all hope that it could achieve any useful work; either it had no real knowledge of the situation or it was a mere tool of the palace, the ultraconservative party and the foreigners. Kemal's brow darkened, not because of the empty threats based on a complete absence of strength, with which the new government was attempting to set itself up as the enemy of the people, but because he realised that when the Turkish people met their enemies they would find them elevated into the position of judges, and themselves weighed down by a ballast which would make it hard for them to remain afloat. This consisted of the Sultan and his government, who were disposed to show themselves compliant, and accept the most disgraceful conditions of peace in the nation's name.

The Minister Damat Şerif began his work in a way which showed his hostility to Kemalism. His first circular set forth principles similar to those expressed by the Grand Vezir; he said that he had detected symptoms of discord in the interior of the country, which could have no other result than to increase the difficulties through which the Empire was passing, and this was, he said, a matter for great grief. Kemal now knew the true worth of this cabinet, and decided that it was better to endure it until the elections were held, when the party which obtained the majority would take over the government, as happens in those countries which give some value to national opinion. However, relations with the capital could not be reopened so long as Ali Rıza failed to recognise openly the aspirations of the revolutionary movement. By the 7th October Ali Rıza had realised that he could not govern without public support, but his olympic pride did not allow him to submit personally to the necessity of this truth, and he charged his Minister of War Mersinli Cemal to accept the conditions.

Kemal immediately sent a favourable reply, and the restrictive measures which he had imposed were abolished. Despite this, the general situation continued to be extremely delicate because of the way in which the cabinet acted, and its lack of resolve; the influence of the foreigners and the Sultan could be seen, as the government delayed in making up its mind to accept the decisions of Erzurum and Sivas. The cabinet claimed that the Representative Committee should be dissolved, on the grounds that its mission had ended now that it had recognised the Central Government, and that that was the only government which should exist. Kemal agreed with that, but he did not find it sufficient reason for the dissolution of the Committee, which represented a national association which from henceforth would operate like any other political party; it would confine itself to watching the actions of the government, and would prepare itself to take part in the parliamentary elections. Neither did he agree to the dissolution of the organisations for defence.

After a long correspondence between the cabinet and Sivas which led to no agreement, the cabinet decided to send Salih Paşa, Minister of the Navy, to Anatolia to talk to Kemal. The two men met at Amasya on the 19th October 1919 and began their discussions on the following day. After three days they agreed upon a plan in which the national wishes were clearly stated; much of the sting had been taken out of the discussions by the fact that the elections had already been announced. This amounted to the acceptance of Kemal's proposals, his "Delenda Carthago," which had been approved by the Congress of Sivas, as the bases for the protocols signed in Amasya.

At the same time Kemal obtained a promise that the Parliament would not meet in Istanbul.

Kemal considered it particularly important that Parliament should meet in a city safe in Anatolia; however this went completely against the wishes of Vahdettin, and more so than Kemal could have imagined, since he did not know that the Sultan had made a secret pact with the British. The Sultan realised that the rebellious Kemal had discovered his trick, and that he would not be able to bring the nationalist ringleaders within his grasp. Yet the Padişah believed that his cleverness would win the day in the last resort, and if it did not, his ally would lend him strength.

The Imperial Cabinet and Court had made a truce with the Kemalists, by which name the revolutionaries were beginning to be called, but it was a truce which would only lead to new clashes. The sides began their election campaign. The government's party was called "the Liberal Entente" (Hürriyet ve İtilâf), and among its ranks could be found all the enemies of Kemalism, members of the court, aged generals, traditionalists, ultraconservatives, the clerics, all of them protected by the Sultan, and forming an alliance with the Friends of Britain. The important issue of the place where Parliament was to meet, on which Salih Paşa had promised to persuade his colleagues to accept the proposal made by Kemal, led to a long struggle in which the Paşa was defeated, since many of his fellow soldiers and sympathisers of the revolutionary movement failed to understand exactly why he was insisting upon it, and took the other side. They were soon to receive a new proof that the Paşa's reasoning had been sound.

Despite the confident arguments defended by important members of the nationalist movement, Kemal's opinion remained unchanged; he saw only too clearly how little the new Parliament would be worth in the corrupt environment of the capital, where it could be threatened by the cannons of the enemy fleets, and the armies of occupation.

Meanwhile the elections took place normally. When the votes were counted the nationalists had a large majority, and Kemal, Rauf, Bekir Sami and other leaders were elected Members of Parliament.

The Paşa set about persuading them to accept some preliminary precautionary measures; for example, the nationalist members were to meet in groups in certain cities before going to the capital, in order to reach agreement amongst themselves to form a powerful bloc in Parliament, which would be capable of defending their wishes there; the Committee would go on doing its job until the Members declared, after Parliament had met, that they were exercising their mandate in complete freedom; if the Peace Conference reached a decision which was contrary to national aspirations, and this were approved by the Government and Parliament, these would be set aside, and with the support of the national will the Committee would seek ways of defending the principles established at the Erzurum and Sivas Congresses.

There was another task of even greater importance to which Kemal was devoting himself with an energy and tenacity unusual even for him: the creation of strength. The word "strength" was to be seen at the root of his programme. Without it the whole edifice would collapse. Kemal's spirit was not fed by illusions, hopes, or mysticism: his thirst was for realities.

The results of Wilson's idealism and the justice of those who set about reforming the world, and who in the name of peace were preparing wars for the future, had already been seen at the Palace of Versailles and the Château of Saint Germain. By some diplomatic acrobatics, the same principles which they had defended, such as the right of each nation to be the master of its own destiny, had come to serve the opposite argument, to the benefit, naturally enough, of the special interests of the victors. It would soon be the Ottoman Empire's turn to be presented before this last judgement, but it could already be seen that it would be dismembered.

Turkey had to realise that if any salvation was possible for her, it had to be based on strength. Kemal trusted the unselfishness of his people, who needed to be organised and armed. Everything was lacking, and the army could be said to exist only in name, but the Paşa thought himself inspired by an inflexible determination. He would create the strength which was indispensable for the presentation of Turkey's rights. Since his arrival in Anatolia he had lost no opportunity of preventing the dispersal of the army, and encouraging in every way the creation of volunteer groups.

The Smyrna front was being held by volunteers commanded by disbanded officers and civilians with experience of fighting; the resistance would achieve other proportions if it were directed by a commander on the orders of the nationalist congresses.

A serious problem had arisen after a new flare-up in the south, in Turkish Cilicia. France and Great Britain, who had not yet definitely decided upon their respective inheritances from the Empire, had reached an agreement about the territories inhabited by Arabs, and Cilicia, the historical name for the provinces in southern Anatolia bordering on the Gulf of Alexandretta. In the middle of 1919, the British troops were relieved by French forces, and Syria and the Turkish provinces included in the designation of Cilicia remained under French influence. Since the French occupation forces in these provinces were not of sufficient numbers, their commanders armed groups of Armenians. Besides, in the French army there were Legion Etrangerè regiments recruited from the Armenian population. This awoke ancient hatreds, incidents became frequent and the anger of the Moslem population produced reactions against the French and their helpers. Once diplomatic representations had been exhausted, Kemal decided to undertake military action. He entrusted some officers whose energy and capacity he knew with the task of organising nationalist forces and moving into the attack. The French oppression was met by force, and her troops found themselves roughly handled along the extended front which they were aspiring to make into a definite boundary, on the grounds that Mr. Lloyd George and M. Clemenceau had thus disposed.

Hardly a year had passed since the armistice with Imperial Germany in November 1918, when France saw her soldiers once again falling on the field of battle, struggling against the same adversaries as she had met in the recent tragedy. Her leaders had been seized with the fever of Imperialism; they seemed to have forgotten the horrors of the invasion which their own country had suffered, since it was now they themselves who were the invaders, and hoping to conquer the land of others. The Turks were giving up the immense regions south of Anatolia without a protest, and confining their ambitions to the nucleus where their own nation predominated, desiring to live in peace. It is a fact that the war of 1914 failed to leave upon the human race, in the midst of its disasters, those spiritual benefits which throughout the succeeding centuries have been laid down upon the consciousness of civilisations by great battles and calamities, and which have caused war to be counted as a decisive factor in their evolution. The war which had just ended was sterile, and European civilisation took no lesson from it. After so many years of sacrifices and pain, the human race remained in a worse moral condition than before, awaiting some new chaos from which illumination might emerge.

One can easily imagine the emotions raised amongst the diplomats who met in Paris, at the Sublime Porte, and in the Imperial Palace at the news of the resumption of hostilities. In all these places the rebellious general was called a madman; the Allies would claim that this affront to the victors would justify them in thrusting their hands into Turkey's very entrails, while the Turks who were opposed to Kemalism thought that they would soon see the moment when they would be rid of Kemal, since the Powers would take measures against him, and the people, who now listened to him as if he were a prophet, would realise the error into which they had fallen.

As for the Turkish people, they realised that the hour for great sacrifices was approaching; they were ready, and turned their eyes upon Kemal; he knew the state of their minds, and had therefore thrown down the first card upon the table of destiny.

The opinion which prevailed was that Parliament should meet in the capital. Kemal did not lose heart from this; as a staunch defender of the nationalists' aims, he decided to go to one of the towns where the members were to gather before leaving for Istanbul, in order to give his instructions to them verbally. It was necessary to move the headquarters of the Representative Committee to a town nearer to the capital than was Sivas, and which had quicker communications than that city. Another important reason was that he wished to be nearer the western and southern fronts, and to give more efficient directions to the war operations, whose future size it was difficult to see. The town of Ankara seemed on all counts to be the place most appropriate to lodge the directing centre of nationalism.

The Paşa set off by car on the third stage of his progress from East to West, along the route of the sun, followed by the Turkish migrations. Sivas disappeared behind a curtain of mountains, but the Red River accompanied the traveller for a long stretch. The poplars whose shade refreshed the white city through the long summer, and which on that winter day were shivering with the cold, maintained their usual appearance. The minarets remained in their ecstasies, the Blue Medrese showed as always its poetic beauty. Physically Sivas was unchanged, but her name and its meaning were now gigantic, as was the conception which there affirmed the destinies of a people.

The principal stage on Kemal's route to Ankara was Kayseri. Kayseri is the Turkish name for Caesarea, an important centre of Cappadocia, which is situated on the plateau more than a thousand metres above sea level. The town seems crushed by the proximity of Mount Erciyas-Argaeus, a colossal pyramid four times higher than the plateau. Some flattish and bare hills of an infinitely sad appearance surround the city, which is built with the same grey stone, as are also its walls and its castle.

In Kayseri it is the mystic art of the Seljuks which predominates, and has frozen in stone its whole religious fervour in the mosques, mausolea and medreses. Religion also ruled its earlier civilisations; by a kind of mimicry, the serene and forceful character of St. Basil, father of the Greek Church, was formed by his childish contact with that desert of stone. In the undulations of those arid hills, pushing and climbing one upon another in their longing to reach the giant extinct volcano, the Saint must have seen the spiritual march of civilisations towards Him who has always been, and whose love created the worlds.

When Kayseri was the capital of the Kingdom of Cappadocia, it was called Mazaca. The Romans took control of it in the year 18, under Caesar Tiberius, and from then onwards the city was called Caesarea. Many centuries later, the Seljuk Turks established themselves there and constructed beautiful buildings, including the Mosque of Huant, which dates from the fourteenth century and is a building of sober and elegant proportions. Kayseri was destroyed by an earthquake; one can visit its ruins, which lie half a kilometre west of the present city, on the road leading to the lake and the marshes.

Nothing could equal the sadness produced by these ruins, as one thinks of the love, happiness, plans, frustrations and grief which filled them along with music and mourning. Today it is only the wind which brushes past the fallen walls and solitary columns. Among these skeletons of stone one cannot even pick out the remains of that palace where Nicephorus Phocas first put on the red boots of the Byzantine Emperors, embroidered with two-headed eagles. The new Ottoman city, surrounded by cemeteries, was concentrated near the castle, the bazaars, the dervish convents and the caravanserais; slow caravans wended their way through its narrow streets. The thousand- year-old city now had a new memory worthy of history. When Mustafa Kemal went from Sivas to Ankara in the first stages of his effort for the salvation of Turkey, he stopped in Kayseri, where the people expressed their enthusiasm to him, so that he went on his way with renewed faith.

CHAPTER 17

ANKARA

The peninsula of Anatolia, also known as Asia Minor, is the bridge which unites Asia and Europe. The plateaus of Tibet, the Pamirs, Afghanistan, Iran and Anatolia follow each other to form one huge mountain system. Three-quarters of Anatolia are covered by great plateaus, those of Central Anatolia reaching an average height of eight hundred metres, and those of Eastern Anatolia over 1500. Each of the plateaus is surrounded by chains of high mountains, which prevent the clouds formed by the evaporation of the surrounding seas, the Black Sea, Marmara, Aegean and Mediterranean, from bringing in their life-giving water. The climate of Anatolia is therefore continental, in spite of its proximity to seas.

On the Aegean side, the plateau breaks up and loses height; the climate of this region is maritime. In the opposite direction the plateaus climb like the steps of a ladder as far as Ararat, 5200 metres high, summit of the mountain massif of Eastern Anatolia. Although the plateaus are generally arid, Anatolia still has fertile lands on her outer slopes, and prolific vegetation grows along the whole coast and in the Aegean region. Great rivers, which are born on the plateaus or in the mountains which cut through them in every direction, laboriously seek their way out to the sea, which they reach only after beating against a thousand obstacles and being forced to follow innumerable meanderings. Two biblical rivers run into the Persian Gulf, the Euphrates and the Tigris; the Black Sea receives the Çoruh the Yeşilırmak and the Kızılırmak, in antiquity known as the Iris and the Halys, and the Sakarya; to the Aegean there flow the Gediz (Hermus) and the Lesser and Greater Meander; in the Mediterranean there die the Seyhan and Ceyhan, formerly the Sarus and Pyramus.

The land of Anatolia is richer in historical events than any other area of the East. It was the cradle of brilliant civilisations, and it was crossed by many migrations and enormous armies; many times it was reddened by the blood of warriors, and it contains a high percentage of human ashes. That grey steppe, like some stone idol of Baal, remains unchangeable and undismayed. Since the end of the quaternary period, during which it suffered dreadful convulsions, it has seen generations disappear and has lost count of them; it has seen the creation of kingdoms and empires and seen them go; religions too have followed each other, offering consolations to the suffering.

The first people of whom we have knowledge, who established themselves in Anatolia in the postglacial epoch, were men whose characteristics suggest that they came from Central Asia. They had noticeable cultural affinities with the Sumerians, the first inhabitants of Lower Mesopotamia. In the postglacial period, the Sumerians left Central Asia, since its climate had seriously altered, turning what had been fertile areas into desert. The cause for the migrations of the Sumerians and the Hittites, who crossed the Caucasus to arrive at Lower Mesopotamia and Anatolia respectively, was the same as that of the Semites, who starting from a different place converged generally towards Mount Ararat; this reason was climatic change.

The Sumerians originated the civilisation of Babylonia, and stopped moving southwards between fiftieth and sixtieth centuries B. C., at the same time changing from a hunting and nomadic way of life to that of agriculture and pasturage. It was at about the same time that the Hittites did the same, following the sun on their migration.

We have no knowledge of the civilisation of the Hittites, who are mentioned in the Bible under the name of Heth, until the year 2700 B. C. They prospered from that date until a thousand years later, when their greatest period began. The plateaus of Central Anatolia saw the flowering of the Hittite Empire, beside which the civilisations of Mesopotamia paled, and the peoples who inhabited the Aegean coast, the Greek peninsula and the island of Cyprus appeared primitive.

The chief divinity of the creators of Anatolia's most ancient civilisation was the mother-goddess Ma; her special rites were in the hands of eunuch priests and priestesses. Tashkhil was the divine protectress of the mountains. The Hittites gave special reverence to the solar divinity Arnena, and to the gods of the sky, the earth, the great sea, the wind and storms, the god Kilpantiris, the goddess Kauka, and Teshub, god of war.

The majority of the peoples inhabiting the Aegean at that time, which corresponds to the first period of Cretan or Minoan civilisation between the thirtieth and twenty-second centuries B. C., were of Asiatic origin, as can be seen from the similarities in style and form which are shown by their pottery and those found in Anatolia. The very gods who were worshipped under the Minoan civilisation, which is known to have been the precursor of the Mycenaean, in turn the origin of Greek civilisation, were of Anatolian, Hittite origin. Beyond the ritual figures on the Cretan monuments, we can see an analogy with the religion based on a female divinity representing nature or the earth. The Hittite mother goddess Ma became later Cybele, who was for the Greeks goddess of the earth; the god of the double axe, the Asiatic Teshub, was the Cretan Zeus, who was given the epithet of Labrandeus, a word derived from "labrys" or "axe." From language and other essential features, there can be ascertained not only influence but also racial affinity between the peoples of the Aegean and those who migrated from Central Asia towards the West.

Teshub was to eclipse the thousand gods of the Hittite pantheon, and lead his people to the conquest of the greater part of the known world. In the eighteenth century they made war against the Semites; up to the decay of the first Babylonian Empire, the Hittites had been vassals of many Semite kingdoms. Now the Hittites not only gained their independence, but by subduing all the peoples of Anatolia and Mesopotamia, established their own Empire. Mursil I was one of the most glorious Kings of the Hittite dynasties, and it was he who seized Babylonia. The Babylonian histories make mention of the Hittites on that occasion. However the city of Babylon did not attract them to move their capital there, nor were they seduced by the fertility of Mesopotamia; they preferred the hard work of the land, and the biting wind of their plateaus, back in the heart of Anatolia. They founded their metropolis, called Hattusas, near the present-day Kızılırmak in the middle of the plateau.

The archaeologists Macridi Bey and Hugo Winckler have found very important remains of solid walls, palaces, temples, sculptures, reliefs and inscriptions left by the Hittites in many places of Anatolia, in Malatya, Zincirli, and especially in the lost city of Hattusas, near the Turkish village of Boğazköy.

In spite of the civilisations which have followed each other in Anatolia, the Hittites still maintain their place as the first civilisation of the Aegean world, thanks to their stone monuments, without even considering their literature. In the citadel of Hattusas, which was a true acropolis, there were found thousands of tablets engraved in cuneiform characters in the Hittite and Babylonian languages. From all these discoveries, found between 1905 and 1908, there was formed an archive which was moved to the Istanbul museum, and which on decipherment threw a clear light upon the history of the great Hittite nation.

The Hittite Empire continually expanded further from Hattusas, taking a large part of Syria and capturing Babylon in the middle of the sixteenth century. In Syria the Hittites were faced by another powerful nation, the Egyptians, and the great conqueror, the Pharaoh Thutmoses III, the most famous King of the eighteenth dynasty. When this King came to power at the beginning of that century, his first task was the total expulsion of the Shepherd Kings, who had ruled

Egypt for five centuries. He then sought possession of Syria, taking it from the Hittites of Kadesh, but to achieve this he needed to make fifteen campaigns.

These episodes speak for themselves of the strength with which the Hittites were organised. The booty which the seventy-year-old Pharaoh captured in the city of Kadesh, today Ain Kadis, amazed him for its richness and artistic value. In the fifteenth and part of the fourteenth centuries, the power of Hattusas was reduced by a rival. This was the Empire of Mitanni, which arose in northern Mesopotamia. However, in 1380 there ascended the Hittite throne the notable administrator and valiant warrior Shubbiluliuma, who caused the arts and sciences to flourish and forced the proud Mitannians to obey him. He was known as the Great King. Moved by ancestral hatred of the Pharaohs, he offered sacrifices to the God Teshub and gathered a mighty army. There was now no room for the glory of both nations under the Sun-God Arnena.

The Pharaohs feared him. As an offer of friendship they proposed to marry Queen Ankhsenpaaten, widow of Tutankhamun, to a Hittite Prince. The King agreed to conclude a treaty, which is the first of its kind known in history.

The war between these mortal enemies was to be revived. Ramses II, the last great Pharaoh, wished to eclipse the glory of his predecessors on the field of battle, and threw himself into the conquest of Syria. He met the army of Mursil II in the valley of the River Orontes. It was Mursil who tasted the sadness of defeat, and returned to Hattusas, where he died of grief, while Ramses, the great builder, thought how future generations would be moved to admiration by his deeds. There can be seen in his palace at Thebes bas-reliefs and accompanying inscriptions, which describe his campaigns against the Hittites in the fifth and eighth years of his reign.

Another Hittite Emperor, Montallu, swore to restore success to the arms of the lords of the steppe, but was beaten by Ramses in the Sinai peninsula. The brother of this Hittite King, Khattusil II, who followed him, offered peace to the Pharaoh. He was glad to accept, since it was practically impossible to achieve a complete victory over the determined northern warriors.

The representatives of both kings met to discuss the conditions of the agreement. The lofty civilisation of these peoples, unequalled until that time, can clearly be seen in the elevated language and humanitarian spirit of the text of the treaty. It is the first treaty of which we know the complete text. This is the year 1279 B. C., yet the treaty can still serve as a model of a diplomatic document. Sesostris, as Ramses is called by the Greek historians, had the treaty inscribed in hieroglyphics on a silver plaque, and also on the walls of Karnak; for his part Khattusil had it kept in cuneiform writing, and it has been found at Boğazköy.

Peace had come too late, since both empires had exhausted their strength in centuries of struggle, and were now on the road to a fatal decline.

The good relations between the Hittites and the Egyptians were not broken. Years later the blood of the imperial Hittite house was mixed with that of the Pharaohs of the nineteenth dynasty. The Emperor Khattusil arrived at Thebes with a brilliant following, to accompany his daughter to whom the Egyptians gave the name of "the Princess who contemplates the beauties of Ra," and who was to be the new wife of the glorious Ramses.

The principal cause of the ruin of Kheta were the migrating Achaeans, who penetrated the Anatolian shore of the Aegean. The Achaeans also caused the ruin of Crete. They invaded that island in the fifteenth century, destroying Cnossos and carrying off her treasures, together with her artistic influence, to the mainland cities of Mycenae and Tiryns. The palaces and diverse buildings with which they enriched these flourishing cities are signs of a powerful connection with Minoan civilisation, itself intimately bound to Anatolian culture. There began the Mycenaean age and the Achaean expansion.

The state archives of ancient Hattusas are rich in documents whose importance for the study of civilisation can scarcely be equalled. E. Forrer and Hrozny have recently found there the cuneiform texts of correspondence between the Achaean vassals and the chancellery of the Hittite Empire. The archives of Mursil II also show his relations with the Achaeans of Greece. However, the extraordinary value of these archives lies in the fact that only from them can proof be found of the historical character of the Greek legends; they make clear the historical basis of lyric poetry, tragedy, and those heroic times which are confounded with fable. We can imagine the intense excitement of those archaeologists as they read texts 200 years older than the Trojan War, and found there events of which Greek civilisation had only a confused notion. According to the archives of Boğazköy, the Hittites and Achaeans were in contact from the reign of Shubbi-luliuma in the first half of the fourteenth century, and on the death of that King, the chief of the Achaeans was King Antaravas, a Hittite. In 1325 the throne of the Achaeans was taken by King Tavagalavas, or Eteocles. This man was already lord of the island of Lesbos and held from Mursil as his feudal lord Pamphylia, a region on the Mediterranean shore of Anatolia.

The cuneiform documents of Hattusas speak of the city of Troy, and also of the Kingdom of the Troad and its inhabitants. They record that amongst the allies of the Hittites in their wars against the Egyptians, there marched the "Dardana." Homer gives the name of "Dardanoi" to the Trojans; in the reign of Dudhalia III, in 1255, the name "Asuva," or "Asia," appears in a list of countries and one of its cities is "Troisa," a name we easily recognise.

Besides texts on politics and administration, these precious archives also show extremely interesting literary writings on religious and historical matters. Hittite literature had three notable writers in the person of three kings who reigned in the fourteenth and thirteenth centuries; Mursil II wrote the annals of his reign; Montallu was a mystic who wrote prayers to the protecting gods of his people, and one of these reads: "Sun of my heaven, Lord, shepherd of humanity! Thou risest over the sea and mountest into the sky. Lord of the heaven, my Lord and Lord of man, of the dog, the pig, the animals and the land. Every day thou judgest at thy judgement seat." From thirty-three centuries ago, Khattusil speaks to us of his life as king and supreme religious leader. His protecting goddess continually appears throughout his biography, in which he sings her praises. Mursil was also dominated by the mysticism of his line, and laid his heart down in adoration before the solar divinity of Arnena.

Under the Atreidae, the pressure and expansion of the Achaeans along the coastal regions increased as the Hittites became weaker; those areas became disturbed. The Achaenans were directly opposed by the Kingdom of the Troad and other peoples living in Anatolia, which gave rise to the famous Trojan War.

In his excavations near the river Scamander in the part of Anatolia nearest to the Dardanelles, Schliemann found successive layers of the ruins of Troy and Ilion. The very myths mention the destruction by Hercules of the city which was protected by walls built by Neptune and Apollo. Schliemann succeeded in identifying the sixth city to be built there as that whose ten-year siege is sung by Homer. The date which the archaeologist gives for the fall of the city agrees with the Hittite documents, since if Atreus, King of Mycenae and father of Agamemnon, was attacking Cyprus in 1225, as we read in the archives, and his son was chosen leader of the Greek coalition against Ilion, then the date of 1183 fixed by Schliemann is very close. Herodotus was at least half a century out.

During the reign of Dudhalia V, which can be placed as contemporaneous with the fall of Troy, the Thraco-Phrygians invaded Anatolia across the Hellespont from Thrace, and destroyed the thousand-year-old Empire. This happened at the same time as the decline of the Achaeans.

The aspect of Anatolia completely changed, and a new epoch began. The Thraco-Phrygian invasion of Anatolia, and that of the Dorians into Greece, uprooted whole nations, and caused mass migration. Others took to the sea and went off to establish themselves in far-off regions along the Mare Internum; Achaeans, Etruscans, Sards, Aeolians, Ionians, and Philistines. Later on, Hattusas was destroyed by hordes of people from across the Caucasus, originating in Central Asia. They were of the same origin as the Hittites, but compared to them they can be considered primitive. The Byzantines later gave the name of "Scythians" without distinction to all the invading peoples who came from Central Asia.

The Phrygians founded their Kingdom in the centre of Anatolia and extended their hegemony over a great part of it. At the same time, other states were formed within the frontiers of the Hittite Empire. The ruling classes of all these might be of foreign origin, but the racial characteristics which were there already had irrevocably established a solid basis for the peoples who successively dominated Anatolia, and their cultural influence remained a model for later civilisations. The use of iron, which had begun amongst the Hittites, became known throughout the known world during the period of the movements of populations, which were caused by the Dorian, Thraco-Phrygian and Scythian invasions. This was the last trace of the Hittites, that Asiatic people who were the fathers of the Greek civilisation.

Phrygia, the enormous state founded by the invaders, which enjoyed good relations with the Kingdom of Urartu, where the Hittite element was in control, did not find the other important countries of Asia Minor, Assyria and Lydia, to be enemies capable of disturbing her. The legendary King Midas was thus able to accumulate his treasures amid a tranquil and wealthy people. But Anatolia was condemned to endure invasions and inevitable wars because of her geographical situation. Central Asia was an enormous breeding-ground of men, and its rough climate provoked successive migrations towards the West by pastoral and nomadic peoples who were seeking better land and a kinder climate. In the seventh century, the Kingdoms of Urartu and Phrygia were utterly destroyed by the tribes known as Cimmerians. Such was the impetus of their conquest that they did not remain long in Anatolia, but crossed the Bosporus, sizeable groups of them reaching Gaul and crossing to Britain where they have left traces of their passage.

Phrygia was unable to recover after this tempest and fell under the overlordship of Lydia; King Croesus was now the happy ruler of a great part of Anatolia. A new kingdom appeared in the East, one of the largest men had seen, that of Persia. Before the end of the first part of the sixth century, Cyrus had reached the Aegean coast. Anatolia had one master for the first time since the days of the Great Kings of Hattusas. His ambition drove him to make Europe a Persian province. He marched against Greece, and watched from his throne as his army passed interminably across the Hellespont. The three Greco-Persian wars brought disasters to Persia, and bring us to the decay of the Empire of Cyrus.

Anatolia was penetrated strongly by Greek influence, preparing the ground for Alexander the Great, who made it one of his greatest conquests. The death of Alexander brought a serious question: who would keep the greatest part of that huge inheritance? His generals fought over it, and Seleucus Nicator defeated Antigonus, another of the successors, and founded a great empire in Syria in 312, the whole of southern Anatolia passing into his power. Other Hellenistic states flourished in the peninsula; there was Pergamon in the western region, Bithynia reaching the "Propontis" or Marmara Sea, and that of Pontus, on the "Euxine" or Black Sea.

The next invasion of Anatolia came, like the previous one, from the West. Brennus and his two hundred thousand Gaulish warriors invaded Macedonia in 281, conquering it and also Thessaly; however, at the moment when they were sacking the temple of Apollo at Delphi a storm of such violence fell upon them that the Gauls ran off in panic. The Greeks took this opportunity to decimate the invaders, and the proud Brennus committed suicide, as they rendered thanks to Athene, Artemis and Apollo of Delphi for the phenomenon which they attributed to these gods.

At that time, Western Anatolia was in a state of turmoil. King Nicomedes of Bithynia was fighting his brother Zibeas, who was claiming part of his Kingdom; the King called in the warlike Gaulish condottieri, and defeated his rival with their help. He gave his thanks by the offer of an area to the south of his Kingdom, the heart of the ancient empire of Shubbiluliuma. The Gauls' main centre was the impregnable fortress of Ancyra.

They fought to expand their territories but with little success, since King Antiochus I of Syria, who had originally been tributary to them, defeated them in the year 275; they then reverted to the practice of their former occupation as mercenaries, serving Ptolemy Philadelphus, King of Egypt, then joining the ranks of Antiochus against Ptolemy, and also entering the service of other kings.

There approached the beginning of a new era in Anatolian history; the Roman Republic had defeated its formidable enemy Hannibal in Africa, in the Second Punic War, saw the world within its grasp, and set its eyes on the East. This has been the aim of the great conquerors, of whom Napoleon was the last; even the discovery of America was due to the desire to reach the East, which was the original plan laid forth by Columbus to Isabel of Castille.

The Republic had plenty of reason to intervene in Asia. Antiochus III, King of Syria, was advised by Hannibal, who predicted that Rome would seek to expand throughout the Mediterranean world, and marched upon Europe to attack the Romans, who threw him back and in their turn invaded Anatolia under the command of Lucius Cornelius Scipio. The Romans completely defeated Antiochus the Great's army at Magnesia, a town near Smyrna, so that he had to give up all his territories northeast of the Taurus mountains. The gates of Anatolia were open to Rome's influence, but in accordance with her custom, she did not directly seize any territory.

Some countries opposed the domination which was hidden behind Rome's apparent disinterest; one of these was Galatia. The Galatians were defeated by the consul Manlius Vulso and reduced to powerlessness, but the consul behaved generously to them, recognising their independence on the condition that they did not molest the allies of the Republic.

There appeared in Anatolia an adversary for Rome who was comparable to Hannibal, Mithridates VI, King of Pontus. This king set out to conquer Asia in the year 88 B. C., leading an enormous army. Pergamon, Bithynia and Cappadocia fell to him. He was an implacable enemy of Rome, and ordered the death of all the Romans and Italians who were to be found in the countries conquered by him. The Republic could not pardon this insult, but Mithridates felt strong enough to supplant Rome as master of the world. He subdued Greece, and Athens enriched the number of the illustrious cities which lent glory to the new Alexander, like so many precious jewels.

The struggle between Mithridates and Rome was a long one. Finally, under attack from Gnaeus Pompeius, defeated and hard pressed by the enemy cavalry, he had himself killed by one of his own soldiers. Now that the Republic's great enemy in the East had disappeared, Anatolia lay at her mercy.

Under the Empire, the Greek provinces of Anatolia, so called because of the characteristics of their culture, were finally annexed to Rome; Galatia became Roman in the year 25 B. C. Anatolia made considerable progress under the pagan Empire; trade flourished, and beautiful temples and other buildings, and public works were constructed in all parts. The Roman frontiers of Anatolia were held constant with small changes, and this was how they were found by Constantine the Great when he made Byzantium capital of the Roman Empire in A. D. 330.

In the first centuries of the Empire, Anatolia was disturbed by an unprecedented commotion; the gods themselves trembled on their marble plinths, for a new religion of one single God was increasing the number of its fervent followers at a prodigious rate. Its apostles claimed that far-off in Palestine, under the rule of Tiberius, the Son of God had died for the love of men, nailed to a cross. The spread of Christianity could not be prevented either by persecutions or any other means. The fight against it was led by the Emperors themselves, since the ancient traditions and beliefs were considered to be one of the bases on which their enormous realm was held together. Constantine recognised Christianity as the state religion at the beginning of the fourth century.

In the year 395, the date which marks the beginning of the Middle Ages, the Emperor Theodosius I divided the Empire between his two sons Arcadius and Honorius. The latter received the Western part whose capital was Rome, while Arcadius received the East, with its capital at Constantinople. The Empire had already been divided in two parts since the reign of Diocletian.

The Eastern Empire, also known as the Later or Byzantine Empire, was to have a brilliant career, both in arts and letters, and in power and longevity. The Western Empire, besieged by barbarians, did not even manage to last another hundred years.

For many centuries, Constantinople was the centre of the cultural world. Under Justinian, in the sixth century A. D., the Eastern Empire reached its highest cultural level and its greatest extension and power. The Roman Empire once more ruled the whole of Italy. It was during his reign, that the name of "Turks" was first heard in Europe, since until then every migration of this people had been known under a different name. The Huns led by Attila had seriously endangered the European world in the previous century, and if the battle of Chalons had not gone favourably to the Christian allies, history would have followed a very different course. The Huns were followed by the Avars, who also brought grave peril to the Western nations, and the later Empire especially suffered from their attacks. The Empire lost part of its conquests with the death of Justinian. The Turks, under various names, were bleeding the Empire's strength on the Eastern frontiers; the Persians seized Egypt and Syria, and reached as far as the shores of the Bosporus. The army was returned to its former discipline by Heraclius, who managed to reconquer a large part of the lost territories during a series of victorious campaigns between 622 and 628.

On the first of these dates there had occurred in Mecca, now the Holy City of Arabia, an event which was to mark the beginning of Islamic power, and which is counted as the starting point of the Moslem calendar. Mohammed, the founder of the third great religion to be based on the existence of a single God, fled during that year from his native city, threatened with death by her inhabitants, who were afraid of the great philosopher. His power was increasing at an extraordinary rate, as was the number of followers of the religion he preached.

The Prophet saw complete victory. Eight years later he entered Mecca in triumph, and threw down her idols; he then succeeded in uniting all the Arabs into a single nation, which he charged with the propagation of the new faith throughout the world, expressly authorising the use of force for its imposition. The Empire succeeded in reaching from France and the walls of Constantinople ill Europe, as far as the River Indus and the Sea of Oman in Asia, and in Africa along the whole Mediterranean coast and Egypt.

Mohammed did not live to see such a great triumph, since he died in 632. The builders of the Empire were his successors, the first four Califs. The Omeyyad dynasty, to which they all belonged, and which ruled the Moslem world from Damascus, was supplanted by the Abbasids, descended from Abbas, the Prophet's uncle. This first cloud brought many others with it to darken the skies of Islam; an Omeyyad, Abdurrahman, founded a second Califate in Spain, dividing the Arab Empire.

A new era of great migrations of Turkish peoples from Central Asia was to begin in the eighth century. Since centuries before then, numerous tribes originating in Turkestan, beyond the Tian Shan and the Altai Mountains had been gathering in the plains of Transoxiana. Other Turkish tribes pressed upon these, and pushed them westwards; waves of men invaded simultaneously to the north and south of the Caspian Sea. Those who followed the first route, called Pechenegs, drove out their blood brothers the Hungarians towards the Carpathians; they then moved down through Serbia and Bulgaria destroying these lands and installing themselves there. Those who followed the southern route poured into Khorasan and Persia, where they exchanged their old faith for Islam.

The Pecheneg and Cuman Turks, who composed these migrations, had been forced to move on by the pressure of the Oğuz Turks, who directly caused the ruin of the great eastern empires, those of Eastern Rome and the Califate. The Oğuz entered the service of the Abbasids as soldiers, but the Turks had not been born for the obscure role of servitors; they soon ousted their feeble commanders, and became the masters themselves, lords in their turn of independent principates. The Turks seized control of Egypt in the nineth century, where Ahmet Ibn Tulun founded the Tulunid dynasty, and in the tenth century, after a short Arab rule, another Turk founded a second dynasty, that of the Ikhshidids. The Ghaznavids achieved great renown in Persia, which they controlled almost completely. Other dynasties reigned in Northwest India and Khorasan.

Turkish power reached its peak under the Seljuk dynasty, whose name was derived from that of a commander who led his troops from Turkestan into fertile Khorasan. By the beginning of the eleventh century they controlled the whole of Iran, Georgia, Armenia, Isfahan and Baghdad. By the end of that century the power of the Turks was indisputable over the majority of the old empire of the Califs, who now only enjoyed spiritual power. Five branches of the family of Seljuk reigned in different areas, in Iran at Kerman, in Aleppo, Damascus, and finally in Konya, in Anatolia, since the Turks had invaded that region in the eleventh century, seizing almost all of it.

The first crusaders fell on the plains of Nicaea in 906, at the hands of the Turks, and these formidable adversaries were to face all the others who followed them. From that time onwards it was clear that the Byzantine Empire was in decay; rebellions, intrigues, theological disputes and attacks from both Europe and Asia had reduced it to a small country lacking in morale.

It was dealt a rough blow by the Latin crusaders. When these gathered in Venice in the year 1203, they hearkened to the fair promises made by Prince Alexis, son of the former Eastern Emperor Isaac II, who had been dethroned by his brother Alexis Angelus in 1195.

In July of the following year, the mighty walls of Constantinople suffered a bold attack by the crusaders. Alexis Angelus considered the internal and external situation to be too dangerous and decided to escape with part of his treasure. The blind Isaac and his devoted son were solemnly crowned, but they had debts to pay to the Latin lords, who demanded an enormous booty. The legendary treasures of Byzantium had melted alarmingly; heavy taxes had to be imposed, which angered the people just as much as the knowledge that now their priests would have to obey the Pope; their general protests led to worse consequences.

This state of affairs was taken advantage of by Prince Alexis Ducas, who himself murdered Alexis IV, proclaimed himself emperor and shut the gates of the city against the crusaders. He tried to negotiate with them, but they had seen in the recent developments the moment they had been waiting for, to satisfy their lust to take possession of the wonderful city. Constantinople fell after three days. It is better not to dwell upon the atrocities committed by the crusaders during the sack of the city.

The commanders of the fourth crusade divided the Empire of the East between them. Baldwin, Count of Flanders, was given the city of Constantine, Thrace and the whole of the coastal region of Anatolia from the river Sangarius to the Aegean Sea. Count Blois received Bithynia, Montferrat Macedonia, and the others also received lands and cities.

The Latin Empire was of short duration, for attacks by Byzantines and Turks reduced it to the capital itself, from which the last Latin Emperor, Baldwin II, was expelled by Michael Paleologus in 1261. The Eastern Empire was never able to recover from the disaster caused by the Latin invasion. When Michael entered the "City guarded by God" after his victory, she presented a very sad appearance; all her works of art, which had made the city a great museum, had vanished in the direction of the West, such as the quadriga which now adorns the façade of the Cathedral of St. Mark in Venice.

The Ottoman Turks, successors to the Seljuks in hegenomy over Anatolia, took the Asiatic provinces of the Byzantines one by one, and surrounded Constantinople. The city did not fall into the hands of Sultan Beyazıt because of the invasion of Tamerlane, who destroyed the Ottoman Army on the plains of Ankara. This defeat set back the newborn Ottoman Empire by many years; if the Turcoman conqueror had not been so ambitious that he did not deign to establish himself in Anatolia in his search for world power, the fortunes of the Ottomans would have been quite different.

Since unknown times, there has existed a fortress city in Central Anatolia, set upon a wide grey plain leading up to a sharp peak. This rock in the middle of the plain is situated about 140 kilometres west of Hattusas, the Hittite capital, and beyond the bend of the great river of Anatolia, the Kızılırmak. It is a natural castle, and was an advanced position and defence for the Hittite capital during the periods of insecurity which afflicted the Empire protected by the Thousand Gods.

The migrations or armies which moved towards Europe from Eastern Anatolia, Lower Mesopotamia, or Syria, or vice versa, have had of necessity to leave their footprints upon the soil of Central Anatolia, and on many occasions they have passed over the plain overlooked by that high mountain fortified by the Hittites. Within that same peninsula where East and West have clashed an unknown number of times, this area had become well- known as a field of battle.

After the fall of Homeric Troy, a new state of Phrygia was founded by the Phrygians on the ruins of the Hittite Empire. Legend says that Phrygia, in which Hittite cultural influence was dominant, flourished artistically and built new and beautiful cities, but since there has not remained in Anatolia anything of the artistic development of the Phrygians which can be compared to the arts and spiritual power of the Hittites, we can conclude that they normally rebuilt Hittite cities.

This is certainly the case with Ancyra, as it was called from the time of the Phrygian domination in Anatolia, and which is the fortress city of which we have been speaking. Legend attributes the foundation of Ancyra to the mythological King Midas. It appears in Hittite texts by the name of Ankuva, although exact proof that this is the same city is lacking. The first name means "anchor" and scholars have not been able to agree upon its origins. Nevertheless, it has been shown that it sounded similar to the name of a river and a region in the Altai, that vast cradle of the Turkish race in Central Asia, which has led investigators to think that the original name of the city is Hittite, and was later modified.

Every invader who sought to possess Central Anatolia had to spend much blood in capturing the proud fortress of Ancyra by assault. The Gauls built fortifications which, starting from the citadel, surrounded the Galatian city which spread down the hillside from it. The Hittite fortress occupied that part of the rock which has the best geographical defences; its walls were built with great stones, scarcely worked, and the remainder of the construction was made with bricks of sun-dried mud.

Rome made Ancyra capital of Galatia. Augustus endowed the city with beautiful buildings, baths, temples, a hippodrome and aqueducts. The Romans extended the city onto the plain and surrounded it with strong walls. Thus Ancyra possessed, like the majority of important cities whether Greek or Roman an outer wall, and another as strong or more so which surrounded its acropolis.

Like the whole of Roman Anatolia, Ancyra was reaching greater prosperity. The city was becoming richer and more famous; it was awarded an honorific title, the name of "Sabaste," in honour of the Emperor. The notables of the town decided to show their gratitude to the Emperor and to Rome. While Augustus was still alive, they built for him a magnificent temple, the Augusteum, whose majestic ruins have survived to this day, unlike the rest of the city's monuments, which have been destroyed through the successive attacks, sackings and fires.

Many cities of the Empire dedicated temples to the cult of the Emperor, deified while still alive, and of Rome. In Anatolia there were such temples in Pisidia, Apollonia and other places, but the temple in Ancyra was the most important for its beautiful architecture. Grandiose festivities took place to celebrate the completion of the temple. In the pronaos we can find the following sentences inscribed in commemoration: "The Galatian priests of the temple of Augustus and Rome, having made the inaugural sacrifices, dedicate this temple to the divine Augustus and the Goddess Rome. Fights against bulls and wild beasts, a public holiday and other spectacles were offered under the presidency of the consul and imperial protector Lollianus."

On Augustus's death, the authorities of Galatia decided to render him a final homage. They copied onto the walls of the temple the titles of the great Emperor's deeds, which have become known as his Testament, which had been inscribed on two bronze tablets in Rome. The inscription, which is on the interior walls of the pronaos, begins with this phrase: "Rerum Gestarum Divi Augusti Quibus Orbem Terrarum Imperio Populi Romani Subjecit"—-"the deeds through which the divine Augustus subdued the world to the rule of the Roman people."

The septuagenarian Emperor's farewell has reached our days, upon the walls which have defeated the attacks of time.

Nero gave the city the title of metropolis; Antonius Caracalla had the walls restored, and the citizens called the city Antoniana in gratitude. The importance of Ancyra was not at all diminished under the Eastern Emperors; on the contrary, it became one of the most important centres of the late Empire, until it fell into the hands of Khosroes II during the Persian invasion of the seventh century, which was opposed by Heraclius.

From the Byzantines, the city passed into the hands of the Arab Califs, then returned to Christian rule, to fall into the hands of the Danishmendid Turks in the eleventh century. The crusaders also held it, but for a short time. From the Danishmendids it passed to the Seljuks of Konya, then back again; then it finally remained in the hands of the Seljuks in the second half of the twelfth century.

Ancyra was conquered by the Mongols of Ghazan Han in 1304, remaining under the Mongol dynasty of the Ilkhanids, who ruled it through governors. The last of these had to leave for Iran because of disturbances there, leaving in his place a Turk called Alaettin Ertena, who declared his independence and took the title of Sultan in 1341.

On the disappearance of Mongol power, the administration of Angüriye, as the Mongols had called the city, were passed to a kind of medieval organisation called that of the "Akhi." This originated in the first centuries of the Moslem middle ages, and was inspired by the mystic brotherhoods, which gave it their rites and method of organisation. Among the Akhi would be found the artisans' guilds, dervishes, tradesmen, and important people; it had a great resemblance to freemasonry. The noble and valiant brotherhood of the Akhi maintained its power at the end of the thirteenth century and at the beginning of the fourteenth; as the central power of the Seljuks weakened, they took over the administration of cities and towns to save them from anarchy. From them, the city passed under the sovereignty of the Ottoman Sultan Murat I in 1362.

The Arab historians and geographers give the city on the plain the name of Ankara, which was adopted by the Turks. Ankara was witness to the defeat of Sultan Beyazıt, by Tamerlane, and heard his laments. Yet it became Turkish once again. History then forgot the city which had filled so many of her pages.

Ankara lived the life of any provincial city, through which long caravans of camels slowly passed. In the last years of the decay of the Ottoman Empire, the city fell into complete ruin; poverty was everywhere to be seen. Even the ruins had lost their majesty, as they were invaded by undergrowth which threatened their complete destruction. At various times, the inhabitants had used the ruined monuments as quarries when they needed to reinforce the defending walls; for this, capitals, carved stones and fragments of columns were pressed into service.

At the beginning of the fifteenth century a pious gentleman called Hacı Bayram built a mosque in Ankara which bears his name, and which bears witness to Turkish artistry at that period. It was the last construction of importance to have been built in Ankara. Most of the houses were built of unbaked clay bricks; these fragile walls soon deteriorated from the winds which blew across the plateau, so that with the cracking produced by the summer sun, they acquired a completely abandoned appearance, which reached its culmination in those quarters which were destroyed by fires, and which consisted only of shapeless burnt ruins. Of the walls built on the level ground, only a few stretches remained standing.

In the Turkish cemetery situated at the point where the level ground begins to climb up towards the hill of Tamerlane, near to the hill which bears the Citadel, one can see the effects of erosion. Gravestones, many of them merely blocks of stone of different shapes, lie on the surface in the older parts of the cemetery. Further off one can see others which are covered by the earth, and further off again it is possible to see that there are others now hidden from view, since time erases everything, even the memory of the dead.

With its double line of walls, the Citadel had kept its grandeur intact. Through its streets women passed like ghosts, wearing the traditional veils which covered them completely. The men went about their business wearing picturesque clothing and red fezzes. Most of them were occupied in the mohair trade, which is supplied from the Angora goat.

It was in this condition that Kemal found the city which he had chosen to be the seat of the Representative Committee, and because it was the terminal of a railway which joined it to the main line from the Marmara Sea to Syria; the railway had not been able to save the old city from its sad state.

It was in the afternoon of the 27th December 1919 that there arrived at Ankara that man who, by uniting his own destiny to that of his people, was to accomplish deeds which would inspire admiration even in Anatolia, which was accustomed to looking with indifference on even the most extraordinary occurrences. It seemed that nothing could now surprise Ankara, since the city had seen everything: wars, epochs of riches, years of hunger, empires which fell after tracing the usual rising and falling curve through history, religions which at one time had millions of followers only to disappear, gods who one day were terrible in their presence at their sacrificial altars, only to be forgotten.

The news of the Papa's arrival had become quickly known among the peaceable inhabitants of Ankara, who all came out to meet him. Sizeable groups went out along the road to meet him before he entered the city, and when he had entered it he was given an enthusiastic welcome, from which there were not absent the ulemas and dervishes.

The man who arrived, in a car which had seen much service, was dressed simply and had the appearance of someone who had passed long hours in hard work. This, they said, was Kemal, the hero of so many battles, who was not afraid by the appearance of the enemies that his attitude would bring upon him, and who had made the choice: either freedom for Turkey or death. He did not admit of any doubt. The people applauded him and all wanted to be the nearest to him, to see him and make him understand by their expressions that they were with him, and that they would not hesitate to follow him when the supreme moment had arrived.

CHAPTER 18

OCCUPATION OF ISTANBUL

On the very day of his arrival at the ancient Ancyra, Kemal had the feeling that there was no city in Anatolia where a man like him, who understood the feelings of the people, and only lived to achieve national independence, would find more suitable surroundings. Throughout the history of the Eastern Question, the Western Powers had many times repeated that the Turks ought to be expelled from Europe, and it was very possible that they still held this idea, and more strongly than before. In that case, the Turkish people would find their true spirit on the plateaus of Anatolia, as a man who draws into himself and seeks himself in the middle of some great misfortune; Turkey would be revived from the fountains of her race.

When referring to the rulers upon whom had fallen the mission of saving Turkey's independence, and who had not given thought to the achievement of this without besmirching national honour, but on the contrary were ready to bow their necks before the desires of the foreigners, Kemal said: "The affairs of the nation and the state cannot be conducted by begging or exciting the pity of others, nor can their independence be assured by such means. Begging for justice and pity cannot be a principle for action. The Turkish nation and future generations must never forget that."

Kemal felt his great will to save his country strengthened in that historic city; familiar as he was with history, he saw from its ruin that all Empires have after a more or less brilliant career come to the same end, a sad decay. Almost no remains could now be seen of the first civilisation which had held Ankara as a city or a fortress. He might have thought of Lucan's words: "etiam periere ruinae"—"even the ruins have perished." However his contact with the people, which he found to be strong, and full of a child's hope, made him see that the Turkish nation of Anatolia was ready to begin its career through the course of civilisation.

The Ottoman Empire had gone through its long decay and could now be considered dead; yet it would not drag down with it the Turkish people, which had never properly shared in the grandiose Califate, which relied on Arab and Perisan traditions.

On his arrival, Kemal sent a circular telegram calling to Ankara those Members of Parliament who had been elected from the Association for the Defence of the Rights of Anatolia and Thrace; this was of course a political party, whose organising committee was the Representative Committee, whose president was Kemal. Kemal believed that as happens in democratic countries, the members of the party who are elected Members of Parliament should follow in Parliament the policies of their party.

Kemal's nerves were continually tested by difficulties. Many members gave an unhoped-for answer to his circular, saying that they had to leave for the city of the Calif, whither they had been urgently called, as it was thought that Parliament ought to open as soon as possible. The Paşa soon understood that there was a trick afoot to prevent the Members from meeting with him. Many of them did not know him personally and were not familiar with his way of looking at the situation. It seemed strange to him that the Sultan and members of the court, who had not worried about leaving the country without a Parliament for several months, should now appear so impatient to open it at an impossibly short notice.

In spite of all this, the Nationalist Members received exact instructions from the Representative Committee that they should first go to Ankara.

The cabinet of Ali Rıza was faced with difficult problems; it could not bring itself to give proper recognition to the nationalist movement as being the true strength and will of the nation, but since it was indeed that, the cabinet lacked authority and was a mere fiction. The Allied High Commissioners passed on to the cabinet the dispositions made by the Supreme Council in Paris; these orders were not carried out, not because the cabinet did not wish to be as obedient as it could, but because the nationalists opposed it, so that the High Commissioners began to bear down heavily upon the feeble imperial government with renewed complaints and threats.

In November, General Sir George Milne drew out on a map the now enlarged zone which the Greeks were to occupy, and ordered the Ottoman Minister of War to have the Turkish irregular forces withdrawn beyond that line. This was naturally resisted by Kemal. Milne was giving his protection to the Greek invaders against the Turkish population who were defending their strips of farmland, gardens and homes; all the same there can be no doubt that the British general must have been aware of the first conclusions made by the international commission who had been sent to the Smyrna area, in order to establish who had been responsible for the disturbances there during the Greek occupation.

The Allied authorities received the official report in October. The members of the commission, who were Admiral Bristol from the United States, and Generals Brunoust of France, Hare of Great Britain and Dall'Olio of Italy, could not avoid recognising that the situation of the Christians before the Greek occupation had been satisfactory and free from any threat. The text of the report, referring to the Greek expeditionary force, is as follows: "The occupation, far from giving the appearance of the accomplishment of a civilising mission, immediately assumed the aspect of a conquest and a crusade." The delegates concluded that the responsibility for the unspeakable cruelties which had occurred on the day of disembarkation rested upon the Greek Commander-in-Chief and his officers, who had failed to do their duty, and that it was the Greek Government that was responsible for the bloodshed which had been caused in the interior of the country during the advance of its forces, which had not been authorised by Paris to go beyond the province of Smyrna; the Greeks were held responsible for massacres such as that at Menemen, which had been committed without any provocation.

If the Peace Conference had the intention of declaring that the Smyrna region should be finally annexed to Greece, such an annexation would be contrary to the principles of nationalities, since it was incontestable that the Turkish population was larger than the Greek. This fact shows clearly enough the complete injustice behind the tragedies of Smyrna, Menemen, Aydın, Bergama and Manisa, where the days of grief were marked on so many white stones, sculpted with dates, dates which were graven even more deeply upon the hearts of those who had suffered hunger and cruelties; those tragic monuments were waiting along with those who had been sacrificed, for the avenger who was to come.

The elements who were opposed to Kemal continued their pernicious campaign; one of their main objectives was to prove that Kemal was arousing the people and inducing them to commit atrocities against the Christians, and that disorganisation and insecurity reigned in all the areas where the rebel leaders exercised power. In order to give real substance to their claims, the bands which were dedicating themselves to criminal acts against the non- Moslems were reinforced, and their deeds were immediately made known to the High Commissioners and foreign correspondents, the blame being put upon the revolutionaries. The detachments which the Paşa created to counteract this campaign worked effectively; the most important of these was commanded by the patriot Yahya Kapdan, who was responsible for invigilating the areas near the Bosporus. He fulfilled his duty with remarkable self-sacrifice, until he was surprised by a large military force and summarily shot. This patriotic figure has a right to a place in that remembrance which the Turks keep for the first martyrs of the revolution.

The Members of Parliament were arriving at the meeting place, in small groups or alone. Kemal spoke to every one of them, trying to make them understand that the moments through which Turkey was passing were of such a painful character that they could only be compared to those suffered by peoples which are passing through the days immediately before their total ruin; if in circumstances as tragic as these, peoples do not courageously take the reins of their own destinies, and themselves assume their own responsibilities, the future which awaits them will certainly be very sad. For the present, said Kemal, it was necessary to unite their forces to one common goal; a group must be created in Parliament of all the patriots, which would be supported by the nationalist organisations. Although Kemal had been elected a member of Parliament, he decided not to go to Istanbul for reasons which are easy to understand; however, he told the most influential members, including Rauf, that he wished to be voted President of the Assembly, and that this would also be a convenient plan; if this was done, and if an attempt were made against the Assembly, as he was in no doubt would be made, he would be able to convoke a new Parliament in a new place.

The last members left for Istanbul, and Parliament was inaugurated in the middle of Januray 1920. However it was unable to begin its work officially until the end of that month.

Before that happened the Allied Representatives presented an ultimatum to the Sublime Porte, in which they demanded the dismissal of the Minister of War and the Chief of the General Staff within forty-eight hours. They accused them of favouring the nationalist movement and disobeying the orders of the High Commissioners. The two men offered their resignations.

Kemal, who heard about this after some delay, discovered that the Powers were angry at the energy with which the revolutionaries were opposing the French and Greeks; he could also see that these countries were pressing harder to make Turkey understand that she must submit to them. It seemed to them that the moment was drawing near when they would be able to bring about the division of the country, so that they now intended to find out how far Turkey was prepared to be sacrificed. They certainly rested easier on being obeyed without question over a matter so delicate as the dismissal of a Government Minister.

On the same day that Kemal heard about this serious incident, he sent a telegram to the Grand Vezir asking him to reject the ultimatum, and assuring him that the nationalists would support him. Any weaker reply would have disastrous consequences. He asked him to reply quickly and declared that if the British attempted to cut communications between him and the capital, the nationalists would launch a war for the independence of the country.

The reply arrived quickly; but in it the Paşa was amazed to read threats against his own person. In fact, Ali Rıza ended his telegram by saying that if Kemal had not informed him by a certain date, which he gave, that he was ending his intervention, the cabinet would resign, and would have no responsibility for the events which would follow.

The Paşa was not interested in continuing a polemic with such people as these. Before answering the gratuitous attack which had been made upon him, he confined himself to asking for the text of the ultimatum, which was never sent to him. It now seemed doubtful whether the Powers who were ordering the dismissal of a Minister and a Chief of the General Staff would allow Parliament to begin its meetings. Kemal decided to remain quiet. The circumstances were extremely grave. He was certain that events were happening in the capital which were more dangerous to the peace, and he employed himself in taking all precautions so that the nationalist forces could intervene in any emergency. He gave a secret order to the military commanders of Ankara, Konya, Sivas and Erzurum, to be ready to arrest the foreign officers who were detached throughout Anatolia, as a reprisal for the possible arrest of Members of Parliament or other persons in Istanbul.

Parliament at last met, amid the clouds that presaged storms. When it came to the election of a president, only one or two members gave their opinion that Mustafa Kemal was the right person, thus publicly claiming that the nation recognised the nationalist movement. However, the members most close to Kemal showed some doubts, and the plenary session elected as President a little-known nationalist, Reşat Hikmet.

Neither did Ali Rıza's cabinet fall, as had been planned, and as was necessary. The worthy Members of Parliament were already under the influence of the situation in the capital; at heart they felt satisfied with the honour conferred upon them, and because they had ceased to be rebels and to live in insecurity. Like the members of the cabinet and the courts, they began to think that it was a good idea to win the good opinion of the Powers and their High Commissioners. They were soon to see their mistake.

So as to avoid arguments, they gave their vote of confidence to Ali Rıza. Fortified by this, he ascended the rostrum and delivered a new attack against the Representative Committee. The essence of a circular which he sent to all the provincial governors was this: "From now on there will be no reason for anyone to speak of claims in the name of the national will, anywhere else but in Parliament," and: "All acts which take the form of interference in the affairs of government will from today be liable to punishment." The Grand Vezir was showing himself diligent in crushing the patriotic movement; however, he was unfortunately doing nothing to defend his country from the invasions and insults which were the consequence of obeying the orders of the foreigners.

On the 28th January, Parliament voted to adopt the principles established in the nationalist Congresses of Erzurum and Sivas. This was in fact the only useful result which could be expected from the Assembly. Kemal had given special attention to the wording of the text of the National Pact, so that it would comprise national aspirations in a few lines, and it consisted of six articles. It was accepted with a short preamble, which stated, amongst other remarks; "The principles which here follow constitute the maximum sacrifices which the nation can agree to with the object of obtaining a just and lasting peace." In the articles it was agreed that the fate of the regions which were inhabited by a majority of Arabs should be resolved according to the desires of their own inhabitants; as for the territory contained within the line established by the Armistice, and which was in fact populated by a majority of Moslem Ottomans, it constituted an indivisible whole. Turkey must possess the capital, the Sea of Marmara and the Straits; the minorities were assured of the rights which would be given to Moslem Turks resident in neighboring countries; the Sixth Article, in which one can see in Kemal's powerful and logical spirit said: "The essential condition for our existence and our future is that we should enjoy, like any other state, complete independence and liberty, so that we can have the possibility of national and economic progress, and create a modern organisation. For these reasons we are against restrictions which compromise our political, judicial and financial development."

A few days before the National Pact was voted on in Parliament, a threatening atmosphere began to surround it. All kinds of rumors were brought to the ears of the Members; for instance, it was said that some of them were to be arrested; that it was necessary to show compliance with certain Powers; and they were reminded of their previous record as rebels. At other times they were flattered, and given enticing visions of favour and fortune. The Powers, especially Great Britain, were employing all their powerful means to ensure that Parliament became a support for the Sultan, so that nationalism would lose its power and influence, and the country would give docile acceptance to the conditions which the Masters of the Peace would dictate in their own good time.

Numerous arbitrary acts made plain the intention of the Powers to bring pressure upon Parliament; they could not have given a clearer warning. From the Members of Parliament there came no reaction; they were beaten. Without Kemal's presence and the direct support of his willpower, the members, weak men, or ambitious and faithless, were no more than a scattered flock.

Kemal's forces continued to battle successfully on the southern front against the French and their Armenian protégés who had caused massacres of Turks. The city of Maraş, which the invaders had destroyed, was recaptured on the 11th February 1920. The French expeditionary force found itself in a serious position; Paris intervened on its behalf to the Sublime Porte, using the British cabinet as intermediary, since it would have been scarcely fitting for a victorious Power to have made the resquest with its own mouth, given the character of the subject. Great Britain's diplomatic representative delivered the following official declaration verbally to the Sublime Porte: Istanbul would remain under Turkish control on the condition that the operations against the French and Greeks ceased; if they did not, "the conditions of peace might be different."

In goes without saying that the Imperial Government hurried to bring presure on Kemal to make him listen to the disposition of the Foreign Office, and it equally goes without saying that the leader of the nationalist forces did not deviate from his line of conduct. If he changed his policy, it would mean that he recognised that he had been wrong, and this was not so: the people had been right through instinct, and Kemal had been so through reasoning. It appeared that in the capital affairs were seen through special windows, which changed the view seen through them, windows through which many Members of Parliament were beginning to view the situation of the country, since they thought that the British offer was a real and promising success.

Thus the Powers had shown that in addition to the zones occupied by the British, French, Italians and Greeks, they had also thought of seizing the capital, but since that city was too important for any of the Powers to let another be its mistress, they decided to offer it generously to the Turks, in exchange for cessation of the Kemalist campaign, which was preventing the peaceful mutilation of Turkey.

From the moment at which the Imperial Government had been unable to give a favourable answer to the British Ambassador's request, British pressure was increased decidedly. The first sign of this was news from Smyrna that the Greeks were disembarking new contingents, transport equipment and abundant munitions; it was clear that a strong offensive was to be expected. Kemal foresaw that the guerrilla war would have to develop into a formal one. He thought that a united front could have been made against the common enemy, given the gravity of the situation, but the lack of understanding between the palace and pro-British party on one hand, and the people's cause on the other, had reached a chronic state.

When the Powers asked the Sublime Porte to hand over to them part of the stores of military equipment, the property of Turkey, which had been warehoused and guarded by inter-allied forces at Akbaş, a small port on the Europen shore of the Dardanelles, the government made no difficulty about agreeing to this. It was explained that the materials in question were needed in order to be sent to Wrangel's White Russian army, as if the victorious Powers, overstocked as they were with war materials, happened to be in need of this Turkish stockpile. Loading was about to begin, when on the night of the 27th of February a group of bold patriots arrived in front of the stores at Akbaş in barges, surprising the guard, whom they shut up in a boat. Then they set about loading the 8.000 rifles, 40 machine-guns and 20.000 boxes of ammunition which were in the store. The barges crossed the Strait, and the precious munitions were taken to the centre of Anatolia, using every imaginable means of transport and travelling by the routes less likely to be frequented by the foreigners and anti-Kemalist bands.

Protests rained down upon the Sublime Porte; in their desperation, the Ministers applied to the nationalist members in the hope that at least a part of the war materials might be returned. These members, who had lost much of their spirit in the ambience of the capital, supported this request. As one may imagine, not a single rifle was returned, since there was even greater need for arms than before, as the Greeks had launched an attack on the 3rd March 1920 and captured several Turkish positions. The war had begun.

Unable to make his country obey the orders of the Foreign Office, Ali Rıza found himself obliged to resign.

The problem of the premiership at such a time was of enormous importance; the political atmosphere became uncomfortably hot, amid the clashes of influential parties; at the palace, the former Grand Vezirs Damat Ferit and Tevfik were talking to His Majesty; Ali Kemal, Pastor Frew and other notable personages on the anti-Kemalist side were holding councils; at Parliament, there were interminable meetings of factions, from which Members went out to intrigue in political circles. It was said that Damat Ferit, a man dear to the Sultan and Great Britain, would return to power. The British advised the Sultan that for the time being, during the period of interesting combinations which was approaching, it was wiser to entrust the government to someone who was acceptable to everyone, as this would leave the Calif seated securely on his throne, so that he could then choose a Grand Vezir to his own taste.

Salih Paşa, Minister of the Navy, was entrusted with the formation of a cabinet, and his appointment was well received. His cabinet contained some of the members of the previous one. On the 9th March, British policy began its operations towards the solution of Ottoman problems by the destruction of the meeting-place of the Turkish Hearth, a patriotic institution, without protest from the cabinet.

On the 10th, Kemal was told that the British had plans to arrest the main nationalist leaders, and he asked Rauf and other able men to arrange to be able to move to Ankara when danger became apparent. Something serious was in preparation, for nearly all the inter-allied forces of occupation had been withdrawn from Anatolia; a large number of ships of the Great Fleet were arriving to augment the already large number anchored in the Bosporus, the Golden Horn and the Sea of Marmara.

In the first hours of the morning of the 16th, and without previous warning, strong contingents of British marines and troops were landed simultaneously in various parts of Istanbul. The inhabitants were awakened by the noise of artillery trains on the march over irregular cobble stones of the street. The troops quickly occupied the strategic places: Galata Bridge, the commissaries, Ministries, telegraph offices and barracks. Their Turkish guards were made powerless and their troops disarmed. There were several clashes. Six Turkish soldiers were killed and fifteen wounded at the Ministry of War. The persons whose names were on the lists given to the officers charged with their arrest were detained in their homes or in Parliament. Rauf, Fethi, and other Members of Parliament, officials, politicians and writers were imprisoned.

At 10.00 o'clock Kemal had his first news of the British intervention. In the confusion of the moment, it either did not occur to any of the nationalist leaders to inform him of what was happening, or they were unable to do so. It was Manastırlı Hamdi, an official of the telegraphic office in Istanbul, who communicated directly with the Paşa. The thin telegraph line carried the succession of dots and dashes which made up these deadly sentences: "The military school has been occupied, there are British soldiers outside the telegraph office in Pera." At that moment another communication arrived from a different place, the Ministry of War. The telegraphist began to give details, and the number of dead, saying that soldiers were attacking the Ministry. "They're coming in! The British are here!" Silence; the capital was lost.

Istanbul had in fact been occupied by the victors in November 1918; However, from the 16th of March 1920, by the proclamation made by the army under the orders of Sir Henry Wilson, decreeing a state of siege, and announcing that any individual who disturbed the public peace would be condemned to death or other punishment, the Allies were assuming rights which left the Imperial capital entirely at their mercy.

In official explanation of the arbitrary punitive measure taken against Turkey, an official communique was issued, given the widest circulation, and signed at the bottom "Occupying Forces." The document listed, from the standpoint of British interest, the events which had brought the Ottoman Empire to an untenable position, upon which it was necessary to take a measure such as the occupation of its capital. It went on to say that on the conclusion of the Armistice, the Powers has assumed the duty "of establishing the basis of a peace which could assure the happiness, future development, social and economic life of all the inhabitants of the Empire," and that while the Allies were engaged in the realisation of these laudable aims, certain "individuals" who were spokesmen for the fugitive Unionist leaders had created a body with the name of "National Organisations," but which were nothing of the kind; those men were merely rebels who had robbed the population by pretending to collect subscriptions to the national cause, and had opened a new period of war.

This communiqué certainly expressed the general opinion of the British, since circles near to Downing Street knew very well who were the true movers of the pressure which was being brought upon Turkey. Lloyd George, like a Jupiter thundering on the destinies of the world, had more and decisive thunderbolts ready to hurl against the unquiet Kemalists, whose moral strength he still did not know. One day he was to realise its true value.

Since it is a basic rule in any dispute that both sides should be heard before giving a verdict to one or the other side, it is sufficient to destroy the pretensions to justice and truth which were made by the occupying forces' communiqué, to listen to the declaration of the Allies themselves through the report of the military commission which made public the events in Smyrna, and to remember the provisional occupation of Egypt by Great Britain.

The official communiqué was unable to reach Anatolia, as the British and the court vehemently desired, since Kemal had ordered that the capital should be cut off from communication, and no news of any kind was received from it, as in the days of Damat Ferit.

CHAPTER 19

A NEW STATE

As a result of the occupation of Istanbul, a measure taken by the Powers to coerce Turkey in her rebellion, Kemal suddenly found himself with the destinies of his country in his hands. Even his own friends had opposed him over the question of calling Parliament to meet in a safe place in Anatolia, and they had happily set off for the capital as lawful members of the Imperial Parliament. Too late they realised the truth contained in the Paşa's words, resulting from his logical reasoning.

Without having made a careful study of the situation, Great Britain, with France, Italy and Greece behind her, was intending to give a severe and decisive warning to Turkey by seizing control of her capital city. Having struck the blow, she found herself with a capital which was not a capital at all: Parliament dispersed, and with the exception of the Sultan, the court and the cabinet, which had no power over the nation, the powers over which the invaders were counting on establishing control slipped through their fingers, and departed by various routes towards Ankara.

The 16th of March was a day of feverish activity for the Paşa and his helpers, an enormous number of decisions being taken. They did not know what the enemy's plans were, and whether the events in Istanbul were going to be the starting point of actions against Anatolia. A formal protest was sent to the diplomatic representatives of the Powers of the Entente, through the Italian representative in Antalya, and by the same means the text of a protest was sent to the Houses of Parliament of Great Britain, France and Italy, and to the Foreign Ministers of the neutral countries. They were told that this attack on the political liberty and the sovereignty of Turkey was a more direct attack against those principles which were considered sacred by the civilised world; those of liberty, nationality and homeland.

Kemal gave instructions to the nationalist authorities to inform the people of every detail of the events of that morning, and published a proclamation to the people. The Moslem world also received abundant news of the attacks suffered by the city which was the Rome of the Moslems.

The Paşa's orders, which were to be carried out if nationalist leaders were arrested, were faithfully obeyed. His orders were that if this happened, the foreign officers who were in Anatolia should be made prisoners. In some places the railway lines were taken up, and the British detachments which were still situated in the cities of Eskişehir and Afyon Karahisar were reduced to powerlessness and their officers taken prisoner. Although this was a flagrant insult to the prestige of the British Army, Great Britain took no steps on this occasion to achieve heroic solutions; her power at the time did not extend to this.

Two disembarkations, two acts of violence, two dates; it was these that had originated the movement for the defence of the Turkish people, and hardened them in their decision to fight for their threatened existence; with these two events, Turkey lost her faith in the justice and equity of the European Powers, in the Peace Conference, and in the gentlemen who sought to reform the world. These two events were the occupation of Smyrna and Istanbul. When the second of these happened, Kemal's words found a louder echo in the spirits of the people; many of those who had at first been undecided or unbelieving now ceased to be so.

"The nation will defend herself against all foreign intervention; if the Central Government should be unable to assure the independence of the country, a provisional government will be created; it is necessary that the national forces should begin action, and that the national will should exercise its sovereignty." It was on these concepts that Kemal was building the new state which he had seen as the only solution for the future of his country. A new Turkish state was about to be born, whose aspiration was that of living freely and in a dignified manner; its strength would rest upon the sovereignty of the people. The moment when it came into the world was a dark one; it saw the light through a chaos of wars, external and internal.

Kemal had made provision for a meeting of a new congress in Ankara, in case the Parliament in Istanbul were dissolved. This congress, however, should have wide powers, and authority to change the regime. Kemal had for some time been convinced that a republican form of government was the one which best suited his country. However his knowledge of the psychology of the people, their fanaticism, their backwardness in basic education, and their lack of instruction in social and political affairs, persuaded him not to publish his democratic and republican opinions, unless very slowly and after considerable calculation.

The words "Sultanate" and "Califate" held a complex significance for the mass of the Turkish people; they were words of divine origin, synonymous with justice, homeland and religion. If the people had understood that anyone had the intention of attacking these sacred institutions, it is almost certain that they would not have followed him. Kemal knew this, and as the events drew nearer which allowed him to see the approaching birth of the Republic, he took the greater care that his words, whether in proclamations or in ordinary conversation, were spoken with a reverential tone towards the temporal and spiritual powers of the "Representative of God upon the earth," and he often recommended the success of his activities and those of the people to God. Kemal's Republic would be essentially secular; but to reach that point he needed the support of the clerics, who would not give it to him if they understood from his intentions that he meant to destroy the Sultanate and consequently the Califate also, since they were intimately linked to such a degree that it was difficult to establish where one finished and the other began.

Kemal went through periods of spiritual withdrawal, when his faculties worked together in complete union and harmony, as he meditated deeply, reviewing all his ideas and the events through which he had lived, before bringing all that to a consideration of history and a cool weighing of his conclusions. "Life," he thought, "means a struggle and clashes, and success in the struggle means success in life. All depends on strength, on moral and material power, and all the things which worry men, the dangers to which they are exposed and the victories which they obtain, are born amid the tumult of the general battle for life." The new state could now be born; but its enemies, selfish interests and unbounded ambitions, all these discordant factors, were crouching in wait and would hurl themselves upon the newborn hope; the clash of battle would be terrible, but Kemal had faith in ultimate victory.

A Turkish Republic would then be established on the ruins of the Ottoman Empire. The Empire had conquered many great countries and united them under a name; however it had only succeeded in achieving a fictitious union, which dissolved of its own accord as soon as the conquering force had disappeared. Kemal thought that the primary basis of stability for the future state should be its homogeneity; it should be guided by a purely national policy, contrary to that followed by the Empire, which at times followed pan-Islamic ideas and at others pan-Turanian.

The Constituent Assembly must meet as soon as possible in Ankara. Kemal continuously used the telegraph to confer with the civil and military leaders. Objections were made to the term "constituent," on the grounds that people were unfamiliar with it. In fact, Kemal did not wish to give a clear explanation of the meaning which he gave to the word, and thus reveal his plans. For this reason, when the circular calling elections was drafted, the Assembly was described as "invested by the people with extraordinary powers."

The majority of the Members of the dispersed Parliament, who had managed to escape British persecution, were beginning to arrive from Istanbul or announcing their intention of making the journey. All of them were assured that they had a seat waiting for them in the Assembly which would meet in Ankara. They gave up their objections before the evidence that the Imperial Government no longer represented any Turkish force, after its disgraceful behaviour during the occupation of the capital; the only hope lay in Anatolian nationalism. The main leaders of that party in Parliament, having examined their consciences during their short stay in the prisons of Istanbul, well stocked with political or ordinary prisoners, had by now realised their error and obstinacy in opposing Kemal in the discussion over the place where Parliament should meet. They were to remain in prison for long months in the gloomy dungeons of the island of Malta, to which Turks considered dangerous were transported in large numbers. Istanbul was left so devoid of enemies of the Sultan and the British, that Ankara remained for some time without any means of discovering what was happening or being planned there.

Seeing their well thought-out plan intended to finish Kemalism frustrated, the Sultan and his allies began a formidable activity towards that end. The first task was to frustrate the meeting of the Assembly. Through their intrigues, Kemal was made to look like an ambitious man who was trying to usurp the sacred right of the Sultan and Calif, and whose evil attitude had caused the occupation of the capital and the harsh conditions which were going to be imposed on the Empire.

The country became infected with spies and agitators; they knew how and to whom to talk, to the Turks, amongst whom respect for the holy institutions was deeply rooted in their consciences. The anti-Kemalist bands, now better armed and generously paid, redoubled their exploits. In some areas the clergy and dervish orders began by their own instinct to show their disapproval of Kemalism.

During the days while the meeting of the Assembly was being prepared in Ankara, reactionary movements appeared in many places, extending from the Marmara Sea up to the environs of Ankara itself. Several bridges were blown up, and public meetings were held at which representatives of the Sultan inflamed the people with arguments of the following kind. What were those men in Ankara trying to achieve with their lies? Were they trying to form a new government? And what right had they to do this, when the Sublime Padişah was ruling from the throne of the Califate, surrounded by his Vezirs and respected by all the foreign Powers? These influences were also able to penetrate the army; in the

Samsun Division, the officers openly declared that they would not obey any order that was contrary to the interests of the Sultan.

The society called "The Resurrection of Islam" multiplied its branches, and the defeatist campaign was fought at full strength. This was the prelude to the civil war which was approaching. Kemal had to arrest the fatal uncertainty which was taking hold of the country. If the Assembly could not meet because of the disorders and dangers which were threatening Ankara, nationalism would lose much of its prestige; for that reason, and because he knew the mentality of the people and did not wish to give foundation to the criticisms made by the opposing propagandists, he inserted into his notes and telegrams words and phrases which showed agreement with religious and holy principles, and the devotion due to the Sultan and Calif.

Thus in the circular in which the date of Friday 23rd of April 1920 was fixed for the opening of the Grand Assembly, it struck the eye that because a Holy Day had been chosen, since Friday is a Holy Day for Moslems, the Assembly would open under divine protection. A reading of the Koran would be begun two days beforehand, and its last verses would be read out before the Assembly building, as soon as the Honourable Members had returned from the mosque of Hacı Bayram, where they would have attended a solemn religious service, "during which the light of the Koran and the call to prayer will be poured forth upon the Faithful." A procession would go from the mosque to the place of assembly, led by the Hacı Bayram's Standard, and outside the building a thanksgiving would be recited and lambs would be sacrificed. Complete readings of the Koran were to be made in all the mosques of Turkey, and at the moment when the name of his Imperial Majesty was pronounced, prayers and oblations were to be made with the hope that his august personage, and those of his humble servants, should recover their liberty in the shortest possible time. They must indeed have been grave moments which were passing, for the secular and republican Kemal to employ terminology worthy of an ulema; to achieve his objectives, all weapons seemed good.

A terrible struggle was approaching. The Anglophile Damat Ferit had on the 5th of April returned to head the government, more determined than ever to destroy Kemalism. His plans were now on a grand scale, as he felt strong through the support of Britain, the Greek invasion, and the French front. If in addition to this the people could be induced to revolt by exciting their rooted fanaticism, and an army created which could attack the Kemalists in the rear, victory would be certain.

He found full cooperation from his brother-in-law Vahdettin, who in his office as high pontiff of the Moslems published a "fetva," a religious decision, in which he described the nationalist movement as being in rebellion against the Sultan, for which reason the Faithful were commanded to take up arms in the Holy War against the unbelievers.

The failure of part of the people to react against the occupation of the capital seems inconceivable, and one must perhaps explain it by their Moslem fatalism. The war was lost, the country invaded and obliged to submit itself to the victors, so why resist? It must be written in the book of destiny, and in the fate of Turkey, that it must be so. For this reason, the propaganda made by the British and the Palace found fertile ground in the hearts of many men who found themselves facing the problems of this century with a mentality appropriate to past ages.

The Paşa found some comforting signs in those days which foreshadowed cataclysms: the majority of the intellectuals in Istanbul, like those of the whole country, espoused his cause and put their pens at his service. They flocked to Ankara, and worked together on the "Hakimiyeti Milliye," "National Sovereignty," the daily newspaper founded by Kemal in that city, and revived the people with their enthusiasm during the years of fighting.

On the 23rd of April, after the completion of the religious observances which had been announced, the Grand National Assembly began its meetings in the place which fortune bad chosen, the former meeting place of the local committee of Union and Progress. The meeting chamber could scarcely contain the Members of Parliament and the group of other personalities and invited journalists. It was a wretched place, without electric light, and the thick chimneys of the coal stoves reached up to a hole in the wall, in search of fresh air, held up by wires fixing them to the ceiling. There is in existence a photograph of the inaugural session, a document of great illustrative value, taken at the moment when Mustafa Kemal was reading his speech. His unmistakable silhouette stands out against the light, while the audience listen to him with complete attention. There are many turbans of religious men, while other members wear fezzes and many of them the kalpak, an astrakhan cap, symbol of the nationalists.

The Members were as if surrounded by semidarkness; they did not know of the future which the new state was to have in history, nor had they noticed its foundation; they were surrounded by obscurity. How can we imagine them looking upon the establishment of a Turkish state where there would be no room for the Sultanate or Califate? Even on that same day they were discussing how to enter into contact with Vahdettin, in order to solve the great problems with his help or under his auspices; he was still considered more of a martyr than what he truly was.

Kemal proved his political dexterity in managing to lead the Assembly in the direction he wanted without arousing suspicion. What, he asked, did they intend to tell the Sultan? That the nation was ready for every sacrifice in order to obtain its independence? The Sublime Calif could not hold views different from that; but he was powerless in the hands of the British and could not do more than hope to help the nation.

Kemal's proposals were approved after a short discussion. They contained the following principles: it was recognised that it was essential to form a government different from that in Istanbul; the national will, concentrated in the Assembly, was considered to be the mistress of the destinies of the country; there existed no power higher than that of the Assembly, which held both legislative and executive power. From the Assembly men would be elected to form the council entrusted with the direction of government; this council would have a president, who would be the same as the President of the Assembly. At the end of the motion there appeared a note of special importance, since it deprived the Sultan of all power. It said: "When he is freed from all pressure, he will occupy his place within the limits which the Assembly shall determine."

On the 24th, Kemal was elected President of the Grand Assembly. From that day, he was in effect the President of Turkey, which now had a new, republican regime, although this was not spoken of.

PART FOUR

TOTAL EFFORT

CHAPTER 20

THE CIVIL WAR

The flames of the civil war were threatening to scorch the whole country. Centres of rebellion were increasing in number, fomented by the agitators paid by Vahdettin, his brother-in-law and the British, who spared no promises and did not bargain over Turkish liras. They preached that the Kemalists were excommunicates; the true Faithful were obliged to fight against them and punish them.

The "Army of the Califate" had begun to be formed in the middle of April. Its good pay had attracted a large number of adventurers who, commanded by good Turkish officers who supported the Sultan, and under the orders of Generals Süleyman Şefik and Süphi, who had been seconded by a well-organised General Staff, itself advised by British officers, soon made themselves into a fighting force worthy to be taken into account, which reinforced and revived the spirits of the anti-Kemalist bands. Anzavur, a bold Circassian, was the leader of the voluntary forces in Northern Anatolia; he achieved a black reputation for his hatred of nationalism and his cruelty.

Counterrevolutionary activity reached a crescendo in the days following the opening of the Assembly. Several towns near the capital of the new state rebelled or fell into the hands of the supporters of the Calif. The twenty-fourth Regular Division had to be sent to that front, to help the nationalist detachments, who were volunteers, in defending the approaches to Ankara. The Division fell into an ambush and was completely destroyed, and this success redoubled the boldness of the Calif's supporters, who were able to extend considerably the area they controlled.

Kemal entrusted the defence operations to leaders of the highest quality, General Ali Fuat and Colonel Refet, whom he had to withdraw, together with regular troops, from the front facing the invaders in order to have them fight against their own fellow citizens. The battle assumed a character of unusual cruelty. The Calif's supporters tried to impose their will by terror, torturing nationalists before executing them, and putting the populations who resisted them to the fire and the sword. It seemed that they were possessed by a bloodthirsty mysticism, such as cannot be found except in wars of religion.

However, although the area of battle to the north of Ankara was in fact the most dangerous, it was not the only one. An armed movement arose in the area of Boğazköy, towards the East, the ancient Hattusas. A nationalist detachment was made prisoner there, at the same time as the capture of another battalion in the vicinity of Tokat. The rebels completely controlled the zone and brought the fire of civil war nearer to Ankara. The fortress of Zile had to capitulate and the towns of Boğazlıyan and Yozgat had to surrender. The troops of the Califate enlarged their ranks from every town which they captured.

The difficult situation of the defenders of Ankara was aggravated by the danger of an attack from the rear. The battle-hardened volunteer troops of Ethem the Circassian, a famous nationalist leader who had been defending part of the front against the Greeks with his brothers, was sent to the Eastern front with all speed. In cooperation with the Third Army Corps at Sivas, which was a grandiloquent name for a meagre force, Ethem succeeded in temporarily halting the victorious march of the counterrevolutionaries on the eastern front. However, the rebellion broke out in other places, such as the neighborhood of the great railway which crossed Anatolia, in Afyon Karahisar and Konya, while the Kurdish tribes on the frontiers with the French and British occupation zones in Turkish Mesopotamia revolted and attacked the nationalist troops.

Damat Ferit believed that he was but a step from victory; he was congratulating himself on his tactics, which were similar to those used when counterrevolution triumphed in 1909, when the Red Sultan speculated with the religious fervour of the people and their ancestral inclination to submission before the Sultan.

Damat Ferit's emissaries, scattered in large numbers throughout the country, incessantly asked the question "Would the faithful subjects of the Sublime Calif expose their country to the suffering of great disasters, to serve the interests and ambitions of Kemal, an undistinguished leader?"

In Paris, the Masters of the Peace were somewhat worried by the news which came of continual disturbances in the Ottoman Empire. Clemenceau found himself in an ever worse situation against those Turks about whom he had made public his very low opinion; the French defeats in Anatolia awoke his impotent rage, but the French people did not even wish to hear of any new warlike expeditions. Lloyd George made the necessary speeches, and the four reformers of the world set about the equitable division of Turkish territory, when they could spare the time, since they gave preference to the delicate problems raised by the dismemberment of Hungary.

The Imperial Government was informed that it could send a delegation to the Paris Conferences. The aged Tevfik, formerly Grand Vezir and now leader of the delegation, heard the conditions proposed by the Powers on the 11th of May. The proposed dismemberment of Turkey was of such a nature that even Tevfik considered it incompatible with the principles of an independent nation. The Lords of the Peace thought his objection ridiculous. The Turks would come to agreement, and the basis which had been established would be accepted by the dying man. They therefore set about trying to make the Sultan and his brother-in-law see reason, and on the other hand thought how they could finally destroy the forces of Kemalism. Where could they find sufficient strength? It seemed that the Imperial Government had not had the expected success in its campaign against Kemal, nor could they count upon a mobilisation of troops from France or Great Britain, since this would give the opposition parties in those countries a magnificent chance to criticize their governments.

Venizelos noted with satisfaction the difficulties which the rebellious Turkey was giving to the Supreme Council, and his suggestions were accepted. Greece offered to make the Kemalist bands, who were causing all the trouble, see reason. Naturally certain territorial concessions would have to be made to her in order to encourage her people. Since this was the only remedy, it was accepted.

It did not please the Great Powers to see Greece too much involved in Turkish affairs, as they knew all about her dearly-held ideas about a Great Greece and her territorial ambitions. It was true that they had allowed the Greeks to disembark in Smyrna as a prize to reward them for taking part in the Great War, but the Greeks' hatred of their former masters, the Turks, turned this occupation into a bloody crusade. In order to halt it, the Allies had created the Milne Line, which they forbade the Greeks to cross. They now gave them leave to cross it and destroy nationalism by force of arms.

In Ankara, the days were passing with an air of intense excitement; counterrevolution was spreading with incredible speed, as new centres appeared on all sides, while the nationalist troops had suffered many defeats, and their authorities had been arrested, dismissed from their posts or executed. It seemed possible that the dark cloud of defeatism could cover the whole country.

The meagre buildings of the capital on the plateau were insufficient to house the extraordinary number of people who had come to offer their services to the nationalist cause. Every corner was used, and not even the most miserable lodging was considered bad, even by men who had been accustomed to live in luxury in the Pearl of the Bosporus. The city was dominated by Kemal's spirit. His way of life gave the example; he dressed simply, wearing suits of a sportive cut, usually eating little, and living in a mere couple of rooms in the railway station. Everyone was equal in Ankara, down from the President of the Assembly, whom one might often find in the streets talking to anyone who came near him, down to the peasant who came along to enlist in the people's army. Intellectuals and professional men, former Imperial civil servants, who had given up their petty jealousies and social pride, characteristics which prosper in the calm atmosphere of great cities and did so particularly in the Ottoman court, considered themselves all brothers within an ideal, pioneers of the new Turkey.

It was in this combative atmosphere, mingled with fear of the rebellion which was gaining successes, that the Assembly took action on the problems of revolution. A law was passed repressing all hostile acts against the new government, declaring them to be treasonable; as a result of this there were later instituted the Independence Tribunals. The Assembly also enacted the appointment of Commissars, eleven in number, chosen from its own members, who were charged with the direction of the war and the various branches of public administration.

In the Council of Commissars, which can be compared to that of the Soviet, the Commissar for the General Staff, the highest military authority, was Colonel Ismet Bey. His career could be considered brilliant, for he was four years younger than Kemal and had occupied high positions in the General Staff. He had served under Kemal in the Caucasus and Syria, and after the Armistice was appointed Secretary of War. In that position he did what he could to further Kemal's plans. When there was no longer any hope that Turkey could be saved by the Sultan, Ismet moved to Ankara, along with the mass of old and new supporters of Kemal and nationalism. History was to record however, that these people nevertheless arrived on the plateau while there was still time for heroism.

The Presidency of the Council of Commissars, and the position of Commissar for National Defence, were given to Fevzi Paşa, a man of military family, calm and strong. He had fought in the recent wars, having taken part in the defence of the Dardanelles after Kemal, and later commanded the Seventh Army in Palestine, winning the rank of divisional commander for his services. After the war had ended, he held the position of Chief of the General Staff and Minister of War. He gave secret help to the nationalist operations, both by sending war materials to Anatolia and by doing whatever he could without arousing suspicions. The other members of the Council of Commissars, whose names frequently appeared during the history of the revolution, were the following: Bekir Sami, Commissar for Foreign Affairs; Dr. Adnan, for Public Health, and for the Economy Yusuf Kemal, a man of deep culture.

Kemal, as President of the Assembly, was also President of the Council of Commissars, since Fevzi had come to be something of a Prime Minister, in relation to the Head of State. The organisation of the government went forward slowly, because of the enormous work it had to accomplish.

The "fetva" of the Calif which excommunicated the nationalists and Kemal, and which was published very widely throughout the country, with the help of Greek planes which brought it to the attention of the Turkish front lines, poisoned the hearts of many people. It was of extreme importance to Kemal that religious feeling, which dominated the way of thinking of the people to a greater of less degree, should not be turned into a weapon against him by the forces of reaction. With his statements referring to the religious framework within which the Assembly was to begin its work, and his words full of respect towards the holy religion, he convinced the representatives of religion in Anatolia to accept his explanation that the Calif's decree had been made under pressure from the foreigners, who were holding the Representative of God prisoner in Istanbul. The ulemas, doctors of the Koranic Law, considered that this was clearly the case, and they managed to find a verse amongst the thousands left by the Prophet which they were able to use in order to declare the Califal Bull invalid. This brought relief in Ankara and help in the counter-propaganda being waged from there.

It was nevertheless but a feeble support, for counterrevolution was advancing, and it seemed that the nationalist forces would be unable to hold it back. Even in Ankara, the citizens began to be afraid of the reprisals which the Calif's cruel soldiers would inflict upon them for having harboured the Kemalists, and these fears were made public. The final misfortune came upon the 11th May, when the Imperial Government condemned the rebel Mustafa Kemal to death for disobedience, the sentence being ratified a few days later by Sultan Mehmet Vahdettin. The Sultan was now confident of victory.

Each day invariably brought sad news to Kemal, an accumulation of reverses which would have disheartened anyone who lacked his force of character. He had to make unheard-of efforts to keep alive the faith of those who accompanied him. His administrative burden was immeasurably increased by the need to put down the revolts which were springing up throughout the country, and to resist the army of the Calif.

The first promising sign was the French request for an Armistice, because of the serious difficulties they faced under siege by the nationalists. Monsieur de Caix, representative of the High Commission in Syria, arrived in Ankara at the end of May. This fact represented a political success, as France's application to the new government, instead of that of the Empire, proved that power lay in the hands of the former. It also gave a glimpse of the difference between the ways in which Britain and France were treating the Ottoman problem, and of the rivalries and envies which existed between them. For example, Great Britain was not supporting her ally against Germany over the question of the Rhineland; France was now showing, by making a move towards the nationalists' side, that the great prize which Great Britain was keeping for herself, the remains of the Ottoman Colossus, might yet escape from her hands. A truce of 20 days was agreed between the French delegation and the new government, which space of time was used by de Caix to inform Paris that the nationalists were demanding the removal of all French forces from Turkish territory, and to obtain an answer.

Kemal turned to face the counterrevolution with the intention of crushing it. As he sat thinking in the shadows in the hall of one of the buildings of the Agricultural School, where he was directing the military operations with Ismet and Fevzi, he looked like a sick man incapable of movement. Fatigue, adversity and his own physical suffering gave his lined features the appearance of resignation to powerlessness. But suddenly his hands would clench, and he slowly straightened himself up; it was not he himself who was at stake, but his country. He wished to save her, and had consecrated his life to this mission. He must win! His face became transfigured, and illuminated by the brilliance of his gaze, bright as a sword of Damascus under the feeble light of a kerosene lamp; his body became agile, his voice clear and authoritative, as Kemal amazed his comrades who had thought him worn out by excessive toil. He looked hard at the maps of the General Staff; then he would ask for facts, read the last telegrams from the front lines which were beating down the rebellion, and discussed the measures which had to be taken, smoking constantly, then remaining silent for a final meditation before issuing orders, short and precise, which admitted no discussion.

The fourth peace treaty had just been imposed on another of the conquered nations. Hungary had to resign herself to undergo horrible mutilation, which her people have never accepted. In the heart of every Hungarian there are written the words: "Nem! Nem! Soha!" "Never! Never! Never again!" the words which they use when speaking of the treaty of Trianon. The next defendant was the Ottoman Empire. The general conditions which had been prepared were already known in Anatolia, and they were unacceptable. Three days after the signature of the Treaty of Trianon, on the 7th of June, the Assembly declared void all the treaties and agreements concluded by the Empire, or which might be concluded by it, after the date on which the allied troops had entered the Ottoman Parliament. In this way the treaty which the Powers were to dictate to Turkey was considered invalid before its signature. When the Turkish people learned of the territorial dismemberment which the Powers were going to inflict upon the Empire and understood the restrictions of all kinds which were to suffocate their nation, they realised that the only hope lay in Kemal, and most of those who had allowed themselves to be convinced by the paid agitators of the Sultan repented of this. The force of reaction was broken. The Kemalist army took advantage of the moment to defeat Anzavur's troops; the Califal army fought a rear guard action without much success, since most of its leaders lost their lives.

Istanbul and the Bosporus lay open to a possible attack by the victorious army. In Thrace, European Turkey, the first Army Corps, under the command of Colonel Cafer Tayyar, had the power to be the decisive instrument in implementing whatever orders Ankara made concerning Istanbul. The leaders of the occupying forces had already taken decisions about the evacuation of the city.

It was then that Venizelos' plan found favour in Paris. It was as follows: the Greek army, which was better armed, would advance towards the centre of Anatolia, and if the Kemalists resisted they would be destroyed. An attack would also be made in Thrace, which would be left free of enemies. As a result, the Empire would be forced to pass through the Caudine Forks and sign the peace treaty. When this last matter had been arranged, the peace of the world would be secure within a framework of justice and general well-being.

Well-known military experts including Marshal Foch were consulted about possible consequences of the Greek plan, from a purely military point of view. Foch approved the plan as being a safe one, as did the British General Wilson.

Millerand and Lloyd George advised immediate action; the former, pained by the loss of military prestige France had suffered in Cilicia, agreed that France should take an active part in the events which were to follow. On the 18th of June, the French occupied Zonguldak, an Anatolian port on the Black Sea and the nearest to Ankara in a straight line; on the 20th, Venizelos was allowed to order the Greek advance; the British fleet concentrated itself on the strategic points which had been agreed, and on the 22nd the Greek army moved on to the offensive.

Six Greek divisions, divided into three columns, moved forward, under the command of General Paraskevopulos. The offensive had unexpected success. Within two weeks the whole Kemalist front was broken up, and the defending troops suffered a great number of losses, retiring in disorder. The northern column occupied Bursa and established contact with the British forces in the port of Mudanya on the Marmara Sea. The centre column reached Uşak and the southern Nazilli. The Greek success was also complete in Thrace. Through an incomprehensible error, Colonel Cafer Tayyar was not at his post of command, which caused the disaster which occurred in that region. Part of the Turkish forces took refuge in Bulgaria and the rest either perished or were made prisoner.

The Nationalist army formed from the remains of the defeated Imperial forces, and lacking in means of transport, adequate munitions, and specialist groups, was unable to organise itself properly despite Kemal's titanic efforts. With Anatolia encircled by enemies and watchful fleets, it was impossible to put together the necessaries for maintaining a formal war; however, it was above all the fratricidal struggle which caused the weakening of the army which was being formed. The front against the French took away thousands of men, while Kâzım Karabekir's Army Corps could not leave the eastern provinces, since these would be left exposed to an Armenian attack.

The Greek army found itself faced by only feeble opposition; the invaders' General Staff also knew perfectly well, through trustworthy information from the British and Califal forces, the respective positions and military strength of all the forces which were set against them, scattered along the front 300 kilometres long. Also, the enemy chose the best places to break through the overextended Turkish front with powerful columns.

In Ankara, the prevailing state of mind was one of despair and fury, for it was not known how far the Greeks would advance, carrying all before them. There was a respite; General Ali Fuat, commander of the Western front, was able to collect together the remains of his divisions near the trans-Anatolian railway, and begin to reorganise them, while the Greeks fortified their positions.

Before the magnitude of the disaster, the members of the Grand Assembly gave free rein to their excitement, and protests and laments filled the Parliament chamber. On the day after the loss of Adrianople, the members met in secret sessions and loudly demanded explanations for what had occurred; they directly accused the military leaders of responsibility and demanded their punishment. Some of the members, by violently criticising the commanders for the army's lack of preparedness, were indirectly extending the criticism, though without naming him, to Kemal himself, who was the Commander-in-Chief of that army.

When their excitement had subsided somewhat, Kemal began to speak; he said that he recognised the patriotism of the Honourable Members; however, he understood that grief and affliction had led them to see what had happened in a special light, to forget the true situation of the nationalist army before the Greek invasion, and, above all, to forget the reasons which had brought it to such a sad condition. The turbulent sea of the Assembly was calmed by Kemal's serenity, eloquence, clear-sounding voice and convincing words. He then gave the members renewed hope: "In history" he said "there is no case of a front which has not or could not have been broken; in particular, the front of which we are speaking, hundreds of kilometres long and defended by insufficient forces, could not have been maintained indefinitely. Fronts are susceptible of being broken: in consequence, the measure which must be taken is to close again that breach which has been opened."

Kemal believed and publicly said that it was impossible to defeat a foreign enemy, while there was no real internal union and national solidarity, and while opposing forces existed in the heart of Turkey. "But if the nation assumes the attitude which I advise, the success which the enemy obtains for a moment, and which may consist of occupying a large area of territory, can be merely temporary. A nation which affirms and maintains its unity and its will, is sooner or later able to make an aggressive and proud enemy repent of his actions." The Assembly once more believed him, since faith returned to its heart amid misfortune, where true value is recognised.

Of the events which happened after his armies had begun to retreat, Kemal was caused most anguish by the tragic loss of Thrace and of the good divisions which he had confided to Cafer Tayyar. This man listened to certain propositions made by the Imperial Government, and went to Istanbul. After his return to the army of corps he was wounded in battle and made prisoner, and Thrace passed into enemy hands without even the gesture which one might have expected from her defender. Kemal gave his opinion on this to the Assembly: "Thrace was certainly in a difficult situation, but there was nothing to prevent the Army Corps from fulfilling its military duty, and the duty which had claims upon the honour of every patriot. If this did not happen, the only man responsible before history is Cafer Tayyar. When the sons of our country are sent against the enemy, exposed to the danger of death, and the country's resources are used in military operations, the only thing which should concern the commanders should be the realisation of the patriotic labour which the nation expects of them by iron, fire and death. Only in this frame of mind and with this conviction is it possible to fulfil one's military duty."

The Lords of the Peace could rejoice, and if Greece had still been a pagan country, Venizelos would have been elevated by his compatriots to the glories of Olympus. Turkey had been destroyed, and would accept the harsh conditions imposed beneath the knee of the victor and by the cold contact of his sword upon her neck.

On the 22nd July, the Sultan called in council all the undistinguished defenders of his policies. They discussed the proposals and counterproposals made by the Supreme Council, and after giving formal discussion to them, they agreed to the peace treaty.

On the 10th August 1920, the representatives of the Imperial Government signed a treaty called the Treaty of Sèvres, by which the ancient Eastern Question was seen to have been cleared up in a manner no one had dreamed of. Not only was the Empire completely dismembered, but even Anatolia, which according to Wilson's principles should have been considered Turkish, since the majority of its population were Turks, was divided up as follows: an extensive region on the Aegean shore, including Smyrna, passed to Greece; in the eastern provinces there was created an independent Armenia and an autonomous Kurdistan under British protection. The southern frontier with Syria was drawn to the north of the city of Urfa, which meant a huge slice being taken from Turkish territory.

Most of the rest of Anatolia was divided into zones of interest for the Great Powers: France was to occupy an enormous triangle, the base of which consisted of the southern frontier of Turkey from the Tigris to a point to the west of the city of Mersin; the peak of the triangle was 75 kilometres north of Sivas. Italy had seen the promises of territory, made by the Allies to induce her to default on the promises uniting her to the Central Powers, only half completed, but was generously rewarded in Anatolia; she received the ancient Mysia, part of Lydia and of Phrygia, the whole of Caria, Pisidia, Pamphylia, Lycia and part of Cilicia and Lycaonia, that is, from the zone of the Straits as far as the Mediterranean. The coastline which she thus acquired in the Mediterranean and the Aegean gave Italy great hopes to achieve a preponderant position amongst the Mediterranean Powers, which would later have given Benito Mussolini a formidable basis from which to realise his imperialist ambitions.

A broad swath of territory surrounding the Sea of Marmara and the Straits was to remain under the "control" of the Powers, and Turkey was to lose all control over them. Thrace would pass to the Greeks, as would the islands of Imbros, Tenedos and the others already occupied. Istanbul, too valuable a prize for the Powers to have agreed which of them would possess her, would continue under the Crescent, as would a corner of Thrace adjoining the city, within the zone of allied control. As for Turkey she was awarded, in an equitable spirit, a third of Anatolia, on the Black Sea.

Having renounced all her rights over the regions occupied by the Allies, the "Empire" was to be disarmed, and her finances entrusted to the Allied Powers; her income would be devoted before all else to meeting the costs caused by the maintainance of the occupying armies and the indemnities for the war. The Empire would recognise the equality of the rights of the Christian minorities, which would have representation in Parliament; the capitulations and other privileges would be restored in totality.

It was to gain this result that the Sultan Mehmet Vahdettin and his Grand Vezir had provoked a civil war, sowing death and discord amongst the "Turks, and had favoured the entry, in crusading style, of enemies who were desolating enormous areas of Anatolia, from which the Empire had taken its origins.

CHAPTER 21

THE ARMENIAN CAMPAIGN

From the upheavals in Russia, Lenin rose to power with the victory of Bolshevism. He believed that the social and political structure of the country must be destroyed, and that the first of the societies of the future would arise from the ashes of the former state. He divided the land amongst the peasants, to whose committees he handed over the property of the church, and recognised the right of the various regions which formed the Empire to govern themselves. Lenin and Wilson had areas in common, both in their ideas and in their failures.

After defeating Kerensky, Lenin's government asked Germany for peace, which was signed in Brest-Litovsk in March 1918. The Allies thereupon broke off diplomatic relations with Russia. After the end of the war, the Allies, who were worried by the Bolshevik revolution, began hostilities against it. Great Britain occupied Arkhangelsk, on the White Sea, and a "cordon sanitaire" was established all along Russia's European frontier. The British were followed by the Finns, Estonians, Latvians, Lithuanians, Poles and the Romanian army, which had joined that in Salonika, which was approaching the Black Sea. The White Russian forces contributed to the general offensive; the army of Admiral Kolchak advanced through Siberia, where there were also Japanese, American and Czechoslovak troops, towards Moscow, and General Denikin was advancing towards it from the Caucasus.

The revolutionary government, whose influence only extended over European Russia, was completely surrounded; the enemy fleets controlled the three seas which washed her shores. In order to counteract the effects of this iron circle, the Soviet Government began an intense Communist propaganda campaign abroad, working behind the backs of the enemy armies and especially in the colonies of the Great Powers, where Soviet emissaries incited the population to fight for the rights of man and liberty; the ideals of universal revolution were threatening the Capitalist and Imperial Powers.

Fighting favoured the Red Army; they recovered Ufa and Orenburg in December 1919; in the interior of the country heroic measures were taken against possible counterrevolution; in April of the following year, the allied army under Franchet d'Esperey was forced to evacuate Odessa; the Red Army was victori-

ous in the West against Poland. Great Britain saw that the cause was lost and
followed her usual tactic of retiring from active part. In September she declared,
along with the other members of the Supreme Council, her intention of not in-
terfering in Russia's internal affairs.

The Soviets openly declared their opposition to the planned division of Turkey and Iran by the Allies. The Straits had the same vital importance for the Soviets as they had had for Imperial Russia. The Tsars had been unable to conquer
them, in cruel wars; the leaders of the new Russia planned to assure themselves of
the advantages of the Straits, through the achievement of a mutual understanding of interests; similar feelings were felt in Ankara. Soviet Russia was the only
country from which necessary help could be obtained.

The good understanding between Russia and Turkey was also to destroy
the ambitious British plan to dominate the Caucasus and Iran. The first act of
foreign policy taken by the Grand Turkish Assembly was to enter into diplomatic
relations with Moscow. The two governments, one of national revolution and
the other for Bolshevik revolution must join hands and help each other against
their common enemies, the Great Imperialist Powers. There was no question of
any likeness between their social ideologies, nor even that these might be adapted: it was merely a political alliance which was sought for. The Assembly chose
a commission which left for Moscow in May 1920. A month earlier the Red
forces had occupied Baku, in Azerbaijan, where the party sympathetic to Communism was placed in power. There only remained between Russia and Turkey
the Armenian republic of Yerevan, which was protected by the Great Powers,
in particular Great Britain, who sent it war materials, coal and food which it
needed. The Armenian people were led to commit serious mistakes through the
limitless confidence which they had never ceased to hold in the Great Powers and
Orthodox Russia. In the end, it was not to be the Powers which would suffer the
consequences of these mistakes, since having incited support they withdrew into
silence, but the Armenian people, who had not taken warning from the harsh
lessons of their history.

The Armenians had complete faith that through the support of the Supreme
Council and Great Britain they could realise their old dream of a Great Armenia, which would be spread over the ruins of the Ottoman Empire. They did
not refrain from giving in to their racial hatred and committing acts of cruelty
and even massacres against the Moslem population, which were encouraged by
the "Tashnak" party, mortal enemies of Turkey. In 1920, the assaults made on
Turks in the eastern provinces and in Armenia decided the Assembly to order a
campaign against Armenia. It had to be conducted as soon as possible, since the

life of Turkey and the Nationalist Government depended for the most part on the material aid, arms, ammunition and money which Russia could send to her. The Armenian danger would finally be ended, and apart from the advantage of bringing the Turkish frontier up to that of Russia, it would be possible for the good divisions kept inactive on the eastern frontier to take part in the defence of the country on the French and Greek fronts.

The farseeing President of the Assembly had ordered partial mobilisation in the eastern provinces in June, so that it was possible to have the army ready three month? later. It proved impossible to solve this issue concerning Turkey and the Soviets by diplomatic means. The Ankara government sent an ultimatum to Yerevan. The Armenians thought themselves very strong and were overconfident of the protection of the Powers, since they replied to the ultimatum by a surprise attack with considerable forces on the 24th of September, against the Turkish army in camp near the frontier. This army withstood the attack and moved to the offensive under the orders of General Kâzım Karabekir.

The army took Sarıkamış, a name of sad memory for the Empire, on the 29th of the same month after a vigorous attack; the next day it captured Merdenek, and Kars was abandoned without a fight. Resistance was made in Gümrü, today Leninakan, but it was beaten down. On the 6th of November the Armenians asked for a halt to hostilities; they had been completely defeated and were now more sceptical and more realistic about the value of the Great Powers' promises. They accepted the Turkish conditions of restoring the frontiers which existed before the Russo-Turkish war of 1877; this included the famous districts of Kars and Sarıkamış. After some time during the invasion of Georgia by the Red Army, the Turks recovered from Georgians parts of the country which had been lost to the Russians in the war of 1877. They were the famous regions of Ardahan and Artvin. Batum was also for a short time in the hand of the Turks.

This victorious campaign blew against the castle of cards dreamt up by Woodrow Wilson, arbiter for the creation of new Armenia, but who could not maintain his own policy, as he was defeated in Congress and lost all his popularity.

The American people rejected the idea of getting mixed up in affairs of Europe and the Middle East, especially when as in the case of Armenia, it meant making themselves the enemy of Turkey, for which there was no reason whatever.

The Armenian campaign proved that insufficient study had been made of the strength of Kemalism, and that this negligence, caused by the pride of the Powers, would produce serious difficulties to oppose their designs. Kemalism required heroic measures to defeat it, and it was an urgent necessity to remove it from Anatolian soil; the Bolsheviks now had access to Turkish ports, and the contagion would pass to the colonies or nearby countries which were under European mandate. In addition, the gold which Russia owed to her former allies would serve to give new strength to Kemalism which, employing good armaments, would become a terrible adversary against those who might wish to destroy it. Again the Greeks were needed.

The Treaty of Gümrü, which brought a brilliant ending to the Armenian war for Turkey, was the first treaty to be concluded by the Government of the Great Assembly. This success brought new enthusiasm to the people, which were now almost unanimous in regarding Kemal as the saviour of of the country; many politicians recovered their faith in the leader of the movement.

Parallel to the events of this campaign were proceeding others of an internal nature which the Paşa had to confront with energy and severity, and at the same time with extreme tact and prudence. After the new state had been created, there were born along with it political and social tendencies, and currents of ideas of every class, some good, some bad, many misguided. The most interesting example, which occupies an important place in the history of the revolution because of its material significance, is that of the "Green Army."

It had its origin in the hearts of certain persons who were connected with revolutionary circles in Ankara, and were considered to be comrades of Kemal. With the intention of defending the nationalist movement from the fiery storms of reaction, they took the initiative in forming new volunteer detachments, which had given excellent results, both on the Greek front and in the civil war. The volunteers enrolled in the defending ranks entirely of their own accord, and thus in full awareness of what they were doing.

Kemal was overwhelmed by his enormous task in the days following the constitution of the Assembly, amid all the horrors of the civil war, and he approved the creation of these detachments, who were administered entirely by those who had initiated them. Kemal was giving his main attention to the regular army, since he was convinced that discipline based on absolute and unhesitating obedience could only be found in such a body, which he was dedicated to creating; it should be a disciplined army, imbued with the ideals of the revolution.

The Central Committee of the Green Army, the name given to the newly created detachments, enrolled a large number of volunteers through the use of Kemal's name. Their success was so great that even those that had started the movement were surprised, and moved on from their original objectives to give a political character to the Association, so that it acquired a half-hidden strength which Kemal perceived when it was already late.

Among the detachments which had been formed, and which had proved most useful as well as gaining the most fame through their intrepid fighting, were those led by the Circassian brothers Çerkes Ethem and Tevfik. Tevfik was a captain in the Ottoman army, but his brother had had no training at all; his ability to command and his nobility towards his men had made him a leader both renowned and respected. These brothers entered into relations with the Central Committee of the Green Army when they were sent to put down the rebellion to the east of Ankara, and therefore passed through that city. Ethem, Tevfik and another brother Çerkes Refit, who was a member of the Grand Assembly, joined the Green Army, and managed to become the masters of it through their influence in the Assembly, the admiration of the people, and the actual forces which they led.

It thus happened that the brothers, now leaders of the secret Association and the Green Army, and backed by people of the same intellectual level as themselves, believed that they had the ability to dictate their will; they loudly denigrated the regular army, upon which they put all the blame for the latest defeats, saying that they, the irregular forces, were the only troops deserving of the national gratitude.

In the area around the Hittite capital of Hattusas, Ethem began to assume the airs of a feudal lord: his gallows were always at work, and he began to give orders to the governors of that province and of the neighboring provinces, which, if they did not obey immediately, he followed by threats of death; he treated the commanders and officers of the regular forces who were cooperating in the repression of the rebellion, with disdain, and his arrogance reached such a pitch that, more as a proof of his power than as the product of any reflection, he demanded that the Governor of Ankara be delivered to him, so that he could hang him for being to blame for the rebellion which had arisen in Yozgat. When Kemal was consulted, he declared that as everybody knew, the governor Yahya Galip had performed great services to the cause and was continuing to do so, so that it was out of the question even to think of giving in to this demand.

When Ethem found himself faced by an opposing force, and in the danger of appearing a fraud before his officers, he became furious. He said to any who wished to hear him: "When I get back to Ankara I will hang the President of the National Assembly in front of its own palace."

Kemal investigated the causes of Ethem's curious attitude. He then became aware of how far the secret society and the Green Army had moved; he foresaw further disagreements, this time within the bosom of nationalism. He interviewed the Secretary-General of the Green Army, Hakkı Behiç, and asked him to dissolve both the society and the army. The Secretary-General said that Kemal's demand was unacceptable and unenforceable, because of the importance of both bodies, and the spirit of their leaders. Kemal decided to leave things apparently as they were, and to use the help of public opinion to frustrate the plans of the unreflecting Ethem. He was still a long way from realising how far the pride of the Commanders of the Green Army would reach, and the form in which the crisis would come to a head.

Since Kemal believed that at the moment it was indispensable to maintain union in the nationalist ranks, and to continue using the detachments of volunteers, he gave advice to the Government which led it to follow a policy which Ethem and his supporters were able to read as a sign of weakness.

Ethem's forces were posted to the Greek front, in the region of Kütahya. His influence and that of the Green Army was growing daily. They began to publish a newspaper called "Yeni Dünya" or "New World," in which Communist propaganda appeared. It was a Communism that had been poorly understood, and which was not consonant with the ideals of the people, which were predominantly nationalistic, in the life and death struggle in which they were engaged. This conflagration of ambition, ignorance and Communism even acquired importance in the Assembly. The favourable current of opinion enjoyed by the Green Party was shown by the election as Commissar for the Interior of Nâzım Bey, who was supported by the Green Party, and was himself the founder of the "Popular Communist Party." Kemal refused to accept Nâzım as a Commissar despite his election. On the 4th of November a motion was accepted, according to which the members of the Council of Commissars would be elected by the Assembly from candidates presented by the President, and chosen by him from amongst the members.

General Ali Fuat, Commander of the western front, proposed to the General Staff as a result of Ethem's influence, that he should be allowed to make a surprise attack on the Greek division situated before Kütahya and which, according to him, was completely cut off. Ismet, Chief of the General Staff, and Kemal disagreed with this view, since if as Ali Fuat said, he was counting on falling upon the Greek division, with two divisions and Ethem's forces, and obtaining an isolated success, the enemy forces were without any doubt much superior in all the rest of the front, so that if they moved into a counteroffensive, as was certainly to be expected, the weak Nationalist Army which was still being reorganised after the June disaster would suffer defeat.

The offensive moved from military to political ground. The project received warm support in the Assembly, where it was said that it was an inconceivable thing to miss such a good opportunity of winning back some of the lost prestige of Turkish arms.

Despite the categorical opposition of the General Staff, Ali Fuat announced that he had decided to move onto the offensive, and without delay, on the 24th of October, he began the attack upon which not only he but the Green Army and half the Assembly counted, to fulfil their greatest hopes.

The disorganised way in which the offensive was made, with little discipline, and Ethem's famous flying columns, which did not behave with the precision which is required by military actions of important size, contributed to the misfortune suffered by the attackers, who were obliged to beat a retreat. As Kemal had predicted, the Greeks attacked in turn, and easily accomplished a new advance towards the railway line, while at the front at Afyon Karahisar they dislodged the Turks from their advantageous positions before Dumlupınar. Fortunately, the Greek General Staff did not receive orders to make a new general advance.

Kemal personally took the measures necessary to repair the faults which had been committed: he removed General Ali Fuat from his command at the front, and offered him in exchange the position of Ambassador in a diplomatic mission which was soon leaving for Moscow; he was replaced by Ismet Bey. The southern part of the western front was given to Colonel Refet Bey, the Commissar for the Interior, and General Fevzi took charge of the direction of the General Staff. Kemal's next action was to give precise orders to the officers who were in charge of the rebuilding of the front, that they should carefully create a strong regular cavalry; the irregular troops must be diverted into the regular army. It was urgently necessary to make an end of them.

Kemal gave these orders the day after the victory at Gümrü, which marked the final defeat of Armenia, and security that he would soon have within his hands the indispensable elements for the creation of a people's army, the only salvation for Turkey.

Mehmet Vahdettin was watching with despair as the problems which were shaking his throne again became serious. For a short time after the Nationalists' defeat before the "Sword of the Entente," the Greek army, he had believed that his worries were over; however, the Armenian campaign was showing that Kemalism was still strong, and that it would be stronger still with the help of Communism, a horrible word to Imperial ears. He drew another conclusion from the campaign, about which, although it was making light of the Treaty Sèvres, the Powers had not shown interest. Had they no strength? If that was so, he was lost.

He was shrewd enough to decide upon a change of policy; among his store of maxims was: "make a friend of the enemy you cannot beat." He would try to get closer to the men of Ankara; that was the best idea; that would not lose him British protection and it might bring him some advantage. The Powers would agree to make some modification to the Treaty of Sèvres, and with this bait he would attract the Kemalists. After that they would see what happened. As a first step in the new policy, the Grand Vezir Damat Ferit was dismissed, and the aged Tevfik Paşa took over that shaky office. The Sultan had the good idea of making the Grand Vezir accept into his cabinet men who, like Marshal Ahmet Izzet and Salih Paşa, were well thought of by the public. In fact, there were people even in the Nationalist camp who began to have ideas of a possible settlement.

Ahmet Izzet, who was a personal friend of Kemal's, was given the job of getting in touch with him. He sent an officer to Ankara bearing a note which hinted that the Allies might perhaps accept some conditions more favourable to Turkey in the Peace Treaty, such as that the Smyrna region might remain under Turkish sovereignty through a special form of government, but that for this it was first necessary to know whether an agreement was possible between Istanbul and Ankara. He then asked for an interview, which would also be attended by Salih Paşa.

The episode which followed this shows the President of the Assembly as a politician of stature; as the day for the meeting which had been arranged grew closer, the British Ambassador made known that the Armenian Question, like that of Smyrna, could be favourably solved, if Turkey could agree on her internal situation. The public saw an easy hope in these promises of small adjustments; however, this current of opinion might prove harmful, and since a cabinet which had been so well chosen was able to foment such opinions, Kemal decided to keep their excellencies Izzet and Salih in Ankara, so that they should change their way of thought, revived by the pure air of the plateau.

The meeting took place on the 5th of December in Bilecik, a town through which the Istanbul-Ankara railway passes. The Imperial delegation arrived, reinforced by the Minister of Agriculture Hüseyin Kâzım as Minister plenipotentiary, and two counsellors. When the two delegations had met in a hall at the railway station, Kemal got up and presented himself as the President of the Grand National Assembly and of the Government. Then he asked: "To whom have I the honour of speaking?" The ministers, whom he knew perfectly well, looked at each other as if to see if any of them had managed to understand what he meant.

Kemal went on: he said that he did not recognise that any government existed in Istanbul or, therefore, that they were Ministers.

It was agreed to begin discussions without discussing qualities or titles. Kemal realised that these personages had really nothing important to say, and he brought the conference to an end by inviting them to come to Ankara where they would be the guests of the Grand Assembly. No one went against such a polite request, and when they reached the nationalist capital Kemal declared to the press that those gentlemen had come animated by the desire to work effectively for the good of the country, and that they wished to enter into contact with the government of the Grand Assembly.

During the time which had passed between the ill-omened offensive by Ali Fuat, and the atrival of the Imperial Ministers in Ankara, the Nationalist Army had achieved great progress, both in its man power and armaments, and above all in the morale which had been inculcated into it. A rational system of requisitioning had been established, and also a more efficient service for provisioning the front. Refet was given the charge of forming the cavalry.

Everything was going well, except for the direction taken by the Green Army and the Circassian brothers. Ethem went to live in Ankara, claiming that he was ill; he there began to direct his moves towards obtaining a greater influence over the Assembly and getting control of the government, helped by his brother the Member of Parliament Refit, and his supporters. His brother Tevfik remained in command of the flying columns and of the front which they had been assigned to. His main occupation was to get together the largest number of men who supported him and arm them; the day when he would move into action was getting closer. He refused to allow the Commander of the Front to inspect his forces, and took no notice of a circular from the Commander in which the various commanders were ordered to refrain from intervening in civil affairs. On the contrary, he continued as Ethem had been, a scourge of the civilian population of the area, where he disposed of lives and property like a feudal lord. He refused to hand over deserters or men accused of treason or espionage to the Independence Tribunals, but judged them himself and sent them to the gallows or pardoned them.

These acts of hostility and insubordination against Ismet, Commander of the Front, decided Kemal to intervene as a mediator. Kemal had no fear of the Green Army from either a military or political point of view; he therefore treated them generously, hoping that they would give up their secret ideas of rebellion, which were not difficult to guess at, and that they would return to their former honest service to their country.

Ethem was aiming high; his slight education and weaker intelligence encouraged him to nourish ideas of absolute power, and these were given greater strength by the flattery of his followers. He encouraged a rumor which claimed that the substance of the disagreement was the defensive struggle of the Green Army against Kemal, who had made a plan to get rid of the Circassian brothers and establish dictatorship once he was in sole power.

As Head of State, it was Kemal's duty to ensure internal order and agreement; the moments through which Turkey was passing were grave, and her future obscure. He invited Ethem and Reşit to go with him to Eskişehir, so that they could meet Ismet and reach a satisfactory agreement. Ethem made objections, but was obliged to agree. At the beginning of the journey the two commanders looked at each other with penetrating and cold regard. Ethem feared an ambush, seeing that the solution of the situation was close and might be a terrible one; nevertheless he would not give up. Facing him, Kemal felt strong and animated by generous sentiments; he wished to reach an agreement, but all the same the army's discipline must be respected. Nothing could stand against that!

When the train stopped in Eskişehir the next morning, Ethem disappeared with the help of some of Kemal's companions. Kemal give no hint of his plans. There dined with the President of the Assembly that same night Ismet, Reşit the Circassian and a group of "comrades," as Kemal called the members of his government. Kemal asked Ethem's brother where he was. "He is in bed, ill," he replied, "but perhaps he may be able to come to the general headquarters later for the discussions."

The group moved in that direction; Ethem however did not arrive. Since the necessary time had now been gained, Reşit remarked with an air of triumph: "Ethem is at this moment at the head of his forces!" Kemal managed to control himself and swallow this insult. Aggressively, almost shouting, Reşit began to defend his brother, and made harsh attacks on those who thought in a different way; even the logical arguments put to him failed to calm him down. Kemal got up and stopped him: "Until now I have spoken as an old comrade, and with the sincere desire to reach an agreement which might have been in your favour, but from this moment our comradeship has ended. In my capacity of Chief of State I order the Commander of the Western Front to use force in the manner which the situation demands."

Ethem took the final measures for his rebellion, gathered his forces and recruited new soldiers. He communicated with his partisans in Ankara through a secret code. The authorities in the towns in his area and adjacent ones received his orders, which admitted no hesitation. It was soon discovered that propaganda was being made in the regular army, and that some people were trying to corrupt it, well supplied with money.

The storm was gathering on the horizon. As a final call to reason, a Commission of Members of Parliament set off to talk to Ethem, and when their task proved useless, Kemal, with the agreement of the Council of Commissars, ordered the Commander of the Front to put down the rebellion of Ethem and his brothers. These men were of the same type as the "Beys," feudal lords, who held Turkish provinces within their grip even in the last century. The only law they knew was caprice, and their most fruitful industry robbery; they were one of the great obstacles to the progress of Turkey, and for that reason Sultan Mahmut waged pitiless war upon them in his efforts to reform the Empire. His wrath was equally aroused by the Janissaries. No confidence could be placed on those troops, led by chieftains who used their ascendency to further their own ambitions, and due to them the Empire suffered many internal misfortunes. In Ethem and his men Kemal saw the possible repetition of the crimes of the Beys and Janissaries, and since it was impossible to make them understand that they were living in a different era, lie had no other choice but to destroy them for the good of the country.

The regular army gave proof of the progress it had made by completely defeating the new janissaries in less than a week. The latter fled, led by Ethem, into Greek territory where they were well received.

During his flight, Ethem sent a telegram to the Sublime Porte announcing his entry into the service of Greece, and that he was already in agreement with the Greek command about the way in which they should proceed; after this news he offered himself to the orders of His Majesty. Betraying his country, Ethem kept his word, by revealing the disposition of the Turkish army and all the details for which Venizelos would have given the gold of Greece. The Greek army moved onto the offensive on the following day.

CHAPTER 22

CONFERENCES AND BATTLES

The precious information given by the deserter Ethem and his valuable followers offered the Greek expeditionary force a unique chance to strike a shrewd blow at the Nationalists. The three pillars which supported the Turkish front were, from north to south, the cities of Eskişehir, Kütahya and Afyon Karahisar, which were all stations on the great railway. As they realised, the Turkish troops had been sent from the first and third of these cities towards the second of them, to attack Ethem. Eskişehir and Afyon Karahisar were therefore vulnerable points. The Greeks would attack them, and their numbers and superiority in arms would inevitably force the Kemalists to send the troops concentrated in Kütahya to the other two towns, by forced marches.

As soon as these detachments had moved, the Circassian brothers would make a direct attack on Kütahya; since the presence of opportunity plays such an important role in military science, the commanders at the front were ordered to follow this fine plan with immediate effect.

After making threatening movements along the whole front, about 20.000 men armed with 150 heavy machine-guns and 50 cannon met the force which Ismet had dispatched with all speed from Kütahya at Inönü, before Eskişehir. The Turkish force was no more than a third of the strength of the attackers. Against their expectation, the latter encountered serious resistance. Throughout the whole of the 9th of January 1921, and the following day, they threw vigorous attacks against the Turkish positions. There were moments at which the Turks seemed to be giving way in some places, but they presented again an immovable front to every new attack. During the night of the 10th the invading army retired towards Bursa. The history of the revolution records this as the first laurel of victory in the war against Greece. Ismet received the title of General.

Ethem attacked the Nationalist Division commanded by Lieutenant-Colonel Izzettin, which was defending Kütahya alone. Thanks to the heroism of this commander and his men, they were able to defeat the traitor Ethem after a bloody struggle, and Ethem was separated from his troops during his retreat. He managed to escape, while his men, who were made prisoners, later recognised the error into which they had fallen.

Very important political events had taken place in the land of Pericles. The young King Alexander, whom Venizelos had placed on the throne from which Constantine I had been deposed in 1917, died on the 25th of October 1920, from infection produced by a monkey bite. During the reign of Alexander, Venizelos was master of the Kingdom; he showed his skill as a political pilot in the way in which he navigated through the seas of intrigue, ambition and hatred which marked the Peace Conferences. He brought his country's armies to the ancient Greek Ionia, and gave hope to his people that they would one day see realised the ideal of the Great Greece for which they worshipped him.

Now that Alexander was dead, who should wear his crown? Venizelos offered it to Paul, the younger brother of the dead King, but he refused it since he considered his exiled father to be the true monarch. It was therefore necessary to resort to a plebiscite. The elections turned up a crushing majority in favour of the return of Constantine I, and the former popular idol, Eleutherios Venizelos, had to begin his journey into exile.

How could his fall have been possible? Had his people so soon forgotten the services given to his country by that man who had been a demigod in their eyes only a few weeks before? We should go back a few paces and view the whole history of Attica at a glance, in order to see other great men who suffered, like him, because of the inconstancy and ingratitude of the people of Athens. Aristides the just, Themistocles the victor of Salamis, Alcibiades, Miltiades the hero of Marathon, Cimon the victor over the Persians, all these learned the bitterness of exile.

Venizelos partly disappointed his people; he was taking too long to give them what he had promised and they were getting impatient. The sons of Greece had conquered at the price of their blood the whole of Thrace and Western Anatolia but yet they had not achieved the fruit which should come from such a victory. The Greek army could make out the domes of the marvellous Byzantium beyond the mouldering walls of Theodosius; Justinian's city was at their mercy; Constantine XIII could be avenged; Christian hymns could resound as never before, echoing in the dome of the great church, that vast holy dome, symbol of the heaven which would cover Greece redeemed. The army was at the gates of Byzantium, and Venizelos, too weak to stand against the Powers, was not brave enough to demand what the people believed belonged to them.

Nor was any solution being reached in Anatolia; always, at the very moment when the Greeks could have pursued and destroyed the Turkish army which they had just defeated, the Powers, who were jealous of Greece, gave orders through Venizelos that they must halt and dig trenches, while the Turks were reorganising themselves at ease. The Greek people no longer wanted to know anything about the "permission" of the Powers. They therefore voted with one voice for the return of King Constantine, a name which found an echo in their hearts, being that of ten Kings of the Byzantine Empire.

Although the Powers of the Entente officially presented a united front, they were in fact far from united. In the first place, France was not satisfied with the division of the corpse of the Empire. Showing the uncomfortable cleverness which had caused her enemies to call her "Perfidious Albion," Great Britain had chosen the areas which were safest, although of less apparent importance; in exchange she had induced her ally to accept, in addition to Syria, the province of Cilicia, which proved to be a truly Greek gift, where the Turks had her in a difficult position.

France now realised too late that all her policy of friendship with Turkey, which had been founded by Francois I and which had brought her a real influence over that country, was now losing it in favour of Great Britain. Two factors had finally decided France to become "a friend of the oppressed peoples": The most important of these was the material and moral strength of Kemalism, supported by the new Russia, which was already growing upon the horizon as a Power to be feared. France felt reborn within her the old sympathy for Turkey, a country beloved by French writers. The second factor, which was the one officially put forward, was what was called "the treachery of the Greek people," which had brought back Constantine to power, although he had been concerned in the murder of the French sailors in Athens. French support was withdrawn from Greece from that moment. Her example was followed by Italy, who had seen that the promises of territory made to her had not been made upon the maps, and who was worried by the rise in the power of Greece, her Mediterranean neighbor. After mature consideration, both Italy and France preferred Ottoman to Greek predominance.

Great Britain's plans were going well, and instead of being upset by the change which had occurred in Greece, she entered into secret agreements with the supporters of Constantine, and everything remained as before with one advantage: this was that the "Sword of the Entente" became the "Sword of Britain."

The attitudes of the Allies clashed on a diplomatic level in Paris, and the practical result of this was that on the 25th of January it was decided to invite both the Greeks and the Turks to discuss matters with the Allies in London in the following month. This time it was specified that Mustafa Kemal or his representatives must form part of the Ottoman delegation. This was the first time that the Powers gave such a mention to this half-mysterious person who was resisting armies attacking him from every point of the compass on the plateaus of

Anatolia. Great Britain thought it was one thing to know how to defend oneself with arms, but another to do so in a diplomatic conference. There she was sure of destroying him.

In the decision made in Paris, it was announced that the delegates were being invited to a conference to make certain modifications to the Treaty of Sèvres, which had been found necessary in view of the events which had happened. It was a very remarkable success for that "rebel general," also branded as a communist, that he should have succeeded by his own efforts to force a revision of the Treaty, which Millerand had officially declared could not have any modifications allowed in it by the Allied Powers.

Vahdettin was more worried than ever; if the Powers were seeking to talk to Kemal, it was because they thought the Sultan and Calif was no more than a puppet which they could no longer use. This meant that they were giving him up to his fate. He had guessed what might happen long before; the victory of Kemal would mean the end of his reign and perhaps that of the dynasty of Osman. He was not wrong, since Kemal was moving the Assembly towards the left, towards a republican regime.

The Grand Assembly began its work by-putting into effect the democratic principles which were contained in the motion presented by Kemal, of which the essence was: the national will, represented by the Assembly, is the effective master of the destinies of the country; there exists no power higher than that of the Assembly. This was equivalent to disowning the authority of the Sultan. On this foundation, a special commission prepared a draft constitution for the new state. When it was submitted for the approval of the Assembly, the attitudes of the various members became clear, from the clerics, who took up a position on the extreme right, across to the democrats who followed Kemal's wishes. The discussions on the new constitution went on for long months, and Kemal used this time to undermine the throne of Osman.

The Constitutional Law was approved at last on the 20th of January 1921. It consisted of eleven articles in which the status, powers, form and character of the Grand Assembly and its government were established. Its essence was as follows: sovereignty belongs to the nation without reserve or restriction; the administrative system rests on the principle that the people controls its destinies effectively and personally; legislative and executive power is concentrated on the Assembly? the Assembly is formed of members elected by the people; elections are held every two years; members may be reelected; the opinion of religious law, and legal judgements most relevant for the needs of the time, will be taken as basis for the preparation of laws and regulations. (The religious law was only mentioned to calm down somewhat the right wing politicians and induce them to agree to the other articles). The Assembly governs the various departments into which the government is divided, through the medium of its Commissars, chosen by the Assembly, to whom it gives the necessary instructions. The President of the Assembly is chosen by the Assembly and holds his office for the period of one legislative session; he is at the same time President of the Council of Ministers.

There existed such a remarkable difference between the constitution of the new state and that of the Empire of the Sultans, that any legal scholar could easily have seen that the victory of one implied the disappearance of the other. This became clear when Tevfik Paşa, the Grand Vezir, having received the invitation made by the Powers, sent the happy news to the President of the Assembly. The latter replied that the only legitimate and independent government in Turkey was the Government of the Grand Assembly, and that for that reason the Powers had made a mistake in sending the invitation to Istanbul. He therefore refused to appoint any delegates.

Kemal suggested to the Grand Vezir that since the union of all the moral and material forces of the country was essential in order to defend Turkey effectively at the London Conference, the Padişah ought to recognise the Grand Assembly. He added that if the Sultan opposed the internal union of the country, he would be directly responsible for the consequences which his action might bring, and that his throne would be endangered.

This was the first occasion that Kemal publicly expressed ideas so far ahead of his general plans. It was still a very bold act to attack the holy person of the Sultan. It was true that the final remnants of the rebellions against the new state had been crushed, and that the government in Istanbul was merely a shadow; nevertheless, as he was constantly reminded, as soon as he touched upon the Sultanate, the Califate, or the religious law, he met a strong and constant opposition, even in the circle of his own friends.

The words "Life means struggle and opposition," are words which apply to Kemal's character and beliefs. He was not going to triumph without effort, risk and struggle; this is the teaching of history.

The Grand Vezir continued to insist that Ankara should appoint delegates which would go to the London Conference together with the Imperial delegation. He put the case to Kemal in every possible light, and gave him some information from trustworthy sources, which predicted that before the Conference the Greeks would make a new attack in Anatolia so that they should be listened to with greater attention, and he also warned him that the Powers would refuse to receive the Ankara delegates separately.

The problem was solved by intervention from Italy. There were good relations between Italy and the Nationalist Government; the Italian authorities in Antalya, the main port of the zone they occupied, allowed the circulars published by Ankara to be sent overseas, and recently, with the political change in Greece, the rapprochement between Italy and the Kemalists had taken a new step forward. Both France and Italy wanted Kemal's representatives to be at the London Conference, for this was in the interests of their policies. Count Sforza, the Italian Foreign Minister, made personal efforts to ensure that the Grand Assembly received a separate invitation, and he passed this to the delegation, which was already in Rome, a few days before the Conference opened.

On the 27th of February 1921, there were seated at the conference table the Allied delegates, the Greeks, and unexpectedly the United Turkish delegation. The famous "Sick Man" was that day to speak his last words to the world, through the mouth of the aged Tevfik. When it was the turn of the Turkish delegation to speak, the Grand Vezir said: "I pass the right of speech to the leader of the delegation of the Grand National Assembly, who is the true representative of the Turkish nation." Bekir Sami, Commissar for Foreign Affairs in Ankara, began to speak, and from that moment defended the cause of Turkey.

Those who were following the discussions immediately saw the difference between the revolutionaries in Anatolia and the delegates of the Sublime Porte. The first were young, vigorous and decisive; the second aged and feeble. Tevfik Paşa was afraid of catching cold in his legs, since his blood did not bring them the necessary heat, and he covered his knees with a woollen rug.

The great allied diplomats felt that they were strong enough to manage to outwit the Kemalists, who were appearing in international conferences for the first time. The Allies' plan was to make them accept the Treaty of Sèvres after making some concessions. France and Italy thought that they would satisfy the Turks at the expense of the Greeks. The delegates of the various countries soon realised that no practical result could come from the Conference, since Turkey was refusing to recognise the Treaty of Sèvres. So that the Conference should not end with that impression, the Great Powers prepared a plan of solution which they presented to the Turks and Greeks. They were to reply within a month

This plan gave Turkey the following niggardly offers: a plebiscite was to be held in Smyrna and the surrounding province after two years, and after five years these areas would pass to the party which had won the plebiscite; it was agreed to make a small reduction in the so-called zone of the Straits, which was under allied control; the number of occupying troops would be reduced; Istanbul was handed back and some promises were made about frontiers, capitulations, and financial matters, all of which naturally depended on the ratification of the Treaty of Sèvres.

During the month of March, on the 12th of which the useless Conference came to an end, the Powers separately tried to obtain some advantage from the Kemalist delegation. Bekir Sami showed readiness to enter into large diplomatic manoeuvrings with the masters of the world on his own account. He signed an agreement with Lloyd George under which Turkey promised to free her British prisoners in exchange for the Turks detained in the prisons of Malta, except those whom Great Britain accused of having cruelly treated British and Armenian persons during the war. He signed a convention with Aristide Briand which he thought was a complete triumph; France declared that she was ready to reduce her pressure over Cilicia to some extent in return for which the Nationalist Government would give France a privileged economic position. Finally he agreed with Count Sforza that Italy's influence should be dominant in the zone which Sèvres had allotted to her.

None of these agreements was accepted by Ankara; Bekir Sami had gone beyond his powers. In the first case, the British Government was assuming the right to judge Turkish citizens, which was unacceptable. The second revived a relic of the spirit of the capitulations, and the third suffered from the same defect. When Bekir Sami arrived in Ankara after rubbing shoulders with the great personages of Europe, he refused to accept that he had been wrong: on the contrary, he attempted to prove the soundness of his high diplomatic vision; however, since his protestations were not accepted, he resigned from his position.

The agreement on the exchange of prisoners, which the Assembly had not thought of admitting, entered into effect in practice. When Great Britain freed a number of prisoners in Malta, the Assembly ordered that an equal number of British should be released. Some months later through an agreement between the Red Crescent, the equivalent of the Western Red Cross, and the British High Commission in Istanbul, all prisoners of both sides were set at liberty.

Four days after the last session of the London Conference, an important treaty was signed in Moscow, which is known by the name of that city, between the Government of the Grand Assembly and the Union of Socialist Soviet Republics, which marked the triumph of the policy of friendship followed by the two sides. The two revolutions were linked by vital interests in the political field. They were both surrounded by enemies, condemned to disappearance by the

Powers of the Entente, and excluded from the world order; at the time when they were as likely to live as to die, the two revolutions met, understood each other and took each other by the hand. To Lenin, Turkey did not mean only security in the Black Sea, the Straits and the Caucasus, but also a powerful weapon in his struggle against British Imperialism in Iran and Afghanistan, whilst the Kemalist revolution, which was standing opposed to European domination, received from its beginnings the support of the oppressed Moslem peoples.

The two revolutions linked hands across Armenia. But there remained a delicate question, that of ideologies. The propagation of Bolshevik ideas could not serve the interests of the new Turkey. Kemalist ideals, if achieved, would amply fulfil national aspirations. It was equally inconvenient to the U. S. S. R. that nationalist movements should penetrate the small states which had been formed during the collapse of Russia, and which were authorised by Lenin's theories. Lenin was unable to apply these fine theories, based on true idealism, which like those of President Wilson produced difficulties and realities which could not be overcome. Lenin was now a statesman, and had to accommodate his ideals to find formulas which would still not depose him from his apostolic pedestal; it was a fine idea that the regions which had formed part of the lost Empire should govern themselves, but it should be through a government chosen by Moscow, which would bring everything back to where it had been.

Bolshevism preached the struggle against oppression, and its propaganda was invading the colonies of the European Powers; it announced: "We shall set alight the world with the fire of the Third International"; however, the propaganda was heard by the peoples of Turkish race and Moslem religion who were Russian subjects. Although the example of Kemalist nationalism was of benefit to the Bolsheviks in the colonies of the Imperialist Powers, it was not such an advantage in Tsarist Russia, whose frontiers the Soviet Government had decided to maintain.

Several of the new Soviet Republics, between the Don and Lake Baikal, were inhabited by Turks. The Turks had previously been masters of Russia, after the descendants of Cengiz Han had conquered her at the beginning of the thirteenth century, and she remained under them, the Golden Horde, for two centuries, until the Grand Duke Ivan the Good broke the chains of servitude. It was then the turn of the Russians to rule their former masters. But could the Turks not become free and govern themselves? This was the danger which the Soviets felt, and also the guarantee for Kemal that the Third International would not settle upon Anatolia.

In September 1920 an Asian Congress met in Baku, organised by Moscow. The peoples of Asia, whom ill-chance had made the plaything of the Western countries, met there. There was within them the seed of Asia's awakening, but feeble and insecure. Nevertheless, Great Britain was losing ground and was forced to withdraw from the Caucasus. Anglophobia gained strength in Iran and Afghanistan, on the road to India.

The leaders in Moscow set limits to Bolshevik expansion in Asia; nationalism was the weapon which could realise the aspirations of those oppressed peoples. Kemal's enemies in ideology tacitly recognised that his policy was good. For Turkey, Kemalism meant strength and faith, while Communism, which Kemal if sorely pressed might possibly have allowed to penetrate into Anatolia, and from which region, the right arm of Asia, it would have continued its progress towards Europe, would have meant nothing for him but weakness or despair.

The Baku Congress was attended by the former triumvir Enver Paşa, champion of pan-Turanism and mortal enemy of Great Britain. After his flight from Istanbul he had gone to Odessa, and got in touch with the Bolsheviks, who welcomed him. It would be very useful for Moscow to have the cooperation of this man, who was so well-known among the Russian Turks, in their negotiations' with the Moslem Russian republics. Enver's fellow triumvir Cemal Paşa was actively working in Afghanistan in the service of the Emir Amanullah, whose army he organised. This was activity against Great Britain, and Cemal was happy to do it. Since 1907, Great Britain had been exercising a disguised protectorate over Afghanistan, a country deep in the Hindu Kush and bordering upon India. Amanullah was one of the fervent standard-bearers of Asian awakening; in his enthusiasm he prepared an army with which he violated Indian frontiers. He then, on the eve of an encounter with the powerful British army, understood that his gesture had been over-romantic, and sued for peace. He achieved some important advantages and dedicated himself to transforming his country into a modern state. He signed a treaty of alliance with Ankara in March 1921.

Iran, closer to Russia, had better fortune and succeeded in shaking off the British protectorate, under Rıza Pehlevi.

Cemal was destined for a tragic end, as were Enver and Talât. The two first named made approaches to return to nationalist Turkey, but were unsuccessful. Cemal was assassinated by an Armenian in Tiflis; Talât died at the hands of an Armenian student in a street in Charlottenburg near Berlin in the same year, 1921. The arm of Armenian vengeance did not reach Enver, who set off for Turkestan as an agent of Moscow. Thus Enver went to meet his destiny. A fine chapter was to end the book of his life, filled with adventures, good fortune and immoderate bursts of glory.

The Emir of Buhara had risen against the new oppressors, the masters who had stepped into the place of the Tsars. His war cry, a Turkish cry, found an echo in Enver's heart, and he rushed to join the rebels. He was soon made their leader. In March 1922 he asked the Red Army to withdraw from Turkestan. It was already too late, for the Red Army was too strong, as the internal situation of the country was now stabilized. In the first days of August, in a battle to the southeast of Samarkand, Enver died facing the enemy, as was shown by the five bayonet wounds which killed him.

The Treaty of Moscow was signed on the 16th of March 1921 by Chicherin, the Soviet Commissar for External Affairs, and Yusuf Kemal in the name of the Grand Assembly. The document states that it is the right of peoples to decide their destinies freely, and recalls the solidarity uniting the two countries in the struggle against Imperialism, which had brought them to conclude a treaty of brotherhood. It recognises Turkey's right to her old Imperial frontiers before the Russo-Turkish war of 1877. The Grand Assembly cedes the city of Batum to the Soviet Republic of Georgia, but Turkey is given the right of free use of that port. The Soviet Government declares that the capitulation system is incompatible with the sovereign right of a country, and therefore considers it invalid in Turkey.

If the London proposals disappointed the Turks, they also disappointed the Greeks in their ambitions of territorial expansion. Greece had embarked on this adventure in Anatolia first, because her participation in the World War had been rewarded by the gift of Smyrna, and then when Turkish nationalism prevented the Powers from effecting the projected division of the Ottoman Empire, Greece was charged with a military operation which would make this possible. Now, because it suited the complex politics of envy between the Powers, the formal territorial promises which had been made to Greece were being called into discussion.

Constantine had been right when he opposed his country's abandonment of neutrality; nevertheless, the Greek army, which was in splendid conditions of materials and morale, would realise the unfulfilled promises; it would march with double enthusiasm to repeat the Achaean conquest and to bring back the Byzantine cross to the orthodox sanctuaries.

Before two of the four weeks' grace agreed in London had passed, the Greek Army, which had been reinforced effectively, began to advance towards the Great Railway, in front of which the Nationalists held their fortified positions. General Papulas ordered the offensive in a simple manner; his army was divided in two parts, to have as general objectives Eskişehir and Afyon Karahisar. Its superiority in numbers and arms would be sure to sweep away the defending forces. The railway, which meant ability to act, would become an advantage for the communications of the attacking army, and allow it to form an unshakeable front.

The Greek divisions began to move on the 23rd of March, the northern group starting from Bursa and the southern from Uşak. The first to establish contact was the southern Greek column, which forced Refet, who was defending that part of the front, to withdraw with more than half his forces towards Eskişehir. The rest moved southwards under the command of Fahrettin Paşa. The defence of Afyon Karahisar was broken and the city was at the mercy of the enemy. However, the Greek commander made a mistake which was immediately noted by Kemal; instead of directing the victorious divisions towards Eskişehir, where the result of the offensive would be decided, since Afyon was already within his power, he moved southeast towards Konya, leaving the real battlefield behind.

The Greek northern group attacked the Turkish lines on the 27th; it redoubled its efforts on the following day, and furiously attacked on the third day; on the 30th the whole defending front withdrew. At times the victory seemed to be inclining towards Greece; however Ismet, who had showed himself to be a soldier of the first rank, in the first battle of Inönü, was as vigilant as ever, and repaired the breached or reinforced the sectors which had been weakened by the shock of an enemy twice as powerful in numbers and armaments. From that day it was seen that the Greek drive was failing, exhausted by the obstinate Turkish resistance; on the following morning, Ismet threw in a formidable counterattack with reinforcements which had arrived from Ankara, destroyed the advantages which the enemy had obtained in the four days of battle, and forced them to retreat.

For the second time the enemy was seen from the hill of Inönü leaving the field of battle, along with their dead and even their wounded, together with plenty of military equipment. For a second time the extraordinary bravery and tenacity of the Turkish race, dominated by the new spirit communicated to it by Kemal, broke the offensive of the powerful invading army.

The hours passed slowly in Ankara, as Kemal observed with visible anxiety the development of the battle on the plan of the western front. It was natural that in days so serious for his country and his work, the direction of the plans of defence were in his hands. His joy was immense when he heard of the victory; his character was not demonstrative, or loud in the expression of his feelings to the outside world, but a clear smile revealed two rows of small white teeth. He composed a telegram for the victors of Inönü and their worthy leader as follows: "In congratulating you upon your great victory, which will write your name in

history's book of honour, and which inspires the whole nation with eternal gratitude, I wish to say that from the height upon which you stand, one can discern
not merely a glorious battlefield covered by thousands of enemy corpses, but a
view upon the horizon of a radiant future of glory for our people and for you."
Kemal did not suffer the malady of Themistocles, whom Miltiades' laurels prevented from sleeping.

On hearing that Ismet's forces were advancing towards Afyon Karahisar, the
Greek command ordered the evacuation of that city. The Greeks dug into positions at Dumlupınar. Refet advanced towards this last place with three infantry
divisions, intending to turn the Greek withdrawal into a flight, but he came up
against an obstacle, for his way was blocked by a battalion. Extraordinary though
it may seem, Refet could not succeed in dislodging it. He allowed so much time
to the enemy, that two reserve divisions were able to arrive and the main part of
the army was able to retreat in a normal way. On the 12th of April, Refet moved
onto the attack with eight divisions, and feeling sure of success he sent two cavalry divisions round by a long detour, to take up positions behind the enemy and
cut off its retreat.

The attack did not give the desired result; however at one moment, because
of the withdrawal of large Greek contingents, who were doing so because they
had been ordered to take up safe positions, Refet believed that the enemy was
really beating a retreat, and he hurriedly sent a telegram to Ankara claiming a
definite victory. Kemal was worried by some details which did not seem to him to
agree with the definite news that had been received, and he asked for clarification
of them. The sad truth was that the enemy had not been defeated; their positions
were excellent, and the attacks of the Turkish divisions had had no effect, though
the latter had suffered serious losses.

Thinking over the results of the Greek offensive, Kemal came to the conclusion that although it had been halted and the railway line was clear of enemies,
the Greeks would return to the attack. He did not waste a single day in the en-
joyments of the delights of victory or in pleasant dreams upon his laurels. The
defence must be reinforced to guard against every eventuality; the curtain had not
yet been raised over the more tragic acts of the drama. The army had lost confidence in Refet, and the safety of the country required that he should be deprived
of his command. Ismet was given complete control of the front, since a single
commander would ensure a better coordination of effort.

The work of the Grand Assembly, upon which rested all power, was being
held up by the disagreement which arose between the members even over the
most simple questions. At the start, the Assembly had the same political ten-

dencies as the "Association for the Defence of Rights"; but when it came to the question of discussing the items contained in the programme point by point, the various political leanings and opinions held by each individual member came into collision, so that the combative legislation needed by the country, and the solution of administrative and other problems, suffered delays or had to be left unresolved.

At the beginning of 1920, it was suggested that groups of members should be created, representing the different opinions which had arisen. Kemal thought that this would allow the Assembly to get through more work. This measure did not give the hoped-for result; on the contrary, whereas previously the members had in an isolated way spoken their own ideas or supported ideas of which they were persuaded by the eloquence of the proposer of this motion or that, they were now merely voting along party lines. Frequently there were turbulent sessions in which one group defended an idea while the other attacked it, while the national interest received no benefit. Kemal thought that as a solution to this state of affairs, there would be no objection to the foundation of a political group, since in all democratic countries the Presidents of Parliament or of the State belonged to political parties. He called it "The Group for the Defence of the Rights of Anatolia and Thrace." Its programme consisted of two points; first, to achieve the principles of the National Pact; the second contained the secret of Kemal's aspirations, to transform the theocratic Empire into a secular republic. It said: "Within the Constitutional Law, the group will spare no effort to prepare and gradually establish the organisation of the nation and the state."

In May 1921, the Assembly almost unanimously joined this new group, and from that moment it began to achieve useful work. Soon the Assembly was split, though not openly, into two great factions; the defenders of the holy institutions which ruled the Empire, and those who followed Kemal in hoping for modern means of government for their country. The second part of his party's programme awoke well-founded suspicions amongst the clerics and monarchists. The campaign against Kemal the "reformer" began quietly. They attacked him because, they said, he was planning to abolish the institutions and make himself dictator. He was preparing the way for this; was he not President of the Assembly, of the Government, and now of the most powerful political group? He was cutting down the prestige of the glorious Sultanate and the Holy Califate; although Vahdettin's conduct was worthy of criticism, to use that to overthrow the institutions which had lasted for centuries could be nothing more than a pretext hiding personal ambitions.

The alarm was given by the cleric Raif Efendi, member for Erzurum. With the agreement of other colleagues of his, he changed the name of the Erzurum Committee from "Association for the Defence of Rights" to that of "Association for the Defence of Holy Institutions." General Kâzım Karabekir, who enjoyed great influence inside and outside the army, took the side of the clerics and shared their fears. He sent Kemal a telegram in code, full of doubts, advice, warnings and questions. It could be seen between the lines that the conqueror of the Armenians suspected that his colleague might seize the place which had hitherto been held by the sons of Osman. Kemal realised that Karabekir, an extreme traditionalist, would become an important adversary at the first false step he made. He therefore used all his persuasiveness in explaining things to him in such a way as to calm him down. The most meaning phrases in his reply were: "The Constitutional Law is not a complete or detailed law; it is limited to introducing into our civil and administrative organisation the democratic principle which we are obliged to adopt by the necessities of the time. The opinion of Raif Efendi, that this law suggests the coming substitution of the monarchical regime by a republican one, is the product of his imagination."

Whether or not these words convinced Karabekir, the fact is that they made him hesitate and wait for the development of events; in other words he gave Kemal what he needed, time. The campaign of the monarchists and clerics did not cease.

The second victory of İnönü marked a greater separation between the Allies, who did not share the same view about the Greco-Turkish war, for which they alone were responsible. France and Italy found in İnönü greater reason to wish to become friends of the unfortunate Turks; Great Britain remained watching, though without interrupting her help to the Greeks.

Briand found a good opportunity to regain some of France's lost prestige in Turkey. He sent a former Minister, Monsieur Franklin-Bouillon, on an official mission to Kemal. Italy for her part also entered into more open relations with the Nationalist Government.

Franklin-Bouillon arrived in Ankara two months after the second victory of İnönü. The occasion favoured good understanding between France and Turkey; neither country wanted to continue the war in Cilicia. France was occupying the whole of Syria, so why should she risk making an enemy such as Turkey over the Turkish provinces of Adana and Antep? These provinces would become the Alsace and Lorraine of Asia, and would beget tragedies for the future. Kemal earnestly desired to reach agreement with some of the Powers of the Entente, since he knew that the greatest chance of victory lay in there being the greatest disagreements existing between the executors of the Treaty of Sèvres.

Kemal and Franklin-Bouillon began their discussions in the room which Kemal occupied at Ankara railway station. There was a difference of opinion when they tried to find a starting point as a basis for their negotiations. Kemal proposed that it should be the National Pact, but his diplomatic adversary said that this would present difficulties, and he therefore advised that it should be the Treaty of Sèvres. "That Treaty," said Kemal, "is a sentence of death, so fatal for the Turkish nation that we request that its name should not be pronounced by mouths which claim to be friends. It is impossible that Europe should be ignorant of our National Pact; perhaps it is ignorant of the text, but Europe and the whole world, seeing us spill our blood for years, must certainly reflect upon the reasons which have provoked such bloody conflicts."

The French government was hesitating before making an agreement with the new Turkish state. Since France was not yet convinced of the Turks' military power, she preferred to wait until she had greater security.

In the first days of May there appeared before the Independence Tribunal in Ankara the Indian Moslem Mustafa Saghir. He had been educated in the best schools of Great Britain, and had been working since years before in the intelligence service of that country in Egypt, Iran and Afghanistan. His last mission had been that of studying and carrying out the assassination of Mustafa Kemal. In the trial of Saghir, the defendant's confession drew away the veils of mystery which had been covering important events in the East, and there appeared in all its nakedness the vast plot which had been contrived against the great obstacle to British policy in Turkey, Mustafa Kemal.

CHAPTER 23

ISTANBUL IN CAPTIVITY

In his palace at Yıldız, which surrounded by its walls occupied the summit of one of those most beautiful hills beside the Bosporus, Sultan Mehmet Vahdettin walked, a tall skeletal figure, through the great halls and corridors, abandoned by the courtiers. The Turks have given Vahdettin the name of the Black Sultan, because of his feeble character and his feudal obedience to the British, and because he took up arms against the struggle which the Turks made against their invaders.

The Calif of hundreds of millions of Moslems was feeling the same sickly fears as his brother the Red Sultan; he was afraid for his life. Those cursed rebels who were penetrating everywhere were capable of making an attempt against him, like those nihilists who had assassinated the Tsar Alexander II, and if the revolution was successful his fate would certainly be that of Louis XVI or Nicholas II; yet he had Great Britain's promise that she would not abandon him. From Yıldız one could see the powerful warships of His Britannic Majesty and his Allies cut out against the view of the Marmara and the Bosporus like Chinese shadow puppets; this sight was enough to calm down the Black Sultan.

The decadence of the House of Osman can be measured by its last descendants, the four sons of Abdülmecit, weakened by the pleasures of the harem: Abdülhamit the murderer, afflicted with that fear known as persecution mania; Murat V, feebleminded; Mehmet Refat, unable to assume responsibility, and Vahdettin, in whose lustreless eyes one could recognise the characteristics of the Imperial family and infer the existence of irresolution, insensitivity and fear. At least the decadence of the Byzantine Emperors produced a noble gesture, in the pride of the defender of Constantinople, Constantine XIII, and his heroic death in the final battle. "I will not hand over the city which God entrusted to me except to God himself," was his reply to the demands of Sultan Mehmet. Vahdettin, however, had not only failed to oppose the occupation of the city and the total dissection of the Empire, but was even allied with the foreigners themselves to fight against the people whose fate had been entrusted to him by his country.

He was afraid even of his own thoughts; shades invaded the palace corridors and with them there arrived furtively the horrible ghosts which populate dark corners, so that they reached up to the Black Sultan's bent shoulders, making him feel the icy breath of their gaping jaws and hurry on ahead of them. He knew who those monsters were who accompanied him as he wandered nightly through the palace, and penetrated his own room: some were begotten by his fear, others by the remorse he did not admit even to himself.

To escape from emptiness and shadows, Vahdettin sought refuge in his harem; there he had beautiful women who sang, played musical instruments and tried to entertain him with sweet voices and reverential manners. Carnal pleasures brought him oblivion for a few moments. To prolong and repeat these, he had to resort to the secrets of the ancient East, but his was a boredom difficult to cure.

It was in those days that he discovered amid the flowers in his garden a flower more beautiful than they, a fifteen-year-old girl, who seemed the incarnation of spring; she was called Nevzat and was the daughter of one of the palace gardeners. The Sultan desired her and possessed her; the youth and innocence of his sweetheart made him live again through his youthful years. Her bed radiated a light which frightened the ghosts way. Vahdettin forgot the horrors of the civil war he had provoked and the endless sufferings of his people; he even momentarily forgot his own future, which was his main worry, and his throne, to which he clung tenaciously.

Istanbul had been changed by almost three years of allied occupation, which had been mitigated at the first, but had become absolute since the British coup. In the blue mists of morning on the Bosporus, the city always offered the unique beauty of her much praised silhouette, but it was only when one came closer to her walls, walked through her streets, and looked into the courtyards of the imperial mosques, that one made contact with the unsuspected life which was animating her.

A thick crowd was choking in the narrow streets, which had become the tributaries of the few avenues which led like rivers to the squares and market places. British patrols cut through the multicoloured multitude, crossing the paths of other groups of soldiers, French, Italians, Greeks and Americans. The occasional Turkish guard, standing by his sentry box, watched the events around him with indifference; he seemed certain that no one was going to ask his advice should any disorder occur.

Since the end of the World War not less than 550.000 people had flocked into Istanbul. The city was capable of housing a maximum of a million inhabitants, so that it was necessary to build barracks, make whole suburbs of tents, and adapt the medreses beside the great mosques, together with their courtyards and dependent buildings, to give shelter to the thousands of Turkish refugees who had fled from the Greek bayonets. The "Muhacir" as were called the refugees of Turkish race, who incessantly moved towards Thrace and the Straits during the dismemberment of the Ottoman Empire, kept an impressive silence, which is characteristic of Turks; in their encampments it was only the song of the shepherds which wept with grief for the dead, and nostalgia for their fields, their lost herds and ruined huts.

It was the White Russians who were the largest group in the foreign quarters of Galata and Pera. There had been constant movement towards Istanbul ever since the outbreak of the storm of revolution in Russia. With the mystical optimism of the Russian nobility, they persuaded themselves that they would not remain there long; however, time passed by, the news was always worse and the number of refugees grew every day. They had hopes of the war which the Powers were making against the Bolshevik Government, under Admiral Kolchak, Denikin, Yudenich and finally in Wrangel and Bahalovich; however the remains of the White Russian armies enormously increased the influx of Russians to Istanbul.

Still wearing their various uniforms, Russian generals, officers and Cossacks elbowed their way through Pera together with princes, beggars, the soldiers of six other armies, officials of the Ottoman and foreign administrations, ambassadorial and consular employees, orthodox priests with statuesque profiles and fine locks of hair tied up in elegant buns, rabbis with beards and ringlets, dressed in loose-fitting taffeta robes, Franciscans, Jesuits and many other orders; nuns in white wimples, philosophical Moslem clerics, Armenian priests with bony and melancholy features; ladies of Levantine society, of extreme elegance, showing off the "dernier cri" of Parisian fashion, and the ordinary population of Greeks, Turks and Armenians.

There was literally no room in the city to contain such an increase in its population. The refugees found it difficult to find work, since the capital was isolated from Anatolia and trade was therefore almost paralysed. The city was living a false life, animated by the money which the foreigners and their armies were spending limitlessly.

The Russians found a solution to this black gloom by opening restaurants and cabarets, in which the services rendered by beautiful and distinguished Muscovite ladies ensured success. Hunger, despair, and everything else which was inseparable from the great poverty which afflicted the city, and on the other side the presence of gold and lust, rapidly delivered the city up to vices. Places providing unconfessable pleasures grew like mushrooms amid the dark shadows; there was no desire, no matter how low, which could not be satisfied in the new Sodom into which European civilisation had turned the seat of the Califate.

In spite of the intense life which seemed to reign in her streets, because of the crowds which frequented them, in spite of the music which could be heard from the places of entertainment, and the tumult amid the brothel quarters frequented by the soldiery, one could feel that there was something tragic beneath all this noise, and in the life of that abandoned city. Diseases which the neglected health control allowed to spread in an alarming way began to exact their payment for indulged vices. Cocaine, hashish and alcohol found thousands of addicts. The lower areas of the town were ruled by criminals. Rape, kidnapping, assault and robbery were the order of the day. What was the allied police doing? Not much, evidently. There is little order where there are many masters. The various police forces, public and secret, were fully occupied in spying on each other, discovering and informing the respective High Commissioners of the plans of the other Allied Powers, and they were all busily watching the Nationalists, who were sending all manner of help from Istanbul to their brothers in Anatolia. Nationalist officers in different disguises daily entered the city, where they had created secret organisations. It was this which interested the feared Allied Police.

And yet there, in the midst of that captive city, there existed a so-called government of the Ottoman Empire. The Grand Vezir Tevfik Paşa presided over the Council of Ministers and presented the affairs of state to the Emperor for his approval. The mentality of the Ottoman court, made up of those ancient Vezirs, was curious indeed; for they were unable to realise what a sad comedy they were playing out, as a government which could not even keep its control over the capital city! This mentality was shared by the Ministers whom Kemal had detained in Ankara, hoping that through contact with the people and understanding of the Nationalists' ideals, they would finally decide to cooperate with the Government of the Grand Assembly. Izzet and Salih were not at ease on the plateau; they wanted to return to Istanbul and rejoin their families. In order to achieve this they promised to resign from their ministries, and happily left for the city where the Moslem Vatican was situated, robbed of all prestige.

It seems incredible that they did not apparently notice the oppression suffered by the Turks in the captive capital, in contrast with the freedom in which the people lived in Anatolia. In Anatolia there were no capitulations, no consular tribunals, no persecutions by the Allied Police, no punishments, no gallows for those forking for their country, and none of the constant insults received by Turks for wearing the fez. The following is a true story which exemplifies the state of Imperial authority; the British police arrested the Grand Vezir in his car, for breaking the rule controlling movement. It was only at the police station that Tevfik Paşa was at last able to make them understand who he was, which had been beyond the understanding of the British policemen, even with the help of the insignia which distinguished his vehicle.

Since Greece was not at war with the Empire, but with the common enemy, the Kemalists, diplomatic relations had not been broken, and a Greek force formed part of the Allied troops of occupation. Their military mission was accommodated in the middle of Pera, beneath the Greek royal flag. It would be a mistake, however, to believe that the Greek colours attracted any attention from the passersby, since the quarters of Galata and Pera were profusely decked with blue and white flags. The Greek orthodox population was living in overflowing happiness, awaiting the triumphal entry of Constantine. The latter's portrait had replaced that of the former idol Venizelos; beneath the King's portrait was written the word "Ergete" — "Come."

Those Turks who felt the imperious voice of patriotism calling them did not hesitate to give up comfort and pleasures for the revolutionary cause, together with its privations and its spartan life. Those who remained amid the foreigners, and were not employed in supplying the Anatolian army or in journalism in defence of the cause, had to endure the daily insults of the foreigners, who treated them like people from their colonies; however we cannot believe that they felt the insults very deeply, despite the tragic days which they later claimed to have lived through.

CHAPTER 24

SAKARYA!

The sun of the Anatolian summer scorches the ground of the high and barren plateaus which descend in prolonged steps from the imposing eastern massifs down to the soft and fertile regions of the Aegean coast. These last areas are a paradise, whilst the plateaus are a desert tortured by their climate.

A heavy heat falls upon the earth, and the cracks in the ground beg for water. Men and animals go in search of refuge in the shade; but hardly have the worst hours of heat passed, when over all the ill-cared-for roads of the plateau there is renewed the monotonous creaking of the solid wooden wheels which turn, complaining sadly, upon the axles, also wooden, of the "kağnı," the ancient two-wheeled carts drawn by oxen or buffaloes. Long lines of "kağnıs" move along the roads on journeys lasting weeks at a time. There are no men to be seen in these strange convoys, for the measured pace of the oxen is led only by women or children. There are also to be seen long caravans of camels or little donkeys moving along the tracks in the same direction.

Night comes as a relief, but the groaning of the solid wheels does not end; now they make an accompaniment to the women's melancholy songs. Where are all these convoys going across the interminable roads of Anatolia? What grief, what pain is it that moves those women to abandon their homes and make these exhausting marches? For what do their voices weep along with the wheels of the "kağnı?"

It is the voice of their country, threatened, which leads them over the burning white roads, carrying ammunition and food to the men at the front who are waiting for the enemy's final assault; perhaps they will not be able to stop him, and then the whole of Anatolia will suffer the devastation which the western provinces have endured. The creaking of the "kağnı" and the song of the women in the night make up a hymn never before heard in Anatolia, which makes the dust of the bones of sleeping generations vibrate with emotion, as they dream of glory beneath the protection of the Moslem minarets, or the stone lions of the Hittites, for it is a hymn to liberty, and to the efforts of the people to defend its right to live. Thirty centuries later, a western people, the Greeks, are following the trail of the Thraco-Phrygians who destroyed the existence of the Hittite Empire; the new invaders are preparing to give the coup de grace to another Asian Empire, that of the Ottomans.

The boats, usually of small tonnage, which managed to escape the allied vigilance, deposited their precious cargo of war materials at the Black Sea ports. The ammunition and arms which had been obtained by those working for the cause in Istanbul were transported from those ports to the front, many hundreds of kilometres away, by an organisation of the people. Fine examples of the people's self-denial appeared daily. No orders from the Nationalist authorities were needed to have the boats relieved of their cargoes, and the contents dispatched in the required direction in hundreds of carts and "kağnıs."

Women showed themselves as active as the men, and it was they who took charge of conducting the "kağnıs." Clothed in their oriental costumes of bright colours, their heads wrapped in yaşmaks, leaving part of the face uncovered, they took an effective step towards their emancipation, by showing their usefulness and their capacity for self-denial.

War materials, which were no longer needed there after the Armenian campaign, were brought from the Russian frontier over a distance of more than a thousand kilometres. In the last stages, because of the lack of roads or other reasons, the porters carried the ammunition on their shoulders, to deposit it right in the trenches or beside the artillery batteries, before turning back to their far-off villages, as usual without a word. The invaders on the other hand were remarkably well-equipped with mechanical means of transport, as with the best ammunition and all the conveniences which a modern army can enjoy. In addition, they were occupying the paradise of Anatolia, its western part, bathed by fresh streams, covered with rich vegetation, and opening onto three seas which kept the expeditionary force in touch with the European world. They lacked nothing, neither the spirit of conquest, mystic fervour or racial hatred. Constantine realised that an even larger army was necessary for the decisive campaign. The two battles of İnönü proved that Turkey was ready for sacrifices, and that the forty-two thousand Greeks who had made the final attack there would have to be doubled in order to make sure of victory. Within three months the number of men rose to a little under a hundred thousand, that of machine-guns to 5.600 and that of cannons to 345. Some of the new soldiers were recruited from among the Orthodox subjects of the Ottoman Empire.

Against such an army as this, Kemal had gathered together 56.000 men. It was impossible to enact a general mobilisation, since it was not that men were lacking but the means of maintaining them, arms and ammunition.

The Nationalist army waited behind the line of the Anatolian railway, in positions to the west of the fortified cities of Eskişehir, Kütahya and Afyon. There was no doubt that the third assault was about to be made.

King Constantine knew his people well; from Venizelos' example, he knew the fate that would await him if he did not obtain victory; he had been forgiven for Inönü, but it was not wise to risk his fortune another time. When everything was ready down to the last detail, and he felt certain of victory, he chose the 10th of July for the decisive attack which Greece had been waiting for anxiously.

General Papulas was in command. He had experience of grief. After being beaten at Inönü, he understood his mistakes and was this time determined to act more cleverly. He concentrated his army into two compact groups; however, instead of directing them against the fortified cities, he ordered them to attack en masse towards the gaps between them. The day dawned when the great Anatolian tragedy would begin, in which two peoples were to bleed to death. The Greeks marched enthusiastically to the attack on the plateau; many of them expected at any moment to see there appear in the sky the cross seen by Constantine the Great, with the words "in hoc signo vinces."

The most violent attack was made against the Turkish left wing between Afyon and Kütahya. The first of these cities fell to the Greeks on the 13th and the second on the 17th. The centre of the Turkish army also began to give way. Only the positions at Inönü, which were only weakly besieged, kept up resistance. It seems that this was part of the Greek plan, to hold the mass of the Turkish army at Eskişehir, and then surround the city and destroy the army finally.

With exemplary calm, General Ismet was passing through the greatest crisis of his life. He was the commander responsible for the front, which had been broken up through the loss of Afyon and Kütahya, and there was a danger that the whole defending army might be annihilated. He could order a general retreat to the east of the railway, abandoning that backbone of Anatolia; this, however, would mean recognising defeat, and losing the army's whole prestige before the European Powers. Ismet's nerves were exhausted by the continual tension; his plain soldier's uniform looked like a borrowed suit on his small body, which had become terribly thin. His generals wanted to resist, each of them having a different opinion. Like the officers and men, Ismet understood that Kemal's presence was essential; at such a time, Kemal's aura of military victory made him into a demigod of war. He had the genius and secret of electrifying the masses of soldiers, and it was he who could give life to that army on the edge of a horrible disaster.

On the day after the capture of Kütahya, the 18th, Kemal arrived at great speed at Karaca Hisar, to the southwest of Eskişehir, where Ismet's headquarters were situated. Ismet's dwelling was in a miserable shack; for furniture, he had no more than a camp bed, a rough wooden table on which the battle plans were laid, and two or three chairs. With a sombre expression, Kemal carefully studied the placement of the little blue and red flags which showed the position of both sides; no tremor showed in his voice as he asked for certain information. Ismet and other high commanders watched him, awaiting his orders; a certain relaxation could be seen in their manner, since they would no longer have to torture their hearts over dilemmas; from now on all they would have to do was to obey.

Kemal spoke; the whole army was to be gathered to the north and south of Eskişehir; that city would have to be abandoned, and contact with the enemy broken off, the army retreating to the east of the river Sakarya, where it would be possible to reorganise it. These wise decisions provoked severe criticism: it was argued that they should not abandon such well-populated regions and important cities while there was still hope. Kemal realised this perfectly well, and considered that this was the greatest disadvantage of his daring tactics, and he therefore added: "Let us unhesitatingly apply the lesson which military science dictates to us. We will take care of the other disadvantages later."

On the evacuation of Eskişehir, it was entered by Constantine's troops on the 19th. The Turks launched a counterattack to the east of the city, to allow enough time for their various formations to put enough distance between themselves and their invaders. The counterattacking troops were the last to break off contact, and make for the deserted plateau. About 150 kilometres of burning plain would have to be crossed before they reached the river Sakarya, beyond which the remains of the army would be united. As the army marched in small formations, and even in isolated groups of men, munition trains, and artillery batteries, it was joined by the Moslem population, who had managed to escape in time from the Greek invasion. The tracks overflowed with an uncountable number of vehicles drawn by various means. The carts which contained the rest of their belongings were attended by whole families, of whom the more fortunate could add a couple of cows, or a few goats and domestic birds.

These rivers of man and animals, converging towards Ankara, resembled the great migrations of the Turkish tribes on the march, but this time they were not marching in search of better lands to conquer and colonise. The great number of wounded men, the general agitation, and the terror of those who were lagging behind, which could be seen reflected on their faces whenever they looked round as if they feared at any moment to see enemies pursuing them, and the disorder among which soldiers and peasants went mingled together, showed that this time it was an exodus.

After the first moment of rejoicing had passed, Constantine realised that his victory had been reduced in effect since the Kemalist army, despite the heavy reverse it had suffered, had managed to retreat and give itself time to reorganise, by placing 150 kilometres of deserted country between it and himself. With the agreement of his generals he decided to make the final attack as soon as possible and capture Ankara.

Kemal moved away from the lost regions, travelling by railway from Eskişehir to Ankara. Enemy planes were bombarding strategic places. The general retreat had begun. There was nothing more for the Paşa to do there; it was in Ankara at the Grand Assembly and before public opinion, which had been frightened by the news of defeat, that his presence was necessary in order to struggle against loss of morale.

Mustafa Kemal was travelling in a compartment reserved for him, which was a carriage lacking in any sort of comfort. His face was contracted, pale to the point of greyness, as he absorbed himself in deep reflection. His companions, who included several high-ranking officers, were talking over the tragic events in low voices and gloomy tones; half Anatolia was lost, including her most important cities and the railway; many thought that this meant the loss of all hope. Kemal heard part of the conversation and raised his eyes towards them: "What can the railway mean," he asked, "or Eskişehir, of any other city? Nothing! For us the army is everything, and we have saved it!"

Outside the window it was night. Beside the tracks the Porsuk river flowed on its capricious course, at one moment beneath the rails, then further off, them coming near again. To the south, a people was marching, exhausted by grief and fatigue, across the deserted plain. The retreat of the Turks, which had begun under the walls of Vienna, had now reached the centre of Asia Minor, where men were trying to enslave them. Kemal looked again at his lamenting companions, and his eyes lit up as he said words which made them doubt his mental stability: "I will defeat the enemy within four weeks!"

Ankara became seized with anxiety as the general retreat began; it was certain that the Greeks were marching towards it, and that the Turkish army in its shattered state could not hold them back. As the first refugees were establishing their camps of carts like a belt around the city, many of Ankara's inhabitants fearfully left for destinations further to the east. Muted reproaches were heard against the Nationalist Government, and against Kemal, who had miscalculated the strength of the Turkish people and those of their adversaries.

The Members of Parliament who opposed Kemal found people to listen to them, even amongst his own partisans. His enemies, after painting a picture of defeat in more tragic colours, insinuated that there must be someone responsible for this most sad situation; that person was now preferring to remain in obscurity, but he must be dragged out and made to face his responsibilities, which he could not escape. Some members poured out their bitter rancor against the creator of the defences. Others gave themselves up to despair, thinking that total disaster was inevitable; the remainder thought that the only salvation lay in nominating Kemal as Generalissimo; up till then, his name had been synonymous with victory in the battlefield.

Kemal waited till the storms of eloquence had passed before presenting himself at the Assembly. As soon as nerves were exhausted and oratory satisfied, public opinion moved to the conclusion that he should be asked to accept the supreme command, and he thereupon appeared in the Assembly during a secret session. He presented a note which was immediately read out, accepting the command under one condition, that he should be given all the powers which the Assembly possessed. This was essential if he was to have speedy obedience to the orders he must give in order to increase his military power and the possibilities for defence. He also stipulated that the powers given to him were to be limited to a period of three months.

The members, who at the beginning had been quite ready to crush him beneath the weight of a huge responsibility, recoiled before Kemal's demand. They thought they could see the spectre of dictatorship behind the dictatorial powers he had asked for. During the two secret sessions, to which the discussion extended, a pretext was made of anxiety for Kemal's own security, while it was also argued that the Assembly would lose all its power. Kemal gave assurances on all counts. On the 5th of August 1921, Kemal was invested with the rank of Generalissimo, and given all the powers of the Assembly, though it was declared that both the title and the powers, which were given for a period of three months, could be withdrawn from him at any moment.

The Law of Dictatorship which had been approved, was similar to that of "dictatore creando" which was promulgated by the Roman senate at the instance of Titus Largius, in the 253rd year of Rome, to be used in case of extreme danger to the state. The dictator was at the same time a magistrate and commander of the army; his power was equivalent to that of the ancient Kings. His power was limited to six months. This law brought great advantages to the Roman Republic.

The Generalissimo remained in Ankara for a week, devoting himself to providing the army with men, clothing, and means of transport and organising its proper supply. The last battle, the retreat, and the abandonment of large stores, had left the army in a lamentable state. Kemal knew those small details with which great things are made; his orders, which had the power of law, followed each other rapidly. A commission for requisition was set up in every part of the country; now that Turkey's destiny depended on the efficiency of her war machine, the whole nation must contribute to the creation of its army.

Refet, who was a better organieer than a soldier, was appointed Commissar for Defence, while Fevzi was given the exclusive responsibility for the General Staff. These two men were placed under the immediate command of the Generalissimo. The country was transformed into a great workshop in which the most varied objects necessary for defence were tirelessly manufactured. The number of decisions issued by Kemal within only a few days would astonish any ordinary army commander; for him, everything was improvisation, from the ensuring of the most insignificant details of the soldiers' clothing up to the provision of artillery ammunition.

On the 12th of August Kemal left for the front accompanied by Fevzi; Ismet was still commander of the front. The disorganised army had halted on the east bank of the Sakarya, the ancient Sangarius, which flows across the plateau over rough ground, before falling towards the Black sea, through defile after defile, with sharp changes of height. It was decided to try to hold the enemy along the Sakarya, on both sides of the bridge which carries the Eskişehir-Ankara railway across the river; the front was about a hundred kilometres long. It would have been an impossible task to fortify such a long front adequately. Kemal's genius perceived that the enemy would try to make an encircling movement around the Turkish left wing, since it would be easier to approach Ankara from that side. He decided to concentrate his best forces on the threatened wing. If he was wrong, all was lost.

The Turks were helped by two geological allies, the river and the steep hills. To cross the first of these, the Greeks would have to brave the Turkish machine-gun fire unprotected; to capture the hills meant assaulting as many fortresses. There was a third ally too, the exhausting temperature of the Asian summer, which was making the areas which the invaders had to cross into deserts where water was scarce.

Kemal suffered a misfortune on the mountain called Karadağ, which dominated the railway crossing over the Sakarya. He had got off his horse to observe some defence works, holding the reins under his arm, and lit a cigarette before remounting. The horse shied, and jumped sideways, knocking Kemal violently to the ground. At his headquarters, which were at Polatlı, behind Karadağ, it was found that he had a rib fractured in such a way that it was pressing sharply against a lung. The pain was terrible, and he could only walk by leaning over towards his wounded side. His doctors advised complete rest, but that was impossible. So many sacrifices were needed to obtain victory in the battle, and he could be one more of them!

The soldiers saw a bad omen in this accident; however, before 48 hours had passed, they again saw the Paşa touring the front defence lines on horseback. He told the groups who came round him, in a voice subdued with pain and exhaustion: "In the same place that one of my bones was broken, the resistance of the enemy will be broken!"

Kemal's desperate resolve to win infected his army. Every resource of man and material was being used up and yet, on the eve of battle, the new army was ten thousand men fewer than that which had awaited the enemy in front of the railway; so great had been its losses.

The headquarters were moved from Polatlı to a village, Alagöz, from which the battle could be directed better, since it was an equal distance from both wings. The writer Halide Edip, a woman emancipated from the old customs, who had come at Kemal's call to fight for the revolution, and inflamed the people with her ardent oratory, entered the army as a private soldier. Later she became a declared political adversary of Kemal, and wrote a book in which she showed her animosity towards him; nevertheless, she could not but recognise on many occasions her admiration as a Turkish woman for that great man. In her book "The Turkish Ordeal" she recounts her first visit as a soldier to the Generalissimo at Alagöz: "The narrow village road is full of holes, muddy and dark. I think it is after midnight. We cross a little bridge and make for the largest of the houses on the other side of the stream. I recognise Kemal's personal guards, with their black tunics, like those worn by men of the Black Sea. It is a half-ruined house. The Paşa's Aide-de-Camp takes me to his room, which is the only one with a gas lamp. Mustafa Kemal stands up. It is clear that his rib is still causing him much pain, as he walks with difficulty and rests himself against the wooden table which is in the middle of the room."

"At that moment I went towards Mustafa Kemal with veneration in my heart. In that humble Anatolian house, he was the incarnation of the decision of young men to die, so that the nation should live. No palace, title, or power would make him as great as he was in that room, from which he was to lead the Turks to their final effort to resist complete annihilation. I went to him and kissed his hand."

Before giving the order to advance on the conquest of the plateau, King Constantine advised his General Staff to take every necessary precaution against the climate and the ground, two dangerous enemies. The transport services were excellent, as a great number of lorries assured the supply of the staging posts, and the provision of water.

The magnificent Greek army began to move on the 13th of August. It consisted of 90,000 perfectly armed men, equipped with 7,000 machine- guns, 300 cannon, and 20 aeroplanes. Their recent victory had given the soldiers calmness and dexterity; no impression was made on them either by the sun or by the rough going. The Mediterranean races are ready to follow great enthusiasms, and if fed by some grand idea, they are able to achieve prodigious things. The Turks are distinguished from them through being more difficult to enthuse, but in compensation they have an extraordinary tenacity, which can only be compared to that of other oriental peoples. Kemal placed much of his confidence upon this difference in temperament.

The Greek army was opposed by the Turks with a total of 40,500 infantry, 4,500 cavalry and about 700 machine-guns; the artillery had only 177 cannon left while the airforce had no more than two planes. Kemal's faith must have rested on factors other than his little army's armaments and numerical strength. History offered examples of greater attempts by the Christian West against the Turks which had been brought to nothing in Anatolia. Had not the crusaders of Peter the Hermit been decapitated to the last man? It is true that the warriors of the Duke of Lorraine defeated the Turks on the plain of Dorylaeum - today Eskişehir, but the privations they had to endure on the desert plateau inflicted great losses upon them; there were days on which 500 men died of thirst. In the twelfth century, the army of the Emperor Conrad succumbed at the hands of the Turks in the defiles of the Taurus. Louis VII had to give up his land expedition after his army had been decimated. He embarked in Antalya to escape from the cursed country of Anatolia, but the thousands of pilgrims who were unable to follow his example were put to the sword by the Turks. When Frederick Barbarossa died in the river Cydnus, his army was left to the mercy of the scimitars.

Constantine's new crusaders might suffer a fate similar to that of their predecessors.

Within ten days, the Greeks had passed the test of sun and terrain, and after studying the Turkish positions, they threw themselves impatiently into the attack. From the mountain where his royal standart billowed, Constantine watched through a telescope as his assault troops crossed the river and broke the Turkish front in several places. The breaches were immediately filled with the troops who had been deployed in the rear guard. Every hill to which the Turks clung savagely cost enormous sacrifices before it could be taken.

The sight of these thousands of heroic men in a titanic struggle was a sublime spectacle; the courage of the fighters on both sides was at the same, very high level. As Kemal had foreseen, the Greeks made their chief efforts against the left wing, which was able to withstand their furious attack without giving way. On the 31st of August, after nine days and nights of uninterruped fighting, that wing was forced to retreat twenty kilometres. The front, which originally faced westwards, was obliged by the Greek pressure to change its position and face southwards.

The battle entered a phase which was bloody in the extreme; there was hand to hand fighting, entire divisions were wiped out, and the generals fell fighting along with their soldiers. The vigorous Greek attacks frequently broke through the Turkish lines, for which circumstance Kemal laid down from the beginning a new tactical rule for military history. Wishing to destroy the belief that success resides in the preservation of lines of defence, he said: "There are no such things as lines of defence, but a surface of defence, which is the entire country. Not an inch of the territory of the country can be abandoned without having first been bathed in the blood of its citizens. Any unit, great or small, may be dislodged from its positions; but it must rebuild its front to face the enemy in the first place where it can maintain itself and continue the fight. Units which see their neighbors orced to retreat must not join their fortunes with them. It is their duty to resist in their positions until the end." The battle continued ferociously, and the Greek assault did not weaken. Every metre of terrain cost them much blood, and nowhere did Kemal's army break. The Turks died, but killed as they died, and the Greek drive finally exhausted itself. In two weeks of fighting they had pushed the Turkish left wing to within only 50 kilometres of Ankara. Without question, the decisive moment was approaching.

Kemal's knowledge of his army was extraordinary; he knew the exact number of men who fought in each division and in the small units, together with the names and abilities of their commanders, while the terrain had no secrets from him. But Kemal could no longer influence the result of the battle; it was the commanders at regimental and battalion level who in fact held the active direction of the battle in their hands.

After 14 days of fighting it was feared that a crisis had arrived, with the fall of some hills called Çaldağ, to which the General Staff attached great importance; they could be considered the last Turkish bulwark in the defence of Ankara. Kemal was in a state of great excitement that night, drinking coffee and smoking continuously. He could not remain seated, in spite of the pain caused by his broken rib whenever he moved, and he walked round the table, bent over and resting himself against the furniture. He looked again at the plan of battle, asking himself again aloud whether he should order the retreat while it was still possible. If he did so, Ankara was lost, the remains of the army would then have to retreat beyond the Kızılırmak, and Nationalism would find it difficult to raise its head again after a blow of that kind. To remain appeared to offer the prospect of total annihilation, but perhaps that was preferable. His last campaign would find him at the head of his men. Then they would see how men of his type died.

Those who saw Kemal during the time of Sakarya, agree in saying that he never at any other time showed as then the depth of his sold. The thought of the thousands of men, whom his policy for saving Turkey was taking to their deaths, the responsibility which weighed upon his shoulders, and the attacks which would fall upon him if he failed, had removed the rigid mask which had covered his face during other battles and while he was performing the task of government. He was like men who are condemned to death, who do not seek to disguise or hide their state of mind.

His work during the recent weeks, his wound, the exhausting climate, his carelessness about eating, since he sustained himself more with coffee than with food, his excessive smoking, the little rest he took sitting in his chair, and above all his nervous exhaustion, all these had made him into a ghost of his own self. A grey shadow covered his wasted face, which was ploughed by deep wrinkles; wide circles surrounded his eyes, which shone as if lit by a fever. He was terrible to look at.

It was at two in the morning when the telephone rang in the next room; an officer told the Generalissimo from the doorway that Fevzi Paşa wanted to speak to him. Kemal went to the telephone as quickly as he could; the officers in the house stood around him; the intense emotion of the moment was shown by their anxious expressions, grimaces which showed ruddy under the lamp-light. "Is that you, Excellency? You say that the day has ended in our favour? How? The Greeks will soon withdraw? ...."

It seemed that Kemal had become years younger in a few minutes. It was suggested that he should take a short rest, but he refused and asked for coffee. The exhaustion which the enemy army had reached must be taken advantage of, and an offensive launched. The plan of attack was the following: as allowed by the reduced scale of the Greek attacks on the left wing, he would take away as many troops as he could from there and from the centre, move them unnoticed by the enemy to the right wing, and launch an attack along the Sakarya which would endanger the enemy's lines of communication and retreat. The Greeks had in fact advanced 75 kilometres east of the river in their desire to outflank the left wing of the Turkish army.

On the following day it could be seen that the Greeks had lost all their reserves of energy in that battle in the heart of the unfriendly plateau; their strength had failed, one step away from victory.

Marching by night, Kemal moved the troops which he had been able to collect to the right wing, where he made a surprise attack. Papulas understood the imminence of danger, and ordered his troops to withdraw towards the river. Then Kemal ordered the general counterattack. He directed the final phase of the battle from Karadağ. Wrapped in his long grey coat, and wearing his astrakhan kalpak with an oriental tilt, he sat cross-legged in the eastern fashion to make the last moves on that gigantic chessboard: checkmate!

Two weeks after that memorable night, Papulas gave the order for retreat. The Turks were also exhausted, and there was no question of a general pursuit.

The Sakarya battle lasted 22 days and nights. It can be considered as one of the great feats of arms in history. This is not only because of the change of fortune it showed and the genius with which it was directed, so as to give the victory to an army only half the size of its adversary, but also for its historical importance. It marks the end of the Turkish decline, which had been marked out by an unending succession of battles, disastrous for the Crescent, stretching from the walls of Vienna until they reached that Anatolian river at which the western advance was halted.

This battle can be considered as being of the same importance as that of Chalons, which saved the European peoples from Asiatic domination, that of Poitiers, where Charles Martel stopped the Arab invasion, and the second siege of Vienna, which marked the end of Ottoman dominance.

On the 17th of September, the Grand Assembly gave Kemal the rank of Marshal and the title "Gazi," the most prized title which is awarded in the Moslem East to a great conqueror.

CHAPTER 25

THE PEACE OFFENSIVE

Greece left behind on the muddy banks of the Sakarya the great dreams which for a moment she had been near to realising. In that terrible battle, the Greeks had fought like heroes; everything pointed to their victory; their failure to achieve it was due only to the strength given to an army by the presence of a great commander. Xenophon Stratikos, Deputy-Commander of the Greek General Staff during the battle, analyses the causes of the defeat as follows: "The nerves of the Greeks were stretched to the utmost, and finally gave way before the trenches dug in front of Ankara. When they realised that Kemal's willpower and energy was stronger than their own, they folded before them, and the final objective could not be reached."

As the Greek army made a clear retreat across the burning desert, it was their turn to feel, in their exhaustion, the whole inclemency of the climate and the terrain. The excellent Turkish cavalry, reinforced by irregular groups, took an active part in the pursuit of Constantine's army, which suffered severe difficulties and a large number of losses. In revenge, and to make it more difficult to provision the pursuing forces, the Greeks burnt all the villages and farms which they found on the way, until they reached the lines which their commanders had prepared to the east of the railway, where they immediately began to fortify themselves.

The Sakarya victory had extraordinary repercussions throughout the Moslem and Eastern world; the warmest congratulations reached the Gazi from every part; the oppressed peoples saw in him the sun of their hopes of liberty.

From the day of victory, the political panorama changed for Ankara. France showed herself favourably disposed to sign an agreement with her, and Moscow authorised the Soviet republics of Armenia, Azerbaijan and the Ukraine to make treaties with Turkey. The Treaty of Kars, signed by Turkey and these republics, gave full validity to the Treaty of Moscow which had been signed earlier.

Five weeks after the victory, the Turkish Chancellor Yusuf Kemal and Franklin-Bouillon signed the Turco-French agreement of Ankara. The French Government no longer had any doubts about the effective solution of the Eastern Question, and congratulated itself upon having been the first to attempt to make official contact with the Ankara Government. The text of the agreement was very favourable to Turkey. The spirit of the National Pact was respected, the state of war between the two countries was declared ended, and the frontier between Turkey and Syria was established. Cilicia remained within the Turkish frontier. The only compensation made by Ankara was the recognition of the rights of the minorities.

Whilst Ankara and Paris were exchanging diplomatic representatives, London, on hearing news of the agreement that had been made, protested to her ally for proposing to break up the eastern front, and threatened her with breaking that of the Rhineland. France was forced to follow the orders of Downing Street, although only in appearance. Lloyd George was still the sworn enemy of Turkish Nationalism, but the latter's side was now stronger; there was now little chance that the "Sword of the Entente" could achieve success, as it had become sadly blunted. The French found it best to count on other factors, such as time and diplomacy, while following the British proposals: in this way they would give them enough rope to hang themselves.

The Gazi saw the sky clearing over his country. Now that the long Cilician war was over, the forces which had been held there would swell the ranks of the decimated central army. Cilicia cost Turkey much blood, with which many fair pages were written in the history of the new republic. The finest is the story of the resistance of the city of Antep, whose heroism was rewarded by the Assembly with the title of "Gazi," so that since then it has been called Gazi Antep, Victorious Antep.

The formation of a powerful army required the conscription of new intakes, and long months had to be given to their training. There was not much available; Soviet loans allowed it to be completed, but this could not be done so quickly. The Gazi's task was long and difficult to accomplish; he realised that it would be a good idea to gain time by listening to the propositions made by the Powers, who were looking for a solution to the Eastern Question which would benefit them.

The opposition had been reduced to silence by the Sakarya victory, but returned to activity three months afterwards. A great contribution to its new strength was made by the arrival in Ankara of a group of persons who had been imprisoned by the British when they occupied Istanbul in 1920. Kemal forgot past misunderstandings, and when Rauf arrived in Ankara he appointed him Commissar for Public Works, and gave equally important posts to other Members of Parliament.

Many members were not in agreement with the antimonarchical tendencies of Kemal's political group in the Assembly, and as the opposition began to take shape, they took the opportunity of leaving his group. A new group was formed, called the "Second Group," which from the beginning took up a combative position. The floodgates of hostilities were opened. What, they asked, did the army mean by such inactivity? In what direction was the state going? Who was leading them, and where to? It was not possible that a whole nation could be dragged towards objectives which were obscure and undefined!

In a secret session, the Gazi made some important statements to the Assembly. He declared his firm decision to attack and defeat the enemy, but said that it was more dangerous to attack if one trusted in half-taken measures, than not to attack at all. The Gazi possessed the precious gift of words, and the clarity in which he explained his reasoning made him an orator of stature; his clear-sounding voice helped him, and his characteristically expressive gaze impressed his personality on his hearers. In earlier days, a speech such as the one he had made would have imposed silence, but this time his opponents answered roughly. One of them had the temerity to tell the speaker that his tone was too commanding, while another cast doubt upon his intentions, and a third threw at him the following: "You will lead the enemy to disaster!" It was useless to reason with the members of the "Second Group," so that the Gazi contented himself with gaining the approval of the majority, which still followed him, and left for the front.

At the beginning of 1922, the opposing parties in that European political arena which concerned the Eastern Question entered into battle with each other. Great Britain had lost confidence in the strength of Greece, and she dragged her Allies to a conference in which it was intended that they should appear as Powers mediating in the Turco-Greek conflict, as if it had not been they themselves who had caused the Greek army to enter Anatolia. The Great Powers had seemed like a tripod, but the French leg was to be the cause of its instability. French public opinion was already decided; it was not going to enter into conflict of any kind with Kemalist Turkey.

The conference of Prime Ministers met in Paris on the 21st of March 1922. The Allies first proposed to the Turks and Greeks that they should make an armistice for a period of three months, with the possibility of renewing it until the establishment of peace conditions. Before Ankara could reply, a new note, which had been composed by the Paris Conference and contained the main lines of the basis for peace, was submitted to both the belligerents.

Once again it was the spirit of Sèvres which was attempting to solve the Eastern Question, since the peace proposals were similar to those in that treaty, with some modifications. The Allied Prime Ministers declared that above all they desired no one to suspect them of partiality; they desired to hold the balance of justice with a firm hand, at the same level for both sides, yet in the same note there appeared this non sequitur: "The Ministers wish to give Greece some compensation for the great sacrifices she has made during the war in order to serve the allied cause." This showed that their pose as arbiters and neutrals was no more than a diplomatic farce. The conference had no practical result, but it confirmed in the mind of the Gazi the belief that justice could only be obtained by force of arms. The Powers' diplomatic offensive failed, and they were left in a difficult situation with regard to Turkey, having shown their hand.

Kemal had moved from the railway station to a private house; he had chosen one in a beautiful place, on a hill which overlooked the city. The hill is called Çankaya, Bell Rock. It rises from some lower spurs, and in places it is quite steep. There could be seen at its foot typical country houses built of stone with their windows painted red. The hill was adorned with small groups of poplars and a few wild roses, together with the green pasture of early spring.

The Commander's house was a modest but solid dwelling, surrounded by aged trees. One could see from the house the half-ruined city of Ankara in its grey Valley, sparsely covered with vegetation. Higher up, as the view stretched out, there were mingled colours which changed according to the hour of the day, until they finally took on a violet shade, on distant mountains, softly silhouetted against the lofty sky of the plateau.

Çankaya-its crystal-pure air and its silence calmed the Gazi's nerves, overstretched by his incessant work. In a short time he had transformed that simple house, furnishing it with taste very personal to himself, and with his own clear lines and sober character. In the central building there was a hall in the oriental style, with a marble fountain in the centre, and covered with fine carpets. From this room one passed into his study, the most personal place of that indefatigable worker, which was a room of ample size; there he had his library, his files, and a number of valuable objects which had been given to him by the various regions of Turkey and by Moslem countries. The bedrooms were on the second floor of the building. Halfway between the house and the road leading to Ankara, there was a much smaller building, divided into two rooms which were used as a dining room and a waiting room. There reigned in these, as in all the rest of this improvised home for a Head of State, the same harmony and comfort which Kemal created for his surroundings, and which revealed his possession of a well-formed taste.

The Gazi, his skin tanned by the soldier's life which he led at the front, lived his life as a politician and administrator in Çankaya; there he received the people whose opinions on matters of the moment he wished to know, and with them he searched, often until the early hours of the morning, for solutions to the transcendental problems which must be solved for the wellbeing of the young state. His exceptional capacity for physical endurance, and his inexhaustible mental strength were unabated; after a night of mental effort, when his companions, members of his government, retired exhausted in every respect, the Gazi frequently felt the desire to go out for a horse ride.

Below him, Ankara was still asleep, filled by an unprecedented multitude. Although by this time one could see some progress in building, the city on the plateau was still far from being comfortable. There was a shortage of water, especially in the summer, but it was all put up with stoically; the hope of seeing their great work realised was enough for the pioneer Nationalists. The example of their leader, and the simplicity of his life, silenced their complaints before they reached expression.

Zübeyde Hanım, Kemal's mother, lived her last years by the side of her beloved son, on whose account she had suffered uncountable griefs, during those long months when no clear news was reaching Istanbul about Kemal's revolutionary activities. At one time she believed that he was dead, and at others, the official press campaign against him caused her periods of fear. Her mental suffering had weakened her, debilitated as she was by age. Her sight was what had most failed, and in Çankaya she was almost completely blind. She had kept her white skin, and had not lost her usual strength of character. Her son's fame, and her chance to live with him made the small but incessant ills of old age, which were torturing her, easier to bear.

The Gazi had not at this time changed his opinions about the policy he should follow with the Allied Powers, and in general to save the country. As he has said: "We had the firm and constant conviction that we could not allow ourselves to be deceived by hopes of success in the diplomatic field, until we had expelled the enemy by force of arms, and shown our existence and our national strength through our deeds. It is useless for an individual to expect consideration if he has not yet proved his capacity; the same is true of nations. Only those who have proved themselves can make claims for humane, just or generous treatment."

The law which had been passed on the 5th of August in the previous year, to give Kemal dictatorial power for a period of three months, aroused criticism in the Assembly, which grew and became more bitter at every renewal of the provisions, until it was rejected in the debate on its third prolongation. The majority who normally supported the Gazi allowed themselves to be persuaded by the opposing speakers, perhaps remembering Sulla and Caesar, who made themselves into perpetual dictators.

The members of the Council of Commissars presented themselves to Kemal, who was ill in Çankaya; they informed him that they intended to resign en bloc. The Gazi asked them not to do so, and to wait forty-eight hours; he would go to Parliament and try to make it change its opinion.

In the Assembly, the opposition roared against Kemal. It was claimed that he was usurping the Assembly's powers, and that by having secret sessions he was trying to keep the truth from the nation, making Parliament merely a pretence; one member, of the group who had invented the suggestive phrase "The Sultans are dead; long live the Paşas," shouted from the rostrum that Kemal would by his conduct make the Assembly an instrument which would disgrace the nation in the eyes of the world, adding that the nation was above individuals.

The Gazi carried his prestige with him to the rostrum, determined to win in this parliamentary battle, the result of which might have a deep effect on the political life of the new state. He was not going to allow the work of revolution to miscarry halfway. In no circumstances would he give up the Supreme Command, and he would rather have taken violent measures than do so. It is interesting to read some of the remarks with which the Gazi tried to defend himself, since they reveal his innermost thoughts: "It is certainly the nation collectively, which constitutes the basis of everything, but it is one man or men who direct the affairs of state. It is useless to try to deny this truth with meaningless theories." He replied to those who were attacking him on financial grounds, saying that the costs of the army were disproportionate to the available resources, as follows: "I do not believe in the argument which says that if we have money we can make an army, but if we have no more money then our army must be disbanded. I assure you that whether we have money or not, the army will continue in existence." Others considered that he had abused his powers in his measures to obtain food and clothing for the army. "Necessity knows no law," he said, "and no law shall make me hesitate in taking the measures I believe necessary to prevent the army from being defeated."

A vote was called after violent debates, and it gave a majority for the extension for the law of dictatorship. It was seen that Kemal's supporters felt their faith renewed when he was with them.

There was no slackening in the peace offensive against Turkey directed by Lloyd George. He was looking for possible points of political weakness in the Kemalist front in order to bring it down. It was first of all necessary to paralyse the Turkish army's offensive, and diplomatic means were the best way to achieve that.

The British Prime Minister took advantage of the Genoa Conference between the European Powers and the U.S.S.R. to try to seduce Russia and separate her from her protégé. Russia was rising as a threatening power, capable of fomenting universal revolution; the East was shaken by her influence and was escaping the grasp of the Great "Western Empires. With the help of Bolshevism, China was beginning to show signs of resenting the grip of foreigners, white or yellow; in Iran, Russian influence had effaced the British, and Turkey was appearing as a serious enemy to Europe of the capitulations and a champion of the other Moslem countries. It was Moscow who was giving her the help she needed.

At the Ligurian city of Genoa there arrived delegates from the Soviets, the Vatican and the Powers. It seemed strange to Italy, where Communist ideas were striving against Fascism, to see Chicherin, dressed with impeccable elegance, raising his glass to the health of the Supreme Pontiff. At that moment, Lenin's Government was in fact more interested in attracting foreign capital and improving its financial position in order to confirm its authority, than to show intransigence, Nevertheless, Llyod George achieved no success.

Downing Street then proposed that a commission should be sent to Kemalist Turkey, to gain information about the atrocities committed against the Christian minorities. France replied that it would be well to send another commission to the zone occupied by the Greeks, and the proposal proceeded no further. When Lloyd George gave an account to the House of Commons for his Eastern Policy, he declared that it was a humanitarian duty to protect the Christians who were persecuted by the cruel Turks. Lloyd George's humanitarianism received an unexpected reply: in a public declaration, Cardinal Logue, the Primate of Ireland, said: "The British Government has decided to send a commission to Turkey to investigate the terrible massacres of Christians. That commission ought to go first to Northern Ireland and make an investigation about the massacres which are being committed there daily. Lloyd George is striving to protect the Christians of Turkey; I wish he would do something for the Christians in Northern Ireland."

In July it was decided to call a new conference, which would be attended by the three Great Powers and both belligerent countries; Beykoz, a place on the Bosporus, was chosen for its venue.

In Ankara, the "Second Group" had won a victory; they had succeeded in getting the Assembly to pass a law which required that the Prime Minister and

Commissars should be elected directly by the Assembly by secret voting. Hitherto, it had been the President of the Assembly who presented his candidates, from whom the Assembly chose its Commissars. Through this new law the Gazi immediately lost the position of Prime Minister, to which Rauf Bey, the real leader of the opposition, although apparently a friend of Kemal, was then elevated.

Kemal was more preoccupied with the preparation of the army, which could be considered ready for the final attack. In July 1922, it consisted of 104.000 perfectly trained men, 2.860 machine-guns and 323 cannon. For its part, the Greek army did not remain inactive, as some have claimed; this is shown by the figures, since their strength was in July 132,000 men, while their armament was 8,060 machine-guns and 348 cannon.

The Greek General Staff were not considering any possibility of an offensive, but they had fortified their positions in such a way as to feel secure that they could frustrate any enemy attack; in the dangerous parts of the front, double and triple defence lines were built. Generalissimo Hadjianestis was passing a pleasant life in the beautiful city of Izmir, the Turkish name for Smyrna, far away from the discomforts of the front; the Greek officers were trying to find distractions from their boredom, and relief from the privations of the interminable campaign. They were all trying to get leave and spend it in Izmir, which, like Istanbul, offered means of satisfying the most varied appetites. Those who were obliged to remain at the front relieved their boredom with alcohol and gambling, and their example was followed by the troops. Greece was certainly counting on a peaceful solution for the war, through Allied intervention.

The spirit reigning in the Nationalist camp was very different, and over it there would beat the wings of victory. Theirs was an army of volunteers, comrades, united by a will stronger than the strictest discipline. Because of their modest dress, the officers could hardly be distinguished from their men; Ismet, Commander of the Front, used to wear his usual worn- out uniform. As those who had ever been under the command of the Gazi affirmed, he behaved in a simple, democratic way during his long visits to the front. He talked to the soldiers and investigated their needs. In the midst of winter, wrapped in his ample cloak with its fur collar, and wearing his kalpak, he toured the front line and watched the units at exercise. An existing photograph has captured him at a moment when he was resting on the snow, covered in his cape.

Greece realised that time was passing without the British Cabinet extracting her from the mire in which she was stuck. Constantine thought that the moment had arrived for him to take the initiative and direct the war in a new direction. Since Thrace was in the power of Greece it remained to round off that conquest with the city of Constantine the Great. In this way, even if the Greek army was forced to give up Anatolia, she would have the certainty of all of European Turkey. The Straits and the Sea of Marmara would become an impassable barrier to the Turks, who had no fleet.

Constantine sent strong contingents to Thrace; however, he did not have the courage necessary to realise his plans and seize Istanbul; he showed timidity before the warnings of the Powers, and contented himself with defending his cause with diplomatic notes. On the 30th of July, Greece declared the autonomy of the ancient Ionia. This was another of the final measures Constantine had thought of.

CHAPTER 26

TO THE MEDITERRANEAN!

The Gazi had his plans of attack already prepared; he would wage an anni-
hilating battle, using the larger part of his army against a single point. He had
chosen the enemy's right wing, to the southwest of Afyon Karahisar. This was the
most important area and at the same time the weakest part of the Greek front.
If they broke through there, the Turkish divisions would find themselves behind
the enemy's fortified lines, which would mean inflicting on them a terrible defeat.

The Gazi, Fevzi and Ismet held a preliminary meeting in Akşehir at which
they decided to hurry forward the preparations, so that the offensive could be
achieved as soon as possible. The success of the attack depended essentially on
its remaining secret, for which reason the Gazi made a pretext that an important
football match was taking place, in order to bring the senior commanders of the
army to Akşehir.

From there he went to Ankara, where he announced his decision to the Assembly, saying: "Six or seven days after the start of operations, I will defeat the
enemy." Halfway through August he left the capital by car without anyone noticing, except for the very few who were in the secret. Life continued at Çankaya
as if the master of the house was still there, but he declined to receive visitors for
reasons of health. Meanwhile, he was crossing the saline desert, across which
small caravans were slowly moving through a monotonous landscape; far off one
could see some ancient "han," a kind of caravanserai which gave hospitality to
travellers. Between the desert and the violet mountains which bound it, there
gradually appeared amidst cheerful greenery the minarets of Konya, that holy city
which had been Iconium in Byzantium times, and which was made the capital of
the Seljuk Turks in the eleventh century; they gave it architectual splendour and
religious fervour. There were twenty medreses to instruct young men in theology,
in which not even Baghdad surpassed her. The Gazi had not given warning of
his arrival at that city, which had given up preoccupations on the life beyond for
real problems. The Gazi put the telegraph office under guard, to make sure that
no news of his passage escaped. On the twentieth he was in the White City of
Akşehir, and in touch with Ismet Paşa.

It was ordered that the attack should begin on the 26th of August 1922; the regiments and artillery batteries marched by night, by long detours, and when dawn broke they took shelter in thickets or villages to escape detection from the air. On the 25th, Kemal and his headquarters established their camp to the southwest of Koca Tepe, a hill situated some kilometres from Afyon and near Greek fortifications. From the summit of that hill the Gazi intended to direct the great battle.

The Greek camp had no suspicion that danger was imminent; Hadjianestis was in Smyrna, 300 kilometres from the front, convinced that the Turks would not attack, and that even if they dared to they would be decimated in front of the formidable fortifications, which the British Military Commission that had just inspected them had declared to be "impregnable."

The occupied zone had been impoverished by the requirements of the invading forces, together with the devastations they had committed and the removal of livestock to Greece, and the fields had not been cultivated as in peacetime. The Moslem population was living in continual fear, and subject to the cruellest treatment; in the areas near the front, the inhabitants were forced to toil in the defence works. The Greeks repeated their threat if they were forced to retreat nothing and nobody would escape them as they destroyed everything in their path. However, the Turks thought that anything was preferable to this heavy slavery.

On the night of the 25th the Turkish forces which were directed to the main part of the attack approached the front lines with caution; the artillery batteries took up the positions made for them by the prodigious efforts of their supporting troops, while the cavalry got ready in the rear. The ghost army made no sound to break the characteristic silence of the plateau.

It was still the dead of night when the Gazi reached the summit of Koca Tepe; around him and in the immense void he felt open before his feet, all was darkness. An imperceptible clarity appeared in the East and gradually the stars lost their brilliance; when the thick shadows had been half dispelled by the light, the gigantic clash of two nations would take place. The Turkish soldiers watched the light as it spread. It was the time of prayer, and their lips moved imperceptibly, their foreheads bent down. What was written for them in the book of fate? How many would never see again the joyful dawn! They turned their gaze towards the enemy lines, which they would soon be able to make out; they had followed their commander to that place, not thinking of themselves, but of their mourning country; they did not count. Let Allah's will be done.

The Gazi was walking like an automaton among the sharp stones as if on sentry-go, to distract himself from his nervousness. With a heavy frown, he reviewed with his extraordinarily clear intelligence the various possibilities of enemy action; he could not find any new possibility; none could exist, since he had foreseen and analysed all of them. His heart was not to be altered by any feeling, either of hatred or of enthusiasm; this was strategy par excellence. At that moment even his men had lost their individual meaning for him; the units were chessmen which he would move in the great battle; his adversary was also playing, and the best player would win.

An impressive view began to be revealed to the eyes of the men who were to die for their ideals; there were colossal rocks in strange shapes rising above the plain, threatening. At the foot of one of these, 1200 metres high, there lies spread like a fan Afyon Karahisar, "Black Castle of Opium," a position of vital importance in the Greek defence. The Gazi looked at his watch again. It was half-past five; at the same moment the artillery announced the beginning of the attack with the roar of their cannon.

The bombardment became more and more intense as their aim became more exact, and did not weaken in intensity for three hours. At the first shots, the Greeks awoke in confusion, hurried to take up their arms, and rushed to defend themselves from an attack whose importance they did not realise.

The Turkish infantry and cavalry poured like a torrent through the fortifications which had been destroyed by the artillery. The Greek lines north of Afyon near Kütahya were also broken, so that there was a danger that the main body of Constantine's forces would be surrounded. The front line of defence, which had been thought impregnable, fell into the hands of the Turks that same day, despite vigorous counterattacks. On the second day Afyon fell and the whole southern front withdrew northwards. The Greek command thought that the large-scale defence works at Dumlupınar would be a breakwater that could hold back this furious sea of attackers, who seemed to be unaware of exhaustion.

Kemal's army did not reduce their pressure, but on the contrary were the more inflamed by the certainty of victory. Their commander advanced along with his troops, and entered Afyon before the smoke had cleared. Chief of the General Staff Fevzi was always at his side, and Ismet was commander of the front. Commanders of the two Turkish armies Nurettin and Yakup Şevki came to the campaign tent to receive orders.

Dumlupınar could not hold. Under pressure from three directions, the main body of the Greek army was forced to retreat towards the mountainous region of

Asilhanlar. On the 30th, the six divisions which were desperately trying to find a way of escape from the iron ring which was being closed around them, tried to do so through a long narrow valley called Kızılca; hut there they found their tomb, The Gazi never lost sight of the enemy's movements, and caught the retreating divisions between the two Turkish armies and the Fifth Cavalry Corps. It was a horrible battle, in which the bad situation in which the Greeks were surprised, and the panic which seized them resulted in the almost complete extermination of the main body of the invading army. The total losses of the beaten army in these last actions were around 50,000.

This battle, after which ne doubt remained that Anatolia would be completely liberated, was often known as the "Battle of the Generalissimo," in honour of the hero.

The Gazi ordered the main body of his army to march towards Izmir and the rest against Eskişehir. In his orders for the day on the 1st of September he said: "Armies! Your first objective is the Mediterranean! Forward!"

The last act of the drama of Anatolia was to have the same characteristics as its beginning and its development: cruelty and hatred. The desire to avenge their defeat gave an inconceivable energy to the Greeks, who had already decided to give no further resistance and were trying to reach the sea as soon as possible. Their passage was marked by thick ruddy clouds of smoke and a chorus of cries of pain; those who had wished to come as saviours met with ruins, corpses, and laments. Anatolia could not remember the sight of such an infernal spectacle.

The Christian families joined the retreating divisions, fearful of reprisals, thus enormously increasing the strength of the torrent which was flowing to the sea under the burning sun of the Asian summer.

The Gazi reached Uşak on the 2nd of September, and found it almost totally destroyed. His heart was tortured by the immensity of the disaster. He passed by uncountable heaps of captured equipment, evidence of British generosity. The same day, the Greek Commander Tricupis, who had succeeded Hadjianestis, was brought to him. Commander-in-chief Hadjianestis left for Izmir just before the Battle of the Generalissimo took place and appointed General Tricupis as his representative. He has fallen prisoner after the battle of the Generalissimo. The Gazi had a lively interest in knowing what had been his opponents' strategy in the battle.

Kemal, Fevzi and Ismet were waiting seated around a table in a large room in the Turkish headquarters. The Greek generals entered accompanied by two Turkish generals. The Gazi and his subordinates got up, and the latter returned the Greek officers' salute by a nod of the head, but Kemal shook them by the hand and invited them to sit down. As the seven generals sat round the table, the Greeks in their generously braided uniforms and nervous manner contrasted with the tranquil Turks, who were dressed with extreme simplicity. The Gazi offered them cigarettes and asked for coffee to be brought.

The conversation moved to a discussion of the various operations performed by both commanders, beginning with an interpreter but soon continuing in French. Tricupis explained a series of movements which he would have advised in order to halt the offensive, and the Gazi in turn explained the way in which he would have reacted had they been taken, since he had foreseen them. In fact the opposing generals were of a very different calibre. Tricupis attacked Dionis for not having obeyed certain orders, and this degenerated into a quarrel between them, which was very out of place. Disappointed as he was with the feeble stature of his opponents, the Gazi got up to bring the interview to an end, asking the Greek Commander if he could be of any service to him. Tricupis asked that news of him should be given to his wife, who was in Istanbul.

As a thoughtful consolation to a fellow soldier in misfortune, the victorious general told his beaten opponent: "War is a game of chance. You have done everything possible for a soldier and man of honour. Fate is to blame. Do not be discouraged." Tricupis thanked him for these words, and in his state of nervous turmoil there came to his lips the feeling that was torturing him most in those days, of guilt at not having made the gesture of dying along with the army he commanded. His officers thought that he should have done that, and he felt humiliated. "Oh! General! I failed in my last duty." "That is a personal matter," answered the Gazi, looking away as if distracted by some detail of the decoration of the room.

Nature has been generous to that paradise of Anatolia, those areas which enjoy perpetual spring, and which descend from the point where the plateau breaks, by leisurely slopes towards the coast. But now there only appeared before the conquering general's eyes, in all the places which had been drowned by the wave of death, only scorched ashes, and people searching for or burying their dead, instead of the villages and cities that had flourished there.

From Uşak the Gazi continued towards Smyrna. He halted 90 kilometres away from that city, at the ruins of Salihli. He was no longer thinking about the military operations, but was weighing the political consequences of his victory, and considering the possible reactions of the Powers. After the Battle of the Generalissimo, the Powers offered an armistice to the Grand Assembly. This was a cheap way of saving the Greek army. In view of the urgency of the situation, they did not wait for a reply, but sent a telegram directly to the Gazi. They informed him that the allied Consuls in Smyrna were authorised to negotiate with him, and asked that he should give an interview to them.

The Consuls offered to surrender the city of Smyrna to the Gazi, and asked him to appoint a general to take charge of it. It was not the time for the Gazi to agree to humanitarian solutions for those who had been destroying the country, and the honourable Consuls' attitude was somewhat ingenuous. After he had read the telegram, Kemal asked, as if he had not understood: "What city are they going to surrender to whom?" It could now be assumed that the Greeks would not offer any serious resistance; what they were desperately trying to do was to reach the sea and save themselves in the ships which had been mobilized to their aid. On their way they continued with their destructive work. The cities of Nazilli, Aydın and Manisa, amongst others, suffered terribly. Later on, a plain column was erected in Aydın, as if a funeral monument for the city, with an epitaph which will serve for the whole afflicted region: "Passerby! Stop a moment at this place and think of those who, for the love of their country, have bade farewell to their love and their dreams. This is the place of the murdered, widows, orphans. It is a monument erected in memory of those who died for their country's independence."

On the 9th of September, the Turkish army made its entry into the Pearl of the Orient. The Greeks had offered a feeble resistance in the outskirts of the town, in order to give time to the embarkation of the main body of the fleeing troops, and the exhausted multitudes which followed them. Their pursuers caught up with them so successfully, that the last Greeks and the first Turks arrived together at the beginnings of the town. To the sea! The fugitives thought of nothing else; to get rid of their weapons and of everything which would prevent them getting to the place of embarkation before the next man. The vanguard of the conquering army made its entry amid the enthusiasm of the Moslem population. There occurred some bloody clashes, provoked by Greeks and Armenians, who fired upon the soldiers at various points of their march, but the conduct of the Turkish officers is worthy of praise, since they managed to quell the rage which their men must have felt from the sight of Anatolia in flames, and prevent them from taking vengeance on the mass of Christians who were waiting in crowds upon the quayside, or sacking the Christian quarters.

Kemal entered the city 24 hours after the arrival of the army, without heeding objections made to him on the grounds that the city was still dangerous for him. Passing along the quayside, which was the only part of the city where the houses did not reach the waters of the gulf, the commander saw the ships of the allied squadrons some distance from the shore, great monsters, powerless witnesses of the defeat of the West. The European Powers and the new Turkey were now face to face. He was going to make Europe understand that a new era had dawned, and that from then onwards they must refrain from getting involved in the life of Turkey.

With his generals, he took the following military measures: first, the remains of the invading army would be expelled, while the Turkish army would set out in two directions, towards the Bosporus and the Dardanelles. He had no worries in the diplomatic field; the Powers who were interested would come to him, the victor.

Unexpectedly there then began for the heroic general a period of sentimental activity. On the day after his arrival, a young Turkish lady who had insistently asked to see him came into his office at headquarters. She presented herself as Latife Hanım. She had recently returned from France where she was studying law, and her parents were still there. She had suffered the Greek oppression in Smyrna, having been suspected of giving information to the Turkish army. She now came to ask the Gazi to accept hospitality at her villa at Bornova, together with his general staff.

Kemal was observing her with pleasure, somewhat surprised by the sure way in which she spoke and the boldness of her manner. Her magnificent eyes, the perfect oval of her face, and determined chin, gave a real attraction to her features which were animated by a strong will and lively intelligence. Her dress showed that she was familiar with the latest ordinances of Parisian fashion; however, although like women of the upper classes she had given up the veil since the World War, she had covered her head with a black scarf, which fell over her shoulders and contrasted with the pallor of her countenance.

With well-chosen words she expressed the admiration inspired in her by the Gazi's achievements, and her thanks as a Turkish woman. She showed him a medallion in which he saw his own face. He was happy to accept the hospitality of such an agreeable person, and some days later was installed in the villa belonging to Latife's parents at Bornova, which is a short distance from the city and is a village favoured by the rich families because of the tranquil beauty of the place, overlooking the last curve of the gulf.

The mistress of the house surrounded her guest with the greatest comfort, and he, exhausted as he was by the soldier's life he had led during the campaign, was properly grateful. He was flattered by Latife's attentions; but what attracted him to her was the breadth of her knowledge, and the accuracy of her judgement.

He enjoyed discussing things with her, and she could follow him on any subject; he could not remember having met any young lady to equal her in education. Her manners were such as one acquires in distinguished families. Thus the Gazi moved from his admiration of his hostess for her intellectual qualities, and without noticing, to seeing her also as a woman, an aspect which offered equal reason to attract-him.

Thousands of Christians, Greeks and Armenians, were flowing into the devastated areas without interruption; they understood that the gulf which had opened between the Turks and themselves would prevent them from living together in the future. These masses of people jostled on the quayside, waiting for the boats in which they could leave the rich and once happy Ionia. They were afflicted with a contagious panic, and nasty scenes occurred as those who had arrived last tried to push into the front ranks; their features acquired a crazed expression from the notion that a general massacre might begin at any moment. The boats available for evacuation were always too few for the human tide which was always growing.

Fires broke out at various places in the city, especially in the Armenian quarter. The flames, helped by the wind, moved from one house to the next, and from one quarter to another; in a short time the larger and most important part of the city was nothing more than a huge bonfire. Voices were raised in Europe accusing the Turks of responsibility for the disaster, and instancing the event as an incontestable proof of Turkish vandalism. This final slander falls before logical thought. "Who was it that devastated Anatolia? Who was it that declared that Smyrna would not be surrendered intact? The answer is too well-known to repeat.

This spectacle worthy of Nero lasted for three days. The Gazi watched the progress of the fire with his face twisted in silent grief. How much evil the Great Powers had caused in Turkey, Kemal thought, through their policy of sowing discord between the various peoples who formed her population, igniting in them the spirit of Nationalism and Religion, and giving them visions of unattainable autonomy! However, with the victory he had gained, and the firm attitude which he would follow, and which had been his invariable way of behaviour towards Imperialist Europe, he would show her the necessity of treating Turkey as a sovereign country, and that the days of intrigues were over. The old story of the Christian minorities threatened by the Turks, and the need to protect them, would end of its own accord, since the minorities had emigrated in the wake of the armies they had helped to enter the country: in the East the Russians, the French in the South, the Greeks in the West.

When the fire was gone, the ruins could be seen; there was a chaos of the skeletons of blackened walls and smoking ashes, all the more horrible and sad because that wide stain lay amid an idyllic scene, under the deep blue coastal sky.

Since all doubts that Kemal had achieved a total victory had been dissipated, the three Powers agreed to deliver a solemn warning to the victorious general that he should not invade the neutral zones of the Straits. They hurriedly sent reinforcements to the Asian parts of that zone and reinforced their fleets. Perhaps fearing that the flags of the Powers, which had for centuries been enough to terrify the Eastern peoples, would not produce their usual effect on this occasion, Lloyd George declared that as Great Britain was desirous of keeping the Straits free at all costs, she was pleased at the perfect harmony which existed between her, France and Italy, "to prevent the danger of the reappearance of a victorious Turkey on the European coast," and called upon the Balkan countries and the Dominions to come together in making a front against the Turks. He announced that Great Britain would significantly increase her forces in the Near East, and that he had ordered the fleet to oppose by all means any Turkish attempt to penetrate the neutral zone. Lloyd George's intention was to drag the Powers, Dominions and the Balkan countries into the accomplished fact of a war with Turkey.

The French and Italian Governments told the Foreign Office that they definitely did not wish to take part in actions against Turkey, either offensive or defensive. France withdrew her troops from the Asian zone of the Dardanelles, and took them to the European shore. Italy followed her example. Neither did the Dominions respond to the call to arms and Great Britain found herself alone against Kemal, whose victorious army was master of Anatolia. Great Britain would naturally have been at an advantage in a confrontation with Turkey, but the British people no longer wished even to hear of new adventures, an attitude which they showed through the press; in addition, the majority of His Majesty's subjects disagreed with the policy of hatred which Lloyd George had begun at the end of the World War. Nationalist Turkey would be supported by Soviet Russia, and the conflict with her might bring the British Empire a colonial rising, as Asia awoke with a formidable explosion.

On the 18th of September there were no longer any remains of Constantine's army in Anatolia, and the two Turkish columns came face to face with the British forces which blocked the entry to the Straits. France asked the Gazi to prevent the neutral zone from being violated, to which he replied that the Nationalist Government did not recognise the existence of such a zone, and that in any case it was impossible to halt the armies until Thrace was freed. In view of this, Franklin-Bouillon was deputed to seek an interview with Kemal at Smyrna. Tension was at its height; every minute was important, since the Turkish vanguard had entered the neutral zone and was taking up positions at a fighting distance from the British; there was reason to fear a crisis at any moment, and the beginning of a war between the two countries.

The Gazi remained enigmatic; he was thinking over the pros and cons of all the decisions he might take. His exact understanding of the true extent of Britain's power and the sympathy shown by France and Italy by withdrawing their troops, decided him not to fear the British bluff, but to keep pressure up until the last moment, and agree to discuss peace as a victor, imposing his own decisions upon it.

On the 23rd of September, the Powers proposed that a conference should be called to discuss the terms of peace, that the restoration of Thrace should be considered, and that there should be a preliminary meeting to establish the line behind which the Greek troops in Thrace must withdraw. The Gazi accepted the idea of a meeting at Mudanya, and for this purpose he appointed Ismet Paşa his representative with full powers.

In Ankara, some people expressed some worries about the Gazi's political activities, declaring that affairs of this kind were within the competence of the Council of Commissars. They asked him to return to Ankara, but he refused to do so. He saw no benefit in his losing touch with the army, just when the final success depended upon the threat which such an armed force represented.

The city of Bursa, founded by Prusias II, King of Bithynia, and which was the first capital of the Ottoman Empire, is joined to the small port of Mudanya on the Sea of Marmara by a short railway. This port acquires its relative importance by the life given to it by Bursa. The representatives of France, Great Britain and Italy were received in Mudanya by Ismet Paşa; as for the Greek representatives, they were advised to remain on the warship which had brought them there.

Ismet presided over the sessions with great dexterity, but there were difficult problems to be solved; Turkey was demanding the immediate return of Thrace, and that Istanbul and the Straits should be evacuated before peace was concluded. The discussions ran their course in a tempestuous atmosphere, until they broke down on the 8th of October and the armistice ended. The Turkish armies again began to move, and there was an imminent danger of war. After two days the British delegate received the decision of his government; Thrace would be evacuated, but Istanbul and the Straits would remain occupied until the conclusion of peace. Lloyd George had hauled down the sails of his intransigence.. The offer made was the most that British prestige could allow without losing face in the eyes of the world. The British delegate Sir Charles Harrington said privately to Ismet: "We shall evacuate, Paşa, but we want to do it honourably." The armistice was signed in Mudanya at midnight on the 11th of October. Just as the generals were signing the various copies of the agreement, the Greek warship carrying its delegation weighed anchor and left. The Greek delegation declared in writing that they did not feel authorised to sign the agreement, since none of the objections they had made had been taken into account. This last gesture of Greece in her crusade for the great ideal was an inglorious one, since later she had to accept the conditions imposed upon her.

CHAPTER 27

ABOLITION OF THE MONARCHY

From Istanbul, there came to greet the Gazi strong delegations from patriotic societies, teachers, and students. The words spoken to them by the Gazi reflected his revolutionary spirit, and through them he appeared as the reformer who was to transform Turkey into a modern country. On one occasion he spoke from the stage of the largest cinema in the city. Standing silhouetted against the red of the national flag, he addressed his words mainly to the women teachers who filled most of the seats: "We have won a very complete victory; yet it represents nothing if you do not help us. Win the battle of education, and you will have done more for our country than we have." He advocated the entry of the Turkish people into the rhythm of Western civilisation, since isolation would bring them nothing but misfortune: "You will be lepers, pariahs, alone in your obstinacy and outdated sentiments. Always be yourselves, but find out how to take from the West whatever is necessary for the life of developed peoples. Let in science and new ideas; if you do not, they will devour us!"

When the results of the Great Offensive and of Mudanya became known, Istanbul lived through days of great animation; the venerable walls of Santa Sophia vibrated with the huge enthusiasm of the multitudes which invaded it on such solemn occasions. Refet Paşa made a triumphal entry into the capital, amidst silence from the foreigners, Vahdettin and the Christian minorities and acclamation from the Turks. The Pera quarter, an essentially foreign area, changed its blue and white clothes for red ones. Those who felt compromised by their anti-Turkish activities preferred to leave the country, together with their capital. As had been laid down in the Armistice of Mudanya, the civil administration of the capital, the zone of the Straits and later that of evacuated Thrace, was to remain in Turkish hands. Refet Paşa took charge of it, and installed himself in the Sublime Porte.

After the stormy military conference at Mudanya, the Gazi returned to the city on the plateau. An internal political problem of essential importance was worrying him deeply: there existed in name two powers in Turkey, the effective one, that of the Assembly, and that of the Sultan and Calif. It was the time to get rid of this division.

The Assembly was of course ready to depose Vahdettin from his throne, but not to abolish the Sultanate. The Turkish people were conservative, traditionalist and religious; throughout the history of the Empire there had never been a single case of an attempt against the monarchy. The most current opinion in political circles was that the present Sultan should be replaced, and a constitutional monarchy like the British should be established. It was expected that the Gazi would be Prime Minister, but the clerical party was afraid that he would try to abolish the Sultanate, and would have preferred to see him as the founder of a second dynasty; the people would have equally welcomed the enthronement of their saviour.

The Gazi, however, saw the situation in a different light; with his revolutionary and progressive ideals, looking towards the future of mankind, he could not be contented with such a reactionary point of view. A weaker spirit than his would certainly have compromised with his principles, in exchange for sitting on the throne of Süleyman and being transformed overnight into the Representative of God, but he found the first of these honours unreal, and the second nonsensical.

He was convinced that the most fitting form of government for a modern state was that of a republic. He knew that the people were not ready to pass from the old regime, which was to blame for the social, material and political backwardness in which they lived, to a republican system in which the individual must be conscious of his existence within the state, and of his political responsibilities. There would have to be a patient educational process; if it triumphed, he could feel proud at having given a real service to his country. He was determined to abolish the Sultanate and Califate, and proclaim a republic when the moment was propitious.

The opposition started rumors that the Gazi had the secret design of abolishing the monarchy. One can imagine the reactions to such news in political circles. The Prime Minister Rauf, acting in concert with some other personalities, determined to get Kemal to make a definite statement about the plans attributed to him. Rauf invited Kemal, Refet and Ali Fuat to meet for a discussion on important matters. In Refet's house there met again the four comrades who had met in Amasya in 1919, at the beginning of the Nationalist Movement.

Neither Refet nor Rauf had ever been committed supporters of the Gazi, but rather tried to reduce his prestige. Although Ali Fuat had not been entirely in agreement with the Gazi, he alone was not actually opposed to him. Rauf immediately raised the reason for their meeting: the Assembly mistrusted its President's attitude concerning the Sultanate; "You ought to calm the Assembly" said Rauf," and through that, calm public opinion."

Before answering, Kemal asked Rauf to give him his opinion on the Sultanate and Califate, which the latter did in exact terms: "I am bound to the Sultanate and Califate heart and sold, because my father received favours from the Padişah; the memory of those favours is rooted within me. As for respect of the Califate, this has been imposed upon me through my education. To abolish that office and attempt to substitute it by an organ of a different character would lead to disaster. That is inadmissable." Refet declared that he was in complete agreement with what Rauf had said. Ali Fuat, however, evaded the question.

If Kemal set forth his reasons then, it would mean raising a storm and delaying the arrival of the republic, and he therefore answered: "The question which we are discussing is an unreal one. There is no reason for the alarm and emotion which has been shown by some members of the Assembly." Rauf would not be satisfied until Kemal promised to make a formal declaration before the Assembly. Kemal promised this and did accordingly.

On the 28th of October, Ankara received the official invitation to the Peace Conference which was to meet at Lausanne in Switzerland. The Sultan's government received a similar invitation. In an attempt to reestablish Imperial rights, the aged Tevfik telegraphed directly to the President of the Assembly, giving himself the proud title of Grand Vezir, and claiming a share of the victory for himself and his colleagues. They naturally expected to go to Lausanne.

The invitation made to Istanbul by the Entente, and the aspirations of the Sultan's Government, gave the Gazi the opportunity to cause the fall of the monarchy; in fact, events were running ahead of his own wishes. Attacks and violent criticisms of Vahdettin arose from the Assembly itself, which shared the general excitement over the issue; the members decided to meet immediately, get rid of the ambiguous situation and wind up the affairs of that so-called government whose death agonies were becoming harmful. During the debate, the Assembly attacked the traitorous Sultan and his Ministers in the pay of Great Britain, and a motion was read requesting that those individuals, whom the people no longer recognised as a government, should be subject to the Law of Treason.

The Sultan's deposition was imminent. The Gazi saw that the long- awaited hour for bringing down the throne of Osman had arrived, and yet still understood that it was necessary to go carefully, since one false step could cause his wishes to miscarry. He thought of a halfway measure so original that the Assembly did not know what to make of it, since no one had thought of such a possibility before;

this was to separate the Sultanate from the Califate and abolish the first; the Califate would remain with the Osmanlı dynasty.

In order to prepare them for it, Kemal presented a motion signed by more than 80 members, which affirmed that the rights of sovereignty belonged to the nation, as was declared in the Constitutional Law. This caused alarm amongst the members of the Second Group, who expressed their conviction that the Sultanate should not be abolished. The discussion began in the Assembly on the 1st of November. The Gazi quoted Islamic and Turkish history to show, with support from facts, that the Califate and Sultanate could be separated in such a way that sovereignty would remain in the hands of the Grand Assembly. As for the spiritual and religious power, the Califate, that would continue in the reigning dynasty.

The Assembly was taken by surprise, and to gain time to think it sent the project to be studied by a commission. The commission met in a neighboring room, and was composed of lawyers and clerics wearing turbans, long beards and ample robes. The Gazi suspected what was going to happen, and foresaw that the clerics would give a negative vote to the motion they were discussing; he therefore went into the crowded room where the discussions were going on, without many people noticing him, and sat down on a bench near the corner furthest removed from the improvised rostrum.

Speakers followed each other without interruption, and all of them found the separation of the two offices to be impracticable. The Koranic Law gave no precedents to show that this could be done and innumerable passages from the Koran were quoted in support of this. It was argued that the Sultanate and the Califate were two almost identical titles, and that it was difficult if not impossible to separate their powers. The first Califs, the successors of Mohammed, possessed temporal power united to the spiritual, and since the Ottoman Sultans were the successors to those Califs, they retained the same characteristics, since on inheriting the Sultanate and Califate from the Arabs, they had founded their state upon Islamic principles. No one had the courage to argue With these savants, whose bombastic phraseology and Arabic and Persian vocabulary gave the impression that they possessed lofty understanding.

Despite the opinions which had been expressed, Kemal's proposal was perfectly feasible. On the death of Mohammed, the founder of the Arab Empire and creator of Islam, in which he was considered the highest religious authority, his father-in-law Abubekir was chosen to succeed him on the double throne with the title of "Califa"-which means "Successor." The Prophet's family lost the Califate before thirty years had passed from his death. It was the Sultan Selim the Grim who had brought back the title of Calif from his Egyptian expedition in the sixteenth century; he had forced the Calif Mutawakkil, a remote descendant of the original Califs who was living off the charity of the Egyptian government, to pass it over to him. The Ottoman Emperors gave themselves the title of Sultan, "Sovereign" in Arabic, which had first been used by the Calif's generals, and then by all the monarchs of Moslem peoples, as the title of King was used in other countries. If therefore, the Ottoman Sultanate had been separated from the Califate up to Selim, and would never have been united to it without Selim's proud whim, the original situation could perfectly well be restored.

The prolonged verbosity of the members of the commission showed no signs of ending very quickly; however, it was clear that the vote would go against the proposal. The Gazi could not allow himself to be defeated at the beginning of his struggle on behalf of the republic, by these men who were the incarnation of Turkey's backwardness. He asked to speak, climbed onto the bench on which he had been sitting, and with a firm voice and an imperious gesture made the following announcement: "Gentlemen : sovereignty and the right to rule cannot be conferred on the first man who comes along, by the disposition of an academic discussion. Sovereignty is acquired by force and violence. It was through violence that the sons of Osman seized power, reigned over the Turkish nation, and maintained their rule over six centuries. Now it is the nation which rebels against those usurpers, and puts them in their right place, taking for itself, effectively, the exercise of its own sovereignty. This is a fact. I think that it would be very opportune if those who are met here, the Assembly, and everyone should regard this as a natural thing. If not, reality will eventually be made clear in the necessary form. But it may be that a few heads will then tumble!" These words were followed by a deathly silence.

Recovered from their transient pallor, the gentlemen of the mixed commission looked at each other and understood. Hoca Mustafa Efendi answered in the name of all: "Excuse us; we now see the situation in a different light. We understand perfectly."

The game was won. The bill was drafted and presented to Parliament that same day. Some members proposed that there should be individual voting, but Kemal took the rostrum and declared, in the same tone of voice that he had used with the clerics and lawyers: "That is useless; I have no doubt that the High Assembly will unanimously accept the principles which are intended to safeguard forever the independence of the nation and the country." The law abolishing the Sultanate was approved by acclamation. Thus ended the Ottoman monarchy, glorious in its beginnings, but which had fallen into the depths of decay under its last representatives.

Vahdettin could not make up his mind to abdicate, not so much from the Imperial Throne which no longer existed, but from the office of Calif, in which he could not remain either. The civil administration of the capital had by now passed into the hands of the representatives of the Grand Assembly; the ex-Sultan was now alone in the midst of men whom he had persecuted with such singular tenacity; however, the Calif could not arrive at any decision, and clung to the feet of his now meaningless throne.

The whole country was waiting for him to leave. On the 7th of November, the newspaper "Yeni Şark" asked: "What is the ex-Sultan waiting for?

When will he decide to render, by his departure, the only service which he is capable of rendering if not to Turkey, at least to the illustrious dynasty of Osman?" He must have been influenced by one event: this was the death of his former minister Ali Kemal, sworn enemy of the Nationalist Movement. Ali Kemal had still been in Istanbul. He had been seized in the middle of the street by a group of nationalists, and taken first by car and then by boat overnight to İzmit in Asia. A rumor went round that the hated Ali Kemal was in the Governor's palace, and the excited people beat upon the doors; when the ex-Minister came out, his guards could not hold back the fury of the multitude, who threw themselves upon him, beating him and stoning him. He fell down and got up again, but he was felled again by stones, and killed there upon the ground.

Now the Black Sultan was trembling for his life. His heart was suddenly seized with the idea of flight. He sought aid from General Harrington, Commander of the Allied forces, asking for Great Britain's protection. The British general prepared his escape in all detail. On the morning of the 17th of November an ambulance stopped near a small gate of the Palace at Yıldız; it was raining. The door was soon opened a little and a head looked out to peer around the empty street. His fear calmed, the Black Sultan quickly went to the ambulance and got in, accompanied by his son, the little Prince Ertuğrul. In the car was waiting General Harrington himself.

The ambulance arrived at the quay of Dolmabahçe on the Bosporus, and a few minutes later the Calif went on board the Admiral's boat, where he was received with all the honours due to his rank. From the Admiral's boat the Shadow of God upon Earth and Rider of the Universal Order went aboard the "Malaya," in which he soon afterwards departed for the island of Malta, along with his little son Ertuğrul and his treasure chest. It was a strange coincidence that the name

Ertuğrul should be born by both the legendary father of Osman, who gave his name to the dynasty, and by the son of the obscure last Sultan.

In making a general assessment of Mehmet Vahdettin's performance as sovereign, the Gazi has said: "What a shameful situation can a people, full of self-respect and with a noble heart, be reduced to by a wretch who has gained a high position and a proud title, thanks to the evil system of succession." He adds: "It must be the sincere desire of the whole civilised world to put an end to the era in which politics are ruled by a system of puppets."

On receiving news of the Calif's flight, the Assembly deposed him and nominated in his stead Prince Abdülmecit Efendi, son of the Sultan Abdülaziz.

Turkey's victory had deep repercussions in the politics of the countries which had been the direct enemies of the new state. Lloyd George resigned from his high position after the failure of his anti-Turkish campaign, and because he felt lack of popular support. Of the four members of the Supreme Peace Council, who were to blame for the Treaties of Versailles, Saint-Germain, Neuilly, Trianon and Sèvres, he was the last to disappear from the forefront of the political scene. His policy, a feudal one of punishment, lost him the support of his people, as was shown to him by later elections.

For Greece the epilogue was tragic, corresponding to the great drama in Anatolia. The people and the army had to find scapegoats for their defeat. They decided that the government was responsible, through its lack of foresight, its confidence in the Powers who had tricked it, and the bad commanders it had placed at the head of the army through sheer favouritism. There were army mutinies in Salonika, Crete and many other places; there were loud demands for Constantine to abdicate, which he did on the 27th of October 1922 in favour of his son George. The revolutionary troops entered Athens the following day. Venizelos had conquered. The people forgot that the Anatolian adventure had been exclusively his work; it was not a matter of achieving justice, but of taking their minds from the pain caused by the great defeat.

Popular vengeance had to be satisfied. Constantine's leading henchmen were tried and condemned, some to death, others to prison, others to exile. On the 17th of November, in spite of Great Britain's diplomatic intervention, there were shot Demetrios Gunaris, former Prime Minister and leader of the royalist party, Nicholas Theotokis, George Baltazzi, a former Minister, Protopapadakis, formerly Prime Minister, and the Generalissimo Hadjianestis.

Chapter 28

THE FINAL VICTORY — LAUSANNE

The work of the Lausanne Conference was not confined to solving the war between Turkey and Greece, but to make peace between the Entente and Turkey, who had been in a state of war since 1914. In addition, the new Turkish state would have to clear up the tragic inheritance left by the Ottoman Empire, an inheritance of debts, capitulations, and mortgages of every sort, beginning with those which affected her honour and pride.

The Gazi had been well pleased by Ismet's wise behaviour at Mudanya, and chose him as the head of the Turkish Delegation to the Peace Conference, which he was to attend as Minister for Foreign Affairs. The Prime Minister Rauf, who thought that he ought to have been the leading delegate, was extremely annoyed by this appointment, as were his followers. The Gazi's responsibility was very great, and his political prestige was at stake; he had made a formal promise to the nation that he would fulfil the National Pact, which included the complete independence and freedom of the country, without political, legal or financial restriction. Could Turkey obtain satisfaction on all the points to be discussed? She had a powerful card in her hand: Turkey was not presenting herself at the Conference as a conquered nation, like Germany, Austria, Hungary and Bulgaria, but as a victor, and she would make this felt. Turkish arms could return to the attack. Liberty or death!

For their part, the Powers were not prepared to lose their centuries-old privileges in Turkey; the capitulations must continue in force, though somewhat reduced. The debts of the Empire provided an excellent motive for the reimposition of the system. Great Britain was aiming for certain important objectives, and it was therefore Lord Curzon, the Foreign Minister and a strong personality, who took the direction of the great British offensive into his hands. It has been said that Great Britain can lose all the battles except the last one; this had now arrived, and Lausanne was to be the last battle in the barely concealed Anglo-Turkish war.

Great Britain had the first success, a united front against Turkey. All the doubtful points were resolved between the Powers, and they left Great Britain at liberty to direct her attack according to her wish. The reparations which had been promised by Germany to France were paid after an excessive delay, so that France intended to take some punitive measures against the Germans, and for this it was important to count on British support. The French press proclaimed the allied union at Lausanne.

The Conference was opened on the 20th of November. The Prime Ministers Poincaré and Mussolini were present. Against Turkey there were ranged France, Great Britain, Italy, Japan, Greece, Yugoslavia and Romania. The U.S.S.R. and Bulgaria took part by virtue of being countries bordering on the Black Sea.

From the first moment Ismet skilfully opposed the idea that the discussions should be conducted as if by conquerors against the conquered: Turkey was ready to speak on equal terms, but in no other way.

The Prime Ministers left Lausanne somewhat surprised; Lord Curzon remained as absolute master of the United Front. He made a rough attack on the Turkish delegation, bringing extreme pressure upon them on every point that had been brought for discussion. Soviet Russia came forward in support of her friend and did so noisily; she proclaimed the Russo-Turkish front as a counterattack to the United Front. Weeks followed each other without seeing any chance of agreement.

The reparations which Greece was to pay for her devastation of Anatolia, and which she was in no condition to afford, were in principle exchanged for the cession of part of Greece at Karaağaç on the left bank of the River Maritza. This question like many others was left hanging fire, since the liquidation of the Ottoman debts was taken up particularly by France as a matter of the first importance. Ismet Paşa, though an intelligent man, and endowed with the finest qualities, was not at the level of his antagonists in the field of Western diplomacy. On occasions he lost his calmness before these chameleons of international politics, but took refuge upon his principles. No, Turkey would accept nothing which was against her complete liberty and independence.

Lord Curzon had his plan to try to impose his will upon the Turks and obtain advantage from them; if these Turks of the new Kemalist school were obstinate about accepting what was imposed on them, they would find out that peace could only be found by bending to the will of the British Empire, after which everything would be easy, provided that the Empire's material interests were attended to. The basic premise must rise to the surface; the oil-rich region of Mosul must be British. Curzon followed his plan methodically; the first part ended when it became clear that Turkey would not accept any clause which compromised her sovereignty. The second act must therefore follow. For the next stage, the British delegation cunningly came closer to the position held by the Turks; they now saw the position more clearly, and an attempt was made on a separate understanding.

The importance and secret nature of the talks begun by Great Britain behind the backs of the much-vaunted United Front, required an appropriate concession on the other side. Ismet was now acclimatised to his surroundings, and for him the answer was simple; it was naturally not within his powers to make a decision, as he must first go to Ankara and get agreement from the Gazi.

After more than two months had passed since the inaugural session, there was presented to the Turkish delegation a plan for a peace treaty, the clauses of which were found unacceptable by Ismet. On the 4th of February 1923, Lord Curzon set off back to the Thames, tired of discussions and in a bad temper; at least he appeared so when leaving Lausanne. Ismet took the opposite road with no less demonstration of disappointment.

After the Sultanate had been abolished and the Califate deprived of all effective power, the opposition had increased their activities. They were extremely alarmed, and thought it necessary to halt the Gazi in his march towards absolute power, since they foresaw that he was going to supplant the Calif. A first attempt at opposition was made in the Assembly at the beginning of December 1922. A bill was read in the following terms: "To be elected a member of the Assembly, it is necessary for a candidate to be a member of the population of the territories which are now within the present frontiers of the country, or to have been domiciled for five years in his electoral district."

Owing to his having been born in Salonika, which was now in Greek territory, and having been unable to establish himself in any electoral district because of having to visit the various battle fronts, Kemal would not be eligible in future elections. "I believed," he said bitterly, "that my services had earned me the sympathy and love of my people." The Gazi had foreseen the possibility that his enemies might make an attempt to prevent him from continuing to serve his country; however he had never expected to find that an attempt to deprive him of his rights would be made within the bosom of the Assembly.

The Assembly rejected the bill, and public opinion showed its support for Kemal, who defended himself from the politicians with the people's help.

The Gazi realised that with that Assembly, which every day was becoming more aggressive and alarming, it would be impossible to reach satisfactory solutions for the great problems still outstanding, such as that of the peace. The present Assembly had been the first to meet under the new state. The Constitutional Law of the 20th of January 1921 laid down that the elections for the Assembly should be made every two years; later on, during the course of the national struggle, the Assembly decided not to dissolve itself until final victory had been achieved. Thus, Parliament could constitutionally be reelected in April of the following year, 1923. The Gazi decided to take the necessary steps for holding the new elections, but determined first to create a political party, which should have essentially democratic foundations, and would be called "The People's Party."

In creating his party he judged it necessary to judge popular feeling, and to enter into contact with the humble classes. With this objective he began a long journey through western Anatolia in January 1923. He gave all his time to talking with the people; on every occasion he collected together several thousand people in places which could contain such crowds, and there expounded his ideas, his party's programme, from which the people would be the greatest beneficiary. The masses, lacking the envy of the politicians, acclaimed him enthusiastically; they recognised in that man Turkey's saviour, and that it was he who would bring new life to their exhausted and ruined country.

The Gazi made the people ask him every kind of question freely. Usually they asked about the result of the Peace Conference, or the position of the Calif in relation to national sovereignty. He answered that the nation could rest at ease; Turkey would obtain satisfaction in Lausanne for her just claims. The difficult question was that referring to the powers of the Calif and his place within the machinery of state, since the clerics had been making an intense campaign in defence of the sacred rights of God's Representative, ever since the abolition of the Sultanate. It should be pointed out that primary and secondary education were for the most part in the hands of the clergy, as were the religious courts. The fantastic number of mosques scattered profusely over the whole country were also as many platforms from which the clergy were making themselves heard. We can thus understand the strength of the opposition which the Gazi had to fight for the support of the people.

The opposition, which could now be identified with the clerical party, presented the political motives which were impelling them as a religious question. The leaders of the religious organisations preached that the Califate and the government were indivisible; the Calif ought to take over from the Sultan as Head of State. A pamphlet published in Ankara was distributed during those days, written by the Member of Parliament Şükrü Hoca, defending the theory that the Calif was ex officio President of the Assembly. The Calif should be not only the sovereign of Turkey, but of all the Moslem populations from China to Morocco. One read in the pamphlet that the sovereign was to "direct those peoples, and ensure the performance of religious ordinances, which should be better adapted to their temporal interests."

The Gazi's opinion on the old question of pan-Islamism with respect to Turkey consisted of the following: "Our nation and its government desire the prosperity of all our fellow Moslems; we desire that the governments formed by them in different countries should live in complete independence, but we cannot from Turkey direct a great Empire including all the Moslem peoples; this is an illusion contrary to science and logic. Every political entity is limited in its power and development; when it exceeds those limits it becomes an anomaly."

The Gazi resisted the claims of the clergy and the opposition, without showing signs of his plan to abolish the Califate at the first opportunity. He declared that the right of watching over the destiny of the new state fell upon the nation, and not on one personage, no matter what kind of titles he might possess, and that it was hardly reasonable to impose the maintenance of a pan-Islamic sovereign upon the shoulders of the Turkish people. It was this wish for temporal power which had caused the greater part of the disasters suffered by the Turks. How many had died in Iraq, Yemen and in Africa, to defend this mirage? "It is time for a truce with those catastrophes," he said, "to which our people have been dragged, through ignorance of our own condition and the state of the world. Now that we have this knowledge, we cannot go on allowing this tragedy to continue."

In Izmit he was interviewed by a group of leading journalists from Istanbul, whose questions included the following: "Would the new state have a religion?" This was another subject about which he had to be careful. "There is one," he answered, "the Moslem religion." He added: "The Moslem religion tolerates freedom of conscience." The Gazi was convinced that freedom of conscience must be respected, especially in Turkey where there were followers of different creeds. The separation of religion and the state was to be one of the first reforms that he planned.

The Gazi passed from Izmit to Smyrna, always in the same close contact with the people. His first duty in the latter city was to visit the grave of his mother, who had died on the 14th of that same month of January. The infirmities natural at her advanced age had led her doctors to advise her removal to a climate less rough than that of the plateau, and the Aegean city had been chosen, but the move had not been able to prevent her death. His mother died happy, since she had been able to witness her beloved son's great victories, and it had been also given to her to see him married and ready to make a home. Kemal bent over the gravestone, and as he saw scenes from his childhood live again in his memory, it seemed that he again felt his mother's caresses, and her good words. Throughout her long journey through life, kindness and nobility were so united to her conduct that they appeared to be an integral part of herself. Kemal's silent grief, shown in his contracted features, was that of a child who had become a man, yet still a child in the depth of his feelings of tenderness towards the mother he had lost.

As we have just said, the Gazi had contracted matrimony; this happened a short time before the death of Zübeyde Hanım; his wife was that young lady who had offered the Gazi her residence at Bornova, and who always wore upon her breast a medal with the hero's portrait. The idyll came to fruition in the villa of Latife's parents; in that beautiful woman, the future reformer believed that he had found the ideal wife. Her conversation was always of interest; she served him as an excellent translator from French and English, which she knew as well as she did Turkish. She would be a true companion for him, and their union would be an example of a western marriage, in which man and wife had equal rights.

Nevertheless, Kemal did not wish to marry yet; he had promised himself not to do so until his work for his country was concluded, so that nothing should distract him from that. When the Mudanya Conference began he left for Ankara, and Latife was left without news of him, though with growing longing. One day after the abolition of the monarchy, Kemal thought a little about himself; the beautiful Latife was attracting him more than he himself could have expected; he told his feelings to Zübeyde, and her happiness moved him to take a decision in the direction which he himself desired.

Without explaining to anybody, he took the first train to Eskişehir, where he continued to Smyrna, never quickly enough for his desire. Extreme must have been the surprise reflected in Latife's magnificent eyes when she saw the Gazi enter her house, his face transformed by happiness-at moments like these he looked no more than thirty-and by way of greeting take her hands and exclaim: "We shall marry! We shall marry!" And as she tried to control her own emotions, he added "Immediately! Without ceremony, without telling anyone!"

Kemal had to allow her a few hours' grace before receiving her answer. The wedding ceremony took place in extreme simplicity, and from then on his wife was also secretary and as she said, aide-de-camp of the Gazi. She appeared beside him on horseback on military parades, and took part in social life as would the wife of a European leader.

During the journey of studies and propaganda which the Gazi had begun, he took advantage of every hour and minute with his usual dynamism; it was a novelty for the people to find a leader asking them their wishes, since there was no precedent for such an action in the history of the Empire. Kemal's prestige was clearly evident, and he drew the conclusion that as soon as he had created his party he would be able to put his planned legislation into practice. On the 18th of February he met Ismet at Eskişehir, as the latter returned from Lausanne, and they continued on to Ankara together.

The opposition was feeling strong; there was free speculation about religion and the divine origins which had instituted the Califate, the plans attributed to Kemal the atheist, and the failure of Ismet, his protégé, at the Peace Conference. Now that the Sultanate had been abolished, they must look for a form of government. Why did the Gazi delay in raising this subject?

Before the Assembly, Ismet explained the situation of the negotiations in Lausanne. The opposition practically threw themselves upon the delegate, accusing him of incompetence, disobedience to the Council's instructions and of having caused the negotiations to get bogged down. Ismet was unable to defend himself, so that the Gazi spoke on his behalf, as he knew well that this new campaign was one of those started by the opposition and directed towards himself. The energy of his opponents did not flag for eight days on end; they shouted their demand that that delegation should not return to Lausanne, whilst the Gazi achieved prodigies of oratory on the other side. He obtained the only success that could have been expected from that Assembly, in that no decision was taken.

Over the issue of the reelection of the Assembly, Kemal acted in his usual way; he examined all the possible objections that could be made to what he wanted, and when he felt secure, took action by surprise. One night he telephoned to Rauf and asked him to bring the members of the cabinet to his house, to hold a discussion at which he would also be present. The cabinet, who were in the majority favourable to the Gazi, made no objections to the dissolution of the Assembly. He then called the leaders of the First Group. He had to use the whole of the night and part of the following morning to convince them. He thereupon called a full meeting of the group for the Defence of Rights, which also agreed. The Assembly voted its own dissolution that same day.

Kemal then began the active organisation of his party, which would be the only party to contest the elections, though individual candidates were not excluded. On the 8th of April 1923, he published a programme which would serve as the basis for the People's Party. There was no reference amongst the nine main principles to the plans which he had decided to carry out, such as the proclamation of a republic, the abolition of the Califate, the separation of religion from the state, the abolition of seminaries and convents, and other reforms.

Thanks to the vigorous defence made by the Gazi, the delegation led by Ismet returned to Lausanne. The Conference began its work again on the 23rd of April; Lord Curzon did not return from London, and sent Sir Horace Rumbold to take his place. Ismet realised from the first meetings that his opponents had not come disposed to make the conclusion of an early peace easy, within the Turkish demands. As had happened in the first part of the Conference, the Allies adopted the policy of interminably prolonging the negotiations on those subjects which were vital to Turkey; they would try to wear her down and extract sacrifices from her, in exchange for the solution of those issues.

The greatest struggles that Ismet had to conduct were against Rauf and the Council of Commissars, who consistently opposed his point of view, and this frequently endangered the favourable development of the Lausanne discussions. The Gazi had to intervene whenever a difference arose between Rauf and Ismet.

The Turkish delegate held firm within the limits indicated by Kemal. France was the main Power to hold out over the economic and legal clauses, but after a prolonged intransigence she gave way before Turkish persistance, and the discussion ended in the middle of July. On the 24th of that month the Treaty was signed, recognising Turkey's integrity and complete independence, so that peace was sealed.

In this Treaty, a victory for Mustafa Kemal's patriotic labours, the frontiers established in the National Pact were respected. The capitulations regime was completely abolished, and no clause appeared which was irreconcilable with Turkey's absolute sovereignty. The Treaty also included the solution of the problems between Turkey and Greece, including the exchange of the Greek population which lived in Turkish territory for Turks living in Greece, which marked a great step forward towards a lasting peace between the two countries.

In Turkey, the elections for the new Parliament had taken place. The new Assembly would support Kemal in carrying out his plans for reform.

It was inevitable that the conflict between Rauf and Ismet should reach a crisis; since the Gazi supported Ismet, Rauf resigned as Prime Minister. Ali Fethi was chosen in his place. The second Parliament of the Grand Assembly met on the 11th of August and there fell to it the honour of ratifying the Treaty of Lausanne. On the 2nd of October 1923, the commanders and last detachments of the occupying forces marched through the Square of Dolmabahçe beneath the Turkish flag, to which they offered military honours; they embarked for their various countries the same day. Great Britain was withdrawing honourably.

That flag is kept in the military museum of St. Irene in Istanbul, as the symbol of the struggle and sacrifices of a people for their independence, memorable events which European writers have described as "The Turkish miracle."

PART FIVE

THE REPUBLIC AND THE SOCIAL REFORMS

CHAPTER 29

THE REPUBLIC

Kemal's patriotic plans were not confined to material victories on the battle fronts and in international politics; he had an intense desire to achieve internal happiness for his country, which could only be brought about by realistic means. Kemal was a modern, positivist philosopher. His doctrines were always aimed at improving the conditions of the people, from whom they were inspired, and drew the strength which was indispensable to carry out reforms.

Kemal's humanitarian and popular principles had existed in his brain in essence since the time before he placed himself at the service of the Nationalist cause; his actions had remained true to these convictions, and whenever he had found the time opportune, he had brought them into practice, a little at a time. Thus it was that in Erzurum in 1919 he caused the following phrase to appear amongst the fundamental principles then adopted: "It is necessary that the National will should exercise its sovereignty"; at the Congress of Sivas: "It is recognised that the National will, concentrated in the Assembly, is the de facto master of the destinies of the country," and in the Constitutional Law of 1921, it is clearly stated that: "The system of administration rests on the principle that the people personally and effectively control their destiny."

The regime towards which he was gradually bringing the country was a republican one. He took advantage of the external danger and the fatal actions of the Black Sultan to gain approval for his reforms and abolish the Sultanate. From that moment the government of the state lay practically in the hands of the people, and this form of government is called a republic; Kemal wished this to be recognised as soon as possible.

In order to pass from one regime to the other it was necessary to pass through a period of transition which might be longer or shorter, during which he would have to fight against a powerful adversary, the temporal master of the theocratic Empire, and whose power had been maintained during the War of Independence; this was the theocratic structure of the state. For centuries the law, the administration of justice, education and the government had been under the immediate influence of religion, with the result that the clergy had ramified prodigiously and sent down deep roots into the life of the Empire. The people received their influence constantly through the mosques, religious tribunals, dervish convents and seminaries.

The Sultans maintained the clergy as an integral part of the regime; amongst other large privileges which they enjoyed, the members of religious orders were exempted from military service, which favoured their survival, especially in the Ottoman Empire with its frequent mobilisations. The Gazi decided to free the people from this influence.

On the abolition of the Sultanate, the royalist-clerical party became alarmed and began to agitate; it was important to give the democratic regime its true name of "republic" as soon as possible, and thus quieten the coming tumult before an accomplished fact.

A certain resistance to the government's proposals soon became evident in the new Assembly, which turned into opposition after Ali Fethi had been Prime Minister for two months. The chief objective of the opposition was to hold back Kemal's work for the people, defend the Califate and ensure that that office was the highest in the state. Some of the generals who had most distinguished them- selves in the Independence War and were old comrades of Kemal, decided to oppose him and went over to the other camp, though not openly. Ali Fuat and Kâzım Karabekir left the Assembly, under the excuse that they were tired of politics, and took up the office of Inspectors of the Second and Third Armies respectively; they did this with the idea of winning over the army to their ideas and gaining its support. Refet and Nurettin joined the military and anti-republic group.

The government was placed in a difficult situation by this continual oppo- sition. On many occasions the Prime Minister Ali Fethi wished to resign, but it was clear that this would not solve the problem. The Gazi thought that it would be wise to declare the republic before the opposition increased their strength. Still without revealing the innermost part of his mind, where he kept what he called his "national secrets," he asked Fethi and the other Commissars to present their resignations, and to refuse to be reappointed, thus provoking a crisis.

When it was announced that the Council had resigned as a body, the various groups of the Assembly attempted the task. Consultations and discussions did not result in the presentation of any list which could win the Assembly's confi- dence.

The Gazi gathered around his table in Çankaya Fethi, Ismet and some gen- erals and Members of Parliament whom he knew well. In the course of that memorable dinner their host remarked: "Tomorrow we will proclaim a republic."

Since all the guests were supporters of the democratic regime, they applauded his decision. Each of them was initiated into the role he would have to play on that historic day. The decision had been taken at the right time, since suspicions of what might happen were already awakened; on the other hand, the absence of the four discontented generals, and also Rauf, Adnan and other leaders, would make the task easier.

On the morning of the 29th, there was a meeting of the parliamentary group of the People's Party, under the presidency of Ali Fethi, to discuss the list of candidates. No agreement could be reached, so that a motion was accepted asking that the Gazi, in his position as President of the party, should be given the task of resolving the problem. The Gazi came to the meeting, and asked for an hour in order to present the means of solution that he had found. During that time he interviewed those people whom it was necessary to inform of the events which were to follow immediately.

Returning to the party meeting, he mounted the platform, and declaring his conviction that the system in operation was the cause of the difficulties which occurred every time it was necessary to form a cabinet. He was submitting a plan for the party's approval to remedy this defect in the system. He came down from the platform and gave the motion to one of the secretaries for him to read aloud.

Those who were not in the secret heard not the names of possible commissars, but a modification of the Constitutional Law. To its first article there was simply added the following: "The form of government of the Turkish state is the republic." In other articles, it was established that the President of the Republic should be elected by the Assembly from its own members, and that it was possible for him to be reelected; he would have the right of presiding over the Assembly and the Council of Ministers. From among the Assembly's members he would choose a Prime Minister who would form the cabinet.

Four and a half hours of discussion were needed to approve the modifications proposed. The session of the Assembly opened at 6 o'clock in the evening. Some unimportant matters were dealt with, while awaiting the report of the commission on the Constitutional Law, which was favourable; only one phrase was added: "The religion of the Turkish state is Islam." Ismet Paşa, who was acting as President of the Assembly, proposed the vote to amend the law, and this was carried.

Thus the Republic was born in Turkey on the 29th of October 1923. The official name of the state was to be: "The Republic of Turkey."

Immediately afterwards, the Assembly was asked to elect the President of the Republic; it could be no other than the man who had been exercising the chief magistracy of the state since its foundation. This transcendental event was announced to the people that night by a 101-gun salute; Ismet formed the first republican cabinet.

The royalist-clerical party sadly saw the disappearance of their hopes of putting a member of the Ottoman family at the head of the state with the title of Calif. In some important Istanbul newspapers the precipitate proclamation of the Republic was harshly criticised; it was asked if the Republic would bring a new mentality with it, whether it would donate the brains of statesmen to its rulers, and if those who had thus baptised the state were able to solve the difficult situation that the country was in, impoverished as it was by so many wars. They declared their disappointment with the National Guide, noting that it was impossible even for well-balanced minds to resist the temptation to acquire power and personal authority.

Some persons including Rauf made statements to the press which were hostile to the new regime and more especially to the man who had succeeded in having it proclaimed. Rauf referred to the Gazi in the plural as "irresponsible persons." In short, Rauf and the other discontented leaders wanted to point out that by his haste, and without consulting any of his oldest revolutionary comrades, the Gazi had succeeded in using the word "republic" to displace the Sultan and place himself on the Sultan's throne.

Kemal was reproached by his old comrades for secretiveness and dissimulation, but as he knew what their ideas were, he could not be frank with them; if he had been, his comrades would have blocked the road towards democracy.

Kâzım Karabekir, Refet, Ali Fuat, Adnan, Rauf and other leading persons, together with the newspapers "Tanin," "Vatan" and "Tevhid," began a campaign for the continuance of the Califate, since the Republic left its fate uncertain. At that time the Calif received a large number of meaningful visits, and gave interviews to several newspapermen. There was a rumor that Abdülmecit was about to resign, but this was then denied. He would not abdicate, it was said, so long as he was not opposed by Islam, whereas at the moment Islam had placed its hopes upon him. The Califate, which was the patrimony of the house of Osman, and a moral treasure of the nation, ought soon to see its powers defined within the state, and rumors which suggested that the Califate might be abolished were antipatriotic, since this would be equivalent to suicide for the Turkish world.

CHAPTER 30

ABOLITION OF THE CALIFATE

The Calif Abdülmecit Efendi, although deprived of temporal power and even of any explicit prerogatives, was making efforts to restore the dignity of the Califate to its past brilliance, in the palace of Dolmabahçe, the most grandiose of the Imperial residences in Istanbul. He brought from the nearby palace of Yıldız all the works of art and value which might enrich the environment of the ostentatious palace at Dolmabahçe; he surrounded himself with chamberlains, aides-de-camp, and the whole apparatus of a court, as far as his reduced income allowed. He received foreign diplomats, retired officials and high clerical dignitaries who grouped themselves around him, in order to revive the importance of the Califate and show that they were ready to maintain it.

The new Calif was a person interested in poetry, and above all in painting, in which he showed a certain skill. He maintained a voluminous correspondence with far-off cities of the Islamic world, and signed his letters: "The Envoy of God, Abdülmecit, Son of Abdülâziz Han"; now possessed by his role, he planned and asked permission to attend the Friday Selamlık wearing a cloak and a turban, both in the style of that used by Mehmet the Conqueror. Naturally he was not permitted to wear this form of dress.

He had himself accompanied to that traditional ceremony by gaudily- dressed guards and a large following. If it was necessary to go by water to arrive at the chosen mosque, Abdülmecit would sit in a luxurious "kayık," or boat, which was gilded, and propelled by several pairs of rowers, dressed in the old gold-embroidered uniforms that he had found in the palace wardrobes. Contrary to the custom of the Sultans closely related to him, he took every opportunity to return paternal salutes and smiles to curious passersby. Pomp had always been appreciated in the East, and this personage with such a fine appearance and proud manners, surrounded by a halo of mystery and mysticism, followed by a reverential group of imposing clerical dignitaries, princes and soldiers, inspired respect and wonder.

At first, Abdülmecit felt quite happy at having obtained the Moslem papacy, but later on he found himself surrounded by intriguers, the clergy, the court, and the powerful reactionary party; but it was certainly the public demonstrations of submission made by famous generals and well-known nationalist leaders which finally awoke in the royal painter the ancestral longing to rule. He must have believed that the moral backing of about 300 million Faithful would give him enough strength to stand up against the atheistic nationalists.

The Gazi had a plan for which he was going to give priority amongst the achievement of his reforms, the abolition of the Califate. This would be followed by the separation of religion from state, and the abolition of the Ministry of Religious Affairs, the religious courts and the Koranic Law.

The matter had to be treated carefully. The Gazi was helped by the intensity of the printed campaign which was kept up by some important newspapers in Istanbul, the ex-capital of Turkey, mirror of the opposing mentality and religious agitation. These newspapers published letters from the Agha Khan and the Emir Ali, in which these Moslem personalities defended Abdülmecit; they lectured to the Turkish Government on Islamic Law, and demanded that the theocratic institution should remain.

These letters produced an effect opposite to what had been hoped for by the Agha Khan, the Emir Ali or those who inspired them to write them. As a result of this, and earlier events, the Assembly decided to send an Independence Tribunal to Istanbul. This is an organ of justice, and is formed in circumstances where the internal stability of the country seems to be threatened.

The Gazi roughly reproved the Agha Khan and the Emir Ali. What right had they to make themselves into mentors of Turkey? What could be the value of the word of an Agha Khan, who was an unconditional servant of the British Empire, which had deprived so many millions of Moslems of their independence? When Turkey had been entering the World War, and the Sultan and Calif Mehmet V. had raised the banner of a Holy War, Agha Khan III had not listened to the call of that Faith and that Califate which he was now defending. On the contrary, he had exhorted the Islamic Councils in India to fight on Great Britain's side, and preached to Moslems that they should enrol in the armies fighting against the Calif. This Indian leader lived a pleasant life, thanks to the favours of his Imperial master; he could be seen amongst the gentlemen of the international Turf Clubs, and he was as well-known in Parisian society as in that of London, where he was in contact with His Majesty's Government.

At the beginning of 1924, the Calif, whose standard of living could not be sustained with the money allowed to him by the government, wrote a communication to the government through his secretary-general, in which he asked for an examination of the "Treasure of the Califate." The tenor of this note was communicated by Ismet to the Gazi, who was in Smyrna taking part in a "Kriegspiel," or war game. The Prime Minister received an immediate reply. This was, that it was considered an insolence that the Calif should make use of a secretary in his correspondence with the national government. The state was not in a condition to feed the Calif's desires for ostentation, but only to assure him a decent standard of living. "For us" he said, "the dignity of the Calif can have no more importance to us in the last analysis than that of a historical memory."

During the military exercises the Gazi was, as was his custom, in close contact with the officers and men; he took advantage of the present occasion to sound out the army's feelings about the possible abolition of the Califate, and he felt that they would not oppose it. Ismet, Fevzi and Kâzım, the Minister of War, were also attending the exercises. Kemal confided in them and explained his way of looking at the Califate and religion. They thus came to the conclusion that the Califate should be abolished as soon as possible.

The Assembly sessions were opened on the 1st of March. The Gazi had already prepared in its main outlines the attack against the religious control of Turkish life, and he made a speech that day in which the main sections promoted the modernisation of law and public education, which until then had been under the direction of the clergy.

In that opening session there was discussion on the budget, and the members were particularly drawn into long discussions on the allowances paid by the government to members of the Ottoman dynasty, and also the budgets of the Ministry of Religious Affairs and the "evkaf," pious foundations. At Kemal's instance, the members charged with speaking on the matter declared these budgets to be excessive.

On the 3rd of March three motions were read to the Assembly for its approval. It was proposed to abolish the Califate and expel all members of the Ottoman dynasty from Turkish territory, to suppress the Ministry of Religious Affairs and the "evkaf," and to unify education. The debates lasted for five consecutive hours and as a result, the important laws were passed which began the era of the great reforms.

The "evkaf" were institutions of a religious nature, responsible for the administration of goods bequeathed by individuals and intended for pious purposes, which were known by the name of "vakfs."

The revenue of these goods, which bore witness to the humanitarian spirit of the Turks, supported asylums, hospitals and other benevolent institutions. The bad administration of the vakfs caused their financial ruin, and as a result, the reduction of the revenue they produced. The "evkaf" now came under the control of the Prime Minister, through a General Directorate.

The medreses, from which graduated large numbers of theologians who occupied teaching positions in primary schools, directed religious observance and handed down justice, were summarily closed. From now on, teaching would be secular, and would be the responsibility of the Ministry for Public Education, using Western methods.

The day after these decisions were taken, the Calif Abdülmecit was crossing the Turkish frontier on his way to Switzerland. Some days later the other members of the dynasty also removed themselves from Turkey. The course traced through history by the descendants of Osman had gone full circle.

After the abolition of the Sultanate, there had reached the Gazi from Moslem countries near and far expressions of the desire of Moslems that he should occupy the Calif's throne. Sheikh Rasih returned from India bringing a similar request from authoritative bodies in the countries he had visited. Kemal was grateful for these demonstrations of affection, but replied to Rasih Efendi: "Are those who want to make me a Calif ready to obey me? In consequence, would it not be ridiculous to perform a role which has no meaning?"

One evening, now far-off, when his friends found the cadet Mustafa Kemal, as often, sitting with a book open on his knees, and asked him why he was sacrificing himself so much to his studies; the blond student answered them: "I would like to become somebody." "You will not hope to become Sultan" they laughingly replied. "No," he answered "I would like to become myself!" Many decades had passed, and through all that time Mustafa Kemal had been true to this principle; no ambition had made him change his way of thinking, or shaken him from his realism.

The new state needed a clearly established constitution. Now that the Republic had been proclaimed this could be done. On the 20th of April 1924, the new Constitutional Law was passed, based on that which had existed since 1921; some principles, which were incompatible with the essentially secular character which the Gazi wanted to give to the Republic, had to be kept in, and new ones were added at the demand of the right wing. There were added the following: "The religion of the Turkish state is Islam," while in the articles concerning the form of the oath taken by Members of Parliament, there appeared the words: "I swear in the name of God." Some years later, in 1928, it was possible to remove those phrases which had had to be kept in the constitution of a secular state because of the exigences of the time.

The striking feature of the Constitutional Law consists of the system called the Unity of Powers, which the Gazi defended: all power is concentrated on the Assembly, which cannot be dissolved, unless the Assembly itself decides to hold new elections in very special circumstances. The Assembly exercises executive power through the President of the Republic, who is chosen by the Assembly, and through the Council of Ministers chosen by the President. The Head of State has only a very limited right of veto.

The reforms which Kemal was to gradually put into practice in the future, needed to be studied with care, as did the way in which they would be most easily adaptable. To this end he began a new tour through the country in the month of August. Beginning with Western Anatolia, he then visited the coast of the Black Sea, and went as far as Erzurum. In every place he spoke to the people, and brought himself close to the humble classes.

He was teaching the people the meaning of the People's Party; he explained that in other countries there existed different social classes, so that there were different parties defending the interests of each of them; in Turkey, however, the huge majority of the people were farmers and there was no class of big landowners. Since great capitalists did not exist either, the real basis of economic activity rested on small businesses and industries. Capitalism in this form could not be the enemy of the people. Factories then employed only a few workers in a thousand, but there would be more and more factories, and then tens of thousands of workers would be required. The working and farming classes would form the basis for the People's Party, together with the businessmen and industrialists. If the nation were seen as Kemal saw it, it could all be part of the People's Party, and that was why a single political party was sufficient; or rather, one school to give political education to the people, which lacked it.

There naturally existed, as in other countries, those classes which took advantage of their superior education to subject those who had been unable to receive it. These classes had no place in the republic which the Gazi was building; the nobility had been expelled, clericalism was systematically being destroyed, and militarism had disappeared, since Kemal had made it one of his first tasks to keep the army completely separate from politics.

The great barrier which still existed was that of education, but that would soon disappear. Kemal did not expect equality, of which nature shows no example, but to reduce the separation between the illiterates and those who have followed higher studies.

On his return to Ankara he was surprised to notice that neither Rauf nor Dr. Adnan had come to meet him at the station as had been their custom. Some days later he heard that General Kâzım Karabekir had given in his resignation from his military duties. Hearing that General Ali Fuat had just arrived in the city, the Gazi sent an aide-de-camp to give him an invitation to dine at Çankaya. The general did not come, but on the other hand had a meeting with Rauf, before going to the General Staff, where he gave in his resignation as Inspector of the Second Army, as he said that he preferred to exercise his functions as a legislator. Both he and Karabekir were Members of Parliament.

These manoeuvrings had a meaning, and followed a thought-out plan. The opposition leaders had thought of founding a political party, and the generals opposed to Kemal believed that their influence over the army was solidly based. They therefore all agreed to return to the Assembly; their civilian friends had made an active campaign within it, and the chance had come for them to start a full attack.

The exchange of populations which had been decided in Lausanne was being carried out in a very imperfect way because of the great difficulties met with in achieving it. There were hundreds of thousands of people who had to be moved from Greece to Turkey, and who had to be supported until they were given land, dwelling, cattle and tools for working the land. The subject gave grounds for criticism of the conduct of the ministry responsible and the cabinet in general.

The opposition put forward a question by the application of the cleric Esat Efendi, which had to be answered on the 1st of November. Before that day, the Gazi took certain measures to keep the army outside the political orbit. He saw that there was an approaching peril that politics, not based on ideals or pro-grammes but on the interests of one or other group, as had happened in the time of the Young Turks, might disturb the progress of republicanism and hold up the enforcement of the reform. The military commanders who were also members of Parliament were told that they must choose between military or legislative duties.

Kemal opened the new Parliament of the Assembly on the 1st of November 1924. The Republican regime was one year old. Thanks to the energetic mea-sures of the Gazi, there had been no serious political disturbance. There are few revolutions which have succeeded in uprooting traditional regimes, and which have not been followed by powerful political upheavals, reactions, and swings of the pendulum until stability has been reached. The French Revolution, to which the Kemalist revolution has some similarities in that it expelled one family and certain classes from power, in the pursuit of democracy and affirming the rights of man, had to pass through the National Assembly, the Legislative Assembly, the Convention which proclaimed the French Republic, the violence of the Terror, the confused years of the Directory, the ascent of Napoleon to the Imperial throne in 1804, then the Second Republic, and the Second Empire, until it reached stability with the Third Republic in 1870, more than 80 years after the start of the Revolution. Neither did the Russian Revolution avoid many changes in power, corresponding to various movements.

The Gazi, who was a careful observer of history, took precautions to avoid such fatal consequences of the great popular revolutions; if he was successful, the nation owed to him its salvation from new sufferings. Later on, during the course of the Republic's history, the Gazi's actions might see sometimes harsh, at times cruel; yet when the reasons which impelled him in those circumstances are analysed, it is recognised that he was guided by the higher interests of the nation and the people, although the people were not able to understand it.

The discussion on the question began on the 5th of November. Rauf, the leading figure in the attack, demanded that the government should give information on the way in which the immigrants were being settled, what was being done for the army, which was then changing from a state of war to one of peace, and what measures had been taken to ensure the maintenance of the heroic fighters. From this question he was able also to move on to say that the country had been bled by so many years of successive wars, and by the administration of previous governments, which was admitted to have been bad. The most fertile regions had been devastated by the invader, the cities had been destroyed, and it was impossible to achieve in such a short time a task so colossal as their reconstruction, and the restoration of production to its former level.

From his detailed discourse, Rauf moved to a higher level, and accused "some comrades" of following a path which would lead them to deprive the Assembly of its rights. He said that he was not a partisan either of the Sultanate or of the Califate, but that he was opposed to any authority which showed signs of taking over the powers of those positions. It was obvious that he was speaking of the Gazi, and wished in this way to bring the country's attention to the danger that he might have ambitions to make himself dictator.

Rauf ended his speech with this sentence: "May God keep our country and all of us beneath His Holy Protection, while we exist."

The orators who spoke for or against the government were many; the President's bell could hardly control the disorders, arguments and insults. Finally, Ismet's cabinet obtained a vote of confidence. Parallel to the struggle in Parliament, those newspapers who favoured the fall of the government attacked it tirelessly;

the members who opposed this were called ingenuous servants, who unthinkingly obeyed the secret orders given to them by hidden forces. Kemal was accused of partiality, and he was reminded of his duties, to which were added threats such as: "Tomorrow may be too late." Ismet Paşa was a special target for the arrows of the press; in "Tanin" one read: "What a vile spectacle is offered to the country by the People's Party and Ismet's government!"

Rauf and his partisans had decided to form a political party. The question they had brought, which placed Ismet's government and Kemal himself in the dock, was the last occasion in which they acted as members of the People's Party. The new party took the name of "Progressive Republican Party," and there fell into it the whole of the reactionary forces and those politicians who, without being declared reactionaries, were opponents of the Gazi. Amongst its principles it was declared that the party respected religious ideas and beliefs.

The step had been taken; now the innumerable mollas, sheikhs, hocas, emirs, and all the orders of dervishes and sects could carry the good news to every corner of the country: a party had been formed which was faithful to religious belief and the Sacred Word. "Was it not that axiom," says the Gazi in his "Speeches," "which was the standard carried for centuries by those who followed their own designs, deluding ignorant, fanatical and superstitious people? Was not this the flag under which the Turkish nation had been dragged for centuries towards innumerable misfortunes and the marshes of obscurantism, from which we have emerged at a cost of great sacrifices?"

The political crisis was acquiring serious outlines, The Gazi thought it was best in such a complex situation to remove Ismet from the arena, as he was a personal enemy of Rauf and many others, and had been accused of every imaginable fault by the opposing politicians and press. The fact that Ismet happened to be ill at the time gave a useful opportunity for the formation of Ali Fethi's cabinet on the 21st of November. Ali Fethi, who had a pleasant personality, and was generally popular, would calm down the political excitement for a while.

CHAPTER 31

FLAMES IN THE SOUTHEAST

Relations between Turkey and Great Britain were extremely strained over the Mosul Question, to such an extent that His Majesty's government sent an ultimatum to the Republic, because of an alleged incursion of Turkish troops to the other side of the "Brussels Line," which had been provisionally agreed by both countries as the frontier between Turkey and Iraq. Turkey answered coldy, and was ready even to go to war if necessary before giving in to British pressure.

Mosul continued to be the cornerstone of Turkish foreign policy. At Lausanne, Great Britain succeeded in having the solution of this question, which was so important for her, left for a later occasion. The disputed area possessed great oil deposits; in addition, that part of Mesopotamia, the centre of the ancient Assyria, had a real strategic value, since it allowed secure communications for the British Empire between Palestine and India. Turkey could therefore expect a tenacious battle from her opponent, who has generally known how to persevere in the realisation of her designs.

From the remains of the Ottoman colossus, Great Britain created after the World War Palestine, Hejaz, Transjordan, Nejd, and Iraq, which she succeeded in having placed under her protectorate. She thus assured herself of free communication between the Mediterranean and the Persian Gulf. Iraq, which included the major part of Mesopotamia, was disputing her northern frontier with Turkey.

It was absolutely necessary that this dispute should be resolved in a way favourable to the interests of Great Britain, although she had to wait. The government of the newborn Turkish Republic would find itself fatally involved in some crisis, on which Great Britain would cleverly capitalise, in order to make the Turks give the desired concession.

The protectors of Iraq had their first opportunity with the revolt of the Nestorians, who lived in a part of Turkish territory beside the provisional frontier. Troops had to be sent to reestablish order. Apparently some of these violated the frontier in pursuit of some guilty persons, and this resulted in the British ultimatum and the Turkish reply.

The Nestorian Christians, Turkish citizens, belong to a sect whose origin goes back to the first eras of Christianity, to the fifth century in which Nestorius, Patriarch of Constantinople, created a system centred upon Christ which forbade the use of the title "Mother of God" for the Virgin Mary, since he considered that Jesus Christ was at once Man and the Word, and not God. These declarations let loose a storm. Nestorius and his system were declared heretical. His followers, who were numerous and not ready to renounce Nestorian theories, were persecuted. They emigrated to Egypt, Southeast Anatolia, where they still survive, and even reached China.

The Republic was to be subjected to the test of fire. On the 17th of February 1925, a serious insurrection broke out in the provinces of Southeast Anatolia, and went forward in an alarming fashion within a few days. The rebellion started in the most backward areas of Turkey, where the Imperial administration had been practically non-existent, because of the great distance from the sea and important towns. This area was part of the ancient Kurdistan.

It was an extremely mountainous region, and its inhabitants, who were mainly nomads, shepherds and warriors, were famous for their ferocity; the tribal chiefs and feudal lords maintained a considerable independence, and collected taxes on their own account. In a word, Ottoman Kurdistan lived completely in the Middle Ages, cut off from the civilized world and ignorant of the advance of science. The fanaticism of its inhabitants was kept awake by the battles they fought against the Armenians and Nestorians, since the Sultans used the Kurds to punish the tricks of their Christian subjects in the eastern provinces.

In the old Ottoman Kurdistan, the inhabitants were generally known as Kurds, when there was in fact an indisputable racial majority of Turks in its Anatolian part, and if the latter called themselves Kurds it was because they came from the region called Kurdistan.

The peace of Lausanne destroyed the dreams of independence which allied propaganda had awakened amongst the feudal lords of southeast Anatolia. Indeed, the republican administration began to take possession of the areas in which the tribal chiefs had never allowed intervention from the state. The secular tendencies of the Ankara government, the abolition of the Monarchy and above all that of the Califate, together with other measures which they considered antireligious, caused indignation amongst the inhabitants of Turkish Kurdistan, which was so far removed from the twentieth century. The complaints of the clergy gained a hearing there; Holy Religion was under attack from the impious men in Ankara, who would undoubtedly go as far as forcing the Faithful to wear hats, transform them completely into "infidel dogs" and compel them to allow their women to show themselves with their faces uncovered.

This hidden excitement came out into the open when the Progressive Republican Party was formed and declared that it respected religious beliefs. The leaders of the new party were men who were very well-known from their leading part in the life of the country in recent years, especially General Kâzım Karabekir, who had gained fame in the Eastern provinces for his campaign against Armenia.

The party sent delegates to the eastern provinces, where they began an intense campaign. In this way, the Progressive Republican Party stood forth as the defender of the mosque, but gave wing to reaction. The movement, which had been started with a great impetus, could have spread through the whole country and placed it in grave danger. Great Britain had found the occasion for which she was waiting, and therefore stirred up the fire which had happened to break out on her frontiers.

The rebellion was led by a sheikh who had much prestige in Kurdistan, called Sait, a man well-versed in theology and Grand Master of an order of dervishes. He was followed by the majority of the feudal lords and tribal chiefs, and they quickly seized important towns. Several divisions of regular troops had to be sent there with all speed, but because of the distance, the inclement weather, since it was midwinter, and the absence of roads, these took a long time in reaching their destination.

Two weaks after Sheikh Sait had raised the banner for revolt, Parliament approved a modification to the Law of Treason; it was forbidden to form societies using religion as the basis for their political activities. Anyone taking part in such associations, or proposing a change in the form of government was declared a traitor to the country.

The Prime Minister Ali Fethi did not act with the energy needed for the situation, and he was criticised for this in the Assembly. He resigned and was replaced by Ismet, who was ready to put radical measures into effect. As in the great social revolutions, it was the more extreme tendencies which successively took charge of the government, opposing not only the rightwingers, but even the moderate revolutionaries; thus it happened to the Kemalists. After Ismet took power for the second time, a struggle began against those opposed to the complete revolution. On the 4th of March, the day after the man who had signed the Lausanne Treaty came to office, there was promulgated the Law for the Maintenance of Order, which authorised the government to take the measures it judged necessary to put an end to the subversive movement. On the 7th, two Independence Tribunals were established: one was to remain in the capital and the other would go to the eastern provinces. Also, partial and urgent mobilisation was decreed.

In the meantime, the rebels continued to hold a large region from the Euphrates to the Iranian frontier. They entered Diyarbakır, the fortress city on the Tigris, to cries of: "Long live the Sacred Şeriat! Death to the atheists of Ankara!" Sheikh Sait promised to restore the Monarchy, the Califate and the Holy Religion.

Diyarbakır is the ancient city of Amida the Black; it is surrounded by formidable walls of black basalt, and in spite of having been possessed by the many invaders of Anatolia, its walls and towers retain their strength intact. The energetic action of the Republic forced the rebels to withdraw from the Black City. They lost all the other cities one by one, including their last strongholds, until they were completely defeated after three months, which saw many a bloody fight.

The sheikhs who had been responsible were captured along with all the leaders of the movement, and suffered the death penalty without delay. Sheikh Sait also became a prisoner. During the trial which followed it was clear how much influence the Progressive Republican Party had exercised over the direction of the rebel movements. Sheikh Sait met his death in the great square of Ankara, hanged from a rope.

Since it fell amongst the organisations mentioned by the Law of Treason, and because of the disclosures which came out during the trials of the rebel leaders, proving the relation between them and some members of the party, the government set about the dissolution of the Progressive Republican Party. The press which supported the "Progressives" was submitted to censorship, some newspapers were closed and a certain number of journalists were condemned to various punishments. The politicians who were active opponents of the republican regime and of Kemal personally were some time afterwards condemned to ostracism. A hundred and fifty of them had to submit to this order, and became known as the "150 undesirables." Among these were men well-known for having taken part in notable deeds during the War of Independence, people of recognised talents and education; and yet for that same reason, they were harmful to the transformation of Turkey as Kemal understood it. They were a hidden obstacle to the moral Westernisation of the Turkish people as it had been left formed by the theocratic Sultans.

Mosul continued in dispute, and it was therefore possible that there might be more disturbances in Kurdistan. In December 1925, the League of Nations gave its verdict in favour of the United Kingdom, awarding it the province of Mosul, to the south of the provisional frontier, without any compensation to Turkey. Turkey had previously declared that she had accepted the intervention of the League as mediator and not as judge, so that the Chancellor Tevfik Rüştü refused to accept the judgement in the name of his country.

Ankara reached a direct understanding with London, and the agreement of Mosul was drawn up and signed in June 1926 between Turkey and Iraq, bringing the dispute to an end. The frontiers were determined with some advantage to Turkey; she gave up the oil of Mosul in return for a large financial indemnity. The agreement of Mosul was the last of the treaties by which Turkey obtained recognition of her frontiers.

CHAPTER 32

THE REVOLUTION IN DRESS

Although the rebellion in the East had been crushed, the Law for the Maintenance of Order still continued in operation, to prevent if possible new disturbances. The Gazi was going to make use of this to put into practice the social reforms on which he had long meditated.

The people said that the Gazi was keeping the Emergency Law, really Martial Law, in order to use it as an instrument of despotism, but he only used it to ensure the stability of the Republic, except also to destroy the people's false beliefs and oblige them to adopt Western dress and customs.

On the 24th of August the Gazi began a journey to the coast of the Black Sea. He left at such an early hour, that only those accompanying him noticed the original manner in which His Excellency the President was planning to travel: instead of the famous astrakhan cap of the Nationalists, he was wearing a panama hat. When he arrived at the city of Kastamonu, the multitude who had come to welcome him were left dumb with amazement when they saw the Liberator salute them with a "hat," and receive their delegations with his head uncovered.

The surprise of the inhabitants of Kastamonu was fully justified, since until that day the hat, as used in Europe, was the distinctive sign of foreigners, of the "Gavur," infidels. The Turks wore the fez, and during the War of Independence, the kalpak began to be worn amongst the Nationalists, but this custom was still very much in the minority in 1925.

The fez, which in Turkey represented the traditionalist and religious spirit, was not of Turkish but of African origin, and bore the name of the city of Fez, where there were the best factories of this kind of headgear. It consists of a cylindrical cap of scarlet or purple felt, ornamented with a tassel of long black cord. Having no peak, it was a great nuisance on sunny days, and since it had to be worn on all occasions, even in closed places, during meals, and in offices, the colour and lower part were deformed by perspiration.

The fez became generally worn amongst the Greeks on the islands and the Anatolian coast of the Aegean. It had been instituted by the Sultan Mahmut II, the reformer who wished to Westernize the Empire but who lacked the moral strength of the Gazi, who was to achieve this later on. The Padişah wanted to make his subjects adopt a uniform headgear, since until that time they had been using the most varied turbans, caps and coiffures. The different parts of the Army and Navy, as also the Imperial Guards and Janissaries, distinguished themselves by their headgear, which was in some cases so large and complicated that it was sometimes a real impediment. Civil servants and administrators showed their rank by the shape and colour of their turbans, as was also the case with the different categories of clergy and dervish sects. It was easy to distinguish a man by his headgear.

At a time when the Empire was still large, and the Padişah had numerous non-Moslem subjects, and while the Great Powers were exercising pressure in favour of non-Moslems' rights, Mahmut's policy of eliminating as far as possible the signs which separated them from the Faithful was an intelligent one. Mahmut tried not only to standardise headgear with the fez, but also to Westernize the form of dress. He himself wore a simple frock coat buttoned up to the neck, and trousers, with a European style cloak over all, capped by the fez. In fact none of his successors went back to using the complicated and sumptuous clothing of the time of Selim III, Mustafa IV and Abdülhamit I.

When Mahmut began his fez campaign in 1829 he believed that it would be accepted by the people without much protest, because of its convenience and because it suited the rules of Moslem ritual, which demand that prayer is made with the head covered, and that the forehead is touched to the ground as a sign of humility. It was in every way a delicate subject. The Sultan wished before all else to attract support from the higher class of what can be called the Moslem clergy, the ulemas, that is the Doctors of Theology and senior priests. He knew that if they accepted the fez, the people would do likewise. However the mosques trembled at the first attempt. What! A hoca, an imam, wearing a fez? The Şeyhulislam, Minister for Religion, categorically refused to obey the Imperial ruling, although he was a liberal man who had often supported the Sultan's reforming ideas; this new proposal, however, went beyond all limits. He declared: "The Sultan can cause the head of his slave to fall, but he must not profane it." The affair reached such dimensions that Mahmut feared revolution, and decided not to insist upon it.

Little by little the fez came into general use, and with the exception of men of religion and those who pretended to be such, who went on using the turban, the country adopted it, so that it came to represent the spirit of the nation and the religion, the opposite of what it had been orginally considered, a symbol of anti-Islamic reforms.

In 1903, the Red Sultan tried to have the cavalry troops adopt the kalpak, which was of Turkoman origin, but the Seyhulislam and his counsellors declared that the sacred fez could not be replaced by the kalpak.

When Kemal began his campaign in 1925 in favour of the hats used in civilized countries, those who defended the fez used the same arguments as had been used in 1829 by those who favoured the turban. The fez, which at that time had meant progress, was now the emblem of reaction.

The Gazi conversed with the inhabitants of Kastamonu and made speeches in favour of the adoption of the hat. He declared that it was necessary for the Turks to reach the level of the civilized peoples from every point of view, and that they must completely change their old mentality. "Look at the Turkish and Moslem world" he said, "and think about the misfortunes which it suffers because it has not adapted its ideas and its mentality to progress, and the changes which civilization ordains. That is the cause of our backwardness and the misfortunes that have happened to us. If we have saved ourselves with the space of a few years, it had been thanks to the transformation of our mentality. We must not stop; we must always go forward. The nation must know that civilization has a strength which destroys everything which remains indifferent to it."

The Gazi tirelessly tried to convert the people to his ideas; he talked to the tailors, and asked them to make cloth caps, since the demand would soon be so great that it would be wise for them to start working right away. The news of the Gazi's promotion of the use of hats flew through the telegraph wires. Thus his speeches were not confined to his hearers in Kastamonu but reached the whole nation. A gasp of horror passed through the mosques and dervish convents. The last warning made to the people by the men of religion had been: "They will even make you wear hats," and this was seen to have happened.

From Kastamonu the reforming President moved on to the port of Inebolu, where he took his reforms of dress a stage further. The costume used by the Turks could not be called national, since it was an amalgam of heterogeneous garments: tunics, wide coloured sashes, the "şalvar" or trousers gathered in half way down the leg, and with an enormous fullness in the upper part, woollen stockings with many-coloured patterns, and shoes of skin with the wool still on, with upturned toes, and tied on with laces. All the women went about wrapped in the "Çarşaf" and their face covered with the "peçe." "Comrades" said Kemal, "the international and civilized method of dress is suitable for our nation, and we shall adopt it. We shall put shoes and boots on our feet; we shall wear trousers, waistcoat, tie, shirt and jacket and naturally to complete this method of dress, I will say frankly, a hat. There are some people who oppose the adoption of a hat; I call them fools and ignorant people. By the side of the power of civilisation, which illuminates, studies and examines, those nations who insist on going ahead with a mediaeval mentality and with primitive superstitions are condemned to disappear, or at the very least to live in slavery."

The Turks had good examples to support the Gazi's claims, in the ruin of the Ottoman Empire and the Moslem peoples who had been enslaved or humiliated by the Europeans. Kemal also spoke of women, and the place which must be accorded to them in the home and the life of the nation; he spoke of the religious orders, and said that it was advisable to close the convents, dissolve the sects and establish rules for the way in which the clergy should dress.

When the reforming President returned to the capital on the 1st of September, a multitude of heads could be seen wearing hats; from then on, the intellectuals and the majority of the populations of the large towns adopted the hat without any law being passed; however news reached Ankara that in the Eastern provinces and generally in the less civilized parts of the country the inhabitants, like a large part of the inhabitants of the large cities, were continuing to use the fez and turban, and roundly refusing to wear the sign of the infidel upon their heads. It was surprising that part of the population should have become so angry over a matter of lesser importance like this, compared to the abolition of the Califate or the proclamation of the Republic.

When the Assembly met again, a bill was passed making the wearing of hats compulsory, on the 25th of November. When attempts were made to put the law into practice, disorders of only moderate importance happened; however, there were demonstrations in several places, led by men bearing the green flags of the prophet, carried from the mosque. Since the movement was daily reaching larger proportions, and like the Kurdish revolt against the reforms from Ankara had already cost a lot of blood and sacrifices, the government decided to put it down with energy. For this it sufficed that the Independence Tribunals began their work, and several dozen instigators were hanged at a time at the doors of mosques.

The Gazi said: "We had to throw off the fez, which sat upon our head as an emblem of ignorance, fanaticism, and hatred of progress and civilisation."

CHAPTER 33

THE CLOSING OF THE "TEKKES".

When he realised the extent of the passionate activity of large sections of the Moslem clergy, not only in opposition to the Republic, but also against the reforms which he was determined to establish in the new secular state, Kemal realised that it was indispensable for his success to put the clergy in the place which belonged to them, that is, not in politics but the field of religion.

Under the theocratic Empire, the priesthood was composed of a higher class called the "ulemas," or doctors of the Holy Law, followed by the "muftis," religious directors of the various parts of the Empire. The ulemas reached that rank after following studies based on the Koran and the Hadith, that is the words and deeds of the Prophet, along with the interpretations of parts of the Koran by learned contemporaries of Mohammed, and the adaptations of the precepts of the Koran to the needs of the times. Those who aspired to the rank of ulemas, completed a period of residence in the medreses with the rank of "softas," or theological students, and were then authorised to conduct religion or be judges; to such an extent were state and religion united.

Religious activity was conducted by "imams" who led the services, "hocas," who were teachers, the "müezzins" who called the Faithful to prayer, the "hafız," who recited the Koran, and the "vaiz," who preached.

In the beginning, the Moslem religion established no priestly hierarchy, but the grades just mentioned were tacitly established over a period of time.

Technically separated from the official religious structure, though bound to it within the service of Allah, there were the orders of dervishes, "tarikatlar," who were inspired by heterodox philosophies within Islam.

During the period when Turkish migratory groups coming from Central Asia began to be converted to Islam, from the eighth century, then penetrated Iran in the next century and from there extended their power over great areas of the Arab and Byzantine world, Sufism attracted many Turks, through its deep and humane hope of self-identification with the Supreme Being, and its doctrine that God is in all things and all things are in God.

The Sufi groups gave the example, and showed the way to the reaction against Islamic scholasticism. Sufis had no need to resort to ulemas or imams as intermediaries between man and Allah; Allah could listen to whoever spoke to Him. Communication was always possible between the Creator and his creatures. Sufism is not a religion, but it is that most intimate mystical feeling which breathes through every religion. It is identified with the term "tassavvuf" the Turkish word for mysticism.

It was Sufism which was the determining factor in the creation of the heterodox congregations or brotherhoods of dervishes. They especially arose in the Turkish East, like an internal process within Islam, with an unorthodox spirit and allowing wide horizons for the individual's experience. In their area of activity and their beginnings, they did not have the same meaning as monastic orders in the Christian or Buddhist sense, but of a path ("tarik" means "path" or "way") to reach God. Sufism was the conceptual mould for the "path" of the dervishes.

The term "dervish" enfolds the quality of a man who is dedicated to the search for the eternal truths, who whether wandering or sedentary, has renounced everything which is not useful to his spirit. In fact, monastic life did not answer an internal need, since the monastery is within the heart of the initiate.

The principal dervish sects, which grew greatly in the Turkish East, were the Rufai, founded in the twelfth century, the Mevlevi, instituted by Celalettin Rumi in the thirteenth century and also known as the Dancing Dervishes, and the Bektaşi and Nakşibendi, which were founded in the next century.

An era of spiritual flowering began in 1097, when the Seljuk Sultan Kılıç Arslan I conquered Konya, which was capital of the Turkish Empire in Anatolia. Learned men, artists, poets and mystics came to Konya from all parts of the Moslem world, and made the city as lofty an intellectual centre as Baghdad, Damascus or Ghazna.

One of the personalities who had most influence in this period of dawn was Bahaettin Velet; born in Turkistan, he came to the Holy City of Konya at the beginning of the thirteenth century with his son Celalettin Rumi, born in Khorasan. The latter, who was a mystic poet of extraordinary lyric intensity, created the Mevlevi sect, whose name was derived from "Mevlana," Our Master, as his disciples called him.

Celalettin preached the way he had chosen to enter ecstasy and approach the Divine: "There are many paths which lead to God, and I have chosen that of the dance, music and poetry." The Mevlevi "tekkes," dervish convents, have kept a record of the circumstances in which the whirling rite was instituted. Celalettin was dancing with his great companion Şemsettin to the rhythm of the flute; he went on turning until he lost consciousness of his material body and exclaimed: "I am rising! I am going to heaven!"

"I did not know that Thou art all the visible and all the invisible; in bodies, in souls, always art Thou." These are words from his "Divan," (the collection of an author's poetry), in which he is inspired by the philosophic idea of "tasavvuf."

There was no other part of the Moslem world where the dervish sects received more consideration or respect. The supreme leaders of the Mevlevi order, who were called "Çelebi," had the privilege of girding each Padişah (Emperor) with the sword of Osman, an act which was equivalent to the coronation of Western kings. The Bektaşi sect, created by Hacı Bektaş, which was the most characteristic of Turkish Islam, practically governed the vast Ottoman Empire from the shadows of its secret mystic sessions. In this as in the other orders, it was not necessary to be a dervish to belong to it. Personalities of the high table of Government and in particular the leaders of the praetorian guard of the Janissaries were affiliated to the Bektaşis. Some Sultans were deposed by decisions taken by that sect.

The Dervish orders fulfilled a powerful role during the Empire, and the Sultans protected them, in order to be protected in their turn.

As the Ottoman Empire declined, its institutions and the "tarikatlar" declined with it. They abused their influence and power. After the great reforming Sultan Mahmut II in the first half of the nineteenth century had carried out the massacre and destruction of the Janissaries, who were opposing the modernisation of the Ottoman army, he energetically persecuted the Bektaşis and some of the sect's members suffered the ultimate penalty.

The Gazi remembered the active participation of the clerical hierarchy and the members of the "tarikatlar" in supporting Sultan Abdülhamit II against the Young Turks. When he himself began the rebellion of the Turkish Nationalists on the 19th of May 1919, when he disembarked at Samsun, he had first received the cooperation of ulemas, hocas, etc., and of the tarikatlar. However, when they suspected that Kemal would destroy the holy institution of the Sultanate, many went over to the Sultan's side, against the national liberation movement directed by Kemal. They approved when Mehmet Vahdettin condemned the rebel general to death, and approved the Fetva of the Şeyhülislam declaring that "It is a sacred duty to kill the nationalists."

Apart from laying down that the state, as a political and temporal entity, and religion, within its own field, are two distinct though naturally not incompatible things, the Gazi believed that the dervish orders were far from continuing to fill the ends which their creators had indicated, with true mysticism, and on the contrary had often harboured procedures and people who were abusing public trust. He considered suppressing these organisations, which had no place in the modern and secular republic for whose existence he was struggling.

On the 2nd of September 1925, two decrees were made by the Council of Ministers under the Gazi's presidency; one laid down the final closure of the "tekkes" and dissolved the congregations; the other designated those members of the clergy who had the right to use clerical garb and to fill positions in the hierarchy of the mosque, and made conditions to which their conduct must conform. Along with the "tekkes," there were also closed the "türbes," or tombs to which votive offerings were made, and which were considered miracle-working.

The Gazi believed that social education in the new Turkey must be completely modern. He declared his opinion that to expect any help from the dead was not enough for a civilised society, and as he analysed the reason for the existence of the dervish orders, he pointed to the better part of them, which was the desire to ensure the happiness of their members. "I will not admit in any way" he said, "the existence in the Turkish community of primitive men who, with the light of science and civilisation to guide them, seek moral and even material happiness in the advice of some sheikh or other. You must know that the Republic of Turkey cannot be the country of sheikhs, dervishes, novices, and members of sects."

The possessions accumulated by the orders were confiscated. Mustafa Kemal was following a perfectly worked-out plan in suppressing these institutions, and his philosophy that fanaticism, though not religious observance, must be extirpated from the heart of every Turk.

In his "Nutuk" ("Speeches"), he summarises the way in which he saw this question: "Could one claim the title of a civilised nation for an accumulation of men dragged along behind a crowd of sheikhs, dedes, seyeds, çelebis, babas and emirs, and who entrusted their fate and their lives to palmists, wizards, soothsayers and sellers of charms? If we had retained these elements and these institutions, would we not have committed the gravest and most irreparable error against the cause of progress and rebirth?"

Earlier on, during the struggle for independence, the Gazi had lost no opportunity of moving the country towards a secular regime. There are many stories told in connection with this, including one which is set in Konya. The ulema in charge came up to Kemal and tried to talk to him separately. Kemal was accompanied by some officials, and told him that this was not the right moment, and that if he had anything to say he should say it before them all. What the Superior wanted was that the old privileges of the seminarists should continue to be respected. "You are excellent schools for deserters," said Kemal. "With two more battalions I would capture Afyon and Izmir." And turning to the people he asked: "Which would you rather have, those cities or this school?" On receiving the answer he wanted, Kemal ordered that those pupils who were of military age should be taken away to receive military instruction.

Another time, the Gazi attended the opening of a hospital at Kayseri, and as it was the custom that clergy should take part in such ceremonies, an imam came forward to deliver a prayer for the occasion. Kemal waved him back: "God can hear my voice just as well as yours," he said, and went on to express in simple language his desire that the new hospital should labour in the fight against pain and sickness.

The Gazi's basic idea was that religion should remain in its true place, that is, in individual consciences, since it was something personal and intimate; for that reason, the external signs of the different religions, which showed Turkish citizens the religious differences which divided them, ought to be removed. The last law aimed at this objective is the one which forbids the representatives of any religion or sect to wear their characteristic vestments outside the places of worship, with the exception of the head of each religion in Turkey.

CHAPTER 34

LEGAL REFORMS

When the Gazi was not travelling he lived in Çankaya. The great reforms, which he was bringing into effect one after the other, forced him to make serious studies, meet specialists on the various subjects, and discuss with them the possible ways of adapting them to Turkish life. He was again living alone now; he had divorced his wife according to the ancient Moslem practice. Kemal had thought that he had found the ideal companion in Latife, because of her education and perfect manners, apart from the happiness which that beautiful young girl would doubtless bring to his new home, but she turned out to be very different from what he had thought on marrying her. Latife's European education caused her to imagine that she was the equal of her husband, and that she could exercise a great influence over him and take an active part in politics. She went beyond her position as wife of the President of the Republic, and her role as collaborator in realising the reforms, especially those concerning the emancipation of women, a mission in which the Gazi was pleased and proud to see her take part.

It is reasonable to suppose that Latife was not as intelligent as she seemed, as she was not content to remain in her place, where she certainly had enough to do. Her parents made more demands than were permissable, asking for sinecure offices and favours, which annoyed the Gazi; however Latife succeeded in obtaining these, thanks to the influence she had acquired over the government. Quarrels and coldness began. His wife became authoritarian, believing that she must be obeyed in everything, and that the life and custom of her husband ought to follow the rhythm she imposed. At last, she thought she understood that the policy followed by Kemal was not that most fitting for Turkey; she repeatedly said as much before outsiders and even in public statements; in short she showed herself to be an opponent of Kemalism. When Kemal's patience was exhausted and he realised his mistake, he first considered the matter in silence as was his custom, and then made a rapid decision. He composed the act of repudiation, read it to Latife, and immediately arranged that she should travel to Smyrna to rejoin her family. They had no children to unite them, and Kemal had been unable to realise the home of which he had dreamed.

After this experience he never tried it again. His mission was infinitely greater than that of forming a home, or a family; it embraced the whole of Turkey, which was his great home, just as the people were his great family, and he was to consecrate all the hours of his life to them.

At the beginning of December 1925, the Gazi was in Konya. Some paragraphs written at this time and taken from his notebook are known, because they were published in facsimile in "Vakit," an Istanbul newspaper. The impressions they give are interesting, since they show his intimate thoughts, being written for himself. Exceptionally, it has been allowed for some of the pages to be published. Amongst other things he noted: "I have no other aim than that of working for the good and the happiness of the country and the nation. Such a task is sufficient to ensure happiness and contentment for a man." This was written after his divorce. "I and those who are with me are certain that our aims are noble, and that we are following the right path. We are in no way exempted from the need to look into the past to find teaching for the present and the future. We take no pride in the services which we have rendered, but we are inspired by the hope that we will be allowed to achieve those which we can yet give. We shall not stoop to attract ephemeral popularity, or deceive the nation with plans which are beyond our intelligence, and which we cannot properly accomplish."

"Konya, 5th December 1925. We find it" (Kemal speaks in the first person plural) "a great injustice that we are represented as acting arbitrarily, like despots. We do not act arbitrarily and we are in no way despots. Our life, and all our activity have been consecrated to the struggle against those who acted in an arbitrary and despotic way in the affairs of the country. Our action has been inspired by logic and intelligence. All the events which fill our life are proof of this truth. It is true that it has happened sometimes that we have appeared disrespectful towards those who have shown themselves harmful to the country's interests by their deeds and ideas. We are always ready to show ourselves severe and implacable against those who make efforts to prevent the nation from advancing along the road of progress. If we cannot give any assurance to those who ask us for proof of magnanimity and impartiality on that subject, it is because we place the interest of the country above everything else."

On the 23rd December, the international calender and time were adopted. This reform ended the complications and difficulties which the use of three different calendars caused Turkey in her international relations and her internal life.

The Ottoman Empire followed the Arap lunar calendar. The lunar month begins when the moon first appeared in the sky as a thin crescent, which is still referred to as "new moon." New moon occurs when the moon lies directly between the earth and the sun and, in consequence, cannot be seen. The cycle of the moon's phases takes a little over 29 1/2 days and therefore in Arap calendar a lunar year contains 354 days and some hours, which show differences from place to place. According to the calendar used in the West, the year is that period of time in which the earth performs one revolution in its orbit around the sun. The year contains approximately 365 days and 6 hours. The lunar year is 11 days and 6 hours shorter than the solar year. The months of the lunar calendar do not keep to the same season in relation to the sun. Therefore in countries where the lunar calendar is used, social gatherings such as the New Year, religious festivities or similar occasions may fall either on winter or summer. Besides the lunar calendar, it was necessary to use the solar calendar, which enabled observation of the growth of plants.

It was also complicated to make the months and days agree. The Imperial Government found it necessary to adopt a solar calendar. From then on, two calendars had been in use; the Turkish solar calendar for official purposes, and the lunar calendar, together with the international or Gregorian calendar, which had to be resorted to in order to find out what day the rest of the world was living in.

Another reform which was approved on the same day abolished the traditional division of the hours in favour of international time. From then on the time of sunset is considered 12 o'clock and afterwards the time runs as 1,2,3,... Thus it had been that in earlier times the Turks had followed the time called "alaturca," while the foreigners had followed the "alafranga" time, which as is easy to imagine, gave rise to frequent misunderstandings.

The ancient Islamic Law, based on the Word of the Prophet, was the most serious obstacle encountered by Turkey's social progress. It had varied little, since the Turkish people had adopted Islam and Arab customs, and begun to govern themselves by the Koranic Law, both in the constitution of their state and in their social regulations.

The foundations of Islamic Law are the dogmas and moral precepts comprised in the Koran, the Word of Mohammed, which is the only fountain of wisdom. In addition to the Holy Book, the preparation and development of the Law had taken into consideration the Hadith, which contains information on Mohammed's way of conduct, and completes and interprets the meaning of the precepts of the Koran. In the time of the first Califs, whenever the Koran left any points not explicitly resolved, when its precepts were to be put into practice, groups of wise men and theologians would gather and find solutions for the difficulties, taking it upon themselves to interpret the hidden wishes of the Prophet.

Moslem Law was therefore rudimentary in its beginnings, which became clear when the Arabs conquered a great Empire in the seventh century and found themselves obliged to govern different peoples with differing customs. To meet the needs arising from this situation, the Arab jurisconsults set to work to perfect Islamic Law, which they did without going beyond the limits and spirit of its original sources, the Koran and the Hadith.

The Law was divided into three parts. The first part was not very different from the principles of present-day European Law. The section on marriage was the one which showed the greatest difference from its European equivalent, allowing polygamy; the system of repudiation, by which the husband had the right to expel his wife from the home, kept women in a state of inferiority. The third part of the Law dealt with punishment, and was inspired by the Lex Talionis, which is based on the Law of Moses.

The Ottoman Empire took the foundations of its code of laws entirely from the ancient Islamic Law, and justice functioned in the following way: first there came the Calif, Supreme Judge and Head of State; in his name, the "kadı's," who were judges graduated from the medreses, administered justice. A characteristic of the Law was its recognition of a judge without assessors. Apart from the kadı's there were the "muftis" or higher jurisconsults, to whom those who did not agree with the kadı's decisions could appeal.

The reforming Sultans had the idea of modernising the law, but prevailing interests opposed this. It would have been necessary to make a total change in the constitution of the theocratic state, and separate civil from religious affairs, which no Sultan could have dared to attempt. Since Ottoman history was full of examples of the danger brought by progress, nothing more than half-measures were taken.

The decline of the "Sick Man," which became more marked in the middle of the nineteenth century, aroused the ambitions of the Great Powers in his respect, and he understood the need to reach the cultural level of his opponents, or die. It was this compelling motive which gave birth to the period of reforms. In the field of law, it was necessary to codify the laws, creating a system which agreed with the social development of the times; this was done, but imperfectly.

The Civil Code was ready in 1868 under the name of "Compilation of Juridical Provisions"; the Penal Code was adopted 11 years later. The whole code was called the "Mecelle," and was based on the civil provisions of Arab and Islamic Law. From the legal reforms of that time there arose, in order to apply them, two kinds of courts instead of what had been before; there were the civil courts called the "Nizamiye," and the religious courts, or those of the "Şeriat." The latter continued to function in their accustomed way; however, their competence was limited to disputes concerning the right of families and the pious foundations. Appeal courts were set above the civil courts.

It was impossible to make any reform in family law, and the Turks continued to obey the laws which had served the Arab community many centuries before.

Apart from this double legal system there existed the various courts of the minorities, which were competent in all matters concerning the rights of families and persons belonging to them. Thanks to the capitulation regime, the foreigners had the right of being judged in their respective consulates.

This was the scene as it was found by the Young Turks' revolution in 1908. There were many plans made to give the Empire a modern code and system of justice, but very little was accomplished.

When the Treaty of Lausanne had been concluded, opening a period of freedom for Turkey, Kemal began to work actively, with a view to suggesting the form in which the legal revolution should operate. Even before that propitious Treaty had been signed, he had announced his revolutionary intentions on the subject, making use of an axiom which appears in the "Mecelle," and which was based on the Holy Law: "The Laws change as things change with time." According to the Gazi, this was the fundamental principle of the legal policy which the new Turkey should follow.

When the secularisation of the state had been decided, the first material step towards legal reforms was the abolition of the religious courts and the Ministry of Religious Affairs; the double legal authority was contrary to modern logic, since there were frequent disputes about respective competences, and the "Şeyhülislamat" or Ministry of Religious Affairs got into conflict with the Ministry of Justice, since there was no relationship between the judges of one side with those of the other.

In his speech on the 1st of March 1924, the Gazi spoke thus about the legal reform, which was a subject on which, he said, faith in mythology was a system preventing the awakening of peoples: "The most important thing is to liberate our conception of justice, and our legal institutions and laws from the bonds which hold us under their influence, consciously or unconsciously, and which are incompatible with the needs of the century."

On the occasion of the opening of the Law School in Ankara in November 1925, the Gazi recalled that the negative force which had been the cause of the decay of the Empire was the Law which had controlled it. Thus the Empire which had been strong enough to control great areas of Europe had been unable to overcome the lawyers, who had resisted the introduction of printing, perfected by Gutenberg in 1436, for three centuries. "The nation believes," he said, "that the rule which says that all laws should be inspired by needs here on earth, is a condition of its existence."

From September 1924 there were meetings of the leading Turkish lawyers to discuss the new legislation. Two parties appeared; one advised that laws should be created in accordance with modern social life, while the other proposed to adopt the European codes of laws which most suited the country. Kemal took the latter side, since studies and discussions would have lost time which was difficult to estimate.

The Swiss Civil Code, which was the most modern and suited to the latest advances of legal law, was adopted as a whole, except for the part concerning trade. With the adoption of that legal corpus, there were effectively abolished the provisions of the old Religious Law, and also the customs which had been erroneously supposed to be based on religion. Polygamy, repudiation of wives, and everything which placed women in an inferior social position were swept away.

The opinions of the Congress of The Hague in 1907 served as basis for the Commerical Law adopted by Turkey; the Law of Judicial Procedures was taken from that of Neu chatel in Switzerland, and at second remove from French and German codes; the Swiss examples served for the Laws of Execution and Bankruptcy, and the Maritime Law was copied from the German Code. The Italian Penal Law was adopted as being the most modern of its kind, while the Law of Procedure for the Penal Courts took the example of those used in Germany.

This task of adaptation was naturally not completed in the year 1926, like the Civil Code, but was finished after 4 years of work.

The organisation of justice received all the attention due to it; the number of Magistrates' Courts was raised to the required number, and they were presided over by judges without assessors; Courts of First Instance were created, to which every legal issue had first to be referred, and which were controlled by three judges, while the Criminal Courts which tried cases carrying serious penalties were presided over by five. The Appeal Courts continue to operate, and there is no jurisdiction higher than theirs. No defendant can be questioned without the presence of his defending lawyer, provided that he has asked for this. The Assembly has the right of pardon.

Special laws and regulations were made to place strict qualifications on the professions of lawyer and judge, whose control had hitherto been extremely lax; during the Monarchy, there had been many members of the Bar who had never been to school.

After the acceptance of the Civil Code, the non-Moslem minorities, to whom Article 48 of the Treaty of Lausanne had recognised legal autonomy in family and personal matters, decided to give up that prerogative, since the ancient Moslem religious legislation had disappeared, and the new laws offered the fullest guarantees.

CHAPTER 35

WOMEN

It was Turkish women who benefited most from the adoption of the Swiss Civil Code; through this, women were placed on the same social level as men, in contrast to the position hitherto reserved for them. In this way women became, in Turkey, an active element in the evolution of the Republic and in national life.

In fact there exists today no difference between the formerly captive Turkish women, and women of countries which are the most socially advanced in the world. Feminine emancipation is one of Kemal's most brilliant humanitarian victories.

Nevertheless, the rights and freedom which have been given to the Turkish women mean no more than a return to the true spirit of the Turkish race. In the centuries when the history of the Turks is known in Central Asia, and in the periods of migrations, women always appear in a powerful position beside their husbands, and there were many who reigned as Queens and led their armies into battle. In the Turkish inscriptions in the region of the Orhon, dating from the seventh century, one reads words such as these: "The Queen who knows the State." There exists many proofs of the rank and equality enjoyed by the Turkish women; in the old edicts of the "Hakans" or Kings, there usually appears the formula "The King and his Lady ordain." Embassies were received by the royal couple.

Although the Turks had been converted to Islam, polygamy and the seclusion of women took centuries to enter the customs of the Turkish people, which was not prepared to deprive women of the freedom they had been accustomed to. The famous Arab traveller and geographer, Ibn Battuta, who toured Anatolia in the fourteenth century, has left some interesting descriptions of the life and customs of the Turkish population of the period. He drew attention to the fact that despite their religion, the women did not cover their faces, and he was surprised by the respect with which they were treated by the men. Identical accounts are given by other travellers in the East. One of these adds that contrary to Moslem custom, husbands and wives in Turkish villages were acquainted with each other before marriage.

Under the Empire, the Koran and mediaeval Moslem philosophers were interpreted in such a way as to bring the situation of women to a state we can hardly conceive of. They did not receive more than the most elementary education, and that only in their childhood. Later, once they had assumed the veil, they were allowed to read sacred works, in particular the "Mevlut," which were poems in honour of the Prophet's birth; it was considered scandalous for them to read anything else. Of course they only read who knew how to, and these were few. The virtue of these creatures, who were denied the honour of belief that they could personally defend themselves from the traps of adulterous love, was protected by strong walls and firm bars, vigilant eunuchs, and by their being forbidden to go out into the street unescorted or unaccompanied. For them, the street had to be seen through the "kafes," a wooden grille placed across the windows of the harem, or through the thick "peçe."

Selim, Mahmut and Abdülmecit, the reforming Sultans, did nothing in favour of women, who only obtained some improvements with the victory of the Young Turks, not so much by the efforts of the latter, as by the penetration of the Western mentality and customs. Girls' schools were opened, and overflowed with pupils anxious to learn. The peçe suffered evolution, and more transparent cloth was used; the "feraçe" was adopted, which left the eyes uncovered. A moderate improvement was also to be seen in the customs under which they lived, which became more marked during the years of the war. Even polygamy was tending to disappear because of the new standard of living.

During the War of Independence, the women of Anatolia once again became fellow workers with their men, as they had been in ancient times; they worked the land, served in hospitals and carried ammunition. The creaking of the kagm, sacred song of liberty, sounded only to the rhythm imposed by those fearless peasant women who, without ceasing to look after their small children, followed the interminable roads which led to the front.

The Gazi gave a special place amongst his plans for reform to the emancipation of women, who had proved their vitality and patriotism before his eyes. However, he did not raise the question while the war was in progress, since such a plan would have favoured the reactionary campaign. In February 1923, he spoke in Smyrna of the necessity for both sexes to take part in progress, since a society was composed of two sexes both of which were indispensible, and if one of them remained backward, society and the country would be incurably weakened. "Women's original duty consists of motherhood," he said. "Let us remember that it is our mother who gives us our first education, and let us recognise the importance of that, at its true value. Our women will be taught all the sciences, and will pass through all the grades of instruction that the men do. The women will go forward to the future together with the men, and will work with them. Ignorance is general throughout our country, and does not affect only our women but our men too. Finally, I will say to our mothers that it is their duty to make us perfect beings; they have achieved their mission in the way they have been able, but from now on we shall need men endowed with another mentality, men who are perfected in a different way. It is the mothers of the future who will educate these men."

This speech marks the beginning of the Gazi's active campaign in favour of women; now he lost no opportunity to try to eliminate negative ideas about women from the people's mind. In August 1924, he said publicly: "I must categorically declare when speaking of civilisation, that family life is the basis of progress and the source of strength. A defective family life begets social, economic and political weakness. It is necessary that the male and female elements which constitute the family enjoy their natural rights, and are in a condition to fulfil their duties in the family."

At Inebolu, he made the people see that it was necessary to do away with all the customs imposed upon women, which could be supported by no serious reasoning. He treated the women as his comrades, and it is interesting to repeat some of his words: "Men comrades: these customs come in some degree from our egotism and from the fact that we are very attached to honour, and very vigilant. Yet our comrades, the women, possess the same faculties of understanding and thought as we do. Let them show their faces to the world and be able to observe it carefully with their eyes; there is nothing in that that can worry us."

He had to face some reaction from the people to the suggestion that women should abandon their customs, the institution of the harem, and the veil; the Gazi therefore spoke very frankly: "Comrades, I repeat: do not fear this change. I will add that we are ready, in order to achieve so important a result, to allow the sacrifice of some lives; that is not important. I draw your attention to the fact that the obstinacy and fanaticism with which we hold on to the present state of affairs cannot save us from the dangers which threaten us, or from all of us becoming mere sheep destined for the "sacrifice."

Turkish women showed themselves less reluctant than men to accept modern life; they did not wait for legalisation before throwing off their ancient yoke. They happily entered the new way of life; thousands of women took employment in various enterprises and factories; they entered the schools and penetrated every level, since no one would have dared to obstruct the will of Turkish women to emancipate themselves, that will being interpreted and maintained by the reforming President with all his strength. When the Civil Code was adopted in 1926, women felt the protection of the law within their homes and outside them. This event marked the free and final collaboration with that precious factor that women truly represent in the life of civilised peoples.

This was the end of the Turkey of the novels, in which foreign writers of great imagination, dealers in exoticism, found subjects for their works. For example, the legend of Aziyade, "Les Desenchantees," and other romantic books about Turkey, had misrepresented the features and spirit of that country as they were published throughout the world.

In the four years following the adoption of the Civil Code, women gave many proofs of their ability; they did useful work in the institutions of medical and social help, in the banks and commercial enterprises. A large number of women entered the university faculties. Kemal was extremely satisfied with the female sex, for which he had made himself responsible before the nation, and considered that women were ready to take part in political life. In 1930 the Assembly gave women the right to vote, and eligibility for municipal elections; this was a step towards complete political equality between the two sexes.

Kemal's philosophy admitted all the natural and political rights of women, and he did not believe that their physical constitution made them unfit to do military service, since they were the equals of men in rough tasks in the fields, and had shown their extraordinary capacity for endurance during the War of Independence. In addition, their behaviour at the front had made him believe that they could give great services on the battlefield itself. Now that women had almost every right, and would soon be given all the rest, it was right that they should not be excluded from any of their obligations.

Those of backward mentality, who were horrified and alarmed by the inconceivable changes in the customs effecting women, were afraid for public morals, since they thought that with the disappearance of the material barriers which had guarded women's honour, they would allow themselves to be drawn into the worst excesses. The paltriness of these thoughts was shown by the excellent behaviour of women in all areas of national life, and in their method of amusing themselves.

The Turkish woman was transformed into a "sports woman" by several institutions for the physical education of women, "girl scout" organisations and the teaching of gymnastics and sport in the schools. From time to time there were held excellent mass displays of gymnastics, in which thousands of men and women took part, while the deportment of girl scout companies was applauded on military parades.

After five more years of observation, the Gazi and the country were confident that women could be admitted to the Grand Assembly. They were therefore given the right to be elected to it and vote in it, and in 1936, 20 female members took their seats in Parliament, not as representatives of their sex, but of the various electoral districts which had voted for them.

In this framework of complete equality, Turkish women did not cease to show their great qualities, and the error of their having been confined in the ignorance of the harem. Finally, in May 1937 a star of diamonds was awarded to the female aviator Sabiha Gökçen who had followed the course of the 'Türk Kuşu' (The Turkish Bird), with complete success, and also the courses of the School of Military Aviation. When she received her award, Sabiha declared that she would go as a military pilot whenever her country called.

CHAPTER 36

POWDER AND BRONZE

On the 13th of March 1926, the Istanbul morning newspaper "Milliyet" ("Nationality") began to publish a series of articles under the title of "Pages from the Memoirs of the Great Gazi." The publication of these memoirs has been a precious aid to those who study Kemal's life. They throw a useful light on his activities from before the Young Turks' revolution, and end with a section about the internal political situation in the days following the Armistice of Mudros. An appendix clears up some points about the conspiracy of Yakup Cemil in 1916, which almost seriously compromised the already famous Mustafa Kemal.

The contents of these pages are of the most vivid interest for their author's biography, and equally for the study of contemporary Turkish history. Kemal did not write them down, but dictated them to the Turkish journalist and writer Falih Rıfkı Atay, at sessions attended also by some intimate friends of the President. The only reason why he did not write them down himself was that he lacked the time, since he was a confident writer, as he showed the following year in his "Speeches." Kemal explained why he had published his memoirs; it was not because he had been seduced by the mania of writing reminiscences, but because he wanted the nation and people to know what his attitude had been in face of the various past circumstances, and so that they would be able to understand him.

In 1927, the Turcologist Jean Deny published, in the "Revue des Etudes Islamiques," a version of the Gazi's "Memoirs," annotated and with an interesting introduction.

The work of building the Republic did not cease. New regulations and laws shaped its already well-formed body. The registry of land, which was in the greatest disorder because of the bad administration of the old regime, was reorganised to conform to the new Civil Code; surveying work had to be carried out.

The transcending religious and legislative reforms of the people's customs were carried out without severe disturbances; the majority of the people either understood Kemal or followed him instinctively; and those upheavals which did occur were due to the influence exercised by agitators and the political opposition. Thanks to the fact that the agitators had been disarmed by a series of draconian measures, the Progressive Party dissolved, the eastern rebellion put down, the group of undesirable politicians expelled, and the press censored, the people ceased to feel influences contrary to the Republic and the reforms. The opposition, which lived in the highest classes, who had formerly been beneficiaries of the theocratic monarchy, understood that any attempt to attract the people would be useless; the only way of changing the state of affairs in their favour was therefore to eliminate Kemal.

This was to be carried out by a group of members of the dissolved Progressive Party, of the old Committee for Union and Progress and other remains of the opposition to Kemalism. Meetings were held with extreme secrecy in private houses and masonic lodges in Istanbul, and a decision was taken: arms were given to some individuals who were sent to the capital, where they were under the protection of the leaders of the Progressive Party. They then looked for the best place in which to eliminate the Paşa. At first it seemed that a place near the club which Kemal used to frequent would serve the purpose, but later there was preferred a turn in the road from Ankara to Çankaya, by which their victim must necessarily pass. At this stage, some of the conspirators in Ankara got frightened of the possible results for them of such a risky adventure, and they brought pressure on the main ringleaders to have the executioners sent back to Istanbul. They no doubt remembered how the planned attack of 1921 had been discovered, in which the leading figure was the Indian Mustafa Saghir. Istanbul was expecting a visit from the Gazi, who had not returned there since his departure in 1919. It was almost certain that he would do so in the year 1926, and in consequence the hidden forces prepared to give him a tragic reception. Their hopes were disappointed, since Kemal began a journey of inspection through Western Anatolia. It was announced that he would visit several cities including Smyrna.

The conspirators lost no time, and sent their murderers to Smyrna; the attempt was to be directed by the former Member of Parliament Ziya Hürşit. In Smyrna, they completed every detail of the proposed plan in collaboration with other individuals, including the means of escape, which was to be by sea to a nearby Greek island, as the first stage; they hired the boats and crew for that purpose. All that remained was for the victim to arrive, as they had agreed upon the place from which the bombs were to be thrown.

The tragedy, whose consequences would without doubt have been fatal for Turkey, was avoided by an accidental detail. Kemal took longer over his journey than had been calculated, waiting in certain towns, so that he arrived at the Pearl of the Aegean one day later than had been fixed. During this space of time, one of the people hired to man the assassins' boat informed the police of the attempt.

On the 16th of June the group were captured with their bombs and revolvers. In a message which the Gazi directed to the nation, he included these words: "One day, my humble body will certainly become dust, but the Republic—its handiwork—will live forever."

Hamdullah Süphi, who was then President of the Turkish Hearths and was a remarkable writer and speaker, has passed on some words of Kemal which he spoke during those epic days of Anatolia: "There are two Mustafa Kemals. There is one Mustafa Kemal of flesh and blood who is now sitting in front of you, who will one day perish, and another whom I cannot call 'I.' He represents a dream, and all that I undertake I do in order to realise the hopes of that dream." He was always accompanied by his vision of the future, and he projected his works and deeds beyond his own death.

The Independence Tribunal immediately began the judgment of the accused and other persons who had been involved, and threw a new light on the plot which had been hatched. Important names were mentioned, and orders went out for the arrest of all of them. The first part of the trial was completed in Smyrna; the minor defenders heard their sentences, which included a very large percentage of capital ones. The second part was carried out in Ankara. Those who were proved guilty or to have taken part in the attempt were condemned to death; those who suffered this sentence included Cavit, Minister of Finance in the Unionist Government, Dr. Nâzım, one of the founders of the Committee of Union and Progress; several ex-Ministers, officers and former Members of Parliament. Rauf was sentenced to 10 years. The judgment was given in default of him. Dr. Adnan was not sentenced. General Kâzım Karabekir and Ali Fuat were not found to be connected with the attempt.

The usual gallows of three beams were set up in the main square of Ankara, and there the principal conspirators paid for their crime. This trial has been criticised for lack of mercy, since some of those who were hanged suffered more because they had been political enemies of the Gazi than because of their connection with the attempt against him. This allegation has not been proved, and it is remarkable that many of the accused who were well- known enemies of Kemalism, and who could have been brought down on this occassion, were acquitted.

Kemal did not allow himself to be swayed by clemency, since the affair went beyond that of an attempt against his own person; it was one of many demonstrations by the reactionary, forces who were now attacking the Republic through its strongest support. The principles defended by these forces had caused the ruin of an Empire, and the backwardness in which the people now were; it was therefore impossible to allow a retreat to such a system as that. Higher interests demanded the highest severity.

There is a precedent for this in the life of Peter I of Russia, known as Peter the Great, and his attitute towards his own son. One can draw parallels between Peter the Great and the Gazi in their great ability to organise their work for reform, their wish to lift their peoples out of backwardness, their struggles against fanaticism, their encouragement of art and science, and their unshakeable energy.

Peter the Great, the most illustrious of the Tsars, reigned at the end of the seventeenth century and at the beginning of the eighteenth, in Russia, scarcely a civilised country at that time. He changed Muscovite customs for European ones, and from then on, Russian women, who because of Byzantine influence had hitherto been kept in seclusion and deprived of their rights, were able to live in relative freedom. He transferred the possessions of the monasteries to the state; he achieved important work in education and social help. Naturally, this reformer had many enemies, since existing interests cannot be touched without winning the hatred of those who used to benefit from them. Peter the Great was forced to crush some reactionary movements, including the rebellion of the "Strelitz," and another in which his son Alexis tried, in the Tsar's absence, to diminish his work. Peter had him condemned to death by a tribunal of dignitaries, together with the other guilty persons.

In October 1926, a simple monument was put up on the peninsula of the Seraglio, Sarayburnu, where the hill of the Byzantine Acropolis descends to the Golden Horn. It shows a walking man, bareheaded and wearing European dress: it is the likeness of Kemal in bronze, standing on a very small base. This was the first statue erected in his honour, but it was to be followed by others, by which the towns, and the people, showed their thanks to the hero and reformer in a material way.

Eight years after he had left it, Kemal returned to Istanbul, the city where he had lived as a prisoner of the foreigners, and where all the intrigues against the Anatolian revolutionaries had been fomented. He arrived at that wonderful city to find it more Turkish than ever before, since the only legal and political authority was now an essentially nationalist government. The capitulations and foreign interference no longer existed. The population gave the liberator an extraordinary reception, showing happiness and emotion comparable to the grief and shame through which they had passed. Kemal's presence brought back to him again the memory of those great days in which the Sakarya victory had been celebrated with indescribable emotion. The Gazi installed himself in Dolmabahçe Palace, which had been declared the presidential residence.

After passing the summer on the shores of the Bosporus, he returned to the austere capital on the plateau, where he completed the monumental speech which he was to make at the second Grand Congress of the People's Party. This began on the 15th of October 1927, in the new Assembly building, a large and comfortable one. The Gazi read out his speech, which lasted for six consecutive daily sessions, and a total of 36 1/2 hours. His gifts as an orator are well-known; his numerous speeches and addresses retain in their essence the convincing force which we can infer that they had when heard from his own mouth. He was in truth the highest exponent of the revolutionary consciousness.

The Great Speech contains the history of Turkey from the 19th of May 1919, the day on which Kemal landed in Samsun, and which marks the beginning of Turkey's struggle for independence. The speech begins with an account of the situation of the country on that date, which it achieves in an excellent synthesis: "The group of Powers of which the Ottoman Empire had been one, had been defeated in the World War. The Ottoman Army was helpless. An Armistice had been signed on harsh conditions. The long years of the World War had left the nation exhausted and impoverished. Those who had dragged the people into this war were concerned with nothing more than their own salvation, and had fled."

The events which form the historical records of the regeneration and liberation of Turkey are reviewed and analysed in chronological succession. The Gazi pays particular attention to internal politics, and the struggle between the two tendencies: the adoption of Westernisation, or the return to the old theocratic systems. He defends the spirit of the reforms energetically, and he makes the preservation of the Republic and its perpetuation an occasion for a moving call to the youth; this is the moral drawn by the speech, and Kemal's political testament, with which he ends an oration which never descends for a moment from the elevated level in which its author began. The mighty speech is characterised by its simplicity, calmness, and lack of artifice.

In the last part of the speech he says: "This long and detailed account, with which I have kept your attention for so many days, is after all no more than the history of an epoch which belongs to the past. I shall think myself happy if I have succeeded in bringing into prominence some points which will be able to awake the attention of my nation and of future generations.

"What I have tried to show in this account is how a great people, whose national life had been considered ended, reconquered its independence, and created a national and modern state based on the latest discoveries of science.

"The result at which we have arrived today is the fruit of the lessons which can be learnt from the misfortunes suffered over the centuries. It has been paid for by the torrents of blood which have irrigated every corner of our beloved country. I commend this sacred possession to the hands of the youth of Turkey. Turkish youth! Your first duty is that of defending forever the national independence and the Turkish Republic. You will find the strength you need in the noble blood which flows through your veins."

The Great Speech was printed in a volume of 543 pages, in large format, with the title of "Nutuk,"—"Speech." Later it was translated into several foreign languages. The French version, which does not give the name of the translator, was printed in Leipzig in 1929, with the title of "Discours du Ghazi Mustafa Kemal," in a volume of 677 pages.

Because of its intrinsic historical value, the "Nutuk" has provided a basis for the Society for the Study of Turkish History in their compilation of the "History of the Turkish Republic," which in its turn is the foundation of history teaching in the schools of Turkey.

Statistics, a science which is indispensable in modern times, and without which the state is condemned to lead a precarious existence, was practically unknown in the Ottoman Empire. There was a lack of data on the economy, agriculture and other assets, while the population was known approximately by rough guesswork rather than by the conduct of censuses. It was estimated that the population of Anatolia and Turkish Thrace was between 6 and 7 millions. The progressive government of the Republic could not be satisfied with approximations.

Kemal gave special attention to statistics, and set up a General Directorate of the subject which he placed under the control of the Prime Minister's office, while each Ministry was provided with a statistics service. The Direction of Statistics held a general census of the population in October 1927, and came up with the figure of 13,660,275. The census not only showed the errors made by the Ottoman calculations, and the defects in the system then employed, but also began a new era in which the population was obliged to declare every birth, marriage or death to the civil registrar.

Another bronze statue was unveiled. This was the monument symbolising victory, set up in the square of Ulus, the Nation. The Gazi, on horseback and standing on a lofty marble plinth from Marmara, looks out westwards over the city of Ankara and the far-reaching plain. Below the monument there are three figures; two are soldiers, one of them keeping vigilant guard, while the other calls his comrades to battle. Behind them is a Turkish peasant woman carrying a great artillery shell on her shoulders; this is the symbol of the heroic actions of Turkish women during the War of Independence. The monument is the work of an Austrian sculptor, Krippel.

Another bronze statue of the Gazi was unveiled in the same year in the open space in front of the Ethnographical Museum of Ankara; this is an equestrian statue of the hero, in military costume, covered by a long cloak. The statue stands on a porphyry base, and can be seen from many points in the city. It is signed by the Italian sculptor Canonica. The statues put up by the Republic broke with Moslem tradition, since that religion prohibited the reproduction of the human figure, whether in painting or sculpture. It must certainly have caused a strange sensation in those people whose mentality was for various reasons evolving slowly, to see a bronze figure of a woman with an unveiled face, in the main square of the capital.

CHAPTER 37

THE ALPHABET

A new measure of undeniable importance, which was intended to get rid of another of the obstacles which hindered the communication of the Turks with the civilised countries, was that concerned with numerals. Turkey was using the Arabic numerals which had been used in Arabia before being introduced into Europe in the tenth century. Europe adopted the system in place of the rather awkward Roman characters; however, the numbers suffered changes that made them unrecognisable at first sight, to such an extent that it was necessary to make a special study to be able to identify the Arabic numerals now in international use, with the old style ones, still used in Turkey. The new figures adopted by the Republic began to be used officially from June 1928.

During the whole of the autumn and winter of 1927, the Gazi concentrated his constructive powers on the preparation of the reform of writing, to which he gave a basic and essential place in the people's efforts to rebuild and progress intellectually; this was Kemal's passion as an administrator.

The Turks had adopted the Arabic alphabet at the same time as their conversion to Islam, about a thousand years before. Under Moslem influence they abandoned their old form of -writing, in which a number of inscriptions have been found in Northern Mongolia, on the banks of the river Selenga, tributary of lake Baikal, and which are known as the Orhon inscriptions. The Arabic alphabet is not convenient or adaptable to the sounds of the Turkish language, which is rich in vowels. Apart from this, there arose another great difficulty; to learn the Arabic script, which was excessively complicated and uncertain, one needed long years of study, which naturally favoured illiteracy, and made knowledge the privilege of the rich classes. Kemal's philosophy could in no way admit this, since he believed that education must be accessible to the whole people. He therefore accused the monarchical regime of having left its people illiterate and ignorant, during centuries of great universal progress.

The Arabic writing was strangling Turkey's desire for international cooperation in intellectual affairs, and hindered her cultural progress. The Gazi had taken upon himself the task of getting rid of the alphabet then in use, and replacing it by one which would not only be easy to teach, but which would also be very similar to the Latin alphabet, used internationally. He therefore got down to work; he called in linguists, historians, grammarians, and intellectuals generally, and after explaining his plans for reforming the alphabet in general lines, he asked their opinion and discussed with them the system which would be most advantageous to introduce. He gave careful study to the various adaptations of the Latin alphabet which were in use for different languages, and the phonetic values given to its signs; then he began to adapt them to Turkish, after a conscientious analysis of the grammar, phonetics and peculiarities of the Turkish language.

The studies presented by the specialists were discussed at special meetings, until the road of reform was gradually marked out. As the work proceeded, Kemal returned again to Istanbul and took up residence in Dolmabahçe Palace, which was transformed into a real academy. The sessions presided over by the reformer were dutifully attended by professors and linguists, Ministers and Members of Parliament.

As one can well imagine, there were some who were doubtful about the proposed reform. Would it not make it necessary to reprint all the books in the Turkish bibliography, dictionaries, and school and university texts? This task, which would certainly take years, together with the learning of the new alphabet which would not take less than that, would mean a serious hold up in the development of public education. People who had already finished school could not return there to learn to write all over again.

The final version of the alphabet was ready in August 1928. The greater part of the success achieved was due to the reformer himself, since it was he who found by tenacity and logic the letters which most exactly represented the sounds of the Turkish language. This Latin-based alphabet, which is called the Turkish Alphabet, as opposed to the Arabic, is not only the most modern known, but is essentially phonetic; there is no letter or sign which is unnecessary, nor are there double letters or any of the hindrances which other languages, such as French and English especially, have preserved through tradition, and which make it difficult to learn them and make confusion easy. The new Turkish alphabet is easy to learn; a foreigner who learns the phonetic value of its letters can read Turkish perfectly in a very few days.

On the night of the 9th of August, a great crowd had gathered in the park at Sarayburnu, formerly the playground of the Sultan, and where the first statue of the Gazi had been erected. The people had been invited to go there by the People's Party, to listen to a speech which the Gazi was going to make, and in which he was going to reveal another of his national secrets. At the announced time the speaker mounted the platform, and explained the necessity of freeing themselves from the Arabic alphabet, which they had never been able to understand properly, and which had for ages been a kind of prison for the Turkish spirit. He assured them that the new alphabet could be learnt in a short time, and even those who had never learnt to read would be able to do this. He issued a call for general mobilisation against illiteracy, which reached the figure of about 90 % of the population.

The mobilisation for the new alphabet had the desired success. The conscript teachers were set before their blackhoards; in towns and villages, in the countryside, and in all places one could see those already initiated into the Turkish alphabet surrounded by those who wanted to learn it. The Members of Parliament went back to their respective constituencies to direct the intensive teaching of reading and writing, but no one equalled the Gazi in his educational activity.

He appeared every day in different places, carrying a portable blackboard in his car, and there he carefully explained the value of the orthographic signs; then like a schoolmaster in class he brought forward one of his pupils, examined him, and made him write some word, such as his name, for example. He checked the level of advance reached in the improvised schools. People called him the "Teacher-in-Chief," and he was never seen as happy and satisfied as on that campaign.

He began a journey along the shore of the Black Sea and through Central Anatolia, in order to teach and activate the teaching of the new alphabet, which he believed was a decisive step towards progress. In Tekirdağ, he expressed his pleasure to the people for the enthusiasm in which they had set about learning the new characters, and the speed at which they had familiarised themselves with them.

"When I shut my eyes," he added, "and I see how lofty and brilliant will be the degree of strength and universal esteem which Turkey's intellectual development will reach thanks to the new alphabet, the sight fills me with ecstasy."

When he was proposing to the Assembly that the Law of the New Alphabet should be accepted, he said: "I am filled with emotion with this success, such emotion that no happiness brought by any victory can even be compared with it. I am filled with the moral satisfaction given by the simple duty of a teacher who will free our fellow citizens from ignorance. Dear comrades, thanks to this immortal measure we have taken, the Turkish nation will enter into a new world of light."

The campaign for education became more organised, and evening classes were opened for workers and people of both sexes who had passed school age. Improvised classes were found in a great many places, and attended by children and elderly people. The new writing was being taught in the mosques and even in the cafes, and it was as if the whole nation had gone back to school. The reforming President went on teaching the humble people with his blackboard.

On the basis of various precedents and opinions, it had been said that it would take about 20 years before this reform could be completely adopted. They talked about the capacity of the people to learn, the evolution which must take place, and other reasons, but none of this convinced the Gazi. There was no reason whatever, that something which an uneducated person could learn in four or six months should take 20 years to be learnt by a people which was after all composed of men. What was necessary was an intensive campaign for public education, so as to bring the benefits of teaching to the largest possible number of citizens.

To print anything in the old Arabic alphabet, the presses needed no less than 612 different characters, which made it very difficult to edit a work; this was the reason for the small advance made by printing in Turkey. The Turkish alphabet, based on the Latin, needed only 70, including the numbers, capitals and signs. It was thus possible to give a great encouragement to the book industry and all kinds of publications, which resulted in a noticeable rise in the country's culture.

The success Kemal achieved in his happiest campaign of all was that completed in the field of public education. If we look for a figure worth quoting especially, and which gives eloquent testimony to that first and most important attempt, we can point to 1 1/2 million illiterates who ceased to be so within a few years.

After the barrier of the Arabic alphabet had been overcome, a new barrier was encountered: this was the excessive number of Arabic and Persian words which had entered the language during the course of eight centuries under the literary influence of those languages; this had given birth to two Turkish languages; the palace language, full of Arabic and Persian words, which Was spoken by the upper classes, and the popular language, or the more pure Turkish, which was despised by the erudite. At the Gazi's instructions, the Republican Government decided to take measures to bring back its ancient beauty and originality to the mutilated national language. As a first measure, from September 1929, the teaching of Arabic and Persian was forbidden in the Lises, which were the last places in which these lessons had remained.

Chapter 38

SOCIAL PRINCIPLES

Kemal now had in his hands supreme authority and absolute power. It would have been easy for him to keep that power; ancient and modern history give us many examples of men who have emerged from the minor bourgeoisie, and who when finding themselves masters of power through any circumstance, have sought means to ensure that power for themselves, without caring what measures they use, even at the price of betraying their conscience and their original political beliefs. Kemal must be given a place among the small number of men who were strong, faithful to their principles and therefore sincere.

His figure moves through the years of the history of its time, always holding the same ideas, never compromising. His actions showed that he was conscious of the road he had chosen and that he would not depart from it. Kemal preached the democratisation of the state, and it was for that reason that he established the republican regime. The Turkish people had never known liberalism, so that they were not prepared, educated or sufficiently well-informed to take over the direction of their own destiny. Kemal knew that, but he decided to educate them and ensure that they gradually understood what democracy was, deriving it from their patriotism, and he made of it a national weapon, a means of progress and well-being.

Since it is the national will which is the master of the country's destiny, the people is sovereign. This was Kemal's "leitmotiv"; however, he was not so foolish as to put his principles into effect from the first moment, before educating the people and assuring himself that they were educated. The opposition parties showed that they had been inspired more by mediocre or low ambitions than by true love for the country and democracy; the rebellion in the East proved the powerful influence of the forces of the past over the ignorant masses. If they were given freedom of action, this would provoke an unending civil war, between those who hankered after the old state of affairs, and those who saw hope in the example of the great democratic nations of Europe and America. Kemal found it necessary to dissolve the parties or groups opposed to him and prevent the formation of new ones; he had to exile undesirable persons and hang those who systematically and violently opposed the march of Turkey towards her new destiny.

It was the Republican People's Party that was to be the school for democracy, and educate the people in political life. The emissaries of the party were given the task of carrying the necessary propaganda to every part of the country. In election campaigns, the candidates for Parliament made political tours, and the citizens were obliged to vote on election day. After Kemal had to provisionally withdraw his first concessions, after the Kurdish rebellion and the activities of the Progressive Party, no candidates were allowed except those of the People's Party; nevertheless the people took advantage of this instruction in voting.

Kemal set up a scene in which there appeared a democratically organised country, and the people were able to see how it worked. It was an ingenious system of transition, until the day when it would face reality. It is certain that it would have been far more comfortable and easy for Kemal, instead of spending a large part of his strength in preparing the people for the regime which he thought was better for them, to have got rid of such worries and governed as a dictator, without bothering about the people, who were sometimes ill-tempered, at others ungrateful, slow to learn and assimilate. But Kemal's greatness and his greatest glory rest precisely on his preoccupation for his people, his infinite patience with them, and his unselfishness in bringing powerful enemies upon himself in their defence. Before any of the laurels, mirages of triumphs and material victories which are within the reach of conquerors, he preferred the role of a schoolmaster, and his strength was channelled towards a primary objective, that of bringing spiritual welfare to his people. In 1930 he had the intention of putting into practice a plan which was now ready and which formed part of the training in liberal politics which the people were following: this was the creation of a second political organisation, an opposition party, on a democratic and secular basis.

Ali Fethi, Kemal's old friend and comrade, who had been Prime Minister in 1924, offered to form the new party; Ismet, who had succeeded him as Prime Minister, had attacked his government during the Kurdish rebellion, so that he had an interest in taking the fight to Ismet in return. So, in August 1930, he founded the party called the Free Republican Party. It differed from the People's Party in its ideas about the economy, public works, and railways; in short, it had a markedly liberal tendency, in contrast to its opponent, which was étatist.

Both Ali Fethi and Ismet began their political propaganda, for which the Gazi gave them complete liberty. The experiment had begun. The newspapers supporting one or the other side began to publish ever more energetic articles. Those supporting the Free Republicans criticised the acts of Ismet's government from its beginning, with complete circumspection; but gradually it was seen that Fethi's party was taking an unexpected direction.

What was happening? Simply that reaction was not under control, nor had the new state of things been truly accepted. The remnants of the Unionists, of the Progressive Party, and those who had promoted the explosion of fanaticism, all clung together behind the banner of the new party, and used the freedom allowed for these first elections to throw themselves into a campaign which was decidedly subversive in character.

Ismet's government was going through the years of the great world economic crisis, whose fatal effects were also felt in Turkey. Turkey was in the midst of reorganisation, but the time for reaping the fruits of this had not yet arrived. Ali Fethi soon lost control of his party; the so-called liberals thought that with the fall of the People's Party the Republic would also totter, and that it would not be very difficult to help it to fall. The founder of the new party realised that it was moving down a dangerous slope, and he dissolved it on the 17th of November of the year it had been founded. It was high time, since many people had come to believe that the creation of the Progressive Republican Party had been a symptom of the decay of the revolution, and that the revolutionary leaders were now divided into two camps. About three weeks after the dissolution of Fethi's party, there occurred in Menemen, a place in the province of Smyrna, some events of the greatest seriousness, which were able to show the temperature which had been reached at that time by the spirit of reaction. Sheikhs and dervishes had been preaching at length in that area, and they thought that the atmosphere was suitable for them to raise the banner of the holy revolution.

Dervish Mehmet entered the town of Menemen at the head of a group of men belonging to the Nakşibendi religious order. Many groups of people joined the procession led by the dervish, who gave a fiery speech in one of the squares, to a growing audience. Just at that moment there happened to pass that way a young officer called Kubilay; he was angered by the dervish's exravagant words, came near to the improvised platform and tried to silence him. The dervish's followers were infuriated, threw themselves on Kubilay and cut off his head, slowly and with a jagged knife, amidst the delirious enthusiasm of their comrades and the hoarse cries of the victim, while the great throng of spectators showed no reaction whatever.

The officer's bloody head was stuck on the pole of a green flag, one of those kept in the mosques, and carried triumphantly through the streets of Menemen. Neither the police nor the gendarmerie were able to put down the revolt, which spread rapidly to neighboring places, until sufficient measures were taken, and the agitators arrested. There were sensational moments during the trial of the guilty men, as the ramifications achieved by the revolt became known. Justice was applied with energy; those convicted of revolt and murder ended their days on the gallows.

The freedom which Kemal had allowed in order to permit his experiment to be carried out had to be suspended; his microscope showed him harmful reactions, which forced him to wait some more years before trying the test again. The Gazi was not as surprised as one might suppose; he was too much of a positivist to be overoptimistic, or believe that every remnant of the old regime had been extirpated in such a short time, and that the mentality of all the inhabitants of the country could be so quickly changed, when there was a difference in the degree to which young or old people could be moulded. Kemal had the courage to seek a clear vision, and to take the nation's pulse. From now on he would know at what pace he could go forward, and he would perfect the nation's political system.

The time was right to penetrate the people's state of mind, and to learn the true state of affairs exactly. He made a journey through the provinces of Central Anatolia and the Mediterranean coast. Guided by his custom and more impelled by curiosity, he talked to the different classes of the people. At times he assumed the appearance of a confessor. When he returned, he advised that the third Assembly should be dissolved, and that when the next Assembly was elected it should contain workers, peasants and independent candidates. One can see from this that the Gazi had not been made timid by the failure of his experiment, but had been able to learn from it, and show that his programme of regeneration and democracy would be applied ever more firmly.

Although Turkey is a country of farmers, the working classes had never been taken into consideration during the time of the Sultanate. The welfare of the peasants, and of the workers and small manufacturers and traders adds up to the national well-being. It was therefore right that the humbler classes should be represented in the Assembly, which ought to be a mirror of the national will. As for the election of independent members, this was a clear proof of the progressive democratisation, which the Gazi had determined to establish under his own protection and that of the party as teacher.

The Fourth Grand Assembly, in which the working classes were represented, opened on the 4th of May 1931. The peasants Halil and Muslihittin, the miners Hasan and Esat, Yaşar the mechanic, Hayrullah the shoemaker and others were able to make their voice heard at the same level of equality as the Members who were intellectuals or factory-owners. In the Kemalist philosophy there exists no difference between classes, nor privileges of any kind; both nature and reasoning continually deny the possibility of absolute equality, yet every person can occupy a place in the community, according to his intelligence and ability, a place which is always useful and necessary, and whoever fulfils his duty is in the eyes of his country equally respectable and worthy to enjoy the fullest rights.

Guided by the political experience of the preceding years, the Third Grand Congress of the Republican People's Party was able to make a final definition of its programme. This Congress met on the 10th of May and was opened by the Gazi.

The programme listed and developed the six advanced principles on which are based the activities of the party, and the reformist policy of its permanent President:

1— Republicanism. This is the first of the six principles, and describes the structure of the political regime which has been adopted, and which is the one which offers the greatest possibility of spiritual development and general progress, among the systems known up to the present time.

2— Nationalism. The Republican government works for the unity of all Turkish citizens, not subjects as in previous times, no matter what their religion may be, within the ideal of the Fatherland, and teaches them that religion is a matter of conscience and does not imply any separation between people of the same country. Kemalism wishes to conserve the characteristics of its people, their ideas and government, but it does not admit in any way the penetration of extraneous political ideas. The political activities of Turkey are limited to within her frontiers. She is not diverted from this principle by her feelings of brotherhood towards the other peoples of Turkish race. The name "Ottoman" which had been applied to the Empire, its government and even to the people itself, has been erased; it was not possible for the name of a family to supplant that of a people. The Republic, the government and the race are properly designated as Turkish.

3— Populism is another of the fundamental principles. This lays down that Turkish society is homogeneous, without castes or privileges.

4— Through "Etatism," the People's Party places the interests of the community on a higher level than those of the individual. The statement on the etatism of the party contains the following ideas: "We believe that individual work and activity are essential, but we hold it as one of our important principles that the state must; effectively participate in the affairs which concern the general and higher interests of the nation, especially in the economic field, in order to lead the nation to prosperity in the shortest possible time."

It was impracticable to hope that in a country which like Turkey had risen from ruins, and where the major sources of wealth and trade were in foreign hands, national reconstruction could be achieved by private initiative, which had lost its bearings; this was clear from the insuperable difficulties, scarcity of capital and lack of direction. The theory of étatism implies that the state should intervene not only in economic affairs, but also in the field of politics and intellectual activity, where relevant to the higher interests of the nation.

5— Secularism. The imposition of this cost the Kemalist movement continual sacrifices. Kemal believed that no religion had brought humanity truth or happiness, and that such things must be looked for in other places. The secularism of the state proves its tolerance in religious affairs, which it limits to the conscience of the individual. The State's judgment is not disturbed by any dogma.

6— Revolution. This principle recognised the great benefits and the great hopes which were opened to the people through the Kemalist revolution, which controls the conception of the Turkish nation's life by its dynamism. The six principles of the programme of the People's Party are symbolised by a red flag adorned with six white arrows, which is used as the party's emblem.

Chapter 39

CULTURE

When the southern branch of the Turks was converted to the faith of Mohammed, they gave up their own culture to adapt themselves to the new rules of that engrossing religion. They became part of Islam, and shared in the revival of Islamic civilisation. The Turkish contributions had a significant value in literature, philosophy and architecture.

The brilliant Islamic civilisation, given its impulse by the Califs both of Baghdad and of Cordoba, based its preservation and development on the different kinds of religious schools. The Seljuk Empire of Anatolia naturally had its Islamic culture. Its capital Konya and other towns became centres of lofty culture and spiritual fervour. There were taught in the Seljukid medreses of higher studies, which can be compared to Faculties, Medicine, Law, Mathematics, Geometry, Architecture and other Sciences, and they were at least at the same level as the schools of Bukhara, Baghdad, Cordoba, Cairo and other cities where the Koran was Law.

In the Ottoman Empire, the heir of the Seljuks, Letters, Sciences and Arts continued to be housed in the medreses, from which there graduated the artists and scientists who contributed brilliantly to the flowering of Turkey in the fifteenth and following centuries, and who supported Mehmet the Conqueror and Süleyman the Magnificent in his works of lawgiving and government. Istanbul was then the true centre of Islamic wisdom and science; students came to its medreses from China, India, Egypt and the whole Moslem world.

Because of the theocratic character of the Ottoman Empire, every branch of learning and teaching converged upon the religious schools; judges and teachers could not be recruited from any other place. With the decay of the Ottoman Empire, which can be seen beginning in the eighteenth century, the medreses ceased to evolve, and lost some of their adaptability. The medreses listened to nothing except the Koran and the Hadith, the oral tradition, and the logic of Aristotle and the old Islamic writers, rejecting everything which meant evolution. This system caused the schools' backwardness.

The passage of time, evolution and their necessary consequences ceased to be taken account of. Dogmatism, and an excessively conservative spirit in the theocratic institutions of learning was the main cause of the spiritual stagnation of the decadent period of the Empire, its Middle Ages. The tekkes, schools of mysticism, followed the same fortune as the medreses: the Turkish nation could no longer expect anything from either.

During the first centuries of the Empire's life, the government did not have an important influence in educational affairs, since these were in the hands of the clergy. The medreses and the teaching profession were maintained by the revenues produced by the "vakfs," pious donations. It was thus the retrograde spirit of the representatives of the "şeriat," the Religious Law, which took control, and this was reflected in the Empire's cultural life. The sciences reached their greatest depth of backwardness in the eighteenth century, and began to revive in the middle of the nineteenth, in the era of the reforms, known as the "Tanzimat."

At the arrival of the Tanzimat there existed the following educational institutions: first there were the medreses, whose important branches of higher education, such as Medicine and Natural Sciences, were in a state of complete neglect. Their students received the title of "softas," wore the classic "cüppe," a wide gown which was the mark of the clergy, and the turban. These were to be the teachers, priests or judges of the future. Their language of instruction was Arabic, in which it was obligatory to read the holy texts; Persian was also studied, whilst Turkish did not deserve the least attention, and was only spoken because it was the language of the country. The second teaching institution was that of the "Children's Schools," which were a kind of rudimentary primary school. Usually it was a place beside the mosque which provided space for these, the most wretched rooms for the most part, and lacking in the necessary hygiene. The pupils used to sit on the floor with their legs crossed in the oriental way, while the teacher, most often one of the less distinguished products of the medreses, was always ready, with ruler in hand, to impose knowledge on them through punishment. The position of teacher was not one of those most sought for, since the vakfs were practically bankrupt, and the revenue which they produced for primary school teachers was so little that the teachers lived off the gifts, both in money and food, which were made to them by the pupils' parents. Apart from religion and morals the teaching consisted of reading and the elements of writing and arithmetic. The system of education was based on memorisation; a pupil was the more highly thought of according to the larger number of Koran verses he could recite. There exists the expression in Turkish "to recite like a nightingale," which was the ideal of Ottoman teaching. It did not matter if the child lost the custom of thinking and received no practical teaching.

A short while before the time known as that of the Reforms, the repeated defeats suffered by the Ottomans obliged the Sultans to take measures to bring their army to a similar level with those of their enemies; this could not be done in any other way than by giving their officers the teaching required by the progress of military techniques of the time. The first school which escaped from clerical control, the Muhendishane, or School of Artillery, was founded in 1797 in the reign of Selim III. In 1827 a School of Medicine was created to fill a need which was abundantly felt; it was followed seven years later by the Military School, while the School of Political Sciences opened a few years after the Crimean War.

The reforms in public education also included the creation of primary schools maintained by the state. Religion occupied an important place in these, but other subjects such as Mathematics, Geography and Natural Sciences were also studied. There were likewise opened secondary schools, the first of their kind. The University of Istanbul was created in 1871, as a separate institution from the Şeyhülislamat, or Ministry of Religion.

The reforms of education produced reactions which were not of the bloody character of the military reforms, but still quite serious. Two kinds of schools, religious and state, produced two kinds of men, with different mentalities, perpetual antagonists. None of the reforming Sultans dared to suppress or reform the religious schools. Mahmut was brave enough to suppress the Corps of Janissaries through spectacular killings; however, he did not dare to face the clergy and the medreses. The turbanned disciples of these, with their rudimentary education, strove to be the true governors of the country, and in pursuit of this they used their powerful weapon, that of religion. They could not endure that the wearers of the fez, that symbol of impious modernism, men educated in schools where they were only taught to despise the sacred precepts, should gradually dislodge them from the best positions. The turbanned classes, dogmatic, ignorant and hostile to progress, systematically opposed any change. The biological theory of the evolution of species was considered to contradict the Bible, and had been forbidden in the higher educational institutions of the Empire, some teachers being stoned for defending it. At the end of the nineteenth century, science was being persecuted in Turkey as Galileo was persecuted by the inquisition in the seventeenth.

When Abdülhamit's bloody autocracy had been ended, and the Constitution restored by the Young Turk movement, Western ideas and teaching penetrated freely. A new drive was made in public education, and there were reforms in the Training Colleges and the University; however, these retouches were not enough to achieve the effective change required by the country.

When Kemal began his movement in Anatolia in 1919, he already had developed ideas about the way in which a people should be educated, if a country wants to be great. When the government of the first Assembly was formed in 1920, he created a Commissariat for Education, and as soon as the new government's prestige was confirmed with the battles of Inönü and Sakarya, he dedicated himself to improving public education, directing it towards nationalism and renewal, using the meagre resources of wartime.

When the war was over, the reformer stated on one occasion: "My dearest wish would be to be the Minister of Public Education, and to work for the development of national culture." Although the post he held was a different one, he was always a great educator, and deserved the name "Teacher-in- Chief." The crusade for education began in 1924, together with the suppression of the,Ministry of Religion, the medreses and religious schools, which was equivalent to unifying teaching within the powers of the Ministry of Public Education. The teachers of the schools which had been closed protested against this measure in a body, since it would not only prevent them from continuing to receive the revenues from the pious gifts, but also dealt a mortal blow to the clergy, since those who in future would aspire to enter that profession would have nowhere to receive religious education. A delegation of clergy had an interview with the Gazi, and tried to achieve the reopening of the medreses. The Gazi's reply was as follows: "You do not want schools, but the nation does. You must finally leave this poor nation and her sons to develop their culture. The medreses will not be opened again; the nation needs schools."

Public education in Turkey made extraordinary progress. In the first ten years of the Republican regime, the number of pupils rose from 358,000, of whom 64,000 were female, to 656,000 of whom 222,000 were female. The number of teachers rose from 12,000 to 19,000 in the same time. A great number of school buildings have been constructed, with the necessary accommodation and hygiene.

The government's education policy, laid down by the Gazi, continued to be the basis; the old Koranic recitation must be replaced by a complete secularism, the best methods of modern pedagogy, scientific principles and the advances of world science. Another principle is that of nationalism; it seeks to make that ideal firm among the youth, to give the Turkish language the place which belongs to it, cleanse it of the long-standing penetrations of Arabic and Persian, and seek renewing vigour in linguistic and racial origins, and in Turkish history. Democracy has been brought into education, without allowing the slightest concession to social position and sex, since all Turks must have the chance of being educated at the level which their intellectual capacity permits. In this way, the whole range of government positions are within the reach of the people; teaching is free, and obligatory at primary level.

The foreign schools, which in the time of the capitulations worked without any state control at all, had been giving an education which hardly conformed with the sovereignty of the country in which they were situated, and were centres of religious proselytism and Great Power politics. After the Assembly's decision in the year of 1924, they were forced to remove all signs and symbols of religion and begin to teach in a secular and national way, using also Turkish teachers.

Children are admitted to the Primary Schools when they are seven. Teaching there lasts for five years. The system of teaching is totally different from that used in the "Children's Schools" in Ottoman times; the teacher and students live in a family-like atmosphere; it is the interest and love which study awakes in the child which make him learn, not fear. On finishing the five years of Primary School, the children begin the first part of Secondary School, or of Professional Secondary School. The latter includes Commercial Schools, Art Schools and Trade Schools, Commercial Lises, Girls' Institutes and others. The Ismet Inönü Girls' Institute can be considered one of the most perfect of its kind. Its splendid building was completed in 1928. One Lise which distinguished itself by its exemplary work has been named "Gazi Lisesi." The Teacher Training Colleges now have appropriate premises, and a body of teachers graduated from Istanbul University or foreign universities.

Istanbul University, reformed in 1933, consists of the Faculties of Law, Medicine, Letters, Science, and lower level Institutes. Kemal established the basis of an independent University in Ankara, and the Faculties of Law, Languages and Medicine have begun work. Apart from these Faculties, one can follow in Ankara courses in Higher Schools of Engineering, Economics and Commerce, Maritime Commerce, and Political Science, the Fine Arts Academy, the Institutes of Agronomy, and the Atatürk Institute of Education, especially meant for Lise graduates, who qualify as Secondary School teachers.

The Gazi spoke to teachers on many occasions, and some of his words show clearly the hope which he placed upon them. In October 1925 he spoke to them as follows, in the Men's Teacher Training College in Smyrna: "It is the teachers, and only they, who save peoples, and turn collections of men into true nations." He also spoke to teachers in Konya at the same time: "Honourable Comrades, I am absolutely convinced that we shall be victorious on that road of renewal, perfection and civilisation which we are following, always so long as we can rely on an army formed by you. We shall continue onwards along the way we have come up to now. The stages through which our nation is forced to pass are considerable, and many are the goals which it is absolutely necessary that we should reach, but we shall reach the brightest goals of all."

Kemal's nationalist and populist theories demanded that the Turkish language should be truly Turkish, with the disappearance of the existing duality of languages, those of the palace and the people: he therefore ordered that all the Arabic and Persian words should be eliminated, since the Turkish language, which had been overwhelmed by such an invasion, had been reduced to merely verbs and suffixes in literary works. In July 1932 the Gazi founded the Association for the Study of the Turkish Language, which was charged with simplifying the language and making it a national one, so as to make it accessible to the masses, and allowing them to receive the benefits of culture.

A great quantity of works began to be translated to the new revolutionary language, and the people were able to understand them; among these should be mentioned the Koran, which was now understood properly by a great majority of Turks for the first time; the prayers, call to prayer and ritual phrases of Islam were translated into Turkish, and it was firmly prohibited ever to pronounce them in a different language again.

Along with the purification of the language, a prohibition was introduced against first names derived from Arabic or Persian, and Turkish names were to be chosen instead of these. It was also decreed that each family must adopt a surname. There had been very few surnames in Turkey, and they had been borne only by a few great families. People usually bore their father's name along with their own, or simply used two names. It was difficult to see the relationship which might exist between people from their names. There were thousands of individuals who had the same names, and to know, for example, which of the General Cemals was being talked about, an explanation was necessary, let alone the confusions which continually happened in every sphere of the national life in cases much more frequent than this example. Naturally the surnames which the families were to choose had to be of Turkish origin. This was invigilated by special commissions of the civil registry. In its session of the 24th November 1934, The Grand Assembly gave Kemal the surname of "Atatürk," which means the Ancestor or Father of the Turks. The word "Ata" is found very frequently in ancient and modem Turkish and always has this same meaning, as for example: "atalar sözleri" which literally means "the word of our grandfathers," or "proverb." In the ancient Turkish states, the Sultans, Grand Vezirs and Princes were given the name of "Atabey." Ismet took the surname of Inönü, in memory of his two victories, while the Chief of the General Staff called himself Fevzi Çakmak, and Ali Fethi adopted the name of Okyar.

One decision which had an obviously democratising tendency was the abolition of the long list of titles which existed, which separated the social classes, such as "Bey," an old honorific title which was later given to men of aristocratic and bourgeois families; "Efendi," first given to Princes but finally to the most humble of classes; "Hazret," meaning "Excellency," "Paşa," a title used by army generals and awarded to civilians by the government; many others could be mentioned, including that of Gazi. From now on, all the Turks would use in civil life the single designation of "Bay" for men and "Bayan" for women. Nevertheless, no title whatever was to be used in any kind of official document or writing; only the person's first and surnames would be mentioned. In the Army and Navy, words from international usage were adopted, such as Marshal, General, and Admiral, which in Turkish are Mareşal, General, Amiral.

Atatürk's greatest care, the educational movement, did not falter for a moment. Now that the country had schools and good teaching methods, now that the national language had been rescued, and the alphabet reformed, there remained the task of rectifying Turkish history, and beginning special studies to clarify and make known the true succession of events which formed the history of the Turkish people from ancient to modern times. At first, until a few years ago, Western historians had not troubled to establish the great history of the Turkish people, since its study had been hindered by legends, errors and groundless opinions; while during the Ottoman period, it was hindered by the servility of the historians in the pay of the Ottoman dynasty, who reversed the truth frequently, merely to satisfy their masters.

Historical studies and investigations began under Atatürk's initiative and aegis; this movement led to the foundation of the Society for the Study of Turkish History in 1929. In July 1932, the first Turkish Historical Congress met in Ankara. The specialists there explained their theories and conclusions, laying a most important basis for the better knowledge of the national history. Atatürk attended every meeting of the Congress, following it with visible interest. Many of the Historical Society's sessions were presided over by him, and the years he had spent perfecting himself bad made him so competent in Turkish history and language that he surprised both the Turkish teachers and the foreign Turcologists.

The societies called Turkish Hearths, "Türk Ocakları," deserve a place of honour in the history of Turkey's cultural awakening. The first group appeared at the beginning of the constitutional monarchy in 1912, expressing the desire of young people for education. There was no place for pan-Islamism or religious exclusivism in this national reawakening; the founders of the Turkish Hearths preached the racial union of all Turks. The Hearths multiplied greatly in a few

years, and their activities covered literature, the arts, education and social assistance. This beneficial institution was presided over for many years by Hamdullah
Süphi, a speaker and prose writer of an uncommonly pure style. The Hearths
were in sympathy with Atatürk's patriotic and nationalist movement from the
first moment, and took a definite part in it. They served as an instrument of the
educational campaign begun by the revolution. In 1931, they were merged with
the People's Party, and took the name of People's Houses, "Halkevleri."

Through the powerful influence exercised upon them by the Kemalist revolution, literature and the arts developed in Turkey. Writers became defenders of
the national cause, and brought the harmonious and purified Turkish language
into use; there was now nothing to prevent the free expression of artistic feeling.

As an institution which indicates the level which has been reached by general
education in this progressive country, we will mention the open door prison of
Imralı. The Ottoman prisons had earned an evil fame for their complete absence
of hygiene; their penal system was exactly the opposite of what is understood by
this today: now it attempts to reeducate the man who has fallen into misfortune,
prevent the appearance or development of antisocial tendencies in him, and make
him into a useful man. These principles had not been heard of in the Ottoman
dungeons; the belief was rather that the condemned man was there in order to
suffer. The inmates were quickly corrupted by evil habits and worse ideas, and
there came out of the prisons no man who had received any instruction or new
direction, but evildoers, infected with vice, enemies of society. Imralı is the first
Turkish penal colony in which the prisoners are not called that, but "colonists."
There they work on farming tasks, receive education and live decently. In this
way there is hope, that those whom justice has separated from society for their
evil actions, will again enter it as good men.

CHAPTER 40

ECONOMIC POLICY

Contemporaneously with its military power and its greatest territorial extension over three continents, the Ottoman Empire experienced a peak of economic prosperity. During the sixteenth and seventeenth centuries, to which we are referring, agriculture was developing in the best way known at that time, and industry was not neglected in comparison. The textile industry led the way, followed by tannery, ceramics and goldsmith work. It can be generally summed up by saying that the 60 million Ottoman subjects supplied themselves with the products manufactured in their own country, and always produced an excess which could be exported.

The political decay of that powerful Empire had deep repercussions on its economy, while there was a corresponding increase in the privileges called capitulations, which placed foreign capital and foreign subjects in an advantageous position compared to those of the Turks, and hindered the normal development of Turkish industry and trade, in favour of the interests of the Great Powers. This situation, with its pernicious results for the Empire, only worsened as the centuries went past.

The effect of the capitulations and the Ottoman decline was increased by the extraordinary development of industry and mercantilism in the Western countries, due to the riches they had found in their colonies and their exploitation of them. The Empire had been left away from the routes between Europe and her colonies, and her fleet remained bottled up in the Black Sea and the Mediterranean.

It was Western mechanisation, and the application of inventions to industrial machinery, which caused the economic ruin of the Ottoman Empire. Having been left behind in the march of civilisation, it could not make use of machinery, while on the other side foreign industrial products entered with complete freedom through the doors opened by the capitulations, and completely ruined the manufacturing industries of the country. In this way the Empire became a wonderful market, which was open without competition to foreign industry and capital.

The Turkish people gradually lost control over the trade of their own country, and were reduced to agricultural production, and that with only rudimentary techniques.

The mentality of the statesmen of the Sublime Porte was remarkably ingenuous. There is recorded a historical event which exemplifies this. A vezir was surprised by the insistence of the French Ambassador, who had just succeeded in obtaining extraordinary trade privileges, and could not resist asking him: "How is it possible that the King of France should be so worried about negotiations of such a mean sort?"

We are now at the time of the Crimean War, in which the Empire was seen in alliance with the Great Powers. This was a chance to take advantage of the new state of affairs in order to make a move towards an economic improvement, but nothing was done; the "Sick Man" made no reaction, since his government lacked the necessary capacity. The most practical step they could think of was to borrow money from the Powers. The first loan was made in 1854 by Palmer's Bank in London, for the sum of 75 million francs; other loans were soon signed, and in a few decades the external debt had reached the figure of 5,200,000,000 gold francs. The interest on this debt at one time reached about 50% of the general income. Yet the truly fatal result of this lack of reasoned administration was the dominant position which foreign capital was achieving in the country. It was natural that the Empire should offer guarantees to those who lent it money, and in this way it became a semicolony of the capitalist powers, giving away concession after concession.

With the coming of the railways, the heavy hand of foreign power penetrated yet deeper, since the concessions made for its construction brought with them interference of a political nature. The first concession was agreed in 1856, in favour of British capital, and was followed by other concessions in 1863, 1869 and subsequent dates. The case of the railway concessions plainly proves the corruption of the Sublime Porte. Baron Hirsch, who held the concession for the Thracian railways, and who cemented his influence by handing out gratuities, records in his memoirs that the Turkish Treasury allowed him to make 270 million francs from those same railways, a sum which went to swell the Ottoman deficit.

On the basis of a general settlement made in 1881, there was set up the so-called "Public Debt," charged with collecting interest on the Ottoman debt and paying off the capital. This institution took over the most secure sources of income.

The Young Turks' revolution, which established the constitutional monarchy, made great efforts to make the finances healthier, and authorised Parliament to "control" the budget; the costs of the Palace and the civil list of the members of the Royal Family, which had been consuming about 15 % of the general income, were reduced. In spite of all the good intentions of the Unionists, they were unable to balance the budget, since it was so weighed down by the interest on the Public Debt.

The Treaty of Lausanne recognised the cancellation of the capitulations and Turkey's complete independence in every respect. The Empire's debts were distributed among the countries into which the Empire had been divided. Atatürk, who was a man of the era of mathematics and machinery, watched the bankruptcy of Turkey with anguish.

On the abolition of the monarchy, Atatürk said in Smyrna in January 1923: "The new Turkish state will base itself not on bayonets but on the economy, upon which even bayonets depend. The new Turkish state will not be a conquering state but an economic state." In the same month of January he told the people in Alâşehir: "Comrades, in the future we shall achieve many important victories. They will not be obtained by arms, but will be economic, scientific and cultural victories. Let us not blow ourselves up with pride for our military triumphs, and let us prepare ourselves for the new conquests."

On the 17th of February, while the Turkish Peace was being debated at Lausanne, Atatürk called an economic conference at Smyrna, the first ever held in the country. Since they now felt sure of many points concerning the economy, which would appear in the Lausanne Treaty, including the suppression of the capitulations and of the customs "control", the Smyrna conference took decisions of great importance, such as that the national industry would be protected. It was also made clear that the policy of loans and concessions was finished.

After the victory, Atatürk expressed his great concern as follows: "He that conquers with the sword is finally condemned to give up his place to him that conquers with the plough. The arm that uses the sword becomes tired, but the arm that wields the plough becomes stronger every day, and affirms its ownership of the soil. The rule of total independence is this: national sovereignty must be consolidated by economic sovereignty."

If one takes into account the fact that the agricultural population of Turkey represents 67.7 % of the total population, and that in some areas this reaches even 81.2%, one understands that agriculture is the centre of gravity of the Turkish economy. However, the Empire had not given agriculture the full attention which that science needs. Since 1890, it had been importing wheat and flour, paradoxically, since the Empire held Anatolia, which has always had the capacity to be the granary of the Near East.

The men of the revolution, under Atatürk's guidance, dedicated those moments which were left to them by the vicissitudes of the war, to try to rebuild the national economy, beginning by the reorganisation and improvement of agriculture. The methods of cultivation were primitive, and the organisation backward, even patriarchal. The lack of railways and roads had serious effects, and the farmers had in some cases to give up even the essential part of their earnings to the "tithe" an arbitrary tax of 10 % on every product obtained by them, whether by tillage or livestock farming.

The tithe, which was officially termed a religious obligation, formed the larger part of the government's income, and its collection was entrusted to tax-farmers, who had obtained the position through bribes, which they then recovered, along with other special benefits, by harassing the defenceless peasants.

At a time when the struggle against the invader had not yet been won, Atatürk explained to the Grand National Assembly his ideas concerning the agricultural economy, and especially the need to protect the peasant and raise his educational and social level; the sincerity of his words deserve the highest of the praises which his admirers have given to his humanitarian works. "The true master of Turkey, her true sovereign, is the peasant," he said, "who is the true producer. It is he who deserves greater well-being and happiness than any other person. Let us finally understand, and maintain with respect and also shame, the treatment we owe to that noble true master of this land, whose blood we have made to flow through the four corners of the world for seven centuries, whose bones we have left in foreign countries, from whom we have seized the fruit of his labours for seven centuries only to squander it, and whose sacrifices we have rewarded with ingratitude, insolence and violence, until he has been humiliated and reduced to the rank of a slave."

In spite of the fact that out of a hundred million liras in the first republican budget, forty were shown as being produced by the tithe, and as one can easily imagine, the financial situation of the newborn state was far from brilliant, Atatürk took the decision to abolish the tithe, which was approved by law in February 1925. The taxes payable by producers were considerably reduced, so that their labours received a just reward, and the agricultural population enjoyed a state of well-being which was reflected in that of the nation.

This, however, was only one of many measures adopted by Atatürk. The small farmers were in a wretched state, as the wars had forced them to give up tilling their land, and they lacked enough working animals, and seeds and especially money were in short supply. The Kemalist government set aside from its weak resources many millions of Turkish liras to help the farmers. The latter were being forced to beg for loans from money-lending capitalists in the towns, and this ruined many of them because of the high interest rates demanded. They were losing their economic independence as they sold their goods, or had them sold for them and had to become wage earners.

The Kemalist government reorganised the Agricultural Bank, whose function it was to give credit to farmers; the Law of "Agricultural Credit Unions" was accepted. In 1925 there was adopted a system of Agricultural Credit Cooperatives. These benefit farmers who have no material guarantees to offer. In 1933 the number of cooperatives was 653, with 2,500 towns and villages taking part in them.

Machinery, new methods of cultivation, and defence against plant diseases and locusts were introduced into the traditional Turkish agriculture. The results have been extremely satisfactory. An idea of this can be gained from the following figures: whereas Turkey was an importer of wheat and flour in 1923, she exported 65,000 tons of that red gold in 1935.

Four Faculties were set up in Ankara, equipped with the last word in scientific systems and methods: these were the Faculties of Natural Sciences, Agronomy, Veterinary Science and Agriculture. Thirteen Agricultural Secondary Schools were set up in different parts of the country.

Atatürk was following the development of agriculture and livestock farming with true passion, and decided to make a personal fight against the problems which the nation had to struggle with in those areas. The hostile natural environment of the plateau was resistant to man, so it was there that the warrior who had been victorious in so many battles would wage war against nature. In the environs of Ankara he acquired two thousand hectares of land, mostly barren and covered with malaria infested marshes, caused by the overflowing of the streams which crossed them.

The only trees in the whole of the area were one pear tree and a few willows; nevertheless, Atatürk named it "Orman," the Forest. One evening in May 1925, three army tents were set up in the "Orman" to cover Atatürk and the agronomists and workmen who accompanied him. Work began immediately on the transformation of that desolate area into a model farm, a place for experimentation in methods of cultivation and animal husbandry, and where candidates for admission to the Agronomy Institute stay for a year working on practical tasks.

Atatürk's useful campaign has had a success beyond all that could have been imagined. The farm has been extended to 15,000 hectares, and now has over six million trees. The marshes have disappeared, and to counteract the disastrous effects of the lack of water at certain times, as happens in many parts of the plateau, Atatürk had a system of dams and centrifugal pumps constructed. In the middle of a period of drought, Atatürk had the satisfaction of sailing on the Marmara pond, which is shaped like that Turkish sea.

Thus Turkey had entered the machine age. Engines roar today over the fields which were once slowly turned at oxen's pace. We seem to hear the poetry of Nazım Hikmet, singing of mechanisation: "This must finally penetrate our minds: the peasant has the love of the land, and the love of the land is the machine."

The machine was to give Turkey powerful help in escaping from her status as a country dependent on the industrial powers. Behind the industrialisation of the new state was a hope for economic independence, which would complete the work of political independence. It was the definite intention of Kemalism to move from the Empire which had been a producer of raw materials, to a Republic based on agriculture and animal husbandry, and also on industry. The difference in technology which had existed between the former state and the industrial nations should be eliminated.

The task needed a great brain, and even more, a great will, both of which were found in Atatürk. From the first moment, the difficulties with which he met were of a kind which would have daunted a man less accustomed to facing problems considered insoluble.

The mechanisation of present day Turkey can be divided into two periods: the first of these covers the period from the year in which the Republic was proclaimed until ten years later. This phase can be described as one of "industrial liberalism": the second period, the "étatist," is still going on.

Although the government's industrial policy, which had been based on respect for private enterprise, had been relatively successful, it was clear after ten years that this was hardly sufficient to supply the internal market, even with state help. A unity of effort was needed, and the government therefore decided to take the industrialisation of the country into its own hands.

During the period of world crisis following the year 1929, Turkish exports, which were in raw materials, suffered a drop in value which affected the internal life of the country as a reflection of the general crisis. Under Atatürk's guidance, the Turkish Government tried to stave off the advance of the crisis by appropriate measures. It appeared that the best way was to make the country into an independent economic unit. To realise this, it was found necessary to create a well-organised industry which should be in the hands of the state. It would buy Turkish agricultural products, and in its turn would be a secure market for the nation's industry.

Etatism, one of the six principles of the People's Party, became government policy. It has a great similarity to Russian étatism, except that the Kemalist version leaves a margin for private enterprise. Etatism is the opposite of individualism; under the latter principle the individual has full freedom to engage in any activity; companies or private enterprises, or even individuals themselves, can establish banks or any other financial or industrial institution, provided always that they observe the law and pay their taxes. The étatist theory considers that the general interest is superior to that of the individual, which is sacrificed.

An étatist government which exploits the mines, forests, railways, public services, navigation and factories, which is the master of all the monopolies and owner of all the banks, is without doubt a strong government which can use its powerful means to build great factories and complete useful work, which private enterprise would find it difficult to achieve. Also, such a government can undertake important work even if it does not give monetary reward, since the state looks to the communal interest, while individuals seek personal interest above all. Of course individuals do not willingly give up their personal interests to become government employees, receiving a salary and occupying posts consonant with their abilities, whether as employees of the lowest rank or as directors of banks, as government executives or merely as working men.

Foreign capital could not reconcile itself to working in Turkey under the new conditions imposed by her after Lausanne; it was not that the Republic did not want the inflow of capital, nor that the conditions for investment were less acceptable than would have been found in other countries, but there was a too obvious difference between the returns which had been possible under the capitulations and those now offered. The U. S. S. R. has always been an eager collaborator with Atatürk's Turkey, and has provided a large part of the machinery needed for her étatist plans. As for capital derived from private local sources, this was practically nonexistent.

The land problem was solved by Atatürk by ensuring that the man who worked the land also possessed it. Kemalism approaches socialism in its étatist policy, but it has a basic originality through its adaptation to the conditions of the country, and its provision of an independent life for the people. The vital problems of the new Turkey, and the road she followed to get over the centuries of stagnation, showed Atatürk the way to a policy that would direct both the economy and life in social, political and intellectual terms; if he had handed over the task of achieving the urgent needs of the nation to the natural evolution of private initiative, he would have acted contrary to the accelerated rhythm of real life.

The government prepared a plan for industrialisation to be completed in five years, and which went into operation in 1934. It was not the intention to establish enterprises which did not suite the requirements of the nation, fictitious industries whose prosperity would be assured by customs protection, but to manufacture within the country those articles which it was importing, and whose raw materials it was producing. The requirements of the home market were taken into account, and the plan was governed by these figures.

Since before the large factories began to be constructed, hundreds of students had been sent to the great industrial countries, in order to specialise in the various branches of industrial technology, while a school for workers specialising in textiles was set up in Kayseri.

The success achieved by the five-year plan, and the start of production in a large number of ultramodern factories has been shown in Turkey's trade balance, and has decided the government to make a second plan, whose main objective will be the electrification of the country.

As we have seen in another part of this chapter, the financial legacy from the Empire could not have been more disastrous. The chronic deficit could not be wiped out by the establishment of the new form of government, since the country was ruined in material terms, devastated by wars and without assistance from foreign capital. Kemalism was guided by three principles in its firm determination to ensure a balanced budget: these were, to refrain from resorting to loans, ensuring an equilibrium in the balance of trade, and strengthening the sources of internal revenue. When these principles were put into practice, they resulted in a reorganisation of the system for collecting taxes; new taxes were introduced and the state monopolies were established. Two years later the first balanced budget was achieved.

At the birth of the Republic, the Turkish currency then in circulation had lost its value, and was backed by no gold reserve; in addition, the trade balance and the country's ability to pay were completely negative. The government real-ised that the only way of supporting its currency was to back it with their own political credit, until the currency achieved a recognised value, by the balancing of the trade account and the building up of a gold reserve to correspond with it. Nevertheless, despite their efforts, the Turkish currency suffered a frightening fall in value. Later on, at the beginning of the world crisis, the government gave the currency a fixed value, thus avoiding the fluctuations which it suffered through external influences.

The government saw that they must create a national bank on which to rest their financial policy. They therefore founded the Central Bank, which is the only bank authorised to issue currency, and which takes charge of the State's financial operations. Having all these reins of control in its hands, the new State was able to withstand the economic storm which afflicted the world. The customs war, trade barriers, quotas, bilateral treaties, and the "clearing" system were all used in external trade, while the situation in the interior was tolerable thanks to the beginning of industrial prosperity. After the storm, during which work continued tirelessly in the industrial field, Turkey emerged with a flourishing industry and no debts. The confidence inspired by the new Turkey, through the way in which she honoured her obligations and efficiently administered her economy, was shown amongst other ways by the agreement on the investment of British capital in the country, which took the form in May 1938 of an agreed credit from the United Kingdom to Turkey for the sum of £ 16,000,000, which was to be partly used for the realisation of the second five-year plan and the building of harbours.

Ancient Anatolia acted as a bridge between Southern Europe and India and China. The Ottoman Sultans took care to build and keep roads and bridges in good order. The Turks deserve to be remembered as great road builders. This is attested by caravanserais and bridges, real works of architectural art, in all the areas which they ruled. The imperial roads were maintained in good condition from the Danube to the Caucasus and Egypt.

The land routes of Anatolia lost all their importance when the Suez Canal opened in 1869. Even before this vital change, the rapid decline of the Empire had left the roads and bridges in neglect. When the Republic was proclaimed there were no more than 18,000 kilometres of roads, of which 40 % were in a terrible state. As for bridges, only a few of the famous ones, built in bygone days, remained standing.

During the Independence War, Atatürk had strategic roads repaired and built, and in 1922 he was again saying in his speeches: "Economic activity and vitality proceed in proportion to the state and development of means of transport, roads, railways and ports."

"Roads and Schools"; that sums up the statesman's general policy; he believed that the economy depended to a large extent on the first of these words, and entirely on the second. After he had pursued this campaign inflexibly for twelve years, the country possessed 30,000 kilometres of good road, and the necessary number of bridges.

It was to be in the building of railways that Kemalism would achieve the greatest fame in public works. The Republic had inherited from the Empire 3,700 kilometres of railways, which had been built by the method of giving concessions to foreign capital, and which belonged to and were exploited by companies of the same origin. Atatürk preached the need to build an enormous railway network; at the economic conference at Smyrna he said: "We are obliged to bring our country together by means of a network of steel and roads, on which trains and automobiles can move, for while the world's means of communication consists of railways and automobiles, it is impossible for us to compete with them by using natural paths and carts pulled by oxen and donkeys."

When the Chester Plan, which was to provide Turkey with the railway network she needed, failed in 1923 through the lack of interest on the part of western capital, Atatürk waited no longer, but ordered that the laying of the rails should begin, using the means at the disposition of the state, and in spite of the financial difficulties. The Prime Minister Ismet Inönü supported Atatürk's creative will with a rare efficiency and tenacity, so that the government of that soldier, who triumphed in the battles whose name he bears, and the diplomatic victor of Lausanne, has passed into history with the name of the "railway government." In 1937 there were 6,737 kilometres of railways, entirely owned by the state.

Ankara is joined by her steel arteries with the great European capitals, Cairo, and the U. S. S. R. Apart from the benefits to the national economy, Kemal's impelling idea was that of bringing education to the scattered regions of Anatolia.

Surrounded as she is by four seas, and possessing the obviously important Straits of the Bosporus and the Dardanelles, Turkey enjoys a particular and exceptional position from the commercial point of view, since it allows her to export her products easily by sea. As in the case of other vital affairs of the country, Atatürk gave his active attention to the development of the merchant marine, and the repair and building of ports.

Following its policy of nationalisation of public services, the Republic took over not only the railways but also running water, telephones and the company holding the concession for the provision of light and motive power, which had all been in foreign hands.

In 1938, Sir John Simon, the British Chancellor of the Exchequer, made the following summary: "The Turkish Government has in the last fifteen years made remarkable progress in the economic field, towards achieving its programme to reshape the economic profile of the country, and has given a clear impulse to industry, through the use of the considerable mineral wealth within its territory. There are few countries in the world who have managed as Turkey has, to keep a balance of payments in these difficult times."

CHAPTER 41

PUBLIC HEALTH

A biography of Atatürk must devote a separate chapter to what this man achieved in the promotion of Public Health, in a country where these words practically lacked meaning.

Ottoman Turkey was devastated by serious diseases, which spread to a fearful extent, without health measures being taken such as are expected by a civilisation which had produced Edward Jenner, Pasteur, Wendell Holmes and Ehrlich. In Turkey, the very existence of these learned men has passed almost unnoticed.

Endemic diseases, of which the first was malaria, reigned over great areas of the country. That fever of the swamps, perhaps the most ancient affliction of Anatolia, shook millions of sick within its grasp, decimated populations, and forced the survivors to flee to the high plateau. This sickness had been attacking Anatolia since ancient times with such severity, that some authors have claimed, and not without reason, that it played an important part in the decay of the civilisations of the Western Anatolian coast. The race was losing strength, while the Imperial Government made no gesture to hold back the advance of malaria. Parents who were themselves physically enfeebled produced children who were feebler still, whilst the sickness germinated unhindered in the swamps. This reached the point when half the population of Anatolia was affected by this dreadful fever.

Another serious disease, common in the provinces bordering on Syria and in the Eastern parts, was trachoma, an eye disease which in acute cases produces blindness in the affected person. Tens of thousands of people were in that melancholy situation, while there were more than two million less severely affected.

Syphilis flourished freely in a country which was ignorant of the most basic hygienic measures, and it claimed a very large number of victims. Following in the list of the great plagues came tuberculosis, ankylostomiasis and typhus. Hydrophobia had spread in Turkey in proportion to the number of dogs, which was large, since as is well-known, they infested the streets of Istanbul and many other cities. Not before time, an Antirabies Institute had been set up in the Imperial capital, but there was no hope of saving anyone who had been bitten in an area distant from Istanbul, since the absence of means of communication prevented them from getting there within the time required for treatment. It would be true to say that in the greater part of Anatolia until recently there was no way of treating hydrophobia except by means known before Pasteur's discovery.

Given the rudimentary state of public health, serious cholera epidemics and outbreaks of plague naturally appeared from time to time, while outbreaks of smallpox were more often seen, though this did not lead to any greater importance being given to vaccination.

Until the eighteenth century, medicine in the Ottoman Empire was at the same level as that in Europe. The famous Medical Faculty of Bursa had existed since the fourteenth century; this, and the schools of medicine which were later established in Istanbul, were centres where medical science possessed all the techniques that could be wished for. Unfortunately the lack of intellectual contact with the West, the Ottoman decline, and the falling of the level of scientific knowledge, turned the medical medreses, like the other medreses, into centres where religious fanaticism and ignorance predominated rather than true learning. The Doctors of Medicine at the beginning of the nineteenth century were merely quacks, who did not hesitate, in difficult cases, to delude their patients with charms and prayers. A rigorous study will allow that religious faith can be a remedy to a sick spirit, but in curing bodily complaints its results are doubtful.

The epidemics which fell upon the helpless people of Turkey at varying intervals, and which in their turn infected the ports of other countries when transmitted by ships, brought the Powers to take a hand in Ottoman Public Health. An international health organisation was set up in Istanbul, to watch over the health of Turkish ports.

Another lamentable side of the backwardness of medical knowledge under the Empire, and the Empire's indifference, was the state of the mental hospitals. Their inmates were treated not as sick men but as men possessed by devils, and the only treatment they received was to be shut up in hospitals like prisoners.

Some progress was made under the Constitutional Monarchy. Amongst other measures contemplated were those of beginning campaigns against malaria and syphilis, at the level which was required; but when this was put into practice, it consisted only of an effort based on primitive methods, and of small extent.

At the transition from the Empire to the Republic, there were in Ottoman territory, counting all the Turkish and foreign hospitals and dispensaries, except the military ones, a total of 7,300 beds. It is enough to reflect that the population at that time was over 13 million. Nothing can be said of the establishments devoted to gynecology and children, since none existed.

In the year 1920, there was created in the first Council of Commissars of the Government of the Grand Assembly, and for the first time in the history of the country, a Commissariat for Public Health and Social Care. This was the first sign of the importance which the Great Inspirer was giving to the health of the race and to social aid. His policy in this respect can be summarised from a part of the speech he made to the Assembly in 1922: "We must protect and ensure the health of our people, lessen the death rate, raise the birth rate, struggle against the effects of contagious diseases and epidemics, and thus allow the members of our nation to become healthy and vigorous individuals, suited for the work."

The Commissariat of Public Health coordinated the efforts, and as soon as the Republic had been proclaimed and when suffcient funds had been found, an enormous campaign was begun in every direction concerning Public Health and Social Assistance, in anticipation of the drawing up of a plan. First, the health control at ports and frontiers passed into state control. It was a question of national honour that the new Turkey was able to fulfil that task in a fully regular and successful way, and this was achieved. From then on cholera, which was lurking on Turkey's frontiers, could not penetrate them in the usual way, and there has been no case of plague in a Turkish port during the last eight years.

The struggle began against the great pestilences; the antimalaria campaign started in 1925. The means adopted consisted of the examination of the sick, their treatment, distribution of medicines, education on treating the disease, and the drying out and drainage of the swamps. Some figures will give a better idea of the importance of the antimalaria campaign: between the years of 1925 and 1932, 7,800,000 people were examined and treated, while 143,000,000 square metres of swampy land were drained. To be efficient, the struggle against malaria must assume gigantic proportions, and must be directed by specialists. For this purpose the Kemalist government set up an Antimalaria Institute in Seyhan, in which the doctors who are assigned to the great campaign spend a period of specialisation.

The continual progress of syphilis was halted by the first attack made on it on a large scale; in the six areas where the disease had the greatest hold, a coordinated attack was made upon it by opening special hospitals and dispensaries; treatment was made compulsory and free throughout the country. Prostitution was controlled, and a medical examination before marriage was made compulsory.

Extraordinary measures were taken against trachoma, which was so widespread in Southern Turkey. Mobile health organisations cooperated with the hospitals and dispensaries which were set up. Over 17,000 patients were operated on in the first years of the health operation, while nearly every sufferer, whether afflicted in a greater or less degree, has received medical attention. An intensive prophylactic .campaign has been carried out in the areas affected by trachoma. Since this eye disease is very contagious, the government tries as far as possible to collect the sufferers together, and isolate them. Thus for example, there are schools where both the students, the teachers and the other staff suffer from trachoma. At present, 12 towns and 426 villages are under strict observation by the health organisations.

Tuberculosis was the last of these diseases to come under attack; however, the Ministry of Public Health and Social Protection has brought into action dispensaries which have the use of the latest equipment for treating tuberculosis. The hospital on Heybeliada, in the favourable climate of the Princes' Islands, is a model of its kind.

When an epidemic of smallpox broke out in Syria in the year 1929, 1,200,000 inhabitants of the frontier area were immunised against that disease; thanks to this, and the creation of a health zone, Turkey was saved from the infection. Vaccination has been compulsory in schools since 1928. In order to establish the mechanism of Public Health, it was necessary to assemble a large number of doctors, and create places which were well supplied with the necessary materials. There was an unimaginable lack of qualified staff; thus, since the state had urgent necessity of large numbers of doctors, the first essential part of the programme was being hamstrung. A law was made compelling every doctor to work for two years paid by the state, but this was far from producing even a moderate sufficiency. It was with the aim of training new doctors that a hostel was established in Istanbul for medical students, in which everything was completely free of charge for them, but which obliged them on graduation to work for the state, for a period equal to three quarters of the time for which they had enjoyed the state's hospitality.

The Central Institute of Hygiene in Ankara is the most important of the establishments created by Atatürk. It began work in its modern buildings in 1931; it is an organisation perfected for conducting experiments, where studies are made to find the most efficient ways of fighting the diseases established in the country, and where vaccine and serum are prepared.

Among the many hospitals built through the tenacity of Atatürk's goverment, following its policy of saving the people from pain, the Ankara Model Hospital, which is equipped with all the advances of science, is considered to be the most modern and best equipped in the Near East and Balkans.

Maternity and the protection of children could not be allowed to go without special attention. In addition to achieving a notable reduction in infant mortality, which had been high because of the people's ignorance and lack of proper care, the government has provided care for those children whose parents cannot look after them, or have been abandoned or orphaned. The "Turkish Association for the Protection of Children" has developed an exemplary work. It was founded in 1921, and took charge of collecting the orphans of soldiers who had fallen on the field of battle; it was continually encouraged by the help of Atatürk and public sympathy. It now has 490 branches in various parts of the country.

The Imperial Government considered both Public Health and Social Assistance to be outside its province. The kindness of the Turkish people had been shown by innumerable donations for welfare purposes, establishing the "vakfs," from which many hospitals were supported. The ruin which overtook the "vakfs" was reflected in the disorganisation, impoverishment and closure of these establishments for the public good.

An important series of laws on Public Health was proclaimed; the Law of Chemists and Laboratories was passed in 1927; in the following year a law was enacted on the Medical Profession and its Auxiliaries, and in 1930 there was passed the important Law of Public Health, which deserves to be counted among the great and assured steps taken by Kemalism for the progress of the Turkish people.

The new Turkey has cooperated, within her capacities, for the welfare of all mankind; an example of this has been the cultivation and export of opium. Anatolia is one of the regions which has produced this drug since the most remote times. Turkish policy concerning opium has followed the Geneva Conventions of 1931; a strict vigilance has been established over the production and export of this product, and although the restrictions which have been imposed have affected the producers and the export trade, humanitarian feelings in favour of international cooperation have prevailed.

CHAPTER 42

FOREIGN POLICY

In the history of the Ottoman Empire, the era of the conquests, reddened by the fire of the Islamic faith and the blood of conquered and conquerors alike, was followed by the period of conservation of the great conquered regions, once the overwhelming driving force had been broken. The terror which the banners of the Prophet and of the Empire inspired in Christian Europe, and especially in the countries which saw their own interests threatened, moved Europe in the century of the Renaissance and the following one, to unite in a common determination to hold back that formidable invader. From the eighteenth century onwards, they succeeded in making her withdraw step by step, but without respite. The same was to happen again later in her African and Asian dominions.

It was therefore an Imperialist policy which predominated in the centuries of Ottoman Power. This can be compared to the policy of all empires, which though motivated by different ideologies, are ultimately moved by the same primitive passion for conquest.

During the period of the Ottoman decline, the growing interference by the Powers in the life of the Empire, the Empire's weakness, and the checks inflicted upon her from time to time by the Western European Powers and others from the East, forced it to follow a policy of self-abasement, to concede capitulations, and to endure the intervention of the Powers; it tried to avoid warfare, at the heavy price of sacrificing honour. Yet this could not prevent her being cut further and further back, until she was reduced to a semicolony. The doctrines of pan-Islamism, pan-Turanism, and Ottomanism were attempts to hold back the final ruin, but they all ended in failure. At last, when Turkey was defeated along with the Central Powers, the Treaty of Sèvres put an end to the Eastern Question and laid down Turkey's liquidation.

It was then that there happened the revolution of the Turkish people, which having been the instrument of Ottoman Imperialism during the course of centuries, was not prepared to be oppressed in its turn. Atatürk, who was the soul of the movement, and a man of entirely modern ideas, phrased the problem in this way: the sad state of the Turkish nation and its doubtful future were due to the Imperialist policy of the Sultans who were called glorious, who thirsted to conquer and accumulate peoples who could never be assimilated to the Turkish nucleus. To a lesser extent, the political mistakes of the Sublime Porte marked the stages of the irresistable decline.

Yet up to a point, Ottoman Imperialism had not been worse than that of other nations; more than on other factors, one can lay the responsibility on the mentality of past ages. Had not Persia, Greece and Rome wished to subdue the known world? Did not France, the United Kingdom, Germany and Italy, base their foreign policies on colonial expansion? And were they not continuing to do so, even after the great conflagration?

It could be seen in the new conditions of life in the postwar period that those nations which were homogeneous, and which had a tradition and culture of their own, would live in freedom; to think of subjecting the Turkish people to semislavery would therefore be to repeat the past, and what had been done by the Empire itself. The Treaty of Sèvres, in other words the will of the Western Powers, was an anachronism and signified a return to violent methods, and to the sowing of hate. Had the four years of tragedy taught nothing?

It was grief which gave Turkey her lesson, which Atatürk used as a basis for his policy. The Turkish people gave up all ideas of domination over the countries which had been subject to the Empire; it recognised freely the right of the various nationalities to exist and govern themselves within their natural frontiers. This was no more than what the Turkish nation asked for itself: the chance to work and progress, in peace with her neighbors and all the peoples of the world.

The war began again. Now the Turks were fighting for something new, the freedom of peoples, and in fact for their own people; but also to give an example to all the others, who in those peaceful years were watching the epic of a people who preferred to die rather than compromise over their liberty. Such an example would give food for thought both to the oppressed and to their oppressors. It was guns that spoke, seeing that the Powers were not bringing themselves to recognise that truth which was ever more affirmed by civilisation, that peoples should live in freedom-at least those peoples that prove that they deserve it.

An age-old and sworn enemy of the Ottoman Empire, Imperial Russia, who was suffering from her own Imperialism, was transformed into Soviet Russia, the new Turkey's first friend. There was nothing to come between the two countries, now that the Soviet leaders had formally declared that they renounced the Tsars' dreams of seizing the Straits. Atatürk was successful because he knew history, and because he exactly knew the capacity of the Powers who were fighting over the remains of the Ottoman colossus; he knew their weaknesses, and he was able to calculate the true practical importance they would have, when Great Britain's threats and France's warlike menaces were brought down to reality. Atatürk made a study of Lloyd George and his position amid the political forces in the United Kingdom. He reached a correct conclusion. Lloyd George did not take the same trouble over his adversary, and the results are well-known.

When the struggle in Anatolia was over, Atatürk began his policy of "Peace in the Country and Peace in the World." The glory of arms is ephemeral, the delirium of conquest fatal; let there be no more wars, no more conquests, and let hatred die out. But how could this be achieved? By eliminating the motives for hatred.

First of all, the situation relating to Turkey's immediate neighbors must be definitively solved. Turkey was able to achieve friendship with Greece, her other great and traditional enemy, thanks to the exchange of populations, and in October 1930 there was signed in Ankara the Turco- Greek Treaty of Friendship and Neutrality, upon which there appeared together the signature of General Ismet, conqueror of the Greeks at Inönü, and that of Venizelos, who was received in Turkey with demonstrations of real friendship. Greece and Turkey would go far along the path of cooperation and peace.

Repeated efforts were needed to solve frontier disputes with Iran, an old enemy for religious reasons, since in that country the Shiite sect of Islam is predominant, in contrast to the Sunnism practiced in Turkey; the Kurds in the areas beside the frontier were continually in a state of disturbance. In 1928, a Treaty of Friendship between Iran and Turkey was signed in Tehran, similar to one previously signed with Afghanistan.

The frontier between Turkey and Syria was ratified through the Treaty of Lausanne, so that there were apparently no reasons for friction between the Ankara and Paris governments.

Another neighbor is the Kingdom of Bulgaria, which had been allied to the Central Powers in the Great War. Discontent with her territory as laid down by the two wars she has lost, the Second Balkan War and the World War, her aspirations to have an outlet to the Aegean Sea, and her irredentism have caused Bulgaria to maintain an isolated attitude in the Balkans. Turkey has done everything possible to bring her into free cooperation, but without success.

The best possible relations have been established with Italy, Turkey's neighbor in the Mediterranean. We must not forget that this country possesses the Dodecanese Islands in the Aegean, and that the chief of the twelve islands, Rhodes, is but a step from Anatolia.

Atatürk could not be satisfied merely by peace with all his neighbors since it was his hope to maintain cordial political and economic relations with all countries of the world, and to take part in any effort which tended to consolidate world peace. The Great Powers concluded treaties of friendship and commercial agreements with Turkey. Turkey joined the multilateral Kellogg Pact of 1928, took part in various political works of the League of Nations, and was invited to join the League on 18th July, 1932.

That ceremony, and the brilliant work of Turkish diplomacy in international affairs, have shown that although Turkey has the larger part of her territory in Asia, she has come so close to Europe spiritually that she can be considered as a European Power. In the days when the Grand Vezir Kara Mustafa was besieging Vienna, the dominions of the Padişah went deep into Europe, without the Empire ceasing thereby to be essentially Asiatic. The Empire's tragic withdrawal was halted just 238 years later by Atatürk on the banks of the Sakarya; that battle marks the beginning of the new Turkish advance towards Europe, a march this time motivated by education and the best humanitarian feelings.

Turkey's geographical position, with one foot in Asia and the other in Europe, straddling the Straits which join the countries of the Black Sea with the Mediterranean world, makes her political situation extremely delicate. An excessive number of interests coincide at that most important crossroads, and compel Turkish diplomacy to remain in continual vigilance. No one knows better than the Turks themselves what dangers arise from the privileged location of their country. It was thanks to that, that the Ottoman Empire achieved the rapid development of its power, but for the same reason it died, and that city which Napoleon said was worth the world to her possessor is a jewel difficult to keep.

Turkey's problem is not that of keeping to her own policy of peace, but of trying to counteract the schemes of those who may have designs on her territory. Since she has a long coastline on the Mare Internum, Turkey is also involved in the question of supremacy in the Mediterranean, another of man's great problems, which has been the cause of bloody struggles in the course of history. In the beginning, Atatürk's government thought that the horizon was completely free of clouds which might presage conflict, since the Great Western Powers had changed their tactics after their rough lesson in Anatolia. After all, the United Kingdom and France, who were already masters of immense colonial Empires, could only have been carried away by a reckless caprice in desiring to acquire more territories. They therefore began a policy of rapprochement with Turkey.

However a first cloud did appear, the expansionist policy of Fascist Italy. Signor Benito Mussolini has been in power since 1922. With his powerful brain and remarkable organising ability, he has brought Italy a rapid rate of progress. The country was poor in raw materials and densely populated, a factor which was made more evident by the restriction of emigration and an extraordinary rise in the birthrate as a result of Fascist propaganda. The Italians began to feel uncomfortable within their frontiers.

Fascism had made Italy into a military power, allowing the Duce to put his expansionist policy into practice. In this, reasons of prestige for the dictator were certainly important, as was the failure to fulfil, according to Italy, the promises of territory made to her to persuade her to enter the war against her former allies; the first demonstration of this was the occupation of Fiume.

Albania fell before Italian pressure, to be used by her in her Balkan politics. She also spread her influence in the countries which wanted revisions of the Peace Treaties, Austria, Hungary and Bulgaria, which were discontented with the situation in which they had remained after the war. Mussolini was dreaming of capturing a colonial Empire for his country. It was rather late in the day; the third decade of the twentieth century seemed ill-fitted to conquests, since all the available territory was already occupied, with the exception of Abyssinia which, though divided between zones of influences since 1906 and a member of the League of Nations since 1932, offered opportunities for conquest.

Before opting for far-off Abyssinia, Signor Mussolini looked around him, investigating the Mare Internum of the ancient Romans; he was seduced by the rich Anatolian coast. Those lands of Caria and Lycia, whose coasts could be easily seen from the Italian islands of the Dodecanese, attracted him, as did Pamphylia and Cilicia; Caria, Lycia and Pamphylia had been partly occupied by Italy after the war, and had been recognised as zones of exclusively Italian influence by the Treaty of Sèvres. Some spying incidents showed signs that there was an investigation going on for a political and military plan against Anatolia. Turkey was immediately on her guard, and diplomatic relations became tense. The Duce said in a speech: "Our future is in the East, the South, in Asia and in Africa." On the following day the Turkish Ambassador asked, in the name of his government, for clarification of what was meant by the words "East" and "Asia." In an evasive answer, he was given to understand that these words did not refer to Turkey. Italy understood that Anatolia, defended by a war-hardened army backed by that of the Soviet Union, was not for her, and took another path.

Normal relations have continued between the two countries. Nevertheless, Atatürk realised that there was an urgent need to emphasise friendship with his neighbors, and achieve practical agreements between those countries which were afraid of the newborn Italian expansionism and German resurgence.

The 27th World Peace Conference suggested to the Balkan countries the idea that they should meet in annual conferences, from which was born the plan for a Balkan Pact; this was signed in Athens in February 1934 by the Chancellors of Greece, Romania, Yugoslavia and Turkey. The Balkan Pact, whose principle aim is that of maintaining the established territorial order, joined Turkey and Greece to the Little Entente. Bulgaria and Albania remained outside the pact, Albania because her movements were limited by her formal treaty relations with Italy, while Bulgaria, who hoped for a revision of the Peace Treaties, refused to sign a document which was equivalent to renouncing her claims.

In 1933, it can be said that the U. S. S. R. finally gave up her offensive attitude, in order to take part in international politics, and adapt herself to their new conditions. Now that Turkey was bound to Soviet Russia by cordial ties, as also to Greece, Romania and the countries of the Balkan Entente, who were themselves united by the Little Entente, Atatürk saw in this state of affairs a secure order in Southeast Europe. Ankara helped to a large extent in solving the problem between Romania and Russia; Romania was afraid that her neighbor would try to dispossess her of Bessarabia, which she had annexed after the 1914 war. When Moscow gave a formal promise to renounce it, they were able to conclude a nonaggression pact. The Balkan Pact, and the entry of the U. S. S. R. into international cooperation were directly motivated by the resurgence of the power of Germany and her expansionist policy, and also by Italian Imperialism.

Although Germany had found herself forced to sue for peace for military reasons in 1918, the nationalist spirit of Germany had not been defeated, which was soon shown by her ambitions to bring back the Reich to its former state as a completely free nation. Pan-Germanism, meaning the union of all those in Europe who were of German race into one Great Germany, was the nationalist movement par excellence. It was an ideal extremely difficult to achieve, since nearly all the countries neighboring Germany have German minorities. If the "Grossdeutschefrage" were solved, it would place Great Germany in a commanding position in European politics.

After the Communist crisis in the last year of the war and the following year, there appeared in 1919, a party which was implicitly dedicated to the resurrection of pan-Germanism. It was founded and led by Herr Adolf Hitler, who gave it the name of the National Socialist Party, abbreviated from its German form into Nazi. After achieving absolute power in 1933, Hitler took effective and energetic measures to fulfil his people's pan-Germanic ambitions. During the fourteen years of the republic, under the governments of Stresemann, Brüning, von Papen and von Schleicher, Germany had managed to gain revision of the Treaty of Versailles in several respects.

The ineffectiveness of the League of Nations at Geneva, and the obvious weakness of the Great Powers, was bound to encourage those rulers who had no constraint or opposition to hold them back in their designs. Whilst Mussolini was conquering in Africa, Hitler sent his troops to occupy the Rhineland in March 1936. This was something which France did not wish to admit; however she had no alternative except to go to war again without knowing which allies she could count on, and the military strength of the German people, soldiers at heart, with the support of 65,000,000 people obeying a single man, forced her to think again.

Hitler rejuvenated the German policy of the "Drang nach Osten," the Drive to the East, which had brought such good results in the hands of Wilhelm II, since it gained the alliance of the Ottoman Empire and Bulgaria; had it been victorious in the world conflict, the oil resources of the Caucasus and Mosul would have been left under German control, as would Turkey herself.

Germany was the best market for raw materials, and the best customer both of Turkey and of nearly all the countries of Eastern Europe and the Balkans. The economic traffic between the Reich and the Balkan countries was without doubt a means through which political penetration also entered. Germany's commercial dominance in Central and Southeast Europe gave her hopes of success in that direction.

The Italian victory in Abyssinia brought to the fore the problem of the control of the Mediterranean, which was disputed by two powers, the United Kingdom and Italy. For the first of these, that sea had the value of a road of enormous importance between the Metropolis and her Asian Empire, to maintain which she required rapid communications. For these reasons, her policy was centred on keeping military dominance along that road, the carotid artery of her organism. The Arab revolt, which Great Britain had stirred up during the years of the World War, brought her very favourable results, since she succeeded in gaining influence over the whole eastern shore of the Red Sea and the Mandate over Palestine, where the port of Haifa was made into a naval base, and together with those of Cyprus and Alexandria formed a powerful triangle in the Eastern Mediterranean.

Italy, which is a power of a truly Mediterranean nature, has a geographical situation of great strategic value, since she cuts the Mediterranean Sea into two parts, leaving only a strait 140 kilometres wide between Sicily and Cape Bon. In the middle of this strait is the Italian island of Pantelleria, which is being armed in such a way as to be a possible obstacle to the passage of any fleet. The strategic road from Tripoli to Tobruk near the Egyptian frontier pointed the way that an army would follow marching towards the Suez Canal. In addition, the bases in the Dodecanese Islands and her strong Air Force with its bases in Marsala, Augusta, Libya and other places, placed Italy in a position where she could aspire to rule the Mediterranean.

The duel for the control of that sea tended to increase after the conquest of Abyssinia, as it appeared that this was but a preliminary to the main struggle. Turkey, as a Mediterranean power, was worried at hearing the sound of arms so near her coast, and took up a defensive attitude, being well aware of the dangers which any international conflict would bring her. As laid down in the Treaty of Lausanne, the Straits remained demilitarised. The Turkish Government put forth its reasons for wishing these treaty clauses to be revised; she declared to the nations which had signed the Treaty her feelings of apprehension over the state of insecurity which existed in the Mediterranean, and asked that she should be permitted to put herself in a state of being able to defend herself alone.

The signatories agreed, and on the 22nd of June 1936, they met in a conference at Montreux, a town on the shores of Lake Geneva. The Government of Italy excused itself from attending; she did not consider that the situation at the time was the right one to examine questions of that nature, and therefore expressed her serious reserves over the Montreux discussions.

The Montreux discussions brought out clearly the rapprochement of France and Britain with Atatürk's Republic, and also with Soviet Russia. Turkey would gain the advantage of making the Straits once more impregnable, while the United Kingdom could find the renewal of friendship with her old rival Turkey an assistance to her in her struggle in the Mediterranean, since Turkey would exercise a very special influence in the solution of the dispute. On the 20th July the treaty was signed authorising Turkey to rearm the Straits.

This Turkish effort had been opportune, since before the Montreux decisions were signed, the Spanish Civil War broke out, and became a war intimately connected with the Mediterranean problem. In the light of the terrible conflagration of the Iberian peninsula, countries looked at their own consciences and grouped themselves into two distinct and opposing camps. The Spanish war was a decisive factor in bringing the German and Italian dictators together. It was to German interest to reach an understanding with the newly-born Spanish revolutionary movement, and help it to win, since in this way she would create for herself a zone of economic and political influence, returning payment in the same coin to France, who had been creating enemy states behind Germany's back.

The dispute over the fate of the Sanjak of Alexandretta passed through stages in which relations between France and Turkey became rather cool. The difficult negotiations finally bore fruit in the reaffirmation of the old friendship between the two countries, which were inheritors of the feelings of Süleyman and Francois I.

The origin of the dispute was as follows: although Syria had been an Ottoman province since 1516, when it was conquered by Selim I, only a few Turks settled there; the reverse occurred in the Sanjak of Alexandretta and Antakya, since one can say that these areas are geologically part of Anatolia. We are speaking of the Ottoman Turks, since the crusaders had already met Turks in that region. The Turkish name of Hatay, which has been given to the districts of Alexandretta and Antakya, is derived from the name of the first Turks who ruled that area. There is therefore no appreciable difference between the Sanjak and Anatolia, either in their general geography or the composition of their population.

Neither the Sanjak nor the other Turkish regions were happy under the foreign occupation which was imposed at the end of the World War; there were frequent armed clashes, and when Atatürk organised the nationalist forces and began the struggle for independence in 1919, remarkable patriotic fervour ran through the whole of Anatolia and the Sanjak. The events of the struggle between Turkey and France on the southern front have been dealt with in another part of this book in their chronological order. The French continually gave arms to the Armenians, enemies of the Turks, as a more efficient way of keeping down the nationalist risings.

When France found that it was difficult and dangerous to continue this struggle against enemies who were so much to be feared, and who were better organised and stronger every day, she decided to enter negotiations with the Atatürk Government, and in October 1921 there was signed the Ankara Agreement, in which the sovereign signatories declared an end to the state of war, and defined the frontier between Turkey and Syria. Unfortunately, the Ankara Government was unable to have the Sanjak included within Turkish frontiers in that otherwise brilliant agreement, and it passed under French Protectorate. However, Ankara succeeded in having certain explicit clauses inserted into the agreement, under which France promised to set up a special administrative regime in the Sanjak, and that the inhabitants of Turkish race would enjoy every facility for the development of their culture. In addition, the French plenipotentiary Franklin-Bouillon promised to persuade his government to allow the inhabitants of Hatay the right to have their own flag, in which the Turkish flag was to be included.

When the frontiers were defined at Lausanne, they laid down as follows: Article Three: "With Syria: the frontier defined in Article Eight of the Franco-Turkish agreement of 20th October 1921." In July 1922 the Letter of Mandate composed by the Council of the League of Nations was delivered to the French Republic. This document does not describe the territory entrusted to France as "Syria," as it had appeared in the agreement of San Remo, but refers separately to "Syria and Lebanon."

The first crisis over the Sanjak question appeared in 1927, when the Turks living there proclaimed the independence of the Government of Alexandretta as a result of the elections held that January. The Members of Parliament elected in April of that year approved the creation of that state, and asked the High Commission to confirm their vote. To recount the successive demonstrations of the Turkish character of the Sanjak's inhabitants, by which we naturally mean the people who were racially, linguistically and sentimentally Turkish, would be long and rather monotonous. One can sum it up by saying that France wished, for the greater success of her Mandate, to prevent any possibility that the Sanjak might return to Turkey or that it should be given independence.

The beginning of the dispute between France and Turkey over the Sanjak dates from the 26th of September 1936, on which day the French representative informed the Council of the Leauge of Nations that an agreement had been concluded under which his country, as the Mandatory Power, would give complete independence to the Republic of Syria at the end of three years. He also declared that discussions of the same nature were being carried on with the Republic of the Grand Lebanon. Hearing this, the Turkish delegate took the platform to repeat his country's satisfaction at such good news, which meant that those regions would now have regimes able to declare self- government; he also added that he hoped that the French Government would give an equal benefit to the Sanjak of Alexandretta by treating it in a similar way.

In October 1936, the Turkish Ambassador in Paris, Suat Davaz, sent the first note concerning the Sanjak question to the Minister of Foreign Affairs, Ivon Delbos. The French position and the opposing Turkish one gave rise to an interesting struggle which shows the diplomatic art at its highest. The Turkish thesis was as follows: at the end of the war, France had been entrusted with the Mandate over an area which had been separated from the Ottoman Empire. Her mission was that of raising the populations entrusted to her to a level of sufficient maturity to be able one day to govern themselves with complete freedom. Experience had shown the French that it was better to give up the idea of a union between Syria and the Lebanon, and adopt a separatist policy. France

had recognised the unity of the Sanjak amongst the territories under her mandate, through the treaties of 1921 and 1926; therefore, if Syria and the Lebanon
were being elevated to the rank of aspirants to independence, the same treatment
ought to be given to the Sanjak. Turkey asked that it should not be forgotten
that the French Mandate covered the whole of the territory within which there
existed some areas of local autonomy, such as Syria, Lebanon, the Alawites and
the Jebel Druz. The Sanjak's autonomy was understood to be within the limits of
the French Mandate, and in some way within that of Syrian independence. The
result of the international responsibility which France had assumed could not
be that of going against the interests of the Turkish population. In a few words,
Turkey was asking for freedom and sovereignty for the Sanjak.

For her part, France maintained that the French Government had negoti-
ated with its Turkish equivalent from its position as Mandatory Power, in the
name of and in the interests of Syria, since she had received the Mandate over
that country in 1920, and the agreement with Turkey was made in 1921. The
1921 agreement was one which laid down frontiers, and in the article referring to
the Sanjak it laid down that the Sanjak should have a special administration. In
practice, when the Sanjak was brought within the framework of the state of Syria,
it was given an administration similar to that of Syria. The Letter of Mandate detailed the obligations and rights of the Mandatory Power. In this it was explicitly
stipulated that the Mandatory Power had the duty of guaranteeing the states of
Syria and the Lebanon against any loss of territory, and also against any control
by a Foreign Power. The act of making the Sanjak independent would therefore
be equivalent to dismembering Syria.

The dispute, which was conducted before the League of Nations, had the
practical result on the 29th of May 1937, that a Commission was sent to the Sanjak with the main objective of preparing the legal framework for elections which
were to be held in the disputed area, to find out the wishes of the majority of the
population. France was to assume the administration of the Sanjak, separately
from her functions as Mandatory Power; order would be maintained under her
authority and responsibility.

The League's Commission went to the Sanjak and after several months produced a plan for an electoral law, which it sent to the President of the League for
official notification to the Mandatory Power, which was to give it legal force. The
Turkish Government was notified only for information. Turkish opinion was
roused against this procedure, and also against the Commission's behaviour in
the Sanjak, as this was alleged to have been onesided. This effectively meant the
failure of the idea of holding elections in Hatay under the aegis of the League, or

at least those elections which the Commission thought possible under the rules they had made.

Turkey then changed her policy a little, and once more came to an understanding with France. The series of incidents which had occurred in the Sanjak and the strained relations between France and Turkey did not hinder the renewal of the discussions. In one of his notes, Camille Chautemps, the French Prime Minister, declared; "I recognise that Franco-Turkish cooperation is a factor of extreme importance in a policy of peace and progress, and all the more so because there is not at present the greatest desire to maintain the relations between the two countries in full friendship and confidence, on this as on every occasion."

Hatay was related to the whole Mediterranean problem. It could not be to France's advantage to have any sort of enmity with Turkey, a power which controlled the Straits, the road uniting France with her ally, the U. S. S. R. In addition, Ankara's influence in the Balkan Entente, allied to the Little Entente, was worth taking into account, as was her powerful army, the work of Marshal Atatürk.

The Third Reich and Nationalist Italy did not retreat from their wish to win the Turkish President's good will; they held the first places in trade with Turkey, and in fact whichever of the Powers fighting for supremacy in the Mediterranean managed to achieve that decisive alliance with Turkey would have won a trick of incalculable importance. The sympathies of Turkey, inspired by her interests and her delicate geographical position, had been generally aligned towards the Paris-Moscow axis, since that of Rome and Berlin caused her apprehensions.

At the end of months spent in negotiations, during which the British Government exercised its influence over the French to persuade it to make a satisfactory solution to the dispute which Turkey considered a national problem, France and Turkey agreed to sign a bilateral pact of friendship, which had decisive political meaning in relation to the support it received from Atatürk. Before the conclusion of the bilateral pact, the Hatay dispute was resolved by a military agreement signed at Antakya on 3 July 1938, under which the territorial integrity of Hatay was guaranteed, and Franco-Turkish military cooperation was arranged to deal with the affairs of that region, until a plebiscite should decide the will of its inhabitants. On the following day the bilateral pact was signed in Ankara. Its most important article is that referring to the political status of the Eastern Mediterranean, since it joins the signatory Powers in the defence of that area, and joins them through their existing treaties to the United Kingdom, the Soviet Union, the Balkan Entente and Egypt, which makes it difficult for any Power to try to alter the terms.

The serious events in Palestine showed that uncertainty had not been re-moved, and that there always existed a threatening situation round Suez; from Gibraltar, the Spanish spectacle spoke with dreadful eloquence of the extremities to which the struggle for leadership in the Mediterranean might be taken.

The agreement with France, Turkey's old ally since the time of Süleyman the Magnificent, or that achieved with the United Kingdom, or Turkey's other alliances did not mean that she was following a policy of strengthening herself with a view to aggressive campaigns. Far from that, it was a policy of international cooperation for peace. She was trying to make aggression and imperialism more difficult, through the union of peoples who were anxious for peace. In short, she wished to give real validity to the first ideals of the League of Nations.

One problem remained at an extremely delicate point; that of curing the injustices which had been done in the treaties which resolved the 1914 war, injus-tices against which the Turkish people under Atatürk's leadership had rebelled, and whose cancellation they had obtained by force of arms. Atatürk, however, believed that with good will and through peaceful means many questions could gradually be resolved in Europe, and that thus peace, a true peace, could be reached; he believed that the articles of the treaties which could not be enforced because of the rapid changes in the complex political appearance of the world, should be revised within the framework of law. Chamberlain thought similarly to Atatürk, believing that it was time to change a state of affairs which could not be maintained, through mutual concessions and goodwill.

CHAPTER 43

ATATÜRK'S ANKARA

Proud and grandiose, the old fortress clings to the rough hillside as if ready to fight the centuries and beat them. The hill whose stones are confounded with those of the citadel is surrounded by a succession of mountainous masses. The plain, divided by several depressions, extends between that hill, other neighboring hills, and the mountains. Amid this rough grey countryside, the ruined city of Ankara, which had known fine days and the favour of Emperors and Princes, was scattered down the hill from the citadel.

When Atatürk reached that provincial city at the end of 1919, with the intention of settling the centre of his revolutionary activity there, there were no more than 25,000 inhabitants in the town, living in the poverty of their dormant industries, and from the sale of raw materials, both operations being almost paralysed by the state of war. There was a great shortage of drinking water, while the small streams which run across the plain overflowed in the spring and autumn, forming marshes, places where the germs of malaria thrived. As far as the eye could see from any part of the city, only one or two stunted trees could be seen. The grey plain, the grey rocks and the dust gave a monotonous picture.

This was the place, where the roughness of the climate was the more apparent through the total lack of comforts, where the Kemalist government established itself. Three consecutive years of war, from which internal strife and political rivalry were not absent, saw those men who believed in Atatürk coming from every quarter to instal themselves however they could in Ankara's wretched houses, packed together but happy to put up with privations for an ideal.

There was not even electric light; motor vehicles could be counted on the fingers of one hand. Commissars and Members of Parliament could be seen going to their offices or the Assembly on horseback. The thousands of refugees who had fled before the Greek advance surrounded the thousand- year-old city with a belt of hunger.

Many people thought that place and that city sad and without hope, as had the War of Independence been thought and indeed as it still was. Both the city and the will to win were in the same state, but they had both obstinately sunk their clenched claws into the hard earth.

This place, which everyone believed to be merely a strategic command post, had been identified in Atatürk's heart as the capital of the new Turkey. His faith had brought a weary people to prefer death to the loss of the smallest part of their freedom; his faith would defeat all obstacles. Down there, on that arid ground, he would make forests grow, and place lakes and gardens. On the plateau, the earth does not give forth her fruits with the ease which is enjoyed by the pleasant valleys of old Ionia; the water courses are few and irregular; the climate is rough, and even the sky is at a higher altitude, and appears pale and unpromising.

What a contrast between Istanbul, resting on the shores of the marvellous beauty of the Bosporus and the blue Marmara, and the burnt and thirsty plateau! The governing classes of the nation were becoming languid in the palaces of the Queen of the East, amid her harems, the voluptuous refinements inherited from the thousand-year-old Persian civilisation, and amid its effeminacy. In Atatürk's eyes, Istanbul was a symbol of a decline of an Empire, but those classes which had been dragged downhill would not drag the Turkish people after them, since it was uncontaminated and strong. On the plateau, he would build the capital city for that people which was being reborn amid battles and poverty, but which had already acquired for itself a precious possession, pain. Ankara was the symbol of the new Turkey, where everything was yet to be made, and which had nothing left but a few grandiose ruins, the ruins of her history.

Ankara had the advantage of being in the heart of Anatolia. In the near future, when the city had been transformed into a centre of modern culture as Atatürk had decided, she would radiate her light and her example throughout Anatolia; also, Turkey's enemies would no longer be able to repeat the words of Lloyd George: "The capital of Turkey must be within range of our cannons."

After the proclamation of the Republic, and when the city on the plateau was raised to be capital of Turkey in 1923, a period of flowering began for her which was to surpass her old golden ages. At the beginning, the buildings which were constructed, the most urgently needed, were put up without any plan; but in 1927 a plan began to be put into effect which had been worked out with the help of foreign city planners of world fame. Atatürk discussed the details of the project point by point in his villa at Çankaya, which was an unrivalled observatory.

Atatürk wanted the plan to embrace all the advances which city planning has gained through experience in the world, and that it should have such a range that it could adapt itself to the size of the city, no matter how large it might grow.

The modern city has been given a general north to south direction, starting from the limits of the old city, and this direction is followed across the plain by the main artery, Gazi Bulvarı, which reaches halfway up Çankaya hill, after passing through the most recent quarters of Yenişehir.

It was, however, the problems of water, fever and lack of trees, which continued to be the main obstacles to the construction of the city of Atatürk's dream. In 1935, therefore, the antimalaria campaign began in Ankara and its surroundings, and the marshes disappeared one by one. In that same year the National Guide caught a carp in the truly sterile area of the plain, which he was to transform into the Orman, a magnificent experimental agricultural station, covered with great areas of woods, nurseries for plants giving shade, fruit trees and others which would ornament the city's gardens.

The insufficient rainfall on the plateaus of Central Anatolia, which does not exceed 250 millimetres a year at the most, is the main cause of its barrenness; in addition to this, the rivers and streams overflow, because of the shortness of the rainy season, whilst in the opposite season, they show dry riverbeds, so that agriculture suffers terribly. In 1936, the Çubuk dam was completed, 12 kilometres north of Ankara, to store the waters of the river of the same name. The volume of water which the Çubuk can provide annually had been calculated at 30,000,000 cubic metres. The natural springs of Elmadag and Koşunlar complete Ankara's water reserves.

All the same, until these works were completed, water was short in the city, especially for irrigation. For that reason, the plants grew with difficulty in the gardens, both private and public, in the parks and boulevards; one saw rows of sickly trees which hardly seemed to grow at all, and flowers which were late in opening their petals. Plants were chosen which were most suited to the area, and when the water arrived in abundance, the new buildings were submerged by a flood of greenery.

The forests of scaffolding competed with the forests of the garden city, the wonderful oasis of the plateau. The number of dwellings finished each year did not reach the requirements of the growing population. By 1927, the number of the city's inhabitants had tripled; the census in that year showed 75,000 inhabitants, and there are now over 130,000.

As happened in America, where there was a considerable majority of males among the immigrants, most of Ankara's new guests were men. After the liberation of women, the first parties began to be given, and Atatürk intended to use these to give the final touch of westernisation to the fair sex; however, women not only came timidly to the dances, but being in the minority, found themselves short of the courage provided by numbers; they remained in a separate group and did not dance. This very understandable diffidence was no sufficient obstacle to Atatürk's civilising plans, since he showed a marked preference for conversation and rendering social respect to those ladies who danced. His behaviour advised the other ladies, and proved successful. Who was going to let herself be left behind?

Comfortable hotels opened their doors, and there began the life of a truly twentieth century city. There were frequent tea and dinner dances, and also receptions in private houses. The life of Ankara today presents a remarkable contrast to that lived by the pioneer Nationalist, in those days, still not far- off, when her epic was being written.

Two stages can be distinguished in the architecture of the city: the first, in which the neo-Turkish style predominates, is exemplified in the palace of the Grand Assembly, while the second, now in fashion, is ruled by the most modern architectural style as used in France, Germany and North America, with sober lines and smooth surfaces, and giving primary importance to ventilation and comfort. The government quarter, bank buildings, and the presidential palace have been built in this style.

Atatürk's dream has been realised; his Ankara has risen from the naked and unfriendly plateau, through the efforts of men, amid trees and flowers. His idea was not to create a great modern city provided with all the benefits of progress, so as to have reason for pride; before all else he wanted the Turkish nation, fallen decades behind the western nations, and made cowardly by her own inferiority of culture, to have a visible example of what her will and awakened spirit could realise; if the Turks could acquire through study a culture similar to that of the most advanced peoples, they could by technology and willpower accomplish works of great importance, and raise cities which should have no reason to envy the most recent cities of the civilised world. In demonstration of this, there was Ankara, with her kilometres of faultless streets, her proud buildings, her parks, her quarters of comfortable houses, her stadia, her airport, her schools and institutes; all this created in the desert, and by their own efforts, without the help of foreign capital.

Ankara has a historical significance, that of the emancipation of the Eastern peoples who were oppressed by the progress and science of the West, by using the West's own weapons, science and progress; it is a lesson which those people who are still living in slavery keep before their eyes.

Atatürk fought against cities which are museums, preferring museums in the cities. The sad spectacle of the picturesque Turkey, in the style of Pierre Loti, which she used to offer to tourists, eager to see in other countries the exoticism and backwardness which they would not allow in their own, has disappeared from civilised Turkey. Falih Rıfkı Atay, the well-known Turkish writer, has expressed graphically the clash of these two mentalities: "There are some people who lament the new state of affairs; they are especially numerous among French writers of the old school. But we should remind them in reply, that if the French walked around the streets of Paris dressed in the garments which are kept in museums, tourism, which has been suffering from the crisis, would receive a new stimulus in France."

Although Atatürk was against "picturesque backwardness," he was passionately interested in history. Archaeology and historical studies have received major protection from the government as never before in Turkey. The historical monuments of every period are carefully preserved, and many excavations have been completed by the Turkish Historical Society. Very important works of art have been discovered, as have the remains of superimposed cities, and excavations have thrown light upon the civilisations which first built and created art in Anatolia, some before the Age of Copper, some from that age, others from the Bronze Age and the Hittite periods.

As is well-known, Central Anatolia was inhabited by the Hittites, and imposing ruins of their famous capital, Hattusas, have been found 185 kilometres east of Ankara, so that it is safe to say that the surroundings of the new capital contain traces of that great people in their soil. Only 14 kilometres south of Ankara, in the excavations at Ahlatlıbel, there were found remains of a fortified tower going back to the Chalcolithic period, between 3,0 and 4,000 B. C. Statuettes of idols, bronze bracelets and skeletons which were found there have been put on display at the Ethnographical Museum in Ankara. This museum, and the temporary museum at the Hacıbayram mosque, contain enough material to claim the title of being the greatest museums in the World for the Hittite civilisation. They possess pottery more than 5,000 years old, objects from the Copper and Bronze Ages, and sculpture from various periods. Galatia, Rome, Byzantium, and the Seljuk and Ottoman Empires are well represented in Ankara's museums.

CHAPTER 44

DEATH

The recrudescence of his old illnesses sent news of his grave condition through the telegraph wires. Atatürk was in his 58th year, but he had aged. His sparse white hair framed his face, in which the features had softened with the arrival of age, brought prematurely by the deprivations of a life spent in struggle.

His sickness took him to his bed for a long last illness, in the overornate palace of Dolmabahçe. His constant worry pressed upon him closer than ever: the future of his people. Had they been educated sufficiently? Would not the same thing happen as with Fethi's opposition party? Would they be able to fight successfully against the forces of the past, and against the ancient spirit of despotism, which had been shown by all Turkey's rulers?

A few days before his death Atatürk told a group of friends that he had faith that his lifelong struggle would be of benefit to future generations, and that after he was dead the people would continue on the road of civilisation and progress which he had marked out. He reminded them of his words spoken at the time of the attempt against his life: "Certainly my body will one day be dust, but the Republic, the work of my body, will live forever."

Paradoxical though it may seem, he was a dictator in spite of his democratic ideas; however, this was because he found himself forced to be one. He realised that the education of his people would not allow a liberal form of government, and that nothing could have been done through that system in Turkey. In his monumental discourse, in which he explained his whole work of government, he said that he had used his strength "in order to lift the nation to that level to which it has the right to aspire in the civilised world: to make ever more firm the basis of the Republic, and thus destroy forever the spirit of despotism."

In 1937 he donated his farms to the state; he had created them with the objective of making agricultural experiments and they had been of great usefulness during the scientific transformation of agriculture and animal husbandry. With this gesture he once more showed his indifference to material wealth.

I have taken the following notes from one of his last conversations, which he held with the Romanian Chancellor, Victor Antonescu, and which show the way in which he ordered his life, being typical of his philosophy. "Because I wanted to know the opinion which philosophers have held about life, I have read many books during my own life. Some of them saw everything darkly. Since we are nothing, they said, and since we will be reduced to nothing, there can be no room in the transitory life of this world for gaiety and happiness. I have read other books, written by more sensible men. Since, say these philosophers, we are nothing and that without remedy we are going back towards nothing, let us be happy during the course of our existence.

"I prefer this last conception of life, but with the addition of these conditions. Those who think they can represent the whole condition of humanity are doomed to failure. Man, as an individual, is condemned to death. To work, not for oneself, but for those who will come after, is the first condition of the happiness that any individual can reach in life. Each person has his own preferences. Some people like gardening and growing flowers. Others prefer to train men. Does the man who grows flowers expect anything from them? He who trains men ought to work like a man who grows flowers.

"I always tell my thoughts to people I respect. I am a man who cannot keep a secret in his heart for no reason. Because I am a man of the people, I always say what I think in front of the people. If I make mistakes, the people can tell me; but it has never yet happened that the people have found me lacking in frankness.

"Nations ought not to experience sadness or affliction. The duty of leaders is to govern them in such a way that they will accept life with happiness and love."

These were the feelings of that man in whose pupils of steel the blaze has now been extinguished.

CHRONOLOGICAL INDEX

27th century B. C.	The Hittites found the first Anatolian civilisation; they originated in Central Asia. Many other migrations have occured over the course of the centuries following the same direction as theirs.
3rd century B. C.	Peak of the Hiung-nu Empire in Eastern Central Asia.
3rd century A. D.	Fall of the Hiung-nu Empire Large tribes begin to emigrate westwards, passing to the north and south of the Caspian Sea.
7th century	Birth of Islam.
7th & 8th centuries	Conversion of the Turks to Islam.
End of 13th century	Osman founds a new state on the collapse of the Seljuk Empire.
1326	Capture of Bursa, the first capital of the Ottoman Empire.
1402	Sultan Beyazit defeated at Ankara by Tamerlane.
29 May 1453	Mehmet the Conqueror captures Constantinople. End of the Middle Ages.
1529	First siege of Vienna.
1535	Süleyman the Magnificent concedes the first capitulations to Francois I.
1571	Sea battle of Lepanto.
1683	Second siege of Vienna. Marks the beginning of the Ottoman decline.
1699	Treaty of Karlowitz, through which Turkey loses Hungary, Transylvania, Podolia, the Morea, and Dalmatia.
1718	Treaty of Passarowitz, disastrous for the Empire.
1809	Accession to the throne of Mehmet II, the reforming Sultan.
1839	Abdülmecit proclaims the Imperial edict of Gülhane, beginning the period of the reforms.
1854-1856	Crimean War.
1877	Russo-Turkish War.
1878	Treaties of San Stefano and Berlin.
1881	Mustafa born in Salonika.

1892	Enters the military training school.
1899	Graduates as sub-lieutenant, moves to Istanbul for the first time.
1904	Receives the diploma of Staff Captain.
1907	Transferred to Macedonia.
1908	Rebellion of the Young Turks.
1909	Deposition of the Red Sultan.
1910	Kemal detailed to follow the French army manoeuvres.
1911	War between Italy and Turkey.
1912	First Balkan War.
23 January 1913	Assassination of Nâzım Paşa. Return of the Young Turks to power.
29 June 1913	Second Balkan War.
12 November 1914	The Ottoman Empire declares war upon France and Great Britain.
18 March 1915	Disastrous attack by the Allied fleet against the Dardanelles.
19 May 1915	Promotion of Kemal to Colonel.
6 & 7 August 1915	Victory of Anafarta, work of Kemal.
8 January 1916	The Allies withdraw, beaten, from Gallipoli.
7 & 8 August 1916	Kemal recaptures the towns of Muş and Bitlis, in the Caucasus.
1918	At the beginning of the year, Kemal accompanies Prince Vahdettin on his journey to Germany.
3 March 1918	Treaty of Brest-Litovsk between Russia and the Central Powers.
3 July	Death of Mehmet V and accession of Mehmet VI, Vahdettin.
30 October	Armistice of Mudros.
13 November	The Allied fleet arrives in Istanbul.
15 May 1919	The Greeks disembark in Smyrna.
19 May	Mustafa Kemal arrives in Samsun.
21 June	Meeting of military commanders at Amasya, presided over by Kemal.
28 June	Signature of the Treaty of Versailles.
8 July	The government ends Kemal's official mission; he resigns from the army.

23 August	The Nationalist Congress of Erzurum begins its sessions.
4 September	Opening of the historic Congress of Sivas.
10 September	Treaty of Saint Germain between the Entente and Austria.
12 September	Sultan Vahdettin concludes a secret treaty with Great Britain.
27 November	Treaty of Neuilly between the Allies and Bulgaria.
27 December	Kemal moves the headquarters of the Representative Committee to the city of Ankara.
28 January 1920	The National Pact is approved by the Chamber of Deputies.
16 March	Occupation of Istanbul by the Allies.
23 April	Opening of the Grand National Assembly in Ankara.
11 May	The Imperial Government condemns Mustafa Kemal to death.
4 June	Imposition of the Treaty of Trianon on Hungary.
22 June	Beginning of the great Greek offensive.
25 July	The Greeks capture Adrianople.
10 August	The Sultan's delegates sign the Treaty of Sèvres.
30 September	Beginning of the campaign in Armenia: the Turkish army enters Sarıkamış.
25 December	Death of King Alexander of Greece. Constantine returns to the throne.
6 January 1921	The Greek army moves onto the offensive all along the line.
9 January	Victory of Inönü.
21 February	Opening of the London Conference.
16 March	Treaty of Moscow between the U. S. S. R. and the Ankara Government.
23 March	New Greek offensive.
31 March	Second victory of Inonu.
28 June	Great Greek offensive.
18 July	Mustafa Kemal orders the Turkish army to withdraw to the river Sakarya.
5 August	Kemal appointed Generalissimo. Approval of the Law of Dictatorship.
13 September	Victory of the Sakarya.
19 September	The Assembly awards Kemal the rank of Marshal and the title of Gazi.

19 October	Signature of the treaty between France and the Kemalist government in Ankara.
6 May 1922	The Law of Dictatorship prolonged for the third time after fierce discussions.
26 August	Beginning of the great Turkish offensive.
30 August	Battle of the Generalissimo.
9 September	Entry of the Turkish army into Smyrna.
11 October	Signature of the Armistice of Mudanya.
1 November	Abolition of the Sultanate.
17 November	Flight of Mehmet Vahdettin.
24 July 1923	Conclusion of the Lausanne Peace Treaty.
9 August	Foundation of the People's Party.
2 October	The allied forces evacuate Istanbul.
13 October	Ankara declared the capital of Turkey.
29 October	Proclamation of the Republic. Election of Atatürk as first magistrate.
30 October	Ismet Paşa forms the first republican cabinet.
3 March 1924	Abolition of the Califate.
8 April	Abolition of the religious courts.
11 February 1925	Revolt in the southeast provinces.
17 February	Abolition of the tithe.
3 March	Ali Fethi's cabinet replaced by Ismet's.
2 September	Decree closing the tekkes and dissolving the religious orders.
25 November	Law compelling the wearing of hats.
26 December	Adoption of the international calendar.
17 February 1926	Adoption of the new Civil Code.
6 June	Agreement of Mosul.
15 June	Discovery of plot to assassinate the Gazi.
3 October	Unveiling of the first statue of Atatürk in Istanbul.
28 October	First population census.
1 May 1928	Adoption of international numerals.
3 November	Reform of the Alphabet
5 June 1929	Law on agricultural credit cooperatives.
17 November 1930	Dissolution of Fethi's party.

23 December	Reactionary disturbances in Menemen.
4 May 1931	Atatürk elected President for the third time. Opening of the Fourth Grand Assembly.
2 July 1932	First Turkish Historical Congress.
18 July	Entry of Turkey to the League of Nations.
26 September	First Turkish Language Congress.
1934	In this year the first five-year plan went into practical application.
24 November	The Assembly gives Mustafa Kemal the surname of "Atatürk."
20 July 1936	Signature of the Montreux Convention.
12 June 1937	Atatürk donates his model farms to the state.
4 July 1938	Franco-Turkish bilateral Pact initialled in Ankara.
10 November	Death of Atatürk in Istanbul.

BIOGRAPHICAL INDEX

A

ABBAS. Uncle of Mohammed (566-652).

ABBASIDS. Califal dynasty which reigned in Baghdad, 762-1258.

ABDERRAHMAN. First Omeyyad Calif of Córdoba (756-787).

ABDÜLÂZİZ I. Sultan, 1861-1876.

ABDÜLHAMİT II. The "Red Sultan," reigned 1876-1909.

ABDÜLKERİM PAŞA. Friend of Kemal, intermediary between him and the court in 1919.

ABDÜLMECİT I. Reforming Sultan, reigned 1839-1861.

ABDÜLMECİT EFENDİ. Last Ottoman Calif, 1922-1924.

ABRAHAM. Jewish patriarch. Old Testament.

ABUBAKR. First Calif, died in 634.

ADNAN, Doctor. Nationalist opposed to Atatürk; husband of the writer Halide Edip.

AEMILIUS PAULLUS, LUCIUS. Roman consul in 181 and 168 B. C.

AGAMEMNON. King of Argos and Mycenae, son of Atreus, 13th century B. C.

AGHA KHAN III. Indian Prince, well-known in aristocratic circles in London and Paris.

AHMET BEY. Commander at Jaffa, helped Atatürk on his journey to Salonika.

AHMET IBN TULUN. Founder of the Tulunid dynasty of Egypt.

AHMET IZZET. Grand Vezir in 1918.

AHMET MUHTAR. Marshal, Prime Minister at the beginning of the Balkan War.

AHMET NESİMİ. Minister of Foreign Affairs during the World War.

ALARIC I. King of the Visigoths, died 410.

ALCIBIADES. Athenian General (450-404 B. C.)

ALEXANDER, The Great. King of Macedonia (356-323 B. C.)

ALEXANDER I. King of Greece, 1917-1920.

ALEXANDER II. Tsar of Russia (1818-1881).

ALEXEIEV, MICHAEL V. Russian General of exceptional note during the World War (1855-1918).

ALEXIS. Son of Peter I of Russia, condemned to death by him.

Alexis III, Angelus. Eastern Emperor, dethroned by the crusaders in 1203.

Alexis IV. Eastern Emperor, 1203-1204.

Alexis V, Ducas. Eastern Emperor in 1204.

Ali. Fourth Calif, 656-661.

Ali (Cenani). Collaborator and friend of Atatürk.

Ali Fethi (Okyar). Prime Minister of the Turkish Republic, November 1924-March 1925.

Ali Fuat. General of exceptional note in the Kemalist Revolution, political opponent of Atatürk.

Ali Galip, Colonel. Attempted to make a coup against the Congress of Sivas in 1919.

Ali Kemal. Minister of Sultan Vahdettin, enemy of Nationalism.

Ali Riza. Grand Vezir from October 1919 to March 1920.

Ali Riza. Father of Atatürk.

Allenby, Viscount. General, commanding the British forces which conquered Palestine and Syria. World War 1918.

Amanullah. King of Afghanistan, 1926-1929.

Anastasia. Wife of Grand Duke Nicholas Nicholayevich.

Ankhsenpaaten. Wife of Tutankhamun.

Antigonus. Alexander the Great's General, King of Syria (301 B. C.)

Antiochus I. King of Syria, 281-260 B. C.

Antiochus III, The Great. King of Syria, 222-186 B. C.

Antonescu, Victor. Romanian Minister of Foreign Affairs, 1937.

Anzavur. Commander of anti-Kemalist volunteers.

Apollo. Mythological divinity.

Arcadius. Eastern Emperor, 395-408.

Aristides. Athenian General and politician (540-468 B. C.)

Aristotle. Greek philosopher, fourth century B. C. Inspired the philosophers of the Middle Ages.

Arnena. Hittite solar divinity.

Artemis. Diana in Greek mythology.

Atay, Falih Rifki. Eminent writer born in Istanbul in 1893.

Athena. Minerva in Greek mythology.

Atif. Nationalist officer.

Atreus. King of Argos and Mycenae.

ATTILA. Famous conqueror, of Turkish race (410-453).

AUGUSTUS, (OCTAVIUS). First Roman Emperor (63 B. C.-A. D. 14).

AURELIAN. Roman Emperor (212-275).

B

BAHALOVICH. Russian anti-Communist General. Russian Revolution.

BALDWIN I. Latin Emperor of Constantinople, 1204-1205,

BALDWIN II. Last Latin Emperor of Constantinople, 1228-1261.

BALTAZZI, GEORGE. Greek Minister, shot in 1922.

BARBAROSSA, HAYRETTİN. Famous Turkish Admiral, died in 1545.

BASIL, St. Father of the Greek Church (329-379).

BEACONSFIELD, Lord.-See Disraeli.

BEKİR SAMİ. Nationalist Commissar for Foreign Affairs in the government of the First Grand Assembly.

BERNARD, St. Preached the Second Crusade (1091-1153).

BEYAZİT I, The Thunderbolt. Sultan, 1389-1402.

BIRDWOOD, Sir WILLIAM. British General who fought in the Dardanelles.

BISMARCK, OTTO, Prince. Chancellor of the German Empire (1815-1898).

BLOIS, COUNT de. One of the leaders of the Fourth Crusade, thirteenth century.

BOUILLON, GODFREY de. Commander of the First Crusade (1058-1100), Duke of Lorraine.

BRENNUS. Gallic chieftain who conquered Macedonia, third century B. C.

BRIAND, ARISTIDE. French politician (1862-1932).

BRUNING, HEINRICH. Chancellor of Germany, 1930-1932.

BRUSILOV, A. A. Russian Generalissimo, of great importance during the World War.

C

CAESAR, JULIUS. Roman General and Dictator (100-44 B. C.)

CAFER TAYYAR. Commander of the Nationalist troops in Thrace. Deserted his post in 1920.

CALTHORP, Sir ARTHUR GOUGH. British Admiral. Signed the Armistice of Mudros.

CANONICA. Italian sculptor who made the Monument of Atatürk in Ankara.

CARACALLA, ANTONIUS. Roman Emperor (188-217).

CARDEN. British Admiral. Refused to attack the Dardanelles, March 1914.

CASTOR. One of the Argonauts. Mythology.

CASSANDER. King of Macedonia and later of Greece, died 297 B. C.

CATHERINE II of Russia. Called "The Great," reigned 1762-1796.

CAVİT. Unionist leader. Involved in the attempt against Atatürk in 1926.

CELÂLETTİN RUMİ. Exquisite Turkish mystic poet, thirteenth century.

CEMAL PAŞA. One of the Unionist triumvirs. Assassinated at Tiflis in 1921.

CEMİL. Second in command in Salonika; helped Atatürk in his journey to Syria in 1907.

CENGİZ HAN. Founder of the Mongol Empire (1154-1227).

ÇERKES ETHEM. Commander of Nationalist irregular forces; betrayed their cause in 1921.

ÇERKES REŞİT. Member of the Assembly, brother of the traitors Ethem and Tevfik.

ÇERKES TEVFİK. Commander of Nationalist irregular forces; betrayed their cause in 1921.

CEVAT PAŞA. Minister of war in 1919.

CHAMBERLAIN, ARTHUR NEVILLE. British Prime Minister, born in 1869.

CHARLEMAGNE. Emperor of the West (742-814).

CHARLES MARTEL. Defeated the Saracens at Poitiers in 723.

CHAUTEMPS,CAMILLE. French Prime Minister during the dispute over the Sanjak.

CHICHERIN, GEORGY VASILIEVICH. Soviet politician, born in 1879.

CHOSROES II. King of Persia, 590-628.

CIMON. Athenian General. Defeated the Persians, died in 449 B. C.

CLEMENCEAU, GEORGES. French politician, Prime Minister during the Great War (1841-1921).

COLUMBUS, CHRISTOPHER. Discoverer of America (1451-1506).

CONRAD III. Emperor of Germany, 1138-1152.

CONSTANTINE I, The Great. Roman Emperor, 306-337.

CONSTANTINE XIII. Last emperor of Byzantium, 1448-1453.

CONSTANTINE I. King of Greece, 1913-1917 and 1920-1922, died in 1923.

CRASSUS, MARCUS LICINIUS. Roman consul and triumvir with Caesar and Pompey (115-53 B. C.)

CROESUS. King of Lydia, fourth century B. C.

CURZON, Lord. Foreign Secretary, leader of the British delegation to the Lausanne Conference.

CYBELE. Goddess of the Earth. Mythology.

CYRUS. Persian King (560-529 B. C.)

D

DAMAT FERİT. Grand Vezir and brother-in-law of Vahdettin. Extremely bitter enemy of Kemalism, Grand Vezir in 1919 and in 1920.

DAMAT ŞERİF. Ottoman Minister in 1919.

DANISHMENDIDS. Turkish dynasty which reigned in Anatolia in the eleventh and twelfth centuries.

D'ANNUNZIO, GABRIELE H. Famous Italian poet (1868-1938).

DAVID. Second King of Israel, eleventh century B. C.

DE CAIX. French delegate to Kemal in 1920.

DELBOS, IVON. French Chancellor during the dispute over Alexandretta.

DENIKIN. White Russian General.

DENY, JEAN. French Turcologist, author of several important works. Contemporary.

D'ESPEREY.-See Franchet D'Esperey.

DERVİŞ MEHMET. Principal figure in the disturbances in Menemen, 1930.

DIOCLETIAN. Roman Emperor, 284-305.

DISRAELI, BENJAMIN. British Prime Minister, Lord Beaconsfield (1804-1881).

DUDHALIA III. Hittite Emperor, thirteenth century B. C.

DUDHALIA V. Hittite Emperor, twelfth century B. C.

DUNSTERVILLE. British General entrusted with a mission in the Caucasus.

E

EDWARD VII. King of England from 1901-1910.

EHRLICH, PAUL. Discovered salvarsan and neosalvarsan (1854-1915).

ENVER PAŞA. One of the leaders of the Committee of Union and Progress. Vice-Generalissimo of the Turkish Armies during the World War (1879-1922).

ERTENA, ALÂETTİN. Governor who proclaimed himself Sultan in Ankara and governed from 1328 to 1336.

ERTUĞRUL. Legendary father of the founder of the Ottoman dynasty.

ERTUĞRUL. Son of the last Ottoman Sultan.

ESAT. Miner, elected Member of Parliament in 1931.

ETHEM.-See Çerkes Ethem.

EUGENE of Savoy, Prince. Famous soldier, General of the Imperial Armies (1663-1736).

EUGENIUS IV. Pope, 1431-1447.

F

FAHRETTİN PAŞA. Turkish General, defender of Medina.

FALKENHAYN, HEINRICH von. German General, commander of the Yıldırım Group in 1917.

FATIMIDS. Moslem dynasty which reigned in North Africa, 909-1171.

FEISAL. Proclaimed King of Iraq in 1921, son of King Hussein.

FERDINAND II. King of Bulgaria, 1908-1918.

FEVZI, Sheikh. Member of the Representative Committee of Erzurum.

FEVZİ ÇAKMAK. Leading personality in the Kemalist Revolution, Marshal and Chief of the General Staff. Born in Istanbul in 1876.

FOCH, FERNAND. Marshal of France (1851-1929).

FORRER, E. Archaeologist, specialising in Hittite history. Contemporary.

FOUCHE, JOSEPH. Duke of Otranto. Minister for the Police during the Empire (1759-1820).

FRANCHET D'ESPEREY. French General commanding the Allied forces which entered Istanbul in November in 1918.

FRANÇOIS I. King of France, 1515-1547.

FRANKLIN-BOUILLON. Signatory of the Franco-Kemalist agreement in 1921.

FRANZ FERDINAND. Heir to the throne of Austria-Hungary. Assassinated at Sarajevo (1863-1914).

FRANZ-JOSEPH I. Emperor of Austria and King of Hungary, 1848-1916.

FRIEDRICH I, BARBAROSSA. Emperor of Germany, 1152-1190.

G

GALILEO. Illustrious Italian scientist (1554-1642).

GENNADIUS. Patriarch of Constantinople under Sultan Mehmet II, fifteenth century.

GEORGE II. King of Greece in 1923 and since 1935.

GEORGE III. King of Great Britain, 1760-1820.

GHAZAN HAN. Turco-Mongol Emperor of Persia (1271-1304).

GHAZNAVIDS. Turkish dynasty which reigned in Khorasan and Afghanistan, 995-1145.

GÖKÇEN, SABİHA. Turkish woman military aviator.

GOREMYKIN, IVAN. Russian Prime Minister during the World War.

GOURAUD, HENRI. General, commanding the French forces at Gallipoli.

GREGORY XIII. Pope, 1572-1585.

GUNARIS, DEMETRIOS. Greek Prime Minister, shot in 1922.

GUTENBERG, JOHANN GENSFLEISCH. Perfected printing (1397-1468).

H

HACI BAYRAM. Builder of a mosque in Ankara, fifteenth century.

HACI BEKTAŞ. Founder of the Bektaşi sect, fourteenth century.

HADJIANESTIS. General, commanding the Greek Army at the start of the Turkish offensive in 1922. Shot in the same year.

HAKIM. Fatimid Calif, reigned in Egypt in the tenth century.

HAKKI BEHİÇ. Secretary General of the Green Army, 1920.

HALIDE EDİP. Turkish woman writer who took part in the Nationalist Movement. Contemporary.

HALİL. Farmer, elected Member of Parliament in 1931.

HALİL PAŞA. Turkish General commanding the Iraq front. World War.

HALİS HAKKI. Turkish Commander on the Caucasus front, 1915.

HAMDULLAH SÜPHİ. Turkish writer who was President of the Turkish Hearths. Born in Istanbul in 1885.

HAMILTON. British General. Commander of the Allied Expeditionary Army at Gallipoli.

HAMZA BIN ALI. Persian prophet, creator of a Moslem sect, eleventh century.

HANNIBAL. Famous Carthaginian soldier (247-183 B. C.)

HARBORD. American General who visited Ankara during the revolutionary period.

HARRINGTON, Sir CHARLES. British General who signed the Armistice of Mudanya in 1922.

HARUN AR-RASHID. Calif of Baghdad (765-809).

HASAN. Miner, elected Member of Parliament in 1931.

HAYRULLAH. Shoemaker, elected Member of Parliament in 1931.

HERACLIUS I. Eastern Emperor (575-641)

HERCULES. Mythological hero.

HERODOTUS. Greek historian (484-406 B. C.)

HINDENBURG, PAUL von BECKENDORFF und. German Marshal, President of the Reich (1847-1934).

HITLER, ADOLF. President of the Third Reich, born in 1889.

HOHENBERG, DUCHESS of. Wife of the heir of Austria-Hungary. Assassinated at Sarajevo in 1914.

HOLMES, OLIVER WENDELL. American doctor, author of a treatise on puerperal fever (1809-1894).

HOMER. Greek poet, nineth to eighth centuries B. C.

HONORIUS, FLAVIUS AUGUSTUS. Roman Emperor, 395-423.

HROZNY. Archaeologist, specialist in Hittite history. Contemporary.

HUNYADI, JANOS. Famous Hungarian warrior (1399-1456).

HUSEYİN HİLMİ. Grand Vezir in the Unionist Government.

HUSSEIN. King of the Hedjaz, leader of the Arab revolt against Turkey in 1916.

I

IBN BATTUTA. Arab geographer and traveller, fourteenth century.

İBRAHİM I. Ottoman Sultan, 1640-1648.

İBRAHİM Paşa. Viceroy of Egypt (1789-1848).

IKHSHIDIDS. Turkish dynasty in Egypt, tenth century.

ILKHANIDS. Turco-Mongol dynasty of Iran, fourteenth century.

ISAAC II, ANGELUS. Eastern Emperor, 1185-1195 and 1203-1204.

ISABEL I. Queen of Castille (1451-1504).

ISMAIL I. King of Persia (1485-1523).

İSMAİL HAKKI Paşa. Inspector of military schools, during the reign of Abdül-hamit II.

İSMET (İNÖNÜ). Atatürk's principal collaborator in the Nationalist struggle and the reforms. Born in Smyrna on 25th September 1884. Elected President on the death of Atatürk.

IVAN III, The Good. Grand Duke of Russia, reigned 1462-1505.

İZZET Paşa. - See Ahmet İzzet.

IZZETTİN. Defender of Kütahya in January 1921.

J

JASON. Leader of the Argonauts. Mythology.

JENNER, EDWARD. British doctor who discovered vaccination (1749-1823).

JOHN VIII. Eastern Emperor, 1425-1448.

JUSTINIAN I. Eastern Emperor, 527-565.

K

KÂMİL Paşa. Grand Vezir in the Young Turks Government.

KARA MUSTAFA. Grand Vezir of Mehmet IV (1634-1683).

KARL von HAPSBURG. Last Emperor of Austria-Hungary, 1916—1918.

KAUKA. Hittite divinity.

KÂZIM (ÖZALP). Important general in the revolution, President of the Grand Assembly.

KÂZIM KARABEKİR. Leading soldier, political opponent of the Reformer.

KELLOGG, FRANK BILLINGS. American politician, author of the Pact which bears his name.

KERENSKY, ALEXANDER. Leader of the provisional revolutionary Russian Government on the fall of Tsar Nicholas. Born 1882.

KHATTUSIL II. Hittite Emperor, thirteenth century B. C.

KILPANTIRIS. Hittite divinity.

KITCHENER, HERBERT, Lord. Commander of the British Army, 1914-1916.

KORNILOV, L. G. Russian General, fought against Bolshevism (1870-1918).

KRIPPEL. Austrian sculptor, who made the Victory Monument in Ankara.

KUBİLAY. Turkish officer murdered by the fanatics at Menemen, 1930.

L

LADISLAS VI. King of Poland and Hungary (1400-1444).

LATİFE HANIM. Wife of Atatürk in 1923; divorced two years later.

LAWRENCE, T. E. Driving force behind the Arab revolt during the Great War.

LENIN (VLADIMIR ILYICH ULYANOV). Russian revolutionary (1870-1924).

LLOYD GEORGE, DAVID. British Prime Minister in 1916. Born 1863.

LORRAINE, DUKE of. - See GODFREY de BOUILLON.

LOTI, PIERRE. Pseudonym of Julien Viaud, French writer (1850-1923).

LOUIS VII. King of France, 1137-1180.

LOUIS IX, (St. Louis). King of France, 1226-1270.

LOUIS XIV. King of France, 1643-1715.

LOUIS XVI. King of France, 1774-1793.

LUCAN. Latin poet (39-65).

LUDENDORFF, HEINRICH von. German Lieutenant-General, Chief of the General Staff during the Great War.

M

MA. Supreme Hittite divinity.

MACRIDI BEY. Turkish Archaeologist. Contemporary.

Mahmut II. Reforming Sultan, reigned 1808-1839.

Mahmut Şevket Paşa. Young Turk Leader, Prime Minister. Assassinated in June, 1913.

Makbule. Atatürk's only sister.

Manlius Vulso. Roman consul; conquered Galatia, second century B. C.

Mehmet, Derviş. - See Derviş Mehmet.

Mehmet I. Fifth Ottoman Sultan, 1403-1421.

Mehmet II, The Conqueror. Ottoman Sultan in 1444 and 1451-1481.

Mehmet III. Sultan, 1595-1603.

Mehmet IV. Sultan, 1648-1687.

Mehmet V, Reşat. Sultan, 1909-1918.

Mehmet VI, Vahdettin. Last Sultan, reigned from 1918-1922.

Mehmet Ali. Viceroy of Egypt (1769-1849).

Mersinli Cemal Paşa. Took part in the Kemalist Revolution, though he had no faith in it.

Michael III, The Drunkard. Eastern Emperor, 842-867.

Michael V, Calaphates. Eastern Emperor, 1041-1042.

Michael VIII, Paleologus. Eastern Emperor, 1259-1282.

Midas. King of Phrygia. Mythology.

Millerand, Etienne Alexandre. President of France, 1920-1924.

Milne, Sir George. British General. Took part in the occupation of Istanbul after the Great War.

Miltiades. Athenian General. Defeated the Persians at Marathon in 490 B. C.

Mithat Paşa. Grand Vezir. Murdered on the orders of the Red Sultan in 1883.

Mithridates, The Great. King of Pontus, enemy of Rome (123-63 B. C.)

Mohammed. Founder of Islam (576-632).

Manastırlı Hamdi. Telegraph operator who informed Kemal of the occupation of Istanbul in 1920.

Montallu. Hittite Emperor, thirteenth century B. C.

Montesquieu, Baron de. Fronch philosopher, forerunner of the revolution (1689-1755).

Montferrat Boniface, Marquis de. One of the leaders of the Fourth Crusade, died 1207.

Murat I. Sultan, 1359-1389.

Murat II. Sultan, 1421-1451.

MURAT III. Sultan, 1574-1595.

MURAT IV. Sultan, 1623-1640.

MURAT V. Sultan in 1876.

MURSIL I. Hittite Emperor, conquered Babylonia.

MURSIL II. Hittite Emperor, fourteenth century B. C.

MUSLİHİTTİN. Farmer, elected Member of Parliament in 1931.

MUSSOLINI, BENITO. Head of the Italian Government from 1922-1924.

MUSTAFA I. Sultan, 1617-1618 and 1622-1623.

MUSTAFA IV. Sultan, 1807-1808.

MUSTAFA BEY. Captain and Atatürk's teacher who gave him the name Kemal.

MUSTAFA SAGHİR. Plotted to assassinate Kemal in 1921.

MUTAWAKKIL. Ceded the Califate to Sultan Selim in the sixteenth century.

N

NACİ PAŞA. Teacher of Atatürk and Aide-de-Camp of Mehmet VI.

NACİYE, Princess. Daughter of Mehmet V, wife of Enver Paşa.

NAMIK KEMAL. Turkish poet and patriot, died 1888.

NAPIER. British General who died at Gallipoli in 1915.

NAPOLEON I. Emperor of France (1769-1821).

NÂZIM BEY. Founder of the "Popular Communist Party" at the beginning of the Government of the Assembly.

NÂZIM, DR. One of the founders of the Committee of Union and Progress; involved in the attempt against Atatürk in 1926.

NÂZIM HİKMET. The most original and vigorous of the Turkish contemporary poets, born 1900.

NÂZIM PAŞA. Minister of War, opponent of the Young Turks. Murdered by them in January 1913.

NEPTUNE. God of the Sea. Mythology.

NERO, L. DOMITIUS CLAUDIUS. Roman Emperor, 54-68.

NESTORIUS. Patriarch of Constantinople.

NEVZAT. Favourite girl and wife of Mehmet Vahdettin.

NICEPHORUS II, PHOCAS. Eastern Emperor, 963-969.

NICHOLAS I. Tsar of Russia, 1825-1855.

NICHOLAS II. Tsar of Russia, 1894-1917, died 1918.

NICHOLAS I. King of Montenegro (1842-1921).

NICHOLAS (NICHOLAYEVICH). Grand Duke, commander of the Russian Armies during the Great War (1856-1929).

NICOMEDES I. King of Bithynia, 279-250 B. C.

NURETTİN PAŞA. Commander of one of the Turkish Armies during the Great Offensive of 1922.

O

OGUZ HAN. Turkish Emperor in Central Asia, end of the third century A. D.

OMAR. Second Calif, 634-644.

OMAR KHAYYAM. Persian poet, twelfth century.

OMEYYADS. Califal dynasty which reigned in Damascus, 661-744.

ORHAN. Sultan, 1326-1359.

ORLANDO, VITTORIO EMMANUELE. Italian politician, Member of the Council of Four, 1918-1919.

ORPHEUS. Mythological personage, poet and musician.

OSMAN I. Founder of the Ottoman dynasty and Empire, reigned 1299-1326.

OTHMAN. Third Calif, 644-656.

OTHO, MARCUS SALVIUS. Roman Emperor, died in the year 69.

OTRANTO, DUKE of - See FOUCHE.

P

PALEOLOGUE, MAURICE. French Ambassador in St. Petersburg during the Great War.

PAPULAS. General, commanding the Greek army at the Battle of the Sakarya.

PASTEUR, LOUIS. French scientist (1822-1895).

PATROCLUS. Greek warrior killed during the siege of Troy.

PAUL. Greek Prince, son of King Constantine I.

PERICLES. Athenian politician, whose name has been given to the fourth century B. C., the most brilliant period in Greek history.

PERSEUS. King of Macedonia, reigned 178-168 B. C.

PETER I of Russia. Called "The Great," reforming Tsar, reigned 1682-1725.

PETER I, KARAGEORGEVICH. King of Serbia (1844-1921).

PETER THE HERMIT. French monk who preached the First Crusade, eleventh century.

PHILIP. King of Macedonia, father of Alexander, reigned 359-338 B. C.

PHILIPPE-AUGUSTE. King of France, 1180-1223.

PHILLIMORE. Commander of the "Inflexible," Battle of the Dardanelles, 1915.

PITT, WILLIAM. British politician (1759-1806).

PLUTARCH. Greek writer, author of the "Lives of the illustrious men of Greece and Rome" (A. D. 50-120).

PLUTO. God of the Underworld. Mythology.

POINCARE, RAYMOND. President of France, 1913-1920.

POLLUX. Mythological hero, one of the Argonauts.

POMPEIUS, GNAEUS. Famous Roman General, Member of the First Triumvirate with Caesar and Crassus.

PROPHET, THE. - See Mohammed.

PROTOPAPADAKIS. Greek Prime Minister, shot in 1922.

PRUSIAS II. King of Bithynia from 186-148 B. C.

PTOLEMY II, PHILADELPHUS. King of Egypt from 285-247 B. C.

R

RA. Personification of the sun. Egyptian mythology.

RAİF EFENDİ. Member of the Representative Committee of Erzurum.

RAMSES II. Pharaoh, fourteenth century B. C.

RAUF BEY (ORBAY). Leading figure in the Kemalist Revolution. Political opponent of Atatürk.

REFET PAŞA. Took part in the Kemalist Revolution. Political opponent of Atatürk.

REŞAT HİKMET. President of the Turkish Parliament in 1920.

REŞİT. - See Çerkes Reşit.

REŞİT PAŞA. Governor of Sivas during the historic Congress, 1919.

RICHARD I. Lion-Heart. King of England, 1189-1199.

RICHELIEU, Cardinal and Duke of. Minister of Louis XIII (1585-1642).

RIZA PAŞA. Director of the Military School of Harbiye.

RIZA PEHLEVİ. Shah of Iran. Ascended the throne in 1925.

ROBECK de. British Vice-Admiral, directed the attack on the Dardanelles in 1915.

ROUGET DE L'ISLE. Author of the Marseillaise (1760-1836).

S

SAİT HALİM. Unionist Prime Minister in 1913.

SAİT, Sheikh. Leader of the Kurdish revolt.

SALADIN. Sultan of Egypt and Syria (1137-1193).

SALİH PAŞA. Ottoman Prime Minister in 1920.

SANDERS, LIMAN von. General, commander of the German Military Mission in Turkey during the World War.

SAVOF, MICHAEL. Commander of the Bulgarian Army in the Balkan Wars.

SCHLEICHER, KURT von. German Chancellor in 1923.

SCHLIEMANN, HEINRICH. Famous German archaeologist (1822-1890).

SCIPIO, LUCIUS CORNELIUS. Roman General (234-183 B. C.)

SEBAHATTİN, Prince. Member of the Committee of Union and Progress.

SELEUCUS NICATOR. Alexander's General. King of Syria (354-280 B. C.)

SELİM I, The Grim. Ottoman Sultan, 1512-1520.

SELİM II. Ottoman Sultan, 1566-1574.

SELİM III. Ottoman Sultan, 1789-1807.

SELJUKS. Name of several Turkish dynasties who reigned in Iran from the eleventh to thirteenth century, in Anatolia from the eleventh to the fourteenth and in Kerman from the eleventh to the twelfth.

ŞEMSİ EFENDİ. Atatürk's teacher in Salonika.

ŞEMSİ PAŞA. Assassinated in Monastir at the beginning of the Young Turks Revolution.

SFORZA, COUNT. Italian Minister of Foreign Affairs in 1921.

SHUBBILULIUMA. Hittite Emperor, called the "Great King," fourteenth century B. C.

SIMON, Sir JOHN. British Chancellor of the Exchequer, 1937.

SOLLY FLOOD. British General. Took part in the allied occupation of Anatolia.

SOLOMON. Hebrew King, son of David (1033-975 B. C.)

SOUCHON. German Admiral, commander of the Turkish fleet. World War.

STANHOPE, Lady HESTER. Protectress of the Druzes (1776-1839).

STRESEMANN, GUSTAV. German pacifist politician (1878-1929).

SÜLEYMAN. Prince wrongly considered by Western historians to have been Sultan.

SÜLEYMAN I, The Law-Giver. Sultan from 1520-1566.

SÜLEYMAN FETHİ. Turkish Colonel murdered by the Greeks during the capture of Smyrna 1919.

SÜLEYMAN ŞEFİK. Turkish General, one of the commanders of the Califal Army, 1920.

SULLA, LUCIUS CORNELIUS. Roman Consul and Dictator (136-78 B. C.)

T

TALÂT PAŞA. Prime Minister during the World War. Assassinated in Germany in 1921.

TAMERLANE (TIMURLENK). Turkish conqueror (1336-1405).

TASHKHIL. Hittite divinity, Goddess of the Mountains. Hittite mythology.

TESHUB. God of War. Hittite mythology.

TEVFİK. — See Çerkes Tevfik.

TEVFİK PAŞA. Grand Vezir in office during the last days of the monarchy.

TEVFİK FİKRET. Turkish poet, director of the review "Servet-i-funun," 1896-1901.

TEVFİK RÜŞTÜ. Turkish Chancellor until 1938.

THEMISTOCLES. Athenian General and politician, victor at Salamis (514-449 B. C.)

THEODORA. Eastern Empress (500-548).

THEODORUS of EPIRUS. Despot of Epirus; conquered Macedonia, thirteenth century A. D.

THEODOSIUS I. Roman Emperor, reigned 379-395.

THEODOSIUS II. Eastern Emperor, 408-450.

THEOTOKIS. Greek Prime Minister, shot in 1922.

THESSALONIKA. Wife of King Cassander and sister of Alexander the Great, fourth century B. C.

THUTMOSIS III. Pharaoh of the 18th dynasty, sixteenth century B. C.

TIBERIUS. Roman Emperor (14-37).

TIMURLENK. - See Tamerlane.

TRICUPIS. Generalissimo of the Greek Army in August 1922.

TULUNIDS. Turkish dynasty in Egypt, tenth century.

TUTANKHAMUN. Pharaoh of the 18th dynasty.

U

URBAN YIII. Pope, 1623-1644.

USEDOM, von. German Admiral, commander of the defences of the Turkish Straits. World War.

V

VENIZELOS, ELEUTHERIOS. Greek politician, Prime Minister on several occasions (1864-1939).

VITELLIUS, AULUS. Roman Emperor (15-69).

VOLTAIRE. French writer (1694-1778).

VULCAN. God of Fire and Metal. Mythology.

W

WILHELM II. Emperor of Germany from 1888-1918.

WILSON, Sir HENRY. British General, commander of the forces which occupied Istanbul in 1920 (1864-1922).

WILSON, WOODROW. President of the United States (1856-1924).

WINCKLER, HUGO. Archaeologist who made important discoveries on the Hittite civilisation. Contemporary.

WRANGEL, G. Russian antirevolutionary General, died 1928.

X

XERXES. King of Persia, 485-465 B. C.

Y

YAHYA GALİP. Governor of Ankara in 1920.

YAHYA KAPDAN. Turkish Nationalist patriot, shot in 1919.

YAKUP CEMİL. Commander who made a plot against Enver Paşa; executed in 1916.

YAŞAR. Mechanic, elected Member of Parliament in 1931.

YUDENICH. Russian anti-Communist General. Russian Revolution.

YUSUF İZZETTİN. Heir to the throne, murdered in 1916.

YUSUF KEMAL. Commissar for Foreign Affairs during the government of the First Grand Assembly.

Z

ZAHAROF, BASIL. Multimillionaire arms salesman, born in Turkey but of Greek origin. Favoured the alliance of Greece with the Entente.

ZENOBIA. Queen of Palmyra, 266-273.

ZEUS. Name given by the Greeks to Jupiter. Mythology.

ZIYA GÖKALP. Turkish poet, defender of the pan-Turanian theory, died 1925.

ZIYA HÜRŞİT. Directed the attempt against Atatürk in 1926.

ZUBEYDE HANIM. Mother of Atatürk, died 1923.

BIBLIOGRAPHY

PRE-OTTOMAN HISTORY

Türk Tarihi Cemiyeti. (Turkish Historical Society). İstanbul, 1931.

Maarif Vekaleti. Birinci Türk Tarih Kongresi. Konferanslar. İstanbul, 1932.

Woolley, L. C. Les Summeriens. Paris, 1931.

Ferrer, F. Vorhomerische Griechen in den Keilschrifttexten von Bogazköi. (Mitteilungen der Vorderasiatisch Gesellschaft. 1913).

Winckler, II. Vorderasien im zweiten Jahrtausend. (Mitteilungen der Vorderasiatisch Gesellschaft. 1913).

Delaporte. L. Les Hettites. Paris, 1936.

Dussaud. R. Les civilisations préhelléniques dans le bassin de la mer Egée. Paris, 1914.

Evans. Essai de classifications des epoques de la civilisation minoenne. Londres. 1896.

Prampolini, G. La mitologia nella vita dei popoli. Milano, 1937.

Cahun, Leon. Introduction à l'histoire de l'Asie. Turcs et Mongols, des origines à 1405. Paris, 1896.

Capus, C. A travers le royaume de Tamerlan. Paris, 1892.

Franke, O. Beiträge aus chinesischen Quellen zur Kentnis der Türkvölker. Berlin, 1904.

Aboul Ghazi Bahadour Khan. A general history of the Turks, Mongols and Tatars. London, 1730.

Le Bas, Phillippe. Asie Mineure, depuis les temps les plus anciens jusqu'à la bataille d'Ancyre en 1402. Paris, 1878.

Vambery, A. Uigurische Sprachmonumenten und der Kudatku Bilik. Innsbruck, 1870.

OTTOMAN EMPIRE

Köprülü, Mehmed Fuad. Les Origines de l'Empire Ottoman. Paris, 1935.

Lavisse et Rambaud. Histoire Générate du IVè. siècle à nos jours. Paris 1893-1901.

Lavallee, Théóphile. Histoire de l'Empire Ottoman. Paris, 1855.

Hammer-Purgstall. Histoire de l'Empire Ottoman, Paris 1844.

Lamartine, A. Histoire de la Turquie. Paris, 1862.

VILLE HARDOUIN, Geoffroi de. La Conquête de Constantinople. Paris, 1872.

CELAL ESSAD. Constantinople, de Byzance à Stamboul. Paris, 1909.

LA JONQUIERE. Histoire de l'Empire Ottoman. Paris, 1914.

UBICINI. La Question d'Orient devant l'Europe. Paris, 1854.

UBICINI. La Turquie actuelle. Paris 1885.

ENGELHARDT. La Turquie et le Tanzimat. Paris, 1883.

ROUSSET, Camille. Histoire de la Guerre de Crimée. Paris, 1878.

MOUZAFFER Pasha. Guerre d'Orient, Defense de Plevna. Paris, 1889.

ARISTARCHI. Legislation ottomane. Constantinople, 1887.

ROUTIER. La Macédoine et les Puissances. Paris, 1904.

BERARD, Victor. La Macédoine. Paris, 1900.

ANCEL, Jacques. Manuel Historique de la Question d'Orient. Paris, 1931.

SANHOURY, A. Le Califat. Paris, 1926.

CHUBBERT, Max. La Question d'Orient depuis le traite de Berlin. Paris 1879.

DOUCHY, W. Guerre turco-grecque. Paris 1898.

DORYS, G. Abdul-Hamit intime. Paris, 1901.

FESCH, Paul. Constantinople aux demiers jours d'Abdul-Hamit. Paris, 1907.

CHOPOV, A. Les reformes et la protection des Chretiens en Turquie. Paris, 1904.

CAHUET. La Question d'Orient dans l'Histoire Contemporaine. Paris, 1905.

PINON, Ren6. L'Europe et l'Empire Ottoman. Paris, 1909.

BERNARD, Victor. La revolution Jeune-Turque. Paris, 1909.

PIERRE LOTI. Turquie Agonisante. Paris, 1913.

PIERRE LOTI. La mort de notre chére France en Orient. Paris, 1920.

ROUMANI, A. Essai Historique et Technique sur la Dette Publique Ottomane. Paris, 1927.

MANDELSTAM, A. Le sort de l'Empire Ottoman. Paris, 1917.

BARCLAY, T. The Turco-Italian War and its Problems. London, 1912.

UN TEMOIN. Histoire de la guerre italo-turque, 1911-12. Paris, 1912.

HANOTAUX, G. La guerre des Balkans en l'Europe. Paris, 1914.

LAMOUCHE, Colonel. Quinze Ans d'Histoire Balcanique (1904-1918). Paris, 1928.

MAHMOUD MOUHTAR Pasha. Mon commandement au cours de la campagne des Balkans. Paris, 1913.

Dreyer, Colonel. La Débâcle Bulgare. Deuxième guerre Balkanique. Paris, 1912.

Moukhtar Pacha. La Turquie, l'Allemagne et l'Europe, depuis le traité de Berlin jusqu'à la guerre mondiale. Paris, 1924.

Morgenthau, Ambassadeur. Mémoires. Paris, 1919.

Paleologue, Maurice. La Rusia de los Zares durante la Gnerra Grande. Buenos Aires, 1930.

Larcher, M. La Guerre Turque dans la Guerre Mondiale. Paris, 1926.

Stienon, Charles. Les Campagnes d'Orient et les intérêts de l'Entente. Paris, 1918.

Delage, Edmond. La Tragédie des Dardanelles. Paris, 1931.

Stuermer, H. Deux ans de guerre à Constantinople. Paris, 1917.

Domergue, Gabriel. La guerre en Orient. Aux Dardanelles et dans les Balkans. Paris, 1917.

Testis. L'expédition des Dardanelles. Paris, 1917.

Lammens, H. La Syrie. Beyrouth, 1921.

Bowman-Manifold. Bosquejo de las campanas en Egipto y en Palestina. Buenos Aires, 1925.

Sarrail, Général. Mon Commandement en Orient. Paris, 1920.

Nogales, Rafael. Cuatro anos bajo la Media Luna. Buenos Aires, 1924.

Grumbach, S. Brest-Litovsk. Paris, 1919.

Ahmet Rüstem Bey. La guerre mondiale et la question turco-arménienne. Berne, 1918.

Türk Tarihi Cemiyeti. (Turkish Historical Society.) Tarih. Yeni ve Yakın Zamanlar. İstanbul, 1933.

Seignobosc, Capitaine. Turcs et Turquie. Paris, 1920.

Lloyd George, David. Mémoires de Guerre. Paris, 1935.

Djemal Pasha. Erinnerungen eines türkischen Staatsmannes. München, 1922.

Mandelstam, A. N. La Société des Nations et les Puissances devant le problème arménien. Paris, 1925.

Lowell, Thomas. El coronel Lawrence. Barcelona, 1936.

ATATÜRK AND THE NEW TURKEY

Hippeau. Les republiques du Caucase. Paris, 1920.

Driault, Edouard. La grande Idée, la Renaissance de l'Hellénisme. Paris, 1920.

GEORGES-GAULIS, Berthe. Le Nationalisme Turc. Paris, 1921.

DRIAULT, Edouard. La Question d'Orient. Paris, 1921.

SCHLICKLIN, Jean. Angora. Paris, 1922.

GEORGES-GAULIS, Berthe. Angora, Constantinople, Londres. Paris, 1922.

KAYSER, Jacques. L'Europe et la Turquie Nouvelle. Paris, 1922.

AHMET RIZA. La faillité morale de la politique occidentale. Paris, 1922.

CASTAGNE. Les organisations bolchéviques de la Russie musulmane. (Révue du Monde Musulman). Paris, 1922.

PAILLARES, Michel. Le Kémalisme devant les Alliés. Constantinople, 1922.

ISMET Pacha. Déclarations. Lausanne, 1922.

HUSSEYN RAGHIP. Le mouvement national turc et Moustafa Kemal. Paris, 1922.

SANDERS, Liman von. Cinq ans de Turquie. Paris, 1923.

PERNOT, Maurice. La Question Turque. Paris, 1923.

GONTAUT-BIRON. Comment la France s'est installée en Syrie. Paris, 1923.

LABONNE, Roger. La Turquie Laique. Le Correspondant. Sept. Paris, 1924.

GEORGES-GAULIS, Berthe. La Nouvelle Turquie. Paris, 1924.

LUQUET, Jean. La Politique des Mandats dans le Levant. Paris, 1924.

HOUTAL, Mosché. L'avenir économiquc de la Turquie nouvelle. Paris, 1924.

HABIB ABI-CHAHLA. L'Extinction des Capitulations en Turquie et dans les régions arabes. Paris, 1924.

ELLISON, Grace. An Englishwoman in Angora. New York, 1924.

DENY, Jean. Moustapha Kémal Pacha. Sa biographie. Paris, 1926.

MARZIO, Cornelio di. La Turchia di Kemal. Milán, 1926.

SAID HIKMET. De l'Empire Ottoman à la République Turque. Lille, 1926.

KIOSSEOGLOU. L'Echange forcé des minorités d'après le traité de Lausanne. Nancy, 1926.

MEYERHOF, M. Le monde islamique. Paris, 1926.

SOUSSER-HALL, G. Introduction à l'étude du nouveau droit civil en Turquie. İstanbul, 1927.

GAZI MOUSTAFA KEMAL PACHA. Souvenirs. Paris, 1927.

MARCHAND, René. Le réveil d'une Race. Paris, 1927.

HALİDE EDİP. The Turkish Ordeal. London, 1928.

MELIA, Jean. Mustapha Kémal. Paris, 1929.

GENTIZON, Paul. Mustapha Kémal ou l'Orient en Marche. Paris, 1929.

Chantitch-chandan. Le Miracle Turc. Paris, 1929.

Castaigne, J. Le mouvement d'émancipation de la femme musulmane en Orient. Paris 1929.

Halide Edip. Turkey Faces West. Yale, 1930.

Bujac, Emile. Les campagnes de l'Armée Hellénique (1918-1922). Paris, 1930.

Tahsin Muhiddine. La réforme financière en Turquie. Paris, 1930.

Pittard, Eugène. Le visage nouveau de la Turquie. Paris, 1930.

Pavlova, Nelia. Au pays du Ghazi. Paris, 1930.

Roger, Noëlle. En Asie Mineure. La Turquie du Ghazi. Paris, 1930.

Wortham, H. E. Mustafa Kemal of Turkey. London, 1930.

Farrere, Claude. Turquie Ressuscité. Paris, 1930.

Mikousch, Dagobert von. Ghazi Mustapha Kémal. Paris, 1931.

Sforza, Comte. Dictateurs et Dictatures de l'après-guerre. Paris, 1931.

Georges-Gaulis, Berthe. Le Question Turque. Paris, 1931.

Vissec, Lucien. La Turquie et les minorités. Paris, 1931.

Labonne, Roger. Les pays turcs et la politique orientale des Soviets. Paris, 1932.

Deny, Jean, et René Marchand. Petit Manuel de la Turquie Nouvelle. Paris, 1933.

Armstrong, Capitaine H. C. Mustafa Kémal. Paris, 193b.

Yusuf Hikmet. Yeni Türkiye Devletinin Harici Siyaseti. Istanbul, 1934.

Aniante, Antonio. Mustafa Kémal. Le Loup Gris d'Angora. Paris, 1934.

Ghali, Paul. Les Nationalités détachées de l'Empire Ottoman à la suite de la guerre. Paris, 1934.

Lamouche, Colonel. Histoire de la Turquie. Paris, 1934.

Direction Generale De La Presse. La Turquie Contemporaine. Ankara, 1935.

Kral, A. Das Land Kamâl Atatürks. Wien, 1935.

Sheridan, Clare. Nuda Veritas. Paris, 1935.

Societe Pour L'Etude De L'Histoire Turque. Histoire de la République Turque. İstanbul, 1935.

Langas-Sezen, Antoine. La vie audacieuse de Gazi Moustapha Kémal. (Les Annales de Turquie). Istanbul, 1935.

Bainville, Jacques. Les Dictateurs. Paris, 1935.

Conker, Orhan. Les Chemins de fer en Turquie et la Politique Ferroviaire Turque. Paris, 1935.

CAFER TAYYAR. L'Ultra Popularisme. Philosophic Moderne de Kamâl Atatürk. Paris, 1935.

BOURGOIN, Marguerite. La Turquie d'Ataturk. Paris, 1935.

FROEMGEN, H. Kamâl Atatürk. Stuttgart, 1935.

RONART, Stephan. Die Türkei von Heute. Amsterdam, 1936.

SAVADJIAN, León. Encyclopédie Balkanique. Paris, 1936.

ZARA, Phillippe de. Mustapha Kémal Dictateur. Paris, 1936.

BISCHOFF, Norbert von. La Turquie dans le Monde. Paris, 1936.

ACTES DE LA CONFERENCE DE MONTREUX. Liége, 1936.

LA QUESTION D'ALEXANDRETTE ET D'ANTIOCHE. Livre Blanc. Ankara, 1936.

SHERRILL, Général. Mustafa Kémal. L'Homme-L'Oeuvre-Le Pavs. Paris, 1934.

SHERRILL, Général. Trois hommes. Roosevelt. Mussolini. Kamal. Paris, 1936.

PRESS DEPARTMENT. MINISTRY OF INTERIOR AFFAIRS.

  Public Instruction in the Republic of Turkey. Ankara, 1936.

  Turkey in the way of industrialisation. Ankara, 1937.

  The Turkish Woman in History. Ankara, 1937.

DIRECTION GENERALE DE LA PRESSE. La Turquie en Chiffres. Ankara, 1937.

ATATURK, Kemal. Discours. Ankara, 1937.

SOCIETE DE L'INDEPENDANCE DU HATAY. Le Calvaire du Hatay. Ankara, 1937.

LA QUESTION D'ALEXANDRETTE ET D'ANTIOCHE. Livre Blanc. Ankara, 1937.

INDEX